Lecture Notes in Artificial Intelligence   1609

Subseries of Lecture Notes in Computer Science
Edited by J. G. Carbonell and J. Siekmann

Lecture Notes in Computer Science

Edited by G. Goos, J. Hartmanis and J. van Leeuwen

T0180229

Springer

Berlin
Heidelberg
New York
Barcelona
Hong Kong
London
Milan
Paris
Singapore
Tokyo

Zbigniew W. Raś   Andrzej Skowron (Eds.)

Foundations of Intelligent Systems

11th International Symposium, ISMIS'99
Warsaw, Poland, June 8-11, 1999
Proceedings

 Springer

Series Editors

Jaime G. Carbonell, Carnegie Mellon University, Pittsburgh, PA, USA
Jörg Siekmann, University of Saarland, Saarbrücken, Germany

Volume Editors

Zbigniew W. Raś
University of North Carolina, Department of Computer Science
9201 University City Boulevard, Charlotte, NC 28223, USA
E-mail: ras@uncc.edu
and
Polish Academy of Sciences, Institute of Computer Science
Ordona 21, 01-237 Warsaw, Poland
E-mail: ras@wars.ipipan.waw.pl

Andrzej Skowron
University of Warsaw, Institute of Mathematics
Banacha 2, 02-097 Warsaw, Poland
E-mail: skowron@mimuw.edu.pl

Cataloging-in-Publication data applied for

Die Deutsche Bibliothek - CIP-Einheitsaufnahme

Foundations of intelligent systems : 11th international symposium ;
proceedings / ISMIS '99, Warsaw, Poland, June 8 - 11, 1999.
Zbigniew W. Ras ; Andrzej Skowron (ed.). - Berlin ; Heidelberg ;
New York ; Barcelona ; Hong Kong ; London ; Milan ; Paris ;
Singapore ; Tokyo : Springer, 1999
  (Lecture notes in computer science ; Vol. 1609 : Lecture notes in
  artificial intelligence)
  ISBN 3-540-65965-X

CR Subject Classification (1998): I.2, H.5, H.3, F.4.1, F.1, H.3.3

ISBN 3-540-65965-X Springer-Verlag Berlin Heidelberg New York

© Springer-Verlag Berlin Heidelberg 1999
Printed in Germany

Typesetting: Camera-ready by author
SPIN 10705068   06/3142 – 5 4 3 2 1 0   Printed on acid-free paper

Preface

This volume contains the papers selected for presentation at the Eleventh International Symposium on Methodologies for Intelligent Systems - ISMIS'99, held in Warsaw, Poland, June 8-11, 1999. The symposium was organized and hosted by the Institute of Computer Science of the Polish Academy of Sciences (ICS PAS). It was sponsored by UNC-Charlotte, ICS PAS, the Polish-Japanese School of Information Technology, and others.

ISMIS is a conference series that was started in 1986 in Knoxville, Tennessee. Since then it has been held in Charlotte (North Carolina), Knoxville (Tennessee), Torino (Italy), Trondheim (Norway), and Zakopane (Poland).

The program committee selected the following major areas for ISMIS'99: Evolutionary Computation, Intelligent Information Retrieval, Intelligent Information Systems, Knowledge Representation and Integration, Learning and Knowledge Discovery, Logic for Artificial Intelligence, Methodologies, and Soft Computing.

The contributed papers were selected from 115 full draft papers by the following program committee: S. Carberry, L. Carlucci Aiello, A. Biermann, J. Calmet, J. Carbonell, N.J. Cercone, S.M. Deen, R. Demolombe, B. Desai, E. Dietrich, J. Eusterbrock, A. Giordana, H.J. Hamilton, A. Jankowski, W. Klösgen, Y. Kodratoff, B. Lowden, M. Lowry, D. Maluf, R.A. Meersman, M. Michalewicz, Z. Michalewicz, R.S. Michalski, M. Mukaidono, S. Ohsuga, L. Padgham, Z. Pawlak, L. De Raedt, V.V. Raghavan, Z.W. Raś, E. Rosenthal, H. Rybiński, L. Saitta, A. Skowron, S. Tsumoto, R. Slowiński, S.K.M. Wong, G.-P. Zarri, M. Zemankova, N. Zhong, and J.M. Żytkow. Additionally, we acknowledge the help in reviewing the papers from: J. Chen, J.W. Grzymała-Busse, M. Kryszkiewicz, M. Merzbacher, S.H. Nguyen, R. Świniarski, A. Wieczorkowska and W. Ziarko.

P. Dembiński was the general chair of the symposium.

We wish to express our thanks to Willi Klösgen, Yves Kodratoff, Robert A. Meersman, V.S. Subrahmanian, and Gio Wiederhold who presented invited talks at the symposium. Also, we are thankful to Z. Michalewicz for organizing two special sessions on Evolutionary Computation. We express our appreciation to the sponsors of the symposium and to all who submitted papers for presentation and publication in the proceedings. Our sincere thanks go to Ewa Gąsiorowska-Wirpszo for her professional help in organizing the symposium. Also, our thanks are due to Alfred Hofmann of Springer-Verlag for his continuous help and support.

June, 1999

Z.W. Raś, A. Skowron
ISMIS'99 Program Co-Chairs

Table of Contents

Invited Papers

W. Klösgen
Applications and research problems of subgroup mining 1

Y. Kodratoff
Knowledge discovery in texts: A definition and applications 16

R.A. Meersman
Semantic ontology tools in IS design 30

V.S. Subrahmanian
Heterogeneous agent systems 46

G. Wiederhold
Information systems that really support decision-making 56

Communications

1A Logics for AI

J. Chen
*A class of stratified programs in autoepistemic logic of
knowledge and belief* 67

A. Giordana, L. Saitta
On-line estimation of matching complexity in first order logic 76

C.-M. Wu, Y. Zhang
Implementing prioritized logic programming 85

A. Badia
Extending description logics with generalized quantification 94

1B Intelligent Information Retrieval

F. Esposito, D. Malerba, F.A. Lisi
Machine learning for intelligent document processing: The WISDOM system 103

A.H. Alsaffar, J.S. Deogun, V.V. Raghavan, H. Sever
Concept based retrieval by minimal term sets 114

P. Lambrix, N. Shahmehri, S. Jacobsen
Querying document bases by content, structure and properties 123

F. Sebastiani
Total knowledge and partial knowledge in logical models
of information retrieval 133

2A Intelligent Information Systems

S.M. Deen, C.A. Johnson
Towards a theoretical foundation for cooperating knowledge based systems 144

B.C. Desai, R. Shinghal, N. Shayan, Y. Zhou
CINDI: A system for cataloguing, searching, and annotating
electronic documents in digital libraries 154

S. Ohsuga, T. Aida
Externalization of human idea and problem description
for automatic programming 163

B. Prędki, S. Wilk
Rough set based data exploration using ROSE system 172

D. Pacholczyk
Towards an intelligent system dealing with nuanced
information expressed in affirmative or negative forms 181

2B Intelligent Information Retrieval

B. Thomas
Logic programs for intelligent Web search 190

R. Basili, M. Di Nanni, M.T. Pazienza
Representing document content via an object-oriented paradigm 199

G. Semeraro, M.F. Costabile, F. Esposito, N. Fanizzi, S. Ferilli
A learning server for inducing user classification
rules in the digital library service 208

S. Kundu
A better fitness measure of a text-document for a given set of keywords 217

G.P. Zarri, E. Bertino, B. Black, A. Brasher, B. Catania, D. Deavin, L. Di Pace,
F. Esposito, P. Leo, J. McNaught, A. Persidis, F. Rinaldi, G. Semeraro,
CONCERTO, an environment for the 'intelligent' indexing,
querying and retrieval of digital documents 226

3A Learning and Knowledge Discovery

H. Wang, H.S. Nguyen
Text classification using lattice machine 235

M. Merzbacher
Discovering semantic proximity for Web pages 244

I. Weber
A declarative language bias for levelwise search of first-order regularities 253

P. Ejdys, G. Góra
The more we learn the less we know? On inductive learning from examples 262

3B Logics for AI

P. Doherty, W. Łukaszewicz, E. Madalińska-Bugaj
Computing MPMA updates using Dijkstra's semantics 271

M. Mukaidono
Several extensions of truth values in fuzzy logic 282

R. Béjar, F. Manyà
Phase transitions in the regular random 3-SAT problem 292

L. Brisoux, E. Grégoire, L. Saïs
Improving backtrack search for SAT by means of redundancy 301

4A Intelligent Information Systems

H.S. Nguyen, S.H. Nguyen, A. Skowron
Decomposition of task specification problems 310

A. An, N.J. Cercone, C. Chan
ORTES: The design of a real-time control expert system 319

B.G.T. Lowden, J. Robinson
A statistical approach to rule selection in semantic query optimisation 330

M.-S. Hacid, C. Rigotti
Representing and reasoning on conceptual queries over image databases 340

4B Learning and Knowledge Discovery

S. Tsumoto
*Knowledge discovery in clinical databases - An experiment
with rule induction and statistics* 349

M. Michalewicz, M.A. Klopotek, S.T. Wierzchoń
Reasoning and acquisition of knowledge in a system
for hand wound diagnosis and prognosis 358

A. Wieczorkowska
Rough Sets as a tool for audio signal classification 367

D. Brindle, W. Ziarko
Experiments with rough sets approach to speech recognition 376

5A Computer Vision

N. Abe, K. Tanaka, H. Taki
A system for understanding a mechanical assembly instruction
manual using virtual space 385

W. Skarbek
Perceptual convergence of discrete clamped fractal operator 395

W. Skarbek, A. Pietrowcew, R. Sikora
Modified Oja-RLS algorithm - stochastic convergence
analysis and application for image compression 402

5B Learning and Knowledge Discovery

K.A. Kaufman, R.S. Michalski
Learning from inconsistent and noisy data: The AQ18 approach 411

J.J. Zhang, N.J. Cercone, H.J. Hamilton
Learning english grapheme segmentation using the iterated
version space algorithm 420

L. Iwańska, N. Mata, K. Kruger
Fully automatic acquisition of taxonomic knowledge from large
corpora of texts: Limited-syntax knowledge representation system
based on natural language 430

6A Learning and Knowledge Discovery

F. Botana
A fuzzy measure of similarity for instance-based learning 439

R. Susmaga
Computation of minimal cost reducts 448

J. Stepaniuk
Rough set data mining of diabetes data 457

D. Michaut, P. Baptiste
Selection of a relevant feature subset for induction tasks 466

6B Knowledge Representation

J. Calmet, P. Kullmann
A data structure for subsumption-based tabling in
top-down resolution engines for data-intensive logic applications 475

M.A. Orgun
Modelling and reasoning about multi-dimensional information 484

M.A. Klopotek, S.T. Wierzchoń
An interpretation for the conditional belief function in the
theory of evidence 494

L.M. Sztandera, C. Bock, M. Trachtman, J. Velga
Artificial neural networks aid the design of non-carcinogenic azo dyes 503

7A Evolutionary Computation

K. De Jong
Evolving in a changing world 512

C. Anglano, A. Giordana, G. Lo Bello
High-performance data mining on networks of workstations 520

J.J. Mulawka, P. Wąsiewicz, K. Piętak
Virus-enhanced genetic algorithms inspired by DNA computing 529

K. Trojanowski, Z. Michalewicz
Evolutionary approach to non-stationary optimization tasks 538

7B Learning and Knowledge Discovery

J. Ćwik, J. Koronacki, J.M. Żytkow
On discovering functional relationships when
observations are noisy: 2D case 547

J.F. Peters, L. Han, S. Ramanna
Approximate time rough software cost decision system:
Multicriteria decision-making approach 556

M.A. de Almeida, S. Matwin
Machine learning method for software quality model building 565

S.H. Nguyen
Discovery of generalized patterns 574

8A Learning and Knowledge Discovery

M. Kryszkiewicz, H. Rybiński
Incomplete database issues for representative association rules 583

S. Puuronen, V. Terziyan, A. Tsymbal
A dynamic integration algorithm for an ensemble of classifiers 592

G. Fiol-Roig
UIB-IK: A computer system for decision trees induction 601

J.W. Grzymala-Busse, L.K. Goodwin, X. Zhang
*Preterm birth risk assessed by a new method of classification
using selective partial matching* 612

J. Dong, N. Zhong, S. Ohsuga
Probabilistic rough induction: The GDT-RS methodology and algorithms 621

8B Evolutionary Computation

C.H.M. van Kemenade, J.N. Kok
Cluster evolution strategies for constrained numerical optimization 630

F. Mansanne, F. Carrère, A. Ehinger, M. Schoenauer
Evolutionary algorithms as fitness function debuggers 639

M. Schmidt
Solving real-life time-tabling problems 648

R. Jonsson
On measures of search features 657

J. Jelonek, M. Komosiński
Genetic algorithms in constructive induction 665

Author Index 675

Applications and Research Problems of Subgroup Mining

Willi Klösgen

German National Research Center for Information Technology (GMD)
D-53757 St. Augustin, Germany
kloesgen@gmd.de

Abstract. Knowledge Discovery in Databases (KDD) is a data analysis process which, in contrast to conventional data analysis, automatically generates and evaluates very many hypotheses, deals with complex, i.e. large, high dimensional, multi relational, dynamic, or heterogeneous data, and produces understandable results for those who "own the data". With these objectives, subgroup mining searches for hypotheses that can be supported or confirmed by the given data and that are represented as a specialization of one of three general hypothesis types: deviating subgroups, associations between two subgroups, and partially ordered sets of subgroups where the partial ordering usually relates to time. This paper gives a short introduction into the methods of subgroup mining. Especially the main preprocessing, data mining and postprocessing steps are discussed in more detail for two applications. We conclude with some problems of the current state of the art of subgroup mining.

1 Introduction

Three main application purposes of a data mining task can be distinguished. The predominant purpose is to use mining results to predict or classify future cases, e.g. classify a client or transaction as fraudulent or predict the probability of a group of car drivers causing an accident.

A second purpose of using data mining results is to describe a domain or, more specifically, the dominant dependency structure between variables of the domain, for instance by a summarized overview on the winners of a planned legislation or the client groups whose market shares decreased.

But data are often inconclusive, because not all relevant variables are available, or the description language to describe, for example, subgroups of objects is insufficient. Then the user is satisfied, if some *nuggets* are identified by a mining method. This means that some single hypotheses are validated as interesting by the KDD system. These results are not complete, because they do not allow to predict all new cases or to summarize the whole dependency. For instance, some single subgroups of patients suffering under a special disease are identified without to derive a complete disease profile. Partial results are produced that can give rise to more detailed analyses to be conducted by the domain experts.

These three main application purposes, i.e. classification and prediction, description, and nuggets detection, roughly determine which data mining methods can be applied. For the selection and parametrization of appropriate methods, more special subgoals of applications must additionally be considered which refer to the application dependent properties the discovery results shall have. Such properties relate, for example, to the homogeneity of subgroups, complexity of results, covering of subgroups, (classification) accuracy. Some examples are discussed in sections 4 and 5.

Subgroup mining is a special, but very broadly applicable data mining approach which can be used for these three main analysis goals and many special data mining tasks. It includes several widely used data mining methods such as decision rules and trees, association and sequence rules, change and trend patterns. Subgroup mining searches for subgroups of analysis units (objects or cases: persons, clients, trans-actions, etc.) that show some type of interesting behavior. The single identified sub-groups are local patterns, but can also be seen as a global model when constituting a consistent and non redundant structured set of subgroups. See [1] for a discussion of distinguishing local patterns and global models.

Statistical findings on subgroups belong to the most popular and simple forms of knowledge we encounter in all domains of science, business, or even daily life. We are told such messages as: Unemployment rate is overproportionally high for young men with low educational level, young poor women are infected with AIDS at a much higher rate than their male counterparts, lung cancer mortality rate has considerably increased for women during the last 10 years.

To introduce the subgroup mining paradigm, one has to deal with types of description languages for constructing subgroups, and to define and specialize general pattern classes for subgroup deviations, associations, and sequence patterns. A deviation pattern describes a deviating behavior of a target variable in a subgroup. Deviation patterns rely on statistical tests and thus capture knowledge about a subgroup in form of a verified (alternative) hypothesis on the distribution of a target variable. Search for deviating subgroups is organized in two phases. In a brute force search, alternative search heuristics can be applied to find a first set of deviating sub-groups. In a second refinement phase, redundancy elimination operators identify a (best) system of subgroups, usually a subset of the first set or a set including some derived subgroups.

An association pattern identifies two subgroups which have a significant asso-ciation. Various specializations can be selected to measure the association between two subgroups, e.g. the confidence and support approach of association rules [2]. A sequence pattern identifies a set of subgroups which are partially ordered according to a given ordering type. Thus the partial ordering must satisfy given constraints, e.g. a serial or parallel ordering. The ordering usually relates to time where each object in the database has a time stamp (e.g. errors in a network, transactions of clients). Typically time windows are regarded that contain objects in a special partial order where each object belongs to a special subgroup. Frequent episodes or episode rules [3] are examples of sequence patterns (80 % of windows that contain an error of subgroup B immediately after an error of subgroup A contain later an error of subgroup C). We will concentrate in this paper on specializations of the first general subgroup pattern class, namely deviating subgroups.

Subgroup patterns are local findings identifying subgroups of a population with some unusual, unexpected, or deviating behavior. Thus a single subgroup pattern does not give a complete overview on the population, but refers only to a subset. Nevertheless these local statements (nuggets) are often useful, either because the interest of the analyst is rather modest, or the available data do not allow to derive the complete description of the behavior for the whole population. In a production control application (see section 4), the analyst may be satisfied, if some conditions for the large number of process variables can be identified that lead to a very high quality of the product. Then these conditions will probably be tried to steer a better production process. In a medical application, the available variables can often not describe the dependencies between symptoms and diagnoses, because only a part of the relevant and typically unknown variables is available. But it is useful to know at least some subgroups of patients that can be diagnosed with a high accuracy.

To be useful, subgroup patterns must satisfy at least two conditions. Subgroup descriptions must be interpretable and application relevant, and the reported behavior for the subgroup must be interesting which specifically means that it is statistically significant. This is achieved by the choice of the syntactical type of the description language and background constraints for valid subgroup descriptions, and of a statistical test measuring the statistical significance of a subgroup deviation. An appropriate test is selected according to the type of the analysis question (which is e.g. determined by type of the target variable and the number of populations to be compared in the deviation pattern) and domain dependent preferences of the analyst that e.g. refer to trade-offs such as size of deviation versus size of subgroup. For a detailed discussion of the role of statistical tests in subgroup mining, a classification of specializations of subgroup pattern types, and an overview on search strategies and visualization and navigation operations, see [4].

2 Data and Domain Knowledge for Subgroup Mining

The application domain of a KDD and specifically of a subgroup mining task is represented by data which may have been collected directly for decision support purposes when e.g. a market research company performs a regular survey on a special market and therefore can usually collect the data that are relevant for the analysis (section 5). But the typical data mining application is a secondary data analysis when the data have been generated during an administrative or transaction process (e.g. client database, production data). Secondary data analyses may include problems of quality and appropriateness of given data for the targeted application question. In addition to data, a knowledge base that holds domain knowledge can be exploited in subgroup mining.

The vast collections of already available operational databases are often the impetus for data mining applications. In this case, typically a lot of preprocessing is necessary to combine data from different sources and to adapt data to various analysis problems (see sections 4 and 5). Then data are transformed into structures suitable for efficient access and operation. In table 1, a classification of data types is given which can be applied to select appropriate mining tasks, analysis methods, and data management solutions for an application.

Subgroup mining methods can operate on observation or tansaction data as well as on textual data. When searching for interesting subgroups of documents [5], each document is represented by a set of terms or phrases that are included or relevant for the document, and a subgroup is described by a conjunction of terms. The statistical evaluations of subgroup patterns rely on simple explorative tests, so that some limited representativity of available data can be handled.

Main data type	observation transaction	textual	multimedia	
Representativity	complete population	sample of convenience	random sample	stratified sample
Variable type	binary	categorical	continuous	mixed
Missing data	no	yes		
Conclusiveness	low	medium	high	
Size	moderate	large	very large	vast
Dimensionality	low	medium	high	
Dynamics	static	timely evolving		
Distribution	local	fixed locations	scattered on net	
Object heterogeneity	one object class	multi-valued attributes	multiple object classes	
Time reference	one cross section	two independent cross sections	series of independent cross sections	longitudinal data
	continuous	time series		
Space reference	point	line	area	surface
Text structure	unstructured	structured parts	hypertext	
Text languages	English	other languages	mixed collection	multilingual text
Hybrid forms	no	mixed obser- vational data	observational & text & multimedia	
Aggregation	micro data	macro data		
Meta data	no	data dictionary	domain knowledge	

Table 1. Dimensions for classifying data and selecting appropriate specializations of subgroup mining patterns

All types of variables can be exploited, using discretization methods for the continuous variables that describe subgroups and different pattern subtypes for categorical, ordinal or continuous target variables. To analyse high dimensional and very large data sets, efficient heuristical search strategies can be selected. For time and space referenced data, special pattern types are used, e.g. for change and trend detection, or by including geographically based clustering methods to derive corresponding selectors for a description. Multi relational description languages can be applied for data with several relations [6].

Subgroup mining methods only exploit some limited form of domain knowledge. Domain knowledge is necessary to achieve a higher degree of autonomy in search and interestingness evaluation of patterns. Current systems typically exploit some metadata and taxonomical knowledge. Taxonomies are hierarchies on the domains of the variables (e.g. a regional classification). They are necessary for describing interesting results on an appropriate aggregation level. For example, a finding which is based on significant cells in a crosstabulation and holds for nearly all provinces, should be generalized to a higher regional level. Other advantages of taxonomies are listed in table 2.

data reduction	very large datasets, categorical analysis methods
interpretability	avoid nonsense groupings of variable(s) (values)
simplicity	avoid repetitions, find appropriate hierarchical level
ordering	general to specific, find deviations and exceptions
search reduction	pruning of subnodes
greediness	expansion by selectors with higher coverage
focusing	support specification of mining task, select aggregation level

Table 2. Advantages of taxonomies

Another technique to deal with interestingness is based on constraining the search space. Constraints, for example on the combinations of variable values that are potentially useful, can be exploited as domain knowledge to exclude non interesting hypotheses. A typical example is an association rule mining task, when sets of products have to be identified that are often jointly bought by clients in mail-orders. The aim of this analysis may be to evaluate the efficiency of the catalogue issued by the mail-order company. Associations between products that appear on the same page of the catalogue may be defined as uninteresting by a relation between products: same-page(product1, product2). By specifying appropriate constraints, uninteresting hypotheses can be excluded from search. Similar techniques are applied when syntactical biases are defined for the hypotheses language, like a conjunctive description language for subgroups. Then similar variables can be put together in a group, and constraints determine, how many variables of a group and which combinations of variables are selected to build patterns or models.

Interestingness can additionally relate to the *novelty* of the results. The system can exploit former discoveries and analyse the reaction of the user (e.g. rejecting or accepting results by including them into reports).

3 Conditions for Successful Subgroup Mining Applications

Based on different emphasis in using approaches from the statistical, database, machine learning, and visualization fields, various KDD systems have been constructed (see: http://info.gte.com/~kdd/siftware.html) that discover interesting patterns in data. What are now the conditions for a successful application of these tools and when do they provide better results than conventional data analysis methods? Primarily, a data rich application is needed. As a common necessary precondition for every data analysis application, this means at first, that the database is sufficiently conclusive containing problem relevant variables for a lot of approximately representative objects of the domain. Provided that these requirements are satisfied, subgroup approaches prove particularly useful in comparison to the standard statistical methods, when an analysis problem includes a large number of potentially relevant variables, multidimensional relations vary in different subpopulations, no proved (statistical) model was already established for the problem, or surprising results can be expected for subgroups.

For example, in the applications on a production control process (section 4), where settings for production parameters that offer good production results shall be found, we had to study more than 100 variables that may influence the quality of a product. On the other side, if the problem is well understood and there is already a proven model to describe or analyse the domain, then there seems to be little need for new methods. Thus for more than 20 years, a market research application analyses surveys on the financial market (section 5). Banks and insurance companies know their own and their competitors´ client profiles, since they have analysed these survey data with conventional data analysis tools for a long time. We recently supported this application additionally with KDD methods of the *Data Surveyor* system [7]. To detect sudden changes in the current year, KDD methods proved useful in this well studied area too. Unexpected changes in special subgroups (e.g. for subgroups that usually are not studied using only the variables of the main model) can be detected by KDD methods that would have been overlooked in traditional analyses. Moreover, it often helps in a KDD application, if some data analysis experience with the problem is already available.

There are several approaches to combine conventional statistical models with the subgroup mining approach. A first option is to use subgroup mining as a preprocessing and exploration task. Then subgroup mining results are used to familiarize with the data and to get an overview on the relevent influence variables and their form of influence. Based on these subgroup mining results, a model (e.g. regression model) can be specified. An alternative option applies subgroup mining in a postprocessing phase to modeling. The residuals of a statistical model are analysed with subgroup mining methods to detect some non-random residual behavior.

Another special combination option applies probabilistic network techniques to subgroup mining results. To elucidate the dependency structure between found subgroups and the target group, probabilistic nets can be generated for the subgroups which are analysed as derived binary variables.

A further necessary condition for useful KDD applications is, that many disaggregated indices or subgroups must be studied (many dimensions can be relevant for the problem). In a political planning application [8], we analysed the results of socio-economic simulation models to study the consequences of new tax and transfer laws. If the analyst or politician is mainly interested in the overall cost of the new legislation and only in a few fixed groups of winners and losers of the legislation, this can be mostly achieved by studying a small set of cross tabulations. In contrast, a typical subgroup mining application analyses a large set of potentially interesting subgroups for which surprising results can be expected.

4 Application: Production Control

We first discuss a production control application with factory data on process conditions and laboratory data on the quality of products. Process conditions are continuously recorded and quality data several times a day. When fixing a data model, it must be decided how to represent time and space related data. The analysis object must be determined, e.g. a production day. In a simple one-relational model, process variables (pressures, temperatures, etc.) are discretized each hour so that separate variables for time points (each hour) and for different locations in the factory are introduced. Additionally, appropriate derived variables capturing time behaviour like maximum, minimum, average, slope are generated for these time or space indexed variables.

Thus data preparation deals with the selection of a data model for the target data to be mined and the construction of this target data base from the raw data followed by data cleaning and reduction. It is an iterative process including feed back loops, as the next preprocessing steps may generate insights in the domain that require additional data preparations, e.g. by evaluating the appropriateness of derived variables.

Because data from several operational or transaction databases have to be exploited, a separate database is constructed to manage the data for data mining purposes. One advantage of a separate mining database is the better performance. Large scale data mining is very computer time intensive, and many queries must be sent to the data base to calculate the aggregates and cross tabulations. There is also the advantage of no interference with the transaction process and of a well defined state of the data when using a separate mining database. Sometimes only a subset of the raw data is needed in data mining which can be more adequately organized for mining purposes (often relying on an variable oriented or inverted data organization). Disadvantages refer to the time effort that may be necessary for importing data to the separate mining data base, and the storage and management overhead for maintaining two data versions. For some applications, an up to date state of the data may be important.

Decision trees can deal with this high dimensional production data application. Execution time is fast, because of the one step lookahead (hill climbing), non-backtracking search through the space of all possible decision trees. However, decision trees cannot spot interactions among two or more variables and typically there exist problems for highly uneven or skewed distributed dependent variables, e.g. a binary dependent variable with nearly all cases in one of the two classes.

Because of the hill climbing, non backtracking approach, only a limited set of all possible conjunctions of selectors that can be built with the (discretized) values of the variables are examined. Often rule based methods overcome these limitations. Various search strategies exist for rule set generating methods, see [9] for more details. Another popular method generates many trees for the dataset, using statistical relevance tests to prune rules and filter them, and thus selecting best rules out of multiple trees to generate a robust, compact and accurate set of classification rules. This goes back to the observation that each tree has a few good rules and many bad ones. Figure 1 and figure 2 show examples of some rule sets that were derived with the subgroup mining system Explora [9] for this production control application.

The results of figure 1 are very untypical for KDD applications. In this case, all four result properties that are important for a rule set could be achieved: A coverage of the whole target group of bad productions with a small number of three disjoint subgroups that are highly statistically significant (exact 100% rules in this case) could be derived. We have found in the example necessary and sufficient descriptions of the target group. Due to the often noisy data situation and the inconclusiveness of the variables used for the description of target groups, such necessary and sufficient conditions for target groups will usually not be derivable.

```
Problem:     Conditions for extremely bad productions
             target group: QKG1 > 0.25,  QKG3 > 0.61

Pattern:     Probabilistic rules

Strategy:    High accuracy, Disjointness, Recursive
             exhaustive search

Production: Plant A, 1995

            1% of the productions are extremely bad

Disjoint subgroups describing this target group:

  100% of PG1 = 0.7, PG9L4 = 0,        PG2 = 0

  100% of PG8 = 0.3, PG3L8 0.28-0.33

  100% of PG2 = 0.2, QKG2  0.47-0.61, PG3 0.3-0.4,
            PG14  0.4-0.5

These 3 subgroups cover 100% of the target group.
```

Fig. 1. Conditions for very bad products

Figure 2 shows an analysis question with more typical results. These were derived in an exhaustive search process of limited depth which was run recursively. This search strategy can be seen as a generalised beam search, where not only a one level exhaustive expansion of the n best nodes is scheduled, but a multi level exhaustive expansion. Thus larger parts of the search space are heuristically processed.

We select a two level expansion procedure. So search in a space of at most two (additional) conjunctions (maximal number of conjunctions selected according to the size of the database, i.e. the number of cases and variable values) is run exhaustively considering however four pruning conditions. A subgroup is not expanded any more, if the statistical significance of the subgroup is already very high, the generality of the subgroup is low (small size), the number of target elements covered by the subgroup is low, or the statistical significance of the subgroup is highly negative. Then a small subset of all found subgroups that exceed a minimum significance level (determined according to the number of statistical tests run in the hypothesis space) is selected that is overlapping below a specified threshold (10% in this case: low overlapping) and covers the target group maximally. This subset selection problem is scheduled as a second search process. Each of the selected subgroups is expanded in a next recursion of this two-phase search and subset selection process with similar prunings and limitations on the number of (additional) conjuncts.

For this application, we use a simple conjunctive description language that does not include any internal disjunctions of values of one variable. Internal disjunctions are often useful for nominal or ordinal variables (section 5). For the predominant continuous description variables of this application, we do not apply a discretization algorithm which is dynamically embedded into the data mining search, but a static generation of taxonomies with hierarchical systems of intervals for the variables in a preprocessing step. Based on visualizations of the variable distributions, appropriate intervals were selected by the domain experts. These static discretizations are much more time efficient than dynamic discretizations, which in this application case and hardware environment (Macintosh) would not have been realizable in an interactive exploration mode with short response times. Some of the drawbacks caused by the fixed static intervals could be mitigated by the hierarchical taxonomical structure.

For a data mining search strategy, in general four components are important. First, the type of the description language has to be selected. Besides simple conjunctive descriptions built with one value selectors (a value is an element of the domain of a variable or an entry in the taxonomy), also negations of one value selectors can be included (marital status ≠ married). A next extension of the complexity of the description language (and search space) allows internal disjunctions of values, such as marital status = married or divorced.

As a second component, a neighborhood operator (expansion operator for general to specific search) generates the neighbors of a description in the partially ordered description space. For a description with internal disjunctions, the neighbors can be constructed by eliminating one of the disjunctive elements in a description.

```
Problem:    Conditions for good productions
            target group: QKG1 < 0.16,   QKG3 < 0.41

Pattern:    Probabilistic rules

Strategy:   High accuracy, Low overlapping, Recursive
            exhaustive search

Production: Plant A, 1995

            20% of the productions are good

Subgroups describing the target group:

      66% of PG2L8 = 0, PG4 <0.18
      94% of PG2L8 = 0, PG4 < 0.18, PG15 > 0.88,
           PG15L8 > 0.88
     100% of PG2L8 = 0, PG4 < 0.18, PG1  = 0.25,
           PG12 0.45-0.55

22% coverage of the target group, 9.8% overlapping

      55% of PG8 = 0.7, PG11L8 0.8-0.85
     100% of PG8 = 0.7, PG11L8 0.8-0.85, PG4 < 0.18,
           PG15L8 > 0.88
     100% of PG8 = 0.7, PG11L8 0.8-0.85, PG1L4 = 0.25

19% coverage of the target group, 5.4% overlapping

      63% of PG1 = 0.5, PG16 0.5-0.6
      90% of PG1 = 0.5, PG16 0.5-0.6, PG15 0.6-0.7,
           PG15L4 0.6-0.7
      86% of PG1 = 0.5, PG16 0.5-0.6, PG8L8 = 0.75,
           PG15L4 0.6-0.7

35% coverage of the target group, 9.4% overlapping

total coverage of target group: 66%
total overlapping: 19%
```

Fig. 2. Conditions for good productions

11

Third, the quality function measuring the interestingness of a subgroup is important. For these production applications we select a quality function that favours large deviations (and not large subgroups). However, the choice of the quality function cannot only be discussed under domain specific requirements (which in this case request large deviations, i.e. high shares of bad or good productions), but also from search aspects. Especially, the greediness of search is important. By favouring large subgroups, the greediness of a hill climbing approach can be restricted. Using taxonomies or internal disjunctions restricts the greediness and provides a more patient search [10], so that in each expansion step the size of a subgroup is not restricted too much.

Fourth, the search heuristic is an important further search aspect. Various heuristic strategies for large scale and refinement search are possible. In this application, we have selected the generalized beam search heuristic.

5 Application: Market Analysis

A next exemplary application refers to the analysis of market research data about the financial market in Germany. All leading financial institutions (banks, insurances) have joined in a common consortium to collect data on the whole market. A market research institute performs surveys by monthly interviewing 2500 persons on their behavior in the market. Several hundreds of variables are collected for each interviewed person. Most of these variables are hierarchically structured, e.g. hierarchical product categories, and have multiple values, e.g. a person can be a client of several banks or use several financial services. Since the data are captured according to a survey plan, each case has an individual weight. Such weighted, multi-valued data provide problems for many data mining systems that only assume simple rectangular one-relational data. This application has been run first with the Explora subgroup mining system and later with Data Surveyor.

Each institution represented in the consortium thus gets survey data on the whole market, included data on the competitors. Therefore the data complement the client databases of each institution. Since the surveys have been regularly collected for some twenty years, the overall database consists of several hundred thousands of cases. It is however an incremental application where the focus is on changes in the current period and in trend detection. Thus the change and trend patterns of subgroup mining are primarily used for the application.

Feature selection techniques are applied to select a subset of relevant independent variables. Sampling methods can select a subset of cases, and missing data treatment clean and amend the raw data. Various techniques to deal with missing data can be used. One possibility is to infer the missing items by exploiting relations with other variables. For example, the gender of a person in a questionnaire could be inferred from other informations (e.g. first name). However, it must be considered whether the fact that a data item is missing (some persons did not fill in their gender in the questionnaire) can provide useful informaton. In another customer retention analysis, the group of clients of a bank that did not fill in this field proved as a client group with a critical tendency that had a high probability to desert to a business competitor.

As the data set is studied for a long time, the overall client profiles are known quite well for the following analytic question: Who does (not) buy product A in the current period (e.g. year)? This question does typically not provide many interesting (novel) answers for any instantiation of A in an institution / product hierarchy. Using the change patterns of subgroup mining [4], one searches for subgroups for which the market share of a product has significantly changed in the current period (month, quarter, year) compared to the previous period. Then quite interesting results are usually detected which belong to two categories.

A first category identifies subgroups which can be explained after some moments of considerations. They are not really novel, since one has found an explanation for the behavior (e.g. some change in legislation, product policy, etc.). But usually one did not think at these subgroups before performing the mining tasks and thus these results are valuable.

A next category identifies subgroups with a behavior change for which one cannot find an easy explanation. These have to be checked in more detail, since they will reveal often errors in the data or some tricky behavior of the interviewers. In one such case, an interviewer could be identified who manipulated the interviews to save his interview time.

Alltogether, these change patterns mainly belong to the nuggets category. Not a whole overview on the change for the current period is derived, but only local subgroups are identified. The change patterns directly identify client subgroups, for which the market share has changed, or in case of trend patterns, show a special type of trend (e.g. linear monotonic increase). This is often more revealing than comparing changes in subgroup patterns that have been statically derived for individual time points. When comparing systems of subgroups (e,g. rule sets derived for several time periods), sensitivity problems of subgroup descriptions usually make the interpretation more difficult.

Good results could also be achieved by combining subgroup mining approaches with conventional modeling techniques. The subgroup mining patterns are inferred for the residuals of a model. Then the model describes the major dependency or trend and the subgroups are identified that deviate from this major line.

Primarily nominal or ordinal variables are applied as explanatory description variables in this application. Thus the type of the description language has been selected to include internal disjunctions. This proved advantageous compared to the simple conjunctive description language, because more general and larger subgroups have been identified which is requested for this application when adjusting the generality-deviation tradeoff. The internal disjunctions further present an overview on the values of a variable that behave similarly (e.g. have an overproportional market share) by including a list of these values and not just the most significant value. In most cases the found internal disjunctions had a clear interpretation. As an example, a list of those German States are identified as an internal disjunction, that constitute the (new) East German States. This disjunction could of course have also been provided as a taxonomical entry in a hierarchy. Internal disjunction languages however contribute to find such groupings dynamically and dependent on a current analytical question. Subsets of values are found that belong together within the context of the current analytic question. These subsets do usually not belong to a fixed taxonomical entry (as the Est German States), but are more loosely connected in the special context. As a special case, missing data is associated to values that play a similar role with respect to the analytic question.

Also for ordinal variables, the internal disjunction approach proved as a competitive alternative to discretization techniques. Thus based on a static prediscretization by a set of intervals, ranges of intervals have been identified that e.g. represent U-form dependencies. For instance in the patient PRIM discretization method [10], such U-form dependencies cannot be detected.

6 Conclusion: Research Problems for Subgroup Mining

The main (data) problems that may occur in a knowledge discovery task are inconclusive data, i.e. the relevant variables are missing, the cases are not representative, there are not enough target cases available, so that the data collected for a primary operational application may not be adequate for the data analysis task. Problems may also exist for redundant data (too many highly correlated data), time and space dependent data, insufficient or inappropriate domain knowledge (no relevant taxonomies to find a good generality level).

The preceding sections have shown that there is already a vast spectrum of subgroup mining variations applied successfully for a broad range of applications. However, KDD is an evolving research area, and some problems have to be solved to provide high quality discovery results.

For the descriptive patterns of subgroup mining, it must be avoided that the descriptions overfit given data. This can mainly achieved with train and test methods which are already successfully applied for classification relying on the evaluation of classification accuracy.

As mentioned in the discussion of figure 2, there are several criteria, e.g. degree of coverage, variance reduction, degree of overlapping, significance, simplicity that are jointly used to assess the quality of a set of subgroups describing a target group. Finding the best set of hypotheses among a large set of significant hypotheses is still a problem. Methods such as tree construction heuristics produce a set of rules arranged as a tree, but usually there may exist better rule sets. One approach for this problem of generating and evaluating a "best" set of hypotheses is discussed in the example of figure 2. Using Bayesian nets for subgroup results is an alternative approach that selects subgroups based on conditional independence.

A next problem area relates to providing adequate description languages. We have already mentioned the limited expressive power of propositional, attributive languages for the production application where additional variables are derived to represent the average or trend in a time or space sequence of measurements. Sometimes *first order language* based approaches can be helpful [11]. Constructive induction is another important approach related to this problem. Here, additional variables are constructed (dynamically during search) that are better suited to describe the given data. Especially for time and space related data, such derived variables can be useful when including descriptive terms based on means, slopes or other (time-) series indicators (see section 4). Dynamically starting a separate search process for finding adequate expressions in a description language is already successfully solved for the problem of discretizing numerical variables and finding geographical clusters of values for regional variables.

Integrating several aspects of interestingness, e.g. statistical significance, novelty, simplicity, usefulness, is a next problem. Future generations of systems will include discovered knowledge in their domain knowledge base to a still higher extent and use these findings for further discovery processes. Thus, they will incorporate more learning and adaptive behavior. Discovery methods could be used to learn from the users by monitoring and analysing their reactions on the discovered and presented findings to assess the novelty facet of interestingness.

For very large datasets including millions of tuples and several hundreds of variables, data reduction is important. Although high performance solutions such as Data Surveyor can extend the applications of KDD methods from the usual boundaries of common KDD systems (10**6 tuples, a few hundreds of fields) by some orders, feature selection and sampling methods are often necessary to provide time efficient interactive discoveries. Interactivity of discovery systems is important because of the explorative nature of the KDD process. Reduction of variables is also important for ensuring clear discovery results.

Explorative data analysis methods often underline the principle of robustness (compare Tukey and other protagonists). This means for KDD that discovery results should not differ too sensitively respective to small alterations of the data, description language or selected values of the dependent variables. As an example, consider the definition of the target group in figure 2. If the specification QKG3 > 0.61 would be slightly changed to QKG3 > 0.62 (assuming no large distributional effects for the variable QKG3), this should not lead to a totally diverse set of rules identified in the discovery process. The main concern in KDD has been on accuracy, whereas robustness until now only plays a minor role in discovery research. Interactive visualization techniques can help to analyse different sensitivity aspects [10].

A variety of patterns is available to execute discovery tasks such as identification of interesting subgroups. *Second order discovery* to compare and combine the results for different patterns could be necessary, especially if many analysis questions are issued to the data. An example refers to combining change patterns with static patterns for the two time periods that define the reference of change.

A next point relates to changing data and domain knowledge. This includes incremental mining methods adapting existing results according to the addition or modification of a small number of tuples and comparing new discovery results (for the new data) with the preceding results. Incremental methods operating on sequential (or also parallel) batches of data are also useful for achieving scalability or anytime data mining.

The role of domain knowledge in KDD is restricting search to exclude uninteresting findings and to increase time efficiency. This technique has been mainly applied in *Inductive Logic Programming* approaches, but should be more extensively applied also for the mainstream KDD methods.

Finally there are a lot of technical challenges to ensure efficient and interactive KDD processes. High performance solutions are necessary for VLDB applications. Other problems relate to the integration of KDD systems with other systems such as database systems or statistical packages. One promising development direction is characterized by incorporating KDD functionality within DBMS systems.

References

1. Hand, D.: Data mining - reaching beyond statistics. Journal of Official Statistics 3 (1998).
2. Agrawal, R., Mannila, H., Srikant, R., Toivonen, H., Verkamo, I.: Fast Discovery of Association Rules. In: Fayyad, U., Piatetsky-Shapiro, G., Smyth, P., Uthurusamy, R. (eds.): Advances in Knowledge Discovery and Data Mining. MIT Press, Cambridge (1996) 307 – 328.
3. Mannila, H., Toivonen, H., Verkamo, I.: Discovery of frequent episodes in event sequences. Data Mining and Knowledge Discovery 1 (3) (1997) 259 – 289.
4. Klösgen, W.: Deviation and association patterns for subgroup mining in temporal, spatial, and textual data bases. In: Polkowski, L., Skowron, A. (eds.): Rough Sets and Current Trends in Computing. Lecture Notes in Artificial Intelligence, Vol. 1424. Springer-Verlag, Berlin Heidelberg New York (1998) 1 – 18.
5. Feldman, R., Klösgen, W., Zilberstein, A.: Visualization Techniques to Explore Data Mining Results for Document Collections. In: Heckerman, D., Mannila, H., Pregibon, D. (eds.): Proceedings of Third International Conference on Knowledge Discovery and Data Mining (KDD-97). AAAI Press, Menlo Park (1997).
6. Wrobel, S.: An Algorithm for Multi-relational Discovery of Subgroups. In: Komorowski, J., Zytkow, J. (eds): Principles of Data Mining and Knowledge Discovery. Lecture Notes in Artificial Intelligence, Vol. 1263. Springer-Verlag, Berlin Heidelberg New York (1997) 78 – 87.
7. Siebes, A.: Data Surveying: Foundations of an Inductive Query Language. In: Fayyad, U., Uthurusamy, R. (eds.): Proceedings of the First International Conference on Knowledge Discovery and Data Mining (KDDM95). AAAI Press, Menlo Park, CA: (1995).
8. Klösgen, W.: Exploration of Simulation Experiments by Discovery. In: Fayyad, U., Uthurusamy, R. (eds.): Proceedings of AAAI-94 Workshop on Knowledge Discovery in Databases. AAAI Press, Menlo Park (1994).
9. Klösgen, W.: Explora: A Multipattern and Multistrategy Discovery Assistant. In: Fayyad, U., Piatetsky-Shapiro, G., Smyth, P., Uthurusamy, R. (eds.): Advances in Knowledge Discovery and Data Mining. MIT Press, Cambridge, MA (1996).
10. Friedman, J., Fisher, N.: Bump Hunting in High-Dimensional Data. Statistics and Computing (1998).
11. Quinlan, R.: Learning Logical Definitions from Relations. Machine Learning 5(3) (1990).

Knowledge Discovery in Texts: A Definition, and Applications

Yves Kodratoff

CNRS, LRI Bât. 490 Univ. Paris-Sud, F - 91405 Orsay Cedex
yk@lri.fr

Abstract. The first part of this paper will give a general view of Knowledge Discovery in Data (KDD) in order to insist on how much it differs from the fields it stems from, and in some cases, how much it opposes them.

The second part will a definition of Knowledge Discovery in Texts (KDT), as opposed to what is known presently under the name of information retrieval, information extraction, or knowledge extraction. I will provide an example of a real-life set of rules obtained by what I want to define as KDT techniques.

1.0 Introduction

KDD is better known in the industry under the name of Data Mining (DM). Actually, industrialists should be more interested in KDD which comprises the whole process of data selection, data cleaning, transfer to a DM technique, applying the DM technique, validating the results of the DM technique, and finally interpreting them for the user. In general, this process is a cycle that improves under the criticism of the expert. Inversely, DM designates a set of information extraction techniques stemming from scientific fields known as Statistics, Machine Learning, or Neural Networks.

Before defining KDT, and since this definition will rely on the one of KDD, I will recall what I believe to be the seven differences between KDD and the existing methods of Data Analysis. In some cases, these differences introduce a new point of view in Science (as for instance, acceptance of the inductive type of reasoning).

2.0 What makes Knowledge Discovery in Data (KDD) different

2.1 The "US" point of view

The first one is the standard of the KDD community that developed in the USA : **KDD extracts potentially useful and previously unknown knowledge from huge**

amounts of data, and creates techniques adapted to such a problem. This definition emphasizes the need for very fast algorithms, which is hardly original ; and, inversely, asking for **previously unknown knowledge** leads us to consider as interesting the topic of finding knowledge that might contradict the existing one. We will elaborate later, in section 2.5, on "**potentially useful**".

Until now, all efforts in Machine Learning (ML) and Statistics have been aimed at finding knowledge that does not contradict the existing one : this is even the principle underlying the development and success of Inductive Logic Programming (ILP), where the new created clauses must not contradict the existing ones.
In KDD, an interesting nugget of knowledge might contradict a large body of knowledge, it will be considered all the more interesting! Inversely, discovering a large number of well-known rules is considered to be the typical trap that KDD systems should be able to avoid.

2.3 The historical point of view

The second one is that **KDD integrates several knowledge acquisition approaches**, and this is not just a concatenation of these approaches. Integrating these methods will generate new solutions, and new scientific problems, imperfectly dealt with until now. The scientific fields to integrate are various, dealing with Machine Learning, including Symbolic, Statistical, Neuronal, Bayesian types of learning, and Knowledge Acquisition, querying Data Bases, Man-Machine Interactions, and the Cognitive Sciences. Until very recently, these fields have developed methodologies that consider a very specific aspect of reality.
A first, still incomplete, instance of such an integrated approach is illustrated by the large KDD systems now found on the market, the most famous of them are: *Intelligent Miner* of IBM, *MineSet* of Silicon Graphics, *Clementine* of ISL, and the new versions of *SAS* that include now a visualization very pleasant to use.

2.4 The user's point of view

The third one is the **importance of the user's goal in biasing the acquisition of knowledge**. Induction is always an intellectually dangerous process if not tightly controlled. It should be obvious that the user's goals are the best of the biases necessary to avoid inventing trivialities. Up to now, academic research neglected this view of the problem, and still too few papers deal with it because existing research fields try to develop techniques that are, as far as possible, universal and that pretend to be useful to every user instead of being specific (if they are, they are called "mere engineering", not "Science"). Some research has been done nevertheless in the KDD community under the name of "rule validation" or "measures of interest," and it tries to take into account the user's requirements.

Besides the classical statistical significance, and the simple coverage and confidence tests, this community has used several other measures of statistical significance, such as "conviction". It has also developed several measures of interest, such as Bandhari's Attribute Focusing [Bhandari, 1994], Gras' intensity of implication [Gras & Lahrer, 1993], Suzuki's exception detection [Suzuki, 1997; Suzuki & Kodratoff, 1998], and Feldman's maximal association rules [Feldman, 1998].

2.5 The scientific point of view

The fourth KDD-specific concept is a kind of intellectual scandal for most scientists: it is the recognition that **validation by measures of accuracy is far from enough.** Up to now, all researchers, including those working on the symbolic aspects of learning, have been measuring their degree of success only by comparing accuracy, and most of them do not imagine that yet another solution might exist. A method is looked at as better if its accuracy is better. KDD, still timidly, but with an increasing strength, pushes forward the idea that there are at least two other criteria of more importance than accuracy, and calls them "comprehensibility" and usability (or simply : usefulness). A positive example of this attitude is the commercial software, *MineSet*, which devoted most of its efforts to providing the user with visual tools to help the user to understand the exact meaning of the induced decision trees.

2.6 The epistemological point of view

Even though the KDD community is very silent about it, this requirement is The fifth one is that the **knowledge extracted will modify the behavior of a human or mechanical agent , it thus has to be grounded in the real world.** Until now, the solutions looked for by computer scientists have been based on providing more universality, more precision, and more mathematical proofs to the "knowledge" they provide to the users. In opposition, the results of a KDD software have to be directly usable, even if they are particular, imprecise, and unproved.

Even though the KDD community is very silent about it, this requirement is linked to the famous Turing problem. Recent discussions about this problem show that ungrounded knowledge is the key to make the difference between a human and a computer (see ["Think", 1994; Searle, 1990, 1984] for a very thorough discussion of this problem). Usable grounded knowledge is exactly what is needed to solve Turing's problem.

2.7 The logical point of view

The sixth one is that KDD relies heavily on the induction process. Most scientists still show a kind of blind faith in favor of deduction. The argument that has been recently presented [Partridge, 1997] against the blind use of deduction is one of efficiency : deductive processes can become so complex that there is no hope of achieving them until their end, and an approximation of them is necessary. If this approximation happens to be less precise (and I'd like to add : or less useful, or less comprehensible

... the last is very often the case) than the model obtained by induction, then there is no objective grounds to stick to deduction. Elsewhere, I have developed [Kodratoff & Bisson, 1992, Kodratoff, 1994], at length, the idea that induction contains complex chains of reasoning steps, and that an analysis of this complexity leads to a better understanding of the conditions into which safe induction can be performed, and safe confirmation procedures can be built, in spite of the famous Hempel paradox.

2.8 The "clean hand" point of view

The seventh one stems more from the practical point of view : specialists in ML and Statistics tend to expect clean data to work upon. They consider that data cleaning and selection is pure engineering that does not deserve their scientific attention. KDD holds that data preparation is an integral part of the KDD process, and holds as much scientific respect as any other step. I must add that most specialists in the KDD field still hate dirtying their hands, but I claim this to be a *passé*-ist attitude that will have to change.

2.9 Conclusion

These seven conditions, and particularly the last four ones, oppose current academic behavior. The argument I meet most often is the following : "Since you ask all these requirements that preclude measurements, and since little can be proved of the processes you are studying, then you are defining an art and not a science". It is true that there does not yet exist an established measure of comprehensibility nor of usefulness, but we just saw that these measures are far from being out of reach. It is also true that, due to its strong industrial involvement, KDD looks forward more eagerly to new applications than to new theories, and therefore it still looks much more like engineering than science but the strong determination of the KDD community to maintain a high scientific level insures that a safe balance will be respected.

3. Existing Natural Language Processing (NLP) tools

The general goal of NLP is to provide a better NL understanding through the use of computers. This seems to contain a contradiction since NL already contains useful and understandable information. It is nevertheless obvious that both comprehensibility and usefulness can be improved in many cases. For instance, a large amount of NL can be much more useful when summarized.

Since the well-known competition organized by the DARPA took place [MUC-n, 199m], Information Retrieval (IR) and Information Extraction (IE) have obtained a large number of results showing the feasibility of what were previously impossible tasks. The progress in these fields is so striking that it cannot be ignored by any one who wishes to work on KDT. This paper intends to show the commonalities and differences (or even, the oppositions) among the problems both fields claim to solve. IR is a well-known research field that provides a user with the best available texts that correspond to key-words given by the user. There is no discussion about this definition, this is why I will not develop this topic here. Inversely, IE is a much newer field, and it might be worth to explain what it is about, especially in view of the fact that it may soon provide the NLP systems from which KDT can start working.

3.1 Information retrieval (IR)

IR is classically defined as selecting the documents relevant to query, and it can be described as: "given a bag of words, find the texts containing the same bag of words." Due to the multiple meanings of a word, this task might become untractable.

Most existing IR systems are based on the assumption of a large query. It happens that most www users query by very few words. In order to improve on this undesirable state, Grefenstette (1997) proposes 3 solutions.
- ☐ The first one is due to Bourdoncle: answer the query by giving the words appearing in the text searched near the original query words, and let the user click on the relevant ones, in order to refine the query.
- ☐ The second one, due to Hearst: answer at first the query by providing not the answers themselves, but clusters of answers characterized by a set of words. The user has to choose which cluster best represents his/her intentions.
- ☐ The third one is due to Grefenstette himself: improve the existing web browsers by including some NLP techniques into them.

3.2 Information extraction (IE)

IE is defined by Wilks (1997, with slightly different words) as follows: "Given a structural template of typed variables, how to instantiate it in a way that fits a text?"
A typical example is given Grishman (1997).

From the purely applicative point of view, IE aims at providing a user with such filled up frames, from texts, in order to highlight some information that might be considered as hidden in the text.

From the purely scientific point of view, IE aims at generalizing the four above steps in order to make them applicable to a wide variety of texts, not to be application specific.

3.3 What is information in IE?

We can propose the following definitions.

☐ Data
Data is a NL text expressing implicit relations among its components.
What is typical about data is that it is only partly understandable by a human, who
needs some machine help to complete understanding.

☐ Information
*Information is one of the relations now given in a machine usable format. It can
also be that a relation implicit in the data has been made explicit for a human.*
Information is thus, on one hand, ambiguously defined, depending on whether it is
addressed to a human or a machine. On the other hand, it is unambiguously defined
as a set of "explicit relations".

☐ Knowledge
Knowledge is the result of processed information, comprehensible by a human.
What is typical of knowledge is that it is the result of a complex processing, not
that it is useful to an agent. From our KDD perspective, knowledge and
information are somewhat confused here.

4. An example of an early attempt at knowledge extraction

This paper presents an analysis of 18 of the texts issued after the 27 attacks by the
"Fighting Communist Cells", Belgium 1984-1985. It uses French adaptation of
Martingale's "Regressive Imagery Dictionary" ("Dictionaire d'Imagerie Régressive")
composed of 3 363 words and roots assigned to 29 categories of primary thinking, to
7 categories of emotions, and to 7 categories of secondary thinking (the last one is a
supertag attached to some categories).

It uses as well a semantic atlas of emotion concepts which scores them along three
dimensions: pleasantness, arousal, emotionality.

It uses also a semantic atlas of aggressiveness concepts, scoring them along four
dimensions: intensity,   institutional/interpersonal,   physical/moral,
acceptable/unacceptable.
The authors created a semantic atlas of terrorist's targets in 7 categories (see infra).
Four experiments are reported
   Analysis 1: rates per category over the 18 texts. Produces a temporal sequence
   looked for regression analysis. It produces patterns; some perhaps are not purely
   random.
   Analysis 2: cuts each text into 20 segments, produces 20 categories over the texts.
   Carries then same analysis as above (variation of the categories over the texts
   themselves). It produces some non random patterns.
   Analysis 3: select the content words more than 50, produces a confusion matrix of
   86 words over 18 texts. Five main "factors" are detected, "marxist ideology",
   "terrorism as a concrete utopia" etc.).
   Analysis 4: *An attempt at KDT: "an exercise in prediction."*, looks for associations
   among factors, e.g., factor 2 predicts factor 1, classes the targets into 7 classes, and

rate the actual attack in these classes: political, military, military-industrial, Belgian/foreign, economic, State buildings, financial, and finds associations among some factors and some next target types.

This last analysis answers the question: what type of target will be attacked knowing the text of the last attack? This looks more like knowledge than information, but the authors seem to be very afaraid to perform this analysis, and they themselves put forward all kinds of disclaimers about it.

Another question they could have been asking the data is: Is there a correlation between some characters of the text and the time clapsed before the next attack, i.e., how to predict the date of the next attack?

5. A definition of Knowledge Discovery in Texts (KDT)

This expression is being used to cover any kind of text analysis, more due to the fashion linked to the word "mining" than for any real progress. I know of at least three different problems, already well known in the NLP community, for which some industrialists claim to be doing "text mining" : syntactical and semantical analysis, information retrieval (i.e., finding the texts associated to a set of key-words ; the French name : "research of documents" is less ambiguous than the American one), and information extraction. As we have seen in section 3, by no means, can it be said that these problems are easy ones, and they even can be part of a general KDT system, but for each of them, it would better to go on being called by its own name.

Rather than giving new names to old topics, I'd like to suggest defining KDT rather as the science that **discovers knowledge in texts,** *where "knowledge" is taken with the meaning used in KDD* (see section 2.5 above), that is: the knowledge extracted has to be grounded in the real world, and will modify the behavior of a human or mechanical agent. This definition introduces in KDT all the problems already described as being proper to KDD, and shows very well how KDT differs from NLP.

a. That KDT **discovers** knowledge means that induction is used, while NLP never had the least interest in inductive processes, except in applying ML techniques to NLP.
b. That knowledge is understandable and directly usable by an agent, qualifies all the statistical tables or principal component analysis, etc. as not belonging to KDT, even though many NLP specialists present them as "knowledge". Those tables transform the text into data, and they can be used as a starting point for KDT. They can thus be very useful for KDT, and be included in the whole KDT process, but they do not constitute a complete KDT system.
c. That knowledge is discovered in (a large amount of) **textS**, instead of in (one or a few) text(s) shows also that KDT does not aim at improving text understanding, but at discovering unsuspected relations holding in a body of texts. I will give an example of this difference just below in section 6: the rule given describes knowledge contained in two years of miscellaneous *"Le Monde"* articles, instead

of showing any kind of deep understanding of one particular article. It must be noticed that a part of the NLP community attacked this problem already (and called it very aptly "knowledge extraction"), but they used statistical tools without interpreting their results, and that did not allow them to go very far in the usefulness nor the comprehensibility of their results as we have seen above, in section 4.

6. An example of KDT

I will give here an example of a set of rules discovered by KDT, without details on the method used (see [Kodratoff, 1999] for details), but with the hope that it illustrates the power of KDT, and that KDT provides knowledge about texts of a striking nature, that has never been discovered before.

Existing NLP systems provide an analysis of the texts contents, with variations depending on the tool which is used. The problem for KDT is to transform these analyses into usable data.

For example, consider the tool named *"Tropes"* (presently available for the French language only), sold by the company Acetic, which executes an analysis of the text. It provides, for each text, a table of syntactic and semantic results. This constitutes a table, the rows of which are the texts, and the column of which are the % of each feature of the text. For instance, the % of temporal junctors is a syntactic feature, and the % of apparition of a given concept in each text, is a semantic feature. An example of such a concept is "catastrophy" in order to give the probability that some of the words that are an instance of a catastrophy, such as 'accident', 'flooding', etc. are met in the text.

We used a set of several thousands of papers found in two years of the French newspaper *Le Monde*, that were selected on the only criterion that they were relatively large papers, in order to allow *Tropes* to work at its best. A preliminary analysis, performed on the output of *Tropes*, and, using the KDD tool *Clementine* of the company ISL, produced the following rules concluding on the fact that *Le Monde* has been largely speaking of the concept catastrophy in one of the texts analyzed.

catastrophy = much-talked-of	IF
North-America = not-at-all-talked-of & Europe = much-talked-of	OR
communication = meanly-talked-of & conflict = much-talked-of	OR
Europe = much-talked-of & family = not-at-all-talked-of	OR
Europe = much-talked-of & woman = not-at-all-talked-of	OR
Economy = not-at-all-talked-of & Europe = much-talked-of	

This set of rules expresses that, in the papers that insist on a catastrophic event, two concepts were also very often talked of. The one of Europe, which underlines an unexpected behavior of this newspaper : when a catastrophy happens in another part of the world other than Europe, the concept of catastrophy is much less strongly evoked. The other is the one of a conflict, in which case, *Le Monde* speaks also of communication. Very interesting is also the analysis of the statistically significant absence of evoked concepts : when speaking very strongly of a catastrophy, *Le Monde* does not speak at all of North America, family, women, and economy. Notice that among the some 300 possible concepts *Le Monde* could avoid speaking of, those are the only ones significantly absent when speaking strongly of catastrophy. A detailed analysis would be necessary to understand why these absent concepts are significant by their absence. It nevertheless shows very clearly that we have here a kind of knowledge that has never before been noticed in this newspaper, nor in any kind of texts. The amount of potential research is enormous.

7. Five examples of topics belonging to KDT research

The goal of this section is simply to illustrate the fact that KDD research might indeed exist, and that it will solve problems that have not yet dealt with by the NLP community, or that have been acknowledged as unsolvable by this community. It should not be used as a definition of what can be KDT research. For instance, I do not evoke the mining that can be done without some text understanding, by a simple analysis of some statistical properties of the text, such as "multigrams" analysis that, I believe, belong also to the KDT field.

7.1 Applying unsupervised rule learning (also called: association detection)

This technique consists of finding relations among the fields of the data. In the domain of DB this phenomenon is called functional dependencies, in Statistics, it is called, correlation, and in KDD, associations. A peculiarity of KDD is that it developed specific techniques to handle Boolean data in a very efficient way. Thus, most "association detection algorithms" ask the user to put the data in the Boolean form. Whatever the form of the data is, unsupervised rule learning always amounts to finding patterns in the data, such that the value of a field implies some knowledge about the value of another field. It is often given the form of a statistical implication, such that

IF field$_i$ = V$_i$ and field$_j$= V$_j$ and ... THEN field$_k$= V$_k$ and field$_q$= V$_q$ and ... (with belief x%)

Starting form texts, it should generate rules an example of which has been already given is section 6. These rules constitute a kind of "intelligent" summary of the set of texts (not of one text only, as already done in NLP).

Using our definitions above, it will be even possible to find surprising rules, or contradictory ones. In both cases, this will constitute a novel way of summarizing a set of texts, as believed impossible until now.

I suggest that an immediate concern for the KDT research should be the discovery of "interesting" rules since texts will be obviously the source of millions of uninteresting rules, especially those that link the concepts that are not spoken of in the texts, which are in a much greater number than the ones that are spoken of. A description of the existing some 8 measures of interest (including measures of statistical significance) is given in [Kodratoff, 1999].

7.2 Applying unsupervised class learning

It creates clusters, also called categories or classes, out of the data. Mainly four different techniques are presently competing, with various successes [Kodratoff, 1999], and up to now, no methodology for measuring the quality of their results has been proposed.

These techniques will cluster together texts, not because of some relatively superficial communality, but because of possibly very deep syntactic and/or semantic resemblance, depending on the choice the user will make of the feature used during the clustering phase.

This will give a large new degree of freedom relatively to existing systems of text clustering Besides, the basis of the clustering will be done on the account of a given NLP system, and independently of it. Any new improvement in the field of NLP can be at once taken into account.

I suggest that an immediate concern for the KDT research should be on the ways to measure the quality of a clustering. When clustering data, it is indeed very hard to have any idea of the experimental quality of an algorithm. Inversely, users are very good at criticizing the clustering of texts, and this should lead to the opportunity to build up test sets, usable later for judging the quality of any data clustering algorithm.

7.3 Applying supervised classification learning

Supervised classification can be defined as follows : given a set of classes and data supposed to "explain" why objects belong to these classes (this is often called a description in extension), find a rule (called a classification function) that recognizes to which class belongs each object (i.e., a description in intention). This is applied to the determination of the class of a new, still unknown example. These techniques thus ask for the designation, by the user, of a target class, and the goal of the system is to find an intentional way to describe the relations between this class and the other features.

The techniques developed by the learning community are fast enough to be used systematically to analyze what a set of texts propose as covert recognition functions for different concepts of interest. For instance, the relation between the press comments and up and down of a company stock can be easily analyzed.

Looking for such sets of rules over time can describe very accurately changes in the way some concepts are perceived in the texts.

7.4 Building ontologies

Nédellec and Faure [1998] have adapted to the automatic building of taxonomies of terms, the approach of Disciple (an early publication is : [Kodratoff & Tecuci, 1987] ; a more modern description is available in [Tecuci, 1998], and an indisputable presentation of the striking results of Disciple is given, in a somewhat hidden way, under the name of "GMU's results", in figures 10-12 of [Cohen et al., 1999]) . Nédellec's results show clearly that hand-built taxonomies as presently done, tend to violate the use of the words as it actually happens in the texts (in other words : it seems that we have a conceptual idea of the relationships among terms that is not reflected in our language, hence the primary importance of automatically building these taxonomies). These authors use an existing syntactical analyzer (presently : Sylex [Constant, 1995]) in order to obtain lists of words belonging to the same subcategorization frame, that is appearing in the same syntactic position relative to a given verb. For instance, in the sentences "Georges goes to Paris," and "The boys go to the lake", Paul and "the boys" belong to the same subcategorization frame of the verb "to go to", and "Paris" and "the lake" belong together to another frame. This provides their system, Asium, with a first set of classes that will be the leaves of the taxonomy. They define a distance measure that allows them to aggregate some leaves into nodes, that can be in turn aggregated until all nouns are in the same large class. The user has to approve all new created clusters, and to approve of the implicit extensions of the subcategorization frames. For instance, suppose that "pot" belongs to the frame of "to cook in" and that "oven" belong to the one of "to broil in". Suppose also that the system proposes to put "pot" and "oven" in the same class. Then the system will ask the user if it is acceptable to cook into an oven (the user can here give a positive answer), and if it is acceptable to broil in a pot, which will be rejected by the user. The system will remember the exact extension for each verb.

It seems that NLP asks also for both generality and part-of relationships. It is thus urgent to improve on Nédellec's work by being able of acquiring part-of relationship in a text.

7.5 Refining semantic nets

Some NLP systems use a semantic net, like the one needed by the apprentice systems aimed at problem solving, such as Apt and Disciple. The systems learn automatically new, more accurate, problem solving rules, but their semantic net is fixed, exactly as is the one of the NLP systems. It is obvious that adding to them some ability to revise their knowledge (as in the AI field called knowledge revision) will increase their ability to better solve problems.

The twist in thinking I propose here is the following : the user's answer, instead of modifying a set of problem solving rules, will be used to modify the semantic net. Knowledge revision has been essentially on the numeric side up to now, that the net has a fixed structure, and only the beliefs attached to each node are modified by learning. In the case of learning form texts, the topic of learning or changing the structure of the semantic net, besides its belief coefficients, becomes the primary one. There is therefore here a gold mine of hard problems, of which it can be said that even little progress will yield large improvements.

A first approach, that can be implemented easily, relies on the fact that the ILP community has been producing a large number of efficient knowledge revision systems. I thus suggest that the semantic net be translated in an equivalent clause form, the revision happen in clause form, and, once the revision executed, the modified set of clauses be back translated as a semantic net.

Let us at first describe how easy some changes that be performed when meeting new information in texts. We shall give then an example which, though relatively simple, cannot happen without rethinking the semantic net.

Example easy to handle Suppose, for example, that one possesses an ontology of cars containing relationships:

Motor -- [PartOf] -- Engine -- [PoweredBy] -- < gas, diesel >
That can be written as the 2 clauses:
Engine (car1, x, y) :- PartOf(car1, x), Motor(x), gas (y)
Engine (car1, x, y) :- PartOf(car1, x), Motor(x), diesel(y)
where car1 is a variable instantiated by the car under study.

Suppose that one meets a text saying that a car works with electricity, the modification of the semantic system is very simple, it amounts to adding an element in the set of allowed energies:

Motor -- [PartOf] -- Engine -- [PoweredBy] -- < gasoline, diesel, electricity >
which is equivalent to adding the clause :
Engine (car1, x, y) :- PartOf(car1, x), Motor(x), electricity (y)

Example hard to handle Suppose now that a text tells that a car works with energy produced by solar cells. It is less easy to modify the semantic net to take into account this information because "solar cell" produces an "energy" that will be used. It could be necessary to refine the definition of energy since, in fact, the energy used in the gasoline engine is of thermal nature, and the heat is produced by the gasoline that burns etc. A human can realize that it is nor really necessary to go into all these details, and that a simplified semantic net can still be useful if taxonomies of energies are introduced, as in the following :

Motor -- [PartOf] — Engine -- [PoweredBy] — Petroleum derivative -- [IsA] -- <gas, diesel>

I

Electricity generator -- [IsA] -- <solar cell>

In clause representation, this new set of relationships is expressed by:

Engine (car1, x, y) :- PartOf(car1, x), Motor(x), petroleum derivative(y)
petroleum derivative(x) :- diesel(x)
petroleum derivative(x) :- gasoline (x)
Engine (car1, x, y) :- PartOf(car1, x), Motor(x), electricity generator(y)
electrical device (x) :- solar cell (x)

The changes are actually standard changes executed by ILP knowledge refinement systems. Nevertheless, we must be aware that the simplification of forgetting the exact role of energy cannot be make automatic. For instance, replace "electricity generator" by "electrical device", and see that you have been introducing a "toaster" as possibly powering a car. This type of mistake is happening often when semantic nets are built, but they are very well dealt with by the generating approach of Disciple and Apt that use their semantic nets in order to generate examples submitted to the user. For instance, after introducing the concept of "electrical device" into the motor of a car, the system would ask the user if a "toaster can provide power to the engine of a car", thus underlining the mistake that has been made previously.

8. Conclusion

This paper discusses some of the most striking features of what I believe to be an entirely new field of research, and which corresponds roughly to what the existing KDD community recognizes as being its problems. This last statement is largely unproved, but at least I can claim, in a somewhat jokingly way, that even though some will disclaim some of the properties I am putting forward, nobody will disclaim all these properties. The most striking instance of the disclaimer that KDD specialists will do is that none of the members of the existing KDD community will acknowledge that they are dealing with the Turing problem. Nevertheless, they will all acknowledge that they want to discover usable knowledge, which means grounded knowledge, which means dealing with the Turing problem, like it or not.

Moreover, the consequences of these definitions are tested by defining, in turn, with their help, yet another new research field, that I name KDT. An example of the kind of knowledge it can yield has been provided. This kind of knowledge is absolutely new, and expresses properties that link a large number of texts together (instead of analyzing one text). It shows that, at least, the definitions proposed can lead to new results, and indeed define a new field of research.

REFERENCES

Bhandari, I. "Attribute focusing: Machine-Assisted Knowledge discovery Applied to Software Production Process Control", *Knowledge Acquisition* 6, 271-294, 1994.

Cohen P., Schrag R., Jones E., Pease A., Lin A., Starr B., Gunning D., Burke M., "The DARPA High-Performance Knowledge Bases Project," AI Magazine 19, vol. 4, pp. 25-49, 1998.

Constant "L'analyseur syntaxique Sylex," in Cinquième école d'été du CNET, 1995.

Darànyi, S., Abrànyi, A., Kovàcs G., "Knowledge Extraction From Ethnopoetic Texts by Multivariate Statistical Methods," in Ephraim Nissan, Klaus Schmidt (Eds.) "From Information to Knowledge" Intellect, Oxford, GB, 1995, pp. 261-268.

Feldman R., Unpublished Communication at ECML workshop on Text Mining, 1998.

Gras R., Lahrer A., "L'implication statistique: une nouvelle méthode d'analyse des données," Mathématiques Informatique et Sciences Humaines 120,:5-31, 1993.

Grefenstette G., "Short Query Linguistic Expansion Techniques: Palliating One-Word Queries by Providing Intermediate Structure to Text," in Maria Theresa Paziensa (Ed.) "Information Extraction," Springer 1997, pp.

Grishman R., "Information Extraction: Techniques and Challenges," in Maria Theresa Paziensa (Ed.) "Information Extraction," Springer 1997, pp. 10-27.

Hogenraad, R., Bestgen, Y., Nysten, J. L. "Terrorist Rhetoric: Texture and Architecture," in Ephraim Nissan, Klaus Schmidt (Eds.) "From Information to Knowledge" Intellect, Oxford, GB, 1995, pp. 48-59.

Kodratoff Y., Tecuci G. : "DISCIPLE-1 : Interactive Apprentice System in weak theory Fields", Proc. IJCAI-87, Milan Aug. 87, pp. 271-273. See also: "What is an Explanation in DISCIPLE" Proc. Intern. Workshop in ML, Irvine 1987, pp. 160-166.

Kodratoff Y, Bisson G. "The epistemology of conceptual clustering: KBG, an implementation", Journal of Intelligent Information System, 1:57-84, 1992.

Kodratoff Y., "Induction and the Organization of Knowledge", Machine Learning: A Multistrategy Approach, volume 4, Tecuci G. et Michalski R. S. (Eds.), pages 85-106. Morgan-Kaufmann, San Francisco CA, 1994.

Kodratoff Y., "Research topics in Knowledge Discovery in Data and Texts," submitted.

MUC-n, 199m; n = 3-6; m = 1, 2, 3, 5; Proceedings of the nth Message Understanding Conference, Morgan Kaufmann, 199m.

Nédellec C., Faure D., "A Corpus-based Conceptual Clustering Method for Verb Freames and Ontology Acquisition," in P. Velardi (Ed.) LREC workshop, pp. 5-12, Granada, May 1998.

Partridge D., "The Case for Inductive Programming," IEEE Computer 30, 1, 36-41, 1997. A more complete version in: "The Case for Inductive Computing Science," in Computational Intelligence and Software Engineering, Pedrycz & Peters (Eds.) World Scientific, in press.

Searle J. R. Minds, brains & science, Penguin books, London 1984.

Searle J. R., Scientific American n°262, 1990, pp. 26-31.

Sebag M., "2nd order Understandability of Disjunctive Version Spaces," Workshop on Machine Learning and Comprehensibility organized at IJCAI-95, LRI Report, Universite Paris-Sud, 1995.

Sebag M., "Delaying the choice of bias: A disjunctive version space approach," Proc. 13th International Conference on Machine Learning, Saitta L. (Ed.), pp. 444-452, Morgan Kaufmann, CA 1996.

Suzuki E. "Autonomous Discovery of Reliable Exception Rules," Proc. KDD-97, 259-262, 1997.

Suzuki E., Kodratoff Y., "Discovery of Surprising Exception Rules Based on Intensity of Implication", in Principles of Data Mining and Knowledge Discovery, Zytkow J. & Quafafou M. (Eds.), pp. 10-18, LNAI 1510, Springer, Berlin 1998.

Tecuci G., Building Intelligent Agents, Academic Press, 1988.

Think, June 1993, a review published by ITK, Univ. Tilburg, Warandelaan 2, PO Box 90153, 5000 Le Tilburg, The Netherlands.

Wilks Y., "Information Extraction as a Core Language Technology", in Maria Theresa Paziensa (Ed.) "Information Extraction," Springer 1997, pp. 1-9.

Semantic Ontology Tools in IS Design

R.A. Meersman[1]

Vrije Universiteit Brussel (VUB)
Building G/10, Pleinlaan 2
B-1050 Brussels Belgium
meersman@vub.ac.be

Abstract. The availability of computerized lexicons, thesauri and "ontologies" –we discuss this terminology– makes it possible to formalize semantic aspects of information as used in the analysis, design and implementation of information systems (and in fact general software systems) in new and useful ways. We survey a selection of relevant ongoing work, discuss different issues of semantics that arise, and characterize the resulting computerized information systems, called CLASS for Computer-Lexicon Assisted Software Systems. The need for a "global" common ontology (lexicon, thesaurus) is conjectured, and some desirable properties are proposed. We give a few examples of such CLASS-s and indicate avenues of current and future research in this area. In particular, certain problems can be identified with well-known existing lexicons such as CYC and WordNet, as well as with sophisticated representation- and inference engines such as KIF or SHOE. We argue nevertheless that large public lexicons should be simple, i.e. their semantics become implicit by agreement among "all" users, and ideally completely application independent. In short, the lexicon or thesaurus then becomes the semantic domain for all applications.

1. Introduction

The formal treatment of semantics in information systems has always been an important and difficult issue -though often implicit or even tacit- in the analysis, design and implementation of such systems. The literature abounds with different ways and attempts to represent the meaning of data and information for use in and by databases and their applications in computerized information systems. We contend that computer-based "ontologies" (we shall make this term precise in what follows, but use it in the meantime to cover lexicons and thesauri) provide a useful way for formalizing the semantics of represented information. In fact we shall argue that such ontologies, in principle, can *actually be* the semantic domain for an information system in a very concrete and useful manner. The caveat "in principle" is needed since current ontologies (lexicons, thesauri) are not (yet) constructed or available in forms that quite suit this purpose.

Modern distributed object (DO) technology such as CORBA [OMG95], DCOM [Red97] etc. makes it ever more likely, and desirable, that objects or agents performing interesting services "meet" interested consumers and applications without

---

[1] This research was partially supported by the ESPRIT Project "TREVI", nr. 23311 under the European Union 4th Framework Programme

prior knowledge of each other's design and precise functionality. Mediators, wrappers and other devices have been proposed to help make this possible, but these are not at present "runtime" solutions. The sheer multitude of such objects/agents in the future dictates that the necessary agreements will have to be negotiated in real-time as the "meeting" occurs. Short of a galaxy-wide standard for programming and data modeling it is hard to imagine that these agreements can occur without the use of sophisticated and general lexicons, thesauri or ontologies. These will need to be (a) very large resource(s), possibly only one per language, but (b) with a rather simple, "semantics-less" structure that makes them nearly completely independent from any domain-specific applications.

Naturally, this necessitates that instead a priori and mostly *implicit* agreements must exist about the contents (individual entries) of such vast natural language-covering ontology, but it is to be expected that this still will be much easier and more stable than dealing with the need for individual and local mini-agreements about the "real world" itself. Even if one fails to reach a complete match between one's terms and those in the ontology, the benefits would likely outweigh the cost of the required compromise. At present, only a few and partial resources of a related kind exist, either as research prototypes (e.g. the very popular [WordNet], see also [Fel98]) or, as is now the case for [CYC], as a proprietary development that does not (yet) constitute a wide standard.

Many efforts and technologies at this moment contribute towards the feasibility of such common ontologies. For instance, DO technology mentioned above has already led to a degree of unexpected standardization of the terminology of business processes –and in fact the processes themselves– as materialized in e.g. [SAP], [Baan] and related products. Another example is XML [BPS98] which may provide a widely used –if limited– vehicle for "semantic" tagging of webpages and -sites. This ability is already being usefully exploited e.g. in [SHOE]; see [HHL98]

The required resource will need to be a (very) large database residing on the Internet; its structure needs to be defined. We argue that it should be as simple as possible to allow a maximum of *application independence*; in fact in a rather precise sense, for communication-based systems this intuitive requirement forms the dual concept to the very well-known concept of *data independence* that drives *all* database technology today.

Needless to say, the increasing availability of very large numbers of data sources, all developed autonomously, and eventually the presence of many software agents on the internet will make common ontological resources attractive for establishing communication on-line without or with a minimum of human interaction. Commercial applications may be imagined in the areas of data warehousing, on-line analytical processing (OLAP), electronic trading and commerce, etc.. See e.g. also [L&G94] for a number of other possible uses for CYC® that apply to all such ontologies.

The rest of this paper is structured as follows. We start in the next section by trying to motivate the need for a common "global" ontology by an example. A general introductory survey in the study of semantics, and notably in the context of information systems is next in Sec.3, followed in Sec.4 by a quick survey of some relevant work in lexicons and ontologies. We then combine this in Sec.5 discussing their use, again, in information systems and methodologies in particular. We conclude in Sec.6 with some comments about possible future research.

2. Motivating Example

A number of distributed software agents are playing around a blackboard communication facility. Some of these agents are **Publisher**, **Categorizer**, **Intaker**, **Matcher**, and **User Agent**. There may be several of each, and others, active at any given time. As we look, **User agent** happens to be servicing a subscriber who wants to set up an on-line news website on basketball, and has selected a suitable website template according to a user profile, and posted a request on the blackboard based on this. **User agent** has a *domain-specific thesaurus* of such templates to choose from. The subscriber wishes to title the website "Hoops Today". For the sake of the example, assume the template (or the subscriber) is somewhat simplistic, and in a fictitious syntax looks like

website

	has	layout = <default>
	has	title = "Hoops Today"
	has	content = on-line_news < stream
	has	subject = basketball+
	not	subject = (basketball_player– , "sex" ~)
	is-a	place < virtual
	part_of	internet

The intended meaning is that the desired website has on-line news content, limited to be a stream; the subject must be "basketball" or maybe something more general (the +); but not containing tidbits involving basketball players or more specific individuals (the –) mentioned together with their favorite pastime or a synonym for it (the ~). A website generalizes to a place that is limited to be virtual, and is in part-of relationship to the notion "internet".

The tokens "has", "is-a", part-of" are called *roles* and they determine how the term following them has to be interpreted; "has content" in our thesaurus means that content is an *attribute* of website. Note the last two items would in general not be application-specific properties of a website; however we didn't find "website" in our favorite lexicon so we had to provide these ourselves in our domain thesaurus. (In fact "web site" surprisingly does not appear today in WordNet, a popular lexicon we use in several examples further on.). We stress again that the syntax above is entirely arbitrary and "constructed" here only for the purpose of illustrating some ideas behind this example.

Clearly the interpretation of roles, and of operators like + when they are domain- or application-specific, is the internal responsibility of the **User Agent**. We say that they belong to its *ontology*. This is a general principle; agents may communicate with each other of course but must do so only through a simple "flat" lexicon devoid of domain specific semantics. The role "is-a" for instance describes in general a domain independent relationship and occurs in almost every known lexicon, thesaurus or "ontology", and should be inherited from and interpreted at that level.

After this intermezzo, let's turn back now to our little system where the agents are waiting, and quickly run through a possible scenario for it. For the sake of further simplicity we shall ignore the "not", "is-a" and "part-of" roles and just concentrate on content type and required subject. The reader may easily imagine scenarios that involve these properties as well.

A **Publisher** in the meantime has triggered on the posted request, knowing it can fulfill it provided it can find the right inputs. It will need to receive these as data coming from other agents; in this case it looks for NITF formatted news text and, since it has experience with the media and news items, also for a relevance ranking with respect to the subject "basketball". Note that **Publisher** needs no specialized basketball knowledge; it only uses the fact that basketball is a subject.

Publisher now posts itself two messages on the blackboard, the first asking for NITF-formatted on-line news, the other asking for a relevance factor of news articles in relation to the subject basketball.

Two agents trigger on these requests. The **Intaker** agent can supply the NITF formatted text, so the agent commits to this. This commitment is accepted by the **Publisher** which removes this part of its request.

The second agent is a **Matcher** who can compute the relevance provided it can receive categorization data on the subject basketball. It posts a request for such categorization on the blackboard.

A rampant **Categorizer** passes by and decides it could partially fulfill this request, given the right inputs. It cannot fulfill the exact categorization required, but after consulting a general-purpose lexicon (such as WordNet for example) it finds it can satisfy a more general categorization on the subject of "sports". Since fulfillment is only partial the posting agents will leave their request on the blackboard until, maybe, in the end the **User Agent** commits if he decides relevance is high enough. For instance, look at Fig.1 which shows the (partially flattened and edited) entry for the specialization hierarchy containing sports and basketball in WordNet. If **Categorizer** would generalize to (another) "court game", the high fan-out under that term might reduce the relevance noticeably.

More requests will be posted until finally **Publisher** can make a partial commitment that is accepted by the **User Agent**, and now a series of parameterized steps is sent to the system for execution. Note that all the steps in the process made use of domain-specific and general "data" knowledge residing in thesauri, while the "operations" knowledge necessary for the use, application or rewriting of the rules was kept inside the agents. This is of course intentional and makes the system flexible and robust, e.g. to allow run-time reconfigurations caused by new (types of) agents appearing at the table (see Figure 1).

Certain aspects of the above system, organization and scenario of operation are currently under investigation as part of a development related to the TREVI Project [TREVI] at VUB STARLab. The current implementation of TREVI (in EU Esprit Project #23311) is a personalized electronic news server system that is designed to operate on a continuous basis, supporting a high volume of subscribers. On the basis of a user profile the system provides the subscriber with a personalized electronic news service through a personalized website, an email message service, or a custom-made client application. The system is unusually modular and a limited ability to process meta-data already presently allows adding new functionality (module types) to the system at runtime. User profiles are mapped onto series of processing steps, each corresponding to a parameterized stateless operation of a module type. The system performs merging and parallelization of the series behind the scenes to achieve an optimized execution scenario. The current system prototype uses a Java/CORBA backbone architecture over a distributed set of (NT) servers.

```
sport, athletics -- (an active diversion requiring physical exertion and competition)
    => contact sport -- (a sport that necessarily involves body contact between opposing players)
    => outdoor sport, field sport -- (a sport that is played outdoors)
    => gymnastics --
        (a sport that involves exercises intended to display strength and balance and agility)
    => track and field --
        (participating in athletic sports performed on a running track or on the field associated with it)
    => skiing -- (a sport in which participants must travel on skis)
    => water sport, aquatics -- (sports that involve bodies of water)
    => rowing, row -- (the act of rowing as a sport)
    => boxing, pugilism, fisticuffs -- (fighting with the fists)
    => archery -- (the sport of shooting arrows with a bow)
    => sledding -- (the sport of riding on a sled or sleigh)
    => wrestling, rassling, grappling --
        (the sport of hand-to-hand struggle between unarmed contestants who try to throw...)
    => skating -- (the sport of gliding on skates)
    => racing -- (the sport of engaging in contests of speed)
    => riding, horseback riding, equitation -- (riding a horse as a sport)
    => cycling -- (the sport of traveling on a bicycle or motorcycle)
    => bloodsport -- (sport that involves killing animals (especially hunting))
    => athletic game -- (a game involving athletic activity)
        => ice hockey, hockey, hockey game -- (a game played on an ice rink by two opposing ...)
        => tetherball -- (a game with two players who use rackets to strike a ball that is tethered ...)
        => water polo -- (a game played in a swimming pool by two teams of swimmers ...)
        => outdoor game -- (an athletic game that is played outdoors)
        => court game -- (an athletic game played on a court)
            => handball -- (a game played in a walled court or against a single wall by two ...)
            => racquetball -- (a game played on a handball court with short-handled rackets)
            => fives -- ((British) a game resembling handball; played on a court with a front wall ...)
            => squash, squash racquets, squash rackets -- (a game played in an enclosed court by two ...)
            => volleyball, volleyball game -- (a game in which two teams hit an inflated ball over ...)
            => jai alai, pelota -- (a Basque or Spanish game played in a court with a ball ...)
            => badminton -- (a game played on a court with light long-handled rackets used to volley
                a shuttlecock over a net)
            => basketball, basketball game -- (a game played on a court by two opposing teams of 5
                players; points are scored by throwing the basketball through an elevated horizontal hoop)
            => professional basketball -- (playing basketball for money)
```

Fig. 1. Sports hierarchy including "basketball" obtained from the [Wordnet] lexicon (partly edited and collapsed for simplification)

[TREVI] is an example of a project that uses lexicon technology in several ways. We may call such systems *CLASS*-type for Computer Lexicon Assisted Software Systems. The design implied in the example above would make such technology fundamental to its operation. As should be immediately obvious, because of the heterogeneous nature of agent technology and the "openness" of possible request, formal agreement on the meaning of the terms (and if possible processes) is indeed primordial. We believe that thesauri (domain-specific ontologies) and the availability of global lexicons will make this possible, by providing a pragmatically usable substitute for a formal, "reductionist" definition of information system semantics. We explain terminology and these principles in the next section.

3. Semantics in Information Systems

For convenience and ease of presentation we shall assume here that an information system is merely defined in a strict model-theoretic paradigm by a pair (S,P) where S denotes a *conceptual schema* and P denotes a *population* of instances that "satisfies" S in an intuitive but well-defined sense (viz. logically P is a *model* for S). Informally speaking, S typically contains "sentence patterns" in terms of types or classes, including constraints or "business domain rules" while P contains instances of these sentences –ground atomic formulas– in terms of proper nouns, numbers and other lexical elements of the universe of discourse. P is typically implemented as a database, for instance. This is further complemented by an active component, the *information processor* which manipulates the instances of P such that consistency, i.e. satisfaction of S, is maintained. A customary implementation of an information processor is by a DBMS, often supplemented by a set of *application programs* that either implement user-desired functionality, or consistency requirements defined in S, or both. While admittedly this is a seriously simplified view (e.g. it ignores most aspects of dynamics and events in the application domain, and is –rather incorrectly– suggestive of a centralized, non-distributed architecture) it will do to illustrate many of the basic issues encountered when dealing with the meaning of the represented and stored information.

Any treatment of semantics will associate the contents of an information system with a "real world" for the purpose of creating an understanding of these contents for the system's users. It will view the entire information system, i.e. both its conceptual schema and its population of instances, as a *language* (of well-formed formulas), and must deal with the following rather obvious but essential principles:

- any semantics formalism for such a language must describe a form of relationship (usually a *mapping*) between the symbols used in the syntactical constructs of this language and the entities (objects, events, relationships, ...) in an observed "real world";
- the "real world" can only enter into the semantics formalism as a *representation* itself, usually under the form of a collection of *signs*. Such a representation is sometimes called a *conceptualization* [G&N87]. This in turn implies an unavoidable a priori choice of alphabet, symbols, etc and dependence from which the formalism however has to abstract;
- any semantics must be the result of an *agreement* among involved domain experts, designers, implementers, and present and future users of the resulting system, which in fact does nothing but *implement* this agreement.

It is especially this last principle that distinguishes semantics in the context of an information system from e.g. the formal treatment of semantics in the context of programming languages [vLe90][Sch86]. The latter is axiomatic and reductionist by the very nature of the interpreter -the computer- which *can* be assumed completely understood. Explicit agreements (except, perhaps, on the machine's axioms and rules of inference) therefore are unnecessary. In the world of information systems, reductionist approaches to semantics do not work so well, as they would necessitate an axioms-plus-logic solution to the "commonsense world" problem in AI [e.g. H&M85]. Indeed, understanding of the operation of the information processor itself becomes largely irrelevant, certainly compared to the need to associate meaning to the input and output streams of the system. These information streams are the very purpose of that system and contain (actually, are constituted of) references to real world entities. In programming terms, it is the *data* manipulated by the program that has the prime responsibility of carrying the semantics, rather than the *program* itself.

Such references therefore, unlike for programming languages, *do* require explicit agreement among the observers of that real world. Obviously, formally registering such agreement in general for any realistic domain is a major undertaking, rapidly becoming more difficult, and even impossible in the usual logical sense, as the number of parties (users, designers, experts, ...) to the supposed agreement grows.

Therefore the information systems community out of necessity (after all, quite many of these systems *do* seem to work usefully) often adopted a pragmatical approach to semantics, giving rise to a large variety of semi-formal or empirical semantic formalisms in the literature [Mee97].

4. Lexicons, Thesauri and Ontologies

"What is an Ontology?" is the title of one of Tom Gruber's Web pages, and the short answer he provides there on the next line is: "a specification of a conceptualization" [Gru93]. This is a rather good and usable definition –although "ontology" strictly speaking as an English word is not a count noun and so in principle we cannot say "an ontology" nor make its plural... It is both simple and precise, if we take a definition of conceptualization in the sense of e.g. [G&N87] or [G&F92]. There, a conceptualization is merely an abstract, very elementary representation of a Universe of Discourse (application domain) in terms of lists of objects, mathematical relationships and functions, denoted in symbols (signs) that correspond one-to-one with "real-world" objects, facts, etc. (In fact the definition used is somewhat more complex, i.e. a conceptualization may be seen as a logical theory, but we shall not adopt that notion here.) See for instance the formal semantics of [KIF] for an illustration of the use of this concept.

Clearly, even if a conceptualization as a substitute for the "real world" is described as independently as possible of a representation formalism, at the very least some –hopefully minimal– kind of modeling, structuring and symbol conventions and denotations must be adopted, i.e. *agreed on*. This however could be relatively easy, at least for the constants of the language. Indeed, computer lexicons, or ontologies, or thesauri (see below), i.e. indexed databases of lexical terms related in context, may form a good basis for a *pre-agreed, common, conceptualization* of the "real world" –if they are properly structured and made sufficiently complete. In other words, when again viewing a semantics for an information system as a mapping (called "interpretation" [G&N87]) from its formal representation language to a "part of the real world", a well-defined lexicon etc. may then be substituted for, and *serve as* the actual semantic domain, becoming the domain (in the mathematical sense) of the semantics interpretation mapping, instead of that "part of the real world".

Notes on Terminology
In the literature on computational linguistics and on ontology in AI the different uses of the terms "ontology", "lexicon", "thesaurus", "vocabulary", "dictionary" etc. give rise to some confusion and incompatibilities. According to the New Shorter Oxford dictionary, and taking the more specific alternatives of each definition, a *lexicon* is "a complete set of elementary meaningful units in a language"; a *thesaurus* is a "classified list of terms, esp. keywords, in a particular field for use in indexing or

information retrieval", and *ontology* (without an article) is "the study of being", "the list of what is/exists" [Bro93]. Both lexicons and thesauri may seem to be special forms of *dictionaries* or *vocabularies*. Most approaches to "ontologies" in the relevant AI literature on e.g. [CYC], [KIF], [SHOE], [ASIS], etc. would therefore seem to lead to tools that are closer to the linguistic concept of thesauri (even if these tools are not a priori domain-specific, such as e.g. [GRASP] is for works of art).

We will therefore for the purpose of this paper say that

- *an ontology* is a specified conceptualization as described above;
- *a thesaurus* is a domain-specific ontology, e.g. Business, Naïve_Physics, Contract_Law, ... or application(s)-specific ontology, e.g. Inventory_Control, Airline_Reservations, Conference_Organization, ...;
- *a lexicon* is a language-specific ontology, e.g. English, Esperanto, Bosnian, ...

All ontologies may therefore be listed as logical theories, or even simply as "dictionaries" in a sense defined below. Admittedly for a thesaurus the distinction between application-specific and domain-specific can be vague and must often be left to intuition, especially since ontologies may cover a *set* of applications. Nevertheless this level-like distinction is a customary one in many IS modeling methodologies where applications are developed within a shared domain (see also the discussion in Sec. 4). So under the definition above a lexicon is more general – encompasses more entries, facts, ...– than a domain-specific thesaurus which is more general than an application-specific thesaurus.

Swartout et al. [SPK96] further distinguish *domain ontologies* and *theory ontologies*, the latter expressing fundamental and unchanging truths about the world such as time, space, mathematics as logical theories while the former are typically large sets of facts about a given (application) domain.

As an example of a (domain specific) thesaurus, we show a small fragment of the one the Reuters news agency uses to classify news items by subject in Fig.2. This ontology is shared by many applications and used in particular in the [TREVI] project (where Reuters plc. is a partner) to enrich news items, after subject identification, with background information based on this classification and according to user profiles. (This was the inspiration for the Motivating Example.)

TOPICS

CORPORATE

...	...
Accounts	Health
Acquisitions	Human Interest
Advertising	International Elections
Annual Results	International Relations
Asset Transfers	Obituaries
Bonds	Religion
Capacity/Plant	Science/Technology
Capital	Sports
Competition/Anti-Trust	Travel/Tourism
/Restrictive Practices	Weather
...	...

Fig. 2. Fragment of Reuters' "Business" Thesaurus: Corporate Topics. ©Reuters plc

Another small fragment is shown in Fig.3 below. Such a thesaurus may actually be seen as composed of elementary entries <context: term-role-term> which we shall define as *lexons* in the next Section. For instance, a lexon in Fig. 3 might be <c-Business t-Industries r-Has_Category t-Brewing>, stating that within the context of Business the term Industries has a relationship with the term Brewing which plays the role of Category in it. Another lexon in Fig.2 would be <c-Business t-Corporate r-Has_Attribute t-Capital>.

INDUSTRIES

...	...
Accountancy	Retail Chemists
Adhesives	Retailer -General
Advertising	Retailer -Specialist
Aerospace	Road Haulage
Agricultural Machinery	Rubber & Plastics
Agriculture	Sales Promotion
Air Transport	Shipbuilding
Aircraft Leasing	Shipping
Airports	Shipping -Support Services
Alarms and Signalling Equipt.	Soft Drinks
Animal Feed	Software (Applications)
Armaments	Software (Systems)
Baking	Sugar
Banking	Telecom Service
Basic Electrical Equipment	Telecoms Equipment
Basic Industrial Chemicals	Textiles
Bread & Biscuit Making	Theatre Venues
Book Publishing	Timber Products
Brewing	Tobacco
Building Products	Tourism
Bus & Coach Services	-(Building Construction)
...	...

Fig. 3. Fragment of Reuters' "Business" Thesaurus: Industries. ©Reuters plc

It will be readily obvious even from these tiny fragments that the roles often are not obvious nor the same for all elements of a sublist, as an information analyst would expect: in fact this poses in general a major problem with many of today's thesauri and lexicons.

It turns out that a rather convenient way of representing the lexons in an ontology during its design phase, is by using the ORM notation (Object-Role Modeling [Hal95], earlier known as NIAM [VvB82]). The NIAM/ORM method has its roots in using natural language agreement as the basis for information analysis, uses mainly binary relationships to represent knowledge and always has had roles as first-class citizens. Commercial design tools are available for it [VISIO], but extensions have to be added to handle large classifications at the "type" level. Another such useful graphical notation, especially for representing theory knowledge in ontologies, are Sowa's Conceptual Structures [Sow84] further elaborated and applied to ontology in [Sow99].

In the case of ORM a small fragment of the above thesauri looks like Fig.4, with a self-understood graphical notation. Each binary relationship corresponds to a lexon in the ontology.

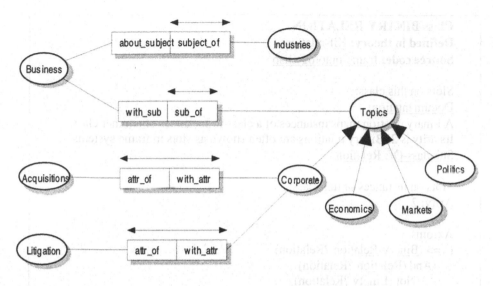

Fig. 4. Example of an ORM binary relationship diagram

Most ontology work in the AI literature so far tends to equip ontologies with fairly sophisticated logical machinery. An elegant example is [KIF] developed at Stanford by a team around Mike Genesereth, and which allowed implementation as an open ontology in the KSL system (a.k.a. Ontolingua). An example of a KIF theory is shown in Fig. 5. (extracted from www-ksl.stanford.edu/knowledge-sharing/ontologies/). The underlined terms denote hyperlinks to other theories or classes. KIF implements an essentially reductionist philosophy but boasts a well-defined formal declarative semantics [G&F92].

The openness of KIF results from a well-defined manner in which (distributed) users may add their own application or "general" domain ontologies to the system and so expand it.

By leaving out this logic machinery we reduce the ontology to a "less intelligent" kind of dictionary (such as in the thesaurus examples in Figs 2. and 3.) and leave the responsibility for handling semantics with the interpreter, viz. the agents that use the ontology. We shall see in the next Section that there are a number of advantages to this "dumber is smarter" principle. CYC® is an example of a (large) instances ontology that operates in this manner, although it is also equipped with a separate limited inference engine, and a manipulation language (CycL) which allows fairly general first order formulas to be stated over CYC®'s *constants*. CYC® is organized in so-called *microtheories* which group related and interacting constants in what is the equivalent of *contexts*. Fig.6 shows the entry for "Skin", and its parent "AnimalBodyPart", both to be interpreted as elements of a microtheory (context) on physiology (copied from the public part of CYC®, www.cyc.com/cyc-2-1/intro-public.html).

Class BINARY-RELATION
Defined in theory: <u>Kif-relations</u>
Source code: <u>frame-ontology.lisp</u>

Slots on this class:
<u>Documentation</u>:
A binary relation maps instances of a class to instances of another class.
Its arity is 2. Binary relations are often shown as slots in frame systems.
<u>Subclass-Of</u>: <u>Relation</u>

Slots on instances of this class:
<u>Arity</u>: 2

Axioms:
(<=> (<u>Binary-Relation</u> ?Relation)
    (And (<u>Relation</u> ?Relation)
        (Not (<u>Empty</u> ?Relation))
        (Forall (?Tuple)
            (=> (<u>Member</u> ?Tuple ?Relation) (<u>Double</u> ?Tuple)))))

Fig. 5. A KIF built-in theory for Binary Relations (a subtype of Relations)

CYC® unquestionably is a massive resource, which has only begun to be mined, and it may even be expected that precisely the simplicity and relative "flatness" of its underlying vocabularies rather than its inferencing capabilities will make it attractive as such. In "flat" ontologies (dictionaries), i.e. devoid of application semantics, the roles (expressing relations, functions) in the lexons become the carriers for most of the application semantics: whenever the using agent "applies" a lexon, it executes the interpretation associated with the role internally (as part of the agent, not as part of any inferencing inside the ontology). In the #$Skin example above, the lexon roles are "isa" and "genls" and are of course interpreted by an internal CYC® "reasoner" which "owns" their semantics. See also for instance again the WordNet example in Sec. 2. for another illustration of this concept.

#$Skin

A (piece of) skin serves as outer protective and tactile sensory covering for (part of) an animal's body. This is the collection of all pieces of skin. Some examples include TheGoldenFleece (an entire skin) and YulBrynnersScalp (a small portion of his skin).
isa: #$<u>AnimalBodyPartType</u>
genls: #$<u>AnimalBodyPart</u> #$<u>SheetOfSomeStuff</u>
#$<u>VibrationThroughAMediumSensor</u> #$<u>TactileSensor</u> #$<u>BiologicalLivingObject</u>
#$<u>SolidTangibleThing</u>
some subsets: (4 unpublished subsets)

> **#$AnimalBodyPart**
>
> The collection of all the anatomical parts and physical regions of all living animals; a subset of #$OrganismPart. Each element of #$AnimalBodyPart is a piece of some live animal and thus is itself an instance of #$BiologicalLivingObject. #$AnimalBodyPart includes both highly localized organs (e.g., hearts) and physical systems composed of parts distributed throughout an animal's body (such as its circulatory system and nervous system). Note: Severed limbs and other parts of dead animals are NOT included in this collection; see #$DeadFn.
> **isa:** #$ExistingObjectType
> **genls:** #$OrganismPart #$OrganicStuff #$AnimalBLO #$AnimalBodyRegion
> **some subsets:** #$Ear #$ReproductiveSystem #$Joint-AnimalBodyPart #$Organ #$MuscularSystem #$Nose #$SkeletalSystem #$Eye #$RespiratorySystem #$Appendage-AnimalBodyPart #$Torso #$Mouth #$Skin #$DigestiveSystem #$Head-AnimalBodyPart (plus 16 more public subsets, 1533 unpublished subsets)

Fig. 6. CYC® constants: #$Skin generalizes to #$AnimalBodyPart. ©Cycorp, Inc.

5. Linking Semantics, Ontologies, and Information Systems Methodologies

As indicated earlier, there are good arguments for keeping ontologies (especially general, global ones such as lexicons) as simple as possible. "Universal truths" could be incorporated in general knowledge bases of this kind, but it is unlikely that they will be used explicitly very often in inferring knowledge that is application-specific, any more than quantum mechanics are needed explicitly to describe material business processes. In relational database theory the distinction between the model-theoretic and the proof-theoretic approaches is well understood since a seminal paper by Reiter [Rei84]. Although Reiter makes a strong and convincing case for the superiority of the proof-theoretic paradigm because of its greater "semantic richness", it is noteworthy that databases today still follow the model-theoretic paradigm. In fact, proof-theoretic (Datalog, or *deductive*) databases, while very elegant and formally satisfying [AHV95] have flared but very briefly in the commercial market-place.

The explanation is rather simple, and methodological in nature. In the proof-theoretic scheme of things rules, constraints, and other ways of representing "more world knowledge" tend to get pushed into the database schema; reasoning with them requires an extension or conversion of DBMS-s with inference capability. However, getting *agreement* among users and designers about so-called "universal unchanging truths" –if such facts can at all be identified in a pragmatical business environment– and locking them into the database schema is exceedingly more difficult, and rare, than obtaining agreement about (static) data structures. In fact often "exceptions become the rule", defeating the purpose of the new capabilities of the DBMS, which are then soon abandoned.

In the model theoretic paradigm, the issue in practice is tackled, but in general not solved, using *layers* (or *levels*) of knowledge representation, rather analogously to the levels of ontology defined above in Sec.4, viz. general > domain > application. In [ISO90] an early case (the "onion model") was made for layering real world knowledge in this manner from the abstract to the specific, even within a domain. While no implementation was given there and then, the resulting architecture relates nicely to some current ontology principles. In particular it leads to a requirement for ontologies to be *extendable* with domain- and application specific thesauri, as for instance is possible in KIF. However, most application specific knowledge in this way ends up in insulated mini-extensions or hard-coded in the application programs. One partial remedy is that the information system's conceptual schema allows for a layer of application- or even domain-specific constraints from which filters may be generated which will screen incoming data for conformance to these constraints. Reasoning about these constraints however is rare in information systems, and at best in some CASE tools a limited constraint consistency check was performed, see e.g. the RIDL* analyzer for NIAM in [DMV88] or a similar module for ORM in InfoModeler [VISIO].

Usable and teachable methodologies for constructing and maintaining consistent, simple and practical lexicons and thesauri are very much lacking at the moment, as well as for designing and developing CLASS-type systems. This is obviously a difficult problem, but "global" lexicons must carry authority if they should be usable as semantic domains. All existing lexicons, especially the larger domain independent ones suffer from important deficiencies, such as the frequently inconsistent semantics of the, in our terminology, implicit classification "roles".

Most modular ontology construction techniques such as the ones proposed by [KIF], [SHOE] and its derivative [ASIS] organize knowledge in fairly small "chunks" to be added to a more fundamental ontology. It is rather striking, but perhaps not so surprising, to see that this requires a kind of modeling which is not unlike the building of a "pattern data model" [Fow97] for the domain or application, and produces similar results. Even the constraints (i.e. mostly *business rules*) find a place there. In the case of a thesaurus, constraints are indeed likely to stay domain- or application specific –as pointed out earlier, ample methodological experience with development of classical information systems –pre-CLASS, so to speak– shows it is usually very hard to get users to agree on business rules, even on relatively mundane things like the unique identification of business objects.

Whichever the ontology construction method, it will in one way or the other need to respect the (coarse) layering into fundamentals, domain and application, and possibly finer layers as well within applications, and eventually within domains. This coarse knowledge layering is symbolically depicted in Fig. 7. Note that the application level (not the domain level) also needs to take care of "local" encodings such as abbreviations used in a particular company etc..

43

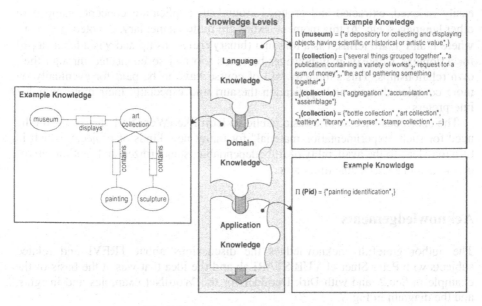

Fig. 7. Knowledge levels in an ontology

In general, and among other issues, the question will arise how to decide in which level to include a certain information occurrence. As a methodological step one could suggest simple abstraction starting from the lowest level: if the lexon is interpreted by different applications, it becomes a candidate for generalization into the domain level, i.e. into a thesaurus for that domain. The language level is a nearly static one and must be kept "completely" domain independent if possible. One of the drawbacks of, for instance, WordNet is the unclear separation between the language level and the domain level there. Some entries contain relations that are domain dependent, whereas this domain information is not included for others.

6. Conclusion and Avenues of Research

Lexicons, thesauri and other ontologies will need to appear to make semantic communication between distributed systems practically possible. The process for reaching agreements needed for establishing meaningful cooperation will at the very least be strongly simplified by the presence of such "universally" accepted resources with nearly implicit semantics. Ideally, domain experts, users and designers will be able to reach *dependable* (even if partial) agreement on concepts used or needed, based on their listed use in context.

In the spin-off research activity from TREVI, loosely described in the Example of Sec.2, we hope to achieve useful feedback from the CLASS prototype to be constructed for some of these ideas. It will provide information on the feasibility of structuring application and domain ontologies (possibly as lexon databases) to be plugged into a very simple, very easy to use but very large and "semantics-less" future lexicon architecture (also implemented as a lexon database, using only "universal" roles). The use of databases allows large collections of lexons to be easily indexed, extracted and grouped around an application concept, mapped to other languages, etc. At this moment lexons are quite elementary, denoted $\gamma(t_1\ r\ t_2)$ where t_1 and t_2 are terms, r is a role in a (binary) relationship and γ is a label (term) for a context. Contexts may however be terms too and so connected through their own relationships. This simplicity will of course have to be paid for eventually by more complex domain and application thesauri and especially their more complex interpreters.

The enormous success of a basic public lexicon like [WordNet] clearly shows the need for such "experimentation material" for many new kinds of projects, which in turn may lead to the availability of truly dependable, standardized and "authoritative" ontologies in a reasonable timeframe.

Acknowledgements

The author gratefully acknowledges the discussions about TREVI and related subjects with Peter Stuer of VUB STARLab and the idea that was at the basis of the example in Sec.2, and with Dirk Deridder for the WordNet examples and insights, and the diagram in Fig. 7.

Literature References

[AHV95]   Abiteboul, S., Hull, R. and Vianu, V.: Foundations of Databases. Addison-Wesley, Reading MA (1995).

[Baan]   R. van Es (Ed.)Dynamic Enterprise Innovation: Establishing Continuous Improvement in Business, , Baan Business Innovation, January 1998.

[BPS98]   Bray,T., Paoli, J. and Sperberg-McQueen, C.M.: Extensible Markup Language (XML). World Wide Web Consortium (W3C). Available at www.w3.org/TR/1998/rec-xml-19980210.html (1998).

[Bri98]   Brinkkemper, S.: Global Process Management. In: [Baan] (1998)

[Bro93]   Brown, L. (ed.): The New Shorter Oxford Dictionary of the English Language. Clarendon Press, Oxford (1993).

[DMV88]   DeTroyer, O., Meersman, R.A. and Verlinden, P.: RIDL* on the CRIS Case, a Workbench for NIAM. In: Computer Assistance during the Information Systems Life Cycle, , T.W. Olle, A. Verrijn-Stuart, and L. Bhabuta (eds), North-Holland, Amsterdam (1988).

[Fel98]   Fellbaum, C.(ed.): WordNet: An Electronic Lexical Database. MIT Press (1998).

[Fow97]   Fowler, M.: Analysis Patterns: Reusable Object Models. Addison-Wesley, Reading MA (1997).

[G&F92]   Genesereth, M.R. and Fikes, R.E.: Knowledge Interface Format Reference Manual. Stanford Computer Science Department Report (1992).

[G&N87]   Genesereth, M.R. and Nilsson, N.J.: Logical Foundations of Artificial Intelligence. Morgan Kaufmann Publishers, Palo Alto CA (1987).

[Gru93]   Gruber, T.R.: A Translation Approach to Portable Ontologies. J. on Knowledge Acquisition, Vol. 5(2), 199-220 (1993).

[Hal95]   Halpin, T.: Conceptual Schema and Relational Database Design. Prentice-Hall (1995)

[HHL98]   Heflin, J., Hendler, J. and Luke, S.: Reading Between the Lines: Using SHOE to Discover Implicit Knowledge from the Web. In: Proceedings of the AAAI-98

Workshop on AI and Information Integration (1998); from webpage accessed Feb.1999 www.cs.umd.edu/projects/plus/SHOE/shoe-aaai98.ps

[H&M85] Hobbs, J.R. and Moore, R.C. (eds.): Formal Theories of the Commonsense World. Ablex, Norwood NJ (1985).

[Hun88] Hunnings, G. The World and Language in Wittgenstein's Philosophy. SUNY Press, New York (1988).

[ISO90] Anon.: Concepts and Terminology of the Conceptual Schema and the Information Base. ISO Technical Report TR9007, ISO Geneva (1990).

[L&G94] Lenat, D.B. and Guha, R.V.: Ideas fr Applying CYC. Unpublished. Accessed Feb. 99 from www.cyc.com/tech-reports/ (1994)

[Mee94] Meersman, R.: Some Methodology and Representation Problems for the Semantics of Prosaic Application Domains. In: Methodologies for Intelligent Systems, Z. Ras and M. Zemankova (eds.), Springer-Verlag, Berlin (1994).

[Mee97] Meersman, R.: An Essay on the Role and Evolution of Data(base) Semantics. In: Database Application Semantics, R. Meersman and L. Mark (eds.), Chapman & Hall, London (1997).

[OMG95] CORBA: Architecture and Specification v.2.0. OMG Publication (1995).

[Red97] Redmond, F.E. III: DCOM: Microsoft Distributed Component Object Model. IDG Books, Foster City CA (1997).

[Rei84] Reiter, R.: Towards a Logical Reconstruction of Relational Database Theory. In: On Conceptual Modeling: Perspectives from AI, Databases, and Programming Languages, M.L. Brodie, J. Mylopoulos, and J.W. Schmidt (eds.), Springer-Verlag, New York (1984).

[K&T98] Keller, G. and Teufel, T.: SAP R/3 Process Oriented Implementation. Addison-Wesley, Reading MA (1998).

[Sch86] Schmidt, D.A.,: Denotational Semantics: A Methodology for Language Development. Allyn & Bacon (1986)

[Sow99] Sowa, J.F.: Knowledge Representation. Logical, Philosophical and Computational Foundations. PWS Publishing, Boston MA (1999) [in preparation].

[SPK96] Swartout, W., Patil, R., Knight K., Russ, T.: Towards Distributed Use of Large-Scale Ontologies. In: Proceedings of the 10th Knowledge Acquisition for Knowledge-Based Systems Workshop (KAW'96), (1996).

[VISIO] Infomodeler, now part of Visio Enterprise Modeler, Visio Corp.

[VvB82] Verheyen, G. and van Bekkum, P.: NIAM, aN Information Analysis Method. In: IFIP Conference on Comparative Review of Information Systems Methodologies, T.W. Olle, H. Sol, and A. Verrijn-Stuart (eds.), North-Holland (1982).

[vLe90] van Leeuwen, J. (ed.): Formal Models and Semantics. Handbook of Theoretical Computer Science, Vol. B. Elsevier, Amsterdam (1990).

Internet References to Cited Projects

[ASIS] The ASIS Project, http://wave.eecs.wsu.edu/WAVE/Ontologies/ASIS/ASISontology.html

[TREVI] The EU 4th Framework Esprit project TREVI, http://trevi.vub.ac.be/

[CYC] The CYC® Project and products, www.cyc.com/

[GRASP] The GRASP Project, www.arttic.com/GRASP/... ...public/News03/News03/GRASP_Ontology.html

[KIF] The Knowledge Interface Format (also as KSL, Ontolingua), http://ontolingua.stanford.edu

[SHOE] The Simple HTML Ontology Extensions Project, www.cs.umd.edu/SHOE/

[WordNet] The WordNet Project, www.cogsci.princeton.edu/~wn/

Heterogeneous Agent Systems (Extended Abstract)

V.S. Subrahmanian[1]

Department of Computer Science
and
Institute for Advanced Computer Studies
University of Maryland,
College Park, Maryland 20742, U.S.A
vs@cs.umd.edu

Abstract. IMPACT (Interactive Maryland Platform for Agents Collaborating Together) provides a platform and environment for agent and software interoperability being developed as a joint, multinational effort with participants from the University of Maryland, the Technische Universität Wien, Bar-Ilan University, the University of Koblenz, and the Universita di Torino. In this invited talk, I will describe the overall architecture of the IMPACT system, and outline how this architecture (i) allows agents to be developed either from scratch, or by extending legacy code-bases, (ii) allows agents to interact with one another, (iii) allows agents to have a variety of capabilities (reactive, autonomous, intelligent, mobile, replicating) and behaviors, and (iv) how IMPACT provides a variety of infrastructural services that may be used by agents to interact with one another.

1 Introduction

Over the last few years, there has been increasing interest in the area of software agents that provide a wide variety of services for human users. Such services are spread over a wide area, and include identification of interesting newspaper articles, software robots that perform tasks (and plan) on a user's behalf, content based routers, agent based telecommunication applications, and solutions to logistics applications. Despite all of this wide interest, the theory of agent systems is remarkably undeveloped. Most existing "intelligent agent" systems are either well-engineered systems that lack a firm theoretical basis, or involve agent theories that are as yet unimplemented.

IMPACT ("Interactive Maryland Platform for Agents Collaborating Together") is a multinational project whose aim is to define a formal theory of software agents, implement it (or carefully specified fragments of it) efficiently, and develop an appropriate suite of applications on top of this implementation. The primary aim of this paper is to provide a brief overview of the IMPACT system. The reader will find full technical details in [1, 3, 4, 2, 5].

2   Goals of IMPACT

To our mind, a software agent consists of a body of software code that:

- provides a set of useful *services* that humans and/or other agents may wish to use;
- a *description* of the above services that allow humans and/or other software agents to assess whether they can use the service and to understand the terms and conditions of using such a service;
- has the ability to *act* autonomously and/or in coordination with a human being or with other similar agents, in accordance with a set of operating principles encoded by a human;
- has the ability to *rationally decide* what actions to take in accordance with a set of operating principles;
- has the ability to *cooperate or interact* with other agents.

While not all agents or agent applications need all the above goals, a platform/environment for deploying agent applications must certainly provide support to an agent developer in endowing his/her agents with the above properties.

The goal of the IMPACT project is to design the basic theory and algorithms needed to build a software platform that allows agent developers to achieve the goals listed above. In the rest of this paper, we will briefly outline software architecture that supports the above goals. The architecture consists of two major parts

1. *What does an agent look like from the point of view of a software developer* ? While past formal descriptions of agents have been largely logic based, and specify the logical behavior of agents, our goal is to specify how to structurally build software agents so that such logical behavior (or well as a variety of other behaviors) can be taken by the agent.

2. *What infrastructural capabilities must be provided on a system-wide basis so that a set of agents of the type described above can meaningfully locate agents providing certain services, comprehend messages received from other agents, etc.?*

3   IMPACT Architecture

Figure 1 shows the overall architecture of the IMPACT system. As the reader can see, IMPACT consists of two kinds of entities — agents, that are newly constructued or legacy codabases that have been converted into agents as described in Section 3.1 below, and IMPACT servers that provide the system-wide infrastructural capabilities alluded to in the previous section. IMPACT Servers can be replicated and/or mirrored across the network.

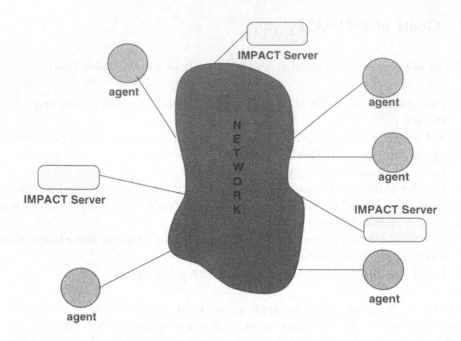

Fig. 1. Overall IMPACT Architecture

3.1 Agents

As different application programs reason with different types of data and as even programs that deal with the same types of data often manipulate that data in a variety of different ways, it is critical that any notion of agent-hood be applicable to arbitrary software programs. Agent developers should be able to select data structures that best suit the application functions desired by users of the application they are building. Figure 2 shows the architecture of a full-fledged software agent. Such an agent contains the components listed below. It is important to note that all agents have the same architecture and hence the same components, but the *content* of these components can be different, leading to to different behaviors and capabilities offered by different agents.

- First, we assume the existence of some set of data types (or data structures) that the agent manipulates. Each data type has an associated space of data-objects — for example, the data type `countries` may be an enumerated type containing names of all countries. At any given point, the *instantiation* or *content* of a data type is some subset of the space of the data-objects associated with that type.
- The above set of data structures is manipulated by a set of functions that are callable by external programs (such functions constitute the *application programmer interface* or API of the package on top of which the agent is being built.

For example, if we have a data type called **quadtree** (which may be managed by a GIS system), examples of functions supported might be **range** (which finds all points within R units of a given point X, Y on a given *map*), **k-nearest-nbr** (which finds the k nearest neighbors of a given point X, Y on a given *map*).

IMPACT builds on the syntax of a previous research effort by our group on heterogeneous data systems called HERMES. Based on knowledge of the data structures and functions supported by a body of code, we may use a unified query language to query them. If p is the name of a package, and f is an n-ary function defined in that package, then $p : f(a_1, \ldots, a_n)$ is a code-call. This code call says "Execute function f as defined in package p on the stated list of arguments." We assume this code call returns as output, a *set* of objects — if an atomic object is returned, it can be coerced into a set anyway. For example, in the previous quadtree example. a code call could be **quadtree:range(20,30,40)** which says "find all objects within 40 units of location $(20, 30)$" — this query returns a set of objects. An *atomic code-call condition* is an expression of the form $\mathtt{in}(X, p : f(a_1, \ldots, a_n))$ which succeeds if X is in the set of answers returned by the code call in question. Code call conditions are boolean combinations of these in-predicates, together with deconstruction and constraint operations. Due to space restrictions, we cannot go into a detailed syntax. An example of a code call condition is

$$\mathtt{in}(X, \mathtt{oracle} : \mathtt{select}(\mathtt{emp}, \mathtt{sal}, >, 100000) \, \&$$

$$\mathtt{in}(Y, \mathtt{image} : \mathtt{select}(\mathtt{imdb}, X.\mathtt{name})) \, \&$$

$$\mathtt{in}(\text{``Mary''}, \mathtt{imagedb} : \mathtt{findpeople}(Y).$$

This code call condition first selects all people who make over 100K from an Oracle database and for each such person, finds a picture containing that person with another person called Mary. It generalizes the notion of join in relational databases to a join across a relational and image database.

- In addition, the agent has a *message management program* that can be used to communicate with other agents.
- At any given point in time, the actual set of objects in the data structures (and message box) managed by the agent constitutes the *state* of the agent. For example, in the case of a quadtree data structure, the state of the agent consists of (i) all the messages in the agent's message box, and (ii) all the nodes and information actually in the quadtree. Likewise, in the case of the image database above, the content of the image database agent is all the image objects in the database.
- The agent has a set of *actions* that can change the state of the agent. Such actions may include reading a message from the message box, responding to a message, updating the agent data structures, etc. Even doing nothing may be an action.

Every action has a precondition, which is a code call condition, a set of effects that describes how the agent state changes when the action is executed, and an *execution script or method* consisting of a body of physical code that implements the action. For instance, when a robotic agent executes the action `move(X,Y)`, not only must its state be updated to reflect the move, but an execution script to actually move the robot to its new location must be executed.

- The agent has an associated body of code implementing a *notion of concurrency*. Intuitively, a notion of concurrency takes a set of actions as input, and returns a single action (which "combines" the input actions together) as output. Three or four examples of such notions of concurrency have been devised in IMPACT. [3, 5] contain further details.
- The agent has a set of *action constraints* which are rules of the form "If the state satisfies some condition, then actions $\{a_1, \ldots, a_n\}$ cannot be concurrently executed. In the case of a robot, an example of an action constraint is:

$$\{move(left), move(right)\} \hookleftarrow$$

says that an agent cannot move both left and right at the same time.
- The agent has a set of *integrity constraints* that states of the agent are expected to satisfy. Such integrity constraints are just code call conditions. For instance, a robotic agent may have an integrity constraint saying it can only be at one point at a given time.
- Finally, the agent has a set of rules called the *Agent Program* specifying the operating principles under which the agent is functioning. These rules describe the do's and dont's for the agent. They specify what the agent may do, what it must do, what it may not do, etc. The Agent Program uses deontic modalities to implement what the agent can and cannot do. Due to space restrictions, we are unable to go into the technical details of agent programs – an example of a rule in an agent program is:

$$\mathbf{P}\alpha(X) \leftarrow in(X, oracle : select(rel1, field1, >, 100)) \, \& $$
$$\mathbf{F}\beta(X.field2).$$

This rule says that the agent in question is allowed to execute the action $\alpha(X)$ if X is in the result of executing a select operation on an Oracle relation, and the agent is forbidden to execute the action $\beta(X.field2)$.

IMPACT provides an environment within which the above parameters can be expressed in a declarative logical manner, even though specialized data structures are used to implement the basic computational operations performed by the agent.

The IMPACT Agent Development Environment (IADE) contains the following important features:

- It provides a simple Java-based, web-accessible interface through which the user may specify all the above parameters. This is shown in Figure 3 below. Using this interface, the agent developer may never need to know that s/he is building logical action rules on top of imperative data structures.

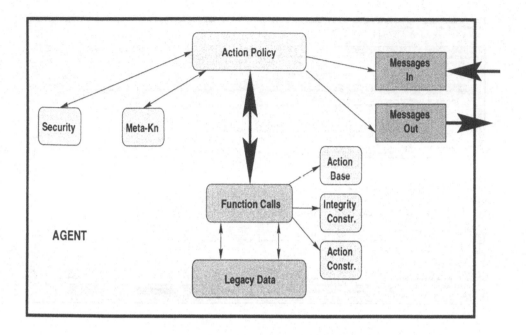

Fig. 2. Architecture of IMPACT Agents

- In addition, using this interface, the agent developer may specify a number of compilation constraints the often make the agent behave much more efficiently at runtime.
- Once the agent developer specifies all the above parameters using the IADE, the IADE automatically creates a body of agent code that behaves in accordance with the semantics of the agent as described by Items (1)–(8) above.
- The agent developer may test the working of his specifications by executing the agent's behavior (cf. Figure 4 below.

3.2 IMPACT Server

Figure 5 shows the architecture of the IMPACT Server. The IMPACT Server provides a variety of services that are required by a society of agents as a whole, rather than by a single agent. Such services include:

- **Registration Services:** When an agent is deployed by an agent developer using the IADE, it automatically provides the agent developer with the option of registering the agent with an IMPACT registration server. This server provides a graphical interface through which the services provided by the agent can be registered. This registration causes certain data structures to be updated with information on the services provided by the agent in

Fig. 3. Screenshot of IMPACT Agent Development Environment (IADE)

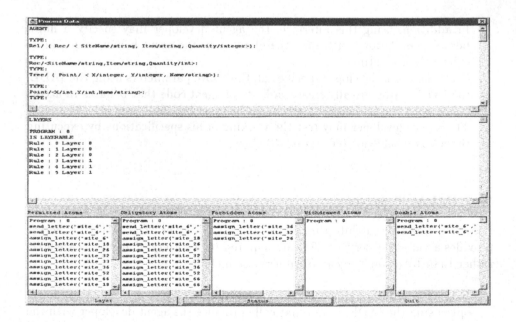

Fig. 4. Screenshot of IMPACT Agent Development Environment (IADE)

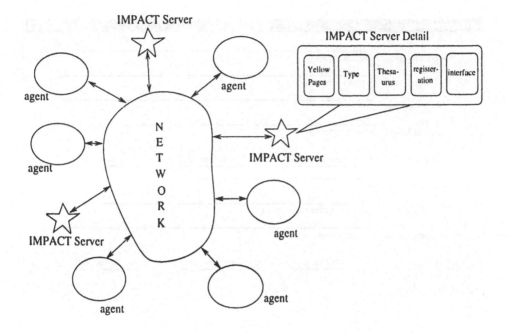

Fig. 5. Architecture of IMPACT Server

question. Changes to service offerings may also be registered with this server (after undergoing an authentication check).

– **Yellow Pages Services:** The IMPACT Yellow Pages Server accesses the data structures created by the registration server in read-only mode. When an agent wants to find another agent offering a desired service, it contacts the Yellow Pages Server and specifies one of two kinds of queries.

 • **Nearest Neighbor Queries** which are queries of the form "Find me the k best matches for a desired service, e.g. `sell:tickets(opera)`?" or

 • **Range Queries** which are queries of the form "Find me all matches for a desired service, e.g. `sell:tickets(opera)`, which are within a given distance of this query?.

– **Type Services:** The IMPACT Type Server allows agent developers to specify types used by them together with relationships between their types and existing types. For example, suppose an agent developer creates a type called `japanese_cars` and an existing type called `cars` is declared in the IMPACT Type server (either by this agent developer or someone else), then the agent developer can state that `japanese_cars` is a subtype of the type `cars`.

– **Thesaurus Server:** The IMPACT Thesaurus Server allows the Yellow Pages Server to expand queries to related queries. For example, if an agent wants to find an agent that offers the service `sell:cars`. Then an agent that offers the services `sell:automobiles` is probably a good match for

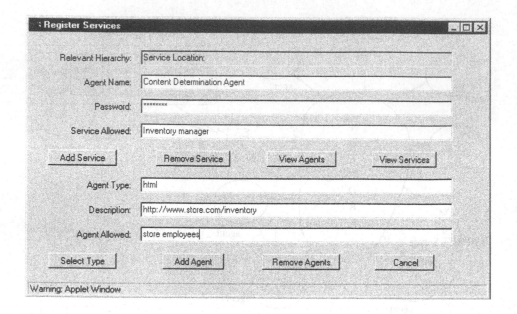

Fig. 6. Agent/Service Registration Screen Dump

this request, but to know this, the Yellow Pages Server needs access to a thesaurus.

- **Ontology/Translation Services:** The IMPACT Agent Development Environment contains facilities to provide ontology services and assumptional information. For example, an agent whose data is stored in English may have trouble responding to a query from another agent phrased in German. The aim of the IMPACT ontology server is to allow the latter agent to reformulate the query in terms it can understand.

Figure 6 shows a screen dump of the IMPACT registration server.

4 Conclusions

In this paper, we have described the overall architecture of the IMPACT System for the development and deployment of multiple agents. As this is an extended abstract, we are unable to go into extensive technical details of the IMPACT Agent Development Environment, and the components of an agent. However, the interested reader will readily find this information in [1, 3, 4, 2, 5].

Acknowledgements

Different parts of this work were supported by the Army Research Office under Grants DAAH-04-95-10174, DAAH-04-96-10297, DAAG-55-97-10047 and DAAH04-96-1-0398, by the Army Research Laboratory under contract number DAAL01-97-K0135, and by an NSF Young Investigator award IRI-93-57756,.

References

1. K Arisha, T. Eiter, S. Kraus, F. Ozcan, R. Ross and V.S.Subrahmanian. IM-PACT: Interactive Maryland Platform for Agents Collaborating Together, IEEE INTELLIGENT SYSTEMS magazine, March 1999, to appear.
2. J. Dix, V.S. Subrahmanian and G. Pick. Meta Agent Programs, Submitted for journal publication, Sep. 1998.
3. T. Eiter, V.S. Subrahmanian and G. Pick. Heterogeneous Active Agents, I: Semantics, accepted for publication in *Artificial Intelligence* journal in Jan. 1999.
4. T. Eiter and V.S. Subrahmanian. Heterogeneous Active Agents, II: Algorithms and Complexity, accepted for publication in *Artificial Intelligence* journal in Jan. 1999.
5. V.S. Subrahmanian, P. Bonatti, J. Dix, T. Eiter, S.Kraus, F.Ozcan and R. Ross. *Heterogeneous Agent Systems: Theory and Implementation*, MIT Press, 1999, to appear.

Information Systems that *Really* Support Decision-making

Gio Wiederhold

Stanford University
Computer Science Department.
Gates Computer Science Building 4A
Stanford CA 94305-9040
650 725-8363   fax 725-2588
<gio@cs.stanford.edu>

Abstract. A decision maker in an enterprise is expected to make decision which have a positive effect on its future. Information systems should support their activities. Today, databases and web-based resources, accessed through effective communications, make information about the past rapidly available. To project the future the decision maker either has to use intuition or employ other tools, and initialize them with information obtained from an information system to such tools. An effective information system should also support forecasting the future. Since choices are to be made, including the case of not doing anything, such a system must also support the comparative assessment of the effects of alternate decisions. We recommend the use of an SQL-like interface language, to access existing tools to assess the future, as spreadsheets and simulations. Making results of simulations as accessible as other resources of integrated information systems has the potential of greatly augmenting their effectiveness and really support decision-making.

1 Introduction

Today rapid progress is being made in information fusion from heterogeneous resources such as databases, text, and semi-structured information bases [WiederholdG:97]. Basic database systems are growing into broader information systems to encompass the communication and analysis capabilities that are now broadly available. In many cases, the objective of the investment in those systems is to support decision-making. However, the decision maker also has to plan and schedule actions beyond the current point-in-time. Databases make essential past and near-current data available, but do not support the essence of decision-making, namely to assess the effect of alternate future courses that can be initiated [Knoblock:96].

To assess the effect in the future of the decisions to be made diverse tools come into play. These tools range from back-of-the envelope estimates, via spreadsheets, to business-specific simulations. The information they provide is complementary to the information about the past provided by databases, and helps in selecting the best course-of-action. The need has been clearly recognized in military planning.

Quoting from "New World Vistas, Air and Space Power for the 21st Century"[McCall:96]: The two 'Capabilities Requiring Military Investment in Information Technology are:
1. Highly robust real-time software modules for data fusion and integration;
2. Integration of simulation software into military information systems.'
Tools for planning and simulation have benefited from substantial research efforts [DeanW:91].

Today planning research includes distributed planning, focusing on interaction with remote participants [SandewallB:94]. The use of databases and or simulations is not well integrated in this research, the focus is on coordination of plans that are put forward by the participants[LindenG:92]. Once the information on costs, delays, and benefits is known, these systems will analyze the alternatives and present optimal plans. Except in handcrafted situations their use has been limited, since gathering all the required information on past and future situations is tedious. The effect is that participants tend to prune the choices prior to the actual planning phase, limiting greatly the alternatives to be analyzed, and reducing the need for the planing algorithms themselves [TateDK:92].

Simulation is a major area of research as well, and much of this work is used in practical settings, as a tool by staff that supports decision-making. Simulation tools often deal explicitly with risks and provide measures of certainty as part of their outputs. The simulation results are analyzed by support staff, and summaries are forwarded to the actual decision-maker. It is rare that the decision maker has the time to go back and request analyses of variations of the choices that have been presented. The predictive requirements for decision-making have been rarely addressed in terms of integration and fusion [Orsborn:94].

Most simulation tools are too complex for direct use by decision-makers. Specifically, many war-gaming simulations are very costly and most are impossible to reuse, so that they are not available in actual emergencies [Zyda:97]. The primary tool actually used by decision-makers is the spreadsheet. Once the formulas are defined, alternate assumptions or allocations are plugged in to provide estimates of future effects. The results are copied out to paper documents. Some 3-D spreadsheets allow on-line flipping through alternatives that have been computed and retained.

2 Infrastructure

Technology has made great strides in accessing information about past events, stored in databases, object-bases, or the World-Wide Web. Data warehouses that integrate data into historic views are becoming broadly available [Kimball:96]. Access to information about current events is also improving dramatically, with real-time news feeds and on-line cash registers. We must still expand the temporal range to project the effect of candidate events into the future. Decision-making in planning depends on knowing past, present, and likely future situations, as depicted in Figure 1. To assess the future we must access simulations which employ a variety of technologies [Burnstein:96]. Many simulations are available from remote sites [FishwickH:98].

Simulation access should handle both local and remote, and distributed simulation services.

Distributed simulations communicate intensely with each other, using interactive protocols [IEEE:98], but are rarely accessible to general information systems [SinghalC:95]. If the simulation is a federated distributed simulation, as envisaged by the HLA protocol, then one of the federation members may supply results to the decision-making support system. To mediate the difference in granularity, such a server must aggregate data from the detailed events that occur many times per second in distribute simulations to the level of minutes or hours that are typical for initiating planning interactions.

3. Concepts

A high-level information system is one that supports decision-making by providing past and future data to a client program. The client program aids the decision maker by incorporating analysis and planning algorithms that assess the value of alternate decisions to be made now or at points in the near future.

During that process effective access is needed to past and current information, and to forecasts about the future, given information about current state and decisions that may be made, typically about resource allocations: money, people, and supplies.

Data covering past information has to be selected, aggregated and transformed to be effective in decision-making. Because of the volume of resources mediating modules are often required. A mediator is a software module that exploits encoded knowledge about certain sets or subsets of data to create information for a higher layer of applications. A mediator module should be small and simple, so that it can be maintained by one expert or, at most, a small and coherent group of experts. The results are most effectively represented by a timeline [DasSTM:94]. The common assumptions is that there is only one version of the past, and that it can be objectively determined.

Recent data may be reported by messages, especially where databases cannot be updated instantaneously. The database paradigm is strong on consistency, but that may mean that recent information, that is not complete or yet verified, may not be retrievable from a formal database. To the decision-maker, however such information is valuable, since any information can lower the uncertainty when one has to project into the future.

Today most simulations are performed in a planner's mind. That is, the planner sketches reasonable scenarios, mentally developing alternate courses-of-action, focusing on those that had been worked out in earlier situations. Such mental models are the basis for most decisions, and only fail when the factors are complex, or the planning horizon is long. Human short-term memory can only manage about 7 factors at a time [Miller:56]. That matches the number of reasonable choices in a chess game, so that a game as chess can be played as by a trained chess master as well by a dumb computer with a lot a memory. When situations become more complex, tools should be used for pruning the space of alternatives, presentation, and assessment. Today, the pruning is mainly done intuitively, the presentations use whiteboards and

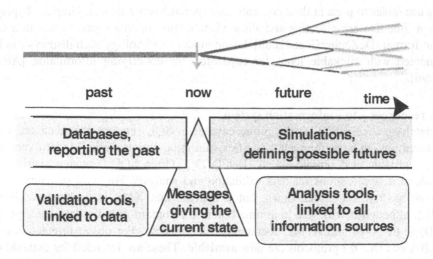

Fig. 1. Components of Effective Information Systems

the available tools are video-conferences and communicating smartboards, perhaps augmented by results that participants obtain from isolated analysis programs. For instance, a participant may execute a simulation to assess how a proposed decision would impact people and supply resources. Financial planners will use spreadsheets to work out alternate budgets.

Computer-based simulations for planning assess resource consumptions, benefits, risks and the like at points in the future. Risks for alternatives may be obtained by mining past data for similar situations. Simulations that incorporate gaming may automatically investigate allocations that can be made by the enemy, select their best choice and continue the projection for multiple plies. Simulations that deal with natural events will incorporate probabilities of weather, floods, or earthquakes. Derived effects, as flight delays, road closures, and the like might also be computed. There are always multiple futures to be considered in decision-making. The combination is depicted in Figure 1.

4. Interfaces

A composed system as we propose has many interfaces. There is the interface to the decision-maker and the tools employed in the process, and there are the interfaces to the databases, their mediators, the message systems, and, finally, to the simulations.

Information system – to - decision maker

To make the results obtained from an information system clear and useful for the decision maker that interface must use a simple model. Computer screens today focus on providing a desktop image, with cut and paste capability, while relational data bases use tables to present their contents, and spreadsheets a matrix. Graphic displays using a time-line are effective and allow visualization of many past events in a coherent format [DeZegherGeetsEa:88]. Using modern technology such displays can be augmented with clickable icons for expansion for underlying information [AberleEa:96].

Data resources – to - information system
For database access SQL is the prime candidate. SQL requires that data are well structured, and this requirement simplifies validation and analysis. Modern versions of SQL provide also remote access [DateD:93]. Often SQL language queries are embedded in applications for data validation and analysis. For semi-structured data the dust has not yet settled down, but it appears that XML is a prime candidate [XML], although it will be a long time before thr domain-specific data descriptions (DTD) settle down and HTML documents are replaced. For object-oriented access CORBA and DCOM protocols are now available. These are intended for embedding in application software and not as flexible as SQL and HTML.

Note that access languages as SQL are interface languages only, they are not the language in which to write a database system; those may be written in C, PL/1, or Ada. The databases themselves are owned and maintained by specialists, as domain experts and database administrators.

Simulation – to - information system
To provide the missing link to simulation systems we have developed a prototype simulation access language, SimQL [WiederholdJG:98]. It mirrors that of SQL for databases. Since we wish to integrate past information from databases with simulation results we started with the relational model. However the objects to be described have a time dimension and also an uncertainty associated with them.

The simulations themselves will be written in their own specialized languages or in common programming languages as Fortran or Ada [INEL:93]. Users of spreadsheets are completely unaware of their source languages.

An ability to access simulations as part of an information system adds a significant new capability, by allowing simultaneous and seamless access to factual data and projections (e.g., logistics data with future deployment projections). Interfaces such as SimQL should adhere closely to emerging conventions for information systems. For instance, they might use a CORBA communication framework, and 'Java' for client-based services. Such use of COTS technology will facilitate the integration of an SimQL interface into analysis applications that also employ access to diverse non-predictive data resources.

5. SimQL Implementation

SimQL provides an interface for accessing information about future events. There are two aspects of SQL that SimQL mimics:

- A Schema that describes the accessible content to an invoking program, its programmers, and its customers.
- A Query Language that provides the actual access to information resources.

Using similar interface concepts for data and simulation result access will simplify the understanding of customers and also enable seamless interoperation of SimQL with database tools in supporting advanced information systems. We focus on accessing pre-existing predictive tools.

Components of the system include four types of software

1. A compiler for the SimQL language, which generates code to access wrapped forecasting resources
2. A repository containing the schemas for the wrapped resources, identifying input and output parameters for each.
3. A wrapper generation tool to bring existing forecasting tools, as simulations, spreadsheets, and dynamic web sources into compliance
4. The actual forecasting tools, spreadsheets, discrete simulations, and web sources

Note that there are significant differences in accessing past data and computing information about the future:
- Not all simulation information is described in the schema. Simulations are often controlled by hundreds of variables, and mapping all of them into a schema is inappropriate. Only those variables that are needed for querying results and for controlling the simulation will be made externally accessible. The rest will still be accessible to the simulation developer. Defining the appropriate schema require the joint efforts of the developer, the model builder, and the customer.
- Predictions always incorporate uncertainty. Thus, measures of uncertainty are being reported with the results.
- Unlike SQL views, which are supported by real underlying SQL tables having static data, SimQL models only keeps information about interfaces to wrapped simulations, which can change constantly.
- We do not expect to need persistent update capabilities in SimQL. Model updates are the responsibility of the providers of the simulations. The queries submitted to SimQL supply temporary variables that parameterize the simulations for a specific instance, but are not intended to update the simulation models.

Wrappers are used to provide compatible, robust, and 'machine-friendly' access to their model parameters and execution results [HammerEa:97]. Our wrappers also convert the uncertainty associated with simulation results (say, 50% probability of rain) to a standard range (1.0 - 0.0) or may estimate a value if the simulation does not provide a value for its uncertainty.

Despite the structural similarity, the SimQL language is different from SQL in several ways, among which the following are the most prominent

1. The SimQL schema and query languages differentiate between IN, OUT, and INOUT variables, restricting the flexibility seen in SQL relational access.
2. The OUT variable in SimQL has two parts of the form of (value, uncertainty).

Our experiments used diverse simulations. They were wrapped to provide information to a SimQL interface.

  a) Two spreadsheet containing formulas that projected business costs and profits into the future. Inputs were investment amounts, and results were made available for years into the future.
  b) A short-range weather forecast available from NOAA on the world-wide web. Temperature and preciptation results were available for major cities, with an indication of uncertainty, which rapidly increased beyond 5 days.
  c) A long-range agricultural weather forecast for areas that overlapped with the cities. The initial uncertainty here was quite high, but increased little over a period of a several months.
  d) A discrete simulation of the operation of a gasoline station, giving required refill schedules and profits.

A customer application can invoke multiple SimQL simulations. Our experiments only combined simulations b) and c), selecting the forecast based on data with minimal uncertainty over a wide range. Still, these experiments with a few real-world simulation convinced us of the applicability of the SimQL concep to a range of settings and provides a foundation for further research in this direction. Details of the prototype are given in [WiederholdJG:98] and on our webpages.

6. Use of Simulation for Current Status

We have focused on using simulation to assess the future. There is however an important task for SimQL in assessing the present state. Databases can never be completely current. Some may be a few minutes behind, others may be several days behind in reporting the state of sales, inventory, and shipments. Information about competitors often lags even further behind, although it is the most crucial element in decision-making.

The traditional, consistency preserving approach in database technology is to present all information at the same point in time, which reduces all information to the worst lag of all sources. It would be better to use the latest data from each source, and then project the information to the current point-in-time. In fact, we are certain that decision maker today will take recent, even if inconsistent data into account when faced with data of varying times of validity. SimQL can support this approach since tot provides an interface that is consistent over databases (assumed to have data with probability 1.0) and simulations, as shown in Figure 2.

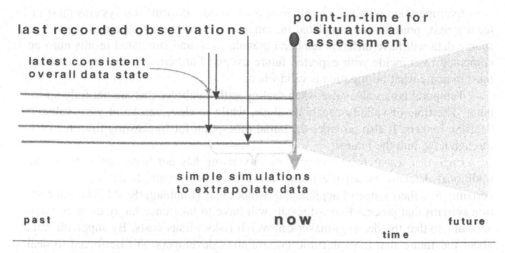

last recorded observations

point-in-time for
situational
assessment

latest consistent
overall data state

simple simulations
to extrapolate data

past   now   future

time

Fig. 2. Even the present needs SimQL

Extrapolation of last know database states to the current point-in-time will help in providing a nearly-consistent, somewhat uncertain picture of, say, where the supply trucks are now. This situational information will be more valuable to a decision maker than a consistent picture that is a week out of date, and would not reflect recent sales.

7. Research Opportunities

The importance of rapid, ad hoc, access to data for planning is well conceptually understood, but not served adequately by existing tools. Our work on SimQL provides the interfaces for tools, but did not extend to implementations of the vision for modern information systems that motivated our research. There are many research opportunities to help bring the vision about, from tool development for understood issues to conceptual research to deal with new issues in computation and representation that will arise.

The focus of traditional database technology has been highly reliable and consistent services for operational systems. As decision-making support has become more important, the constraints due to this emphasis have restricted the services needed for effective decision-making support.

Specifically, information systems should not be limited to reporting of historic data. Already, when historic records are a bit out-of-date, planners routinely make undocumented projections to extrapolate to the current situation and obtain an approximate current picture. Extrapolating further into the future increases the uncertainty. Furthermore, alternate decisions, or acts-of-nature, lead to alternate future scenarios. When the simulations incorporate alternate assumptions, they will produce alternate futures, so that an information model that supports planning must not only incorporate uncertainty, but also alternatives.

Interoperation with past information is required. Information systems must integrate past, present, and simulated information, providing a continuous view. The source data will have different temporal granularities, and simulated results must be computed to coincide with expected future events. Furthermore, the representation must indicate what information is valid when.

Temporal issues also arise when dealing with databases that are not fully up-to-date. The time-of-validity capability alone, while modest, can be of great value to decision-makers. It also provides the initial time-point for forecasting from the past, through now, into the future.

Important research into uncertainty processing has not been applicable in the traditional database model [Pearl:88]. There have been multiple definitions of uncertainty and their range of applicability is not clear [BhatnagarK:86]. The information systems that process forecast results will have to take uncertainty explicitly into account, so that the decision-maker can weigh risks versus costs. By supplying data about the future that have intrinsic uncertainties developers will be forced to deal with the issue explicitly, and we expect that new research will evolve to deal with the scalability and robustness of such applications.

The data stored in many databases are also not always certain. Mediators may report such data, using their own knowledge, once analysis tools have reached the maturity to deal with uncertainty over large datasets [GarciaMolinaBP:92].

The information systems must support comparison of the results for multiple courses-of-action (CoAs). These CoAs branch out, although sometimes the results of two distinct sequences of CoAs may merge at a future point. Queries directed to a future point in time will hence provide a list of value-sets. Each set is valid, although the system may impose that the some of the certainties of the sets be equal to 1.0. Labeling of the branches, so that their provenance is clear is open research issue.

As time passes, opportunities for choosing alternatives disappear, so that the future tree is continuously pruned as the *now* marker marches forward. At the same time, the uncertainties about future events should reduce, so that the tools that provided the information about the future should be re-invoked.

Keeping the results in an information models for planning up-to-date requires continuous re-evaluation. It makes little sense to warehouse all future CoAs and their results. Keeping the system content current is unlikely to happen without tools that automate the integration of information about the future into decision-support systems.

8. Conclusion

We have described issues that decision makers face when using the current information processing tools that computer scientists, system designers, and implementors provide. We find that integration of databases and forecasting tools is poor. To investigate the feasibility of improving the situation we defined and implemented a new interface language, SimQL. This language provides access to the growing port folio of simulation technology and predictive services maintained by others. We have some early results, indicating that highly diverse predictive tools may be accessed in an integrated fashion via a language as SimQL.

We expect that interfaces as SimQL will enable information systems to become much more effective and really support realistic decision making processes. Most importantly, having a language interface will break the bottleneck now experienced when predictions are to be integrated with larger planning systems. Because of the importance of forecasting to decision-making, we expect that concepts as demonstrated will in time enter large-scale information systems and become a foundation which will make a crucial difference in the way that spreadsheets, simulations and computational web resources will be accessed and managed.

Acknowledgments

This research was supported by DARPA DSO, Pradeep Khosla was the Program Manager; and awarded through NIST, Award 60NANB6D0038, managed by Ram Sriram. The original SQL compiler was written by Mark McAuliffe, of the University of Wisconsin - Madison, and modified at Stanford by Dallan Quass and Jan Jannink. James Chiu, a Stanford CSD Master's student, provided and wrapped the gas station simulation. Julia Loughran of ThoughtLink provided useful comments to an earlier version of this paper [WiederholdJG:98].

References

[AberleEa:96] Denise Aberle, John Dionisio, Michael McNitt-Gray, Rickt Taira, Alfonso Cardenas, Jonathan Goldin, Kathleen Bown , Robert Figlin, and Wesley Chu: "Integrated Multimedia Timeline of Medical Images and data for Thoracic Oncology Patients"; *Imaging and Therapeutic Technology*, Vol. 16 No.3; May 1996, pp.669-681.

[BhatnagarK:86] Bhatnagar and L.N. Kanal: "Handling Uncertain Information: A Review of Numeric and Non-numeric Methods"; in Kanal and Lemmer(eds.): *Uncertainty in AI*, North-Holland publishers, 1986.

[Burnstein:96] M. Burnstein & D. Smith: "ITAS: A Portable Interactive Transportation Scheduling Tool Using a Search Engine Generated from Formal specifications"; in B. Drabble (ed.): *Proceedings of the Third International Conference on Artificial Intelligence Planning Systems,*: AAAI Press: 1996.

[DasSTM:94] A.K. Das, Y. Shahar, S.W. Tu, and M.A. Musen: "A temporal-abstraction mediator for protocol-based decision support"; *Proceedings of the Eighteenth Annual Symposium on Computer Applications in Medicine*, Washington DC, 1994, pp.320-324

[DateD:93] C.J. Date and Hugh Darwen: *A Guide to the SQL Standard, 3rd ed*; Addison Wesley, June 1993.

[DeanW:91] Thomas Dean and Michael Wellman: *Planning and Control*; Morgan Kaufmann, 1991.

[DeZegherGeetsEa:88] IsabelleDeZegher-Geets, Andrew G. Freeman, Michael G. Walker, Robert L. Blum, and Gio Wiederhold: "Summarization and Display of On-line Medical Records"; *M.D. Computing*, Vol.5 No.3, March 1988, pp.38-46.

[FishwickH:98] Paul Fishwick and David Hill, eds: *1998 International Conference on Web-Based Modeling & Simulation*; Society for Computer Simulation, Jan 1998, http://www.cis.ufl.edu/~fishwick/webconf.html.

[GarciaMolinaBP:92] Hector GarciaMolina, D. Barbara, and D. Porter: "The Management of Probabilistic Data"; *IEEE Transactions on Knowledge and Data Engineering*,Vol. 4, No. 5, October 1992, pp. 487-502.

[HammerEa:97] J. Hammer, M. Breunig, H. Garcia-Molina, S. Nestorov, V. Vassalos, R. Yerneni: "Template-Based Wrappers in the TSIMMIS System"; *ACM Sigmod 26*, May 1997.

[IEEE:98] *P1561, Draft IEEE Standard for Modeling and Simulation (M&S) High Level Architecture (HLA)*; IEEE, 1998.

[INEL:93] Idaho National Engineering Laboratory: "Ada Electronic Combat Modeling"; *OOPSLA'93 Proceedings*, ACM 1993.

[Knoblock:96] Craig A. Knoblock: "Building a Planner for Information Gathering: A Report from the Trenches"; *Artificial Intelligence Planning Systems: Proceedings of the Third International Conference (AIPS96)*, Edinburgh, Scotland, 1996. .

[LindenG:92] Ted Linden and D. Gaw 1992: "JIGSAW: Preference-directed, Co-operative Scheduling," *AAAI Spring Symposium: Practical Approaches to Scheduling and Planning*, March 1992

[Kimball:96] Ralph Kimball: *The Data Warehouse*; Wiley, 1996.

[McCall:96] Gene McCall (editor): *New World Vistas, Air and Space Power for the 21ˢᵗ Century*; Air Force Scientific Advisory Board, April 1996, Information Technology volume, pp. 9.

[Miller:56] George Miller: "The Magical Number Seven ± Two"; *Psych.Review*, Vol.68, 1956, pp.81-97.

[Orsborn:94] Kjell Orsborn: "Applying Next Generation Object-Oriented DBMS for Finite Element Analysis"; ADB conference, Vadstena, Sweden, in Litwin, Risch *Applications of Database'*, Lecture Notes In Computer Science, Springer, 1994.

[Pearl:88] Judea Pearl: *Probabilistic Reasoning in Intelligent Systems*; Morgan-Kaufman, 1988.

[SandewallB:94] E. Sandewall and C. Backstrom (eds.): Current Trends in AI Planning, IOS Press, Amsterdam, 1994.

[SinghalC:95] Sandeep K. Singhal and David R. Cheriton: "Exploiting Position History for Efficient Remote Rendering in Networked Virtual Reality"; *Teleoperators and Virtual Environments*, Vol.4 No.2, pp.169-193, Spring 1995.

[TateDK:92] Tate,A; Drabble,B; Kirby,R : O-Plan 2: the Open Planning Architecture 1992, AAAI Spring Symposium.

[WiederholdG:97] Gio Wiederhold and Michael Genesereth: "The Conceptual Basis for Mediation Services"; *IEEE Expert, Intelligent Systems and their Applications*, Vol.12 No.5, Sep-Oct.1997.

[WiederholdJG:98] Gio Wiederhold, Rushan Jiang, and Hector Garcia-Molina: "An Interface for Projecting CoAs in Support of C2; *Proc.1998 Command & Control Research & Technology Symposium*, Naval Postgraduate School, June 1998, pp.549-558.

[Zyda:97] Michael Zyda, chair: *Modeling and Simulation, Linking Entertainment and Defense*; Committee on Modeling and Simulation, National Academy Press, 1997.

A Class of Stratified Programs in Autoepistemic Logic of Knowledge and Belief

Jianhua Chen

Computer Science Department

Louisiana State University

Baton Rouge, LA 70803-4020

E-mail: jianhua@bit.csc.lsu.edu

ABSTRACT

Przymusinski proposed [11] *AELB*, the autoepistemic logic of knowledge and belief. The AELB logic is a very powerful and expressive formal system which isomorphically contains various major non-monotonic knowledge representation formalisms and major logic program semantics. Thus AELB can be used as a unifying framework for non-monotonic knowledge representation formalisms, which allows us to compare and better understand different formalizations of common-sense knowledge.

The notion of "static autoepistemic expansion" forms the semantic basis for reasoning in AELB logic. However, not all AELB theories have *consistent* static expansions. In this paper, we identify a class of AELB theories, namely, the stratified AELB programs, and show that every stratified program has a unique consistent least static expansion. The existence of the consistent least static expansion is an important property which assures the usefulness of inferencing in such AELB theories.

1. Introduction

Przymusinski developed [11] AELB, the autoepistemic logic of knowledge and belief, and showed that AELB is a powerful, unifying non-monotonic knowledge representation framework, containing various major non-monotonic formalisms [2, 4, 6, 11] and major semantics for normal and disjunctive logic programs [9-10, 13]. The AELB logic is a propositional modal logic, obtained by adding the belief operator "B" to Moore's autoepistemic logic (AEL) [8] which already has the knowledge operator "L". Thus AELB has two modal operators, "B" and "L". The semantic basis for inferencing in AELB logic consists in the notion of "static autoepistemic expansions". Namely, given a theory Δ in AELB, we consider a formula ϕ to be a logical consequence of Δ if and only if ϕ is contained in a static autoepistemic expansion of Δ. The notion of static autoepistemic expansion (static expansion for short) generalizes the "stable autoepistemic expansion" in AEL logic.

One problem with inferencing in AELB logic is that not all AELB theories have *consistent* static expansions. Przymusinski has shown [11] that for the logic

AEB, the restriction of AELB to the language with only the "B" operator, every AEB theory has a unique least static expansion. Such least static expansion is *consistent* for the class of *affirmative* theories. However, it is well known that in Moore's AEL logic, which can be seen as the restriction of AELB to the language with only the "L" operator, not every theory has stable expansions. Therefore, when we consider AELB theories with both the "B" and "L" operators, we cannot expect the existence of consistent static expansions for every theory. On the other hand, in representing common-sense knowledge, we may often need to explicitly represent both what is "known" and what is "believed", which are modeled by the "L" and "B" operators. Therefore it is important to identify interesting subclasses of AELB theories with both the modal operators, which are guaranteed to have consistent static expansion.

In this paper, we characterize a class of AELB theories involving both modal operators and having the desired property, namely, the existence of consistent static expansions. This class is defined by its syntactical structure of the clauses in a theory, in the form of a "stratification" among the propositions occurring in the theory. Thus we term this class of AELB theories as "stratified programs" in the spirit of stratified normal and disjunctive logic programs [9]. The nice thing about this class of AELB theories is that every theory Δ in the class has a unique consistent least static expansion (in the sense defined in Sec. 3) which can be computed efficiently.

The rest of this paper is organized as follows. In Section 2, we briefly review the AELB logic and its relevant properties. In Section 3, we introduce the class of stratified programs and present the main theorem that every theory in this class has a unique consistent least static expansion. We also present in Section 3 the algorithm for computing the consistent least static expansion. We present examples of applying stratified programs in knowledge representation and reasoning in Section 4. We conclude in Section 5. Due to space limit, we omit the proofs of the lemmas and the main theorem, which will be presented in the full paper elsewhere.

2. The Autoepistemic Logic of Knowledge and Belief

AELB is a propositional modal logic with two modal operators "B" and "L". The language of AELB is obtained by augmenting Moore's AEL logic (which already has a modal operator "L") with another "belief" modal operator "B". A formula is called *objective* if it does not involve any modal operators. An objective atom (often called atom when no confusion is likely) and its negation are called (objective) *literals*. A *belief atom* is a formula of the form $B\phi$ where ϕ is any formula in AELB; similarly, a *knowledge* atom is a formula $L\phi$. Belief atoms and knowledge atoms are called *modal atoms*. Modal atoms and their negations are called *modal literals*. A clause in AELB is a disjunction of literals and modal literals. A theory Δ in AELB is a set of clauses of the form

$$b_1 \wedge ... \wedge b_m \wedge B\phi_1 \wedge ... \wedge B\phi_n \wedge L\psi_1 \wedge ... \wedge L\psi_k \rightarrow$$
$$B\alpha_1 \vee ... \vee B\alpha_s \vee L\beta_1 \vee ... \vee L\beta_t \vee a_1 \vee ... \vee a_l$$

Here each a_i, b_j is an objective atom, and each ϕ_i, ψ_j, α_i, β_j is an arbitrary formula in the language of AELB. A theory Δ is called *affirmative* if $l > 0$ for each clause in

Δ; Δ is called *rational* if $s = 0$ for each clause in Δ. The following two axiom schemata and the necessitation rule of inference are assumed for the logic:

(D) Consistency Axiom:

$$\neg B\square$$

(K) Normality Axiom: For any formulas ϕ and ψ in the language:

$$B\phi \wedge B(\phi \rightarrow \psi) \rightarrow B\psi$$

(N) Necessitation Inference Rule: For any formula ϕ in the language:

$$\frac{\phi}{B\phi}$$

Here "$\square$" stands for the logical constant "false".

Before we present the definition for static expansions, we need to introduce several notions. First, an *interpretation I* is a mapping from the set of objective atoms and modal atoms to the set $\{True, False\}$. Here by modal atoms we mean the union of the set of belief atoms of the form $B\phi$ and the set of knowledge atoms of the form $L\phi$, where ϕ is any formula. An interpretation I is extended to a mapping from all AELB formulas to $\{True, False\}$ in the obvious way. Note that the truth value assignment by an interpretation I to a belief (knowledge) atom $B\phi$ $(L\phi)$ is independent of its assignment to ϕ. Given an AELB theory Δ, an interpretation I is called a model of Δ if I assigns *True* to all formulas in Δ. For two models M and N of Δ, we say M is smaller than N (in symbols $M < N$), if (1) M and N coincide on the truth assignment for modal atoms, and (2) the set of objective atoms assigned to be true in M is a proper subset of the true objective atoms in N. A *minimal* model M of Δ is a model such that there is no model N of Δ which is smaller than M. A formula ϕ is said to be *minimally entailed* by Δ, written as $\Delta \models_{min} \phi$, if ϕ is true in all minimal models of Δ. We write $\Delta \models \phi$ to denote that every model of Δ satisfies ϕ, i.e., assigns *True* to ϕ.

Given an AELB theory Δ, we say a formula ϕ is derivable from Δ (written $\Delta \vdash \phi$) if ϕ is obtained from Δ by using axiom schemata (D), (K), necessitation rule (N), and ordinary propositional inference. The set of all formulas derivable from Δ is denoted as $Cn_*(\Delta) = \{\phi: \Delta \vdash \phi\}$.

An AELB theory Δ models the knowledge and beliefs that an ideally rational, introspective agent will hold, given the initial knowledge Δ. Such knowledge and beliefs are characterized by the *static autoepistemic expansion* Δ^* of Δ, which is defined through a fixed-point equation.

Definition (Static Autoepistemic Expansion). Let Δ be an AELB theory. A set Δ^* of AELB formulas is a static autoepistemic expansion of Δ, if it satisfies the following equation:

$$\Delta^* = Cn_*(\Delta \cup \{L\phi: \Delta^* \models \phi\} \cup \{\neg L\phi: \Delta^* \not\models \phi\} \cup \{B\phi: \Delta^* \models_{min} \phi\}).$$

Note that the above equation has Δ^* on both sides of the equality and thus it is a fixed-point equation.

There are several important properties of static autoepistemic expansions. When restricted to the language with only the "L" modal operator, static expansions of Δ coincide with stable autoepistemic expansions of Moore's AEL. When restricted to the language with only the "B" modal operator, the resulting logic AEB is a new logic which has several important and nice characteristics. In particular, Przymusinski has shown that every AEB theory has a unique least static expansion which can be obtained by fixed-point of an iterative monotonic operator. In addition, it is shown [1] that for finite theories, the fixed-point is always achieved with only one iteration. Moreover, for *affirmative* AEB theories, the least static expansion is always consistent. In [11], Przymusinski has shown a number of interesting applications of AELB for modeling common-sense knowledge.

3. Stratified AELB Programs

The general AELB language allows one to express both knowledge and beliefs, which is a desirable feature. However, with both "B" and "L" present, a theory Δ may or may not have *consistent* static expansions. This poses a problem to using the AELB logic for modeling common-sense knowledge. Thus it is important to identify non-trivial classes of AELB theories which allow both the "B" and "L" operators, and guarantee the existence of consistent static expansions. We characterize a class of *stratified* AELB theories called *stratified programs* that satisfy the above criteria.

A stratified program Δ consists of a set of clauses of the following form:

$$D_1 \wedge \cdots \wedge D_p \wedge B\neg A_1 \wedge \cdots \wedge B\neg A_n \wedge \neg Lb_1 \wedge \cdots \wedge \neg Lb_m \rightarrow C_1 \vee \cdots \vee C_k \qquad (1)$$

where each b_i, C_j, D_l is an atom, each A_j is a conjunction of atoms, $k > 0$, m, $n \geq 0$. Here $C_1 \vee ... \vee C_k$ is called the *head* of the clause and $D_1 \wedge ... \wedge D_p \wedge B\neg A_1 \wedge ... \wedge B\neg A_n \wedge \neg Lb_1 \wedge ... \wedge \neg Lb_m$ is called the *body* of the clause. A clause of the above form is called a *definition* for each of the head atoms $C_1, ..., C_k$. The clauses in Δ has a stratification Σ as defined below. A stratification Σ of Δ is a partition of the objective atoms in Δ into disjoint sets (called strata) $S_0 \cup S_1 \cup ... \cup S_l$ such that the following conditions are satisfied:

(a)   For each clause (1) in Δ, the head atoms $C_1, ..., C_k$ belong to the same strata S_j;

(b)   For each clause (1) in Δ, with head atoms in S_j, each of the atoms $D_1, ..., D_p$, and each of those in $A_1, ..., A_n$ belongs to some strata S_i, $i \leq j$; and each of the atoms $b_1, ..., b_m$ belongs to some strata S_t, $t < j$.

It should be pointed out that the class of stratified programs form a proper superset of the affirmative *super logic programs* developed in [1], on substituting **Not** for **B**¬ in the body of each program clause. The stratified programs are more expressive, as they allow both the belief and knowledge operators in the language, which is often necessary for modeling common-sense reasoning. Another nice feature of the stratified programs is that the existence of a consistent static expansion is guaranteed, similar to the corresponding result about the affirmative super logic programs (or more generally, affirmative AEB theories). We also note that the notion of stratified AELB programs is a generalization of the original notion of stratified disjunctive logic programs as in [9].

Let Δ be a stratified program and let $\Sigma = S_0 \cup S_1 \cup ... \cup S_l$ be its stratification. Here we assume the *tightest* stratification in the sense that for each strata S_j, $j \geq 1$, there is at least one clause (1) in Δ with head atoms in S_j such that the "knowledge part" $(\neg \mathbf{L}b_1 \wedge ... \wedge \neg \mathbf{L}b_m)$ of the clause body is non-empty, i.e., $m > 0$. It is easy to see that we can partition the program clauses in Δ into disjoint sets $P_0 \cup P_1 \cup ... \cup P_l$ such that the clauses with head atoms in strata S_j form P_j.

From now on, we denote by B_0 the AEB language with objective atoms only from S_0, and by B_j the AEB language with objective atoms only from $S_0 \cup ... \cup S_j$. Similarly, we denote by L_j the AELB language with objective atoms only from $S_0 \cup ... \cup S_j$. We use "$\Delta|_{B_j}$" to denote the restriction of an AELB theory Δ to the language B_j; similarly, "$\Delta|_{L_j}$" denotes the restriction of Δ to the language L_j.

Let Δ be a stratified AELB program with stratification $S_0 \cup ... \cup S_l$ and let Δ_1, Δ_2 be two static expansions of Δ. We define a "preference" relationship (written "$\leq$") between Δ_1 and Δ_2 as follows. We say Δ_1 is preferable over Δ_2 ($\Delta_1 \leq \Delta_2$) if for each formula ϕ in B_j such that $\phi \in (\Delta_2 - \Delta_1)$, there is a formula ψ in B_i, $i < j$, such that $\psi \in (\Delta_1 - \Delta_2)$. In other words, $\Delta_1 \leq \Delta_2$ if and only if one of the following two situations is true:

(1) $\Delta_1|_{B_j} = \Delta_2|_{B_j}$ for $0 \leq j \leq l$, or

(2)   There is $0 \leq k \leq l$ such that $\Delta_1|_{B_j} = \Delta_2|_{B_j}$ for $j < k$ and $\Delta_1|_{B_k} \subset \Delta_2|_{B_k}$.

Δ^* is called a *least* static expansion if Δ^* is preferable over every other static expansion Δ_i of Δ. Note that this notion of least (AELB) static expansion is a generalization of the notion of least static AEB expansion of an AEB theory.

Theorem 1 (Main).

Every stratified program Δ has a unique consistent least static expansion. Moreover, the least static expansion of Δ can be obtained iteratively using the stratification of Δ.

Definition (Reduction of a stratified program P w.r.t. theory Q). Let P be a stratified program and let Q be an AELB theory. The reduction of P w.r.t. Q, written P/Q, is obtained from P by the following two steps:

(1)   Remove from P any clause (1) such that the negation of some modal atom/literal in the clause body is contained in Q.

(2)   Simplify the body of the remaining clauses in P by removing the modal literals $\neg \mathbf{L}b_j$ and $\mathbf{B}\neg A_r$ which are contained in Q.

Sketch of Proof for Theorem 1. Let Δ be a stratified program and let $\Sigma = S_0 \cup S_1 \cup ... \cup S_l$ be its stratification. Let $P_0 \cup P_1 \cup ... \cup P_l$ be the corresponding partition of the program Δ. The existence of a consistent static expansion Δ^* can be shown by induction. First, by results in [11], each affirmative AEB theory W_j has a unique consistent least static expansion in AEB denoted $\overline{W_j}$; moreover, W_j has a unique consistent static AELB expansion W_j^* which extends $\overline{W_j}$. Now we define two sequences of theories Q_j and W_j for $0 \leq j \leq l$ as follows. $Q_j = P_0 \cup \cdots \cup P_j$. $W_0 = P_0$, W_0^* is the unique consistent static expansion which extends $\overline{W_0}$. For $j \geq 1$, W_j is defined as $W_{j-1} \cup P_j/W_{j-1}^*$. Noticing that each W_j is an affirmative AEB theory, the existence and consistency of $\overline{W_j}$ and W_j^* for $j \geq 0$ can be shown by induction. And then we can show by induction that Q_j has a consistent static expansion Q_j^* which equals W_j^*. We can also show that W_l^* is the unique least static expansion of Q_l (which equals Δ).

Now we are ready to present the algorithm for computing Δ^*, the consistent static expansion guaranteed by the main theorem. In the following, the notation $STAT0(W_j)$ for the AEB theory W_j denotes the unique AELB static expansion extending $\overline{W_j}$.

Algorithm STAT

Input: A stratified program Δ with stratification $\Sigma = S_0 \cup S_1 \cup ... \cup S_l$ and the corresponding program partition $\Delta = P_0 \cup P_1 \cup ... \cup P_l$.

Output:

The least static expansion Δ^* of Δ.

(1) $W_0 = P_0$, $W_0^* = STAT0(W_0)$.

(2)   For $j = 1$ to l do

        (2.1) $W_j = W_{j-1} \cup P_j/W_{j-1}^*$.

        (2.2) $W_j^* = STAT0(W_j)$.

(3)   Output $\Delta^* = W_l^*$.

4. Knowledge Representation by Stratified Programs

Example 1. This example is from Przymusinski's paper [11]. Consider a scenario in which:

(1)   You will rent a movie if you believe that you will neither go to a baseball nor to a football game;

(2)   You do not buy tickets to a game if you do not know that you will go to watch the game.

This scenario can be modeled as the following stratified program P:

$$(1) \quad \mathbf{B}\neg baseball \wedge \mathbf{B}\neg football \quad \rightarrow \quad rent\_movie$$
$$(2) \quad \neg Lbaseball \wedge \neg Lfootball \quad \rightarrow \quad dont\_buy\_tickets.$$

This program has a stratification $\Sigma = \{baseball, football, rent\_movie\} \cup \{dont\_buy\_tickets\}$. In terms of program clause partition, we have $P = \{(1)\} \cup \{(2)\}$. It is easy to follow the STAT algorithm outlined in the previous section for this simple program. We have $P_0 = \{(1)\}$. First we calculate $\overline{P_0}$. Since P_0 does not contain any clause with *baseball* or *football* in the head, it is clear that $\neg baseball$, $\neg football$ is true in all minimal models of P_0. Hence $\mathbf{B}\neg baseball$ and $\mathbf{B}\neg football$ are in $\overline{P_0}$. Subsequently we have $rent\_movie$ in $\overline{P_0}$. From $\overline{P_0}$, we can easily get P_0^*, the unique extension of $\overline{P_0}$ in AELB, which should contain, among others, the modal literals $\neg Lbaseball$, $\neg Lfootball$. The reduction of $P_1 \ (= \{(2)\})$ by P_0^* will produce the clause "$\rightarrow dont\_buy\_tickets$". Then we can compute P^*, the least static AELB expansion of P as guaranteed by Theorem 1, which contains all the literals and modal literals in P_0^* mentioned above, and the atom $dont\_but\_tickets$.

Now assume that the original scenario is changed slightly: you learn that you will either go a baseball game or a football game. The following program clause
$$(3) \ baseball \vee football$$
will be added to the program P. After this modification, the stratification among the atoms remains unchanged whereas the program clause partition becomes: $P = \{(1), (3)\} \cup \{(2)\}$. The least static AELB expansion of P now will not contain $rent\_movie$, because $\neg baseball \wedge \neg football$ is no longer true in all minimal models of P. In fact P^* will contain $\mathbf{B}\neg rent\_movie$. But the literals $\neg Lbaseball$, $\neg Lfootball$ and $dont\_buy\_tickets$ will still be in P^*.

Example 2. In the following scenario, you are trying to set up the drinks on the dinner table:

(1) You will go swimming after dinner if you believe that you have neither disease1 nor disease2.

(2) You will drink water at dinner if you will go swimming after dinner.

(3) You do not take any medicine if you do not know you have disease1 and you do not know you have disease2.

(4) You will drink water at dinner if you believe that you need to take medicine.

(5) You will drink beer or wine at dinner if you do not take medicine and you believe you will not go swimming after dinner.

(6) You will wait to set the drink if you do not know exactly which one (water, beer, wine) that you will drink at dinner.

The above scenario can be modeled by the following stratified program P:

$$(1) \quad \mathbf{B}\neg d_1 \wedge \mathbf{B}\neg d_2 \qquad\qquad \rightarrow \quad swim$$
$$(2) \quad swim \qquad\qquad\qquad\qquad\quad \rightarrow \quad water$$

(3)	$\neg Ld_1 \wedge \neg Ld_2$	$\rightarrow$	*no_med*
(4)	$\mathbf{B}\neg no\_med$	$\rightarrow$	*water*
(5)	$no\_med \wedge \mathbf{B}\neg swim$	$\rightarrow$	*beer* $\vee$ *wine*
(6)	$\neg Lbeer \wedge \neg Lwine \wedge \neg Lwater$	$\rightarrow$	*wait*

This program has the stratification $\Sigma = \{d_1, d_2, swim\} \cup \{no\_med, beer, wine, water\} \cup \{wait\}$. The program clause partition is $P = \{(1)\} \cup \{(2), (3), (4), (5)\} \cup \{(6)\}$. Given the current scenario, it is easy to see that $\neg d_1 \wedge \neg d_2$ is true in all minimal models of P and thus $\mathbf{B}\neg d_1 \wedge \mathbf{B}\neg d_2$ is in P^*. Therefore according to P^* you will go swimming after the dinner, you will drink water (and no beer/wine) at dinner, and you will not take any medicine. The least static expansion P^* contains, among others, the following set of atoms and modal literals: $\{\mathbf{B}\neg d_1, \mathbf{B}\neg d_2, swim, \mathbf{B}swim, Lswim, \neg Ld_1, \neg Ld_2, no\_med, \mathbf{B}no\_med, Lno\_med, water, \mathbf{B}water, Lwater, \mathbf{B}\neg beer, \mathbf{B}\neg wine, \mathbf{B}\neg wait\}$.

Suppose now you have the additional knowledge that you have either *disease1* or *disease2*, but not sure which one. This will be encoded as

$$(7) \quad d_1 \vee d_2.$$

The revised program P still has the same predicate stratification, and the program clause partition becomes $P = \{(1), (7)\} \cup \{(2), (3), (4), (5)\} \cup \{(6)\}$. Due to the presence of the clause (7), $\neg d_1 \wedge \neg d_2$ is no longer true in all minimal models of P and thus $\mathbf{B}\neg d_1 \wedge \mathbf{B}\neg d_2$ is not in P^*. So *swim* is not derivable. However, since you still do not know exactly which illness you have, no medication will be taken, according to (3), i.e., *no_med* is derivable. According to (5), you will derive *beer* $\vee$ *wine*. Since there is no definite knowledge on exactly what you will drink at dinner, you will wait to set the drink, according to (6). The least static expansion P^* contains (among others) the following set of formulas and modal literals: $\{d_1 \vee d_2, \mathbf{B}(d_1 \vee d_2), L(d_1 \vee d_2), \mathbf{B}\neg swim, \neg Lswim, \neg Ld_1, \neg Ld_2, no\_med, \mathbf{B}no\_med, Lno\_med, beer \vee wine, \mathbf{B}\neg water, \neg Lwater, \neg Lbeer, \neg Lwine, wait, \mathbf{B}wait, Lwait\}$.

5. Conclusions

Przymusinski's autoepistemic logic of knowledge and belief (AELB) has been shown to be a powerful and expressive formal system for common-sense reasoning which contains various major non-monotonic knowledge representation systems and major logic program semantics. An important issue regarding AELB is that not all AELB theories have consistent static expansions which form the semantic basis for query-answering in AELB. In this paper, we address this issue by identifying a class of AELB theories named *stratified AELB programs* and proving that each stratified AELB program has a unique least consistent static expansion which can be computed via an iterative procedure. The class of stratified AELB programs is quite expressive, including both the knowledge operator L and the belief operator $\mathbf{B}$, and containing the class of *super logic programs* previously studied in the literature [1]. The ability to express both knowledge and belief in the same logic program is important, as it allows us to represent both "well-founded negation" and "stable negation", and thus significantly increases the expressive power of logic programs. The existence of the least consistent static expansion in stratified programs and its iterative computing procedure facilitate the application of logic programs for knowledge representation and reasoning.

References

[1]   S. Brass, J. Dix, T. Przymusinski. Super Logic Programs. *Proceedings of the International Conference on Principles of Knowledge Representation and Reasoning (KR'96)*, Vancouver, Canada, Morgan Kaufmann, 1996.

[2]   M. Gelfond. Logic Programming and Reasoning with Incomplete Information. *Annals of Mathematics and Artificial Intelligence*, **12**: 89-116, 1994.

[3]   M. Gelfond, V. Lifschitz. The Stable Model Semantics for Logic Programming. In R. Kowalski and K. Bowen, editors, *Proceedings of the Fifth Logic Programming Symposium*, Cambridge, MA, 1988, pp. 1070-1080.

[4]   M. Gelfond, H. Przymusinska, T. Przymusinski. On the Relationship between Circumscription and Negation as Failure. *Artificial Intelligence*, **38**: 75-94, 1989.

[5]   V. Lifschitz, Minimal Belief and Negation as Failure. *Artificial Intelligence*, **70**: 53-72, 1994.

[6]   J. McCarthy. Circumscription - A Form of Non-monotonic Reasoning. *Artificial Intelligence*, **13**: 27-39, 1980.

[7]   W. Marek and M. Truszczynski. *Non-Monotonic Logic*. Springer-Verlag, 1994.

[8]   R. Moore. Semantical Considerations on Non-Monotonic Logic. *Artificial Intelligence*, **25**: 75-94, 1985.

[9]   T. Przymusinski. On the Declarative Semantics of Deductive Databases and Logic Programs. In J. Minker, Editor, *Foundations of Deductive Databases and Logic Programming*, Morgan Kaufmann, Los Altos, CA, 1988, pp. 193-216.

[10] T. Przymusinski, Semantics of Normal and Disjunctive Logic Programs: A Unifying Framework. *Proceedings of the Workshop on Non-Monotonic Extensions of Logic Programming at the 11th International Logic Programming Conference*, Springer-Verlag, 1995, pp. 43-67.

[11] T. Przymusinski. Autoepistemic Logic of Knowledge and Beliefs, *Artificial Intelligence*, In Press.

[12] R. Reiter. On Closed World Data Bases. In H. Gallaire and J. Minker, Editors, *Logic and Data Bases*, Plenum Press, New York, 1978, pp. 55-76.

[13] A. Van Gelder, K.A. Ross, and J.S. Schlipf. The Well-Founded Semantics for General Logic Programs. *Journal of the ACM*, **38**(3): 620-650, 1991.

On-Line Estimation of Matching Complexity in First Order Logic

Attilio Giordana and Lorenza Saitta

Dipartimento di Scienze e Tecnologie Avanzate
Università del Piemonte Orientale "Amedeo Avogadro"
Corso Borsalino 54, 15100 Alessandria, Italy
{attilio,saitta}@di.unito.it

Abstract. The expressiveness of First Order Logic (FOL) languages is severely counterbalanced by the complexity of matching formulas on a universe. Matching is an instance of the class of Constraint Satisfaction Problems (CSP), which have shown to undergo a phase transition with respect to two order parameters: *constraint density* and *constraint tightness*. This paper analyzes the problem of satisfying FOL Horn clauses in the light of these recent results. By means of an extensive experimental analysis, we show how Horn clause verification exhibits a typical phase transition with respect to the number of binary (or greater arity) predicates, and with respect to the ratio between the number of constants in the universe and the cardinality of the basic predicates extension.

1 Introduction

Recent investigations have uncovered that several classes of computationally difficult problems, notably NP-complete problems, show a "phase transition" with respect to some typical *order parameter,* i.e., they present abrupt changes in their probability of being solvable, coupled with a peak in computational complexity [Cheeseman, Kanefsky & Taylor, 1991; Williams & Hogg, 1994; Hogg, Huberman & Williams, 1996; Selman & Kirkpatrick, 1996; Gent & Walsh, 1996; Zhang & Korf, 1996; Walsh, 1998]. This is typically true for search problems, and the phenomenon seems to be largely independent from the specific search algorithm used [Hogg, Huberman & Williams (Eds.), 1996].

The identification of a phase transition may have important consequences in practice. In fact, the standard computational complexity of a class of problems is a pessimistic evaluation, based on worst-case analysis. Actually, many instances of the class can be solvable (or proved unsolvable) with reduced computational efforts. The investigation of phase transitions can provide information on single instances of the class, moving the focus from the maximum complexity to a "typical" complexity of instances. The location of the phase transition divides the problem space in three regions: One in which the probability of the existence of a solution is almost zero, and then it is "easy" to prove unsolvability. Another one, where many alternative solutions exist, and then it is "easy" to find one, and, finally, one where the probability of solution changes abruptly from almost 1 to almost 0, potentially making very difficult to find one of the existing solutions or to prove unsolvability.

Goal of the present work is to investigate the emergence of phase transition phenomena in matching First Order Logic (FOL) formulas. The ultimate goal is to apply the results to the problem of learning concepts from a set of classified positive and negative examples [Michalski, 1980]. In fact, during learning, matching candidate hypotheses to examples is repeated thousands of times, constituting thus the main source of computational complexity [Anglano et al., 1998; Giordana et al., 1998]. Then, reducing the complexity of matching may have substantial benefits in FOL learning, because more interesting hypotheses can potentially be found with less effort.

2 Phase Transitions in the Matching Problem

In this paper we are interested in the satisfiability of existentially quantified, conjunctive formulas, $\exists x \, [\varphi(x)]$, with n variables (from a set X) and m atomic conjuncts (predicate names from a set P). Given a universe U, consisting of a set of relations (tables) containing the extensions of the atomic predicates, the considered formula is satisfiable if there exists at least one model of $\varphi(x)$ in U.

In order to simplify the problem, still retaining its essence, we have adopted the following assumptions:

- Each variable $x_1, x_2, \ldots, x_n$ ranges over the same set Λ of constants, containing L elements.
- Only binary predicates are considered.
- Every relation in U has the same cardinality, namely it contains exactly N tuples
  (pairs of constants, in this case).

In order to perform experiments in a controlled way, a large number of matching problems have been generated according to a specified procedure described in the following subsections. The generation of a matching problem concerns both φ and U.

Given X and P, with the additional constraint $m \geq n-1$, the generation of a formula φ involves two steps. First, a *skeleton* φ_s is constructed deterministically, using (n-1) predicates from the set P:

$$\varphi_s(x) = \varphi_s(x_1, \ldots, x_n) = \alpha_1(x_1, x_2) \wedge \ldots \wedge \alpha_{n-1}(x_{n-1}, x_n) \equiv \bigwedge_{i=1}^{n-1} \alpha_i(x_i, x_{i+1}) \tag{1}$$

The skeleton structure guarantees that the resulting formula is not disjoint. Afterward, all the remaining (m-n+1) predicates in P are added to φ_s, selecting randomly, uniformly, and without replacement (inside each predicate), their arguments from the set X. With this procedure we obtain a formula:

$$\varphi(x) = \varphi_s(x) \wedge \varphi_a(x) \equiv \varphi_s(x) \wedge \bigwedge_{i=n}^{m} \alpha_i(y_i, z_i). \tag{2}$$

The variables y_i and z_i belong to the set $\mathbf{X}$, and are such that $y_i \neq z_i$. The generated formulas contain exactly n variables and m conjuncts, and the same pair of variables may appear in more than one predicate.

Every relation in U is constructed by creating the Cartesian product $\Lambda \times \Lambda$ of all possible pairs of values, and selecting N pairs from it, uniformly and without replacement. In this way, a same pair cannot occur two times in the same relation.

In summary, the matching problems we consider are defined by a 4-tuple (n, m, L, N). Several thousands of matching problems have been generated, choosing different values of n, m, L, and N.

2.1 Search Tree for Matching

Given a formula $\varphi(\mathbf{x})$ with the structure (2), the search for its models involves the construction of a tree τ, whose levels correspond to the assignment of values to the variables, considered in a given sequence. The search proceeds through the construction of partially satisfied subformulas of $\varphi(\overset{\bullet\bullet}{\mathbf{X}})$, until either the whole $\varphi(\overset{\bullet\bullet}{\mathbf{X}})$ is satisfied or unsatisfiability is proved. We start with a subformula

$$\varphi_2(x_1,x_2) = \underset{\bullet\bullet}{\alpha_1(x_1,x_2)} \wedge \beta_2(\{x_1,x_2\}),$$

where β_2 is the subformula of $\varphi_a(\overset{\bullet\bullet}{\mathbf{X}})$ that contains those predicates with arguments $\{x_1,x_2\}$. Obviously, the subformula β_2 may not exist, if the pair $\{x_1,x_2\}$ does not occur in $\varphi_a(\overset{\bullet\bullet}{\mathbf{X}})$. If $\varphi_2(x_1,x_2)$ is satisfiable, we consider the variable x_3 and the subformula

$$\varphi_3(x_1,x_2,x_3) = \varphi_2(x_1,x_2) \wedge \underset{\bullet\bullet}{\alpha_2(x_2,x_3)} \wedge \beta_3(\{x_1,x_2\},\{x_1,x_3\},\{x_2,x_3\}),$$

where β_3 is the subformula of $\varphi_a(\overset{\bullet\bullet}{\mathbf{X}})$ containing the predicates with arguments $\{x_1,x_2\}$, $\{x_1,x_3\}$ or $\{x_2,x_3\}$. The process goes on in the same way until the variable x_n is considered.

In order to investigate the emergence of phase transitions, two sets of experiments have been performed with different values of the parameters.

2.2 Effect of the Structure of the Formula

In a first set of experiments, the dependency of the matching cost and of the probability of solution upon the formula's syntactic complexity has been investigated. Parameter L and N have been set to constant values (L = 50, N = 100), and n and m have been varied. More specifically, three series of runs have been performed with n = 8, n = 10, and n = 12, respectively. In every series of runs, m assumed all the integer values from (n-1) through (n-1+30). For every assignment to n and m, 50 independent matching problems have been generated (4650 matching problems in all).

A stochastic search algorithm, implementing a random backtrack search without replacement, has been used. The cost C of the search has been defined as the total number of explored nodes in the tree, until either a first solution is found, or unsatisfiability is proved. For unsatisfiable problems it may be necessary to explore the whole tree.

In Fig. 1, the graph of the matching cost, $C_m(m)$, as a function of the total number of predicates in the formula φ, is reported, for a fixed value n = 10. Every point represents the average over the 50 individual matching problems. In the same figure, also the graph $P_m(m)$, corresponding to the probability of solution, is reported. P_m has been computed as the fraction of solvable problems among the 50 generated ones. A phase transition, with an average complexity rising up to 24,000 steps, occurs when the predicate number m reaches the value m = 19. The same experimentation has been repeated with n = 8 and n = 12 variables, obtaining similar behaviours. Whereas for n = 8 the obtained peak is considerably smaller than the one reported in Fig. 1, for n = 12 the matching algorithm ran, in several cases, out of memory.

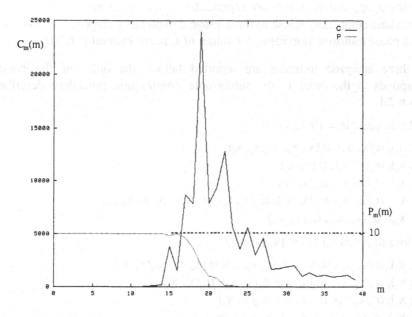

Fig. 1. Complexity $C_m(m)$ of the matching problem, and solution probability $P_m(m)$ as functions of the number m of predicates in a conjunctive formula, with n = 10, L = 50 and N = 100. Each value of $C_m(m)$ is an average over 50 runs. In every run a different universe has been randomly generated, but L and N have been kept constant. The probability of solution, for a given m, has been computed as the fraction of solvable problem instances among the 50 ones.

As previously observed [Hogg, Huberman & Williams, 1996], the location of the 1/2-probability of solution point coincides with the location of the complexity peak. Moreover, there is a large variability in complexity among individual instances. The region below the peak, where the sharp change in solvability occurs, is called the "mushy" region [Smith, 1994; Prosser, 1996], and is defined as the interval in which the probability of a solution existing changes from 0.01 to 0.99 (or vice versa). Inside the phase transition region there is a large variability in the computational complexity of matching, ranging from around one hundred steps to more than 270,000.

2.3 Effect of the Structure of the Universe

A second set of experiments was aimed to test the dependency of the complexity on the structure of the universe U. The experimentation has been done as described in the following. First, ten formulas with m = 19 predicates have been generated (in the region of the "hardest" cases). Then, the parameter L has been varied from 11 to 60, while keeping the size of the relations constant at N = 100.

The number of variables is again n = 10. For every value of L, 50 different universes have been generated, and the 10 formulas have been matched against all of them (a total of 25,000 matching problems). Fig. 2 reports the average complexity for the formulas φ_8, φ_9, and φ_2, which are representative for the maximum, minimum, and intermediate complexity (close to the average complexity), respectively. Also in this case, a phase transition is evident, for values of L in the interval [17, 24].

The three analyzed formulas are reported below; the order of the conjuncts corresponds to the order in the subformula construction procedure described in Section 2.1.

φ_8 (Maximum) : m = 19, L_{cr} = 20

$\alpha_1(x_1, x_2), \alpha_2(x_2, x_3), \alpha_3(x_3, x_4), \alpha_4(x_4, x_5)$
$\alpha_5(x_5, x_6), \alpha_{10}(x_3, x_6), \alpha_6(x_6, x_7)$
$\alpha_7(x_7, x_8), \alpha_{11}(x_5, x_8), \alpha_{12}(x_7, x_8)$
$\alpha_8(x_8, x_9), \alpha_{13}(x_1, x_9), \alpha_{14}(x_4, x_9), \alpha_{15}(x_5, x_9), \alpha_{16}(x_8, x_9), \alpha_{17}(x_8, x_9)$
$\alpha_9(x_9, x_{10}), \alpha_{18}(x_8, x_{10}), \alpha_{19}(x_4, x_{10})$

φ_2 (Close to Average) : m = 19, L_{cr} = 22

$\alpha_1(x_1, x_2), \alpha_2(x_2, x_3), \alpha_3(x_3, x_4), \alpha_{10}(x_1, x_4), \alpha_4(x_4, x_5), \alpha_5(x_5, x_6)$
$\alpha_6(x_6, x_7), \alpha_{11}(x_2, x_7), \alpha_{12}(x_6, x_7), \alpha_7(x_7, x_8), \alpha_{13}(x_7, x_8)$
$\alpha_8(x_8, x_9), \alpha_{14}(x_1, x_9), \alpha_{15}(x_4, x_9), \alpha_{16}(x_1, x_9)$
$\alpha_9(x_9, x_{10}), \alpha_{17}(x_3, x_{10}), \alpha_{18}(x_4, x_{10}), \alpha_{19}(x_5, x_{10})$

φ_9 (Minimum) : m = 19, L_{cr} = 22

$\alpha_1(x_1, x_2), \alpha_2(x_2, x_3), \alpha_3(x_3, x_4), \alpha_{10}(x_1, x_4), \alpha_4(x_4, x_5)$
$\alpha_5(x_5, x_6), \alpha_{11}(x_2, x_6), \alpha_{12}(x_3, x_6), \alpha_6(x_6, x_7)$
$\alpha_7(x_7, x_8), \alpha_{13}(x_4, x_8), \alpha_{14}(x_1, x_8)$
$\alpha_8(x_8, x_9), \alpha_{15}(x_1, x_9), \alpha_{16}(x_2, x_9)$
$\alpha_9(x_9, x_{10}), \alpha_{17}(x_8, x_{10}), \alpha_{18}(x_1, x_{10}), \alpha_{19}(x_6, x_{10})$

Fig. 3 shows the probability of solution $P_L(L)$ versus L, for the three selected formulas. Again, the 1/2 probability point and the complexity peak coincide. Also in this case, a wide variability in the complexity is evident. Unsolvable problems exhibit a much higher average complexity, because the whole search tree has been visited for them.

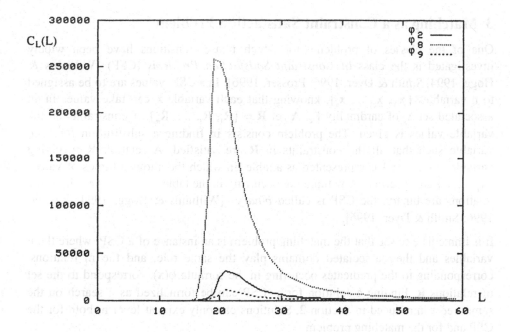

Fig. 2. Average matching complexity $C_L(L)$ versus the cardinality L of the set of constants, for three formulas φ_2, φ_8, and φ_9 selected among a set of 10. Every point corresponds to an average over 50 runs, each one with a different universe.

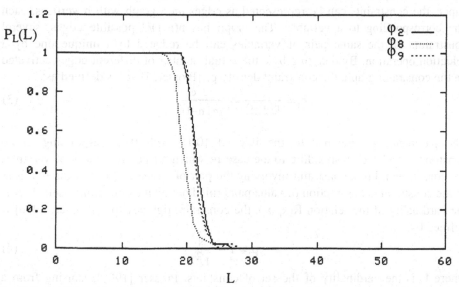

Fig. 3. Probability of solution $P_L(L)$ for the three formulas φ_2, φ_8, and φ_9, versus the cardinality L of the set of constants.

3 Matching as a Constraint Satisfaction Problem

One of the classes of problems for which phase transitions have been widely investigated is the class of *Constraint Satisfaction Problems* (CSP) [Williams & Hogg, 1994; Smith & Dyer, 1996; Prosser, 1996]. In a CSP, values are to be assigned to n variables $\{x_1, x_2, ..., x_n\}$, knowing that each variable x_k can take values in an associated set Λ_k of cardinality L_k. A set $\mathbf{R} = \{R_1, R_2, ..., R_m\}$ of constraints on the variable values is given. The problem consists in finding a substitution for each variable such that all the constraints in $\mathbf{R}$ are satisfied. A relation R involving variables $\{x_i, ..., x_j\}$ is represented as a table, in which the allowed tuples of values $\{a_i, ..., a_j\}$ are specified. Any tuple not occurring in the table is not allowed. If all the relations are binary, the CSP is called *binary* [Williams & Hogg, 1994; Prosser, 1996; Smith & Dyer, 1996].

It is immediate to see that the matching problem is an instance of a CSP, where the n variables and their associated domains play the same role, and the m relations, corresponding to the predicates occurring in the formula $\varphi(x)$, correspond to the set of relations $\mathbf{R}$. Finding a solution for a CSP can be formalized as a search on the same tree τ introduced in Section 2. Solutions can only exist at level n, both for the CSP and for the matching problem.

In this section, previous theoretical results are applied to the experimentation performed in Section 2. Two parameters are usually defined in order to account for the constrainedness degree of a CSP: *constraint density* and *constraint tightness* [Prosser, 1996]. When dealing with a binary CSP, as in the case considered in this paper, the constraints can be represented as edges on a graph with n vertices, each one corresponding to a variable. The graph has $n(n-1)/2$ possible edges; several constraints on the same pair of variables can be reduced to a unique one by a selection operation. By denoting by c the actual number of different edges activated on the constraint graph, the constraint density p_1 [Prosser, 1996] is defined as:

$$p_1 = \frac{c}{\frac{n(n-1)}{2}} = \frac{2c}{n(n-1)} \tag{3}$$

The parameter p_1 belongs to the interval [0,1], with 0 corresponding to no constraints, and 1 corresponding to the case in which all possible pairs of variables are constrained. For a constraint involving the pair of variables $\{x_i, x_j\}$, the tightness of the constraint is the fraction of value pairs ruled out by the constraint itself. If N is the cardinality of the relation $R(x_i, x_j)$, the constraint tightness p_2 [Prosser, 1996] is defined by:

$$p_2 = 1 - \frac{N}{L^2} \tag{4}$$

where L is the cardinality of the set of constants. Prosser [1996], starting from a theoretical analysis presented by Williams and Hogg [1994], derives an estimate for the critical value of p_2:

$$\hat{p}_{2,cr} = 1 - L^{-\frac{2}{p_1(n-1)}} = 1 - L^{-\frac{n}{c}} \tag{5}$$

The same estimate $\hat{p}_{2,cr}$ has been obtained by Smith and Dyer [1996], using a slightly different approach.

Using (3) and noticing that p_2 does not depend on m, we obtain from (5):

$$\hat{m}_{cr} = \frac{\hat{c}_{cr}}{\rho} = \frac{n \ln L}{\ln\left(\frac{L^2}{N}\right)},\qquad(6)$$

where the symbol ρ denotes the probability (averaged over m) that exactly c different edges on the constraint graph are activated, given that the formula to be matched (built up as described in Section 2) has m predicates. In fact, given the way we generate the formulas to be matched, our parameter m does not coincide with c in (3), because some of the m predicates may have the same set of arguments. The average value observed in the experiments summarized in Fig. 3 has been $\rho = 0.89$.

Using (4), we can compute a corresponding estimate for the critical value of L, keeping all other parameters constant (including p_1, which does not depend on L); it must be:

$$1 - \frac{N}{L_{cr}^2} = 1 - L_{cr}^{-\frac{2}{p_1 (n-1)}}$$

The predicted critical value of L is then:

$$\hat{L}_{cr} = N^{\frac{1}{2-\frac{n}{c}}}\qquad(7)$$

For the three formulas φ_8, φ_2, and φ_9, discussed in Section 2, formula (7) gives the values $L_{cr} = 19.14$ for φ_8 (actual value $L_{cr} = 20$), $L_{cr} = 19.14$ for φ_2 (actual value $L_{cr} = 22$), and $L_{cr} = 22.9$ for φ_9 (actual value $L_{cr} = 22$). As we can see, formula (7) is close enough to the observed average values, with a slight tendency to overestimate L_{cr}. The accordance with the experimental results is good, considered that our generation model of the problem instances is slightly different from Prosser's.

4 Conclusions

In this paper we focused the attention on works related to the appearance of phase transitions in constraint satisfaction problems, the matching problems being a subset of them. In the phase transition region the matching complexity exhibits a very high variability, so that many matching problems can still be answered within acceptable complexity limits.

For this reason, on-line techniques, based on Monte Carlo sampling, can be used to decide, very early in the search, whether a specific matching problem is likely to be too hard, or can be afforded within the granted computational resources. The results open a real perspective of using weaker language biases, so that more complex structural properties could be discovered by learning in a relational framework.

References

1. Anglano C., Giordana A., Lo Bello G., and Saitta L. (1998). "An Experimental Evaluation of Coevolutive Concept Learning". In *Proc. 15th Int. Conf. on Machine Learning* (Madison, WI), pp. 19-27.
2. Cheeseman P., Kanefsky B., and Taylor W.M. (1991). "Where the *Really* Hard Problems Are". In *Proc. 12th Int. Joint Conf on Artificial Intelligence* (Sidney, Australia), pp. 331-337.
3. Gent I.P., and Walsh T. (1996). "The TSP Phase Transition". *Artificial Intelligence, 88,* 349-358.
4. Giordana A., Neri F., Saitta L., and Botta M. (1998). "Integrating Multiple Learning Strategies in First Order Logics". *Machine Learning, 27,* 209-240.
5. Hogg T., Huberman B.A., and Williams C.P. (Eds.) (1996). *Artificial Intelligence, Special Issue on Frontiers in Problem Solving: Phase Transitions and Complexity, 81 (1-2).*
6. Hogg T., Huberman B.A., and Williams C.P. (1996). *Artificial Intelligence, 81,* 1-15.
7. Michalski R.S. (1980). "Pattern recognition as a rule-guided inductive inference". *IEEE Trans. on Pattern Analysis and Machine Intelligence, PAMI-2,* 349-361.
8. Prosser P. (1996). "An Empirical Study of Phase Transitions in Binary Constraint Satisfaction Problems". *Artificial Intelligence, 81,* 81-110.
9. Selman B., and Kirkpatrick S. (1996). "Critical Behavior in the Computational Cost of Satisfiability Testing". *Artificial Intelligence, 81,* 273-296.
10. Smith B.M. (1994). "Phase Transition and the Mushy Region in Constraint Satisfaction". In *Proc. European Conf. on Artificial Intelligence* (Amsterdam, The Netherlands), pp. 125-129.
11. Smith B.M., and Dyer M.E. (1996). "Locating the Phase Transition in Binary Constraint Satisfaction Problems". *Artificial Intelligence, 81,* 155-181.
12. Walsh T. (1998). "The Constrainedness Knife-Edge". In *Proc. 15th National Conf. on Artificial Intelligence* (Madison, Wisconsin, USA), pp. 406-411.
13. Williams C.P., Hogg T. (1994). "Exploiting the Deep Structure of Constraint Problems". *Artificial Intelligence, 70,* 73-117.
14. Zhang W., and Korf R.E. (1996). "A Study of Complexity Transition on the Asymmetric Travelling Salesman Problem". *Artificial Intelligence, 81,* 223-239.

Implementing Prioritized Logic Programming

Cheng-Min Wu and Yan Zhang*

School of Computing and Information Technology
University of Western Sydney, Nepean
Kingswood, NSW 2747, Australia
E-mail: {cwu,yan}@cit.nepean.uws.edu.au

Abstract. Conflict resolution is an important issue in knowledge representation and reasoning. A common idea of solving conflicts in reasoning is to introduce priorities in the underlying reasoning mechanism. This paper describes an implementation of prioritized logic programs (PLPs) proposed by Zhang and Foo recently [4]. PLPs is a non-trivial extension of Gelfond and Lifschitz's extended logic programs [3] by associating preferences to the program, where answer sets provide a semantics of PLPs. As a central part of the implementation of PLPs, we present major algorithms of computing answer sets of PLPs. We show how answer sets of a PLP can be computed efficiently based on previous Niemelä and Simons' method of computing stable models of logic programs [2].

1 Introduction

Conflict resolution is an important issue in knowledge representation and reasoning. A common idea of solving conflicts in reasoning is to introduce priorities in the underlying reasoning mechanism. This paper describes an implementation of prioritized logic programs (PLPs) proposed by Zhang and Foo recently [4]. PLPs is a non-trivial extension of Gelfond and Lifschitz's extended logic programs [3] by associating preferences to the program, where answer sets provide a semantics of PLPs. As a central part of the implementation of PLPs, we present major algorithms of computing answer sets of PLPs. We show how answer sets of a PLP can be computed efficiently based on previous Niemelä and Simons' method of computing stable models of logic programs [2]. The paper is organized as follows. Next section briefly reviews the syntax and semantics of PLPs. By illustrating several typical examples, this section also shows how conflicts are resolved in PLPs. Section 3 proposes several key algorithms for computing answer sets of PLPs. Finally, section 4 concludes this paper with some remarks.

2 Prioritized Logic Programs (PLPs)

In this section we introduce the syntax and semantics of prioritized logic programs (PLPs).

* The first author is supported in part by a Logic Programming Research Scholarship from the University of Western Sydney, Nepean.

2.1 Syntax of PLPs

Our language $\mathcal{L}$ includes the following vocabulary:

- *Variables*: x, y, z, $\cdots$.
- *Constants*: C, C_1, C_2, $\cdots$, including logical constants *True* and *False*.
- *Predicates*: $P, Q, R, \cdots$.
- *Names*: $N, N_1, N_2, \cdots$.
- A strict partial ordering (i.e. antireflexive, antisymmetric and transitive) $<$ on names.
- A naming function $\mathcal{N}$, which maps a *rule* (see below) to a name.
- A symbol $\leftarrow$, which is used to represent a rule.
- Connectives $\neg$ and *not*, where $\neg$ represents the classical negation (strong negation), and *not* represents *negation as failure* (weak negation).

We also require that the sets of variables, constants, predicates and names be disjoint. A *term* is either a constant or a variable. An *atom* is $P(t_1, \cdots, t_k)$, where P is a predicate of arity k and $t_1, \cdots, t_k$ are terms. A *literal* is either an atom P or a negation of an atom $\neg P$. A *rule* is a statement of the form

$$L_0 \leftarrow L_1, \cdots, L_m, not\ L_{m+1}, \cdots, not\ L_n,$$

where L_i $(0 \leq i \leq n)$ is a literal. L_0 is the *head* of the rule, while $L_1, \cdots, L_m, not$ $L_{m+1}, \cdots, not\ L_n$ is the *body* of the rule. Obviously, the body of a rule could be empty. iA term, an atom, a literal, or a rule is *ground* if no variable occurs in it.

For the naming function $\mathcal{N}$, we require that for any rules r and r' in a PLP (see the following definition), $\mathcal{N}(r) = \mathcal{N}(r')$ iff r and r' indicate the same rule.

An *extended logic program* Π is a collection of rules [3]. A *prioritized logic program* (PLP) $\mathcal{P}$ is a triplet $(\Pi, \mathcal{N}, <)$, where Π is an extended logic program, $\mathcal{N}$ is a naming function mapping each rule in Π to a name, and $<$ is a strict partial ordering on name. The following is an example of prioritized logic program.

$\mathcal{P}_1$:
$N_1 : P \leftarrow not\ Q, not\ R,$
$N_2 : Q \leftarrow not\ P,$
$N_3 : R \leftarrow not\ P,$
$N_1 < N_2, N_2 < N_3.$

We also use notations $\mathcal{P}_1(\Pi)$, $\mathcal{P}_1(\mathcal{N})$, and $\mathcal{P}_1(<)$ to denote the sets of rules, naming function's values and $<$-relations of $\mathcal{P}_1$ respectively.

A prioritized logic program is defined as an extended logic program by associating with a partial ordering $<$ to it. Intuitively such ordering represents a preference of applying rules during the evaluation of a query of the program. In particular, if in a program $\mathcal{P}$, relation $\mathcal{N}(r) < \mathcal{N}(r')$ holds, rule r would be preferred to apply over rule r' during the evaluation of $\mathcal{P}$ (i.e. rule r is more preferred than rule r'). Consider the following classical example represented in our formalism:

$\mathcal{P}_2$:

$N_1 : Fly(x) \leftarrow Bird(x), \; not \; \neg Fly(x),$
$N_2 : \neg Fly(x) \leftarrow Penguin(x), \; not \; Fly(x),$
$N_3 : Bird(Tweety) \leftarrow,$
$N_4 : Penguin(Tweety) \leftarrow,$
$N_2 < N_1.$

Obviously, rules N_1 and N_2 conflict with each other as their heads are complementary literals, and applying N_1 will defeat N_2 and *vice versa*. However, as $N_2 < N_1$, we would expect that rule N_2 is preferred to apply first and then defeat rule N_1 after applying N_2 so that the desired solution $\neg Fly(Tweety)$ could be derived.

2.2 Semantics of PLPs

In this subsection, we develop the semantics of PLPs. Our method is based on an extension of answer set semantics for extended logic programs [3]. Before we present our idea in detail, we need to introduce this answer set semantics first.

Let Π be an extended logic program. For simplicity, we treat a rule r in Π with variables as the set of all ground instances of r formed from the set of ground literals of the language of Π. We will also adopt this assumption in our prioritized extended logic programs. In the rest of paper, we will not explicitly declare this assumption whenever there is no ambiguity in our discussion.

Let Π be an extended logic program not containing *not* and *Lit* the set of all ground literals in the language of Π. The *answer set* of Π, denoted as $Ans(\Pi)$, is the smallest subset S of *Lit* such that

(i) for any rule $L_0 \leftarrow L_1, \cdots, L_m$ from Π, if $L_1, \cdots, L_m \in S$, then $L_0 \in S$;
(ii) if S contains a pair of complementary literals, then $S = Lit$.

Now consider Π be an extended logic program. For any subset S of *Lit*, let Π^S be the logic program obtained from Π by deleting

(i) each rule that has a formula *not* L in its body with $L \in S$, and
(ii) all formulas of the form *not* L in the bodies of the remaining rules.

We define that S is an *answer set* of Π, denoted $Ans(\Pi)$, iff S is an answer set of Π^S, i.e. $S = Ans(\Pi^S)$.

Consider $\mathcal{P}_2$ presented in last section. It is not difficult to see that extended logic program $\mathcal{P}_3(\Pi)$ has two answer sets: $\{Bird(Tweety), Penguin(Tweety), \neg Fly(Tweety)\}$ and $\{Bird(Tweety), Penguin(Tweety), Fly(Tweety)\}$.

In program $\mathcal{P}_2$, we have seen that rules N_1 and N_2 conflict with each other. Since $N_2 < N_1$, we try to solve the conflict by applying N_2 first and defeating N_1. However, in some programs, even if one rule is more preferred than the other, these two rules may not affect each other at all during the evaluation of the program. In this case, the preference relation between these two rules does not play any role in the evaluation and should be simply ignored. This is illustrated by the following program:

$\mathcal{P}_3$:

$\quad N_1 : P \leftarrow not\ Q_1,$
$\quad N_2 : \neg P \leftarrow not\ Q_2,$
$\quad N_1 < N_2.$

Although heads of N_1 and N_2 are complementary literals, applying N_1 will not affect the applicability of N_2 and *vice versa*. Hence $N_1 < N_2$ should not be taken into account during the evaluation of $\mathcal{P}_3$. The following two definitions formalize this intuition.

Definition 1. Let Π be an extended logic program and r a rule with the form $L_0 \leftarrow L_1, \cdots, L_m, not\ L_{m+1}, \cdots, not\ L_n$ (r does not necessarily belong to Π). Rule r is *defeated* by Π iff for any answer set $Ans(\Pi)$ of Π, there exists some $L_i \in Ans(\Pi)$, where $m + 1 \leq i \leq n$.

Definition 2. Let $\mathcal{P} = (\Pi, \mathcal{N}, <)$ be a prioritized extended logic program and $\mathcal{P}(<^+)$ denote the $<$-closure of $\mathcal{P}$ (i.e. $\mathcal{P}(<^+)$ is the smallest set containing $\mathcal{P}(<)$ and closed under transitivity). $\mathcal{P}^<$ is a *reduct* of $\mathcal{P}$ with respect to $<$ iff there exists a sequence of sets Π_i ($i = 0, 1, \cdots$) such that:

(i) $\Pi_0 = \Pi$;
(ii) $\Pi_i = \Pi_{i-1} - \{r_1, \cdots, r_k \mid$ (a) there exists $r \in \Pi_{i-1}$ such that $\mathcal{N}(r) < \mathcal{N}(r_i) \in \mathcal{P}(<^+)$ ($i = 1, \cdots, k$) and $r_1, \cdots, r_k$ are defeated by $\Pi_{i-1} - \{r_1, \cdots, r_k\}$, and (b) there does not exist a rule $r' \in \Pi_{i-1}$ such that $N(r_j) < N(r')$ for some j ($j = 1, \cdots, k$) and r' is defeated by $\Pi_{i-1} - \{r'\}\}$;
(iii) $\mathcal{P}^< = \bigcap_{i=0}^{\infty} \Pi_i$.

Example 1. Using Definition 2, it is not difficult to conclude that $\mathcal{P}_1$ and $\mathcal{P}_3$ have unique reducts as follows respectively:

$\quad \mathcal{P}_1^< = \{P \leftarrow not\ Q,\ not\ R\},$
$\quad \mathcal{P}_2^< = \{\neg Fly(x) \leftarrow Penguin(x),\ not\ Fly(x),$
$\qquad\quad Bird(Tweety) \leftarrow, Penguin(Tweety) \leftarrow\},$
$\quad \mathcal{P}_3^< = \mathcal{P}_3(\Pi).$

Now it is quite straightforward to define the answer set for a prioritized extended logic program.

Definition 3. Let $\mathcal{P} = (\Pi, \mathcal{N}, <)$ be a PLP and Lit the set of all ground literals in the language of $\mathcal{P}$. For any subset S of Lit, S is an *answer set* of $\mathcal{P}$, denoted as $Ans^P(\mathcal{P})$, iff $S = Ans(\mathcal{P}^<)$, where $Ans(\mathcal{P}^<)$ is an answer set of extended logic program $\mathcal{P}^<$. A ground literal L is *derivable* from a PLP $\mathcal{P}$, denoted as $\mathcal{P} \vdash L$, iff L belongs to every answer set of $\mathcal{P}$.

Example 2. Immediately from Definition 3 and Example 1, we have the following solutions:

$\quad Ans^P(\mathcal{P}_1) = \{P\},$
$\quad Ans^P(\mathcal{P}_2) = \{Bird(Tweety),\ Penguin(Tweety), \neg Fly(Tweety)\},$
$\quad Ans^P(\mathcal{P}_3) = Lit,$

which, respectively, are also consistent with our intuitions.

Example 3. Let $\mathcal{P}_4$ be:

$\mathcal{P}_4$:
$\quad N_1 : P \leftarrow not\ Q,\ not\ R,$
$\quad N_2 : Q \leftarrow not\ P,$
$\quad N_3 : R \leftarrow not\ P,$
$\quad N_1 < N_2.$

$\mathcal{P}_4(\Pi)$ has two answer sets $\{P\}$ and $\{Q, R\}$. Obviously, N_2 is not defeated by $\mathcal{P}_4(\Pi) - \{N_2\}$ as P only belongs to one of two answer sets $\{P\}$ and $\{R\}$ of $\mathcal{P}_7(\Pi) - \{N_2\}$. Therefore, the unique reduct $\mathcal{P}_4^<$ of $\mathcal{P}_7$ is the same as $\mathcal{P}_4(\Pi)$. So $\mathcal{P}_7$ has two answer sets $\{P\}$ and $\{Q, R\}$.

It is worth observing that if we add $N_1 < N_3$ to $\mathcal{P}_4$, $\mathcal{P}_4$ will then has a unique answer set $\{P\}$. On the other hand, if we add $N_3 < N_1$ instead of $N_1 < N_3$, the unique answer set of $\mathcal{P}_4$ will then have $\{Q, R\}$.

3 Computing PLP Answer Sets

In this section we develop algorithms for computing answer set of PLPs. We first describe our basic ideas of computing answer sets of PLPs and then present formal algorithms to implement our ideas. However, the detailed algorithms presented only deal with PLPs without any variables appeared within them and only produce one reduct (answer set). Further discussion will be followed to explore it in more detail.

3.1 Basic Ideas

From concepts introduced earlier in this paper, PLPs will eventually reduce to extend logic programs (ELPs) by eliminating the partial ordering in PLPs and any rules which are defeated during the process.

Several functions are introduced here in order to do such transformation: **Closure_plus**, **Defeatness**, and **Reduct**. Using Definition 2, function **Closure_plus** is to produce all possible partial ordering relations among rules under the transitivity of $<$. Function **Defeatness**$(\Pi, test\_rule\_set)$, on the other hand, is to test a set of rules $test\_rule\_set$ whether is defeated in Π, it either returns true (defeated) or false (not defeated) (see Definition 1).

For function **Defeatness**, it is required to compute an answer set for a given ELP. Firstly, ELPs are to be transformed to NLPs (normal logic programs). We then employ an algorithm proposed by Niemelä & Simons [2] to compute the stable model for NLPs, and then change it back to ELPs in order to determine the defeatness of ELPs. Once the original program and consecutive program reach a fixed point (after the process of **Defeatness**), it is straightforward to compute the reduct. From Definition 2, reduct is simply taking an intersection of the original and consecutive programs.

3.2 Algorithms

In this subsection, we present formal algorithms of computing answer sets of PLPs together with some examples to explain them.

function **Closure_plus**(plp_set)
    DOWHILE NOT end of plp_set input ordering
        Test transitivity of the input ordering
        DOWHILE transitivity exists
            IF transitivity creates an infinite loop
                Display error message
                Terminate program process
            ENDIF
            IF new transitivity ordering not duplicated
                Create new entry in **Closure_plus**
            ENDIF
            Test transitivity on newly created ordering
        ENDDO
        Read input ordering from plp_set
    ENDDO
END

Example 4.   Program $\mathcal{P}_1$ revisited.
    $N_1 : P \leftarrow not\ Q,\ not\ R,$
    $N_2 : Q \leftarrow not\ P,$
    $N_3 : R \leftarrow not\ P,$
    $N_1 < N_2, N_2 < N_3.$

Under transitivity, a new ordering relation $N_1 < N_3$ will be derived. Function **Closure_plus** would generate a set: $\{N_1 < N_2, N_2 < N_3, N_1 < N_3\}$. To prevent an error which may cause an infinite loop when computing the closure, a test is necessary in place to avoid such error. Adding ordering $N_3 < N_1$ or $N_3 < N_2$ into the original $\mathcal{P}_1$ will cause an infinite loop, program will terminate abnormally.

function **Defeatness**($\Pi, test\_rule\_set$)
    IF any ordering in test_rule_set **NOT** in Π
        Return false
    ENDIF
    Compute Π's answer sets
    IF answer_set is empty
        Return false (not defeated)
    ENDIF
    DO all rules in test_rule_set
        DO all answer_set entries
            IF body of the rule (with not atom) not in answer_set entry
                Return false (not defeated)

```
      ENDIF
    ENDDO
  ENDDO
  Return true (defeated)
END
```

It is necessary to mention that the process of "Compute Π's answer sets" in above algorithm needs to call three functions **Elp2nlp, Smodel** and **Nlp2elp** in function **AnswerSet** described by the end of this section. Note that Π is an ELP, and with some modification on Π (i.e. functions **Elp2nlp** and **Nlp2elp**, we can compute its answer sets by using function **Smodel** proposed in [2].

Note that all testing rules (with *not* atom) have to be considered with all answer set entries. Consider that $\mathcal{P}_4$ is the case, while answer sets of $\mathcal{P}_4(\Pi) - \{N_2\}$ are $\{P\}$ and $\{R\}$, and testing rule is N_2 which has only one (*not* P) in the body. P is covered by the first answer set $\{P\}$ but second answer set $\{R\}$, therefore N_2 is not defeated by the $\mathcal{P}_4(\Pi) - \{N_2\}$.

```
function Reduct(plp_set)
    plp_set= (Π, N, <)
    reduct = Π
    DO all rules in original Π
        temp_reduct = Π
        Π₀ = Π
        Create tempset (set of ordering belongs to <⁺ with head = rule)
        defeat_flag = 0
        IF tempset is not empty THEN
            i = 0
            Test(tempset, i)
        ENDIF
        reduct = temp_reduct ∩ reduct
    ENDDO
END
```

Π_i in function **Reduct** is created by function **Test** (see below). Function **Reduct** is to compute reduct of Π, all rules in Π will be processed but only one reduct will be generated from this based algorithm. We will discuss how to generate all reducts and deal with variables later in this paper.

Refer to definition 2 (ii): $\Pi_i = \Pi_{i-1} - \{r_1, \cdots, r_k \mid \cdots\}$, expression in curly brace is created as **tempset** here. Then if **tempset** is not empty, it would be the first argument pass to function **Test** which calls itself to do the defeatness test on Π_i. Once all rules have been processed, reduct is simply a $\bigcap_{i=0}^{\infty} \Pi_i$.

Example 5. Consider a program containing rules N_1, N_2 and N_3 while its closure $<^+$ is a set $\{N_2 < N_1, N_2 < N_3\}$. In function **Reduct**, the tempset for N_1 and

N_3 is empty, then its reduct is $\Pi_0 = \Pi$. Note that in the first call, tempset for $N_2 = \{N_1, N_3\}$.

```
function Test(tempset, i)
    IF defeat_flag = 1 THEN
        Return
    ENDIF
    IF Defeatness(Π, tempset) THEN
        defeat_flag = 1
        create Π_{i+1} = Π_i - tempset
        temp_reduct = Π_{i+1} ∩ temp_reduct
        new_tempset = all rules in Π_{i+1} appear in tail position of
                        ordering from closure_plus <⁺
        IF new_tempset is empty THEN
            Return
        ELSE
            Test(new_tempset, i+1)
        ENDIF
    ELSE
        DO all possible combination of tempset
            new_tempset = one combination
        IF new_tempset is empty THEN
            return
        ELSE
            Test(new_tempset, i)
        ENDIF
        ENDDO
    ENDIF
END
```

Function **Test** is a recursive call, only one reduct is produced, defeat_flag is used to determine termination of the function **Test**. As long as no defeatness is encountered, it will do all possible combination of tempset until empty tempset is encountered.

```
function AnswerSet(plp_set)
    elp_set = Reduct(plp_set)
    nlp_set = Elp2nlp(elp_set)
    sm_set = Smodel(nlp_set)
    answer_set = Nlp2elp(sm_set)
END
```

In function **AnswerSet**, a function named **Elp2nlp** is needed to translate an extended logic program (elp_set) to a normal logic program (nlp_set) and a function named **Nlp2elp** to convert nlp_set back to elp_set. The detail of

Elp2nlp is omitted here since it is straightforward to present it according the procedure described in [3] (only a matter of changing names in the process). Function **Smodel** for computing stable models was proposed in [2], which is based on bottom-up backtracking search. It works in linear space and employs a powerful pruning method based on an approximation technique for stable-models which is closely related to the well-founded semantics. The implementation has been tested extensively and compared with a state of the art implementation of the stable model semantics, the SLG system. The algorithm was found to compute stable models significantly faster than the SLG system.

For program $\mathcal{P}_1$, we have known that closure $<^+ = \{N_1 < N_2, N_2 < N_3, N_1 < N_3\}$ produced by the function **Closure_plus**. Then by calling function **Reduct**, a reduct of $\mathcal{P}_1$, that is $\{P \leftarrow not\ Q, not\ R\}$ generated. Therefore, function **AnswerSet** will return an answer set for $\mathcal{P}_1$ which is $\{P\}$ for testing $\{N_1\}$.

The algorithm only needs a small modification if one wants to produce all reducts. By ignoring the **defeat_flag** within function **Test** and keeping record of all reducts been produced, all reducts can then be generated based on this algorithm. For programs which have variables associated in rules, by replacing all instances of variables with appropriate places in corresponding atoms, one can easily generate answer sets of the program by this algorithm.

4 Conclusion

In this paper, we have proposed and discussed a prioritized logic programming and its implementation algorithms. Due to space limitation, we did not go to details to analyze our algorithm complexity. But it has been shown in our full paper that the cost of computing answer sets of a PLP, approximately, is polynomial times of the cost of computing stable models of extended logic programs. A prioritized logic programming compiler has been implemented. Readers are referred to http://www.cit.nepean.uws.edu.au/~yan/project.html for more detailed issues on implementation and applications of PLPs.

References

1. G. Brewka, Well-founded semantics for extended logic programs with dynamic preferences. *Journal of Artificial Intelligence Research*, 4 (1996) 19–36.
2. I. Niemelä and P. Simons, Efficient implementation of the well-founded and stable model semantics. *International Joint Conference and Symposium on Logic programming (IJCSLP '96)*, pp 289–303, 1996.
3. M. Gelfond and V. Lifschitz, Classical negation in logic programs and disjunctive databases. *New Generation Computing*, 9:365-386, 1991.
4. Y. Zhang and N.Y. Foo, Answer sets for prioritized logic programs. In *Proceedings of the 1997 International Logic Programming Symposium (ILPS'97)*, pp69-83. MIT Press, 1997.

Extending Description Logics with Generalized Quantification

Antonio Badia

University of Arkansas
abadia@godel.uark.edu

Abstract. In this paper we show an extension of DLs with Generalized
Quantifiers (GQs). Unlike the work of [QUA], we introduce an infinite
set of GQs to the language by giving a language in which to define quantifiers. We also introduce structural or typeless quantifiers and polyadic
quantifiers. Each one of these extensions greatly enhances the expressive
power of the original DL beyond first order logic, while keeping a very
simple syntax.

1 Introduction

Description logics (DLs) are a family of logical formalisms that has its roots
in earlier Artificial Intelligence work (the KL-ONE language ([BS])). There has
been lately a surge of interest in DLs in the area of Databases, as their usefulness
as information modelling formalisms has been recognized. DLs have been used
for tasks like reasoning about schemas (both for design and integration), queries
(both intensional and extensional) and view definition. Semantically, most DLs
have limited expressive power; [BOR] shows that they are essentially equivalent
to a fragment of First Order logic. In [QUA] it is shown how to add *generalized
quantifiers* to DLs in order to improve on their ability to succinctly express
complicated constraints. Here we continue that line of research by showing how
to add sets of GQs that take the resulting logic beyond the expressive power
of First Order logic and facilitate the task of reasoning about data models. In
section 2 we introduce some background concepts and notation; in particular we
describe DLs and GQs. In section 3 we describe successively more sophisticated
classes of GQs that can be added to the basic language, and give several examples
of their use. Finally, in section 4 we consider some further work.

2 Background

2.1 Description Logics

We assume three disjoint sets of symbols, called *atomic concepts, atomic roles*
and *constants*. Constants denote domain objects, concepts denote sets of domain
objects, and roles denote binary relations on the domain. For a given object, the
objects related to them by a role are the *fillers* of that role. When the role relates

only one object to another (i.e. there is one single filler), the role is usually called an *attribute* or a *feature*. Complex concepts are formed recursively as follows. Let P be an atomic concept, R a role, o a constant and n a natural number. Then P, $\neg P$, $C \sqcap D$, $C \sqcup D$, $\forall R.C$, $(\leq n\,R)$, $(\geq n\,R)$ and $(fills\ R\ o)$ are concepts, where C and D are already defined concepts[1]. Two special concepts, $\top$ and $\bot$, called *top* and *bottom* respectively, are also used. A constraint (or formula) is defined as $C_1 \sqsubseteq C_2$, where C_1 and C_2 are concepts. Some formalisms also allow for any role R, the inverse role R^{-1}.

The semantics of the language is given by interpretations $\mathcal{I} = (\Delta^{\mathcal{I}}, \cdot^{\mathcal{I}})$, which consist of a set $\Delta^{\mathcal{I}}$ (the *domain*) and a function $\cdot^{\mathcal{I}}$ (the *interpretation*) from language expressions to the domain, which obeys the following constraints[2]:

1. for every concept C, $\cdot^{\mathcal{I}}(C) \subseteq \Delta^{\mathcal{I}}$.
2. for every role R, $\cdot^{\mathcal{I}}(R) \subseteq \Delta^{\mathcal{I}} \times \Delta^{\mathcal{I}}$.
3. for every constant o, $\cdot^{\mathcal{I}}(o) \in \Delta^{\mathcal{I}}$.
4. $\cdot^{\mathcal{I}}(\top) = \Delta^{\mathcal{I}}$.
5. $\cdot^{\mathcal{I}}(\bot) = \emptyset$.
6. $\cdot^{\mathcal{I}}(\neg P) = \Delta^{\mathcal{I}} - \cdot^{\mathcal{I}}(P)$.
7. $\cdot^{\mathcal{I}}(C \sqcap D) = \cdot^{\mathcal{I}}(C) \cap \cdot^{\mathcal{I}}(D)$.
8. $\cdot^{\mathcal{I}}(C \sqcup D) = \cdot^{\mathcal{I}}(C) \cup \cdot^{\mathcal{I}}(D)$.
9. $\cdot^{\mathcal{I}}(\forall R.C) = \{a \in \Delta^{\mathcal{I}} \mid \forall b(a,b) \in \cdot^{\mathcal{I}}(R) \to b \in \cdot^{\mathcal{I}}(C)\}$.
10. $\cdot^{\mathcal{I}}(\leq nR) = \{a \in \Delta^{\mathcal{I}} \mid |\{b \mid (a,b) \in \cdot^{\mathcal{I}}(R)\}| \leq n\}$.
11. $\cdot^{\mathcal{I}}(\geq nR) = \{a \in \Delta^{\mathcal{I}} \mid |\{b \mid (a,b) \in \cdot^{\mathcal{I}}(R)\}| \geq n\}$.
12. $\cdot^{\mathcal{I}}(R^{-1}) = \{(a,b) \in \Delta^{\mathcal{I}} \times \Delta^{\mathcal{I}} \mid (b,a) \in \cdot^{\mathcal{I}}(R)\}$.

The semantics of constraints (formulas) is given by the following: an interpretation $\mathcal{I}$ satisfies $C_1 \sqsubseteq C_2$ iff $\cdot^{\mathcal{I}}(C_1) \subseteq \cdot^{\mathcal{I}}(C_2)$.

2.2 Generalized Quantifiers

In the past, GQs have been a subject of interest mostly for logicians. Seminal work was carried out by Mostowski ([MOS]); the original motivation was to be able to talk about properties that are not first order logic-definable. Lindstrom ([LIN]) refined the concept and studied logics with GQs in a general setting[3]. The publication of [BC] made their importance evident in linguistics, and was followed by a wealth of research in the area ([TM] is one example of that research). We argue that the insights of the theory may also illuminate some aspects of knowledge representation languages.

A *type* $t = [t_1, \ldots, t_n]$ is a finite sequence of natural numbers. Given a set M, a *Generalized Quantifier* of type $t = [t_1, \ldots, t_n]$ on M is an n-ary relation between subsets of $M^{t_1}, \ldots, M^{t_n}$ (i.e. a subset of $\mathcal{P}(M^{t_1}) \times \ldots \times \mathcal{P}(M^{t_n})$, where $\mathcal{P}(A)$ denotes the *powerset* of set A). The arity of a quantifier of type $t = [t_1, \ldots, t_n]$ is $max_{i=1}^{n} t_i$ and its argument number is n. A GQ is called *monadic* if it is of arity

---

[1] Note that $(= n\,R)$ can be defined as $(\leq n\,R) \sqcap (\geq n\,R)$.
[2] In the following, $|A|$ denotes the cardinality of set A.
[3] Generalized quantifiers are sometimes called *Lindstrom quantifiers*.

1, *polyadic* if it is of arity > 1, and it is called *unary* if its argument number is 1, *binary* if its argument number is 2, etc. Quantifiers of type $[1,1]$ are called standard, as this type has been found to be the most common type of GQs for natural language analysis ([TM]) and for use in query languages ([BAD], [HSU]). We use Q as a variable over GQs, and write $Q(A,B)$ to indicate that sets A,B belong to the extension of Q, i.e. that they are in the relation denoted by Q.

Below we give a few natural examples (we will write particular quantifiers in boldface). In each case, the GQ is standard, and it corresponds directly to conventional English usage. $Q(A,B)$ is read as "Q As are Bs", as in "all As are Bs", for the quantifier **all**.

$$\textbf{all} = \{A,B \subseteq M | A \subseteq B\}$$
$$\textbf{some} = \{A,B \subseteq M | A \cap B \neq \emptyset\}$$
$$\textbf{no} = \{A,B \subseteq M | A \cap B = \emptyset\}$$
$$\textbf{at least n} = \{A,B \subseteq M | |A \cap B| \geq n\}$$
$$\textbf{at most n} = \{A,B \subseteq M | |A \cap B| \leq n\}$$
$$\textbf{more} = \{A,B \subseteq M | |A| > |B|\}$$
$$\textbf{most} = \{A,B \subseteq M | |A \cap B| > |A - B|\}$$
$$\textbf{H} = \{A,B \subseteq M | \ |A| = |B|\} \ (Hartig's \ quantifier)$$

Observe that the last three GQs are not first order logic-definable. The concept of GQ is an extremely powerful one; GQs can be added to a logic to extend greatly its expressibility, although there are limits to what can be expressed with GQs ([DH]).

Not every relation between subsets of the domain is considered a GQ. Intuitively, we would like a GQ to behave as a *logical* operator, in the sense that it should not distinguish between elements in the domain, and nothing should be dependent on the domain M chosen. Logicality and other requirements are usually expressed by *axioms*, which in this context are constraints put on the definition of the quantifier. The following one has been deemed fundamental by most authors:

Definition 1. *(ISOM) A quantifier Q follows ISOM if, whenever f is a bijection from M to M', then $Q_M(A,B)$ iff $Q_{M'}(f[A],f[B])$*[4].

This constraint appears in the classical papers by Mostowski and Lindstrom ([MOS],[LIN]). Both make it part of the definition of *generalized quantifier*, since it implies, as explained above, that GQs are *logical*.

There have been several other axioms considered. Some of them imply that the behavior of a quantifier is independent of the context, as is the case for the usual logic constants. This seems, therefore, a desirable property. There is an axiom that makes context independence a characteristic:

---

[4] ISOM stands for *isomorphism*, since when M and M' are monadic structures f is an isomorphism ([WE1]).

Definition 2. *(EXT) Quantifier Q follows EXT if for all M, M', all A, B such that $A, B \subseteq M \subseteq M'$, $Q_M(A, B)$ iff $Q_{M'}(A, B)$*[5].

There are still other axioms that have been proposed, mainly to capture *semantic universals* (i.e. rules that seem to be followed by all natural language determiners). We will not develop this issue here.

3 Extensions

In [QUA], Quantz shows how to add GQs to description logics. Quantz only considers standard (i.e. binary monadic) quantifiers, which are assumed to have a language-independent meaning (i.e. quantifier Q has assigned to it a relation in $\Delta^{\mathcal{I}} \times \Delta^{\mathcal{I}}$, called the meaning of Q -in symbols $[\![Q]\!]$). In this context, the formula $Q(C_1, C_2)$ where Q is a GQ and C_1, C_2 are concepts, is a straightforward addition to the language. Thus, $C_1 \sqsubseteq C_2$ can now be expressed as **all**(C_1, C_2). However, Quantz notes that GQs already exist in description logics, in concepts like $\forall R.C$ and in number restrictions like $(\geq nR)$. Thus the syntax rules introducing $Q(R, C)$, $Q(R, R)$ and (C, R), where C is a concept and R a role, are also acceptable. However, these quantifiers remain monadic, as the semantic rules make clear:

1. $\cdot^{\mathcal{I}}(Q(R, C)) = \{a \mid < \cdot^{\mathcal{I}}(R)(a), \cdot^{\mathcal{I}}(C) > \in [\![Q]\!]\}$.
2. $\cdot^{\mathcal{I}}(Q(C, R)) = \{a \mid < \cdot^{\mathcal{I}}(C), \cdot^{\mathcal{I}}(R)(a) > \in [\![Q]\!]\}$.
3. $\cdot^{\mathcal{I}}(Q(R_1, R_2)) = \{a \mid < \cdot^{\mathcal{I}}(R_1)(a), \cdot^{\mathcal{I}}(R_2)(a) > \in [\![Q]\!]\}$

Quantz adds a finite number of GQs to the language; concretely, the set {**all**, **at most n**, **at least n**, **n**}. All these quantifiers are first-order definable; however this extension allows expression of properties of sets of objects.

Example 1. This and the following examples are from [CL]: assume a database that handles information about the organization of a conference. To state that *more than three authors are German*, we can write

    at least 3(Author, (fills country Germany)).

While [QUA] is a step in the right direction, it does not fully exploit the power of the concept of GQ. The GQs added are a small, fixed set, and are all monadic. In the next subsections we will show how to add a potentially infinite number of GQs to the language; how to define *structural GQs*, that allow us to express structural properties of data models, and how to add polyadic quantifiers.

3.1 Monadic Quantifiers

In subsection 2.2 we noted that standard GQs are the most commonly used in queries. These quantifiers can be defined by certain numerical properties. First, we note that a quantifier Q can be identified with a class of structures

---

[5] EXT stands for *extensionality*.

$< M, A, B >$, where M is our universe of discourse and $A, B \subseteq M$, by defining
the class as follows: $\mathcal{K}_Q = \{< M, A, B >| Q_M(A, B)\}$

We will assume from this point on that the universe under consideration, M,
is finite, and that GQs respect ISOM. Since Q is invariant under isomorphism,
the class $\mathcal{K}_Q$ is closed under isomorphisms too.

Let $\mathcal{M} = < M, A, B >$ be a standard structure with $A, B \subseteq M$. We define,
for any $X \subseteq M$, $X^1 = X$ and $X^0 = M - X$. Let s be a function from $\{A, B\}$
into $\{0, 1\}$, and let $\mathcal{S}$ be the set of all such functions. Define $P_s^M = A^{s(A)} \cap B^{s(B)}$
for any $s \in \mathcal{S}$. Then the set $\{P_s^M\}_{s \in \mathcal{S}}$ is a *partition* of M. This partition is all
that can be said about $\mathcal{M}$ from a logical point of view; that is, for any two
monadic structures $\mathcal{M}$, $\mathcal{M}'$ (of the same type), for all $s \in \mathcal{S}$, if $|P_s^M| = |P_s^{M'}|$,
then $\mathcal{M}$ and $\mathcal{M}'$ are isomorphic ([WE1]).

Since Generalized Quantifiers, as classes of structures, are closed under isomorphism, we have the following:

Proposition 1. *If Q is a standard GQ and $\mathcal{M} = < M, A, B >$ and $\mathcal{M}' = < M', A', B' >$ are such that for all $s \in \mathcal{S}$, $|P_s^M| = |P_s^{M'}|$, then $Q_M(A, B)$ iff $Q_{M'}(A', B')$.*

For structures of type $< M, A, B >$, the elements of the partition defined
above are $A \cap B$, $A - B$, $B - A$, and $M - (A \cup B)$. Thus, any two structures
(quantifiers) $< M, A, B >$ and $< M', A', B' >$ are isomorphic (and therefore
define the same quantifier) iff these four elements have the same cardinality.
Note that the above only requires that GQs respect ISOM. When, in addition to
ISOM, a quantifier respects EXT, the definability conditions are more restricted,
as the following points out:

Lemma 1. *If Q is a standard GQ that respects EXT, and $\mathcal{M} =< M, A, B >$,
$\mathcal{M}' =< M', A', B' >$ are such that $|A - B| = |A' - B'|$, $|B - A| = |B' - A'|$
and $|A \cap B| = |A' \cap B'|$, then $Q_M(A, B)$ iff $Q_{M'}(A', B')$.*

Intuitively, EXT allows us to ignore the context (anything outside) of A and
B.

For the rest of this paper we will consider only quantifiers that obey ISOM
and EXT. Most GQs in query languages seem to fall into this category ([GGB],
[HSU])[6]. From the above lemma it follows that any monadic quantifier in the
category is determined by a relation between the cardinalities of the elements
of the partition, in the following sense (this concept is called *number-theoretic
definability* in [WE1]).

Definition 3. *Let Q be a standard GQ. The corresponding numerical quantifier
(in symbols Q_N) is the natural number predicate defined as follows: for any
M, A, B with $A \subseteq M$ and $B \subseteq M$, $Q_M(A, B) \Leftrightarrow Q_N(x_1, x_2, x_3)$, where $x_1 = |A - B|$, $x_2 = |B - A|$, $x_3 = |A \cap B|$.*

---

[6] This is not surprising if one interprets those conditions from a database perspective -ISOM ensures that GQs are *generic* operators, while EXT ensure that they
are *domain independent*, both properties usually associated with query languages
([AHV]).

For example, we can redefine some GQs introduced in subsection 2.2 in this manner:

- **all** is defined by the formula $x_1 = 0$ (i.e. $|A - B| = 0$). Definition 3 simply asserts that $A \subseteq B$ iff $|A - B| = 0$. It is trivial to see that if $A \subseteq B$ then $|A - B| = 0$. On the other hand, assume that $|A - B| = 0$ but $A \not\subseteq B$. Then there is an element $x \in A$ such that $x \notin B$. But then $|A - B| \geq 1$. Absurd.
- **some** is defined by the formula $\neg(x_3 = 0)$ and **no** is defined by the formula $x_3 = 0$. Clearly $|A \cap B| = 0$ and $A \cap B = \emptyset$ ($|A \cap B| \neq 0$ and $A \cap B \neq \emptyset$, respectively) are two equivalent ways to define the same property.
- **at least n** is defined by $x_3 = 0 \lor x_3 = 1 \lor \ldots \lor x_3 = \mathbf{n}$, since for natural numbers $|A \cap B| \leq \mathbf{n}$ is equivalent to $|A \cap B| = 0 \lor |A \cap B| = 1 \lor \ldots \lor |A \cap B| = \mathbf{n}$[7].
- **H** is defined by the formula $x_1 = x_2$, since $|A - B| = |B - A|$ implies that $|A| = |B|$, and vice versa.

Since monadic quantifiers are determined (in the sense formalized above) by numerical properties, we can define families of quantifiers by defining properties on numbers. However, giving a (fixed, finite) list of number formulas would only add another way to define a (fixed, finite) set of quantifiers. Instead, we define a *language on numbers* which allows us to generate an infinite number of formulas, and therefore, an infinite number of quantifiers. This framework allows us to define new GQs as needed, instead of having a finite, fixed set.

Definition 4. *The* proportional language *(PL) is the set of formulas on natural numbers obtained under the following syntax:*

1. *Terms and variables*
   (a) $0, 1, 2, \ldots$ *are numerals.*
   (b) *If m, n are numerals, $m + n$ is a numeral.*
   (c) *If m, n are numerals, $m \times n$ is a numeral*
   (d) $x, y, z, \ldots$ *are domain variables.*
   (e) *Numerals and variables are terms.*
2. *Formulas*
   (a) *If t_1 and t_2 are terms, $t_1 = t_2$ is a (atomic) formula.*
   (b) *If φ, ψ are formulas, then $\neg\varphi$, $\neg\psi$, $\varphi \land \psi$, $\varphi \lor \psi$ are formulas.*
   (c) *If φ is a formula of PL where the symbol $\times$ does not appear, and x is a variable, $\exists x \varphi(x)$ is a formula of PL.*

Nothing else is a formula[8].

---

[7] Note that this is a *finite* disjunction.

[8] A very similar family of quantifiers is called the *properly proportional* quantifiers in [KM]. A *properly proportional* quantifier $Q^\Theta_{m,n}(A, B)$ is defined by an equation of the form

$$\frac{|A \cap B|}{|B|} \; \Theta \; \frac{m}{n}$$

where m, n are natural numbers, $n \neq 0$ and Θ is one of $=, \neq, \leq, \geq$. Since $x_3 = |A \cap B|$ and $x_2 = |B - A|$, $x_3 + x_2 = |B|$, and we can write the equation as $x_3 \times n \; \Theta \; (x_3 + x_2) \times m$.

We say that a quantifier Q is definable in PL iff it is number-definable, in the sense of definition 3, by a formula $\varphi(x_1, x_2, x_3)$, where φ is in PL.

The quantifiers definable in PL can express some important properties that are not first order logic-definable. All examples of the previous section are expressible in PL. In fact, it is proven in [BAD] that PL can define the same quantifiers as first order logic extended with counters and arithmetic ([GT]).

Some quantifiers expressible in PL are[9]:

1. All standard first order quantifiers. Westerstahl has proved that a sublanguage of PL can express all standard first order quantifiers ([WE1]) (see how to express **all, some, no** in the previous example).
2. the *counting* quantifiers: for any n natural number, **exactly n, at most n** and **at least n** are expressible in PL by formulas $x_3 = n$, $x_3 \leq n$ and $x_3 \geq n$, respectively.
3. the *comparison* quantifiers, like **H, more** (with the formula $x_1 < x_2$[10]); **most** (with the formula $x_3 > x_1$).
4. the *proportional* quantifiers. PL can express formulas like
   $$\tfrac{n}{m} \text{ of } (A, B) = x_3 \times m = (x_1 + x_3) \times n$$
   with the meaning $\tfrac{n}{m}$ *of As are Bs*. When $m = 100$, we have the *percent* family of quantifiers. This also allows PL to express *proportional* GQs, like **one half of, one third of....**

Example 2. One of the strengths of DLs is the ability to express negative information. We can state that the sets of instances for two entities are disjoint: *no author is a referee* is expressed as
Author $\sqsubseteq \neg$ Referee
Now it simply becomes **no(Author, Referee)**.

3.2 Structural Quantifiers

In [CLN], DLs are used to represent information expressed in other data models, and a translation is shown between a powerful DL and the relational data model, the object oriented data model and a frame system. A vital part of this modelling is the ability to express structural information. Thus, to say that A and B are subclasses of C we use the formula $A \sqsubseteq C \sqcap B \sqsubseteq C$. With GQs, we can express the same information with $all(A, C)$ and $all(B, C)$. But we can also express that the subclasses are disjoint by stating $no(A, B)$. However, to express that A and B are a partition of C we have to add the fact $A \cup B = C$. This can be paraphrased in DLs -with and without GQs. The problem is, how to express that we have a partition with n elements, for arbitrary n? To solve this problem, we introduce the notion of *typeless* or *structural* GQs.

---

[9] To simplify the examples, we note that $|A|$ and $|B|$ are available in PL, since $|A| = |A - B| + |A \cap B| = x_1 + x_3$, and $|B| = |B - A| + |A \cap B| = x_2 + x_3$. Also, note that $x \leq y$, for x, y natural numbers, is expressible in PL as $\exists n(x = y + n)$, and $x < y$ is expressible as $\exists n((x = y + n) \wedge \neg(x = 0))$.

[10] As pointed out in the previous footnote, the formula should be $x_1 + x_3 < x_1 + x_3$.

Definition 5. *An extended type is a finite sequence* $t = [t_1^{i_1}, \ldots, t_n^{i_n}]$, *where each* t_j *($1 \leq j \leq n$) is a natural number and each* i_j *is either a natural number or the cardinal number* ω *(when* $i_j = 1$ *we will not write it). A GQ of extended type* t *is defined as before, with the* j-th *term contributing* i_j *terms of the form* M^{t_j}, *except that if* $i_j = \omega$, *an infinite family of GQs is introduced, with each one having* M^{t_j} n *times, for* $n > 0$.

Example 3. The GQ $\mathbf{P}(A, A_1, \ldots, A_n)$, which has type $[1, 1^\omega]$, is defined by
$$\bigcup_{j=1}^n A_j = A \wedge \bigwedge_{j \neq k} A_k \cap A_j = \emptyset \wedge \bigwedge_{j=1}^n A_j \subseteq A$$
for arbitrary n. Thus, it is defined for types $[1,1]$, $[1,1,1]$, $[1,1,1,1]$,.... Note that when the type is $[1, 1]$, this GQ reduces to the GQ **all**.

Example 4. The fact that *persons are either male or female* is expressed as
    Person $\sqsubseteq$ Male $\sqcup$ Female
If we wanted to express that concepts Male and Female are a partition of Person, we would need to add
    Male $\sqcup$ Female $\sqsubseteq$ Person $\wedge$ Male $\sqcap$ Female = $\perp$
This now becomes simply $\mathbf{P}$(Person, Male, Female).

Note also that the definition of $\mathbf{P}$ can be seen as set of logical rules to be used in reasoning about the quantifier. That is, we could infer, from $\mathbf{P}$(Person, Male, Female), that **all**(Male,Person), **all**(Female,Person), **no**(Male,Female) and Male $\sqcup$ Female = Person.

3.3 Polyadic Quantifiers

All the quantifiers defined so far are monadic. However, GQs can be defined over arbitrary arguments. Since DLs have also binary relations (roles) on them, we could consider GQs of arity 2. Having quantifiers of arity 2 would allow quantification over roles. A GQ of type $[1, 2]$ could express relations between concepts and roles.

Example 5. The GQ $\mathbf{D}$(A,B,R) = $\{A, B \subseteq M, R \subseteq M^2 \mid R \subseteq A \times B\}$ of type $[1,1,2]$ expresses the fact the A is the *domain* of binary relation R, and B is the *range*.

The GQ $\mathbf{W}$(A,R) = $\{A \subseteq M, R \subseteq A^2 \mid$ R well-orders A$\}$, of type $[1,2]$, can express the fact that there is a well-order for the domain.

The GQ $\mathbf{T}(R_1, R_2)$ = $\{R_1, R_2 \subseteq M^2 \mid R_2$ is the transitive closure of $R_1\}$ of type $[2,2]$ expresses a property not definable in first order logic.

4 Conclusion and Further Work

We have shown an extension of DLs with generalized quantifiers. Unlike the work of [QUA], we introduce an infinite set of GQs to the language. We also introduce structural or typeless quantifiers and polyadic quantifiers. Each one of these extensions greatly enhances the expressive power of the original DL beyond first order logic. Other means of defining GQs and adding them to the language should be investigated.

In this research we have focused on increasing the expressive power. There is an obvious trade-off with complexity which we have not pursued. It is an open question whether standard operations on DLs (like subsumption) are decidable in this new framework and if so, what the exact complexity is.

References

[AHV] Abiteboul, S., Hull, R. and and Vianu, V. *Foundations of Databases*, Addison-Wesley, 1994.

[BS] Brachman, R. and Schmolze, J. *An Overview of the KL-ONE Knowledge Representation System*, Cognitive Science, vol. 9, 1985.

[BAD] Badia, A., *A Family of Query Languages with Generalized Quantifiers: its Definition, Properties and Expressiveness*, Ph.d. thesis, Indiana University, 1997.

[BC] Barwise, J. and R. Cooper, *Generalized Quantifiers and Natural Language*, Linguistic and Philosophy, volume 4, 1981.

[BOR] Borgida, A. *On the Relative Expressiveness of Description Logics and Predicate Logics*, Artificial Intelligence, vol. 82, 1996

[CLN] Calvanese, D., Lenzerini, M. and Nardi, D. *A Unified Framework for Class-Based Representation Formalisms*, Proceedings of the Conference on Principles of Knowledge Representation, Bonn, 1994.

[CL] Catarzi, T. and Lenzerini, M. *Representing and Using Interschema Knowledge in Cooperative Information Systems*, International Journal of Intelligent and Cooperative Information Systems, vol. 2, n. 4, 1993.

[DH] Dawar, A. and Hella, L., *The Expressive Power of Finitely Many Generalized Quantifiers*, in Proceedings of the 9th IEEE Symposium on Logic In Computer Science, 1994.

[GT] Grumbach, S. and Tollu, C., *Query Languages with Counters*, in Proceedings of the International Conference on Database Theory, Lecture Notes in Computer Science, number 333, Springer-Verlag, 1992.

[GGB] Gyssens, M., Van Gucht, D. and Badia, A., *Query Languages with Generalized Quantifiers*, in *Application of Logic Databases*, Ramakrishnan, Ragu ed., Kluwer Academic Publishers, 1995.

[HSU] Hsu, P. Y. and Parker, D. S., *Improving SQL with Generalized Quantifiers*, in Proceedings of the Tenth International Conference on Data Engineering, 1995.

[KM] Keenan, E. and Moss, L., *Generalized Quantifiers and the Expressive Power of Natural Language*, in [TM].

[LIN] Lindstrom, P., *First Order Predicate Logic with Generalized Quantifiers*, Theoria, volume 32, 1966.

[MOS] Mostowski, A., *On a Generalization of Quantifiers*, Fundamenta Mathematica, volume 44, 1957.

[QUA] Quantz, J. *how to Fit Generalized Quantifiers into Terminological Logics*, Proceedings of the 10th European Conference on Artificial Intelligence, 1992.

[TM] *Generalized Quantifiers in Natural Language*, van Benthem, J. and ter Meulen, A., eds. Foris Publications, 1985.

[WE1] Westerstahl, D., *Quantifiers in Formal and Natural Languages*, in *Handbook of Philosophical Logic*, volume IV, Gabbay, D. and Guenther, F., eds., Reidel Publishing Company, 1989.

Machine Learning for Intelligent Document Processing: The WISDOM System

Floriana Esposito   Donato Malerba   Francesca A. Lisi

Dipartimento di Informatica, Università degli Studi di Bari
via Orabona 4, 70125 Bari, Italy
{esposito I malerba I lisi}@di.uniba.it

Abstract. WISDOM is a intelligent document processing system that transforms printed information into a symbolic representation. Its distinguishing feature is the use of a rule base which is automatically built from a set of training documents using two inductive learning techniques: Decision tree learning for the blocks classification, and first-order rule induction for the document classification and understanding. In the paper, advances made with respect to previous studies on this application domain are illustrated and a complete set of experimental results is reported.

1 Introduction

Recent advances in the information and communication technologies have increased the need for tools that are able to transform data presented on paper into a computer-revisable form [17]. This transformation requires a solution to several problems, such as the separation of text from graphics, the classification of the document, the identification (or semantic labelling) of some relevant components of the page layout and the transformation of portions of the document image into sequences of characters. In the literature, the process of breaking down a document image into several layout components is called *document analysis*, while the process of attaching semantic labels to some layout components is named *document understanding* [18]. Furthermore, the term *document classification* has been introduced to identify the process of attaching a semantic label (a class name) to the whole document on the ground of its layout alone [3].

WISDOM (Windows Interface System for DOcument Management) is a paper-computer interface that can transform printed information into a symbolic representation [12]. This is done in four steps: Document analysis, document classification, document understanding and, finally, text recognition with an OCR. The distinguishing feature of WISDOM is the use of a rule base that is automatically built from a set of training documents using two inductive learning tools and techniques. Each authenticated user of the interface has his/her own rule base.

The paper describes how the rule base is built in order to support the tasks of document analysis, classification and understanding. The main novelties with respect to the predecessor system PLRS [4] are two:

1. The application of decision tree learning techniques to the *block classification* problem, which consists in discriminating text blocks from both pictures and drawings and horizontal/vertical lines.
2. The extension of the first-order learning method in order to handle both numeric and symbolic data in the document classification and understanding steps.

The main functions performed by WISDOM are illustrated in the next section. In

Section 3, some machine learning issues in the block classification problem and the solutions adopted in WISDOM are discussed. Finally, in Section 4 the extension of the first-order learning method is briefly explained and some experimental results are reported for the problems of document classification and understanding.

2 Functional architecture of WISDOM

The tasks performed by WISDOM and the intermediate results produced at each processing step are reported in Fig. 1.

Initially, each page is scanned with a resolution of 300 dpi and thresholded into a binary image. The bitmap of an A4-sized page takes 2,496×3,500=1,092,000 bytes and is stored in TIFF format. Actually, WISDOM can manage multi-page documents, each of which is a *sequence* of pages. The definition of the right sequence is responsibility of the user, since the scanner is able to scan a single page at time. Pages of multi-page documents are processed independently of each other in all steps, therefore the document processing flow is described for single pages only.

The document analysis process is quite complex and includes:

1. *Preprocessing*, that is the evaluation of the skew angle, the rotation of the document, and the computation of a spread factor. In particular, the skew angle is estimated by analyzing the *horizontal projection profile*, that is a histogram reporting the total number of black pixels for each row of the bitmap. The histogram shows sharply-rising peaks with base equal to the character height when text lines span horizontally, while

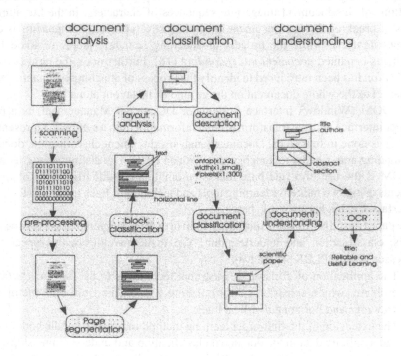

Fig. 1. Functional architecture of WISDOM.

it is characterized by smooth slopes in the presence of a large skew angle. This observation can be mathematically captured by a real-valued function, called *alignment measure*, that returns the mean square deviation of the histogram for each orientation angle θ. Thus finding the actual skew angle is cast as the problem of locating the global maximum value of the alignment measure. Since this measure is not smooth enough to apply usual gradient ascend techniques, the system adopts some peak-finding heuristic [1]. Once the skew angle is estimated, the document is rotated. The loop "skew estimation - document rotation" terminates when the estimated skew angle is zero. At that point WISDOM estimates the *spread factor* of the document image as the ratio of the mean distance between peaks and the peak width. Such a ratio is greater than (lower than) 1.0 for simple (complex) documents.

2. *Segmentation*, that is the identification of rectangular *blocks* enclosing content portions. The page is segmented by means a fast technique, called Run Length Smoothing Algorithm (RLSA) [21], that applies four operators to the document image: 1) Horizontal smoothing with a threshold C_h; 2) Vertical smoothing with a threshold C_v; 3) Logical AND of the two smoothed images; 4) additional horizontal smoothing with another threshold C_a. The novelty of WISDOM is that the smoothing parameters C_v and C_a are adaptively defined on the ground of the spread factor. It is worthwhile to observe that the RLSA operates on a document image with a lower resolution (75 dpi is considered a reasonable trade-off between the accuracy and the speed of the segmentation process).

3. *Blocks classification*, which aims at discriminating blocks enclosing text from blocks enclosing graphics (pictures, drawings and horizontal/vertical lines).

4. *Layout analysis*, that is the perceptual organization process that aims at detecting structures among blocks. The result is a hierarchy of abstract representations of the document image, called the *layout structure* of the document. The leaves of the layout tree (lowest level of the abstraction hierarchy) are the blocks, while the root represents the set of pages of the whole document. A page may include several layout components, called *frames*, which are still rectangular areas corresponding to groups of blocks. An ideal layout analysis process should produce a set of frames such that each frame can be associated with a distinct semantic label (e.g., title and author of a scientific paper). WISDOM extracts the layout structure by means of a knowledge-based approach: Generic knowledge and rules on typesetting conventions are used in order to group basic blocks together [9]. An example of output of the document analysis process is shown in Fig. 2. The level of the layout hierarchy to be displayed is chosen by clicking on the radio buttons 'Frame 2', 'Frame 1', 'Set of Lines', 'Lines' and 'Basic blocks'.

While the layout structure associates the content of a document with a hierarchy of layout objects, such as blocks, frames and pages, the *logical structure* of the document associates the content with a hierarchy of *logical objects*, such as sender/receiver of a business letter, title/authors of a scientific article, and so on. The problem of finding the logical structure of a document can be cast as the problem of defining a *mapping* from the layout structure into the logical one. In WISDOM this mapping is limited to the association of a page with a document class (document classification) and the association of page layout components with basic logical components (document understanding). The mapping is built by *matching* the document description against models of classes of documents and against models of the logical components of interest for that class.

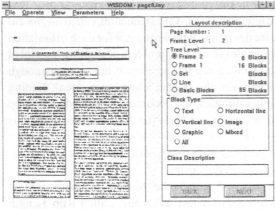

PART_OF(X1,X2), ..., PART_OF(X1,X9),
WIDTH(X2)=66.0, ..., WIDTH(X9)=986.0,
HEIGTH(X2)=34.0, ..., HEIGTH(X9)=306.0,
TYPE(X2)=text, ..., TYPE(X9)=text,
X_POS_CENTRE(X2)=246.0, ...,
X_POS_CENTRE(X9)=686.0,
Y_POS_CENTRE(X2)=386.0, ...,
Y_POS_CENTRE(X9)=3162.0,
TORIGHT(X9,X7),
ALIGNMENT(X2,X3)=only_left_col, ...,
ALIGNMENT(X6,X8)=only_middle_col

Fig. 3. A partial description of the page layout of the document in Fig. 2. Distinct constants (X2, ..., X9) denotes distinct layout components of a page layout. The constant X1 denotes the whole page.

Fig. 2. The output of the document analysis process.

The descriptions of both documents and models are expressed in a first-order language, where unary function symbols, called *attributes*, are used to describe properties of a single layout component (e.g., height and length) while binary predicate and function symbols, called *relations*, are used to express interrelationships among layout components (e.g., contain, on-top, and so on). Attributes and relations can be both symbolic (i.e., categorical and ordinal) and numeric (see Fig. 3).

Models are represented as rules. Typically, such rules are handcoded for particular kinds of documents [13], requiring much human tune and effort. WISDOM uses rules that are automatically generated from a set of training examples for which the user-trainer has already defined the correct class and has specified the layout components with a logical meaning (logical components). The first-order learning system used to generate such rules is INDUBI/CSL [10], which has been extended in order to handle both symbolic and numeric data, as described in Section 4.

Finally, WISDOM allows the user to set up the text extraction process by selecting the logical components to which the OCR has to be applied.

3   Decision tree learning for block classification

Page segmentation returns blocks that may contain either textual or graphical information. In order to facilitate subsequent document processing steps, it is important to label these blocks according to the type of content. Labels used in WISDOM are *text block*, *horizontal line*, *vertical line*, *picture* (i.e., halftone images) and *graphics* (e.g., line drawings). Each block can be associated with only one label, so that the labeling problem can be cast as a classification problem where labels correspond to classes.

A method for document block classification was proposed by Wong *et al.* [21]. The basic features used for classifying blocks are four: 1) the height of each block, 2) the eccentricity of the rectangle surrounding the block, 3) the ratio of the number of black pixels to the area of the surrounding rectangle, and 4) the mean horizontal length of the black runs of the original block image. Additional features concerning the texture of the blocks were proposed by Wang and Srihari [20]. A common aspect of these works is the use of linear discriminant functions as classifiers. An exception is the work by Fisher *et al.* [7], who resort to a rule-based classification method, where rules are hand-coded.

In WISDOM, block classification is performed by means of a decision tree automatically built from a set of training examples (blocks) of the five classes. The choice of a "tree-based" method instead of the most common generalized linear models is due to its inherent flexibility, since decision trees can easily handle complicated interactions among features and give results that are simple to interpret. The numerical features used by the system to describe each block are ten, namely 1) height; 2) length; 3) area; 4) eccentricity; 5) total number of black pixels in the reduced bitmap; 6) total number of black pixels in the segmented block; 7) number of white-black transitions in the reduced bitmap; 8) percentage of black pixels in the reduced bitmap; 9) percentage of black pixels in the segmented block; 10) mean horizontal length of the black runs in the reduced bitmap. The data set considered is a collection of 5473 examples of pre-classified blocks obtained from 53 documents of various kinds. It is available in the UCI Machine Learning Repository (http://www.ics.uci.edu/~mlearn/MLRepository.html).

Two different decision tree learning systems have been considered: C4.5 [15] and ITI 2.0 [19]. The former is a *batch* learner, that is it cannot change the decision tree when some blocks are misclassified, unless a new tree is generated from scratch using an extended training set. On the contrary, ITI 2.0 allows *incremental* induction of decision trees, since it can revise the current decision tree, if necessary, in response to each newly observed training instance. There are several reasons for choosing these two systems. First of all, C4.5 is considered a yardstick for most studies on decision tree learning. Moreover, in a previous study on decision tree pruning we extended C4.5 by embedding several pruning methods [5]. Finally, ITI 2.0 is the only incremental system able to handle numerical attributes as those used to describe the blocks.

Actually, ITI 2.0 can operate in three different ways. In the *batch* mode, it works in a way similar to C4.5. In the *normal* operation mode, it first updates the frequency counts associated to each node of the tree as soon as a new instance is received. Then it restructures the decision tree according to the updated frequency counts. When working in this mode, ITI builds trees with almost the same number of leaves and the same predictive accuracy of those induced with C4.5 (see Table 1). In the *error-correction* mode, frequency counts are updated only in case of misclassification of the new instance. The main difference between the two incremental modes is that the normal operation mode guarantees to build the same decision tree independently of the order in which examples are presented, while the error-correction mode does not.

Table 1. Experimental results for a ten-fold cross-validation performed on the data set of 5473 examples. Both systems are allowed to prune the induced trees using their default pruning method (error-based pruning for C4.5 and MDL pruning for ITI 2.0).

	C4.5	ITI 2.0
average no. of leaves	89.8	92.4
predictive accuracy	96.8	96.88

ITI has been embedded in WISDOM and two new functions have been added to the interface: The interactive correction of the results of the block classification, and the updating of the block classifier. The preference for ITI 2.0 is due to the possibility of on-line training the document processing system: When users are dissatisfied with the classification performed by the induced decision tree, they can ask the system to revise the classifier without starting from scratch. In this way, some blocks (e.g., the logo of a business letter) can be considered text for some users and graphics for others.

From the practical point of view, the main problem we observed is that ITI creates large files (more than 10Mb) when trained on the data set of 5473 instances. The reason of this space inefficiency is due to the need of storing frequency counts of training examples in each node of the induced tree. This inefficiency can be contained (about 1.5Mb) when the system operates in the *error-correction* mode, since frequency counts are updated only in case of misclassification. Luckily, we noticed that a single user can obtain satisfying results with a lower number of training instances, since printed documents managed in a specific application often have a similar layout. For instance, on a set of 112 documents used in an experimentation explained later, a high predictive accuracy is obtained with decision trees smaller than 80 Kb.

4   Handling numeric and symbolic data

In a previous work on the problem of processing paper documents, a multistrategy learning approach was proposed to learn a set of rules for both document classification and document understanding [4]. In particular, a learning methodology that integrates a parametric and a conceptual learning method was adopted. In fact, the application required the management of first-order representations with both numeric and symbolic data, while the conceptual learning method was able to deal exclusively with symbolic data. The integrated learning methodology committed the management of all numeric attributes to the parametric method and the handling of symbolic attributes and relations to the first-order conceptual method. The main limitation of this approach is that the parametric method can manage only zero-order (i.e., non-structural) representations. Thus numeric attributes can concern only "global" properties of the whole document, while "local" properties of a component of the document (e.g., height, width and position) have to be discretized before starting the conceptual learning process.

Preliminary results obtained with the integrated approach were encouraging, but not totally satisfying. This prompted the investigation of an extension of the first-order learning method such that the following conditions are satisfied:

1. On-line discretization of numerical descriptors should be performed by a specialization operator, since the learning algorithm performs a general-to-specific (or top-down) search. The specialization is obtained by adding literals of the type $f(X_1, \dots, X_n) \in [a..b]$ to the clause.
2. The heuristic function used to choose among different intervals [a..b] should satisfy a property that reduces the computational complexity of the operator.
3. The operator should always guarantee to cover the *seed* example that guides the induction process.

4.1 The learning algorithm

This operator has been embedded into INDUBI/CSL, which solves the problem of inducing a set of hypotheses $H_1, H_2, ..., H_r$, from a set E of training examples. Each hypothesis H_i is the description of a concept C_i.

The representation language adopted by the system has two distinct forms of *literals*:

$f(t_1, ... ,t_n)=$Value (*simple literal*)   and $f(t_1, ... ,t_n)\in$Range   (*set literal*)

where f is an n-ary function symbol, called *descriptor*, t_i's can be either variable or constant terms, Value is the value taken by f when applied to $t_1, ... ,t_n$, and Range is a set of possible values taken by f. Some examples of literals are the following: height$(x_2)\in[1.1 .. 2.1]$, color$(x_1)=$red, distance$(x_1, x_2)\in[0.0 .. 1.0]$. Literals can be combined to form *definite clauses*:

$$L_0 :- L_1, L_2, ..., L_m$$

where the simple literal L_0 is called *head* of the clause, while the conjunction of simple or set literals $L_1, L_2, ..., L_m$ is named *body*. Definite clauses of interest for classification problems satisfy two different constraints: *Linkedness* [8] and *range-restrictedness* [2].

Each training example is represented as a single ground, linked and range-restricted definite clause. On the contrary, a hypothesis H is a set of linked, range-restricted definite clauses, called *rule*, such that all clauses have the same head and no constant terms. Permitted literals in H can be either single-valued or range-valued.

At the high level INDUBI/CSL implements a separate-and-conquer search strategy to generate a rule. The *separate* stage of the algorithm is a loop that checks for the completeness of the current rule and, if this check fails, begins the search for a new consistent clause. The search space for the separate stage is the space of rules. In contrast, the search space of the *conquer* stage is the set of clauses. The conquer stage performs a general-to-specific beam-search to construct a new consistent, linked and range-restricted clause. The separate-and-conquer search strategy is adopted in other well-known learning systems, such as FOIL 6.2 [16]. On the other hand INDUBI/CSL bases the conquer phase on the concept of *seed* example, whose aim is that of guiding the generalization process. Indeed, if e^+ is a positive example to be explained by a hypothesis H, then H should contain at least one clause C that generalizes e^+. C is obtained from e^+ by applying the *drop-literal* and *turn-constants-into-variables* operators.

In the conquer stage, INDUBI/CSL starts with a seed example e^+ and generates a set *Cons* of at least M, if any, distinct range-restricted clauses which are consistent and cover e^+. The best generalization is selected from *Cons* according to a user-defined preference criterion, and the positive examples covered by such a generalization are removed from the set of examples to be covered. The conquer stage terminates, and if there are still some positive examples to be covered, a new seed will be selected for the next conquer stage.

The M clauses are searched in the *specialization hierarchy* rooted into a definite clause with empty body,

$$f(X_1, ..., X_n) = \text{Value} :-$$

obtained by applying the operator *turn_constants_into_variables* to the head of e^+. All specialized clauses, which cover e^+ and possibly other positive examples, are ranked according to a user-defined preference criterion. The first P generalizations are selected for the next specialization step. Consistent generalizations are copied into *Cons*.

4.2 The specialization operator

In order to specialize a clause G, INDUBI/CSL has to choose some literals to be added. Both numeric and symbolic data are handled in the same way. The only difference is that numeric literals already present in G can be reconsidered later on. In this case, the best (sub-)interval is recomputed, since it may be influenced by the addition of further literals. All selected literals are generalizations of literals in the seed, e^+, obtained by turning distinct constants into distinct variables (algorithms are reported in [11]).

In order to compute the interval for numerical literals the system builds a table associated to the term $f(X_1, \ldots, X_n)$ by matching the specialized clause

$$G': \quad G, f(X_1, \ldots, X_n) \in [-\infty .. +\infty]$$

against positive and negative examples. Each example produces as many entries as the number of unifiers. The table, initially empty, contains pairs $\langle Value, Class \rangle$, where $Class$ can be either $+$ or $-$ according to the sign of the example e from which $Value$ is taken, while $Value$ is determined by considering the literal of e that unifies with $f(X_1, \ldots, X_n) \in [-\infty .. +\infty]$.

Then the problem is finding the interval that best discriminates positive from negative examples. Any threshold value α lying between two consecutive distinct values defines two disjoint intervals: The left interval $[l_1, l_2]$ and the right interval $[r_1, r_2]$. The lower bound l_1 of the left interval is the smallest value in the table with a $+$ sign, while the upper bound l_2 is the largest value in the table that does not exceed the threshold α. On the contrary, the lower bound r_1 of the right interval is the smallest value in the table that exceeds α, while the upper bound r_2 is the largest value with a $+$ sign. When one of the two intervals contains no positive value, then it is set to *undefined*. At least one of the two intervals must be defined, since the table contains at least one entry $\langle Seed\_value, + \rangle$ for the value taken by $f(X_1, \ldots, X_n)$ in the seed. Not all defined intervals are to be considered, since the specialized clause $G, f(X_1, \ldots, X_n) \in$ Range for a given Range might no longer cover the seed example e^+. Those intervals that include the $Seed\_value$ are said to be *admissible*, because they guarantee that the corresponding specializations still cover e^+.

The best admissible interval is selected according to an information-theoretic heuristic. By looking at the table as a source of messages labeled $+$ and $-$, the expected information on the class membership conveyed from a randomly selected message is:

$$\text{info}(n^+, n^-) = -\frac{n^+}{n^+ + n^-} \log_2 \frac{n^+}{n^+ + n^-} - \frac{n^-}{n^+ + n^-} \log_2 \frac{n^-}{n^+ + n^-} \tag{1}$$

where n^+ and n^- are the number of values in the table with a positive and a negative sign, respectively. If we partition the table into two subsets, S_1 and S_2, the former containing values falling within an admissible interval and the latter containing the remaining $n_1^+ + n_1^-$ values, the information provided by S_1 will be close to zero when almost all cases have the same $+$ or $-$ sign. Although the information prefers partitions that cover a large number of cases of a single class and a few cases of other classes, we must bias such a preference towards intervals with a high number of positive cases, as well. The following *weighted entropy*:

$$E(n_1^+, n_1^-) = \frac{n_1^-}{n_1^+} \text{info}(n_1^+, n_1^-) \tag{2}$$

penalizes those admissible intervals with a low percentage of positive cases. A heuristic criterion is that of choosing the admissible interval that minimizes the weighted entropy. It differs from that adopted in C4.5, where the entropy is not weighted, and in FOIL where only the information content of the positive class is considered.

The following theorem states that only cut points between two consecutive distinct values with a different sign (*boundary points*) should be considered.

Theorem. If a cut-point α minimizes the measure $E(n_1^+, n_1^-)$, then α is a boundary point.

The proof is available at http://lacam.uniba.it:8000/pagine/proof.html. This result helps to reduce computational complexity of the procedure *determine_range* by considering only boundary points. Actually, the theorem above is similar to that proved by Fayyad and Irani [6] for a different measure, namely the "unweighted" class information entropy computed in some decision tree learning systems.

4.3 Experimental results

In order to test the efficiency and the effectiveness of the proposed operator, an experiment on the domains of document classification and understanding has been organized. INDUBI/CSL has been applied to the problems of classifying and understanding a set of 112 real, single-page documents distributed as follows: Twenty-eight articles of ICML'95, thirty articles of ISMIS'94, thirty-four articles of IEEE Transactions on Pattern Analysis and Machine Intelligence (TPAMI), and twenty documents of different type or published on other proceedings, transactions and journals. All documents of the first three classes are first-pages of articles. For ICML'95 papers, four logical components are of interest, namely page number, authors, (body of the) paper, and title. For ISMIS'94 papers the following logical components are considered: Title, authors, abstract and (body of the) paper. Finally, for TPAMI papers only five logical components are defined, namely running head, page number, title, abstract, and (body of the) paper. For the remaining documents it was not possible to define a set of logical components because of the high variability. Thus there are four learning problems to be solved: learning to classify documents in the classes ICML'95, ISMIS'94, TPAMI and Reject, and learning to identify logical components in ICML'95 / ISMIS'94 / TPAMI papers. In document understanding problems each document generates as many training examples as the number of layout components (in this experiment, only components at the 'Frame 2' level are considered).

The experimental procedure followed is ten-fold cross validation. At each trial three statistics are collected: Number of errors on the test cases, number of generated clauses, and learning time. Results for the document classification are reported in Table 2, while results for the document understanding are reported in Table 3. The entries labelled 'mixed' refer to symbolic/numeric representation and on-line discretization.

In the document classification problem, the average number of errors for mixed data is significantly lower than the average number of errors for symbolic data. Indeed, the p-value returned by the non-parametric Wilcoxon signed-ranks test [14] is 0.0144. Moreover, the introduction of numerical descriptors simplifies the classification rules, although the learning time is doubled (time is in prime minutes and refers to a SUN 10).

As expected, the choice of the representation language for the page layout is a critical factor for the document understanding problems. For these problems, indeed, satisfactory error rates have been obtained only with numeric/symbolic representations. For all classes

112

Table 2. Experimental results for document classification.

class	Av. Number of Errors		Number of Clauses		Av. Learning Time	
	symbolic	mixed	symbolic	mixed	symbolic	mixed
ICML'95	1.4	0.8	4.8	2.0	4:42	9:54
ISMIS'94	1.3	0.2	5.7	1.0	5:30	9:18
TPAMI	1.0	0.7	4.4	1.9	5:06	10:06
TOTAL	3.7	1.7	14.9	4.9	15:36	29:30

Table 3. Experimental results for document understanding.

class	Av. Number of Errors		Number of Clauses		Av. Learning Time	
	symbolic	mixed	symbolic	mixed	symbolic	mixed
ICML'95	6.6	3.2	31.6	8.4	44:30	26:00
ISMIS'94	6.3	3.2	43.8	10.8	50:36	25:24
TPAMI	9.2	2.0	39.5	9.0	30:24	32:00

the average number of errors for mixed data is significantly lower than the average number of errors for symbolic data (the worst p-value of the Wilcoxon test is 0.0072). Once again, the introduction of numerical descriptors simplifies significantly the classification rules and decreases the learning time for two classes.

5   Conclusions

In this paper new results on the problem of intelligent document processing have been reported. In particular, the effective application of decision tree learning techniques to the block classification problem is described. Moreover, a specialization operator for the on-line discretization of numeric data has been presented and the empirical proof of the importance of handling both numeric and symbolic data in document classification and understanding is given.

These results also prove the applicability of machine learning techniques to the intelligent document processing task in order to make data capturing from document images more flexible. Indeed, only a minor intervention of the user is required to correct decisions taken by the experimental system WISDOM described in the paper.

Acknowledgments

The authors would like to thank Luca De Filippis and Daniela Gay for their collaboration in conducting the experiments. Thanks also to the authors of the systems C4.5 and ITI 2.0.

References

[1]   Ciardiello, G., Scafuro, G., Degrandi, M.T., Spada, M.R., Roccotelli, M.P.: An Experimental System for Office Document Handling and Text Recognition. *Proc. of the 9th Int.Conf. on Pattern Recognition*, IEEE Computer Society Press, Los Alamitos (1988) 739-743.

[2] De Raedt, L.: *Inductive Theory Revision*, Academic Press, London (1992).
[3] Esposito, F., Malerba, D., Semeraro, G., Annese, E., Scafuro, G.: Empirical Learning Methods for Digitized Document Recognition: An Integrated Approach to Inductive Generalization. *Proc. of the 6th IEEE Conf. on Artificial Intelligence Applications*, IEEE Computer Society Press, Los Alamitos (1990) 37-45.
[4] Esposito, F., Malerba, D., Semeraro, G.: Multistrategy Learning for Document Recognition. *Applied Artificial Intelligence*, **8**(1) (1994) 33-84.
[5] Esposito, F., Malerba, D., Semeraro, G.: A Comparative Analysis of Methods for Pruning Decision Trees. *IEEE Trans. on Pattern Analysis and Machine Intelligence*, TPAMI-**19**(5) (1997) 476-491.
[6] Fayyad, U.M., Irani, K.B.: On the Handling of Continuous-Valued Attributes in Decision Tree Generation. *Machine Learning*, **8** (1992) 87-102.
[7] Fisher, J.L., Hinds, S.C., D'Amato, D.P.: A Rule-Based System for Document Image Segmentation. *Proc. of the 10th Int. Conf. on Pattern Recognition*, IEEE Computer Society, Los Alamitos (1990) 567-572.
[8] Helft, N.: Inductive Generalization: A Logical Framework. In: Bratko, I., Lavrac, N. (eds.): *Progress in Machine Learning - Proc. of the EWSL87*, Sigma Press, London (1987) 149-157.
[9] Malerba, D., Semeraro, G., Bellisari, E.: LEX: A Knowledge-Based System for the Layout Analysis. *Proc. of the 3rd Int. Conf. on the Practical Application of Prolog* (1995) 429-443.
[10] Malerba, D., Semeraro, G., Esposito, F.: A Multistrategy Approach to Learning Multiple Dependent Concepts. In: Taylor, C., Nakhaeizadeh, R. (eds.): *Machine Learning and Statistics: The Interface*, Wiley, London (1997) 87-106.
[11] Malerba, D., Esposito, F., Semeraro, G., Caggese, S.: Handling Continuous Data in Top-Down Induction of First-Order Rules. In: Lenzerini, M.(ed.): *AI*IA 97: Advances in Artificial Intelligence*, Lecture Notes in Artificial Intelligence, Vol. 1321, Springer-Verlag, Berlin Heidelberg New York (1997) 24-35.
[12] Malerba, D., Esposito, F., Semeraro, G., De Filippis, L.: Processing Paper Documents in WISDOM. In: Lenzerini, M.(ed.): *AI*IA 97: Advances in Artificial Intelligence*, Lecture Notes in Artificial Intelligence, Vol. 1321, Springer-Verlag, Berlin Heidelberg New York (1997) 439-442.
[13] Nagy, G., Seth, S.C., Stoddard, S.D.: A Prototype Document Image Analysis System for Technical Journals. *IEEE Computer*, **25**(7) (1992) 10-22.
[14] Orkin, M., Drogin, R.: *Vital Statistics*, McGraw Hill, New York (1990).
[15] Quinlan, J.R.: *C4.5: Programs for Machine Learning*, Morgan Kaufmann, San Mateo (1993).
[16] Quinlan, J.R., Cameron-Jones, R.M.: FOIL: A Midterm Report. In: Brazdil, P.B. (ed.): *Machine Learning: ECML-93*, Lecture Notes in Artificial Intelligence, Vol. 667, Berlin: Springer-Verlag, Berlin Heidelberg New York (1993) 3-20.
[17] Srihari, S.N., Lam, S.W., Hull, J.J., Srihari, R.K., Govindaraju, V.: Intelligent Data Retrieval from Raster Images of Documents. In: Fox, E.A. (ed.): *Source Book on Digital Libraries*, ftp://fox.cs.vt.edu/pub/DigitalLibrary (1993).
[18] Tang, Y.Y., Yan, C.D., Suen, C.Y.: Document Processing for Automatic Knowledge Acquisition. *IEEE Trans. on Knowledge and Data Engineering*, **6**(1) (1994) 3-21.
[19] Utgoff, P.E.: An Improved Algorithm for Incremental Induction of Decision Trees. *Proc. of the 11th Int. Conf. on Machine Learning*, Morgan Kaufmann, San Francisco (1994) 318-325.
[20] Wang, D., Srihari, R.N.: Classification of Newspaper Image Blocks Using Texture Analysis. *Computer Vision, Graphics, and Image Processing*, **47** (1989) 327-352.
[21] Wong, K.Y., Casey, R.G., Wahl, F.M.: Document Analysis System. *IBM J. of Research Development*, **26**(6) (1982) 647-656.

Concept Based Retrieval by Minimal Term Sets

Ali H. Alsaffar[1], Jitender S. Deogun[1], Vijay V. Raghavan[2], and Hayri Sever[3]

[1] The Department of Computer Science & Engineering
University of Nebraska
Lincoln, NE 68588, USA
[2] The Center for Advanced Computer Studies
University of Southwestern Louisiana
Lafayette, LA 70504, USA
[3] Department of Computer Science & Engineering
Hacettepe University
06532 Beytepe, Ankara, Turkey

Abstract. The problem of bridging the terminological gap between the way users prefer to specify their information needs and the way queries are formulated in terms of words or text expressions is of considerable interest. The central ideas of existing approaches based on expert systems technology were introduced in the context of a system called RUBRIC. In RUBRIC, user query topics (or concepts) are captured in a rule base and the rule base is represented as an AND/OR tree. Determining the retrieval output by evaluation of the AND/OR tree is exponential in m, where m is the maximum number of conjunctions in the DNF expression associated with a query topic. In this paper, we propose a method of computing retrieval output that involves the preprocessing of the rule base to generate what we call Minimal Term Sets (MTS) that enhances the computations needed for retrieval. The computational complexity associated with the proposed approach is polynomial in m. We also show that MTSs can provide additional advantages for the users by enabling them to (i) choose query topics that best suit their needs from among existing ones and (ii) use retrieval functions that yield more refined and controlled retrieval output than is possible with the AND/OR tree.

1 Introduction

One of the issues involved in designing this application is that the current search engines do not honor user preferences properly. The advanced query interfaces approximate user preferences by allowing weights for terms and a limited specification of display format for the retrieval output. There is, however, still a considerable gap between the terminologies in defining queries and representing documents. This situation becomes worse in Web catalogs due to the fact that individual vendors use different structures, names, formats and abstractions for products. There are a number of approaches in closing the terminological gap between users and authors of indexed documents, namely extension of queries by the use of thesaurus, the inference models that cluster either index terms or

```
PROCESSOR & RAM & CACHE & HARD_DRIVE & VIDEO => DESKTOP
(PENTIUM | AMD) & "MMX"                => PROCESSOR
["P2/233",0.8] | "P2/266"             => PENTIUM
["K6/233",0.6] | ["K6/266", 0.9]      => AMD
["32MB",  0.5] | "64MB"               => RAM
"512KB"  | "Cache"                    => CACHE
"6.4GB"  & "EIDE"                     => HARD_DRIVE
("ATI" | ["AGP",0.7]) & "4MB/3D"      => VIDEO
```

Table 1. A Rule Base for a Desktop Concept

documents, or a number of feedback techniques that may be used in conjunction with previous two approaches. We chose to adopt *Rule Based Information Retrieval by Computer* (RUBRIC) model on top of descriptor-level retrieval such that our retrieval engine supports concept based retrieval with moderate increase of complexity in defining queries as well as in responding to these queries [1]. We use rules to specify a query topic. As an example, a set of rules for Desktop query is shown in Table 1. In informal syntactical definition of a rule, the derived terms (or subtopics) are represented in capital letters and explicit terms (or text references) thought to be present in documents are represented in double quotation. Both "and" or "or" operators have the same priority level and the association is from left to right. These rules can be suppressed by using parentheses.

A set of rules for a query topic constitutes a goal tree involving AND/OR arcs. Furthermore, to interpret weights across AND or OR arcs and implication nodes we use the functions minimum, maximum, and product. In next section, we discuss the generation of AND/OR goal tree and its evaluation. As seen from this discussion, the time complexity of AND/OR evaluation is exponential in the order of the maximum number alternative definitions for a (sub) query topic.

The concept-level module was implemented on top of the descriptor-level retrieval. This is because a rule base for a query topic is converted to a disjunctive normal form (DNF) made up of conjunctions of explicit terms, called minimal term set (MTS). Such conversion of the desktop concept is shown in Table 2. Each conjunct in MTS is treated as an independent query and submitted to the retrieval system. In section 3, we introduce how to generate an MTS and analyze its evaluation. The MTS evaluation is a polynomial-time look-up operation depending on the number of conjunctions, the number of explicit terms and the computational effort in intersecting two term lists. The MTS of a query topic comes handy in extracting the relevant concepts for a given description of a user's need.

2   AND/OR Goal Tree

Let $W(D_i, T_j) = w_{ij}$ be a weight assignment function indicating the significance of jth term in i^{th} document. An auxiliary structure realizing the weight assignment function is called index file or inverted-index file, if weights are accessible

```
[{"P2/233", "MMX", "64MB", "512K", "6.4GB", "EIDE", "ATI", "4MB/3D"}, 0.8]
[{"P2/233", "MMX", "64MB", "Cache", "6.4GB", "EIDE", "ATI", "4MB/3D"}, 0.8]
[{"P2/233", "MMX", "64MB", "512K", "6.4GB", "EIDE", "AGP", "4MB/3D"}, 0.7]
[{"P2/233", "MMX", "64MB", "Cache", "6.4GB", "EIDE", "AGP", "4MB/3D"}, 0.7]
[{"P2/233", "MMX", "32MB", "512K", "6.4GB", "EIDE", "ATI", "4MB/3D"}, 0.6]
[{"P2/233", "MMX", "32MB", "512K", "6.4GB", "EIDE", "AGP", "4MB/3D"}, 0.5]
[{"P2/233", "MMX", "32MB", "Cache", "6.4GB", "EIDE", "ATI", "4MB/3D"}, 0.5]
[{"P2/233", "MMX", "32MB", "Cache", "6.4GB", "EIDE", "AGP", "4MB/3D"}, 0.5]
```

Table 2. Minimal Term Set of the P2/233 Desktop Subconcept

by term names. In the Prolog database we represent the inverted-index file by a set of facts described as follows. The fact $T_i(D_j, w_{ji})$ exists in Prolog database, if the presence of term T_i in document D_j has a significance of w_{ji}.

The algorithm *Generate_AND/OR* produces a Prolog-like code for a given query topic such that the retrieval output, a list of documents and their retrieval status values (RSV), is obtained as a result of processing AND/OR goal tree. It takes two input files: A set of facts corresponding to the inverted index file, and a set of rules for a query topic. The output of the algorithm is simply a Prolog-like code that is used for evaluating AND/OR goal tree for a given query topic. The critical steps of the algorithm are given as follows.

Step 1. First we combine the rules with the same head using "or" operator, and then for each rule, we create its disjunctive normal form, where the query topic appears as a set of conjunctions of one or more terms, each conjunction being connected to the next one by an "or" operator, as shown below.

$$QueryTopic = \{CF_1, CF_2, \ldots, CF_i, \ldots, CF_m\},$$

where "QueryTopic" is the head of a rule, and CF_i is the conjunction of its term conjuncts, which can be either *structure* or *functor*. If a subquery or text word is paired with a user-supplied weight, we call it structure; otherwise we name it as functor. Since the default weight for a functor is one, an explicit weight of one is assigned when constructing disjunction of conjunctions, QueryTopic. In Table 3, we show intermediate form of the rule set given in Table 1. Our notation in assigning weights to terms in body of a rule differs from the notation of RUBRIC in which the single weight is associated with the head of a rule, but notice that both become semantically equivalent expressions once the calculus for interpretation of weights and propagation of intermediate results is fixed.

Step 2. Let "QT" denote the rule "QueryTopic." We say the rule QT_i is dependent on the rule QT_j if there exists a reference in the body of QT_i to QT_j. This stratification defines a partial order on the rule set (or DNFs.) Furthermore, we define a total order on the rule set by requiring $QT_j \leq QT_i$, if QT_j is in lower stratum than QT_i or QT_j and QT_i are in the same stratum, but QT_j is lexicographically smaller than QT_i. We evaluate the rule set by forward chaining. As seen in Table 3, we have three classes of the rules for Desktop Concept and all rules in a stratum are in lexicographical order.

```
Stratum 0:
  AMD         = {{["K6/233", 0.6]},{["K6/266", 0.9]}}
  CACHE       = {{["512KB", 1]},{["Cache", 1]}}
  HARD_DRIVE  = {{["6.4GB", 1], ["EIDE", 1]}}
  PENTIUM     = {{["P2/233", 0.8]}, {["P2/266", 1]}}
  RAM         = {{["32MB", 0.5]},{["64MB", 1]}}
  VIDEO       = {{["ATI", 1],    ["4MB/3D", 1]},
                 {["AGP", 0.7], ["4MB/3D", 1]}}

Stratum 1:
  PROCESSOR   = {{[PENTIUM, 1],["MMX", 1]}
                 {[AMD, 1], ["MMX", 1]}}

Stratum 2:
  DESKTOP     = {{[PROCESSOR, 1], [RAM, 1], [CACHE, 1],
                 [HARD_DRIVE, 1], [VIDEO, 1]}}
```

Table 3. Disjunctive Normal Forms of Rules – defined in Table 1

Step 3. Assume that the rules in regard to a query topic is ordered as described in Step 2. Starting from the first rule, Step 3 will be repeated until each rule in totally ordered rule set is considered. Let CF_{km} be a mth conjunction in k^{th} rule. Let $CF_{km} = \{[T_1, w_1], \ldots, [T_n, w_n]\}$, where the pair $[T_i, w_i]$ is i^{th} term with weight w_i. We verbally say that a document represented by $ID\#$ and RSV is in the predicate set $CF_{km}(ID\#, RSV)$ if it satisfies the predicate $CF_{km}(ID\#, RSV)$. A similar interpretation is valid for $T_i(ID\#, RSV)$, where the term T_i is either a subordinate query topic or a text reference. The generation of a prolog-like rule indicates that if a document contains all terms T_i, $1 \leq i \leq n$, then it is in CF_{km} with RSV computed as follows. T_i has two significant roles in evaluating RSV of a document in CF_{km} : one as a document term denoted by RSV_i, and the other as a search term in a user query, denoted by w_i. These two significance factors are multiplied and the resulting value is denoted by N_i as the overall effect. If we have only one term in CF_{km} then N_i is enough to determine the RSV of a document. In case we have multiple terms in defining CF_{km}, we take minimum of all $N's$ which means that a common effect of all terms in determining RSV of a document in CF_{km} is reduced to the overall effect of a term with minimum N among the others.

Each conjunction in a given query topic is treated as an independent subordinate query topic such that it offers an alternate path in arriving at the query topic. In case we have multiple conjunctions, the overlapping cases, i.e. a document might be present in more than one predicate set, must be considered to avoid from duplicated documents in the retrieval output of QT_k. For m conjunctions $C(m, i)$ gives the number of combinations for which a document satisfies i conjunctions, Therefore we need in total to consider as many as $\sum_{i=1} C(m, i) = 2^m - 1$ cases to avoid duplication. We encode each region using a binary string of size m which is a set generated by the regular expression

$\{0,1\}^m - \{0^m\}$, and for each region r we generate the corresponding QT_k^r. The RSV of the document with $ID\#$ in the predicate set $QT_k^r(ID\#, RSV)$ equals to the maximum of $RSVs$ of the document satisfying alternative definitions in the region r for the QT_k. For $m = 3$, we have, for example, seven regions and the encoding value $(101)_2 = 5_{10}$ indicates a predicate QT_k^5 whose evaluation contains the documents satisfying only the first and third conjunctions.

Here we described three critic steps of the algorithm that generates a Prolog-like code for a given rule set. Considering time complexity of $Generate\_AND/OR$ algorithm, we see that Step 3 is the most time consuming step. Let k, m and n be the number of subordinate query topics plus the query topic, the maximum number of conjunctions in a (subordinate) query topic, and the maximum number of terms in a conjunction, respectively. Then Step 3 takes at most $O(km(n+2^m))$. This is because (1) we have k DNFs, and for each DNF we have at most m conjunctions, and finally we need to specify at most n term predicates for each conjunction; and (2) the evaluation of a DNF without duplication requires to consider 2^m cases each with m conjunctions. ¿From this explanation it is easy to deduce that the time complexity of AND/OR evaluation is bounded by $O(km(n+2^m)J)$, where J is computational effort to compute a predicate set.

3   Minimal Term Set

Two points need addressing in the evaluation of AND/OR goal tree. First, the algorithm $Generate\_AND/OR$ can handle vector based models (VSMs). Actually there is nothing in the algorithm need be changed to accommodate real values of document terms. There is, however, one issue which seems awkward to VSM: the query processing in AND/OR evaluation makes impossible for a document to be in the retrieval output, if it does not satisfy any conjunction of the rule set in DNF form. This sounds like a Boolean query model rather than a VSM. The second point is the exponential nature of AND/OR evaluation which depends on m in a (subordinate) query topic. It is reasonable to expect that the average value of m may be small. In this section, we address these two points from the perspective of the MTS evaluation following its description.

The minimal term set is the result of the process of expressing a query topic in terms of its text references (or index terms) as shown in Table 2. The essence of our discussion here is to show that both AND/OR goal tree and MTS evaluation end up with the same retrieval output, provided that term weights are Boolean.

Generate_MTS. The input of the algorithm is just a syntactically correct and acyclic query topic definition. First two steps of $Generate\_AND/OR$ algorithm, converting rules into their DNFs and defining a total order on the rules with respect to dependency relationship, are repeated in $Generate\_MTS$ algorithm. The third step is sketched in Table 4. The time complexity of this algorithm in worst case is in $O(k^2 m^n)$, where: k is the number of rules (or DNFs); m is the maximum number of conjunctions; and n is the maximum number of terms in a conjunction.

```
/* Let the total order on DNFs be {QT₁, QT₂, ..., QTₖ} */
for l = 1 to l <= k − 1 do
    let QTₗ = {CFₗ₁, CFₗ₂, ..., CFₗₘ};
    for u = 1 to u <= m do
        let CFₗᵤ = {[T₁, W₁], [T₂, W₂], ..., [Tᵢ, Wᵢ], ..., [Tₙ, Wₙ]},
            where each Tᵢ is a text word;
        find the minimum weight, say mw, of terms in CFₗᵤ;
        for each QTₐ depending on QTₗ, where d > l, do
            let QTₐ = {CFₐ₁, CFₐ₂, ..., CFₐᵧ};
            let CFₐᵥ = {[T₁, W₁], [T₂, W₂], ..., [Tⱼ, Wⱼ], ..., [Tₓ, Wₓ]}
                such that v <= y and Tⱼ = QTₗ;
            for each such CFₐᵥ do
                if u < m then
                    Create CFₙₑᵥ as a duplicate of CFₐᵥ
                    QTₐ = QTₐ ∪ {CFₙₑᵥ}
                end if
                CFₐᵥ = CFₐᵥ − {[Tⱼ, Wⱼ]};
                for each [Tᵢ, Wᵢ] in CFₗᵤ do
                    CFₐᵥ = CFₐᵥ ∪ {[Tᵢ, mw * Wⱼ]}
                end do
            end do
        end do
    end do
end do
convert each conjunct
    CFₖᵢ = {[T₁, W₁], [T₂, W₂], ..., [Tₙ, Wₙ]} of QTₖ to
    CF'ₖᵢ = [{T₁, T₂, ..., Tₙ}, min(W₁, W₂, ..., Wₙ)], and then
sort the conjunctions in descending order of their search weights.
```

Table 4. Third Step of MTS Generation

Theorem 1. *Let QT be a query topic that is syntactically correct and acyclic. Let $QT_{AND/OR}(ID, RSV)$ and $QT_{MTS}(ID, RSV)$ be the set of pairs of documents and their retrieval status values, when evaluated by AND/OR goal tree and MTS, respectively. Assume that term weights are binary. We claim that $QT_{AND/OR}(ID, RSV) = QT_{MTS}(ID, RSV)$, if the evaluation model of MTS is realized in two phases: (1) For each conjunction of text references, use Boolean query processing and then associate the conjunction weight with each document in the retrieval output; and (2) When all conjunctions are exhausted, eliminate duplicated documents by keeping the one with maximum weight.*

Remark 1. Evaluation of the MTS is simply a table lookup operation. If the MTS evaluation is realized in two phases as described in Theorem 1, the time complexity of the first phase of MTS evaluation is of $O(m * [(n − 1) * J])$, where J is the computational effort to evaluate term lists in inverted index file and to intersect two term lists. The time complexity of the second phase is bounded by that of sorting algorithm for documents in the retrieval output.

Remark 2. Let $CF_i = \{[T_1, T_2, \ldots, T_m], c_i\}$ and $CF_j = \{[T_1, T_2, \ldots, T_n], c_j\}$, where CF_i and CF_j, $i \neq j$, are conjunctions in a given MTS form. Furthermore let us introduce following handy functions.

1. $t(CF) =_{def.} \{T_1, T_2, \ldots, T_m\}$ is a function that returns a set of terms included in a given conjunction CF in MTS form.
2. $tt(D) =_{def.} \{T_1, T_2, \ldots, T_n\}$ is a function that returns a set of terms representing a given document.
3. $\gamma(CF) =_{def.} c$ is a function that returns the constant value associated with a given conjunction CF in MTS form.

For a given conjunction and document, a Boolean retrieval function based on term matching can be defined by the following characteristic function.

$$\beta(CF, D) = \begin{cases} 1, \text{ if } t(CF) \subseteq tt(D); \\ 0, \text{ otherwise.} \end{cases}$$

Let $\alpha(CF, D) =_{def.} \beta(CF, D) * \gamma(CF)$ be a retrieval function of the MTS evaluation. Then it is easy to see that

$$\alpha(CF_i, D) \geq \alpha(CF_j, D) \quad \text{if } \gamma(CF_i) \geq \gamma(CF_j) \text{ and } t(CF_i), t(CF_j) \subseteq tt(D).$$

Remark 2 allows us to impose a limit on the number of documents in the retrieval output, provided that the conjunctions in MTS form is sorted in descending order of search weights. We guarantee that further evaluation of subsequent conjunctions would not retrieve a document with higher retrieval value than the ones in the retrieval output. This is a nice property, i.e., partial evaluation of MTS conjunctions, that reduces the time complexity of MTS evaluation. For example, the number of conjunctions for Desktop concept in Table 1 is 32; that is, a full-shot evaluation of the MTS requires to run the retrieval function for each conjunction over inverted index file. Instead, as a result of remark 2, whenever we get top n distinct documents, we stop retrieving other documents.

A conjunction in the form of MTS consists of conjuncts of explicit terms and its interpretation for a given document requires that terms of the document subsume explicit terms of the conjunction, but this a quite strong provision for information retrieval systems, even if each conjunction presents an alternative specification of a query topic. Considering other retrieval functions under the assumption we view a conjunction as a list of terms, for example,

$$\beta(CF, D) = \frac{|t(CF) \cap tt(D)|}{|t(CF) \cup tt(D)|},$$

is a cosine function of Boolean terms. With this retrieval function, Remark 2 does not necessarily hold any more. However we can still have the means to identify a subset of documents in the evaluation set of the CF_i such that their RSVs are at least greater than or equal to the maximum RSV which can be obtained by evaluating the CF_{i+1} – note that $\gamma(CF_i) \geq \gamma(CF_{i+1})$. The means comes from the fact that the cosine retrieval function has the maximum value of one. The *MTS_Evaluation* algorithm given below is general enough to work with other retrieval functions as long as they have an upper bound value. The essence of this algorithm is to append a pair of document and its RSV to the list of retrieval output if and only if it is guaranteed that the RSV of that document is at least as big as the RSVs of all remaining documents that will be appended to the retrieval output.

MTS_Evaluation($QueryTopic, n$)
// $QueryTopic$ is a set of conjuncts sorted in descending order of their
// search weights, and n is the maximum size of retrieval output. Assume
// that $\gamma(null) =_{def} 0$. Furthermore, the $TempList$ is an ordered set of
// pairs of documents and their RSVs. This descending order of RSVs is
// assumed to be kept during the application of union operation. Projection
// of a relation $R(A_1, A_2, \ldots A_n)$ onto some attributes $X \subseteq \{A_1, A_2, \ldots A_n\}$
// is denoted by $\pi_X R(A_1, A_2, \ldots A_n)$.

$m \leftarrow |QueryTopic|$; // Number of Term Lists
$RetrievalOutput \leftarrow \emptyset$;
$TempList \leftarrow \emptyset$;
$MaxRetVal \leftarrow 1$;
$MaxTempRSV \leftarrow 0$;
for $i = 1$ to m do
   $MaxRSV \leftarrow MaxRetVal * \gamma(CF_{i+1})$
   for each document D of the collection do
      $RSV \leftarrow \beta(CF_i, D) * \gamma(CF_i)$;
      if $RSV > MaxRSV$ and $RSV > MaxTempRSV$ then
        $RetrievalOutput \leftarrow RetrievalOutput \cup \{(D, RSV)\}$,
           provided that $D \notin \pi_D RetrievalOutput(D, RSV)$;
      else
        $TempList \leftarrow TempList \cup \{(D, RSV)\}$;
        if $RSV > MaxTempRSV$ then $MaxTempRSV \leftarrow RSV$;
   end do
   for each $(TempD, TempRSV) \in TempList$
      such that $TempRSV > MaxRSV$ do
      $TempList \leftarrow TempList - \{(TempD, TempRSV)\}$;
      $RetrievalOutput \leftarrow RetrievalOutput \cup \{(TempD, TempRSV)\}$,
          provided that $TempD \notin \pi_D RetrievalOutput(D, RSV)$
   end do
   $MaxTempRSV \leftarrow \max(RSVs \in TempList)$;
   if $|RetrievalOutput| \geq n$ then exit the loop;
end do
for each $(D, RSV) \in TempList$ do
   if $|RetrievalOutput| \geq n$ then exit the loop
   $RetrievalOutput \leftarrow RetrievalOutput \cup \{(D, RSV)\}$,
      provided that $D \notin \pi_D RetrievalOutput(D, RSV)$;
end do
sort $RetrievalOutput$ in descending order of RSVs;
return $RetrievalOutput$;

Assuming that a rule itself corresponds to a concept, we organize concepts into a concept hierarchy (specifically AND/OR goal tree) which actually yields a user view. This is because, when a user defines a concept and s(he) wants it to be persistent, we keep them in her/his profile. In other words, to honor users' preferences, it is natural to allow them to define their own views of concepts which may not necessarily coincide with others' views. It is, however, feasible to provide means to users to share local knowledge bases. To do this, there is no need to integrate local views. Assume that each user incorporates the sharing process by allowing some or all her/his persistent concepts to be exported (or to be opened to external world). Furthermore, assume that for each concept we keep its intensional definition, e.g., the MTS in Table 2 constitutes the intension of the P2/233 Desktop concept. If a new user wants to browse a concept list, he/she is asked to roughly define the concept in terms of index terms, which are called text references in RUBRIC, using a query interface. The user's definition is matched against the MTSs of persistent and exported concepts and the resulting set in the form of rules is returned to the user. This scheme of course requires to keep one-to-one correspondence between a rule and its MTS in the rule base.

4 Conclusion

Earlier expert systems approach to information retrieval, where query topics (or concepts) are represented by a rule base, the degree to which a document satisfies the user concept is determined by evaluation of the AND/OR. We propose an alternative method of determining the retrieval output in which the rule base is preprocessed to derive what are called minimal term sets. We provide an algorithm for computing the MTSs and derive the associated complexity. We also show that the complexity of determining the retrieval status values of documents in a collection is much more efficient, when the method based on MTSs is adopted. Besides giving the advantage of more efficient processing, the availability of MTSs can enable user to select query topics best suited to their needs among those available in the system. We provide an illustration of how the RUBRIC approach can be generalized to obtain more refined retrieval output, under the assumption that MTSs are already available. In the future, this work will be extended to the case that the document representations are non-binary.

Acknowledgment: This work is supported by the Army Research Office of USA, Grant No. DAAH04-96-1-0325, under DEPSCoR program of Advanced Research Projects Agency, Department of Defense. Hayri Sever is a visiting assistant professor at Department of Computer Science & Engineering, University of Nebraska, Lincoln, NE 68588, USA.

References

1. B. P. McCune, R. M. Tong, J. S. Dean, and D. G. Shapiro, "RUBRIC: A system for rule-based information retrieval," *IEEE Trans. on Software Engineering*, vol. 11, no. 9, pp. 939–944, 1985.

Querying Document Bases by Content, Structure and Properties

Patrick Lambrix and Nahid Shahmehri and Svend Jacobsen

Department of Computer and Information Science
Linköping University
S-581 83 Linköping, Sweden
e-mail: {patla,nahsh}@ida.liu.se

Abstract. Much information is nowadays stored electronically in document bases. Users retrieve information from these document bases by browsing and querying. While a large number of tools are available nowadays, not much work has been done on tools that allow for the use of the characteristics of documents as well as background knowledge during the search for information. In this paper we propose a query language that allows for querying documents using content information, information about the logical structure of the documents as well as information about properties of the documents. We also present a prototype implementation that supports the query language as well as search that takes background knowledge into account.

1 Introduction

More and more information is nowadays being stored in electronic form. For users it becomes more and more difficult to find information. Essentially, there are two different ways for a user to find information in document bases. The first way is to browse. The user starts with a particular document and follows links from that document to other documents until her information need is satisfied. However, the user may also not find the desired information and give up, or become distracted and follow other paths that are considered interesting. The second way is to query the documents using a search engine. The most common kind of search engine is based on an index that relates keywords to documents. The index is created based on an analysis of the text in the documents. The search is then essentially a table lookup in the index. An example of such a search engine is Altavista. This kind of engines is widely used nowadays. They are easy to use and fast and often give the user at least an approximate answer to the query. Therefore, these systems perform well when a user only needs a crude answer to a query or when a user only needs a starting point from which to browse or query further.

Searching for information using this kind of search engines has, however, a number of drawbacks. The query language for these search engines is usually quite simple allowing in most cases for search using keywords and boolean operators (**and, or** and **and-not**) only. The more advanced search engines of this type may allow for queries involving keywords in some predefined parts of documents such as titles, but usually the engines do not support the use of more advanced information about the logical structure of the documents. However, this would be needed when a user, for instance, wants to find a document with a figure that contains certain information in the figure heading or in the notes section. Also, the user cannot use information about properties of documents, such as file size or author information. This may be interesting when a user only wants to load documents to her own workspace with size smaller than a certain maximum size. Therefore, the ability to use logical structure and properties in the query language together with information about the contents of a document, would allow a user to more precisely specify her query needs.

Another drawback is the fact that a user needs to know the exact term that she is looking for. The documents that are returned for a query are the documents that contain exactly the query term (except for possible stemming). The search engine does not take any advantage of general domain knowledge or additional knowledge that a user may have about the domain. For instance, as the laboratory for intelligent information systems is a research laboratory of our computer science department, when a user is searching for documents from our computer science department, also the documents from the research laboratory should be retrieved. The general knowledge may be stored in the form of ontologies or be commonly available. A user or organization may also have her own preferences or classifications of query terms. For instance, both our computer science department and system engineering department do research on security. However, they work within different frameworks. Therefore, when they are looking for information related to their work, they have their own intuitions and preferences on what kind of information they want to obtain. Background knowledge may also be used to reduce ambiguity in the query terms. In all these cases the use of additional knowledge results in the retrieval of fewer non-relevant documents with respect to the user's information need and therefore in a better quality of the answer to the query.

In this paper we define a query language that allows a user to query a collection of documents using information about content, logical structure and properties of the documents (section 2). Then, in section 3, we describe a prototype implementation that supports the query language and allows for the use of background knowledge during the search. Further, the user can browse through the available information (documents as well as background knowledge) and use this to interactively modify queries. We also report on test results. The paper concludes with a discussion of related work in section 4 and a conclusion in section 5.

2 Queries

In general, the user lacks the flexibility to state queries involving all the characteristics of a document. This is needed, for instance, in a query to retrieve all documents with a specific word (e.g. "retrieval") in the title or any sub-title of the document, belonging to the documentation of a specific project (e.g. DL-project) and with a specific author (e.g. John). This query contains content information (*with a specific word in the title*), information about the logical structure of the document (*in the title* and *belonging to the documentation of a specific project*) as well as other information (*with a specific author*).

A query language supporting all the different kinds of information allows for more precise queries and therefore less documents that are not relevant to a query are retrieved. We define here a base query language that deals with these different kinds of information. Based on a study of current practice and research on structured documents we introduce constructs that should be available in any language that allows for queries using the different kinds of information about documents. The base query language can be extended and for such an extension we refer to section 3. We introduce the syntax and give examples and intuitions. For the semantics of the (extended) language we refer to the appendix.

Queries about Properties. Queries about properties of documents can be asked using a select-from statement. For instance, to find all documents from a research department we write the following: **select * from** *department-document*. These properties can be combined by boolean operators **and**, **or** and **and-not**. We also introduce a construct **fills** that allows for searching for specific values of a document property. For instance, one could ask for the documents for which John is an author: **select * from** (*document* **and fills** *author John*). In this query the property of the document is represented by an attribute (author) and we search for a specific value (John).

Content-based Search. The most common way to search for content information is to use keyword search. In our base language we introduce the **occurs** construct to support this kind of search. For instance, to retrieve the documents that contain the word "retrieval", we write the following: **select * from** *document* **where** *'retrieval'* **occurs**. We also allow to specify directly in the **occurs** construct which type of parts of documents that we wish to search. For instance, the query **select * from** *document* **where** *'retrieval'* **occurs in** *heading*, retrieves all documents that have a heading part (on arbitrary level) containing the word "retrieval".

Queries about Structure. According to recent research in structured documents (e.g. [12]) there is a need for querying and retrieval restricted to parts of a document, for access to documents by their structure and for querying which combines structural data and non-structural data. The logical structure of a document can be seen as defining a part-of hierarchy over the document and its parts. For instance, this document contains among others a title, an abstract and sections while the sections contain sub-sections. We introduce the **includes-some** and **within-some** constructs to allow for traversal of a part-of hierarchy of documents and their parts where the type of the parts is of importance. This allows, for instance, for expressing queries where the scope of the query is not a complete document but only a part of a document. For instance, to find a document where some paragraph contains the word "retrieval" and a figure with "model" in the caption, we perform the following query: **select * from**

document **where includes-some (select * from** *paragraph* **where (** *'retrieval'* **occurs and includes-some (select * from** *figure* **where** *'model'* **occurs in** *caption*))). It is also possible to just retrieve parts of the documents such as in the query to find the sections that are about logic: **select * from** *section* **where** (*'logic'* **occurs and within-some** *document*). We can use specific documents in a query as well using variants of the constructs that deal with objects rather than types: **includes-object** and **within-object**. The following query finds all paragraphs of the particular document ISMIS-proceedings that are about logic: **select * from** *paragraph* **where (** *'logic'* **occurs and within-object** *ISMIS-proceedings*). Further, we allow queries based on the structure of the document that require traversing a part-of hierarchy. For instance, the following complex query finds the sections that together with a particular abstract (paper121-abstract) and title (paper121-title) make up a document: **select * from** *section* **where within-some (select * from** *document* **where (includes-object** *paper121-abstract* **and includes-object** *paper121-title*)).

Combining Query Types. The different kinds of queries can be combined. As an example we translate the query: find all documents with the word "retrieval" in the title or any sub-title of the document, belonging to the documentation of the DL-project and with John as author. We obtain: **select * from** (*document* **and fills** *author John*) **where (** *'retrieval'* **occurs in** *title* **and within-object** *DL-project-documentation*).

3 Prototype Implementation

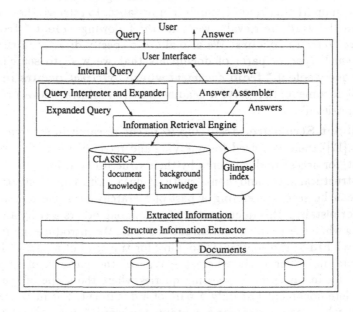

Fig. 1. Prototype system.

The architecture of our system is shown in figure 1 and is an instantiation of the model in [8]. In our prototype implementation the user can query the system using the language described in the appendix. This language is an extension of the language defined in section 2. The query is translated into a internal language query. The internal query language can be seen as an extension of the representation language of the description logic system CLASSIC-P [6, 7]. The query interpreter and expander receives as input a query formulated in the internal query language and may expand the query to take background knowledge into account. The expanded query is then sent to the information retrieval engine which interacts with a number of knowledge bases.

In our prototype the knowledge base component of the system consists of two parts: the description logic system CLASSIC-P [6] and the information retrieval system GLIMPSE [13]. The information about documents resides partly in CLASSIC-P and partly in GLIMPSE. The system creates a GLIMPSE index over the collection of searchable documents, thereby allowing for keyword search. Further, for each document and document part an individual is automatically created in the CLASSIC-P system and the part-of relations between these individuals are instantiated. The addresses of the documents are stored as well. The actual documents reside in a document base which may consist of heterogeneous distributed databases, world-wide web servers or different machines in an intranet. The documents may have different formats. During the testing of our prototype we have concentrated on HTML documents. The logical structure is extracted automatically from the documents by the structure information extractor [9]. Other information about the documents is currently added by a human user. However, one could imagine that a large part of this information could be extracted from the documents automatically using information extraction or document analysis techniques. The background knowledge is stored in the CLASSIC-P system as well. The background knowledge may be general knowledge as well as individual or organizational domain knowledge that may be used to tailor search to the needs and preferences of the individual or organization. It may be new knowledge that is added manually or stored knowledge that can be loaded into the system. This is also true for the information about document types as well as for the properties of actual documents. We note that it is possible to use certain background knowledge in one session and other background knowledge during another session.

The information retrieval engine decides on which parts of the queries are sent to the description logic system and which parts to the information retrieval system. The result of the description logic part is a set of individuals representing documents and document parts. Due to the functionality of the description logic system, relevant background information is taken into account during the search. The result of the information retrieval part is transformed into a list of individuals as well. The answer assembler combines the results. The result of the query is presented as a page containing a list of pointers to the documents satisfying the query.

We implemented a number of interfaces to the system. The expert user interfaces require knowledge about the end-user query language. The novice interface presents the user with a template for a query. The user instantiates the template to pose a query. The interface helps the user by showing for each template item the different syntactically correct possibilities (see, for instance, figure 2). In addition, the interfaces allow for retrieval of information about the different types of documents and about the background knowledge. The information that can be retrieved is the definition of document types and concepts in the background knowledge, as well as information about the more specific and more general concepts and the individuals that belong to the concept. We can browse the information in knowledge bases and use it for interactive querying. For instance, when more answers are desired a query may be made more general, and when less answers are desired the query may be made more specific.

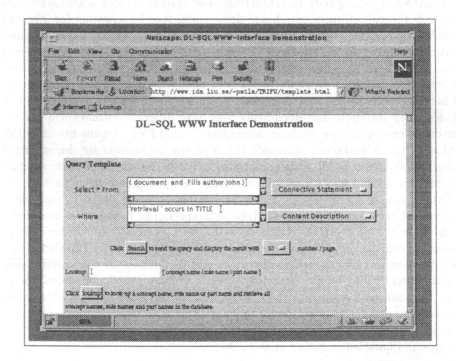

Fig. 2. Interface

We have tested our prototype system on a collection of 180 HTML documents arbitrarily taken from the web pages of our department. The web pages included information about research and education as well as some other activities at the department. We created a description logic representation of the documents using the method in [9]. This program was run under Allegro Common Lisp Version 4.2. We partitioned the document collection into seven parts where part two contained part one, part three contained part two and so on. For each part a GLIMPSE index was created and a description logic knowledge base was instantiated. The background knowledge used in the test contained a description of the structure of the department such as information on the research laboratories and the course leaders.

With respect to the representation of the documents we found that the number of CLASSIC-P individuals grows more than linear with respect to the number of documents. (In our experiments we found a ratio between 1.1 and 1.6.) The conversion program as described in [9] creates a new individual for every HTML tag found in an HTML document and considers this as a part of the document. A less naive approach would decide on a number of tags that can be considered as parts and only store information about these tags.

The loading of the information about the documents in CLASSIC-P took about 20 seconds per document for the largest document base. This may be explained by the fact that the system infers possible new information about the documents and classifies each document under the most specific class (concept) to which it belongs. Also, we did not address any optimization issues and used a research prototype implementation of CLASSIC-P where efficiency was not a main issue. There is thus room for improvement in the sense of optimizing our prototype as well as in the sense of using faster description logic systems.

We tested the system with a number of different queries involving the different kinds of information. The response time for most queries was at most a few seconds on the collection of 180 documents. As expected, the information that had the most influence on the response time are the queries involving logical structure. These queries require a traversal of a part-of hierarchy of the parts of the documents.

The expressive power of our query language allows for expressing information about content, logical structure and properties of documents. Therefore, the users could state their queries more precisely than with other search tools that allowed, for example, only for keyword search. The answer sets contained therefore less irrelevant information. Finally, as expected, the use of background knowledge improved the recall of the system.

4 Related Work

Due to space limitations we only briefly mention related work. For more information we refer to [6, 7]. In [11] a model for information retrieval using keywords as well as structural information is described. The approach requires a keyword index and a number of structural indexes. These indexes are assumed to be given.

A number of other authors propose query languages for structured documents. In [10] a query language is specified for retrieving information from hierarchically structured documents. Four different categories of search capabilities are considered: simple selection and navigation, simple object selection conditions, contextual conditions and object specification. In [3] the object-oriented database management system O_2 is extended to handle SGML documents. The query language O_2SQL is extended with new constructs among which the notion of path variables. In [5] SQL is extended to provide access to structured text described by SGML in text-relational database management systems.

Another kind of related work are the query languages for semi-structured data and web query languages (e.g. [1, 2, 4]). One of the main features of these proposals is that the underlying data and their logical structure can be modeled using graphs. To traverse the graphs and thus to query the logical structure of the documents, the query languages support the notion of path expressions. We note that we can model most of the path expressions in our internal language.

5 Conclusion

In this paper we described a query language that allows for querying document bases using information about contents, structure and other properties of the documents. Further, we described a prototype implementation of a knowledge-based information retrieval system that supports this query language and that allows for the use and browsing of background knowledge during the querying.

The background knowledge and knowledge about documents can be specified for individual users or organizations. In this case the document knowledge base is used to find and retrieve documents that are tailored to the needs of the individual or organization. In future work we will investigate how background knowledge should be organized to obtain the best query results. We will also investigate on the automatic creation of domain knowledge for particular users.

Another important direction for further work is the extraction of information from documents. Our current implementation deals mainly with the extraction of the logical structure and keywords from documents.

Acknowledgements. This research has been supported by the Swedish Foundation for Strategic Research and the Swedish Research Council for Engineering Sciences.

References

1. Abiteboul, S., Quass, D., McHugh, J., Widom, J., Wiener, J., 'The Lorel Query Language for Semistructured Data', *International Journal on Digital Libraries*, Vol 1(1), pp. 68-88, 1997.
2. Buneman, P., Davidson, S., Hillebrand, G., Suciu, D., 'A Query Language and Optimization Techniques for Unstructured Data', *Proceedings of SIGMOD*, 1996.
3. Christophides, V., Abiteboul, S., Cluet, S., Scholl, M., 'From Structured Documents to Novel Query Facilities', *Proceedings of SIGMOD*, pp 1-22, 1994.
4. Fernandez, M., Florescu, D., Levy, A., Suciu, D., 'A Query Language for a Web-Site Management System', *SIGMOD Record*, Vol 26(3), pp 4-11, 1997.
5. Kilpeläinen, P., Manilla, H., 'Retrieval from Hierarchical Texts by Partial Patterns', *Proceedings of SIGIR*, pp 214-222, 1993.

6. Lambrix, P., *Part-Whole Reasoning in an Object-Centered Framework*, Lecture Notes in Artificial Intelligence, 1999. to appear.
7. Lambrix, P., Padgham, L., 'A Description Logic Model for Querying Knowledge Bases for Structured Documents', *Proceedings of ISMIS*, pp 72-83, 1997.
8. Lambrix, P., Shahmehri, N., 'TRIFU: The Right Information For yoU', *Proceedings of the 31st Hawaii International Conference on System Sciences*, pp 505-512, 1998.
9. Lambrix, P., Shahmehri, N., Åberg, J., 'Towards Creating a Knowledge Base for World-Wide Web Documents', *Proceedings of the IASTED International Conference on Intelligent Information Systems*, pp 507-511, 1997.
10. MacLeod, I., 'A Query Language for Retrieving Information from Hierarchic Text Structures', *The Computer Journal*, Vol 34(3), pp 254-264, 1991.
11. Navarro, G., Baeza-Yates, R., 'Proximal Nodes: A Model to Query Document Databases by Content and Structure', *ACM Transactions on Information Systems* Vol 15(4), pp 400-435, 1997.
12. Sacks-Davis, R., Arnold-Moore, T., Zobel, J., 'Database systems for structured documents', *Proceedings of the International Symposium on Advanced Database Technologies and Their Integration*, pp 272-283, Nara, Japan, 1994.
13. Wu, S., Manber, U., 'Fast Text Searching Allowing Errors', *Communications of the ACM*, Vol 35(10), pp 93-91, 1992.

Appendix

The syntax of the query language is as follows:

```
<query> :: select <selection-list> [from <from-list>] [where <where-list>]
<selection-list> :: *
<from-list> :: <concept-name> | <concept-description>
    | (<from-list> and <from-list> {and <from-list>})
    | (<from-list> or <from-list> {or <from-list>})
    | (<from-list> and-not <from-list>)
<where-list> :: <structure-description> | <content-description>
    | (<where-list> and <where-list> {and <where-list>})
    | (<where-list> or <where-list> {or <where-list>})
    | (<where-list> and-not <where-list>)
<structure-description> :: [directly] includes-some <sub-query>
    | [directly] within-some <sub-query>
    | [directly] includes-object <individual-name>
    | [directly] within-object <individual-name>
<content-description> :: '<string>' occurs [in <concept-name>]
<concept-description> :: top
    | all <role-name> <concept-name>
    | all <role-name> ( <concept-description> )
    | all <part-name> <concept-name>
    | all <part-name> ( <concept-description> )
    | atleast <non-negative integer> <role-name>
    | atleast <non-negative integer> <part-name>
    | atmost <non-negative integer> <role-name>
    | atmost <non-negative integer> <part-name>
    | fills <role-name> <individual-name> {<individual-name>}
```

```
        | fills <part-name> <individual-name> {<individual-name>}
        | parts-constraint <role-name> <part-name> <part-name>
<sub-query> :: ( <query> )
        | (<sub-query> and <sub-query> {and <sub-query>})
        | (<sub-query> or <sub-query> {or <sub-query>})
        | (<sub-query> and-not <sub-query>)
<concept-name> :: <string>
<individual-name> :: <string>
<role-name> :: <string>
<part-name> :: <string>
<string> :: <symbol>[<string>]
<symbol> :: A | B | .. | Z | a | b | .. | z
```

The semantics of the query language is defined in a model-theoretic way. An interpretation for the language consists of a tuple $< \mathcal{D}, \varepsilon >$, where $\mathcal{D}$ is a domain and ε an extension function. The extension function maps part names and role names into sub-sets of $\mathcal{D} \times \mathcal{D}$, concepts into sub-sets of $\mathcal{D}$ and individuals into elements of $\mathcal{D}$ such that $\varepsilon[i_1] \neq \varepsilon[i_2]$ whenever $i_1 \neq i_2$. The semantics for the different constructs are as follows. For convenience we write $y \lhd_n x$ for $<y,x> \in \varepsilon[n]$ where n is a part name which means then that y is a direct part of x with name n. We say that y is a part of x (notation $y \lhd^* x$) if there is a chain of direct parts from x to y.

$\varepsilon[\text{select * from } A \text{ where } B] = \mathcal{D} \cap \varepsilon[A] \cap \varepsilon[B]$

$\varepsilon[A \text{ and } B] = \varepsilon[A] \cap \varepsilon[B]$

$\varepsilon[A \text{ or } B] = \varepsilon[A] \cup \varepsilon[B]$

$\varepsilon[A \text{ and-not } B] = \varepsilon[A] \setminus \varepsilon[B]$

$\varepsilon[\text{top}] = \mathcal{D}$

$\varepsilon[\text{all } r \ A] = \{x \in \mathcal{D} \mid \forall y \in \mathcal{D}: <x,y> \in \varepsilon[r] \to y \in \varepsilon[A]\}$

$\varepsilon[\text{all } n \ A] = \{x \in \mathcal{D} \mid \forall y \in \mathcal{D}: y \lhd_n x \to y \in \varepsilon[A]\}$

$\varepsilon[\text{atleast } m \ r] = \{x \in \mathcal{D} \mid \sharp \ \{y \in \mathcal{D} \mid <x,y> \in \varepsilon[r]\} \geq m\}$

$\varepsilon[\text{atleastp } m \ n] = \{x \in \mathcal{D} \mid \sharp \ \{y \in \mathcal{D} \mid y \lhd_n x\} \geq m\}$

$\varepsilon[\text{atmost } m \ r] = \{x \in \mathcal{D} \mid \sharp \ \{y \in \mathcal{D} \mid <x,y> \in \varepsilon[r]\} \leq m\}$

$\varepsilon[\text{atmostp } m \ n] = \{x \in \mathcal{D} \mid \sharp \ \{y \in \mathcal{D} \mid y \lhd_n x\} \leq m\}$

$\varepsilon[\text{fills } r \ i_1 \ ... \ i_m] = \{x \in \mathcal{D} \mid <x,\varepsilon[i_1]> \in \varepsilon[r] \land ... \land <x,\varepsilon[i_m]> \in \varepsilon[r]\}$

$\varepsilon[\text{fills } n \ i_1 \ ... \ i_m] = \{x \in \mathcal{D} \mid \varepsilon[i_1] \lhd_n x \land ... \land \varepsilon[i_m] \lhd_n x\}$

$\varepsilon[\text{parts-constraint } r \ n_1 \ n_2] =$
$\qquad \{x \in \mathcal{D} \mid \forall y_1,y_2 \in \mathcal{D}: (y_1 \lhd_{n_1} x \land y_2 \lhd_{n_2} x) \to <y_1,y_2> \in \varepsilon[r]\}$

$\varepsilon[\text{directly includes-some } C] = \{x \in \mathcal{D} \mid \exists y \in \mathcal{D}, \exists n: y \lhd_n x \land y \in \varepsilon[C]\}$

$\varepsilon[\text{includes-some } C] = \{x \in \mathcal{D} \mid \exists y \in \mathcal{D}: y \lhd^* x \land y \in \varepsilon[C]\}$

$\varepsilon[\text{directly within-some } C] = \{x \in \mathcal{D} \mid \exists y \in \mathcal{D}, \exists n: x \lhd_n y \land y \in \varepsilon[C]\}$

$\varepsilon[\text{within-some } C] = \{x \in \mathcal{D} \mid \exists y \in \mathcal{D}: x \lhd^* y \land y \in \varepsilon[C]\}$

$\varepsilon[\text{directly includes-object } i] = \{x \in \mathcal{D} \mid \exists n: \varepsilon[i] \lhd_n x\}$

$\varepsilon[\text{includes-object } i] = \{x \in \mathcal{D} \mid \varepsilon[i] \lhd^* x\}$

$\varepsilon[\text{directly within-object } i] = \{x \in \mathcal{D} \mid \exists n: x \lhd_n \varepsilon[i]\}$

$\varepsilon[\text{within-object } i] = \{x \in \mathcal{D} \mid x \lhd^* \varepsilon[i]\}$

$\varepsilon[s \text{ occurs}] = \{x \in \mathcal{D} \mid x \text{ contains } s \lor (\exists y: y \lhd^* x \land y \text{ contains } s)\}$

$\varepsilon[s \text{ occurs in } C] = \{x \in \mathcal{D} \mid (\exists y: y \lhd^* x \land y \in \varepsilon[C] \land y \text{ contains } s)\}$

Total Knowledge and Partial Knowledge in Logical Models of Information Retrieval

Fabrizio Sebastiani

Istituto di Elaborazione dell'Informazione
Consiglio Nazionale delle Ricerche
Via S. Maria, 46 – Pisa, Italy
E-mail: fabrizio@iei.pi.cnr.it

Abstract. We here expand on a previous paper concerning the role of logic in information retrieval (IR) modelling. In that paper, among other things, we had pointed out how different ways of understanding the contribution of logic to IR have sprung from the (always unstated) adherence to either the *total* or the *partial knowledge assumption*. Here we make our analysis more precise by relating this dichotomy to the notion of *vividness*, as used in knowledge representation, and to another dichotomy which has had a profound influence in DB theory, namely the distinction between the *proof-theoretic* and the *model-theoretic* views of a database, spelled out by Reiter in his "logical reconstruction of database theory". We show that precisely the same distinction can be applied to logical models of IR developed so far. The strengths and weaknesses of the adoption of either approach in logical models of IR are discussed.

1 Introduction

Logical models of information retrieval (IR) have been actively investigated in the last ten years. The reason behind this interest in logic on the part of IR theorists springs from a substantial dissatisfaction with the insights into the very nature of information, information content, and relevance, that mainstream IR research gives. We indeed think that there are two main IR-related issues to which logic might provide better answers than current approaches.

The first issue has to do with the *quantitative* view of information content that the received wisdom of IR embodies. According to this view the degree of similarity (or the probability of relevance, depending on the adopted model) of a document to a given request may be estimated, by and large, by computing the occurrence frequency of words in the request, in the document candidate for retrieval, and in the collection of documents being searched. If on one hand these quantitative methods are still unsurpassed in terms of effectiveness (i.e. in terms of their ability to weed the irrelevant documents from the relevant ones), on the other hand they do not constitute, in all evidence, a satisfactory explanation of the fundamental notions of IR. In other words, it is implausible that the very notion of information content of a document may ultimately come down to word counts, irrespective of the syntactic, semantic and pragmatic role that each individual word occurrence plays; the dominant view in linguistic semantics is that information content *must* be more than that, even if we are not yet able to put our fingers on it. Quantitative models thus provide a *phenomenology*, rather than a theory, of information content and relevance. It is exactly the search for a *theory* that has driven many IR "theorists" to logical models of IR. Far from believing that the ultimate IR system will be a theorem prover, many of these investigators are convinced that logic, by its strong reliance on the semantics of the formulae it deals with, may foster our understanding of the fundamental (and inherently semantic) notions of information, information content and relevance.

The second issue has to do with the separation of concerns that current practice in IR has *de facto* established between the issues of 1) *representing* the content of documents and requests (*indexing*), and 2) *reasoning* with such representations in order to establish the relevance of the former to the latter (*matching*). In fact present-day indexing techniques are only loosely bound to the matching techniques that use the representations built by them; for instance, the same method for computing the representations of documents/requests (e.g. $tf * idf$ weighting) is being used in conjunction with widely different matching techniques, and the same matching technique (e.g. the cosine measure) is being used in conjunction with representations of documents/requests obtained by widely different methods (see [19] for an example of this "combinatoric" coupling of indexing and matching). In logic, IR theorists find instead a framework in which representation and reasoning are not independently motivated, but are, in some sense, one and the same thing. Logic prompts IR theorists not only to clearly specify the semantics of the representation language for documents/requests and the semantics of relevance, but also to ensure that the way actual representations are arrived at is consistent with this semantic specification.

In a previous paper [23] we analysed the literature on logical models of IR from the point of view of their compliance with the well-formedness criteria that are standard in applied logic. In [23, Section 6.1] we argued that, from this literature, two different ways of understanding the contribution of logic to IR modelling emerge, and that each of them is based on the (unstated) adoption of either the *total knowledge* or the *partial knowledge* assumption.

At a first approximation, the total knowledge assumption means that *everything about the problem domain is assumed to be known*. Although this characterisation may look a bit strong at first sight, it is not once one interprets "everything" as "everything that can be stated in the logical language used for the representation of the problem domain". For instance, the traditional Boolean model of IR (in which the logical language for the representation of documents is that of Boolean conjunctions of propositional letters) is a model in which total knowledge is implicitly assumed. To see this, assume that the set of propositional letters (i.e. the controlled indexing language) is $\mathcal{L} = \{t_1, \ldots, t_n\}$. If a document d_i is represented e.g. by the conjunction $t_2 \wedge t_5 \wedge t_7$, this is assumed to mean not only that d_i is about t_2, t_5 and t_7, but also that d_i is *not* about t_i for $i \neq 2, 5, 7$. In other words, the truth value of *everything that can be specified in the language about d_i* (i.e. whether, for a given t_j, d_i is or is not about t_j) *is assumed known*.

The total knowledge assumption is present, although better hidden, also in models that make use of formal tools traditionally viewed as means of representing uncertainty (even though uncertainty is closely associated to the notion of the partiality of knowledge!). For instance, in the *extended Boolean model* of [20] or in the *probabilistic model* of [16], documents are represented as conjunctions of *weighted* terms, where the weight $w_{ij} \in [0,1]$ of term i in document j is taken to represent the "importance" of i in j or the probability of relevance of j to a generic query consisting of i, respectively. Here, the key observation is that the weight of any term, whatever its interpretation, *is always assumed known*. In other words, the presence of uncertainty in these models is, in the precise sense exposed above, only apparent: every sentence that can be expressed in the representation language is either known to be true or known to be false.

The partial knowledge assumption, instead, makes explicit the fact that not all that is representable in the chosen logical language is assumed to be known. For instance, one may conceive a variant of the Boolean model of IR in which, given the usual set of propositional letters $\mathcal{L} = \{t_1, \ldots, t_n\}$, a document representation $t_2 \wedge t_5 \wedge t_7$ for document d_i is taken to mean, among other things, that *it is not known* whether d_i is or is not about t_j for $j \neq 2, 5, 7$. Adherence to the partial knowledge assumption entails reasoning in the presence of incomplete information, which is the standard way of performing inference in logic.

For what we have said up to now (and, for that matter, for what we had said in [23, Section 6.1]), the distinction between total-knowledge and partial-knowledge models of IR might as well come down to the better known distinction between the *closed world assumption* (CWA) and the *open world assumption*, respectively (see e.g. [9, Chapter 7]). In this paper we argue that our distinction amounts to more than that, in that total-knowledge models of IR assume not only that everything about the problem domain is known, but also that it is represented in *vivid* form [6,7]. The consequence is that adopting either assumption means taking an implicit stand as to what, logically speaking, a (representation of a) document collection is: more precisely, the two different positions relate to the dichotomy between the *model-theoretic* and the *proof-theoretic* models of databases, exposed in a paper by Reiter [14]. The aim of this paper is to show how this latter dichotomy may usefully be applied to the case of logical models of IR, and how advantages and disadvantages of either approach that have already been discussed in the DB literature apply, and to what extent, to the IR case.

The paper is structured as follows. In Section 2 we briefly discuss the notion of "vividness", and how it relates to the model-theoretic and the proof-theoretic views of DBs. In Section 3 we discuss how this dichotomy applies to IR too, show how proposed logical models of IR have *de facto* adhered to either camp, and discuss the advantages and disadvantages that these models incur into by way of this adherence. Section 4 discusses the issue of how "model-theoretic" models may be recast in proof-theoretic form. Section 5 concludes.

2 Vividness, the model-theoretic, and the proof-theoretic models of databases

2.1 Vivid knowledge bases and total-knowledge models of IR

Implicit in the discussion of the previous section is the fact that partial-knowledge models of IR implicitly assume that the problem knowledge *cannot* be encoded by means of a *complete theory* of the chosen logic, and therefore tend to rely on reasoning methodologies involving deduction (possibly of a probabilistic kind) that make use of a knowledge base representing the incomplete theory (see e.g. [10,21]). Such a theory has more than one model, and deduction may as usual be seen as a compact way of handling them all.

Total-knowledge models of Ir (see e.g. [2–4,12,13]) are instead built along the assumption that the problem knowledge can be encoded by means of a *complete theory* of the chosen logic. However, a key point that we missed to observe in [23, Section 6.1] is that these models assume that, of this complete theory, *the simplest representation possible is always available*, where this representation is what Levesque [6,7] calls a *vivid* knowledge base, i.e. a set of (possibly negated) *ground*, *atomic* statements. An example of a vivid KB for the language of propositional logic built upon the alphabet $T = \{t_1, t_2\}$ is the set $KB = \{t_1, \neg t_2\}$: it is a complete theory, and it also vivid, unlike e.g. its equivalent $KB' = \{\neg(t_1 \supset t_2)\}$. Levesque observes that, when a KB is in vivid form, it basically consists in an "analogue" of its unique satisfying interpretation, and therefore may be reasoned upon by methods quicker that theorem proving, much in the same way in which a photograph of a tree in front of a house immediately allows us to reach the conclusion, with no complex chains of either disjunctive or implicational reasoning, that there is a tree in front of a house[1].

It is exactly the vividness of the representations upon which total-knowledge models are built that allows them to disregard proof theory and theorem proving, favouring instead approaches to document relevance estimation based on the explicit manipulation of the vivid data structure that represents the complete theory. For instance, in the "imaging" models of [2–4] documents are represented as in the Boolean model, but the problem domain is additionally represented by a probability density function $\mu(t)$ on the set of n terms occurring in the document collection, taken to represent the "importance" of the term relative to other terms in the collection, and by a real-valued function $\sigma(t_1, t_2)$ on the set of pairs of terms, taken to represent the "semantic relatedness" between the two terms. Here, not only the "importance" of all terms is always assumed known, but it is represented *explicitly* as a vector of weights of length n; not only the "semantic relatedness" between any two terms is always assumed known, but it is represented *explicitly* as an $n \times n$ bidimensional matrix of weights. Should any of these items of knowledge be not explicitly available, and therefore be inferred

---

[1] To take propositional logic as an example, deciding whether α logically follows from a KB Γ in vivid form may be achieved by checking whether Γ is a satisfying truth assignment for α, a substantially easier task that doing unrestricted theorem proving.

on demand from the application of inference rules to other items of knowledge, we would still be in the presence of a complete theory but the vividness property would be lost, and the methods for reasoning on vivid representations would no more be applicable[2].

2.2 Vivid knowledge bases and data bases

Levesque [6] observed that a vivid KB, being free from disjunctive, implicational or quantified knowledge, is akin to a relational DB, where reasoning is basically achieved simply by the lookup of the required information in a table where all available information is stored in ready-to-use form. This suggests the existence of a connection between total-knowledge logical models of IR and DBs. This connection may be better appreciate in the context of the distinction between the *proof-theoretic* and the *model-theoretic* view of DBs exposed by Reiter in [14]. According to

1. the model-theoretic view, a DB is an interpretation I of a first-order logical language L, a query is a formula α of L, and query evaluation may be seen in terms of checking the truth of α in I;
2. the proof-theoretic view, a DB is a set Γ of formulae of a first-order logical language L, a query is a formula α of L, and query evaluation may be seen in terms of proving that α belongs to the deductive closure of Γ.

Reiter argues that the proof-theoretic view of DBs is more fruitful than the model-theoretic one. The latter, in fact, shows its limits in the impossibility of dealing with incomplete knowledge (since first-order interpretations are complete specifications of a state of affairs), null values (since no "undefined" truth value is catered for by first order semantics), and, above all, domain knowledge. In the next section we will discuss how these issues impact on logical models of IR.

3 Model-theoretic and proof-theoretic models of information retrieval

The very idea of a logical model of IR, put forth by van Rijsbergen in [25], relies on the estimation of the formula $P(d \rightarrow r)$, where d and r are logical formulae representing the document and the request, respectively, $P(\alpha)$ stands for "the probability of α", and $\rightarrow$ is the conditional connective of the logic in question. As discussed in [23], this proposal has been interpreted by researchers

[2] Interestingly enough, an analysis of the major traditional (non-logical) models of IR (e.g. [17,20]) reveals that the total knowledge assumption (or its non-logical equivalent) seems to be "wired" into IR since its very inception, no doubt because of its greater computational tractability. This does not mean that the designers of IR models or systems are unaware of the fact that the basic quantities of IR, such as the "importance" of a term, cannot be determined with certainty; it means that the systems (viewed as cognitive agents) are!

to mean widely different things, and has originated two broad classes of models, total-knowledge models and partial-knowledge models. It is the contention of this paper that the difference between total-knowledge and partial-knowledge models may exactly be seen in terms of Reiter's distinction between viewing DBs model-theoretically or proof-theoretically.

Let us discuss total-knowledge models first. It suffices to analyse any model in this category (we will use as examples the "imaging" model developed in [3]) to recognise the basic traits of Reiter's model-theoretic view:

- the reliance on a logic $\mathcal{L}$ endowed with a model-theoretic semantics for its language L. In [3], $\mathcal{L}$ is the **C2** conditional logic, L is the language of propositional letters[3], and the semantics is a model-theoretic semantics based on possible worlds and the "imaging" principle (see e.g. [8]);
- the "representation" of the data encoding the problem domain (i.e. documents, requests, terms, ...) not by the exclusive means of formulae of L, but also by means of a data structure representing a semantic interpretation I of L, similarly to Point (1) in Section 2.2. In [3] documents (and requests) are represented by propositional letters, terms are represented by possible worlds, their importance relative to other terms in the collection is represented by a probability density function $\mu(t)$, and the semantic relatedness between terms is represented by a real-valued function $\sigma(t_1, t_2)$;
- a reasoning method not aimed at determining validity in $\mathcal{L}$, but aimed instead at determining truth in the unique satisfying interpretation I, usually by the explicit manipulation of I itself[4]. In [3], $P(d \to r)$ is computed by revising $\mu(t)$ in a d- and σ-dependent way to yield $\mu'(t)$, and to subsequently compute $P(r)$ on $\mu'(t)$; no use of the proof theory of **C2** is made.

Partial-knowledge models follow instead not only the fundamental traits of Reiter's proof-theoretic view of DBs, but also the standard guidelines of applied AI-style knowledge representation. We will take as example the model presented in [21] to illustrate the following basic features:

- the reliance on a logic $\mathcal{L}$ endowed with a model-theoretic semantics for its language L. In [21], $\mathcal{L}$ is the $\mathcal{P}$-MIRTL probabilistic description logic, L is its language of "concepts" and "roles", and the semantics is, again, a model-theoretic semantics based on possible worlds;
- the representation of the data encoding the problem domain by the exclusive means of formulae of L, similarly to Point (2) in Section 2.2. In [21] documents, requests and terms are represented by concepts, and their relative "importance" is represented by qualifying concepts probabilistically;

---

[3] The **C2** logic was originally defined on a full propositional language [24].

[4] The total knowledge assumption is so widespread in IR (see Footnote 2) that these two notions are often collapsed in IR models: Wong and Yao [26], for instance, state that "The notion of relevance in the Boolean model is interpreted as a strict logical implication: a document is retrieved only if it logically satisfies a request." See [23] for a thorough discussion of this point.

– a reasoning method aimed at determining validity in $\mathcal{L}$. In [21], $P(d \rightarrow r)$ is computed by finding the real number $v \in [0,1]$ for which $P(d \rightarrow r) = v$ is valid in the theory representing the problem domain[5].

At this point, a discussion of the relative advantages and disadvantages of the two opposing views is in order.

The advantage that accrues from the adoption of the model-theoretic perspective is of a "berry-picking" nature: rather than exploiting *logic* (and the tools provided by meta-logic such as the notions of logical consequence, validity, and the like), one picks *one particular intuition* embodied by *one particular logic* and applies it in what is essentially an extra-logical context. This is the case of [3], that, rather than exploiting the inferential power of the **C2** conditional logic in performing inference, borrows the particular graph-theoretic topology of **C2**'s semantic structures and applies it to the revision of a probability density function for establishing relevance. This is also the case of [12], that equates the distance that separates a document from "perfect" relevance to a request, to the distance that separates the nodes representing the document and the request, respectively, in a graph that resembles the "Kripke structures" used for giving semantics to modal logic. In not making use of proof-theory (and, hence, of inference) these approaches exploit the underlying total knowledge assumption, thus avoiding the added computational burden that the existence of multiple interpretations, which would accrue from the partiality of knowledge, brings about.

Another advantage that should be mentioned is the fact that insights from more traditional (non-logical) models of IR may be incorporated in a total-knowledge model without effort, as these other models are also based on the total knowledge assumption. For instance, the *idf* measure of the discrimination power of terms may be incorporated in any total-knowledge model that requires relative term importance to be measured, as both the former and latter models are based on the common premise that the "weight" of a given term, whatever its interpretation, is always known.

The advantages deriving from the adoption of a proof-theoretic perspective, instead, are due to the fact that this perspective opens the way to the *exploitation of domain knowledge in establishing relevance*. As explained by Reiter [14, page 193], the very possibility of a proof-theoretic view of DBs "by itself (...) would not be a very exciting result. (...) The idea bears fruit only in its capacity for generalization". And the usefulness of opening up the retrieval process to the incorporation of additional sources of information is amply recognized also from the IR community: Wong and Yao [26, page 41], for instance, champion

---

[5] The Datalog-inspired approach of Fuhr [5] is a particular case of the proof-theoretic approach, because its semantics, being informed by the closed world assumption, is such that the theory that represents the problem domain is complete, as in the model-theoretic approach. In Reiter's scheme, the approach of [5] would thus be classified as proof-theoretic with *absence* of incomplete information, while the above-discussed approach of [21] would be labelled proof-theoretic with *presence* of incomplete information. A position similar to the one of [5] is adopted in [11].

the adoption of the "subjective" view of probability also on the grounds that "it provides an effective means to incorporate semantic information into the retrieval process".

We think that the importance of incorporating domain knowledge becomes especially evident once one considers that the knowledge that should be brought to bear in the retrieval process may either be

- *endogenous*, i.e. with an internal origin. This is the case of knowledge that can be *estimated* (rather than computed deterministically) through a process of automatic information extraction from the document or from the document collection. Examples of this are the discriminating power of a term (in textual retrieval), the shapes of objects portrayed in photographs (in image retrieval), or the individual words uttered by speakers (in speech retrieval);
- *exogenous*, i.e. with an external origin. This is the case of knowledge that, either inherently or due to the limitations of current technology, cannot be extracted automatically, but have to be provided "manually", i.e. from an external source; examples of this are the author of a photograph (in image retrieval) or the nationality of a non-native speaker (in speech retrieval).

Traditional IR research has assumed that retrieval should be based on endogenous knowledge only. Today, this assumption is increasingly challenged by the emergence of novel applications such digital libraries and multimedia search engines, and by the increasing convergence of research fields that had traditionally led a separate existence, such as IR, DBs, and on-line library catalogues. In these newer contexts, the integration of different sources of knowledge is essential. Resource discovery and multimedia IR cannot rely exclusively on endogenous knowledge, but need to be supported by additional, exogenous information, supplied either by the authors themselves (e.g. under HTML "META" tags), or by third-party cataloguers. To address requests such as

black and white photographs of successful actors of silent movies

an IR system should rely both on endogenous knowledge (knowing whether the image is a black and white one; knowing whether a person is portrayed) and exogenous knowledge (knowing whether the portrayed person was an actor; whether he/she was successful; whether he/she has played in silent movies). To allow the integration of exogenous and endogenous knowledge, a proof-theoretic approach is essential, as its fundamental assumption that knowledge is incomplete allows different sources of knowledge to be smoothly integrated, by simply adding together the corresponding sets of formulae in an incremental fashion.

4 From model- to proof-theory

Is it possible to recast in proof-theoretic terms a model of IR originally designed along model-theoretic guidelines, and viceversa? Is it worthwhile? An answer to the latter question is implicit in our discussion of the "berry-picking" advantages of the model-theoretic approach and of the "exogenous knowledge" advantages of the proof-theoretic one: one might want to embody in one's model the intuitions coming from the model-theoretic semantics of a given logic (e.g. the "imaging" principle exploited in [3]) and, at the same time, want to incorporate exogenous knowledge in the model. The former question then becomes crucial. It should be clear that the first option (i.e. model → proof) is possible, while the latter (i.e. proof → model) is not, the reason being that total knowledge is just a particular case of partial knowledge, but not vice-versa; a situation in which the knowledge of the domain is only partial is far more complex from the reasoning viewpoint, and this is well reflected in the smaller computational complexity of model checking with respect to theorem proving[6].

In the case of DBs, the feasibility of the "model → proof" option is well shown by Reiter [14], who describes a mapping from an interpretation I of a first order language to a first order theory Γ such that I and Γ provide model-theoretic and proof-theoretic characterisations, respectively, of the same DB. Reiter's move is well-known in logic (although the relationship was apparently not noticed by Reiter himself), as it is an instance of what is called a *standard translation*. In general, a standard translation may be seen as the representation of the model theory of a logic $\mathcal{L}$ in the language (hence, in the proof theory) of a logic $\mathcal{L}' \neq \mathcal{L}$. In the IR literature, a mapping conceptually similar to Reiter's (again, the relationship with standard translation, and with Reiter's work, was not noticed by the authors) is present in [1,18] and [22], each dealing with recasting the **C2**-based "imaging" models of [2-4] in terms of a probabilistic logic. As shown in [14], in order for these mappings to be faithful, it is necessary to introduce various axioms whose aim is to restrict the number of satisfying interpretations of the resulting theory to just one, i.e. the interpretation I from which the whole process began. Similarly to the Reiter case, [22] introduces the following (1) domain closure axioms (saying that the only existing individuals are those referred to from within the DB), (2-3) unique names axioms (saying that different individual constants refer to different individuals), and (4) completion axioms (saying that the only individuals that enjoy a given property are those for which this property is explicitly predicated):

$$Term(t_1) \wedge \ldots \wedge Term(t_n) \wedge Doc(d_1) \wedge \ldots \wedge Doc(d_m)$$
$$\forall x.[x = t_1 \vee \ldots \vee x = t_n \vee x = d_1 \vee \ldots \vee x = d_m] \tag{1}$$
$$t_1 \neq t_2 \wedge t_1 \neq t_3 \wedge \ldots \wedge t_{n-1} \neq t_n \tag{2}$$
$$d_1 \neq d_2 \wedge d_1 \neq d_3 \wedge \ldots \wedge d_{m-1} \neq d_m \tag{3}$$
$$\forall x. \neg (Document(x) \wedge Term(x)) \tag{4}$$

Interesting to our purposes is to note that by removing (or "typing") one or more of these classes of axioms from the theory, one may let exogenous knowledge in. For instance, typing our domain closure axioms means substituting (1) with (5)

---

[6] This is basically the same difference between (a) a problem in P and (b) one in NP, as these may be characterized as (a) one in which a solution may be found polynomially, and (b) one in which a candidate solution may be checked polynomially.

and/or (6):

$$\forall x. Doc(x) \supset (x = d_1 \vee \ldots \vee x = d_m) \qquad (5)$$
$$\forall x. Term(x) \supset (x = t_1 \vee \ldots \vee x = t_n) \qquad (6)$$

which would allow other non-term and non-document entities (i.e. authors) to be talked about, thus enabling exogenous knowledge to be plugged in.

5 Concluding remarks

In this paper we have elaborated on one of the findings of [23], arguing that the distinction between total-knowledge and partial-knowledge models of IR may more fruitfully be interpreted in terms of Levesque's notion of vividness and Reiter's distinction between the model-theoretic and the proof-theoretic models of DBs. This finding has several implications, especially for the possibility of incorporating knowledge originating from different sources into IR systems, a necessity rather than a possibility in advanced information seeking environments such as multimedia document retrieval systems.

Quite independently of the practical impact on these advanced applications, we think that the present findings contribute in shedding light on some of the current theorizing on IR. To quote Robertson, we need to spell out the assumptions that underlie systems and models "not because mathematics *per se* is necessarily a Good Thing, but because the setting up of a mathematical model generally presupposes a careful formal analysis of the problem and specification of the assumptions, and explicit formulation of the way in which the model depends on the assumptions. (...) It is only the formalization of the assumptions and their consequences that will enable us to develop better theories." [15, page 128]

References

1. F. Crestani and T. Rölleke. Issues in the implementation of general imaging on top of Probabilistic Datalog. In M. Lalmas, editor, *Proceedings of the 1st International Workshop on Logic and Uncertainty in Information Retrieval*, Glasgow, UK, 1995.
2. F. Crestani, F. Sebastiani, and C. J. van Rijsbergen. Imaging and information retrieval: Variations on a theme. In F. Crestani and M. Lalmas, editors, *Proceedings of the 2nd International Workshop on Logic and Uncertainty in Information Retrieval*, pages 48–49, Glasgow, UK, 1996.
3. F. Crestani and C. J. van Rijsbergen. Information retrieval by logical imaging. *Journal of Documentation*, 51:3–17, 1995.
4. F. Crestani and C. J. van Rijsbergen. A study of probability kinematics in information retrieval. *ACM Transactions on Information Systems*, 16(3), 1998. Forthcoming.
5. N. Fuhr. Probabilistic Datalog: a logic for powerful retrieval methods. In *Proceedings of SIGIR-95, 18th ACM International Conference on Research and Development in Information Retrieval*, pages 282–290, Seattle, US, 1995.
6. H. J. Levesque. Making believers out of computers. *Artificial Intelligence*, 30:81–108, 1986.

7. H. J. Levesque. Logic and the complexity of reasoning. *Journal of Philosophical Logic*, 17:355–389, 1988.
8. D. K. Lewis. Probabilities of conditionals and conditional probabilities. *The Philosophical Review*, 85:297–315, 1976.
9. W. Łukaszewicz. *Nonmonotonic reasoning: formalization of commonsense reasoning*. Ellis Horwood, Chichester, UK, 1990.
10. C. Meghini, F. Sebastiani, U. Straccia, and C. Thanos. A model of information retrieval based on a terminological logic. In *Proceedings of SIGIR-93, 16th ACM International Conference on Research and Development in Information Retrieval*, pages 298–307, Pittsburgh, US, 1993.
11. C. Meghini and U. Straccia. A relevance description logic for information retrieval. In *Proceedings of SIGIR-96, 19th ACM International Conference on Research and Development in Information Retrieval*, pages 197–205, Zürich, CH, 1996.
12. J.-Y. Nie. An information retrieval model based on modal logic. *Information Processing and Management*, 25:477–491, 1989.
13. J.-Y. Nie. Towards a probabilistic modal logic for semantic-based information retrieval. In *Proceedings of SIGIR-92, 15th ACM International Conference on Research and Development in Information Retrieval*, pages 140–151, Kobenhavn, DK, 1992.
14. R. Reiter. Towards a logical reconstruction of relational database theory. In M. L. Brodie, J. Mylopoulos, and J. W. Schmidt, editors, *On conceptual modelling*, pages 191–233. Springer, Heidelberg, DE, 1984.
15. S. E. Robertson. Theories and models in information retrieval. *Journal of Documentation*, 33:126–148, 1977.
16. S. E. Robertson, M. Maron, and W. S. Cooper. Probability of relevance: a unification of two competing models for document retrieval. *Information technology: research and development*, 1:1–21, 1982.
17. S. E. Robertson and K. Sparck Jones. Relevance weighting of search terms. *Journal of the American Society for Information Science*, 27:129–146, 1976.
18. T. Rölleke. Does Probabilistic Datalog meet the requirements of imaging? In *Proceedings of SIGIR-95, 18th ACM International Conference on Research and Development in Information Retrieval*, page 374, Seattle, US, 1995.
19. G. Salton and C. Buckley. Term-weighting approaches in automatic text retrieval. *Information Processing and Management*, 24:513–523, 1988.
20. G. Salton, E. A. Fox, and H. Wu. Extended Boolean information retrieval. *Communications of the ACM*, 26(12):1022–1036, 1983.
21. F. Sebastiani. A probabilistic terminological logic for modelling information retrieval. In *Proceedings of SIGIR-94, 17th ACM International Conference on Research and Development in Information Retrieval*, pages 122–130, Dublin, IE, 1994.
22. F. Sebastiani. Information retrieval, imaging and probabilistic logic. *Computers and Artificial Intelligence*, 17(1):35–50, 1998.
23. F. Sebastiani. On the role of logic in information retrieval. *Information Processing and Management*, 34(1):1–18, 1998.
24. R. C. Stalnaker and R. H. Thomason. A semantical analysis of conditional logic. *Theoria*, 36:23–42, 1970.
25. C. J. van Rijsbergen. A non-classical logic for information retrieval. *The Computer Journal*, 29:481–485, 1986.
26. S. M. Wong and Y. Yao. On modeling information retrieval with probabilistic inference. *ACM Transactions on Information Systems*, 13(1):38–68, 1995.

Towards a Theoretical Foundation for Cooperating Knowledge Based Systems

S M Deen and C A Johnson

Computer Science Department, University of Keele, Staffs, ST5 5BG, England

Abstract. A theoretical grounding is provided for a cooperating knowledge based systems architecture, which is based upon cooperation blocks and cooperation block hierarchies. The architecture describes the requirements for task decomposition, negotiation, cooperation and coordination, fault tolerance and recoverability. A description of behaviour is given in terms of state transition diagrams.

1 Introduction

In recent years agent technology has become an important area of research and development in distributed applications. Cooperating Knowledge Based Systems (CKBS) is a subarea in which each autonomous knowledge based system, known as an agent, cooperates (or even competes) to solve tasks in a distributed environment. As such, a CKBS is close to a multi-agent system (MAS) of distributed AI (DAI) [5], except that whereas MAS/DAI draws its concepts from AI, CKBS uses a more open approach with ideas drawn from the experience and requirements of real world distributed applications, where effectiveness, performance, reliability and usability are of paramount importance.

In [1,2] we described an architectural framework for CKBS applications based upon the concept of a cooperation block. This framework, although developed independently, is very close to the IMS/HMS reference model [4,6] for holonic manufacturing systems, provided that an atomic holon is interpreted as a CKBS agent, and a cooperation domain as a CKBS cooperation block. Both of these frameworks are somewhat informal, and hence the purpose of the current paper is to provide them with a precise and rigorous grounding, thus yielding a firm theoretical foundation for the implementation and study of CKBS and HMS systems.

We first give an overview of our architecture. In order to process a request for task execution, a coordinator agent forms a *cooperation block*, this being a temporary and dynamic alliance between agents allied to the processing of the given task request. Within the block, negotiation firstly involves the decomposition of the task into (possibly interdependent) subtasks and the allocation of these subtasks to agents (cohorts) with the suitable skill to carry out (or coordinate) subtask execution. Following this allocation, a further negotiation phase attempts to generate an execution plan which determines how the cohorts will coordinate their individual executions in order to ensure that the relevant interdependencies are satisfied.

Any cohort A may in turn form a lower-level cooperation block with other agents for the execution of a subtask. In this case agent A acts as a cohort in the upper-level block and as the coordinator of the lower-level block. Cooperation blocks thus form hierarchies which parallel the hierarchy of task decompositions.

The operation of cooperation blocks and their hierarchies should be tolerant to failure, with failures being handled locally as far as is possible, and with recovery mechanisms that ensure that such failures do not leave the system in an unacceptable state. In this respect, the behaviour of a cooperation block hierarchy is similar to that of a holon [4,6].

2 Agents

As in [1], we assume that an agent is a large grain entity having a compulsory software component and an optional hardware component. We assume that agents are cooperative, in the sense that they participate in joint task processing, but that they are autonomous, in the sense that agents decide independently which joint tasks to participate in, and negotiate their own involvement in such task processing.

Agents possess skills, these skills being represented by their membership in *skill classes*. For each *task class* there are two skill classes: one for processing, and one for coordinating tasks in the task class. Each skill class may have many agents (called twins) offering that same skill. In particular, if one twin breaks down, then another twin can replace it. Twins in a given class may be supervised by a class agent called the (skill-class's) *minder* [3].

There is a very wide literature surrounding agents, a reasonable starting point being [5].

3 Tasks

3.1 Task schemata and requests

We assume that a finite number of task classes are known to the system, and that the general description of a task class is given by a *task schema* describing the task procedure and the task parameters.

The task procedure itself does not play a major role in what follows. We assume that agents with the appropriate skill know how to process (or coordinate) the task procedure, and moreover are able to report whether the procedure was carried out successfully.

A (*task*) *parameter* is any value associated with the execution of the task procedure which is externally visible (i.e. public). Any parameter value can in theory be output from one task, and input into another. Two obvious parameters are *start-time* and *end-time*. A pre/post condition is a Boolean condition over the task parameters.

A *task request* (for a particular schema) consists of the task schema, values for some, all or none of the task parameters, and a set of pre/post conditions. Notice that the task request may not include full details of the actual task itself (e.g., input values), as these may not be available until the start of task execution.

The resulting task execution is said to be an *instance* of the task request, and must clearly satisfy the pre-conditions if execution is to commence, and the post-conditions if the instance is to be regarded as successful.

3.2 Task decomposition

A task decomposition intuitively breaks a task into subtasks. Note however that an agent might wish to decompose a task prior to execution (for example during consideration of the task proposal, or during pre-execution planning), thus it is actually the task *request* that is to be decomposed. In general the subtasks within a decomposition will be interdependent. Such interdependencies are expressed by *dependency rules*, these being Boolean conditions defined on the task parameters of a set of task requests. A *decomposition* $\mathcal{D}_t$ of task request t thus consists of
(i) a set of task requests $\{t_i \mid i \leq n\}$, (i.e. t_i are the subtasks of t), and
(ii) a set of dependency rules over $\{t_i \mid i \leq n\}$.

The decomposition should *satisfy* the task request t in that successful instances of the task requests t_i satisfying the dependency rules should result in the successful execution of an instance of t.

We expect that dependency rules capture only the *essential* (i.e. logical) interdependencies. A decomposition $\mathcal{D}_t$ can thus be thought of as a logical specification for accomplishing the given task (request) t. It does not prescribe how the individual subtasks are to be carried out so as to satisfy the dependency rules: such details are contained in the cooperation plan (cf., Section 4.2).

We generally expect that decompositions would be derived from a set of pre-existing decompositions.

4 Cooperation

Cooperation, in the present context, is the process by which the agents in a cooperation block accomplish a task, through all its processing stages, using negotiation and coordination as appropriate. These processing stages include decomposition, planning, scheduling and execution.

4.1 Cooperation blocks

A *cooperation block* $\mathcal{CB}$ is a temporary and dynamic alliance between agents allied to the processing of a specific task request. Each cooperation block has a coordinator agent $coord(\mathcal{CB})$, which is (at least initially) the agent allocated the task request. Agents may join the cooperation block subject to the consent of the coordinator, and may leave the block if they have no uncompleted contract with the block. We can identify the following phases and events in the life of a cooperation block:
(i) cooperation block creation and pre-execution (static) negotiation,

(ii) invocation (of the underlying task),
(iii) (dynamic) negotiation,
(iv) execution,
(v) log results and commit,
(vi) cooperation block destruction.

Cooperation blocks will form hierarchies, and a cooperation block persists through (i) - (vi) above unless it is terminated by its parent. Creation of a child block occurs as a result of a proposal (see Section 4.2.2 below) within the parent block. Static/dynamic negotiation may be absent (and in the case of a trivial cooperation block (see Section 4.3 below) both would be absent). The pattern of negotiation and execution may be iterated in response to failure, and later phases may be absent if negotiation fails. Negotiation within a block is referred to as *internal*, whilst negotiation between the block and its parent block (via the child block's coordinator) is referred to as *external* (to the child). External negotiation might take place at any point as a result of failure. These details are elaborated in the remaining sections.

During the life of the cooperation block its underlying task may be amended as a result of negotiation between the block and its parent block (see Sections 5/6), whence a cooperation block CB whose currently assigned task (request) is t may be written as CB_t.

4.2 Negotiation and coordination

Negotiation, in the present context, is the process whereby the agents in a cooperation block CB_t arrive at a decomposition, a plan and a schedule for the task request t. This negotiation is internal to CB_t. In contrast we shall define coordination as the process whereby the executions of subtasks by different agents in CB_t are synchronised so as to satisfy the dependency rules associated with the current decomposition and to prevent undue delays and deadlocks. In this sense coordination is a system property, rather than an activity of the coordinator as such.

The first phase in negotiation is for $coord(CB_t)$ to invite, and subsequently admit, a set of agents to participate in the block. Negotiation then proceeds as follows.

4.2.1 Decomposition. A decomposition $\mathcal{D}_t$ is chosen for t. Each subtask request t_i in $\mathcal{D}_t$ is allocated to an agent A_i in CB_t.

In this paper it is not our purpose to describe methods for decomposition (or planning/scheduling), thus $\mathcal{D}_t$ might be chosen either unilaterally by $coord(CB_t)$, or by a subset of those agents in CB_t. The allocation may involve any appropriate negotiation strategy. In this respect we note that the contract net protocol [8] in its basic form is probably inappropriate in view of the interdependencies between subtasks.

4.2.2 Planning. Each agent A_i may decompose its allocated subtask t_i still further. These further decompositions are then used to create, via negotiation, a *cooperation plan* for $\mathcal{CB}_t$ consisting of a (finite) set of *action elements*. An action element request a_s consists of a task request s together with a set of input/output rules. An input rule specifies what inputs the action element expects from other action elements in $\mathcal{CB}_t$ and from $coord(\mathcal{CB}_t)$ before processing should start. Output rules dictate what data is output from the action element, and the conditions under which this data is sent to other action elements in $\mathcal{CB}_t$ and to $coord(\mathcal{CB}_t)$. Post-condition checking can be thought of as an output rule, since post-condition failure results in an error message being sent to the coordinator (see Sections 5/6). In order to avoid deadlock, we must clearly ensure that the dependency relationship between action elements defined by the input/output rules is not cyclic.

The proposal of an action element a_s in $\mathcal{CB}_t$ results in the creation of a child cooperation block of $\mathcal{CB}_t$ for the processing of the underlying task s. Each such action element in $\mathcal{CB}_t$'s plan should be a blackbox *as far as the parent block $\mathcal{CB}_t$ is concerned*.

The execution of an action element consists of a pre-condition phase (in which the input rules and pre-conditions are checked), task processing (which terminates when the task's lower-level cooperation block commits), a post-condition phase (in which the output rules are fired, output messages are logged and sent), and finally acknowledgements are received from recipients, and the action element terminates (see Section 6, Figures 1-3).

Thus a cooperation plan can be thought of as a network of lower-level task requests, together with details as to how these lower-level task requests "fit together". Viewed another way, it defines how the agents in the cooperation block intend to cooperate and coordinate their activities in an attempt to achieve both their respective subtasks and the given dependency rules. Thus clearly the plan should satisfy the task request t and the chosen decomposition $\mathcal{D}_t$, in that successful execution of the plan should result in the execution of successful instances of the subtasks in $\mathcal{D}_t$ satisfying the dependency rules (cf., Section 3.2).

4.2.3 Scheduling. Finally a *schedule* is formed by adding timing constraints to some, all or none of the action elements within the cooperation plan.

4.3 Cooperation block hierarchies

In accepting a subtask t_i in $\mathcal{D}_t$, an agent A_i is also implicitly accepting the role of coordinating (within a lower-level cooperation block) each action element a_s within the breakdown of t_i. However, if A_i has the required skill, then A_i might process a_s itself, whence any decomposition, planning and scheduling relating to a_s are internal to A_i. We regard this as the creation of a *trivial* cooperation block.

A *cooperation block hierarchy* is a finite non-empty tree of cooperation blocks. The root block is created by a "user agent", acting on behalf of a user as a result of a user request. If $\mathcal{CB}_t$ is a non-trivial block in such a hierarchy and a_s is an action element (in which s has not yet committed) in the current plan of $\mathcal{CB}_t$, then CB_t has a child node of the form CB_s (and these are the only child nodes of CB_t). CB_t is said to be the *parent* of CB_s. $coord(CB_s)$ is a *cohort* in CB_t, and (amongst other things) is responsible for performing the following on behalf of a_s:

(i) receiving inputs from other action elements in CB_t and from $coord(CB_t)$, checking the input rules and pre-conditions in a_s, and directing the inputs to the relevant cohorts in CB_s,

(ii) collecting output data from cohorts in CB_s, firing the output rules, logging outputs, sending outputs to (and receiving acknowledgements from) the relevant action elements in CB_t and $coord(CB_t)$, and

(iii) negotiation with CB_t on behalf of CB_s, in response to failures in a_s and proposals from CB_t.

During its existence, the child blocks of a given block may change (as may the agents participating in the block). In particular, a cooperation block may change from trivial to non-trivial, and vice versa. This dynamism is necessary if autonomy, in this case fault tolerance, is to be achieved.

5 Failure and recovery

5.1 Failure

Let a_s be an action element in CB_t, then $coord(CB_s)$ can issue a *failure message* to $coord(CB_t)$. Such a failure message would typically contain information about the reasons for failure. Given such a message, the agents in CB_t attempt to negotiate (internally within CB_t) an appropriate recovery and amendment to their plan/schedule so as to enable t to be completed (on time).

Only if this internal negotiation is unsuccessful, does $coord(CB_t)$ report a failure to the coordinator of CB_t's parent block. If $coord(CB_t)$ is a user agent (cf., Section 4.3) then $coord(CB_t)$ would have to report the failure to the user who would negotiate with $coord(CB_t)$ either an amendment (such as a new deadline), or tidy-up (using rollback and/or abort as described below). Thus we see that failures are handled as locally as possible.

Notice that the original failure in a_s might either have been internal to CB_s (such as a resource failure at some cohort in CB_s), or external to CB_s (such as the failure to receive an essential input).

If the coordinator agent $coord(CB_s)$ itself fails, then we assume that the skill minder (cf., Section 2) is employed to replace the agent with a twin (the skill in question being that of coordinating s).

Failure to receive an essential input obviously causes the recipient to delay the start of its execution. Such a failure should result in a failure message being sent to the coordinator as described above, although in practice a query message might be first directed to the sender. We assume that the sender adopts some protocol for resending messages until either an acknowledgement arrives or a timeout occurs (the latter case resulting in a failure message).

The response to the failure message thus consists of (i) the recovery of the failed action elements in the old plan, and (ii) the formation, by negotiation, of the amended plan/schedule. These issues are discussed in the following two sections respectively.

5.2 Recovery

If a_s is an action element in the current plan of $\mathcal{CB}_t$, then $coord(\mathcal{CB}_t)$ can instruct $coord(\mathcal{CB}_s)$ to either rollback, abort, or amend the execution of a_s. We assume in addition, that such instructions are first proposed by $coord(\mathcal{CB}_t)$ to $\mathcal{CB}_s$ (via $coord(\mathcal{CB}_s)$), and that $\mathcal{CB}_s$ is able to decide if such a proposal is feasible.

5.2.1 Rollback means to undo changes made to-date. If $coord(\mathcal{CB}_s)$ receives a rollback(a_s) instruction from $coord(\mathcal{CB}_t)$, then this requires $coord(\mathcal{CB}_s)$ to send either rollback or abort messages to the action elements in $\mathcal{CB}_s$.

Notice that rollback is not an issue if it occurs prior to invocation, in which case rollback and abort (below) are one and the same. Note also that rollback is not possible if failure occurs once task processing (i.e. $\mathcal{CB}_s$) has committed.

5.2.2 Aborting an action element means to cease processing at the current position. The action element's underlying cooperation block itself takes no recovery action. For example if we are discarding an entire physical part in a manufacturing process, then the state of an action element's work on that part is irrelevant, whence under such conditions the inability to rollback is not important.

More generally abort is employed if the coordinator is itself able to resolve the rollback issue, or is able to plan further action elements which will compensate for the abort. Such compensating actions may only be possible via human intervention, which we regard as taking place via "participant agents". Needless to say abort simply cascades down the cooperation block hierarchy. In particular, proposed aborts are not crucial, since abort is always possible by cascading.

5.2.3 Amend. On the other hand, if the coordinator still wishes the work to be completed and/or rollback/abort are not possible, then we must rollforward. This involves $coord(\mathcal{CB}_t)$ and $\mathcal{CB}_s$ negotiating an amendment (of say the task parameters, input and output rules and timing constraints), possibly with the help of a skill-minder (cf., Section 2).

5.2.4 Commit and termination. An action element whose underlying task (i.e. lower-level cooperation block) has committed cannot be rolled back. It may be possible to amend the output rules, and abort may still be a viable possibility (say in response to post-condition failure). An action element that has terminated cannot be rolled back, aborted or amended.

5.3 Dynamic negotiation, planning and rescheduling

A *rescheduling* of a cooperation plan involves assigning new timing constraints to those action elements that have not yet terminated. Rescheduling clearly cascades down the cooperation block hierarchy.

Replanning is the development of an amended cooperation plan. This involves (i) deciding whether to rollback/abort/amend executing action elements from the old plan that have not reported failure. (We would normally expect that such action elements would not be rolled back or amended if at all possible, although abort might be applied as part of a larger scale abort), (ii) deciding whether to discard (i.e. abort) action elements from the old plan which had not yet been invoked, or whether to include them (possibly amended) into the amended plan, and (iii) the creation of new action elements.

The amended plan should be *consistent* with the old plan in that it, together with the completed (recovered) portion of the old plan should satisfy a decomposition of the task (as in Sections 4.2.2 and 3.2). Some of the new action elements might consist of "complementary actions" to compensate for the inability to complete previous action elements as originally specified. Replanning clearly requires rescheduling.

As in Sections 4.2.2 and 5.2, proposals for new action elements are considered by their relevant lower-level blocks. Only if there is unanimous acceptance (to the rollback/abort/amend/create proposals) can the amended plan be accepted as a whole, in which case the coordinator confirms its acceptance of the action elements to the cohorts.

6 Cooperation block/action element life cycle

Figures 1-3 describe the combined life cycle of an action element $a = a_s$ and its underlying cooperation block $\mathcal{CB} = \mathcal{CB}_s$.

Note that amend/abort/rollback instructions (and the corresponding proposals) can arise as a result of the negotiation following either a failure within a, or a failure elsewhere in the cooperation block hierarchy. Transitions related to the latter case are omitted in the interests of simplicity.

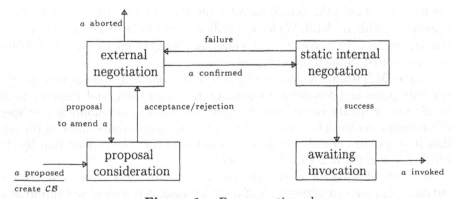

Figure 1: Pre-execution phase

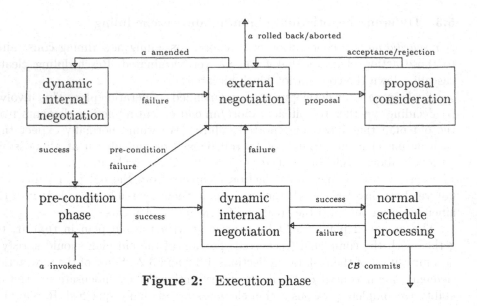

Figure 2: Execution phase

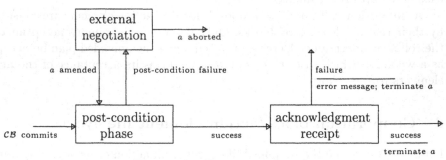

Figure 3: Post-execution phase

7 Conclusions and further research

We have presented a theoretical basis for the cooperation block architecture and behaviour within a CKBS. We have specified the lifecycle of a cooperation block, the requirements for negotiation and planning, and the manner in which failures are propagated through the hierarchy.

In the IMS/HMS reference model [4,6] *autonomy* is defined as the ability to generate plans and schedules, to monitor task execution, and respond to and rectify failure. In the current architecture, this form of autonomy is a property of a cooperation block hierarchy. Indeed this unit is also cooperative in the sense that it cooperates (via the top-level coordinator) with the cooperation block of which it is a child. It is thus *holonic* [4,6].

In terms of providing a solid theoretical basis for the architecture, the most outstanding issues concern proofs of completeness, correctness and termination.

Completeness in the current context could be interpreted in a number of ways. For example we might insist that any task (that is input from the user) is successfully completed given sufficient skill availability, time, and a sufficiently low rate of failure. Correctness requires that a task is successfully completed if it is reported as being successfully completed.

Termination and finiteness are also important properties. These are trivial if the top-level user task is given a deadline (since all lower-level blocks must certainly adhere to it or report failure). If no such deadline exists however, various features need attention in order to avoid termination problems, in particular dynamic behaviour, and the growth of the cooperation block hierarchy.

In terms of failure, we also expect that the top-level user task should be completed successfully on time, or that a failure message should be generated to the user - whence the user can either amend the request, or abort/rollback. In either case, the system needs to ensure that all action elements are either committed, aborted, or rolled back, and moreover that aborted elements satisfy an appropriate property of recoverability.

Without a precise definition of the architecture and behaviour, such proofs would certainly be impossible. We intend to pursue these issues in a sequel.

Acknowledgement. This research was partially supported by the European Union and by the Royal Society. Thanks are also due to Martyn Fletcher, Mike Brough, Peter Granby and three anonymous referees for their helpful comments.

References

1. S M Deen, An architectural framework for CKBS applications, IEEE Transactions on Knowledge and Data Engineering, **8** (1996), 663-671
2. S M Deen, A database perspective to a cooperation environment, in P Kanzia and M Klusch (eds.), Proceedings of CIA'97, (Springer, 1997), 19-41
3. S M Deen, A fault tolerant cooperative distributed system, in R Wagner (ed.), IEEE DEXA Workshop, Vienna (1998)
4. M Fletcher, A critique of holonic manufacturing systems: Architectural requirements and standards, Computer Science Department, Keele University (1998)
5. M Huhns and M Singh, Readings in Agents, Morgan Kaufmann (1998)
6. The IMS (Intelligent Manufacturing Systems) is an international programme with the participation of major industries, universities and research institutes world-wide. It has several projects, one of which is the Holonic Manufacturing Systems (HMS) programme for high-variety low-volume manufacturing in a largely un-manned environment, and of which Keele is a partner
7. F P Maturana, MetaMorph: An Adaptive Multi-Agent Architecture for Advanced Manufacturing Systems, PhD thesis, Department of Mechanical Engineering, University of Calgary, Canada, 1997
8. R G Smith, The contract net protocol: High level communication and control in a distributed problem solver, IEEE Transactions on Computers, **C-29**, no. 12 (1980), 1104-1113

CINDI: A System for Cataloguing, Searching, and Annotating Electronic Documents in Digital Libraries

Bipin C. Desai, Rajjan Shinghal, Nader Shyan, and Youquan Zhou

Department of Computer Science,
Concordia University,
1455 de Maisonneuve Blvd West,
Montréal,
CANADA H3G 1M8
Email contact: bcdesaics.concordia.ca
http://www.cs.concordia.ca/~faculty/bcdesai

Abstract. This paper describes a system called CINDI for cataloguing, searching, and annotating electronic documents in a digital library,
the library being distributed over a computer communication network.
A document is catalogued both on its syntactic and semantic content.
This makes later searching for the document easier and more precise.
On accessing a document, a reader can make annotation about it. Such
annotations are recorded in the semantic header and are accessible to
future searchers. Graphical user interfaces are provided for each of cataloguing, searching, and annotating. The user of CINDI is helped by an
expert system that mimics the basic expertise of professional librarians.

1 Introduction

The electronic documents distributed over a computer communication network
in a digital library must be catalogued properly so *searchers* can easily locate
them. Many systems (Koster, 1994; Mauldin, 1995; Pinkerton, 1994; Kahle, 1991)
catalogue a document on words selected from it. A program (known in the
literature as a *robot*, *worm*, *spider*, or *crawler*) traverses the network accessing
the documents to be catalogued. Such a program, of course, adds to the traffic on
the network. A number of systems use a document's semantics to catalogue it, for
example, CORE (Cromwell, 1994), MARC (Petersen and Molholt, 1990) MLC
(Horny, 1986), and TEI (Gaynor 1994). These systems can be used optimally
only by professional cataloguers, who are usually expensive.

In this paper, we describe a system called CINDI (Concordia INdexing and
DIscovery System), for cataloguing, searching and annotating electronic documents in a distributed digital library. A professional cataloguer is not needed,
since the cataloguing is done by the *provider* of the document, as it is she (we are
using *she* in a generic sense for both males and females) who knows her document
best. A searcher can then locate and access the document. After accessing, the

searcher may annotate it for the convenience of those who may want to access the document later. CINDI provides a graphical user interface (GUI) for each of cataloguing, searching and annotating. The overall structure of CINDI is shown in Figure 1. The details of CINDI's cataloguing, searching, and annotating are given, respectively, in Sections 2, 3, and 4. Concluding remarks are in Section 5.

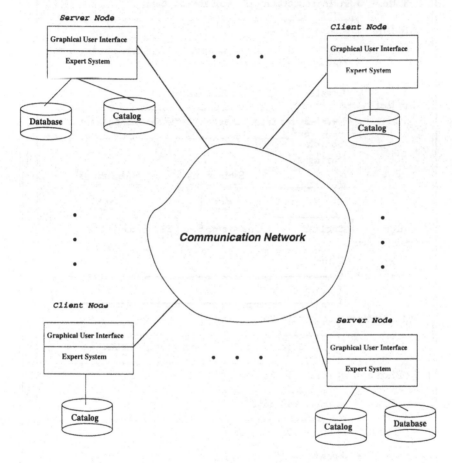

Fig. 1. Overall structure of CINDI.

2 Cataloguing

When a person puts a document on the net, she is the one who can best describe its syntactic and semantic contents. Accordingly, she fills in the slots of a meta data structure called the *semantic header* (Desai, 1997), part of whose GUI is shown in Figure 2; space restrictions prevent us from showing the full semantic header. Since the semantic header is designed to help searchers later looking

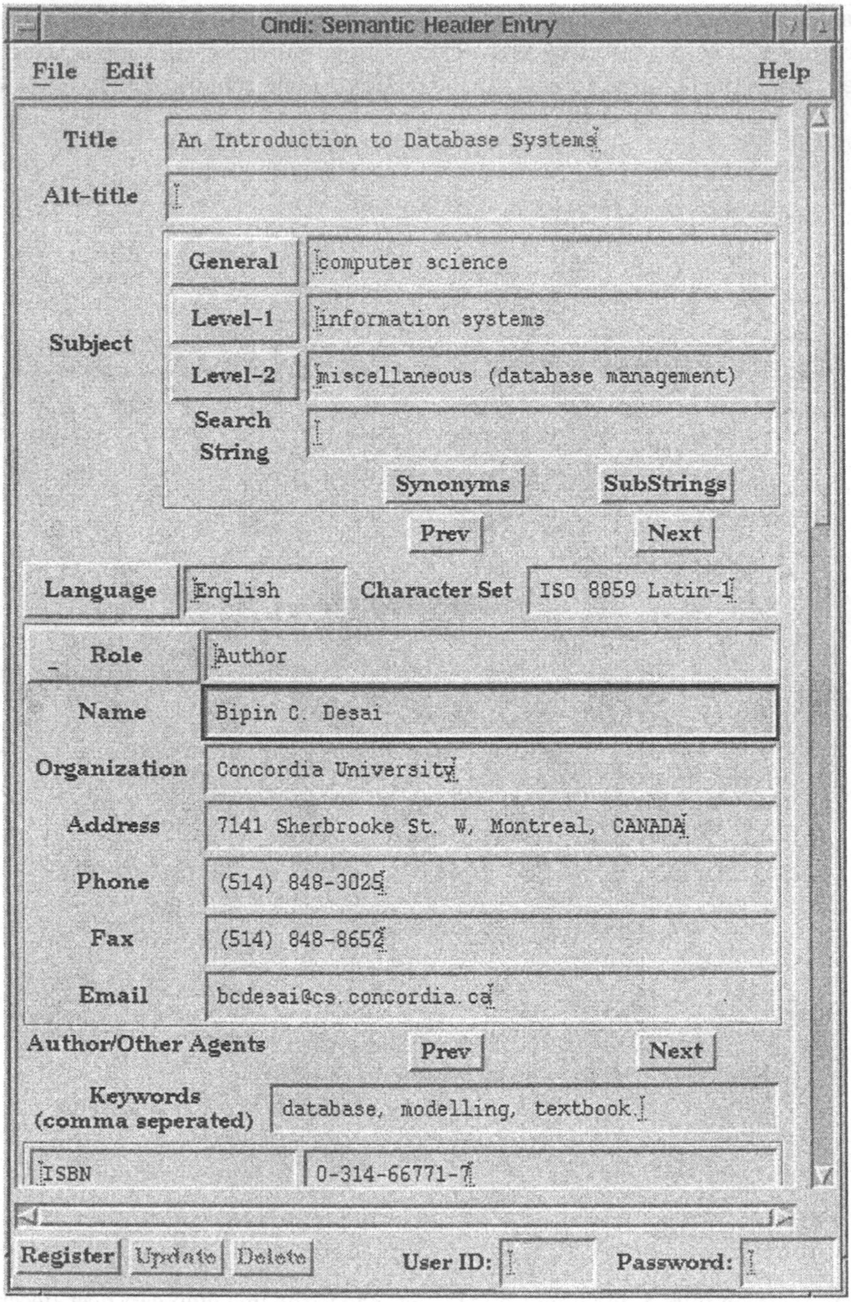

Fig. 2. Part of the semantic header GUI for cataloguing.

for the document, its slots contain those values that are most often used by searchers. An expert system—whose details are described by Chander, Desai, Shinghal, and Radhakrishnan (1997) and Desai and Shinghal (1996a)—mimics the expertise of a cataloguing librarian as it guides the provider in filling the slots of the semantic header. The semantic header has the following slots:

1. The **Title** of the document and its **Alternate–title**, if any.
2. The **Subject** area to which the document belongs. The subject areas are derived from the Library of Congress Subject Headings. CINDI maintains a database containing subject area hierarchies at three levels; for instance, game playing is a sub-area of artificial intelligence, which in turn is a sub-area of computer science. Thus computer science is at zero (or general) level, artificial intelligence at level-1, and game playing at level-2.

   When the provider wants to enter the subject area of the document being catalogued, CINDI offers her with a list of the possible general level subjects. She selects one subject, say computer science. The expert system then employs the stored subject area hierarchies to guide her in selecting first a level-1 subject and then a level-2 subject. If the provider changes the general level subject, then the old level-1 and level-2 subjects are erased, and she can select new level-1 and level-2 subjects. The provider is restricted to entering words from the control terminology standard in library practice. The provider can click on the Synonyms button to map her terminology, perhaps informal, to the control terminology.

   If the provider does not know the full name of the subject area, she can enter the partial name she knows and CINDI will help her find the full name. Suppose the provider enters 'com' and then clicks the SubStrings button in the GUI of the semantic header. A window displays the number of items that match 'com' at different subject levels. If the provider clicks on the General button, another window displays the list of general level subjects matching 'com'. The item selected from the list fills the slot for the general level subject, its level-1 and level-2 subjects being set to empty. Proceeding similarly, the provider fills the slots for the level-1 and level-2 subjects.

   A document may belong to more than one subject area. After entering one value in the subject slot, if the provider wants to enter another value, she clicks on the **Next** button. She then enters another value in the subject slot. If she want to modify the previous entry, he clicks on the **Prev** button and then enters the modified value. Corresponding Next and Prev buttons are similarly provided for all slots that can have multi-values.
3. The language of the document: English, French, Spanish, etc.
4. The characters used in the document: Latin, Cyrillic, Greek, etc.
5. The role of the person associated with the document, for instance, author, editor, and compiler. Then the provider enters the person's name, postal address, telephone number, fax number, and email address. Since this is a multi-valued slot (there can be more than one author), appropriate Prev and Next buttons are available.
6. One or more keywords for the document.

7. Identifiers for the document, for example a URL (Universal Resource Locator). This is a multi-valued slot (in case the document is at more than one node of a distributed virtual library or is available in more than one format) and appropriate Prev and Next buttons are available.
8. The date on which the document was catalogued, and the date on which the document will expire. Moreover, there is information on the version number of the document and whether it supersedes any earlier version.
9. Does the document have a copyright? If the document has a copyright, a later searcher would not be able to down load the document without contacting the author and perhaps paying a fee.
10. The classification of the documents: usual type would be legal status of the document, its level of security or dissemination (general, specialist, adult audience).
11. The nature of the document.
12. The coverage indicates the targeted audience of the document or it may indicate cultural and temporal aspects of the document's contents.
13. If the semantic header pertains to a collection of work, then its components and other related material may be specified in this slot.
14. System Requirements: The hardware and software required to access the document.
15. The Source indicates the documents being referenced by the current document or which were required in its preparation. It could also be the main component for which the current document is an addendum or attachment. The identifier of the source would be URLs, ISBNs, etc.
16. An abstract of the document.
17. Annotations put in by readers of the document.
18. A Provider ID of at least six characters and a password of four to eight characters. More than one semantic header by the same provider can have the same ID and password.
    After the semantic header is completed, the provider registers it with CINDI by clicking on the **Register** button. CINDI then checks to see whether all the essential entries have been made. If any value is missing, CINDI asks the user to make the required entries. Once all the essential entries have been made, the semantic header is registered in the CINDI database.
    Later if the provider wants to update her semantic header, she needs to first supply her ID and password. Other users cannot make any changes in the entries made by the provider since they do not know the provider's ID and password. Other users, however, can make entries in the annotation slot since this slot gives users a forum for discussing the corresponding document. When updating her semantic header, the provider cannot change the contents of the annotation slot. By clicking on the **Delete** button in the GUI of her semantic header, a provider can delete her semantic header in case she wants to withdraw her document from the digital library.

The provider must fill at least the following information in the semantic header: title, general level subject, name of the author, at least one keyword, the date the document is catalogued, and at least one identifier such as an URL, an ISBN, or a FTP address to locate the document. Information in the remaining slots is optional. The name of at least one author is mandatory, or in the case the source is a corporate body, name of the organization is required.

3 Searching

A searcher looking for documents, first looks for the appropriate semantic headers in the CINDI registry. Once the appropriate semantic headers are located (Desai and Shinghal, 1996b), the actual documents are accessed. Since the registry for the semantic header is smaller than the collection of documents, searching becomes faster.

An expert system (Chander, Desai, Shinghal, and Radhakrishnan, 1997), mimicking the expertise of a reference librarian, helps the searcher formulate her query. For instance, if the searcher enters a general level subject, the expert system employs CINDI's stored subject area hierarchies to guide her in selecting level-1 and level-2 subjects. Overall, the searcher may formulate her query employing terms such as document title, author name, subject at different levels, keywords in the document, range of the dates when the document was put in the digital library, and language of the document. Moreover, these query terms can be nested in formulae using the logic operator AND. The graphical search interface is shown in Figure 3.

If the searcher makes a mistake in her query, CINDI issues an appropriate message asking the searcher to make corrections. Once the query is found to be correctly formulated, CINDI transforms it into a database query in reverse postfix. Then the CINDI client process at the searcher's workstation communicates with the nearest CINDI catalogue to determine the appropriate site(s) where the required semantic headers can be found. Subsequently, the client process communicates with the site(s) and retrieves one or more semantic headers.

The result of the search is returned to the searcher's site and displayed in her search GUI. Using the **Prev**and **Next** buttons, the searcher can scroll through the list of semantic headers displayed. To view the semantic header, the searcher clicks on its name in the list. By clicking on the **Access** button, the searcher invokes the Netscape browser to reach the document associated with any of the semantic headers. If the provider of the document has placed no restrictions (some providers, for instance, may ask for a fee to be paid) the searcher is able to access the document.

4 Annotation

The research community depends on peer review of documents submitted for publication. Such reviews are often not published. Nevertheless, comments to the journal editor made by readers of published papers are usually published and are accessible to the community. Many of the documents in a digital library will tend not to be reviewed. It would, however, be beneficial for the new reader of

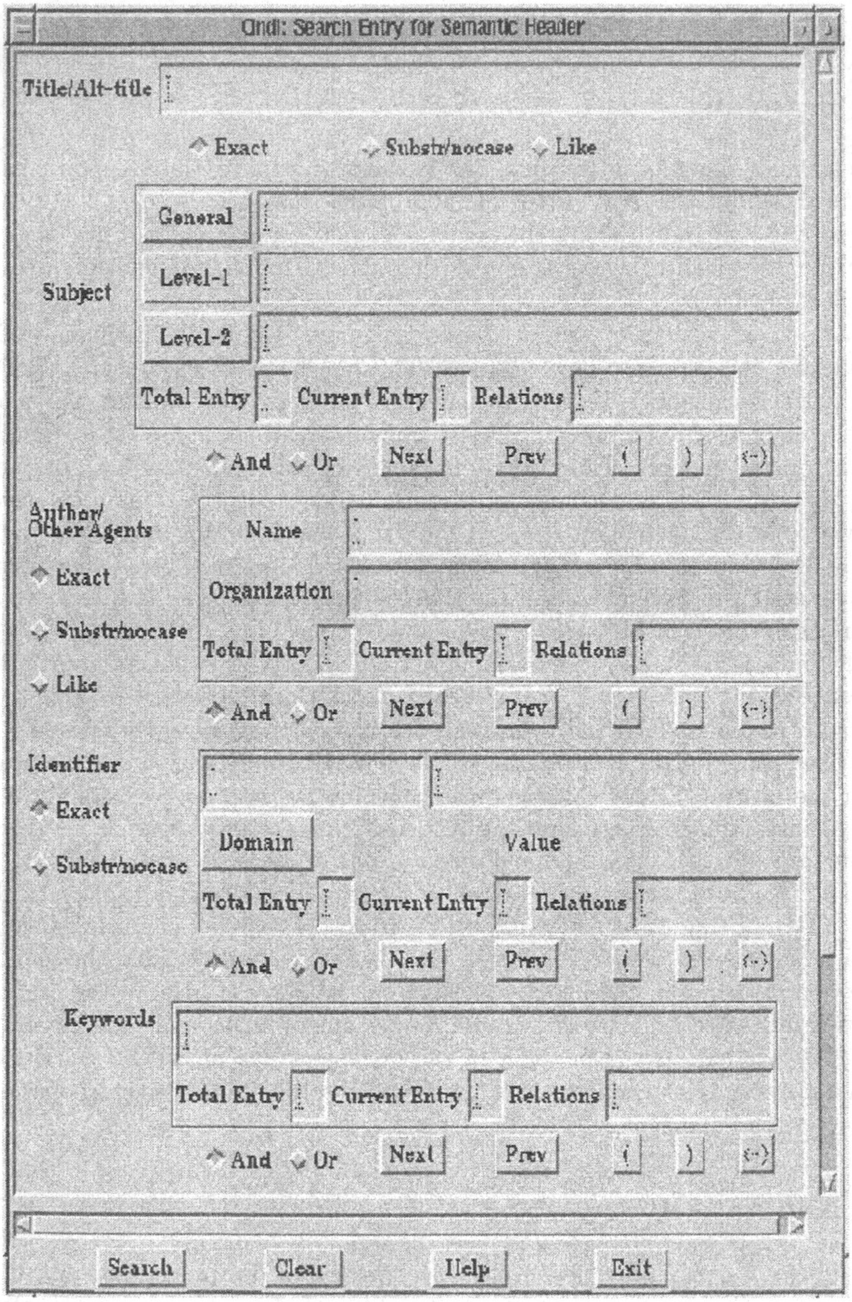

Fig. 3. Graphical interface for searching.

a document to see what past readers have said about it. CINDI allows searchers to add their annotations about a document in the **Annotations** slot of its semantic header. The annotations are stored together with the identity of the person who wrote the comments. The identity of the person includes her full name and email address. The identity must match her profile associated with her login name. Identifying the commenter is aimed at preventing frivolous and libelous annotations.

5 Conclusion

In the CINDI system described in this paper, the provider of a document is the one who catalogues it. Such cataloguing is more reliable than one made by somebody else or the one obtained by scanning the document. By including the document's abstract in the cataloguing information, the provider is able to highlight the nature of the document. The provider uses a GUI to enter her cataloguing information. A GUI is similarly made available to the searcher of documents. Furthermore, a person who reads a document can make annotations available to later readers of the same document.

Acknowledgements

We express our gratitude to the following: Concordia University librarians Carol Coughlin and Lee Harris provided us with the expertise in cataloguing and searching documents. Their expertise was coded in the knowledge base of the expert system, earlier versions of which were developed by Dao Nguyen and Gokul Chander. Seagrams gave us a grant to fund this project.

References

1. Brody, H.: Internet@crossroad. *Technology Review*, 98(4), (1995) pp. 24–31, also at URL
   http://web.mit.edu/afs/athena/org/t/techreview/www/articles/may95/
2. Cromwell, W.: A New Bibliographic Standard, The Core Record. *Library Resources and Technical Services*, 38(4), (1994) pp. 415–424.
3. Chander, P. G., Desai, B. C., Shinghal, R., and Radhakrishnan, T.: An Expert System to Aid Cataloging and Searching Electronic Documents in Digital Libraries. *Expert Systems with Applications*, 12(4), (1997) pp. 405–416.
4. Desai, B. C.: Supporting Discovery in Virtual Libraries. *Journal of the American Society of Information Science*, 48(3), (1997) pp. 190–204.
5. Desai, B. C. and Shinghal, R.: Modeling Expert Search of Virtual/Digital Libraries. In *Poster Proceedings of the Ninth International Symposium on Methodologies for Intelligent Systems (ISMIS'96)* (Oak Ridge National Laboratory, UNC-Charlotte), Zakopane, Poland, (1996a) pp. 41–52.

6. Desai, B. C. and Shinghal, R.: Resource Discovery: Modelling, Cataloging, and Searching. In *Proceeding of the Seventh International Conference and Workshop on Database and Expert Systems Applications (DEXA'96)*(IEEE Press), Zurich, Switzerland, (1996b) pp. 70–75.
7. Gaynor, E.: Cataloging Electronic Texts: The University of Virginia Library Experience. *Library Resources and Technical Services*, 38(4), (1994) pp. 403–413.
8. Horny, K. L.: Minimal–level Cataloging: A Look at the Issues. *Journal of Academic Librarianship*, 11, (1986) pp. 332–334.
9. Kahle, B.: *An Information System for Corporate Users: Wide Area Information Servers*, Thinking Machines Technical Report TMC-199, CA. (1991)
10. Koster, M.: Aliweb: Archie Like Indexing the Web.(1994) URL *http://web.nexor.co.uk/aliweb/doc/aliweb.html*.
11. Mauldin, M. L.: Measuring the Web with Lycos. *Poster Proceeding of the Third International WWW Conference*, Darmstadt, Germany, (1995) pp. 26–29.
12. Petersen, T. and Molholt, P. (eds): *Beyond the Book: Extending MARC for Subject Access*, G. K. Hall, Boston, MA. (1990)
13. Pinkerton, B.: *WebCrawler*, (1994) URL http://webcrawler.cs.washington.edu/WebCrawler/Home.html

Externalization of Human Idea and Problem Description for Automatic Programming

Setsuo Ohsuga and Takumi Aida

Waseda University,
Department of Inf. and Comp. Science
3-4-1 Ohkubo Shinjuku-ku, Tokyo 169-8555, JAPAN

Ways of building a problem model including an object and persons and of specifying programs in this model is discussed. It enables automation of the following programming process. A high-level intelligent system is needed for the purpose. A new modeling scheme named multi-strata modeling is introduced as a key concept to make computer system intelligent. This approach of specifying and generating program was applied to a car electronic system.

1. Introduction

Problems that arise in the future in many areas of human activities are expected to glow very large and complex [GIB94]. Development of information systems to manage these problems becomes more and more difficult. Traditional human-centered method of developing systems can no more be suited for this environment because of the limit of the capability of human being, such as the limits of the manageability of scale, of reducing error, of adaptability to speed, etc. A new method of using computer power in development in wider range than ever are needed. It must be a computer-centered method in contrast to the traditional human centered method. It is necessary to make computers more intelligent having an autonomous problem-solving capability. The term problem is used in a very wide sense in this paper. It is equivalent to mean what a person wishes to know or wants to do. For example, a requirement for making computer program is a problem and a direct objective of this paper.

In section 2, a concept of model building as program specification is discussed and multi-strata model is discussed as a key concept of intelligent systems in section 3. Then it is shown that a problem-specific, problem-solving system can be generated by using this model in section 4. Externalization as a stage of building up a problem model and specifying programs on the model is discussed in section 5. In section 6 an application of this idea to a car electronic system is discussed. Section 7 is a conclusion.

2. Model Building as Problem Representation

A problem solving begins from the creation of a problem in a person's brain and ends when the person obtains what he /she wishes to on the problem, i.e. solution of the problem. Roughly this process is formalized as problem creation, problem model building, making a plan of problem solving, finding problem-solving method, (translating the method into a program if necessary), <u>execution of the method (or program) in computer, displaying the result</u> and acceptance of the solution by the person. Currently computers can commit only a small part of this process (underlined) around program execution because of the difficulty of specifying and solving problem. Since every problem is created originally in person's brain, problem-solving process is divided into two stages; one is person's creation and representation of problem and the other is computer's problem solving. Let the formal representation of problem by person be called the problem model. The first part and last part of problem solving are connected by the problem model and called here externalization of person's idea, or simply externalization, and exploratory problem solving, or simply exploration, respectively as is shown in Figure 1.

The location of problems being transferred from person to computer depends on the problem solving style. In the conventional style, the problem model is represented in the form of program. Making program is a large burden to persons. In order to reduce it, it is necessary to change this style and to put the location of problem transfer to the uppermost position as far as possible. The location of the transfer, and accordingly the representation of problem model, must be decided depending on the problem solving style and problem-solving capability of computers. In this paper a knowledge-based, exploratory problem solving is considered. It must also be considered to give computers a method for supporting persons with which every person can express his/her idea and can represent it as the problem models in the easiest way.

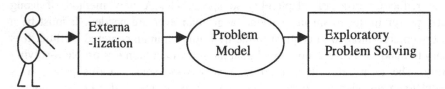

Fig. 1. Human-computer relation at problem solving

In many cases it is required to the exploratory problem-solving system to generate programs instead of generating solution directly. The problem model representation becomes a program specification in this case. Thus the followings are the major issues to be discussed.
1. How to represent the problem model.
2. How to support persons to externalize his/ her idea (Externalization).
3. How to deal with the problem model to get solution and generate program (Exploration).

The requirement for externalization is easiness of describing problem by person while that of exploration is autonomy of problem solving. In fact, not only autonomy but also generality and practicality are required to exploration [ROS97].

Generally speaking, an exploratory problem solving method has wider applicability potentially than the ordinal method. Generality requires the system not only to cover different domains of problems but also to deal with different types and maturity of problems. The different type of problem, e.g. analysis, design, control and so on, requires the system the different method of problem solving. For some type of problems an exploratory problem solving is indispensable. A design is a typical example. It is to find an object structure that satisfies the given functional requirement in an open space. Usually it is impossible to make a procedural program to execute this operation.

Maturity of problems depends on the problem domain. Problems of different maturity require the different approaches for problem solving.

Problem solving is a sequence of model transformations. What transformation is effective for a given problem is decided by knowledge. A problem domain in which various concepts have been established and enough amount of such knowledge is accumulated is a matured domain. Users can use the knowledge to represent and solve problems autonomously. Then it is possible to translate a trace of this process to a computer program. In an immature domain on the other hand, even the basic concepts are not made clear nor knowledge is made. A problem requires persons to take a larger part in problem-solving tasks. The user has to start to build up a concept by articulating the ideas in the field of interest. Even if the concept could have been made in order to represent a problem, the way to find its solution may not be discovered yet. The user has to find it him-/herself. This process cannot be written in the form of program either.

Generality contradicts very often to practicality. A new method to assure the practicality preserving generality becomes necessary. If only a necessary set of rules are provided in advance for solving the given problem instead of using large knowledge base, then this problem can be resolved. Ohsuga proposed a way of generating a problem solving system that is specific to the problem in [OHS96]. It leads us further to generation of programs because program is a special form of an automatic problem solver. This issue has been discussed in [OHS98] using an enterprise modeling as an example. In this paper, a control system for a car-electronics is discussed as another example. A problem model is built in the same principle as the enterprise model and programs are specified based on this model representation. It enables automation of the following programming process.

3. Multi-Strata Model as Problem Model and its Characteristics

Problem model plays many roles. First of all, it is a representation of a problem as a requirement to be satisfied. It must be comprehensive for persons. It is modified in a computer system until a solution is reached and must be computer readable. Thus the model represents a state of problem solving process at every instance of time and a solution in its final state. Every decision is made on the basis of the model representation.

In general problem is created concerning with an object by person who has some interest in it. Thus it is necessary to describe the object precisely for representing the problem. It is not to represent everything of an object but of some aspects in which the person has interest. It is called an object model. Even with the same object, the object model can be different by the view of the person to the object. Hence, the view must also be included in the problem model as well as an object model.

3.1 Object model

Every object model is represented as a related collection of the conceptual constituents included in this scope. There are two types of constituents; a structural component and functionality. The former forms a structural organization of the object. A structural component and a structure of the components are called here the conceptual entity or simply entity. An entity is not always a physical object but also can be a non-physical one. The term functionality is used to mean inclusively attribute, property, function, behavioral characteristic of the object and of its components, relation with the other objects/components. Every entity has some functionality. In other words, functionality is defined with respect to some entity and is represented by a predicate. Let such an entity in the predicate be called an argument. A functionality of an entity can be related with the functionality of the other entity either directly or through the structural relation of the entities that they contain as arguments. Thus there are two different structures closely related to each other, the structures of entities and functionality. To represent an object model is to write down these structures correctly to the detail. If some part of the model is left unspecified, it is a problem representation and problem solving is an activity to complete the model.

3.2 Multi-strata model (MS-model) as problem model

An object model is sufficient when it includes sufficient information to achieve the goal of solving problems given by user. Otherwise it is an insufficient model. Whether a model is sufficient or not depends not only on the amount of knowledge but also on problem type. For example, only a set of predicates as functional requirements without any entity structure is insufficient for the analysis problem to obtain some functionality of a given structure of entities. But it can be a sufficient model for a design problem because the goal of the design is to find a structure of components to satisfy the given requirements. Therefore in order to define a problem precisely, it is necessary to include user's intention in the model. A modeling scheme that describes not only an object but also a subject in the context of a relation between subjects and object is necessary.

Moreover, everything in the world can be an object of human interests. The object can be a problem solving process by others. Then a problem solving process is represented as a nested structure. This stratification can be more than one depending on the situation. The innermost problem is to obtain a solution directly on the lowest level object and its outside problem is to obtain a way of obtaining the solution in the inside process (Figure 2(a)). Let it be called a multi-strata object. A new modeling scheme is necessary to represent such multi-strata objects as shown in Figure 2(b).

Requirements are given not only to object but also to subjects at any stratum in this model. For example, "design an object to satisfy the given object-level requirements" may be given to S1 of Figure 2. It specifies the activity of S1 to find an object model structure satisfying the requirement. Modeling of automatic programming is a typical example. A program is what generates a solution (output) to a given problem (input) in relation with an object. It is therefore a special type of automatic problem solver that is equivalent to a task of a lower stratum subject who has been responsible to this work and programming is an activity of a higher level subject to create such an automatic problem solver. An automatic programming is an activity by a still higher level subject to generate automatically an automatic problem solving system. It corresponds to a person who makes the program. Thus a multi-strata-model is necessary for representing automatic programming.

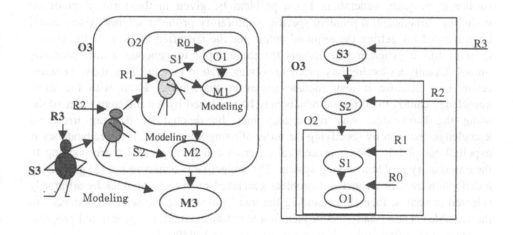

Fig. 2. Multi-strata object and multi-strata modeling

4. System Generation Based On Multi-Strata Model

4.1 Generation of problem solving systems

Among a number of possibilities realized with this scheme, an attempt to generate autonomous systems has been described in [OHS98].

Every problem requires its own problem solving method. It is defined and can be represented by means of a problem-specific structure of knowledge chunks. If this structure is generated before going into problem solving, a problem-specific, exploratory problem solving system is generated. It is achieved by retrieving selectively a problem specific knowledge structure from a large knowledge base including various knowledge chunks for the different types and domains.

Let a lower stratum subject be given a problem and a higher stratum subject be given a requirement for generating a problem-specific, exploratory problem solving system for the problem of the lower stratum subjects. Because of its problem dependency, the key information to generate this structure must be derived from the problem representation. Problem type and domain are found by interpreting the requirement for the lower subject. Knowledge for generating the specific problem solving system must be prepared. It has been discussed in [OHS98] and is not repeated here.

4.2 Program generation

Generation of problem-specific, exploratory problem solving system extends further to program generation. Let a problem be given in the form of predicate including variables. If a problem-specific, exploratory problem solving system could be generated for getting the required output for the specified input, then the system behaves like a program that accepts the same input to generate a corresponding output. Usually an exploratory problem solving system generated as above contains redundancy because it may include irrelevant knowledge. Even with the same knowledge chunk, the different results may be produced by the different order of the using the knowledge. Any redundancy may be deleted by deleting irrelevant knowledge and then by specifying the order of using knowledge. If the redundancy is expelled completely, then a procedural program can be generated corresponding to the exploratory problem solving system. This objective is achieved by, (1) generating a deduction tree for an instance problem generated by fixing variables by arbitrarily selected constants, then (2) expanding the tree by restoring the selected instances to the variables. Then finally this deduction tree is transformed to a procedural program according to the fixed rules. This is also discussed in [OHS98].

Thus a computer program can be developed according to the following processes. (1) A problem model is built (externalization) using knowledge established in the domain. (2) A scope of programming is specified by a set of predicates in a functionality structure. (3) The selected set of predicates is classified into classes of related functionality. (4) A new predicate is generated corresponding to every class. It represents a program to be generated corresponding to the class. (5) To every class a rule is made of which the conclusion is the new predicate and the premises are the predicates in a class. This is a program specification. (6) A problem solving starts assuming that a question on this new predicate is given. (7) A succeeded path to solution is recorded tracing the exploratory problem solving in the form of a deduction tree as mentioned above. (8) The deduction tree is converted to a program.

5. Externalization as Model Building

Externalization is a cooperative work of person and computer to build up a problem model in the form of multi-strata model. The method of building a problem model is different by the problem domain and its maturity. From the programming point of view, it is required to make such a sufficient model that specifies program and also the deduction tree can be generated therefrom. Since a program is a part of the object in which the program is used and represents its activity, its logical structure is specified as a part of its functional structure. The data structure is specified as a part of entity structure that is referred by the functionality included in this part.

When the problem domain is matured enough, the set of primitive functionality and the functional structure of them have already been defined and prepared as the domain-specific knowledge. The problems that can be the object of automatic programming are mostly of this class. For example, it is possible to make such a (case-) knowledge base for business system. Various functions that are needed for businesses have been defined formally with their relations. This knowledge base is made as general as possible so that it covers various specific cases. A problem model is a representation of a specific case. It is created referring to the knowledge, i.e. by selecting the only necessary functionality and the scopes of variables included therein. For example, an enterprise can be modeled as a subset of these functions. Since an enterprise includes many persons of the different roles working there, a multi-strata modeling scheme is indispensable in order to make a precise model. Some function is defined formally to the detail. It can be performed in a computer. The other functions that cannot be defined precisely to the detail are left to persons.

6. Modeling Engine Control System and Automatic Programming

As an example of automatic program generation, a control unit for car electronic systems is presented. Computer control is a recent tendency for not only car electronics but also many other industrial products such as home electronics, various industrial machines, communication terminals like telephone and facsimile system, and so on. Accordingly this type of software development is rapidly increasing. Since the software is a part of the parent machine in which it is embedded, the software must be specified at the design of the parent machine. Even though the scale of the program is rather small, its development accompanies difficulties because an interdisciplinary knowledge is required to a person, real-time operation and high reliability is required for the program and the program must frequently be renewed according to a rapid change of the parent machine. A formal procedure for the program development is desired.

The control unit consists of a set of programs. Some of them are inter-related. Every program is evoked by the external devices such as the sensors embedded in the parent machine to measure the physical conditions of the machine and/or switches operated by driver, and generate information to drive actuators to control the operation of the machine. There must be an interface to every external device for connecting the program therewith. For example, analog-digital converter must be provided. These interfaces are developed depending on the devices independent of the control program development. It is therefore assumed that every program receives output information from the interfaces as inputs and generates outputs as the input to the interfaces of actuators.

Today technology to control the operation of machine based on sensor signal is well advanced and knowledge is accumulated. Some knowledge is obtained through experiment and saved in the form of database. For example, the best timing for ignition of combustion engine has been obtained as depending on the amount of airflow and the rotation speeds of an engine (rpm). An independent function to represent and use this relation is made. A knowledge base has been constructed with these functions. A set of control programs to control an engine operation was specified as the sets of related functions. The best structure of the functions in order to define a program to assure the engine an optimal (at least near optimal) operation is also obtained. This knowledge is used to decide the program structure.

These functions and the structures are different by the different engine types. When a new engine is designed, their different combination is used. Correspondingly a new program is generated. It may be necessary sometimes to discover the new functions and/or the program structure for a new case. This is a part of whole engine design. Program development must be able to follow the speeds of trial-error process of the engine design. A new program generation system is required. The major objectives of this system are, (1) to make an automatic or semi-automatic programming system and (2) to make the car electronic system comprehensive to engine designers.

The first objective is to enables programmers the rapid development of programs so that they can join the engine design. It is expected that, after the user specifies the structure of the functions, a program is made automatically. In general there is a strict requirement on the processing time for this kind of control programs. Usually the program execution must finish in a strictly specified time limit, for example in a 1/n rotation of the engine where n is the number of cylinders. Knowledge based generation of program meets the logical condition but it does not say anything about the processing time required by the program. In order to meet the time requirement, a special method is necessary in addition to the program generation method discussed so far. The starting time and the time limit must be added to the definition of a program as the requirement. Based on this requirement a time chart is made. Every program execution time is written on this chart to specify the time limit. Some programs have the dependency relation with respect to the start and end times. The dependency relation between programs is written into the time chart. In order to satisfy these requirements on the physical performance, it is necessary, (1) to make a program for every function optimal, (2) to generate as many as possible solutions for satisfying the logical requirement, and (3) to select one among them to satisfy the physical requirement.

The second objective is to provide a convenient human interface in order to let users come to understanding easily the meaning, objective and the method of making control program.

It is expected that this technique can be used widely for making the class of programs that are embedded in the large systems to work as the parts. Control programs in a computer system are the ones in this class.

7. Conclusion

A way of building a problem model and of specifying programs with this model was discussed. It enables automation of the following programming process. A high-level intelligent system is needed for the purpose. A new modeling scheme named multi strata modeling was introduced as a key concept to make computer system intelligent. This approach of specifying and generating program was applied to a car electronic system in cooperation with a car production company.

References

[GIB94] W. Wayt Gibbs; Software Chronic Crisis, Scientific American, Volume 18, No.2, 1994
[OHS96] S. Ohsuga; Multi-Strata Modeling to Automate Problem Solving Including Human Activity, Proc.Sixth European-Japanese Seminar on Information Modelling and Knowledge Bases,1996
[OHS98] S. Ohsuga; Toward Truly Intelligent Systems - From Expert Systems to Automatic Programming, Knowledge Based Systems, Vol.10, No. 3, 1998
[ROS97] F. H. Ross; Artificial Intelligence, What Works and What Doesn't ? AI Magazine, Volume 18, No.2, 1997

Rough Set Based Data Exploration
Using ROSE System

Bartłomiej Prędki, Szymon Wilk

Institute of Computing Science
Poznan University of Technology
Piotrowo 3A, 60-965 Poznań, Poland

Abstract. This article briefly describes the process of data exploration based on rough set theory and also proposes ROSE system as a useful toolkit for doing such data analysis on PC computers.

1 Introduction

Today, when the cost of acquiring and storing data is so low, many people keep electronic track of their activity. Doctors write down information about their patients in databases, sellers record transactions, etc. After accumulating all this information, the owners of data become interested in exploring it . Usually, they aim for the following goals:

- checking the consistency of data,
- reducing superfluous information,
- transforming data to knowledge, i.e. discovering interesting and useful information patterns hidden in data.

Currently, there are many techniques that can be used to achieve the above goals, including statistics, data mining and machine learning. If the objects in a database can be described using attributes and it is possible to discern condition and decision attributes then the data can be structured in, so called, information table, whose rows are objects and columns are condition and decision attributes. Each entry object-attribute is a value called descriptor. One of the methodologies gaining popularity during the last decade that can analyze data stored in information table, is the rough set theory, proposed by Pawlak [6]. It is especially useful with inconsistent data. This methodology is implemented in our software system called ROSE (Rough Set Data Explorer). In this article we present a data exploration process using the ROSE system.

2 ROSE system

ROSE is a software package developed in the Laboratory of Intelligent Decision Support Systems, Institute of Computing Science, Poznan Technical University. It implements the rough set based data exploration methodology with variable precision model and similarity relation extensions. It works on PCs running 32-bit operating systems (Windows 95/98/NT). It is a successor of the RoughDAS system - one of the first successful implementations of rough set theory [10].

ROSE is designed to be easy in use, point and click, menu-driven, user friendly tool for exploration and data analysis. It is meant as well for experts as for occasional users who want to perform the data exploration. System communicates with users using dialog windows and all the results are represented in the environment. Data can be edited using spreadsheet like interface.

ROSE is built using modular architecture. It means that every task is performed by standalone program module. For ease of use all modules are integrated in single environment - user interface.

ROSE was written and designed in C++ language. We have tried to obtain maximum transferability between operating systems. All computational modules can be compiled on platforms containing ANSI C++ compiler. So the engine of the system can be moved to more powerful UNIX machines. Only Graphical User Interface (GUI) and visualization modules are bound with Microsoft Windows systems.

To simplify management of the data exploration process ROSE uses special structures called projects. Project contains information concerning not only data file, but also current computational engine options, for example like α and β parameters of variable precision model.

We have decided to store all data and results in plain text files. It guarantees better reusability and allows easier import from databases or spreadsheets. We've introduced new file format called ISF. It supports better syntax checking and allows extended definition of attributes which can have real, coded or even lexical values. The import/export mechanism to other formats is also included (RoughDAS, LERS, etc.) as well as possibility to obtain data from commonly used database formats (dBase and Paradox).

3 Exploration process using ROSE

Data exploration process using ROSE system can be broken up into several phases, represented in Figure 1.

At first, a user of the system has to convert data to the information table and save it in ISF file. For ease of use import mechanism from several sources is provided.

If there are missing values the user should perform preprocessing phase. This phase is also necessary when there are continuous attributes and indiscernibility relation is to be used later in the exploration process.

Next, the user is obliged to select the model of data exploration. Currently ROSE supports three independent models described in detail in Section 5. Model selection may imply inavailability of some phases in data analysis process.

Depending on the earlier choice, the user can select following stages of data exploration: rough approximations, reduction of attributes, rule induction and classification.

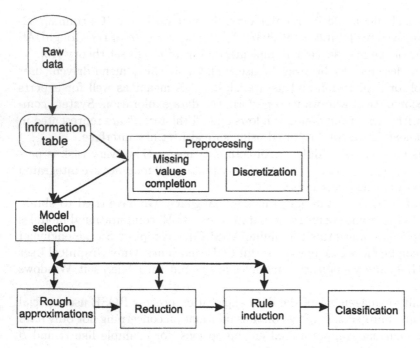

Fig. 1. Scheme of data exploration in ROSE

More information about each phase can be found in the following sections.

4 Preprocessing

The goal of preprocessing phase is to prepare data for further analysis to make it appropriate for used methodology.

In real life applications missing values are usually found in collected data. They pose a real problem for data exploration. The method implemented in module *completer* is based on statistical analysis of most frequent values (usually used in machine learning). In the future we plan to add more advanced methods, dealing with incomplete information [12].

When user selects exploration model based on indiscernibility relation it is suggested to replace continuous domain attributes with discrete ones. Such process is called discretization and there are two available approaches: discretization based on expert's knowledge and automatic discretization based on information theory. We have implemented both methods in ROSE system. To be more specific, automatic discretization uses algorithm based on entropy measure, introduced by Fayyad & Irani [1]. User driven discretization includes possibility to create discretization table or to visually divide attribute domain into intervals.

5 Available models

Currently, there are three data exploration engine models available in ROSE system: classical rough set model, variable precision rough set model and similarity-based rough set model.

Rough set theory was developed by Pawlak in 1982 [6] and since then it was successfully used in many applications. However, there are data sets that are more demanding, for example containing continuous values. That is the reason for research to expand the capabilities of this methodology. One of such extensions is variable precision model introduced by Ziarko [16]. It changes the definition of approximations (see Section 6). A different approach is used in similarity relation model introduced by Slowinski & Vanderpooten [13][14]. Similarity substitutes indiscernibility relation and keeps reflexivity as the only property from among reflexivity, symmetry and transitivity characterizing the indiscernibility. It allows analysis of numerical attributes without earlier discretization. It is also possible to induce rules with an extended syntax employing similarity.

In the near future we plan to include very new exploration models adapted to an understanding of some or all attributes as criteria with preference-ordered scales. The key element of these models is the dominance relation used instead of indiscerniblity or similarity [2]. These new exploration models proposed by Greco, Matarazzo and Slowinski can be combined with fuzzy logic in order to handle uncertainty and imprecision.

6 Approximations

The most important part of the rough set theory is approximation. The first step to find approximations is creating elementary sets (also called atoms). An elementary set contains objects indiscernible on all condition attributes, it means these objects have identical values on all condition attributes. When using similarity relation model, elementary sets are substituted by similarity classes.

When the cardinality of an elementary set is larger then one it is probable, that its objects will belong to different decision classes, so we have an ambiguity. Because of that we define two approximations:

1. Lower approximation with respect to the exploration model being used:
   - in the classical model - it contains all the elementary sets included in the decision class,
   - in the variable precision model - it contains all the elementary sets that have at least $\beta * 100\%$ objects belonging to the decision class,
   - in the similarity relation model - it contains all objects whose inverse similarity classes are included in the decision class,
2. Upper approximation with respect to the exploration model being used:
   - in the classical model - it contains all elementary sets that have a non-empty intersection with the decision class,

- in the variable precision model - it contains all elementary sets that have at least $\alpha * 100\%$ objects belonging to the decision class,
- in the similarity relation model - it contains all objects whose inverse similarity classes have a non-empty intersection with the decision class.

ROSE implements all of the above approximations.

Based on the approximations some measures are calculated, including accuracy of approximation, accuracy of classification, and most important in rough set theory, quality of classification.

7 Reduction

One of important properties of rough set theory is reduction of attributes. We want to check if some of the attributes are not redundant in the information table. There are usually many possibilities of selection of such attributes so the main goal of the reduction phase is looking for all the subsets of attribute set, which guarantee the same value of quality of classification as the complete set (it means they approximate the data in the same way). Those subsets are called reducts and the set of most significant attributes is called a core (it is also the common part of all reducts).

Beacuse the problem of finding all reducts for given information table is NP-hard, it is important to develop methods that, if possible, find all reducts in a reasonable time or introduce heuristic approaches generating some reducts. ROSE is currently equipped with four reduct generation methods.

Historically the first is an algorithm based on lattice search introduced by Romanski [7] which tries to reduce the search space by cutting-off some part which has no potential of including a reduct. It is useful, when the number of reducts is rather small (less then 1000), because of memory requirements.

The nowadays most efficient algorithm for reduct generation was developed by Skowron [8], based on discernibility matrix. It is very fast, although the initial cost of building the matrix can be a disadvantage for datasets having only a couple of reducts. For example, it is possible to generate 809 reducts in ESWL information table, containing 500 objects described by 26 attributes in 2 seconds on PC with Pentium 166MMX processor). The main limit of the algorithm is the memory requirement depending on the size of the information table.

For even larger datasets it is possible to search for some of the reducts using the heuristic approach. It implements strategy based on adding the attributes to the core. It is useful only when other methods fail.

The last option of ROSE concerning reducts is manual generation of reducts. The set of attributes is presented to the user together with possible increase or decrease of quality of classification and he/she can decide which attributes to add or to remove from a set. This approach is meant especially for experts who have also background knowledge about the meaning and possible coalitions of attributes.

Of course, there is an option to generate the core of attributes. Due to its properties it can be found in linear time.

8 Rule induction

The knowledge contained in the analyzed data set can be expressed in form of decision rules, i.e. *if ... then ...* statements. A decision rule consists of a condition part – conjunction of elementary tests on attribute values, and a decision part – an assignment to one or more decision classes.

One should note, that the induction of decision rules is a stand-alone problem, which can be considered independently of the Rough Sets theory. Rule induction algorithms generate rules for a given set of objects. In the simplest case such set consists of all objects from a given decision class. The Rough Sets methodology is useful if the data set is inconsistent and objects described by the same values of condition attributes belong to different decision classes. In such situation decision rules can be generated from approximations or from boundaries of decision classes.

The user can choose one of three schemes of rule induction [15]:

1. Minimal description.
   The resulting description is a minimal set of rules (i.e. the smallest set of rules) that cover all objects from the given set (a rule covers an object when all conditions in the rule's condition part are true for object's attribute values).
2. Satisfactory description.
   The resulting description contains only rules that satisfy requirements specified by the user (e.g. rules that are strong enough or that have good discriminating capabilities).
3. Exhaustive description.
   The generated description contains all possible rules that can be induced from the given set of objects.

8.1 Minimal description

The minimal description is generated by the LEM2 algorithm [3].

Depending on the definition of the set of objects, for which rules are generated, LEM2 induces two types of rules:

- exact rules are generated for the set of objects defined as the lower approximation of a given decision class,
- approximate rules are generated for the set of objects defined as a boundary of a given decision class (a difference between a lower and an upper approximation of the class).

Beside the original LEM2 algorithm, ROSE contains two modified versions:

- the LEM2 algorithm with interval extension,
- the LEM2 with similarity extension [4].

8.2 Satisfactory description

Within this scheme ROSE contains the implementation of Explore algorithm [5]. This algorithm is based on the breadth-first search strategy. It starts the generation with the shortest rules (containing one condition in their conditional part), and then gradually increases the length of generated rules. The search space is limited by thresholds defined by the user:

1. Maximal rule length – i.e. the maximal number of conditions in a condition part of the rule.
2. Minimal rule strength – i.e. the minimal number of objects covered by the rule, that belong to the decision class pointed by the rule.
3. Minimal discrimination level – i.e. the ratio of the number of objects covered by the rule, that belong to the class pointed by the rule to the number of all objects covered by the rule.

8.3 Exhaustive description

The Explore algorithm is also able to generate the exhaustive description consisting of all possible rules for the given set of objects. To achieve this, the maximal length should be equal to the number of attributes and the minimal strength should be set to 1. One should stress however, that generation of all rules can be extremely time and memory consuming, even for data sets of medium size.

9 Classification

In this phase, the decision rules generated in the previous phase are used for classifying objects (i.e. assigning them to decision classes). The assignment process is performed in the following steps:

1. if an object is covered by exactly one rule, then the object is assigned to the decision class pointed by this rule,
2. if there are several rules covering an object, then the conflict is resolved by assigning the object to the class with the highest number of votes or to the class pointed by this of the considered rules, that has the highest value of Laplace correction; the proper conflict resolution strategy is chosen by the user,
3. if no rule covers an object, then the object is assigned to the decision class pointed by the nearest rule, i.e. nearest according to the selected distance metric (the Lp-metric or valued closeness relation [11]). If there are several rules with the minimal distance to the object, the the same conflict resolution strategy as described in step 2 is applied.

The classifier implemented in ROSE can be used for two different tasks:

1. Classification of a new object, which membership to decision classes is unknown.

2. Classification of an already classified object (so called reclassification).

The first of the mentioned tasks is performed in the interactive way for single objects. After the classification, the user is presented the assigned decision class and the detailed information considered during classification process.

The second task is a single step of a reclassification test. The results are presented to the user after performing the whole test ROSE offers two scenarios of such tests:

- Living-one-out – suggested to be used in case of small data sets (smaller than 100 objects).
- K-fold cross-validation – intended to be applied in case of larger data sets. The user can choose random or stratified division into folds (in the latter division the distribution of number of objects from decision classes in each fold is the same as in the whole data set).

After the test a detailed statistical information about the classification accuracy (i.e. average values, standard deviations, distribution in decision classes) is presented. It is supplemented by a confusion matrix.

10 Availability

Demonstration version of ROSE is available on our WWW server at address: http://www-idss.cs.put.poznan.pl/rose. It is limited to information systems, that contain less then 200 objects and 5 attributes. Otherwise it is fully functional, so users can try it on several popular data sets available in the scientific community.

11 Summary

We have presented the process of data exploration based on rough set theory using ROSE software system. ROSE is 32-bit application implementing classical rough set theory as well as new extensions based on variable precision model and similarity relation. Further development of ROSE is in progress.

12 Acknowledgments

Authors of this paper would like to acknowledge the financial support from State Committee for Scientific Research, KBN research grant no. 8T11C 013 13 and from CRIT 2 - Esprit Project no. 20288. We would also like to thank Prof. Słowiński for his support and remarks to the earlier version of this paper and J. Stefanowski, R. Susmaga and R. Mieńko for their cooperation in development of ROSE system.

References

1. U.M. Fayyad, K.B. Irani. On the Handling of Continuous-Valued Attributes in Decision Tree Generation, Machine Learning, Vol 8, 1992, 87-102.
2. S. Greco, B. Matarazzo, R. Slowinski: A new rough set approach to multicriteria and multiattribute classification. [In] L. Polkowski, A. Skowron. (eds.), Proc. of the First Internat. Conference on Rough Setc and Current Trends In Computing - RSCTS'98, Warsaw, Springer-Verlag, 1998, 60-67.
3. J.W. Grzymala-Busse. LERS - a system for learning from examples based on rough sets. In R. Slowinski, (ed.) Intelligent Decision Support, Kluwer Academic Publishers, 1992, 3-18.
4. K. Krawiec, R. Slowinski, D. Vanderpooten. Learning of decision rules from similarity based rough approximations, [In] A. Skowron, L. Polkowski (eds.), Rough Sets in Knowledge Discovery vol. 2, Physica Verlag, Heidelberg, 1998, 37-54.
5. R. Mienko, J. Stefanowski, K. Tuomi, D. Vanderpooten. Discovery-Oriented Induction of Decision Rules. Cahier du Lamsade no. 141, Paris, Univeriste de Paris Dauphine, spetembre 1996.
6. Z. Pawlak - Rough sets. Int. J. Computer and Information Sci., 11, 1982, 341-356.
7. S. Romanski. Operation on families of sets for exhaustive search, given a monotonic function. In W. Beeri, C. Schmidt, N. Doyle (eds.), Proceedings of the 3rd Int. Conference on Data and Knowledge Bases, Jerusalem 1988, 310-322.
8. A. Skowron, Rauszer C. The discernibility matrices and functions in information systems in: Slowinski R. (ed.) Intelligent Decision Support. Handbook of Applications and Advances of the Rough Sets Theory. Kluwer Academic Publishers, 1992, 331-362.
9. R. Slowinski. Rough sets learning of preferential attitude in multi-criteria decision making. In Komorowski J., Ras Z.W. (eds.), Proc. of Int. Symp. on Methodologies for Intelligent Systems, Springer Verlag LNAI 689, 1993, 642-651.
10. R. Slowinski, J. Stefanowski. 'RoughDAS' and 'RoughClass' software implementations of the rough set approach. In R. Slowinski (ed.) Intelligent Decision Support. Handbook of Applications and Advances of the Rough Sets Theory. Kluwer Academic Publishers, 1992, 445-456.
11. R. Slowinski, J. Stefanowski. Rough classification with valued closeness relation. [In] E. Diday, Y. Lechavalier, M. Schrader, P. Bertrand, B. Burtschy (eds.), New Approaches in Classification and Data Analysis. Springer-Verlag, Berlin, 1994, 482-489.
12. R. Slowinski, J. Stefanowski. Rough set reasoning about uncertain data. Fundamenta Informaticae, 27 (2-3), 1996, 229-244.
13. R. Slowinski, D. Vanderpooten: Similarity relation as a basis for rough approximations [In] P.P. Wang (ed.): Advances in Machine Intelligence & Soft-Computing. Bookwrights, Raleigh, NC, 1997, 17-33.
14. R. Slowinski, D. Vanderpooten: A generalized definition of rough approximations based on similarity. IEEE Transactions on Data and Knowledge Engineering (to appear).
15. J. Stefanowski. On rough set based approaches to induction of decision rules. [In] A. Skowron, L. Polkowski (eds.), Rough Sets in Knowledge Discovery Vol. 1, Physica Verlag, Heidelberg, 1998, 500-529
16. W. Ziarko. Analysis of Uncertain Information in The Framework of Variable Precision Rough Sets. Foundations of Computing And Decision Sciences Vol 18 (1993) No. 3-4, 381-396.

Towards an Intelligent System Dealing with Nuanced Information Expressed in Affirmative or Negative Forms

Daniel Pacholczyk

LERIA, University of Angers,
2 Boulevard Lavoisier, 49045 Angers Cedex 01, France
pacho@univ-angers.fr

Abstract. In this paper, we present a new intelligent system dealing with affirmative or negative information. We propose a formalization of linguistic negation in the context of fuzzy set theory based upon a compatibility level and tolerance threshold. Their combination allows us to choose the reference frame from which the intended meanings of "x is not A" will be extracted. The plausible interpretations of denied properties are obtained as the result of the different scoping of a negation operator. Moreover, a choice strategy computes, if needed, an intended meaning of each linguistic negation.

1 Introduction

In this paper, we present a new intelligent system dealing with nuanced information expressed in affirmative or negative forms as they may appear in knowledge bases including, rules like "If Jack *is not small* then he *is visible* in the crowd" or "if the wage *is not high* then the summer holidays *are not very long*" and facts like, "Jack *is really very tall*" or "the wage *is really low*", for example. This problem is threefold and implies *(1)* the representation of *nuanced properties*, *(2)* the representation of strengthening or softening effects resulting from *adverbial modifiers* bearing on properties, and *(3)* the association of different interpretations due to *different scope* of a *negation operator* on a compound linguistic element expressing a *nuanced property*.

Our main goal has been to define a *general model* dealing with affirmative or negative information *(1) based upon the models* proposed in ([11-14]), *(2) improving* theirs abilities in the management of knowledge bases, and *(3) including* the main results of linguistic analysis of negation ([9], [3], [4], [1]). In Section 2, we present the initial representation of nuanced information based on an automatic process defining the L-R functions associated with *nuances of properties* ([2]). Section 3 points out the fact that *a modelisation implying denied properties must be viewed as a one to many correspondence,* called here *multiset function.* Section 4 is devoted to the linguistic analysis developed in ([14]) which improves the formalization of linguistic negation proposed in ([11], [12]) by an explicit taking into account the different *scopes* of the linguistic negation in accordance with linguistic theories ([9], [3], [4], [1]). In Section 5 we propose a formalization of linguistic negation based upon a *compatibility level* ρ and a *tolerance threshold* ε to rend nuanced strength values of modified properties in the *scope* of a linguistic negation of A appearing in "x is not A". A combination of ρ and ε allows to define a *reference frame*, denoted as $Neg_{\rho,\varepsilon}(A)$, from which the possible values of linguistic negation of A will be extracted. In Section 6, we specify the links between the different definitions of linguistic negation proposed in ([11-14]). In Section 7, each *scope of a negation operator* is associated with a reference frame subset, denoted as $neg_{\rho,\varepsilon}(x, A)$, which constitutes the *intended meanings of the linguistic negation ρ–compatible with A for x with a tolerance threshold ε.* We propose in Section 8 *a choice strategy leading to an intended meaning of the linguistic negation.* In Section 9 we state new properties of the linguistic negation which improve the abilities of previous models.

2 The Initial Frame of Information Representation

We suppose that our discourse universe is characterised by a finite number of *concepts* C_i. A set of properties P_{ik} is associated with each C_i, whose description *domain* is denoted as D_i. The properties P_{ik} are said to be the *basic properties* connected with concept C_i. For example, the concepts of "height", "wage" and "appearance" should be understood as qualifying individuals of the human type. The concept "wage" can be characterized by the basic fuzzy properties ([16]) "low", "medium" and "high". *Linguistic modifiers* bearing on these basic properties permit to express *nuanced knowledge*. This work uses the methodology proposed in ([2]) to represent affirmative information like « x *is* $f_\alpha m_\beta P_{ik}$ » or « x *is not* $f_\alpha m_\beta P_{ik}$ » in the case of negation. In this context, expressing a property like "$f_\alpha m_\beta P_{ik}$" called here *nuanced property*, requires a list of linguistic terms.

Two ordered sets of modifiers are selected depending on their modifying effects:
- The first one groups *translation modifiers* resulting somehow in both a *translation and an eventual precision variation* of the basic property: For example, the set of translation modifiers could be M_7={extremely little, very little, rather little, moderately (∅), rather, very, extremely} totally ordered by the relation: $m_\alpha < m_\beta \Leftrightarrow \alpha < \beta$ (*Cf.* Figure 1).

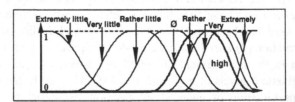

Fig. 1. Translation Modifiers applied to the basic property "high"

- The second one consists of *precision modifiers* which make possible to modify the precision of the previous properties (*Cf.* Figure 2). For example, F_6={vaguely, neighboring, more or less, moderately, really, exactly} totally ordered by $f_\alpha < f_\beta \Leftrightarrow \alpha < \beta$.

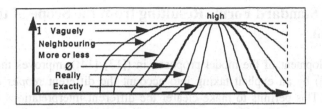

Fig. 2. Precision Modifiers applied to the basic property "high"

3 The Linguistic Negation as a Multiset Function

Utterances like "John is tall" or more generally "x is A" are ways, *natural languages* (henceforth NL) permits to confer some property A to an x. As simple as they could appear at a first glance, their interpretations raise, nevertheless, a lot of difficult problems as soon as the goal is to give them a translation in a formal model entity ([17]). It is well known that first order logic ([8], [5]) appears to be a poor candidate for that, even for these simple utterances, and a formula like A(x) resulting from their translation appears to be far from encompassing linguistics properties of what could inferred from original NL utterances ([6]). Properties of A(x) greatly depends on what A denotes in NL, and modelisations should take all of them into account. This is particularly the case when A is a vague property and fuzzy set theory is generally considered as well suited to cope with this kind of characteristics ([7]). Furthermore, some properties which are generally considered as precise such as *to be closed* gain some vagueness when they are denied. It's the case in particular when the negation of the property is lexicalized through an antonym ([5]). So, for example, *the door in not closed* is not equivalent to *the door is open*. The negation introduces some nuances on the property and in using *not open* instead of *closed* a speaker may exclude *fully open* to mean *half-open*. Moreover, negating some property *introduces a reference frame* from which possible values of the negated property can be extracted. In a sentence like *my hat is not red*, *not red* may refer to some other color for the hat, but also to some nuance of red. It appears clearly that *a modelisation implying denied properties cannot be viewed as a one to one correspondence but as a one to many one*, called here *multiset function*. Some classical approaches to negation fail to embed all desirable negation properties illustrated in our examples. In the fuzzy context ([16]), "x is not A" receives a unique interpretation "x is ¬A" with $\mu_{\neg A}(x)=1-\mu_A(x)$. In a similar way, within a *qualitative context*, one can refer to a set of linguistic labels denoted as $L=\{u_0, ..., u_n\}$ totally ordered: $u_i<u_j \Leftrightarrow i<j$ ([10]). But, the linguistic negation verifies $Neg(u_i)= u_{n-i}$ where here also u_{n-i} denotes a sole value in L. In order to remedy to this deficiency, Torra ([15]) has defined a new *concept of linguistic negation in a totally ordered set L of linguistic labels*. He has proposed a multiset function Neg of L into $\mathcal{P}(L)$ which among the conditions to be satisfied by Neg(A) implies for it to be convex and not void. Unfortunately, these conditions are not totally suited to the representation of linguistic negation ([11, 12]). It is clear that the definitions of linguistic negation proposed in ([11-13]) are based upon multiset functions which alleviate the difficulties of Torra's approach.

4 The Standard Forms Resulting from the Scope of the Linguistic Negation

The development of the model proposed in ([13] [14]) improves the previous ones ([11] [12]) by an explicit taking into account the different *scopes of the linguistic negation*. This permits to make clearer the different interpretations of "x is not A" resulting from scoping effects in accordance with linguistic theories ([9], [3], [4], [1]). In this context, the intended meaning of "x is not A" is conceived as a compositional function applied to the compounds of the denied statement.

Within the discourse universe, let us denote as: $\mathcal{C}$ the set of distinct concepts C_i, $\mathcal{D}_i$ the domain associated with the concept C_i, $\mathcal{M}$ the set of modifier combinations, $\mathcal{B}_i$ the set of associated basic properties P_{ik} defined on $\mathcal{D}_i$, $\mathcal{N}_{ik}$ the set of all nuances of the basic property P_{ik}, $\mathcal{N}_i$ the set of all nuanced properties associated with C_i. Then let : $\mathcal{D}=\cup_i\mathcal{D}_i$, $\mathcal{B}=\cup_i\mathcal{B}_i$, $\mathcal{N}=\cup_i\mathcal{N}_i$, $\mathcal{E}=\mathcal{M}\cup\mathcal{D}\cup\mathcal{B}\cup\mathcal{N}$.

We define the *reference frame of linguistic negation* as follows.

Definition 4.1. Let Neg a multiset function Neg : $\mathcal{E}\rightarrow\mathcal{P}(\mathcal{E})$ verifying the conditions:
L1: $\forall n_\gamma \in\mathcal{M}$, $Neg(n_\gamma)=\mathcal{M}\backslash\{n_\gamma\}$, **L2**: $\forall P_{ik} \in\mathcal{B}_i$, $Neg(P_{ik})=\mathcal{B}_i\backslash\{P_{ik}\}$, **L3**: $\forall x\in\mathcal{D}_i$, $Neg(x)=\mathcal{D}_i\backslash\{x\}$, **L4**: $\forall n_\gamma\in\mathcal{M}$, $\forall P_{ik}\in\mathcal{B}_i$, $Neg(n_\gamma P_{ik})=\mathcal{N}_i\backslash\{n_\gamma P_{ik}\}$, **L5**: $\forall n_\gamma\in\mathcal{M}$, $\forall P_{ik}\in\mathcal{B}_i$, $Neg(n_\gamma(P_{ik}))=\mathcal{N}_{ik}\backslash\{n_\gamma P_{ik}\}$, **L6**: $\forall n_\gamma\in\mathcal{M}$, $\forall Neg(P_{ik})$, $n_\gamma(Neg(P_{ik}))=\mathcal{N}_i\backslash\mathcal{N}_{ik}$.

The negation is characterized as an operator which refers to a subset of values from a set of possible ones. Each condition will be associated with a possible scope of the negation operator which characterizes the reference frame of its intended meaning and the set of values that the choice of this particular scope excludes. From a linguistic point of view "x is not $n_\gamma P_{ik}$" can generally express something corresponding to a nuanced utterance like "y is $n_\delta P_{ij}$". Following are the different *standard forms* resulting from each possible scope.

Depending of the scope of the negation operator, saying "x is not $n_\gamma P_{ik}$", for this x, the speaker may refer to:
- *Another object instead of x belonging to the same domain and satisfying the nuanced property.* [F1]
So, "x is not $n_\gamma P_{ik}$" means "not(x) is $n_\gamma P_{ik}$" or in other words, not(x)=y$\in$ Neg(x) (cond. **L3**). As an example, "Jack is not guilty" since it is John that is guilty.
- *Another nuance of the same property.* [F2]
So, "x is not $n_\gamma P_{ik}$"$\Leftrightarrow$"x is not($n_\gamma(P_{ik})$)"$\Leftrightarrow$"x is $n_\delta P_{ik}$". So, not($n_\gamma(P_{ik})$)=$n_\delta P_{ik}\in$ Neg(n_γ (P_{ik})) (cond. **L5**). As an example, "Jack is not small" since "Jack is extremely small".
- *A nuanced property except $n_\gamma P_{ik}$ which is nonetheless associated with the same concept.* [F3]
So, "x is not $n_\gamma P_{ik}$" means "x is not($n_\gamma P_{ik}$)" which is equivalent to "x is $n_\delta P_{ij}$". In other words, not($n_\gamma P_{ik}$)=$n_\delta P_{ij}$ with $n_\delta P_{ij}\in$ Neg($n_\gamma P_{ik}$) (condition **L4**). For example, "the wage being not very high" can be "really low", "medium" or "rather little high".
- *A nuance of another basic property associated with the same concept.* [F4]
So, "x is not $n_\gamma P_{ik}$" means "x is n_γ(not(P_{ik}))" that is to say "x is $n_\delta P_{ij}$". Here, n_γ(not(P_{ik}))=$n_\delta P_{ij}$, with $n_\delta P_{ij}\in n_\gamma$(Neg($P_{ik}$)) (cond. **L6**). For example, "John is not small" since he is at least "medium".

- A new basic property of the same concept [F5]

In this case "x is not A" means "x is not-A": a new basic property denoted as "not-A" is associated with the same concept. As an example, "this wine is not bad" can induce the new basic property "not-bad".

- Remark. In the following, we do not refer any longer to the first standard form **F1** which seldom occurs in knowledge-bases and suppose that the new property introduced in the last form **F5** appears among other basic properties.

Definition 4.2. We denote as Neg*(u) the subset of Neg(u) leading to one of the previous standard forms defining intended meanings of a linguistic negation.

5 A Negation ρ–compatible with A according to a Tolerance Threshold ε

Linguists ([9], [3], [4], [1]) have pointed out that, asserting that "x is not A", a speaker characterises as negation *i)* the *judgement of rejection* and *2)* the *pragmatic means* exclusively used to notify this rejection. Within the fuzzy context ([11-13]), we have to make explicit the adequacy of the affirmative statement "x is A" with the universe. Intuitively, the speaker considers that this assertion possesses a significant degree of truth. In other words, the membership degree to the fuzzy set associated with A must be greater than a compatibility level with the discourse universe. We can also consider that this value defines the strength with which the assertion is denied. So, *a first parameter* ρ, with 1≥ρ≥0, has been introduced *to take into account this compatibility level and this negation strength.* Then, the judgement of rejection receives as an interpretation: Rejection of "x is A"⇒$\mu_A(x)$<ρ. Moreover, asserting that "x is not A", *if necessary the user refers* to "x is P" as the intended meaning of his negation. It is obvious that any element of Neg*(u) cannot lead to the intended meaning of "x is not A". Intuitively the speaker understands a real difference between the membership degrees belonging to A and P for their significant values, that is to say: $\mu_A(x)$ *(resp.* $\mu_P(x)$*) is greater than* ρ⇒$\mu_P(x)$ (resp. $\mu_A(x)$) *is rather close to* 0. It is obvious that the expression "rather close to" can receive different translations, each of which is defining the threshold tolerance to which the speaker can accept "x is P" as the intended meaning. So, *a second parameter* ε, with 1≥ρ≥ε≥0, *has been introduced to define the negation strength* ρ *according to a tolerance threshold* ε. We can now put down a formal context making it possible to define a linguistic negation ([13]).

Definition 5.1 Let ρ, ε such that: 0≤ε≤ρ≤1. Let us define the multiset function Neg$_{\rho,\varepsilon}$: $\mathcal{U}\rightarrow\mathcal{P}(\mathcal{U})$ as follows: **CD0**: ∀A∈$\mathcal{U}$, Neg$_{\rho,\varepsilon}$(A)⊂Neg*(A), **CD1**: ∀P∈Neg$_{\rho,\varepsilon}$(A), ∀x, {$\mu_A(x)$≥ρ ⇒ $\mu_P(x)$≤ε}, and **CD2**: ∀P∈Neg$_{\rho,\varepsilon}$(A), ∀x, {$\mu_P(x)$≥ρ⇒$\mu_A(x)$≤ε}. Then, Neg$_{\rho,\varepsilon}$(A) is said to *be the linguistic negation* ρ*-compatible with* A *with the tolerance threshold* ε. Moreover, any P∈Neg$_{\rho,\varepsilon}$(A) is said to be a linguistic negation ρ–compatible with A with the tolerance threshold ε.

Example. We have collected in Figure 3 Neg$_{0.75,\,0.35}$ ("low") a set of negations 0.75–compatible with "low" with tolerance threshold 0.35, knowing that Neg*("low") refers to the standard form **F3**.

Remark. As noted before, in some cases a linguistic negation is restricted to a *simple rejection*. So, we add the *new standard form* defined as follows:

For this x, the user does not refer to an affirmative translation of the negation   **[F0]**

We can put $Neg^*(A)=Neg_{\rho,\varepsilon}(A)=\varnothing$. For example, "Smith is not guilty" since his alibi is confirmed. This simple rejection only gives us $\mu_{guilty}(Smith)<\rho$.

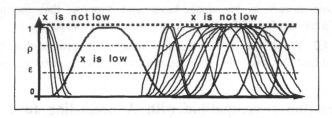

Fig. 3. Negations 0.75–compatible with "low" with tolerance threshold 0.35.

6   Comparison with Previous Models

We can recall the definition (denoted as **DefI**) introduced in the initial model ([11]). Let ε be a real such that $0.33 \geq \varepsilon \geq 0$ and P a property defined in the same domain as A. If P satisfies the conditions: **C0:** P and A are θ_i-similar with $\theta_i<$ moderately, **C1:** $\forall x$, $\mu_A(x) \geq \rho = 0.67 + \varepsilon \Rightarrow \mu_P(x) \leq \mu_A(x) - 0.67$, **C2:** $\forall x$, $\mu_P(x) \geq 0.67 + \varepsilon \Rightarrow \mu_A(x) \leq \mu_P(x) - 0.67$, then "x is P" is said to be a ε-*plausible Linguistic Negation* of "x is A". The definition (denoted as **Def II**) proposed in ([12]) is completely founded upon a neighborhood relation V. So, conditions **CN1** and **CN2** stand for previous ones : **CN1:** $\forall x$, $(\mu_A(x) \geq \rho) \Rightarrow V(\mu_P(x), \mu_A(x)) \leq 1 - \rho + \varepsilon$, **CN2:** $\forall x$, $(\mu_P(x) \geq \rho) \Rightarrow V(\mu_A(x), \mu_P(x)) \leq 1 - \rho + \varepsilon$. Then "x is P" is said to be a linguistic negation ρ–compatible with "x is A" with tolerance threshold ε. It is possible to establish the links between solutions P satisfying the conditions 1 and 2 in these definitions (denoted as **Cond₁=C1+C2** and **Cond₂=CN1+CN2**) and the solutions P satisfying the conditions 1 and 2 (denoted as **Cond₃**) appearing in the definition 5.1. Let us choose the neighborhood relation V_L defined as follows (*Cf.* [11], [12]): $V_L(u, v)=Min\{u \rightarrow_L v, v \rightarrow_L u\}$ where: $u \rightarrow_L v=1$ if $u \leq v$ else $1-u+v$. In this case, we have proved the following results :

1 : if P satisfies **Cond₁** then $V_L(\mu_A(x), \mu_P(x)) \leq 1 - \rho + \varepsilon$ for $\rho \geq 0.67$, $0 \leq \varepsilon \leq 0.33$ and $\varepsilon \leq \rho$. In other words, there exist ρ and ε such that : **Cond₁⇒Cond₂**.

2 : if P satisfies **Cond₂** then $\mu_A(x) \geq \rho$ (resp. $\mu_P(x) \geq \rho) \Rightarrow \mu_P(x) \leq \varepsilon$ (resp. $\mu_A(x) \leq \varepsilon$) for any $\rho \geq 0.5$ and $\varepsilon \leq Min\{\rho, 2\rho-1\}$. So, there exist ρ and ε such that: **Cond₂⇒Cond₃**.

3 : if P satisfies **Cond₃** then $V_L(\mu_A(x), \mu_P(x)) \leq 1 - \rho + \varepsilon$ where $0 \leq \varepsilon \leq \rho \leq 1$. So, given ρ and ε such that $0 \leq \varepsilon \leq \rho \leq 1$, we have: **Cond₃⇒Cond₂**.

4: if P satisfies **Cond₃** then $\mu_A(x) \geq \rho = 0.67 + \varepsilon \Rightarrow \mu_P(x) \leq \mu_A(x) - 0.67$ for any $0 \leq \varepsilon \leq 0.33$. So, given ρ and ε such that $0 \leq \varepsilon \leq 0.33$ and $\rho = 0.67 + \varepsilon$ we have: **Cond₃⇒Cond₁**.

It appears clearly that, given the neighborhood relation V_L, the conditions are not equivalent. Generally, the definition 5.1 leads to more restrictive conditions **Cond₃** defining the linguistic negation. But, for any $\rho \geq 0.5$ and $\varepsilon \leq Min\{\rho, 2\rho-1\}$ **Cond₂** and **Cond₃** are equivalent. Let us now examine the first condition in the definitions **Def I** and **Def II**. **C0** accepts P when P and A are globally less than moderately similar. We can note that, given V_L this condition is satisfied if: $0 \leq \varepsilon \leq \rho - 0.67$. In other words, the definition 5.1, which does not implicitly refer to neighborhood and similarity relations, fulfills this condition in this case. Moreover, the condition **CD0** in the definition 5.1 defines the reference frame Neg*(A) connected with a precise standard form **Fi** of the linguistic negation of "x is A". This condition is in accordance with the linguistic analysis of negation (*Cf* § 4). But, it is not the case with **Def I** and **Def II**. In other words, the set $Neg_{\rho,\varepsilon}(A)$ can be viewed as the reference frame of the linguistic negation corresponding to all standard forms **Fi**. It can be noted that the definition 5.1 leads to this set if Neg*(A) refers to the standard form **F3**. As a result, this comparison points out the fact that the definition 5.1 can induce previous definitions and realize a better accordance with the linguistic analysis of the negation.

7 The set of Intended Meanings of "x is not A"

The set $Neg_{\rho,\varepsilon}(A)$ defines the reference frame from which we have to extract the intended meanings of the linguistic negation. This comes down to defining explicitly a subset of $Neg_{\rho,\varepsilon}(A)$, denoted as $neg_{\rho,\varepsilon}(x, A)$, which consists of the intended meaning of "x is not A". The following definition proposed in ([13]) is more useful that the previous ones ([11, [12]) since a precise set of intended meanings is computed.

Definition 7.1 Put $neg_{\rho,\varepsilon}(x, A) = \{P \in Neg_{\rho,\varepsilon}(A) \mid \mu_P(x) \geq \rho\}$. Any $P \in neg_{\rho,\varepsilon}(x, A)$ is called an *intended meaning for x of the linguistic negation ρ–compatible with A with tolerance threshold ε*. We say also that "x is P" is an intended meaning with the tolerance threshold ε of the linguistic negation ρ–compatible of "x is A". If no confusion is possible, we simply say that P is an intended meaning of the linguistic negation of A for x.

Example. By using previous solutions (*Cf.* Figure 3), we have collected in the Figure 4 the intended meanings of "x is not low" for the values a (3 solutions based upon "low") and b (4 solutions based upon "medium" and "high").

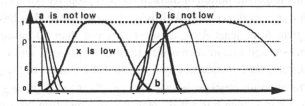

Fig. 4. Negations 0.75–compatible with "low" with tolerance threshold 0.35.

8 A Choice Strategy of an Intended Meaning

If the user wishes only one interpretation of the linguistic negation, it is possible to use the *choice strategy* proposed in ([13]). A particular choice can be done among the

188

plausible solutions leading to the most significant membership degree and having the weakest complexity.

Definition 8.1 The *complexity* of the nuanced property A, denoted as comp(A), is equal to the number of nuances (different from $\emptyset$) required in its definition.

Definition 8.2 A choice of a nuanced property P satisfying the following conditions: I1 : P∈ neg$_{\rho,\,\varepsilon}$(x, A), I2 : $\mu_P(x)$= Max{$\mu_P(x)$│P∈ neg$_{\rho,\,\varepsilon}$(x, A)}., and I3: ∀Q∈ neg$_{\rho,\,\varepsilon}$(x, A), {$\mu_Q(x)$=ξ(x, A) $\Rightarrow$ comp(P) ≤ comp(Q), defines "x is P" as the intended meaning of "x is not A".
Example. By using the solutions collected in Figure 4, "b is not low" receives as internded meaning "b is really medium".

9 Basic Properties of the Linguistic Negation

We can *recall* the initial properties of linguistic negation presented in ([11-14]).

Property 9.1 "x is A" doesn't automatically define the knowledge about "x is not A".

Property 9.2 The double negation of A does not generally lead to "A".

Property 9.3 {$\rho\leq\rho$', ε'$\leq\varepsilon\leq\rho$}$\Rightarrow$Neg$_{\rho',\,\varepsilon'}$(A)$\subseteq$Neg$_{\rho,\,\varepsilon}$(A).

Property 9.4 There exists ρ and ε such that the negation ρ-compatible with the tolerance threshold ε takes into account all previous interpretations of "x is not A".

We can now *enrich* the previous set of properties of the linguistic negation. Indeed, it is easy to prove the following new properties.

Property 9.5 P∈ Neg$_{\rho,\,\varepsilon}$(A)$\Rightarrow$A∈ Neg$_{\rho,\,\varepsilon}$(P).

Property 9.6 ¬(P∈ neg$_{\rho,\,\varepsilon}$(x, A)$\Rightarrow$A∈ neg$_{\rho,\,\varepsilon}$(x, P))

Property 9.7 neg$_{\rho,\,\varepsilon}$(x, A) can be an empty set

Property 9.8 neg$_{\rho,\,\varepsilon}$(x, A) can be a no-convex set.

Property 9.9 The model can deal with boolean basic properties without nuances by choosing ρ=1 and ε=0. In this case, the standard forms defining the set Neg*(A) can correspond with the linguistic notion of marked (or not) property (*Cf.* [9], [3]).

Property 9.10 For any fuzzy property A, it is possible to define five basic properties (denoted as less_than A, at_least A, A, at_most A, more_than A) based upon A and its fuzzy negation ¬A, and this in such a way that, if we put ρ=1 and ε=0, and if we do not refer to nuances, the negation of any P consists of elements of the previous set.

Property 9.11 The previous strategy defines P∈ neg$_{\rho,\,\varepsilon}$(a, A) and Q∈ neg$_{\rho,\,\varepsilon}$(b, B) such that the rule "if a is not A, then b is not B" receives as translation "if a is P, then b is Q".

10 Conclusion

We have presented a new model dealing with linguistic negation within a fuzzy context. The possible interpretations of a denied nuanced property are extracted from a reference frame depending on a compatibility level and a tolerance threshold. The model emphasizes the role of the different scopes of the negation operator and negation appears in it as a multiset function bearing on the different elements of the original NL utterance. Moreover, this new intelligent system improves the abilities of the previous ones in that the linguistic negation possesses a more powerful set of properties. In particular, classical deductive processes can be maintained since the intended meanings of negative information can be explicitly expressed in affirmative form.

References

1. Culioli, A.: Pour une linguistique de l'énonciation: Opérations et Représentations. Tome 1 Ophrys Eds. Paris (1991)
2. Desmontils, E., Pacholczyk, D.: Towards a linguistic processing of properties in declarative modelling. Int. Jour. of CADCAM and Comp. Graphics **12:4** (1997) 351-371
3. Ducrot, O., Schaeffer, J.-M.: Nouveau dictionnaire encyclopédique des sciences du langage. Seuil Paris (1995)
4. Horn, L.R.: A Natural History of Negation. The Univ. of Chicago Press (1989)
5. McCawley, J. D.: Everything That linguists Have always Wanted to Know about Logic (2nd ed.), Chicago University Press (1993)
6. Dermott, D.: Tarskian Semantics, or no Notation Without denotation, Cognitive Science **2(3)** (1978) 277-282
7. Mel'cuk, I. A.: Dependency Syntax: Theory and Practice, State University of New York Press (1988)
8. Moore, R. C.: Problems in logical Form. Proc. of the 19th Annual Meeting of Association for Computational Linguistics, Standford, California (1981) 117-124
9. Muller, C.: La négation en français. Publications romanes et françaises Genève (1991)
10. Pacholczyk, D.: Contribution au traitement logico-symbolique de la connaissance. Thèse d'Etat (1992)
11. Pacholczyk, D.: An Intelligent System Dealing with Negative Information. Proc. of Int. Conf. ISMIS'97, Charlotte, U. S. A, Lecture Notes in A. I. **1325**, (1997) 467-476
12. Pacholczyk, D.: A New Approach to the Intended Meaning of Negative Information, Proc. of 13th European Conf. on Art. Int., ECAI98, Brighton, UK, 23-28 August 1998, Pub. by J. Wiley & Sons (1998) 114-118
13. Pacholczyk, D.: A New Model dealing with Linguistic Negation within the Fuzzy Set Theory Context, Proc. of 6th European Congress on Intelligent Techniques and Soft Computing, EUFIT'98, Aachen, Germany (1998) 573 – 577
14. Pacholczyk, D, Levrat, B.: Towards a General Model for the Representation of Negated Nuanced Properties in a Fuzzy Context, Proc. of 5th Workshop of Logic, Language, Inform. and Computation, WOLLIC'98, Sao Paulo, Brazil, 28-31 July 1998, (1998) 169-177
15. Torra, V.: Negation Functions Based Semantics for Ordered Linguistic Labels. Int. Jour. of Intelligent Systems **11** 975-988 (1996)
16. Zadeh, L.A.: Fuzzy Sets. Information and Control, **8** (1965) 338-353
17. Zubert, R.: Implications sémantiques dans les langues naturelles, Editions du CNRS, Paris, France (1989)

Logic Programs for Intelligent Web Search

Bernd Thomas

Universität Koblenz, Institut für Informatik, Rheinau 1, D-56075 Koblenz, Germany
Email: bthomas@uni-koblenz.de

Abstract

We present a general framework for information extraction from web pages based on a special wrapper language, called *token-templates*. By using *token-templates* in conjunction with logic programs we are able to reason about web page contents, search and collect facts and derive new facts from various web pages. We give a formal definition for the semantics of logic programs extended by *token-templates* and define a general answer-complete calculus for these extended programs. These methods and techniques are used to build intelligent mediators and web information systems.
Keywords: intelligent information systems; intelligent information retrieval; WWW; information extraction; template based wrappers; mediators; logic programming; theory reasoning; deductive web databases; softbots.

1 Introduction

Our goal is to develop techniques for the process of information extraction (IE), locating specific pieces of text in a document, from semistructured documents like web pages. In the last few years many techniques have been developed to solve this problem [1, 6, 7, 9, 16], where *wrappers* and *mediators* fulfill the general process to retrieve and integrate information from heterogeneous data sources into one information system.

We focus our work on a special class of wrappers, which extract information from web pages and map it into a relational representation. We call this information extraction process *fact-retrieval*; due to logic programming the extracted information is represented by ground atoms. In this paper we present a general framework for the fact retrieval from arbitrary, semistructured documents based on our special wrapper language, called *token-templates*.

We assume that, normally, the user is guided by his own domain specific knowledge when searching the web, manually extracting information and comparing the found facts. It is very obvious that these user processes involve inference mechanisms like reasoning about the contents of web pages, deducing relations between web pages and using domain specific background knowledge. This user processes can be modeled by deduction, based on a set of rules, e.g. which pages to visit and how to extract facts. The logic programming paradigm allows us to: model background knowledge to guide the web search and the application of extraction templates; reason about web pages; collect relevant facts. In the context of *wrappers* and *mediators* [16], *token-templates* are used to construct special wrappers to retrieve facts from web pages. Logic programs in addition with token-templates offer a basis to construct wrappers and mediators, which search the web with deductive methods.

2 A Wrapper Language for Semistructured Documents

We assume the reader to be familiar with the concepts of *feature structures* and *unification* The process of fact-retrieval is separated into two major steps:

(a) The source code of a web page as shown in Figure 1 is transformed into a list of tokens (Section 2.1), by using an arbitrary lexical anlayser, like *FLEX* or *LEX*[1]. (b) Extraction templates built from tokens and special operators are applied to the tokenized document. According to the successfull matching of these templates the relevant information is extracted by means of unification techniques and mapped into a relational representation.

```
<P><IMG SRC=img/bmp_priv.gif><B>286 AT</B>,
1 MB Ram, 60 MB FP, 2 Disklaufw., Bigtower,
100 DM, 4 x 1 MB SIMM 30 Pin, 50 DM.
Tel.: 06742/ 5926
<P><IMG SRC=img/bmp_priv.gif><B>Pentium 90</B>
48 MB RAM, Soundblaster AWE 64, DM 650,-.
Tel.: 06743/ 1582
```

Fig. 1. HTML source code of an online advertisment

2.1 The Token

We call a *simple* and acyclic feature structure a *token*, if and only if it has a feature named type and all feature values consists either of variables or constants. That is, no feature value consists of another feature. We write variables in capital letters and constants quoted if they start with a capital letter. Furthermore, we choose a term notation for feature structures (token), that is different from that proposed by Carpenter in [2]. We do not code the features to a fixed argument position, instead we extend the arguments of the annotated term, by the notation Feature = Value (extended term notation). This offers us more flexibility in the handling of features. For example the text Pentium 90 may be written as the list of tokens:[token(type=html, tag=b), token(type=word,txt='Pentium'), token(type=wspace,val=blank), token(type=int,val=90), token(type=html_end,tag=b)].

2.2 Token Matching

Let us assume, that an arbitrary web page transformed into a token list is given. The key idea is now to recognize a token or a token sequence in this token list. Therefore we need techniques to match a token description with a token. For feature structures a special unification was defined in [12]. For our purposes we need a modified version of this unification, the *token-unification*.

Definition 1 (Token-Unification). *Let* $T_1 = token(m_1 = w_1, m_2 = w_2, \ldots, m_j = w_j)$ $j \geq$ *1 and* $T_2 = token(m'_1 = w'_1, m'_2 = w'_2, \ldots, m'_k = w'_k)$ $k \geq 1$ *be tokens.*

Let $A_1 = \bigcup_{i=1}^{j} \{(m_i, w_i)\}$ *and* $A_2 = \bigcup_{i=1}^{k} \{(m'_i, w'_i)\}$ *be the feature-value sets of the tokens* T_1 *and* T_2. *It must hold that* $\{m_1, \ldots, m_j\} \subseteq \{m'_1, \ldots, m'_k\}$. *If this is not the case, we call* T_1 *and* T_2 *not token-unifiable, written* $T_1 \not\sqcup T_2$.

Let $F = \{m \mid (m, w) \in A_1\}$ *be the set of features* T_1 *and* T_2 *have in common. The terms* T'_1 *and* T'_2 *are defined as follows:* $T'_1 := token(m_1 = w_1, \ldots, m_n = w_n)$ *and* $T'_2 := token(m_1 = w'_1, \ldots, m_n = w'_n)$ *with* $m_i \in F \wedge (m_i, w_i) \in A_1 \wedge (m_i, w'_i) \in A_2 \wedge 1 \leq i \leq n \wedge n = |F|$. T_1 *and* T_2 *are token-unifiable iff* T'_1 *is unifiable with* T'_2. *The most general unifier (mgU)*

---

[1] This method allows us to apply our techniques not only to *HTML*-documents, but also to any kind of semi-structured text documents.

σ *of T_1 and T_2 is the mgU of T_1' and T_2' wrt. the usual definition [11]. We write $T_1 \sqcup_\sigma T_2$ iff T_1 is token-unifiable with T_2 and σ is the mgU of the unification from T_1' with T_2'.* ∎

The motivation for this directed unification[2] is to interpret the *left* token to be a pattern to match the *right* token. This allows us to set up feature constraints in an easy way, by simply adding a feature to the *left* token. On the other hand we can match a whole class of tokens, if we decrease the feature set of the *left* token to consist only of the *type* feature. For example: *token(tag=X,type=html,href=Y)* $\sqcup_\sigma$ *token(type=html, tag=a,href='http://www.bmw.de')* with $\sigma = [X/a, Y/'http://www.bmw.de']$

For ease of notation we introduce an alternative notation t^k for a token of type k (type feature has value k), that is given by k or $k(f_1 = v_1, f_2 = v_2, \ldots, f_n = v_n)$ with f_i and v_i are the features and values of t^k where n is the number of features of t^k. We call this notation *term-pattern* and define a transformation $\mathcal{V}$ on *term-patterns* such that $\mathcal{V}$ transforms the *term-pattern* into the corresponding token. This transformation exchanges the functor of the *term-pattern*, from type k to *token* and adds the argument *type* $= k$ to the arguments. Now we can define the basic match operation on a *term-pattern* and a token:

Definition 2 (Term-Match). *Let t^k be a term-pattern and T a token in extended term notation. The term-pattern t^k matches the token T, $t^k \sqsubseteq_\sigma T$, iff $\mathcal{V}(t^k)$ is token-unifiable with T: $t^k \sqsubseteq_\sigma T \iff \mathcal{V}(t^k) \sqcup_\sigma T$ where σ is mgU.* ∎

Example: *html(href=Y)* $\sqsubseteq_\sigma$ *token(type=html,tag=a,href='http://www.bmw.de')*
       with $\sigma = [Y/'http://www.bmw.de']$

2.3 Token Pattern

If we interpret a token to be a special representation of text pieces, the definition of term-matching allows us to recognize certain pieces of text and extract them by the process of unification. This means the found substitution σ contains the extracted information. Therefore we developed the language of *token-pattern*, to define extraction templates, which are used to match sequences of tokens in a tokenized web page. *Token-patterns* are based on similiar concepts as regular expressions. The difference is, that additional operators for iteration, exclusion, enumeration, unification and negation are defined on *tokens* and *token-pattern*. Assume that a tokenized document D is given. A match of a *token-pattern* p on D, written $p \triangleright D$, returns a set of triples (MS, RS, σ), where MS is the matched token sequence, RS is the rest sequence of D and σ is the *mgU* of the token unifications applied during the matching process. We emphasize, that we compute all matches and do not stop after we have found one successful match, though this can be achieved by the use of the *once* operator. The following table gives a brief description of token-pattern.

---

[2] In the sense that the feature set of the *left* token must be a subset of the feature set of the *right* token.

pattern	semantics
p	If $p \sqsubseteq_\sigma D(1)$ holds, then the matched sequence is the list containing exactly one element $D(1)$ and RS is D without the first element. $D(n)$ denotes the n-th element of the sequence D.
$?p_1$	Matches the pattern p_1 once or never; first the match of p_1 then the empty match sequence is enumerated.
$!p_1$	Matches the pattern p_1 once or never; first the empty match sequence then the match of p_1 is enumerated.
$+p_1$	Matches the pattern p_1 arbitrarily often but at least once; uses a decreasing enumeration order of the matches according to their length, starting with the longest possible match.
$-p_1$	Matches pattern p_1 arbitrarily often but at least once; uses an increasing enumeration order of the matches according to their length, starting with the shortest possible match.
$*p_1$	Matches the pattern p_1 arbitrarily often; uses a decreasing enumeration order of the matches according to their length, starting with the longest possible match.
$\#p_1$	Matches the pattern p_1 arbitrarily often; uses a increasing enumeration order of the matches according to their length, starting with the shortest possible match.
$not(t_1,\ldots,t_n)$	The *not* operator matches exactly one token t in D, if no $t_i \in \{t_1,\ldots,t_n\}$ exists, such that $t_i \sqsubseteq_\sigma t$ holds. The token $t_1 \ldots t_n$ are excluded from the match.
$times(n,t)$	Matches exactly n tokens t.
any	Matches an arbitrary token.
$once(p_1)$	The *once* operator 'cuts' the set of matched tokens by p_1 down to the first match of p_1; useful if we are interested only in the first match and not in all alternative matches defined by p_1.
$X = p_1$	Unification of X and the matched sequence of p_1; only successful if p_1 is successful and if MS of p_1 is unifiable with X.
$p_1 \, and \, p_2$	Only if p_1 and p_2 both match successfully, this pattern succeeds. The matched sequence of p_1 and p_2, is the concatenation of MS of p_1 and MS of p_2.
$p_1 \, or \, p_2$	p succeeds if one of the pattern $p1$ or p_2 is successfully matched. The matched sequence of p is either the matched sequence of p_1 or p_2. The *and* operator has higher priority than the *or* operator, (e.g. *a and b or c* $\equiv$ (*a and b*) *or c*)

Fig. 2. Token-Template for advertisment extraction

2.4 Token-Templates

A *token-template* defines a relation between a tokenized document, extraction variables and a *token-pattern*. Extraction variables are those variables used in a *token-pattern*, which are of interest due to their instantiation wrt. to the information we want to extract. They *contain* the extracted information we are interested in.

Definition 3 (Token-Template). *Let p be a token-pattern, D an arbitrary tokenized document and $v_1,\ldots,v_n \in \mathcal{V}ar(p)$ variables in p. For $v_1,\ldots,v_n$ we write v and v_σ for applying the substitution σ to v. A token-template r is defined as follows:*

$$r(D,v,p) := \{(D, v_\sigma, p_\sigma) | (MS, RS, \sigma) \in p \rhd D\}$$

194

Template definitions are written as: $\underline{template}\ r(D, v_1, \ldots, v_n) := p$
r is called the template name, v_σ is the extraction tupel and $v_1, \ldots, v_n$ are called extraction variables. ∎

Figure 2 depicts a *token-template*[3] for the extraction of advertisments as shown in Figure 1.

$\underline{template}\ advertise(Doc, Item, Description) := $ #*any and* $html(tag = img)$ *and* $html(tag = b)$ *and* $Item = *not(html\_end(tag = b))$ *and* $html\_end(tag = b)$ *and* $once(Description = *not(html(tag = p)))$

3 Logic Programs and Token-Templates

The basic idea of the integration of *token-templates* and LPs is to extend a logic programm with a set of *token-templates* (extended LPs), that are interpreted as special program clauses. Intuitively *token-templates* provide a set of facts to be used in logic programs. From the implementational point of view these *token-template* predicates may be logical programs or modules that implement the downloading of web pages and the token matching. From the theoretical point of view we consider these template sets to be axiomatizations of a theory, where the calculation of the theory (the facts) are performed by a background reasoner. In the following we refer to *normal logic programs*[11] when we talk about logic programs. We assume the reader to be familiar with the fields of *logic programming* [11] and *theory reasoning* [13].

3.1 Template Theories

A *token-template theory* $\mathcal{T}_T$ is the set of all template ground atoms, that we obtain by applying all templates in T. For example, consider the template set $\{t(D, v, p)\}$. Assume p to be an arbitrary *token-pattern* and v an extraction tupel. A *template theory* for T is given by $\mathcal{T}_{\{t(D,v,p)\}} := \{t(D, v', P')|(D, v', p') \in t(D, v, p)\}$. This interpretation of *token-templates* associates a set of ground unit clauses with a given set of *token-templates*. The formal definition is as follows:

Definition 4 (Template-Theory, $\mathcal{T}_T$–Interpretation, $\mathcal{T}_T$–Model). *Let* $G(t(D, v, p)) = \{t(D, v', p')|D$ *is a ground term and* $(D, v', p') \in t(D, v, p)\}$ *be the set of facts of a template* $t(D, v, p)$ *and* $T = \{t_1(D, v_1, p_1), t_2(D, v_2, p_2), \ldots, t_n(D, v_n, p_n)\}$ *a set of token-templates. Then* $\mathcal{T}_T = \bigcup_{i=1}^n G(t_i(D, v_i, p_i))$ *with* $t_i(D, v_i, p_i) \in T$ *is the token-template theory for* T. *Let* P *be a normal logic program with signature* Σ, *such that* Σ *is also a signature for* $\mathcal{T}_T$:

- *A* Σ–*Interpretation* I *is a* $\mathcal{T}_T$–Σ–*Interpretation iff* $I \models \mathcal{T}_T$.
- *A Herbrand* $\mathcal{T}_T$–Σ–*Interpretation is a* $\mathcal{T}_T$–Σ–*Interpretation, that is also a herbrand interpretation.*
- *A* $\mathcal{T}_T$–Σ–*Interpretation* I *is a* $\mathcal{T}_T$–*Model for* P *iff* $I \models P$.
- *Let* X *be a clause, wrt.* Σ. X *is a logical* $\mathcal{T}_T$–*Consequence from* P, $P \models_{\mathcal{T}_T} X$, *iff for all* $\mathcal{T}_T$–Σ–*Interpretations* $I : I \models P$ *follows* $I \models X$.

∎

---

[3] For a more detailed description of the *token-template* language (e.g. recursive templates, code calls) the reader is refered to [15].

The corresponding *template theory* for the token-template depicted in Figure 2 and the document of Figure 1 is the set: {advertise('286 AT', '1 MB Ram, 60 MB FP, 2 Disklaufw., Bigtower, 100 DM, 4 x 1 MB SIMM 30 Pin, 50 DM. Tel.: 06742/ 5926'), advertise('Pentium 90', '48 MB RAM, Soundblaster AWE 64, DM 650,-. Tel.: 06743/ 1582')}

3.2 The $\mathcal{T}_T$–Calculus

So far we have shown when a formula is a logical consequence from an extended logic program. Next the definition of a general calculus for *extended logic programs* based on an arbitrary sound and answer complete calculus is given.

Definition 5 ($\mathcal{T}_T$–**Derivation**). *Let $\mathcal{K}$ be a sound and answer-complete calculus for normal logic programs and $\vdash$ is the derivation defined by $\mathcal{K}$. Let P be a normal logic program, T a set of token-templates and $\mathcal{T}_T$ the template theory for T. A query $\exists Q$ with calculated substitution σ is $\mathcal{T}_T$–derivable from P, $P \vdash_{\mathcal{T}_T} Q\sigma$, iff $Q\sigma$ is derivable from $P \cup \mathcal{T}_T$, $P \cup \mathcal{T}_T \vdash Q\sigma$. A calculus $\mathcal{K}$ with $\mathcal{T}_T$–Derivation is called $\mathcal{T}_T$–Calculus.* ∎

Theorem 1 (**Soundness $\mathcal{T}_T$–Calculus**). *Let $\mathcal{K}$ be a $\mathcal{T}_T$–Calculus and $\vdash_{\mathcal{T}_T}$ the derivation relation defined by $\mathcal{K}$. Let T be a set of token-templates, $\mathcal{T}_T$ the template-theory for T and Q a query for a normal program P. Further let σ be a substitution calculated by $\vdash_{\mathcal{T}_T}$. Then $\forall Q : P \vdash_{\mathcal{T}_T} Q\sigma \Rightarrow P \models_{\mathcal{T}_T} \forall Q\sigma$* □

Theorem 2 (**Completeness $\mathcal{T}_T$–Calculus**). *Let $\mathcal{K}$ be $\mathcal{T}_T$–Calculus and $\vdash_{\mathcal{T}_T}$ the derivation relation defined by $\mathcal{K}$. Let T be a set of token-templates, $\mathcal{T}_T$ the template-theory for T and Q a query for a normal program P. Let θ be a correct answer for Q, σ a calculated answer and γ a substitution.*
Then $\forall \theta : P \models_{\mathcal{T}_T} Q\theta \Rightarrow P \vdash_{\mathcal{T}_T} Q\sigma$ where $\theta = \sigma\gamma$ □

By Definition 5 we can extend any arbitrary sound and answer-complete first order predicate logic calculus with template theories and use this retrieved information from the WWW for further deductive processes. That means, existing theorem provers or logic programming systems can be used to query the web and reason about its contents. Therefore a calculation procedure is needed to calculate the according template theories. In this paper we neither describe such a procedure in detail nor do we show how the calculation of a template theory can be efficiently integrated in the derivation process of a calculus. The proofs of the soundness and completness theorem are given in [15].

4 Deductive Techniques for Intelligent Web Search

Logic programming and deduction in general offer a wide variety to guide the web search and fact-retrieval process with intelligent methods and inference processes. The following sections describe some of these techniques.

4.1 Deductive Web Databases

Assume we know two web pages of shoe suppliers, whose product descriptions we want to use as facts in a deductive database. Additionally we are interested in some information about the producer of the product, his address and telephone number that can be retrieved from an additional web page. Therefore we define two *token-templates*, *price_list* and *address*. To simplify notation we leave out the exact *token-pattern* definitions. The following small deductive database allows us to ask for articles and to derive new facts that provide us with information about the product and the producer. We achieve this by the two rules *article* and *product*, which extract the articles offered in the web pages and will derive new facts about the article and the producer.

$web\_page('shoes\ online', http://www.sh-online.com/offer.html) \leftarrow$
$web\_page('Land\ of\ Shoes', http://www.shland.com/products.html) \leftarrow$
$article(Supplier, Article, Price, ProducerUrl) \leftarrow$
$\quad web\_page(Supplier, Document), price\_list(Document, Article, Price, ProducerUrl, Pattern)$
$product(Supplier, Producer, Article, Price, Str, Tel, City) \leftarrow$
$\quad article(Supplier, Article, Price, ProdUrl), address(ProdUrl, Supplier, Str, Tel, City, Pattern)$

Example query: Select all products with article name *"Doc Martens"* that cost less than 100: $\leftarrow Article = "Doc\ Martens", product(Supplier, Article, Producer, Price, Str, Tel, City),$
$\qquad Price < 100$

4.2 Conceptual Hierachy Guided Search

Many information systems lack the ability to use a conceptual background knowledge to include related topics of interest to their search. Consider the case that a user is interested in computer systems that cost less than 1000 DM. It is obvious that the system should know the common computer types and descriptions (e.g. IBM, Toshiba, Compaq, Pentium, Notebook, Laptop) and how they are conceptually related to each other. Such knowledge will assist a system in performing a successful search. One way to represent such knowledge is by concept description languages or in general by means of knowledge representation techniques. Extended logic programs offer powerful means to set up ontologies. For example a simple relation *is_a* can be used to represent conceptual hierachies to guide the search for information. Consider the following small knowledge base:

$\quad notebook('ThinkPad') \leftarrow \qquad\qquad notebook('Satellite') \leftarrow$
$\quad is\_a(notebook, computer) \leftarrow \qquad\quad is\_a(desktop, computer) \leftarrow$
$\quad is\_a(X, notebook) \leftarrow notebook(X)$
$\quad relevant(Q, Z) \leftarrow is\_a(Z, Q)$
$\quad relevant(Q, Z) \leftarrow is\_a(Y, Q), relevant(Y, Z)$

Assume our general query to search for computers less than 1000 DM is splitted into a sub-query like $\leftarrow relevant(computers, X)$ to our small example knowledge base; which results in a set of answers: $\theta = \{[X/notebook], [X/desktop], [X/'ThinkPad'],$ $[X/'Satellite']\}$. This additional inferred query information θ can be used in two different ways: (a) Use it to search for new web pages, e.g. by querying standard search engines with elements of θ as search keywords and apply further extended logic programs on the returned candidate pages. (b) Enhance the information extraction process with the derived information θ by reducing the constraints on special token features in the token-templates to be applied, e.g. $word(txt=Q)$ or $word(txt=\theta_1)$ or ... or $word(txt=\theta_n)$ where θ_i are computed answers and Q is the original object to search for. That means in general the search is extended with all *known* sub-concepts (e.g. $computer \to notebook \to ...$) or instances (e.g. *'ThinkPad'*) of the query concept.

4.3 Optimizing Web Retrieval

To avoid fetching of irrelevant web pages and starting a *fact-retrieval* process we know for certain to fail, Levy suggests in [10] the use of source descriptions. For the fact retrieval from the WWW this might offer a great speed up, because due to the network load the fetching of web documents is often very time intensive. We can easily apply these methods to *extended logic programs*, by the definition of rules, whose body literals define constraints on the head arguments expressing our knowledge about the content of the web pages. The following example illustrates these methods:

$$offer('http://www.autos.de', Price, Country) \leftarrow Price < 40000, Country = 'Deutschland'$$
$$offer('http://www.cars.com', Price, Country) \leftarrow Price > 40000, Country = 'USA'$$
$$product(Car, Price, Country) \leftarrow offer(Url, Price, Country),$$
$$template\_cars(Url, Car, Price, Country)$$

Assuming we are interested in american cars that cost 50000 dollars, the query *product(C,50000,'USA')* will retrieve the according offers. Because of the additional constraints on the price and the country given in the body of the rule *offer*, the irrelevant web page with german car offers is left out. By simple methods, provided by the logic programming paradigm for free, we are able to guide the search and fact retrieval in the world wide web based on knowledge representation techniques and we are able to speed up the search for relevant information.

5 Related Work and Conclusion

Several web information systems have been developed in the last few years. One class of applications is called *Softbots* [4], which are domain specific automated search tools for the WWW. Such existing systems use either tailored extraction techniques (*Ahoy!*) that are very domain specific or their extraction techniques are based on highly restrictive assumptions about the syntactical structure of a web page (*Shopbot*). Both systems do not follow the concept of a general purpose extraction language like *token-templates*. *Token-templates* are applicable to any kind of semistructured text documents, and hence not restricted to a specific domain.

Systems like *IM* [10] or *W3QS* [8] also provide means to query web information sources. Though Levy *et al.* also choose a relational data model to reason about data, and show several techniques for source descriptions or constructing query plans, they leave the problem of information extraction undiscussed in their work. We showed solutions for both the extraction of facts and reasoning by extended logic programs. The *W3QS* system uses a special web query language similiar to the relational database query language *SQL*. Though an additional construction kit for IE processes is given, this seems to be focussed only on the detection of hyper links and their descriptions. The concept of database views for web pages is also introduced, but no information about recursive views is provided, whereas extended logic programs offer these abilities.

Heterogeneous information systems, like *HERMES* [14], *Infomaster* [5] or *TSIM-MIS* [3] all use special mediator techniques to access web information sources among other data sources. These systems use their own mediator model (language) to interface with the special data source wrappers. The system *HERMES* for example is based on a declarative logical mediator language and therefore is similiar to our approach using extended logic programs as mediators and *token-templates* as a special wrapper language. The advantage of our presented approach is simply that the above named systems, except *TSIMMIS*, do not incorporate a general purpose wrapper language for text documents.

Different from the template based extraction languages described in [1] and [7] or the underlying language used in the wrapper construction tool by Gruser et. al. [6], *token-templates* incorporate the powerful concepts of recursion and *code calls* [15]. These concepts allow the recognition and extraction of arbitrary hierachical syntactic structures and extend the matching process by additional control procedures invoked by code calls. Logic programs used as *code calls* can guide the extraction process with a manifold of AI methods. Our methods presented have been successfully implemented as a search-engine for private advertisments [15] and a meta online-encyclopedia.

References

1. M. E. Califf and R. J. Mooney. Relational Learning of Pattern-Match Rules for Information Extraction. In *Working Papers of the ACL-97 Workshop in Natural Language Learning*, 1997.
2. B. Carpenter. Typed Feature Structures: an Extension of First-order Terms. In *Proceedings of the International Symposium on Logic Programming*, 1991. San Diego.
3. S. Chawathe, H. Garcia-Molina, J. Hammer, K. Ireland, Y. Papakonstantinou, Y. Ullman, and J. Widom. The TSIMMIS project: Integration of heterogeneous information sources. In *Proceedings of IPSJ*, 1994. Japan.
4. O. Etzioni. Moving Up the Information Food Chain. *AI Magazine*, 18(2):11–18, Summer 1997.
5. M. R. Genesereth, A. M. Keller, and O. Duschka. Infomaster: An Information Integration System. *Proceedings of ACM SIGMOD Conference*, May 1997.
6. J. Gruser, L. Raschid, M. Vidal, and L. Bright. A wrapper generation toolkit to specify and construct wrappers for web accesible data. Technical report, UMIACS, University of Maryland, 1998.
7. J. Hammer, H. Garcia-Molina, J. Cho, R. Aranha, and A. Crespo. Extracting semistructured information from the web. In *In Proceedings of the Workshop on Management of Semistructured Data*, May 1997.
8. D. Konopnicki and O. Shmueli. W3QS: A query system for the world-wide web. In *Proceedings of VLDB'95*, 1995.
9. N. Kushmerick, D. S. Weld, and R. Doorenbos. Wrapper Induction for Information Extraction. In M. E. Pollack, editor, *Fifteenth International Joint Conference on Artificial Intelligence*, volume 1, pages 729–735, August 1997. Japan.
10. A. Y. Levy, A. Rajaraman, and J. J. Ordille. Querying Heterogeneous Information Sources Using Source Descriptions. In *Proceedings of the 22nd VLDB Conference*, 1996. Mumbai(Bombay), India.
11. J. Lloyd. *Foundations of Logic Programming*. Springer-Verlag, 2 edition, 1987.
12. S. M. Shieber. *An Introduction to Unification-Based Approaches to Grammar*. CSLI, Leland Stanford Junior University, 1986. CSLI Lecture Notes 4.
13. M. Stickel. Automated Deduction by Theory Resolution. *Journal of Automated Reasoning*, 1:333–355, 1985.
14. V. Subrahmanian, S. Adali, A. Brink, R. Emery, J. J. Lu, A. Rajput, T. J. Rogers, R. Ross, and C. Ward. HERMES: A Heterogeneous Reasoning and Mediator System, 1996. http://www.cs.umd.edu//projects/hermes/overview/paper/index.html.
15. B. Thomas. Intelligent Web Querying with Logic Programs. In J. Dix and S. Hölldobler, editors, *Proceedings of the Workshop on Inference Systems in Knowledge-based Systems, preceding the national German AI conference KI '98, Bremen, Germany*. University of Koblenz, TR 10/98, August 1998.
16. G. Wiederhold. Mediators in the architecture of future information systems. *IEEE Computer*, pages 38–49, March 1992.

Representing Document Content via an Object-Oriented Paradigm

Roberto Basili, Massimo Di Nanni, Maria Teresa Pazienza

Department of Computer Science, System and Production
University of Roma, *Tor Vergata*
Via di Tor Vergata, 00133, Roma, ITALY
e-mail: {basili,dinanni,pazienza}@info.uniroma2.it

Abstract. Efficient software infrastructures for the design and implementation of Intelligent Information Systems (IIS) are very important, especially in the area of intelligent NLP-based systems. Recently several approaches have been proposed in literature. However, the emphasis is usually centred on the integration of heterogeneous linguistic processors and the problem of the representation of linguistic data *in vivo* is left in the shadow. In this paper an object oriented architecture for a NLP-based IIS devoted to information extraction tasks will be discussed. An application of this model to a distributed document categorisation framework, employed within an existing system, TREVI [9], will be discussed as a relevant case study.

1 Introduction

NLP-based Intelligent Information Systems are particularly challenging with respect to software infrastructures supporting reuse and adaptation of processors and resources. These classes of systems in fact are characterized by complex architectures for the linguistic processing and push for high modularity: underlying algorithms, methods are not completely understood and different architectures are possible, relying on different modules, to be integrated in a variety of ways. From one side systematic abstraction mechanisms are required to offer to the different linguistic processes a transparent access to linguistic data, usually characterized by a variety of properties. On the other side, the required flexibility of the application architectures pushes in the direction of client-server paradigms for the distribution of the overall NLP tasks. Moreover, complex language processing tasks require extensive resources (e.g. dictionaries, corpora, lexicons). In general such source data are extremely heterogeneus with respect to underlying linguistic theories as well as implementation formats. Then, a good modeling process should guarantee a transparent approach to this information. Effort in this direction has been recently spent in several research centres and the issue is becoming increasingly important in the area of Language Engineering.

Several projects (Tipster [10], GATE [6], CORELLI [11]) concentrated on the definition of software architectures to support the management of complex information in Natural Language Processing (NLP) systems. However, the emphasis is usually centred on the integration of heterogeneous linguistic processors. This is only a partial answer to the above problems as the representation of linguistic data *in vivo* is left in the shadow. Important factors, like robustness, flexibility, portability, scalability and multilinguality, strongly push for data independence, abstraction and reusability of the variety of information related to a given document (i.e. words, structures and content). For example, a linguistic processors (e.g. a POS tagger) may be exploited within several application scenarios (e.g. language understanding as well as information retrieval). Thus, although a lemma (with its own part-of-speech) may well be described systematically in a lexicon, as a static information, something more is needed: the property the lemma shows a unique part-of-speech in a given context (i.e *in vivo*) is worth of a separate, independent (and possibly optimized) representation, transparent for different consumers and thus reusable. Thus, such a *in vivo*representation should be carefully distinguished from its counterpart in a lexicon. This last aspect will be the focus of this paper for which an original proposal is discussed. In the next section different approaches to design of software infrastructure to support NLP-based applications will be briefly discussed. In section 3, a model focused on textual phenomena (i.e. properties of linguistic structures *in vivo*) is suggested and its relationships with language resources discussed. Section 4 describes an existing architecture based on the suggested approach and actually prototyped within the TREVI [9] European project.

2 Software Infrastructure for Natural Language Processing

The relevance of the "so called" *software infrastructures for NLP* problem is well documented by the growing number of research works that are populating the literature (e.g. [10], [6], [11], [12], [2]). The common aim of these works is the attempt to define support architectures for complex information management based on Natural Language Processing (NLP) techniques.

The shift from *Computational Linguistic* to *Language Engineering*, as discussed in [11], is an evidence of the maturity of NLP systems. In particular the concept of reuse in NLP is widely studied.

Sharing NLP software components (e.g. a morphological analyser) remains much more underestimated. The co-operation among different components requires an integration at three different levels: the *process or communication layer* (the two components could be written in different programming languages or can run on different nodes in a computer network), the *data layer* (that defines a general data representation formalism to store linguistic information) and the *linguistic layer* (that characterizes the interpretation of data to be exchanged with respect to a common linguistic theory).

The Corelli Document Processing Architecture take in account all above mentioned issues as well as some problems related to the area of *software-level engineering*, like robustness, portability, scalability or inter-language communication. An Object-Oriented approach is used to design the overall architecture while the CORBA [1] services architecture is used to support distributed processing.

An architecture to build corpus processing systems using a SGML data formalism is described in [2]. The proposed architecture uses pipes to connect different Unix linguistic processes (process or communication layer). This kind of infrastructure requires that the information related to a text is represented in a linear sequence of characters. For this reason an SGML formalism is used to augment text with the linguistic data detected by each processing module (Data Layer). This strategy has different advantages: avoids a proliferation of formalisms for different kind of linguistic data, agrees to a well known standard, exploits the availability of corpora in the SGML format (e.g. British National Corpus) and supports the input/output procedures across implementations of different linguistic modules. This infrastructure does not specify the Linguistic Layer nor linguistic knowledge representation formalisms.

In [6] an alternative approach based on GATE (General Architecture for Text Engineering) is described. The concept of *textual annotation* is used to supply a method to associate information to spans of text during a document analysis. An annotation is characterised by an unique identifier, a type, a set of spans and a sequence of attribute-value pairs. No assumption is made either at the process level or at the linguistic level. However, at the data level, NLP components exchange data reading and writing annotations or attributes related to documents and document collections. The Gate Document Manager (*gdm*) component is devoted to support the reading and writing of annotation. So, specifying a processing module interface is sufficient to define its requirement and contribution in terms of involved annotation and attributes. GATE also provides a graphical user interface to define complex NLP systems by combining different components. In contrast to the previous approach, the added information are stored independently from the source document and each linguistic processing module can recall only the useful information instead of the whole information already associated to the document.

With respect to the problem of sharing and reusing language resources (e.g. dictionaries), in [12] is reported a proposal for a common object-oriented model for language data resources in order to encapsulate the union of available linguistic information. All available resources are represented in a hierarchy where the top level contains very general abstractions shared by different resources while the leaves hold the resource-specific information. The object-oriented design allows a conceptual view of the resources by abstracting from the structure and the typology of the database used to store specific information, e.g. concept and relations. We can also note the attention to follow standards either in the area of software design with UML [8] or in the knowledge representation with EAGLES [4].

In table 1 the properties of each refered infrastructure are summarised.

It should be noted that, the emphasis of the described architectures is mainly focused on the integration of heterogeneous linguistic techniques/processors and the problem of the representation of linguistic data *in vivo* is left in the shadow. In fact the information related to the third column of Table 1 (i.e. the Linguistic Layer) is left unspecified by all the current proposals. On the contrary, as pointed out above, it plays a crucial role in a real NLP-based application.

Table 1. Software Infrastructure features

Sofware Infrastructure	Data Layer	Linguistic Layer	Process or Comunication Layer	Language Resource
GATE [6] Tipster	Annotation	Unspecified (Tipster-based)	User-dependent NLP chain	Unspecified
CORELLI [11] Tipster/CORBA	Annotation	Unspecified (Tipster-based)	Client Server using CORBA	Resource Server
SGML [2]	SGML Mark-up	Unspecified	Pipe of Unix processes	Unspecified

3 Representing linguistic information *in vivo*

A computational representation of linguistic knowledge deals with at least two main aspects. The first is the representation of *textual information*. A lemma or a syntagmatic structure is to be represented as it is going to be used by several consumers: an information retrieval system, for example, may require (possibly comlex) *lemmas* for indexing, mostly in the same way a machine translation system does. The representation of lemmas in their context (i.e as they are derived from a document) is independent from their representation as linguistic items in a lexicon. We will use the notion of *textual information* for this kind of input that a variety of applications (or consumers) need. Textual information is produced during the linguistic processing of the text. Each linguistic module in a NLP system usually needs part of it as a requirement, and produces its extension/enrichment as contributions.

A second aspect deals with the representation of resource information. Usually NLP components need different linguistic knowledge bases to accomplish the analysis. Morphological dictionaries or POS tagger lexicons are simple instances. Lexical knowledge bases are more complex examples, where committments to linguistic theories become a relevant source of difficulties for usage/integration.

As a consequence an architecture to efficiently manage textual information with respect to available linguistic processors and resources should provide a systematic abstraction to serve as a high-level interface among language processors. Moreover, it should provide a set of primitive (i.e. atomic) linguistic objects (e.g. a lemma object) to support their mapping into existing resources (e.g. the set of lemma's senses in a dictionary).

The following section discusses an Object-Oriented model for textual information, its advantages and the role of external language resources with respect to this representation. The UML [8] standard is adopted to avoid misunderstanding in the formal representation of the object model.

3.1 Representing Textual Information

The problem of linguistic information representation can be discussed at different levels ([11]). The data layer specification is devoted to define the data structure used to store the linguistic information. At the same level we need to establish a standard mechanism to link this information to the text. Formalisms proposed in [10] and [2] are generally independent from the underlying linguistic theory because they are defined to support general NLP systems. However the textual information requires a characterization within the linguistic level specification usually based on some linguistic theory formalisms. It is thus necessary, in order to build an NLP application, to firstly define the model of textual information with respect to the adopted linguistic layer and map it into the available data level formalism (Tipster or SGML). A strict seperation between the data and the linguistic layer implies two complex problems with respect to the model definition phase. First, it is the difficult to represent complex linguistic information by using too simple constituents or blocks (annotations or markers). Second, NLP components need systematically wrapper interfaces that are the responsibles for the data-to-linguistic level translations.

Our aim is thus to define the design of a formal representation for textual information at the linguistic level by adopting the Object Oriented paradigm. The result is a set of *object interfaces* to represent, for example, *lemmas* (i.e. output of a specific lemmatisation module), simple or complex *proper noun* and application related information, like *events*. The advantage is that these latter pieces of linguistic information can be easily derived from the former. Events, for example are defined in term of their participants (i.e semantically typed lemmas) or, recursively, other events (see section 4 for an instance).

The main advantage of the OO paradigm is the possibility to hide the data level representation of the textual information in the *implementation* supplied for the linguistic level interfaces. Another important benefit is the capability to explicitly define in the OO model the relations between different objects to represent the linguistic motivated linkage across two or more textual information. For example a complex term, that can be associated to a compound terminological expression, is explicitly related (via a *composition* relation) to the atomic terms representing its constituent. This feature guarantees an easy and efficient access to the textual information within a linguistic module implementation. This because each linguistic feature or property, useful for any NLP consumer module, is accessed directly by invoking specific methods in the textual object.

Our proposal is a set of specific object interfaces to represent the most common textual information, eventually by agreeing to a specific linguistic theory when it cannot be avoided. Section 4 will discuss an instance of a general representation for textual information, as it has been exploited within a NLP-based categorisation system.

The Role of External Language Resources

The same approach described for textual information representation is already adopted to design high level interfaces for language resources in [12], where an OO infrastructure where several language resources can be combined is proposed. An ongoing cooperation with these authors resulted in the definition of the object model for Wordnet, as one instance of integrated resources. The linguistic level class diagram for the data model of Wordnet is reported in Fig. 1.

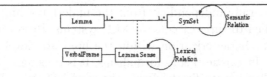

Fig. 1. Linguistic level class diagram for Wordnet resource

It includes only the main concepts expressed in Wordnet. We refer to [5] for the linguistic description of the depicted concepts. Our interest in this context is to describe how the concepts expressed above, at different levels of specification, influence the software design of this specxific language resource.

The implementation level class diagram, reported in Fig. 2, emphasises the distinction between the two specification levels.

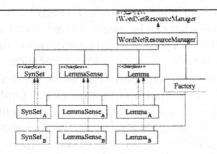

Fig. 2. Data level class diagram for Wordnet resource

The interfaces correspond to a linguistic level specification for *Lemmas*, *SynSet* and *LemmaSenses*. A well known design pattern called *Factory Pattern* [3] is used to realise the software independence between the interfaces and the classes, that implement the interfaces, used to create the linkage with the data level formalism. The Factory object allows the use of several groups of classes, that implement the same interfaces, in order to create, for the same linguistic specification, different data level formalisms.

4 A case study: an NLP based Document Classification System

This section is devoted to underling how an OO data model of *textual information* can be used in a real NLP-based application. A distributed system for document categorisation and enrichment of thematic texts is the current case study within the proposed design methodology. The first prototype of the system has been fully designed and partially integrated within the TREVI (Text Retrieval and Enrichment for Vital Information) european project (see [7])

In TREVI a stream of incoming documents is processed in a distributed environment. A client server approach is adopted where each system component co-operate to the information flow to provide several classes of final users with those documents matching their needs (expressed via general profiles), enriched with structural information and possibly linked to existing (user-owned) repositories of previous texts.

In TREVI, the specific emphasis on linguistic content rather than on simpler retrieval procedures resulted in the definition of a complex architecture for multilingual natural language processing. In 3 is represented a functional specification of the NLP engine integrated within the TREVI architecture. A main

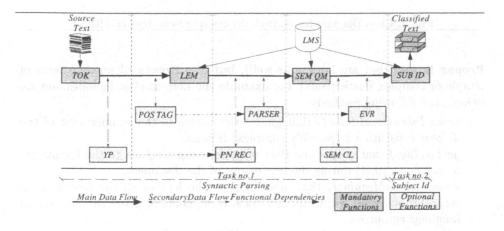

Fig. 3. Functional architecture of the NLP engine in TREVI

data processing chain is extended by several optional linguistic processing modules every time the support resources are available. The data model proposed in the previous section has been adopted to create an high level interface and access the textual information created and consumed during the parsing activity. The approach supports a transparent access to the information the NLP engine produces, i.e. *Contributions*, consumed by the later components in the TREVI information processing chain.

The UML class diagram representing the data model for the *Contribution* of the NLP component is reported in Fig. 4. A set of classes and their relationships are defined and represent both atomic and structured linguistic information extracted during the document analysis. The *ParsedArticle* class is defined to represent documents. All the articles are composed of at least one *ParsedText* object. A ParsedText object contains all the linguistic information related to a text field of a structured article. A set of specialised ParsedArticle(s) is introduced to represent different article types: a given formatted text, in fact, can contain several ParsedText objects related to textual components (i.e. title vs. abstract or sections) absent in other article types. The same figure also shows a set of classes defined to represent textual information like Tokens, Lemmas,

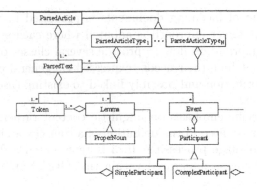

Fig. 4. Class Diagram for textual objects representation in TREVI

Proper Nouns (that are **Lemmas** as well), but also **Events** (defined in term of simple or complex **Participants**). For example the **Lemma** class includes, among others, the following methods:

- *enumTokenConstituent()* that guides the access to the enumeration of the Tokens constuting a (possibly complex) lemma.
- *getPosTag()* that output the Part of Speech tag assigned to the lemma (in a specific context) during the processing of the document.
- *enumLemmaMeaning()* that associates to the lemma all the semantic interpretations valid within the lemma specific context, given the underlying language resources.

Another example is represented by the class *Event*. A potential event (e.g. *management succession*) can be described in terms of its parteicipants (a leaving manager (L), the incoming manager (N), their position (P) and the reference industry (I)). As an example a method like *enumParticipant()* that gets the enumeration of the event participants (e.g. the set of information associated with the lemmas L, N, P and I) is a crucial to any event, and it has been defined for this class. It is worth noticing that the **Lemma** representation can be entirely reused in different application scenarios without any specific change. This is generally true for a non trivial sub-set of classes related to textual information. This is no longer true for more complex classes, e.g. **Events**, although, in TREVI, more then one linguistic task is related to event recognition and management. The idea is that the set of available methods should cover the most common textual information requested by a consumer (i.e. a linguistic or non-linguistic module, e.g. a parser vs. a publisher module).

5 Discussion

The presented OO model for sharing contributions of a NLP component within a complex Intelligent Information System provides an explicit representation of textual information. The proposed model aims to: (1) define a set of object interfaces to represent the textual information at a linguistic level, (2) hide the data level specification inside the objects that are defined to implement these interfaces and (3) guarantee an high level interaction with the linguistic information to better support the design and implementation of linguistic computational modules. The medium term research target is the definition of a framework where the design of a target NLP application reduces to a composition of existing objects models for textual information. The case study discussed in section 4 embodies the suggested principles and demonstrates the advantages of these design choices. Several kinds of textual information (like token or lemmas) are general enough to be fully reused within newer NLP-based applications. However, in a newer and specific application scenario the data model may suffer of specificity. Although further work in this direction is needed, the availabilty of large classes of linguistic objects and the support to the customization of unsatisfactory definitions (i.e. complex concepts like events, or other theory specific information) constitute an important result. The role of textual information in the research on software infrastructures for NLP systems should thus play a major role, in view of the fortcoming NLP applications.

References

1. The common object request broker: Architecture and specification, ver. 2.0. Technical document ptc/96-03-0, OMG, 1995.
2. McKelvie D., Brew C., and Thompson H. Using sgml as a basis for data-intensive nlp. In *ANLP97*, 1997.
3. Gamma E., Helm R., Johnson R., Vlissides J., and Booch G. (Foreword), editors. *Design Patterns : Elements of Reusable Object-Oriented Software.* Addison-Wesley Professional Computing, October 1994.
4. EAGLES. Evaluation of natural language processing systems. In *EAG-EWG-PR.2*, 1994.
5. Miller G. Wordnet: an on-line lexical database. *International Journal of Lexicography*, 3:656–691, 1994.
6. Cunningham H., Humphreys K., Gaizauskas R., and Wilks Y. Software infrastructure for natural language processing. In *ANLP97*, 1997.
7. Mazzucchelli L. and Marabello M.V. Specification of the overall toolkit architecture. In *EP 23311 TREVI Project Deliverable 7D1*, 1997.
8. Fowler M., Scott K. (Contributor), and Booch G., editors. *Uml Distilled : Applying the Standard Object Modeling Language.* Addison-Wesley Object Technology Series, June 1997.
9. Basili R., Mazzucchelli L. Di Nanni M., Marabello M.V., and Pazienza M.T. Nlp for text classification: the trevi experience. In *Proceedings of the Second International Conference on Natural Language Processing and Industrial Applications, Universite' de Moncton, New Brunswick (Canada)*, August 1998.
10. Grishman R. and CAWG. Tipster text phase ii: Architecture design. Technical report, New York University, 1996.
11. Zajac R., Carper M., and Sharples N. An open distributed architecture for reuse and integration of heterogeneous nlp component. In *ANLP97*, 1997.
12. Peters W., Cunningham H., McCauley C., Bontcheva K., and Wilks Y. Uniform language resource access and distribution. In *ICLRE98*, 1998.

A Learning Server for Inducing User Classification Rules in a Digital Library Service

G. Semeraro, M.F. Costabile, F. Esposito, N. Fanizzi, S. Ferilli

Dipartimento di Informatica, Università di Bari
Via Orabona 4, 70125 Bari, Italy
{semeraro, costabile, esposito, fanizzi, ferilli}@di.uniba.it

Abstract. IDL (Intelligent Digital Library) is a prototypical intelligent digital library service that is currently being developed at the University of Bari. Among the characterizing features of IDL there are a retrieval engine and several facilities available for the library users. In this paper, we present the learning component, named *Learning Server*, that has been exploited in IDL for document analysis, classification, and understanding, as well as for building a user modeling module. This module is the basic component for providing IDL with a weak form of user interface adaptivity. Indeed, IDL is equipped with a web-based visual environment, which is primarily intended to improve the interaction of inexperienced users with the library.

1 Introduction and motivation

IDL (Intelligent Digital Library) is a prototypical intelligent digital library service that is currently being developed at the University of Bari [13]. Among the characterizing features of IDL there are a retrieval engine and several functionalities that are available to the library users. IDL exploits machine learning techniques for document analysis, classification, and understanding, as discussed in previous works [3; 5].

One of the goals of our work is to investigate effective ways for endowing the interaction environment with appropriate representations of some meta-information, particularly concerning document content, in order to provide users with proper cues for locating the desired data. The various paradigms for representing content range from a textual description of what is stored in the information source to structured representations using some knowledge representation language. Our choice is to exploit visual techniques, whose main advantage is the capability of shifting load from user's cognitive system to the perceptual system.

In the description of the IDL web-based visual environment, we will essentially focus on the user modeling module, that is the basic component for providing a weak form of user interface adaptivity. This feature is achieved by automatically classifying the user by means of machine learning techniques based on decision trees.

Indeed a key issue in digital libraries research is the support for functions allowing access, retrieval, and organization of information, in order to make rapid decisions on what is relevant and which patterns exist among objects. In this context, conventional interfaces, based on information retrieval viewed as an isolated task in which the user formulates a query against a homogeneous collection to obtain matching documents, are completely out of date. For example, users may realize what they are trying to ask and how to ask it by interacting with the system (*iterative query refinement*) [11].

Several authors agree that users interacting with a huge amount of (unknown and various) information find extremely useful some *meta-information* on different aspects of the stored data, such as: 1) *content*, that is, what information is stored in the source; 2) *provenance*, which refers to how the information in the source is generated and maintained, whether it is a public source or a personal archive, how frequently it is maintained, etc.; 3) *form*, i.e. the schemes for the items in the source, including their attributes and the types of values for these attributes; 4) *functionality*, that concerns the capability of the access services, such as the kinds of search supported with their performance properties; 5) *usage statistics*, that is statistics about source usage, including previous use by the same user or other ones.

The paper is organized as follows. An overview of the main features and architecture of IDL is in Section 2. Section 3 presents the visual interaction environment of IDL, while Section 4 illustrates how the adaptivity of the interface is achieved through machine learning techniques. Section 5 concludes the paper and outlines the future work.

2 IDL: a general view

According to Lesk, a digital library is "a distributed technology environment that dramatically reduces barriers to the creation, dissemination, manipulation, storage, integration and reuse of information by individuals and groups" [7]. On the ground of this definition, we developed IDL as a prototypical digital library service, whose primary goal is to provide a common infrastructure that makes easy the process of creating, updating, searching, and managing *corporate* digital libraries. Here, the word *corporate* means that libraries share mechanisms for searching information, updating content, controlling user access, charging users, etc., independently of the meaning and the internal representation of information items in each digital library.

Indeed, IDL project focuses on the development of effective *middleware services* for digital libraries, and on their interoperability across heterogeneous hardware and software platforms [2]. The main features of IDL are strictly related to the library functions of 1. collection, 2. organization, 3. access:

1. support for information capture - supervised learning systems are used to overcome the problem of cheaply and effectively setting information items free of the physical medium on which they are stored;
2. support for semantic indexing - again, supervised learning systems are used to automatically perform the tasks of document classification and document understanding (reconstruction of the logical structure of a document) [4], that are necessary steps to index information items according to their content;
3. support for content understanding and interface adaptivity - IDL provides users with an added value service, which helps novice users to understand the content and the organization of a digital library through a suitable visual environment, and supports skilled users (supposed to be familiar with the digital library) in making an easy and fast retrieval of desired information items by means of an appropriate interface modality. As to the interface adaptivity, it is achieved through automated user classification based on machine learning techniques.

The architecture of IDL is the typical client/server architecture of a hypertextual service on the Internet. More specifically, the current version of IDL adopts a *thin-client stateful* architecture [9]. In such a model, the application runs with only a Web browser on the user's PC. Moreover, there is no need of storing data locally: no DBMS is present on the client-side of the architecture. Data are simply *grabbed* from the library host, and then presented to the user through HTML screens, which are dynamically generated by means of Java applets, since their content must *mirror* the current content of the repository in the library host or simply they must be generated according to the user choices. Furthermore, the architecture is called *stateful* since it is characterized by the presence of a *Learning Server* that, besides the other services related to document management, is able to infer *interaction models* concerning several classes of users from data collected in *log files* and managed by the *IDL Application Server*. A description of how the IDL Learning Server performs this task is given in Section 4.

Several reasons justify such architecture, rather than a *fat-client* one: 1) low cost of using IDL for dial-up connections (a telephone call to the Internet Service Provider, instead of the remote host of the library); 2) no software to be downloaded, maintained, updated on the user's PC, except a browser; 3) no need to download/upload data from/to the server of the library; 4) access to IDL from any personal computer connected to Internet.

A thorough description of the architecture of IDL is reported in [13].

IDL is programmed in several languages, ranging from C, C++ to Java, and it exploits the various services offered by the World Wide Web.

3 Web-based interaction environment of IDL

Three different kinds of roles have been identified for the interaction with IDL [5]: 1) the *Library Administrator*, allowed to create/delete a digital library; 2) the *Librarian*, in charge of managing specific digital libraries; and 3) the *Generic User*, that interact with IDL for browsing/querying a selected digital library. In this section we present the interaction environment of IDL, that is adapted according to the classification of the generic users, as explained later.

A *Generic User* (user for short) is any person entering the system from the WWW to consult the available digital libraries. The user can query the libraries to retrieve the documents he is interested in. Then, he may display/view, in a digital format, any of the documents found.

Initially, the interface developed was *form-based* [13]. Even though such an interface turns out to be powerful and flexible, it is more appropriate for users who are already acquainted with the library structure and also who have some information about its content. Casual users often perform queries whose result is null, just because they did not have any idea of the kind of documents stored in the library. Therefore, the IDL interaction environment was enriched with some novel visual tools, namely the *topic map* and the *tree-based interface*, allowing users to easily grasp the nature of the information stored and the possible patterns among the objects, so that they can make rapid decisions about what they really need and how to get it.

One of the new features of the IDL environment is the possibility of getting an overview of the library data through the *topic map* or *interactive dynamic map* [15], which gives a global view of either the semantic content of a set of documents or the set of documents itself (*document map* – currently under development) by exploiting a geographic metaphor. A collection of items (topics or documents) is considered to be a territory containing resources (the items themselves); maps of these territories can be drawn, where regions, cities, and roads are used to convey the structure of the set of items: a region represents a set of items, and the size of the region reflects the number of items in that region. Similarly, the distance between two cities reflects the similarity relationship between them: if two cities are close to each other, then the items are strongly related (e.g., documents have related contents).

In order to generate the topic map in IDL (see Fig. 1), we need to identify the set of topics or descriptors defining the semantic content of the documents stored in one of the corporate digital libraries; such topics constitute the library *thesaurus*. When building the library thesaurus, we have used standard techniques, also taking into account the type of documents currently stored in the library [14].

Documents and keywords (topics) have been represented by vectors, that is a common practice in information retrieval [6; 12]. A number of correlations can be computed from these vectors, and then visualized in the topic or document map. The thesaurus is then partitioned in a set of classes A_1, A_2, ..., A_p, where each A_i contains descriptors that are similar (p is a user-settable parameter). A *centroid* is chosen for each class, among the topics. For any other topic, its similarity with the centroid of

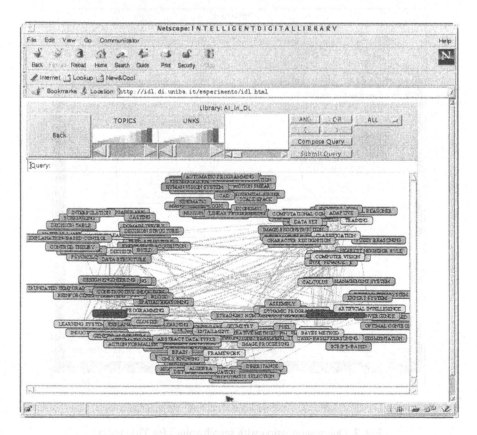

Fig. 1. Topic Map

each class is computed, and it is assigned to the class with the highest similarity.

Color-based coding techniques (to represent the importance of a topic or a link) and widgets make more effective the overall visualization and provide mechanisms for flexible interaction in this data intensive context. Range sliders give the possibility of filtering the information on the map. The topic map is visualized in a small window; hence, in a general overview many topics are hidden. A zoom mechanism facilitates a proper browsing.

The tree-based interface provides another visual modality to both browse IDL and perform queries. The user navigates into IDL along a tree structure, starting from the root and expanding the tree step by step, so that at each node the user can decide if further exploring that path. By selecting any node, a pop-up menu appears with two items: the former explodes the selected node, the latter provides an explanation of the meaning of the node, in order to support the user in his choice. The expandable nodes are shown as labeled rectangles. In Fig. 2 the user has expanded the library node AI_in_DL and the document-class node "icml", so that all available indexes on this class of documents are displayed. The user may now perform a query by entering appropriate values for one or more of such indexes through pop-up windows, that appear when the user clicks on specific index nodes. Once he has inserted the search values, he can submit the query by clicking on the button "Submit".

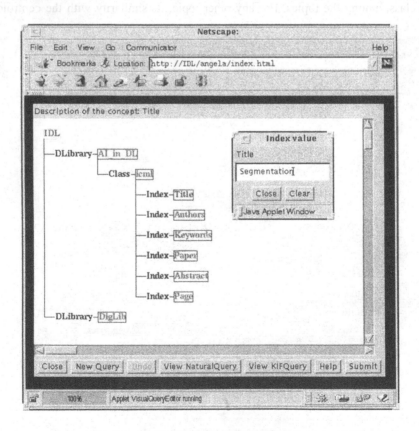

Fig. 2. Query submission with search values for Title index

4 Interaction Modeling through IDL Learning Server

A fundamental problem to cope with when developing a system exploited by several users is to make it *adaptive* to the various kinds of users that can be recognized, with the aim of improving the overall *usability* of the system. A prototype of an intelligent component, working in a client/server way and able to automatically classify a user, is currently embedded in the Application Server of IDL. In the overall architecture of IDL, such a prototype is part of the *Learning Server*.

IDL Learning Server can be defined as a suite of learning systems that can be exploited concurrently by clients for performing several tasks, such as document analysis/classification/understanding and inference of user models. Here we focus on this last task, intended as inferring user profiles through supervised learning methods.

In fact, each user of a system has special capabilities, skills, knowledge, preferences and goals. This is particularly true in the case of a service meant to be publicly available on the WWW like IDL. The reasons why users consult IDL may range from real needs of bibliographic search to checking the orthography of a word.

Indeed, each user has his own profile, thus, when using the system, he will behave differently from any other user. Of course it is impossible, even for an intelligent system, to recognize each single user in order to adapt its behavior to him. Nevertheless, it is desirable that an intelligent system is able to understand which kind of user it is interacting with and tries to help him by making the accomplishment of his goal easier (through contextual helps, explanations, suitable interaction modalities etc.). As a consequence, one of the main problems concerns the definition of classes of users meaningful for the system, and the identification of the features that properly describe each user and characterize the kind of interaction.

As to the task of inferring user models, the main function of the Learning Server is to automatically assign each IDL user to one of some predefined classes, on the ground of information drawn from real interaction sessions with IDL. In the literature of human-computer interaction, this activity is known as interaction modeling [1]. This approach takes advantage of Machine Learning methods [8], since interaction modeling can be cast as a supervised learning problem by considering some user interactions with IDL as training examples for a learning system, whose goal is to induce a theory for classifying IDL users.

The classification performed by the learning server can be exploited in several ways. In IDL, it is used to associate each class of users with an interface that is adequate to the user's degree of familiarity with the system, aiming at speeding up the process of understanding the organization and the content of the chosen digital library and properly assisting the user in retrieving the desired information.

Among all the possible IDL generic users, we defined three classes of users, namely *Novice*, *Expert* and *Teacher*. It is possible that, during the time, the user acquires familiarity in the use of the system, which must be able to track out potential changes of the class the user belongs to. This problem requires the ability of the system to register and identify the user. Each new user is required to fill in a digital form with personal data, then he receives an identity code - User ID - that he will use whenever he will enter IDL again. Correspondingly, IDL Application Server creates and associates a log file to each User ID, in which all the interactions of that user with IDL are stored.

By examining the data stored in the log file generated for each user during the interaction session, it is possible to extract some characteristics useful to recognize the users. Most of the identified characteristics turned out to be application dependent, while only few showed to be system dependent. For instance, relevant characteristics are those concerning the way users exploit the capabilities of IDL search engine, such as date and time of session beginning, class of documents chosen, search indexes chosen, criterion for sorting the search results, number of documents obtained as results of the search, types of errors performed during the interaction with IDL.

Data stored in the log files are then exploited to train a learning system in order to induce a decision tree and a set of rules that makes up the theory used by the system to autonomously perform a classification of the users interacting with IDL.

Fig. 3a illustrates IDL Learning Server that, when a user connects to IDL, consults the available rules and compares them to the set of characteristics extracted from the log file. Fig. 3b shows the scheme of IDL Learning Server that is based on C4.5/C4.5RULES [10]. It has been customized in order to work in a batch way to infer the classification theory from the log files, concerning the set of users whose interactions are selected to train the system. Furthermore, we are currently investigating the possibility of using incremental learning systems [4] that avoid the drawback of starting over from scratch the learning process each time new log examples become available.

A preliminary experiment concerning the classification of IDL users consisted in collecting 500 examples of interactions and generating from them a training set for the system component C4.5. As previously told, we identified three fundamental classes of users, namely Novice, Expert and Teacher. Each log file was used to draw the values taken by the attributes that describe user interactions. We considered 126 attributes. Therefore, each training example is made up of a set of 126 values and is labeled with one of the three classes Novice, Expert, Teacher.

The system component C4.5RULES examines the decision tree produced by C4.5 (depicted in Fig. 4) and generates a set of production rules of the form $L \rightarrow R$, where the left-hand side L is a conjunction of boolean tests, based on the attributes, while the right-hand side R denotes a class. One of the classes is also designated as a default, in order to classify those examples for which no rule's left-hand side is satisfied. Rule generation aims at improving the comprehensibility of the induced results. Indeed, in our experiment, C4.5RULES produced only 4 rules from the 7-node decision tree, that seem to be more *readable* than the original tree-structured classification model. After the training phase, whenever any user accesses

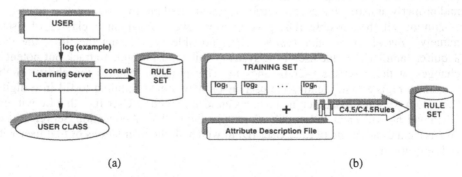

(a)   (b)

Fig. 3. (a) IDL Learning Server, and (b) its scheme

```
C4.5 [release 5] decision tree generator   Sun Jun  2 16:04:09 1997
-------------------------------------------------------------------
Read 500 cases (126 attributes) from DF.data
Decision Tree:
  Average daily connection <= 0.09 : Novice (67.0)
  Average daily connection > 0.09 :
  |  Freq of BadQuery on class Springer of DB AI_in_DL > 0.5 : Expert (122.0)
  |  Freq of BadQuery on class Springer of DB AI_in_DL <= 0.5 :
  |  |     Freq of BadQuery on class Pami of DB AI_in_DL <= 0.5 : Teacher (244.0)
  |  |     Freq of BadQuery on class Pami of DB AI_in_DL > 0.5 : Expert (67.0)
Tree saved
```

Fig. 4. The decision tree induced by C4.5

IDL through a client, the log file generated during the interaction session is exploited to provide a new example that the learning server will classify on the ground of the inferred rules. The way in which rules are consulted by the learning server (and the existence of the classification rules itself) is completely transparent for the user. To validate the obtained rules, an experiment was run with 30 people (15 new students with no experience about the Internet, 5 students with average experience and 10 computer science teachers), and 89% of the cases were correctly classified.

On the ground of the performed user classification, the Learning Server selects a distinct type of visual user interface, regarded as the proper one for that group of users. Specifically, the Learning Server *prompts* any user recognized as a member of the class *Novice* with the topic map interface, the tree-based interface is proposed to a user in the class *Expert* and *Teacher* users have the form-based interface as a default.

The main idea underlying the mapping between user classes and types of interfaces is that users being unfamiliar with the system need an environment that allows them to preliminarily understand the content of a (probably unknown) digital library, just like a fellow that goes into a library for the first time. More *skilled* users are supposed to already know both the organization and the type of content in the digital library, thus they want a powerful tool that allows them to speed up the process of search and retrieval of the specific data they are looking for. However, the choice performed by the Learning Server is not mandatory for the user, hence he is allowed to choose another interface.

The system is able to follow up the user's evolution since a single user is classified whenever he enters IDL. Thus, after a certain number of interactions, it is foreseeable that IDL will propose a different interface to the same user. In particular, we found that, after an average number of 25 interactions, the 30% of novice users were shifted to an upper class.

5 Conclusions and future work

Online digital libraries pose several demands due to the large number and variety of its users, and also to the nature of the stored data, that is distributed on autonomous information sources that differ in content, form, and type. One of the consequences is that digital libraries must be equipped with environments that permit a new style of rich interactions with such information-dense systems. The work presented in this paper is a contribution in this direction. More specifically, we have provided the digital library service with a web-based environment that allows the users to visualize some meta-information about the document contents in order to facilitate the task of retrieving documents of interest.

As a further step to user modeling, we are going to design a framework that allows us to add information about user's topics of interests to the log files. Such additional information items will allow the IDL learning server to infer user profiles that will be profitably exploited both by personalized components for information filtering and by modules based on *push* technology.

As to the learning server, in the next future we intend to complete its development in order to integrate inductive reasoning capabilities in first-order logic.

References

1. Banyon, D., and Murray, D.: Applying User Modeling to Human-Computer Interaction Design. Artificial Intelligence Review, 7 (1993) 199-225.
2. Bernstein, P. A.: Middleware: A Model for Distributed System Services, Communications of the ACM, 39(2) (1996) 86-98.
3. Esposito, E., Malerba, D., Semeraro, G., Fanizzi, N., and Ferilli, S.: Adding Intelligence to Digital Libraries: IDL. In: Proceedings of the IJCAI-97 Workshop W3 "AI in Digital Libraries - Moving from Chaos to (More) Order", Nagoya, Japan (1997) 23-31.
4. Esposito, E., Malerba, D., Semeraro, G., and Ferilli, S.: Knowledge Revision for Document Understanding. In: Ras Z. W. and Skowron A. (eds.), Foundations of Intelligent Systems. 10th International Symposium, ISMIS'97, Charlotte, NC, USA, October 1997. LNAI 1325. Springer (1997) 619-628.
5. Esposito, F., Malerba, D., Semeraro, G., Fanizzi, N., and Ferilli, S.: Adding Machine Learning and Knowledge Intensive Techniques to a Digital Library Service. International Journal of Digital Libraries 2(1), Springer (1998) 3-19.
6. Larson, R.R.: Evaluation of retrieval techniques in an experimental on-line catalog. JASIS, 43 (1991) 34-53.
7. Lesk, M.: The Digital Library: What is it? Why should it be here? Source Book on Digital Libraries. Technical Report TR 93-35, Virginia Tech, Dept. of Computer Science, Blacksburg, VA. Edited Volume (Ed. E. A. Fox). (1993).
8. Moustakis, V. S., and Herrmann, J.: Where Do Machine Learning and Human-Computer Interaction Meet?. Applied Artificial Intelligence, 11 (1997) 595-609.
9. McChesney, M. C.: Banking in Cyberspace: An Investment in Itself. IEEE Spectrum, February (1997) 54-59.
10. Quinlan, J. R.: C4.5: Programs for Machine Learning. Morgan Kaufmann (1993).
11. Rao, R., Pedersen, J.O., Hearst, M.A., Mackinlay, J.D., Card, S.K., Masinster, L., Halvorsen, P.-K., and Robertson, G.G.: Rich interaction in the digital library. Communications of the ACM, 38 (4) (1995) 29-39
12. Salton, G., and McGill, M.J.: Introduction to Modern Information Retrieval, New York, NY, McGraw-Hill (1983).
13. Semeraro, G., Esposito, F., Malerba, D., Fanizzi, N., and Ferilli, S.: Machine Learning + On-line Libraries = IDL. In: C. Peters C. and Thanos C. (eds.), Research and Advanced Technology for Digital Libraries. First European Conference, ECDL'97, Pisa, Italy, Sept. 1997. LNCS 1324. Springer (1997) 195-214.
14. Soergel, D.: Thesauri for knowledge-based assistance in searching digital libraries, First European Conference, ECDL'97, Tutorial Notes, Pisa, Italy (1997).
15. Zizi, M., and Beaudouin-Lafon, M.: Hypermedia exploration with interactive dynamic maps. International Journal on Human-Computer Studies, 43 (1995) 441-464.

A Better Fitness Measure of a Text-Document for a Given Set of Keywords

Sukhamay Kundu

Computer Science Department, Louisiana State University

Baton Rouge, LA 70803-4020, USA

E-mail: kundu@bit.csc.lsu.edu

ABSTRACT

We present a new fitness measure $B_W(D)$ for a text-document D against a set of keywords W. The fitness evaluation forms a basic operation in information retrieval. $B_W(D)$ differs from other measures in that it accounts for both the frequency of the keywords and their clustering characteristics. It also satisfies the properties of *monotonicity* and *super-additivity*, which do not hold for either of the well known Paice-measure and the mixed-max-min measure.

Keywords: Information retrieval, Fitness measure, Clustering.

1. Introduction

A key operation in information retrieval is the evaluation of the fitness of a document D against a set of keywords W. Let $\Omega = \{w_1, w_2, \cdots, w_K\}$ denote the universe of keywords (or essential words) that can be used in evaluating D. We assume that D has been preprocessed to remove all non-essential words, and the remaining words have been reduced to their basic forms, say, via a stemming algorithm [2]. We regard D as a sequence $D = a_1 a_2 \cdots a_N$, where $a_j \in \Omega$. A more general case is where D is represented by a tree, say, but we do not consider this here. It is clear that a fitness measure $0 \le m_W(D) \le 1$ should have the properties (P.1)-(P.4) below. The property (P.2) can be shown to be equivalent to (P.1); the property (P.3) implies $m_\varnothing(D) = 0$ and (P.1), and hence (P.2) as well.

(P.1) *W-monotonicity*: If $W \subseteq W' \subseteq \Omega$, then $m_W(D) \le m_{W'}(D)$.

(P.2) *D-monotonicity*: If D' is obtained from D by replacing one or more occurrences of keywords in $\Omega - W$ by those in W, then $m_W(D) \le m_W(D')$. (In this case, we write $D <_W D'$.)

(P.3) *W-superadditivity*: $m_{W \cup W'}(D) \ge m_W(D) + m_{W'}(D)$ if $W \cap W' = \varnothing$. (The inequality "$\ge$" is motivated by the fact the co-occurrences of two keywords w_1 and w_2 should make D at least as valuable as that when all occurrences of w_1 are replaced by w_2 because of the synergistic effect of co-occurrences.)

(P.4) *D-superadditivity*: If $D = D_1 D_2$, i.e., D is obtained by appending D_2 at the end of D_1, then $m_W(D) \ge m_W(D_1) + m_W(D_2)$. (The inequality "$\ge$" is motivated by the fact that D should be at least as valuable as the sum of its parts. Otherwise, combining D_1 and D_2 into a larger document may not be justified.)

For $w \in \Omega$, let positions$(w) =$ positions$(w, D) = \{j: a_j = w\}$ and for $W \subseteq \Omega$ let positions$(W) = \bigcup\{$positions$(w_i): w_i \in W\}$. We refer to a subset of positions of the form $\{i, i+1,$

$\cdots$, j}, $1 \leq i \leq j \leq |D|$, as an *interval* $I = [i, j]$; we write left(I) for i and right(I) for j. Let size(I) = $|I| = j - i + 1$ = the number of positions covered by I, $f_i = f_{w_i} = |\text{positions}(w_i)|$ = the number of occurrences of w_i in D, and $N = f_1 + f_2 + \cdots + f_K = |D|$ = the size of D. It is convenient to define the binary string bin(W, D) whose ith item is 1 if $a_i \in W$ and 0 otherwise; the length of bin(W, D) is $|D|$. If D_1 and D_2 are two documents over Ω, then their *concatenation* $D_1 D_2$ denotes the combined document D_1 followed by D_2. For example, if $D_1 = aba$ and $D_2 = bbbc$, then $D_1 D_2 = ababbbc$. Clearly, bin(W, $D_1 D_2$) is the concatenation of bin(W, D_1) and bin(W, D_2), and positions(W, $D_1 D_2$) = positions(W, D_1) $\cup$ positions'(W, D_2), where positions'(W, D_2) = {$|D_1| + j$: $j \in$ positions(W, D_2)}. If $D <_w D'$, then positions(W, D) $\subseteq$ positions(W, D').

The frequency measure of fitness [2] is defined by the ratio $F_W(D)/|D|$, where $F_W(D) = \sum f_i$ (summed over $w_i \in W$) = |positions(W)|, the frequency of the keywords W in D. The mixed-max-min measure [2] uses a linear combination of the maximum and the minimum of the frequencies {f_i: $w_i \in W$} in place of $F_W(D)$. For $|W| = 1$, the mixed-max-min measure and the Paice-measure [2, 5] coincide with the frequency measure. A major drawback of these measures is that they fail to account for the "pattern" of the occurrences of W in D. Fig. 1 shows three documents with the same frequencies f_i of the keywords $\Omega = \{a, b, c, d, e\}$; the second document is an extreme case where all a's appear clustered together and the third document is the other extreme case where the a's are least clustered. We clearly perceive these documents differently in regard to the keyword a; for example, the second document is likely to have a more focussed discussion on the topic a than the third document. This shows the need for a fitness measure to account for both the pattern of occurrences of the keywords and their frequencies. The measure $F_W(D)/D$ satisfies the properties (P.1)-(P.4); the mixed-max-min measure and the Paice-measure do not satisfy any of the properties (P.1)-(P.4).

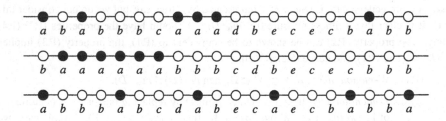

Figure 1. Three documents having the same frequencies f_i of
the keywords and different clustering characteristics of the keyword a.

We present here two new fitness measures $A_W(D)/|D|$ and $B_W(D)/|D|$. The measure $A_W(D)$ approximates $F_W(D)$ from above and the measure $B_W(D)$ approximates $F_W(D)$ from below (A = above and B = below): $0 \leq B_W(D) \leq F_W(D) \leq A_W(D) \leq |D|$. For any given $W \neq \emptyset$, the range of possible values for both $A_W(D)$ and $F_W(D)$ is the interval $[0, |D|]$. However, $A_W(D)$ is more powerful in distinguishing among various documents D than $F_W(D)$ because given the basic frequencies f_i, $w_i \in \Omega$, the measures $F_W(D)$ are uniquely determined for all $W \subseteq \Omega$ by the f_i's. That is, there is only one combination of the values $F_W(D)$, $|W| \geq 2$, for a given collection of basic frequencies f_i. As we will see, this is not so for $A_W(D)$, $|W| \geq 2$, and there can be many combinations of the values of $A_W(D)$. This gives $A_W(D)$ the extra power to distinguish among the documents. A similar remark holds for $B_W(D)$.

We first present $A_W(D)$ because of its simplicity and its important role as a point of contrast for $B_W(D)$, which is superior to the measure $A_W(D)$. We also present several generalizations of $B_W(D)$ to account for the effect of paging within a document and to reduce the impact of small changes in D. We point out that although $A_W(D)$ and $B_W(D)$ are defined in terms of positions(W), these positions themselves are not significant in that if we shift the positions of the keywords W by a fixed amount, for example, then there is no change in $A_W(D)$ and $B_W(D)$. We omit the proofs of the theorems here for want of space.

2. The Measure $A_W(D)$

Consider the document D in Fig. 2(i), where the positions of $w = a$ are shown as solid circles; $F_a(D) = 6$. Suppose we partition positions(a) = $\{1, 3, 8, 9, 10, 18\}$ into three disjoint subsets P_1, P_2, and P_3 in some way. Let I_j be the interval which covers the items in P_j, i.e., I_j extends from the smallest item in P_j to the largest item in P_j. If we choose the partition positions(a) = $P_1 \cup P_2 \cup P_3$ such that $|I_1| + |I_2| + |I_3|$ is minimum, then we get positions(a) = $\{1, 3\} \cup \{8, 9, 10\} \cup \{18\}$, giving $I_1 = [1, 3]$, $I_2 = [8, 10]$, and $I_3 = [18, 18]$; the minimum total length = 3+3+1 = 7. See Fig. 2(i). Let g denote the number of subsets in a partition. For $g = 2$, the optimal partition is positions(a) = $\{1, 3, 8, 9, 10\} \cup \{18\}$, giving $I_1 = [1, 10]$, $I_2 = [18, 18]$, and the minimum total length = 10+1 = 11 > 7.

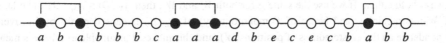

(i) Optimal grouping of the positions of $\{a\}$ into ≤ 3 groups; $A_a(D) = 7$.

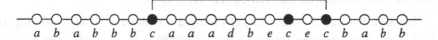

(ii) Optimal grouping of the positions of $\{c\}$ into ≤ 1 groups; $A_c(D) = 10$.

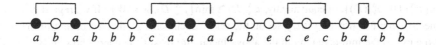

(iii) Optimal grouping of the positions of $\{a, c\}$ into ≤ 4 groups; $A_{\{a, c\}}(D) = 11$.

Figure 2. Illustration of $A_W(D)$ using $g(a) = 3$, $g(c) = 1$, and $g(\{a, c\}) = 4$.

We are now ready to formally define $A_W(D)$ by (1) below. Note that for an optimal set of intervals $I = \{I_1, I_2, \cdots, I_n\}$, $n \leq g$, we necessarily have $I_i \cap I_j = \emptyset$ for $i \neq j$. For the special case $W = \{w\}$, $A_w(D)$ reflects the portion of D that would be referred by an optimal index-set (like that at the end of a textbook) of size ≤ g for w such that each item in the index refers to an individual occurrence of w or a range of occurrences of w (with possible gaps among those occurrences) and these references cover all occurrences of w. We will say more about the choice of g shortly. It is clear that $A_W(D) \geq F_W(D)$; for $g \geq F_W(D)$, each $|I_i| = 1$ in an optimal partition of positions(W), giving $A_W(D) = F_W(D)$. In general, the optimal partition corresponding to $A_W(D)$ is not unique. It is easy to see that more clustered the occurrences of the keywords W are, the closer is the approximation $A_W(D)$ to $F_W(D)$.

$$A_W(D) = \min_{n \leq g}\{|I_1| + |I_2| + \cdots + |I_n|: I_1 \cup I_2 \cup \cdots \cup I_n \supseteq \text{positions}(W)\} \tag{1}$$

Throughout this paper, we choose g for a keyword $w \in \Omega$ according to $g = g(w) = \lfloor F_w(D)/k \rfloor$, for some fixed constant $k \geq 1$ (where $\lfloor x \rfloor$ denotes the largest integer $\leq x$). This amounts to saying that on the average each interval of an optimal partition of positions(w) contains $\geq k$ occurrences of w. For $W \subseteq \Omega$, we then take $g = g(W) = \sum g(w)$, summed over $w \in W$. The reason for allowing a larger number of intervals for a larger set of keywords is that otherwise $A_W(D)$ tends to be too large when the sets positions(w), $w \in W$, are dispersed too widely, which is typically the case for a large document. This can be seen by using $g = 3$ for each of $W = \{a\}$, $\{c\}$, and $\{a, c\}$ for the document in Fig. 2. The optimal set of intervals for $W = \{a, c\}$ is now $\{[1,3], [7, 10], [14, 18]\}$, giving $A_{\{a, c\}}(D) = 12$, which is much larger than $A_a(D) + A_c(D) = 7+3$. However, if we take $k = 2$ and hence $g(a) = 3$, $g(c) = 1$, and $g(\{a, c\}) = 3+1 = 4$, then we have $A_{\{a, c\}}(D) = 11 \leq A_a(D) + A_c(D) = 7 + 10$.

One price we pay for using a larger g for a larger W is that we no longer have the W-monotonicity of $A_W(D)$, i.e., we do not always have $A_W(D) \leq A_{W'}(D)$ for $W \subset W'$. For example, if $D = ababccbccb$ and we take $k = 2$, then we have $g(a) = 1$, $g(b) = 2$, $g(\{a, b\}) = 3$, $A_{\{a, b\}}(D) = 6 < 7 = A_b(D)$. The reverse inequality $A_W(D) \geq A_{W'}(D)$ for $W \subset W'$ does not always hold either. If we use the same g for both W and W', then $A_W(D) \leq A_{W'}(D)$. The lack of W-monotonicity (and hence of D-monotonicity) of $A_W(D)$ is caused partly by its over-dependence on the clusteredness of positions(W), and this makes it unsuitable as a fitness measure. The following theorem summarizes some other properties of $A_W(D)$ (cf. (P.3)-(P.4)).

Theorem 1. If $W \cap W' = \emptyset$, then we have the W-subadditivity $A_{W \cup W'}(D) \leq A_W(D) + A_{W'}(D)$ and the D-subadditivity $A_W(D_1 D_2) \leq A_W(D_1) + A_W(D_2)$. $\square$

Let $M_W^A(D) = A_W(D)/F_W(D)$, if $F_W(D) > 0$ and $= 1$ otherwise. If $M = \max\{M_W^A(D), M_{W'}^A(D)\}$, then it follows from Theorem 1 that for $W \cap W' = \emptyset$, $A_{W \cup W'}(D) \leq M(F_W(D) + F_{W'}(D)) = MF_{W \cup W'}(D)$ and hence $M_{W \cup W'}^A(D) \leq \max\{M_W^A(D), M_{W'}^A(D)\}$. Let $\mu_W^A(D) = 1/M_W^A(D)$ so that $0 \leq \mu_W^A(D) \leq 1$. We can restate the above inequality as $\mu_{W \cup W'}^A(D) \geq \min\{\mu_W^A(D), \mu_{W'}^A(D)\}$, or equivalently, $\mu_W^A(D) \geq \min\{\mu_w^A(D): w \in W\}$. If we regard $\mu_W^A(D)$ as a membership function of a fuzzy set on the set of documents D, then according to the fuzzy set theory [3] the min-operation in the above inequality makes the query "how fit is D to W" look like an and-combination of the elementary queries "how fit is D to w_i", $w_i \in W$. (The abstract fuzzy and-operation gives equality in the above minimum.) Note that although the union in positions(W) = $\bigcup$positions(w_i) (over $w_i \in W$) may suggest that the query corresponding to W is an or-combination of the elementary queries for $w_i \in W$, the above discussion shows that this is an incorrect interpretation. The measure $B_W(D)$ in the next section also supports the and-combination view of the query for W. From Theorem 1, one can also show that $\mu_W^A(D_1 D_2) \geq \min\{\mu_W^A(D_1), \mu_W^A(D_2)\}$. We note in passing that the fuzzy membership function $\mu_W^A(D)$, which is well-behaved in view of the above inequalities, is somewhat unusual in that it is the ratio of the probability $F_W(D)/|D|$ and the approximation $A_W(D)/|D|$ to that probability. In [4], the leftness-measure between two intervals was another example of a well-behaved fuzzy membership function that resulted in an unusual way (from the difference of two probabilities).

3. The Measure $B_W(D)$

We define the measure $B_W(D)$, which is closely related to $A_W(D)$, by (2). The main difference between (2) and (1) is the restriction $I_i \subseteq \text{positions}(W)$ for each i, and the replacement of "min" by "max". The intervals I_i in (2) are taken to be disjoint to avoid duplicate count of the occurrences of the keywords W.

$$B_W(D) = \max_{n \leq g} \left\{ \begin{array}{c} |I_1| + |I_2| + \cdots + |I_n|: \text{ each } I_i \subseteq \text{positions}(W) \text{ and} \\ I_i \cap I_j = \varnothing \text{ for } i \neq j \end{array} \right\} \qquad (2)$$

For $g = 3$ and the document D in Fig. 2, we get $B_a(D) = 5$, $B_c(D) = 3$, and $B_{\{a, c\}}(D) = 6$. As in the case of $A_W(D)$, a larger value of g tends to make $B_W(D)$ larger and hence make $B_W(D)$ approximate $F_W(D)$ more closely. In the extreme case of $g \geq \max\{F_w(D): w \in \Omega\}$, we have each $B_w(D) = F_w(D)$ and for $g = |D|$ each $B_W(D) = F_W(D)$. The measure $B_W(D)$ approximates $F_W(D)$ poorly when positions(W) are least clustered (cf. the third document in Fig. 1). This is also the case for $A_W(D)$.

Theorem 2. The measure $B_W(D)$ satisfies the properties (P.1)-(P.4). □

Let $\mu_W^B(D) = B_W(D)/F_W(D)$ if $F_W(D) > 0$, and $= 1$ otherwise; clearly, $0 \leq \mu_W^B(D) \leq 1$. If we now write $M = \min\{\mu_W^B(D), \mu_{W'}^B(D)\}$, then it follows from Theorem 2 that for $W \cap W' = \varnothing$, $B_{W \cup W'}(D) \geq M(F_W(D) + F_{W'}(D)) = MF_{W \cup W'}(D)$ and hence $\mu_{W \cup W'}^B(D) \geq \min\{\mu_W^B(D), \mu_{W'}^B(D)\}$. We can restate this as $\mu_W^B(D) \geq \min\{\mu_w^B(D): w \in W\}$. As in the case of $\mu_W^A(D)$, we can regard $\mu_W^B(D)$ as a membership function of a fuzzy set on the set of documents D, and the above inequality supports the view that the query "how fit is D to W" is an and-combination of the elementary queries "how fit is D to w_i", $w_i \in W$. We also have $\mu_W^B(D_1 D_2) \geq \min\{\mu_W^B(D_1), \mu_{W'}^B(D_2)\}$. We point out that although neither of $\mu_W^A(D)$ and $\mu_W^B(D)$ may have the W-monotonicity property, this in itself does not indicate a shortcoming of $A_W(D)$ or $B_W(D)$. The subadditivity of $A_W(D)$ suggests that the co-occurrence of two keywords w_1 and w_2 in D may reduce the importance of each w_i in some way. This would be the case if in some way we tend to perform excess "counting" in $A_W(D)$ for each w_i. Indeed, this excess counting is caused by the fact that the intervals I_i may contain positions not occupied by keywords in W.

4. Generalization of $B_W(D)$

The condition "$I_i \subseteq \text{positions}(W)$" in (2) is in a sense too strict in that a small change in few positions of the keywords W may affect the value of $B_W(D)$ in a significant way. One way to reduce this impact is to relax the condition (2) to the weaker form (3) shown below and define the new measure $B_W^\alpha(D)$ by (4). The assumption $\alpha \geq 0.5$ in (3) is clearly meaningful from the practical considerations; it also plays a critical role in the proof of Theorem 3 which is not shown here. The need to assume the disjointness of the intervals I_i in (4) arises because of the pathological situation illustrated in Fig. 3, which shows that if I_i's are not disjoint, then a large block of occurrences of the keywords in W may be accounted for more than once, giving too large a value for $B_W^\alpha(D)$. One way to avoid this problem is to replace the sum in (4) by $|(\bigcup I_j) \cap \text{positions}(W)|$, but this does not properly reflect our intuition about the role of α and hence we do not consider this variation (although Theorem 3 below would remain valid).

$|I_i \cap \text{positions}(W)| \geq \alpha |I_i|$, where $0.5 \leq \alpha \leq 1$ is a fixed constant. (3)

$$B_W^\alpha(D) = \max_{n \leq g} \left\{ \sum_{1 \leq i \leq n} |I_i \cap \text{positions}(W)| : \begin{array}{l} \text{each } I_i \text{ satisfies (3) and} \\ I_i \cap I_j = \varnothing \text{ for } i \neq j \end{array} \right\}$$ (4)

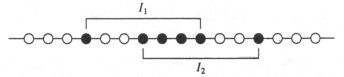

Solid circles corresponds to the positions of the keywords W.

Figure 3. For $g = 2$ and $\alpha = 2/3$, the use of non-disjoint I_1 and I_2 would give $B_W^\alpha(D) = 10$, which is too large compared to $F_W(D) = 6$.

The condition (3) has the effect of allowing many more alternate choices for the intervals I_i in (4) when $\alpha < 1$, and hence $B_W^\alpha(D) \geq B_W(D)$. The intersection $I_i \cap \text{positions}(W)$ in the rightside of (4) together with the disjointness of I_i's ensures that $B_W^\alpha(D) \leq F_W(D)$. It is clear that $B_W^\alpha(D) = B_W(D)$ for $\alpha = 1$. Note that if V is a maximal block of consecutive 1's and I_i belongs to an optimal set of intervals for (4), then either $V \subseteq I_i$ or $V \cap I_i = \varnothing$.

Theorem 3. For $\alpha \geq 0.5$, $B_W^\alpha(D)$ satisfies the properties (P.1)-(P.4). □

As one might expect, the computation of $B_W^\alpha(D)$ is substantially more complex than that of $B_W(D)$ due to the fact that there are many more intervals I_i that need to be considered now. An efficient method for computing $B_W^\alpha(D)$ is obtained by converting the problem to a shortest-path computation problem in a special directed graph $G = G(\alpha, W, D)$, which is constructed as follows. Consider the successive blocks of consecutive 0's and consecutive 1's in $\text{bin}(W, D)$. Let Z_i, $1 \leq i \leq n$ (say), be the 0-blocks which have 1-blocks on its left and right; let $[\text{left}(Z_i), \text{right}(Z_i)] \subseteq \text{positions}(W)$ denote the interval for the 0-block Z_i. We consider two other imaginary 0-blocks Z_0 and Z_{n+1} in the following sense. If the first position in $\text{bin}(W, D)$ equals 1, then Z_0 is an imaginary 0-block preceding the leftmost 1-block; otherwise, Z_0 is the 0-block starting at the first position of $\text{bin}(W, D)$. We define Z_{n+1} in a similar way by considering the last position of $\text{bin}(W, D)$. If Z_0 is an imaginary 0-block, then we take $\text{left}(Z_0) = 0 = \text{right}(Z_0)$ and similarly if Z_{n+1} is an imaginary 0-block then we take $\text{left}(Z_{n+1}) = N + 1 = \text{right}(Z_{n+1})$, where $N = |D|$. The digraph G has $(n + 2)$ nodes $Z_0, Z_1, \cdots, Z_{n+1}$. There are two kinds of arcs in G:

cover-arcs: Each cover-arc corresponds to a group of consecutive 1-blocks (together with their separating 0-blocks) that can be accounted by a single interval satisfying the condition (3) and that can potentially contribute to $B_W^\alpha(D)$. Such an interval will necessarily contain all of an 1-block or be disjoint from it, and hence we represent it as an arc (Z_i, Z_j), $0 \leq i < j \leq n + 1$. Here, Z_i is the 0-block to the left of the first 1-block included in the interval and Z_j is the 0-block to the right of the last 1-block in the interval. The interval for this cover-arc is $I(i, j) = [\text{right}(Z_i)+1, \text{left}(Z_j) - 1]$ and the condition (3) for $I(i, j)$ can be rewritten as (5) below. Note that (Z_i, Z_{i+1}) is a cover-arc for each i, $0 \leq i \leq n$. In general, there will be many other cover-arcs.

skip-arcs: Each skip-arc correspond to an 1-block. The word "skip" means that we may not use this 1-block in $B_W^\alpha(D)$. The only skip-arcs are (Z_i, Z_{i+1}), $0 \le i < n+1$.

We consider paths π in G from Z_0 to Z_{n+1} which consists of at most g cover-arcs. We define the cost of each cover-arc (Z_i, Z_j) to be 0 and the cost of the skip-arc (Z_i, Z_{i+1}) to be the size of the 1-block between Z_i and Z_{i+1}, namely, $\mathrm{left}(Z_{i+1})-\mathrm{right}(Z_i)-1$. Fig. 4 shows the digraph $G(4/5, \{b\}, D)$ for the document D in Fig. 2.

$$\text{Cover-arc } (Z_i, Z_j): \quad (1-\alpha)[\mathrm{left}(Z_j) - \mathrm{right}(Z_i) - 1] \ \ge\ \sum_{i<k<j} |Z_k| \tag{5}$$

$$\text{Cost:} \begin{cases} \text{for a cover-arc} & cc(Z_i, Z_j) = 0 \\ \text{for a skip-arc} & cs(Z_i, Z_{i+1}) = \mathrm{left}(Z_{i+1}) - \mathrm{right}(Z_i) - 1 > 0 \end{cases} \tag{6}$$

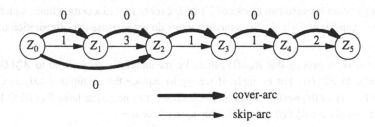

The optimal Z_0-Z_5 paths using $\le g$ arcs of cost 0.

g	Paths	Cost	$B_b^{0.8}(D)$
4 or more	$Z_0 \Rightarrow Z_2 \Rightarrow Z_3 \Rightarrow Z_4 \Rightarrow Z_5$	0	$8-0 = 8$
3	$Z_0 \Rightarrow Z_2 \Rightarrow Z_3 \to Z_4 \Rightarrow Z_5$	1	$8-1 = 7$
	$Z_0 \Rightarrow Z_2 \to Z_3 \Rightarrow Z_4 \Rightarrow Z_5$		
2	$Z_0 \Rightarrow Z_2 \to Z_3 \to Z_4 \Rightarrow Z_5$	2	$8-2 = 6$
1	$Z_0 \Rightarrow Z_2 \to Z_3 \to Z_4 \to Z_5$	4	$8-4 = 4$

Figure 4. The digraph $G(\alpha, \{b\}, D)$ for $\alpha = 4/5 = 0.8$ and D as in Fig. 2, and the measure $B_b^\alpha(D)$ for different values g.

The cost of a path π is then the sum of the costs of its skip-arcs. Let $\pi(Z_{j+1}, k) =$ the shortest length of a Z_0-Z_{j+1} path using at most k cover-arcs. The connection between $\pi(Z_{n+1}, g)$ and $B_W^\alpha(D)$ is given by (7).

$$B_W^\alpha(D) = |\text{positions}(W)| - \pi(Z_{n+1}, g) \tag{7}$$

The equation (8) gives a method for computing successively $\pi(Z_{j+1}, k)$, $0 \le k \le g$, for increasing j. The first term on the rightside in (8) corresponds to the case where the last arc on the optimal Z_0-Z_{j+1} path is the skip-arc (Z_j, Z_{j+1}). The second term in (8), i.e., the nested min corresponds to the case where the last arc (Z_i, Z_{j+1}), $i \le j$, on the optimal path is a cover-arc. It is not hard to show that one can construct the digraph G in time $O(n^2)$ and compute $B_W^\alpha(D)$

in time $O(gp)$, where $p = \#(\text{arcs in } G) = O(n^2)$. The total computation time is therefore $O(gn^2)$, where $n \leq F_W(D) \leq N$.

$$\pi(Z_{j+1}, k) = \min \left\{ \begin{array}{l} \pi(Z_j, k) + cs(Z_j, Z_{j+1}), \text{ and} \\ \min_{k-1 \leq i \leq j} \{\pi(Z_i, k-1): (Z_i, Z_{j+1}) \text{ is a cover-arc}\} \end{array} \right\} \tag{8}$$

We remark that although $B_W^\alpha(D)$ is a significant improvement over $B_W(D)$, it still has some drawbacks in that if we have a very large block of 1's in bin(W, D), then $B_W^\alpha(D)$ will account also any nearby isolated small groups of 1's and thereby tend to increase the value of W. This may not be always desirable because the isolated (groups of) 1's may be quite far from the main block of 1's if the size of the later is large. This can be avoided, however, by putting additional restriction on the intervals I_i in (4); for example, we may require that the maximum separation between two blocks of 1's in I_i cannot exceed a certain limit, which may depend on the number of 1's in I_i. Such modifications do not increase the computation time of $B_W^\alpha(D)$.

We remark in passing that $A_W(D)$ cannot be meaningfully generalized to $A_W^\alpha(D)$ in a fashion similar to $B_W^\alpha(D)$. For example, if we try to replace the condition $I_1 \cup I_2 \cup \cdots \cup I_n \supseteq$ positions(W) in (1) by the weaker condition (9), then we may no longer have $F_W(D) \leq A_W^\alpha(D)$ although we would have $A_W^\alpha(D) \leq A_W(D)$, with equality for $\alpha = 1$.

$$|(I_1 \cup I_2 \cup \cdots \cup I_n) \cap \text{positions}(W)| \geq \alpha|\text{positions}(W)| \tag{9}$$

5. Effect of Paging

We briefly consider two ways to account for the effect of paging in D. The effects of other structures in D such as paragraphs or chapters can be handled in a similar manner. The paging basically means that the keywords in D are now grouped by pages. In Fig. 5, we use the marker 'I' to separate the successive pages. For simplicity, we consider a page which does not contain any keyword from Ω as a blank-page and ignore such pages. We now replace the binary vector bin(W, D) by an integer vector pagewise-counts(W, D), whose ith term is the count of the keywords in W in page i of D; in particular, pagewise-counts(W, D) = bin(W, D) if each page of D contains at most one occurrence of the keywords in W. We write page-sizes(D) = pagewise-counts(Ω, D). We write pagewise-probs(W, D) for the vector of probabilities of the keywords in W in the various pages of D; see Fig. 5. Finally, the vector cond-probs(W, D) gives the conditional probability of each page, given that it contains a keyword from W. The ith term in cond-probs(W, D) is given by the ratio of the ith term in pagewise-counts(W, D) and |positions(W)|. Note that |positions(W)| is the sum of the terms in pagewise-counts(W, D).

One way of handling the effect of paging is to first convert the vector cond-probs(W, D) to a binary vector by thresholding, i.e., replacing each probability by 1 if it is $\geq \tau$ and 0 otherwise, where τ is the threshold value. Then, use the resulting binary vector in the same way as in $B_W^\alpha(D)$. Yet another possibility is to use the vector cond-probs(W, D) directly in place of bin(W, D) with size(I) of an interval $I = [i, j]$, where i and j are page numbers, being defined by $\sum$cond-prob$_k(W, D)$ (summed over pages k, $i \leq k \leq j$). In this way, we focus on the pages that are relatively important in terms of the keywords W

themselves, disregarding the role of other keywords $\Omega - W$. The use of pagewise-probs(W, D) instead of cond-probs(W, D) is not appropriate here; likewise, the use of thresholding with pagewise-probs(W, D) is not appropriate.

$$\text{page-sizes}(D) = \langle 2, 3, 5, 3, 4, 3 \rangle$$

$$\text{pagewise-counts}(a, D) = \langle 1, 1, 3, 0, 0, 1 \rangle$$
$$\text{pagewise-probs}(a, D) = \langle 1/2, 1/3, 3/5, 0, 0, 1/3 \rangle$$
$$\text{cond-probs}(a, D) = \langle 1/6, 1/6, 3/6, 0, 0, 1/6 \rangle$$

$$\text{pagewise-counts}(\{a, b\}, D) = \langle 2, 3, 4, 1, 1, 3 \rangle$$
$$\text{pagewise-probs}(\{a, b\}, D) = \langle 1, 1, 4/5, 1/3, 1/4, 1 \rangle$$
$$\text{cond-probs}(\{a, b\}, D) = \langle 2/14, 3/14, 4/14, 1/14, 1/14, 3/14 \rangle$$

Figure 5. The page-sizes(D), and pagewise-counts(W, D) and pagewise-probs(W, D) for $W = \{a\}$ and $\{a, b\}$ for a document with 6 pages and length 20.

6. References

1. B.Everitt, *Cluster analysis* (2nd ed.), Halsted Press, New York, 1980.

2. W.B.Frakes and R.Baeza-Yates (eds.), *Information Retrieval - data structures and algorithms (1992)*, Prentice-Hall, NJ.

3. G.J.Klir and B.Yuan, *Fuzzy sets and fuzzy logic - theory and applications*, Prentice Hall, New Jersey, 1995.

4. S.Kundu, Min-transitivity of fuzzy leftness relationship and its application to decision making, *Fuzzy Sets and Systems*, 86(1997), pp. 357-367.

5. C.P.Paice, Soft evaluation of boolean search queries in information retrieval systems, *Information Technology Res. Dev. and Appl.*, 3(1984), pp. 33-42.

CONCERTO, An Environment for the 'Intelligent' Indexing, Querying and Retrieval of Digital Documents

Gian Piero Zarri[1], Elisa Bertino[2], Bill Black[3], Andrew Brasher[4], Barbara Catania[2], Diana Deavin[4], Luigi Di Pace[5], Floriana Esposito[6], Pietro Leo[5], John McNaught[3], Andreas Persidis[7], Fabio Rinaldi[3], Giovanni Semeraro[6]

[1] Centre National de la Recherche Scientifique (CNRS), Paris, France
[2] Dipartimento di Scienze dell'Informazione dell'Università degli Studi, Milano, Italy
[3] Department of Language Engineering, UMIST, Manchester, United Kingdom
[4] Pira International, Leatherhead, United Kingdom
[5] Java Technology Center, IBM Semea Sud, Bari, Italy
[6] Dipartimento di Informatica dell'Università di Bari, Italy
[7] ASSETT, Athens, Greece

Abstract. We give a general overview of the European Esprit project CONCERTO. The central idea of CONCERTO is to represent the 'meaning' of digital documents making use of their associated 'conceptual annotations' : a conceptual annotation is intended to supply a computer-usable description of the main information elements of the whole document or of a part of it. We evoke first the general context ('metadata') of CONCERTO ; we describe then its architecture, and we give a concrete example of conceptual annotation.

1   Introduction

The CONCERTO project (Esprit P29159) aims to improve the current techniques for indexing, querying and retrieving textual documents stored in any sort of digital repository, from the World Wide Web (WWW) to digital libraries, by taking into account, at least partly, the semantic content (the 'meaning') of these documents. CONCERTO is an acronym for : CONCEptual indexing, querying and ReTrieval Of digital documents. The central idea of CONCERTO is to represent the meaning making use of 'conceptual annotations' linked with the textual documents : a conceptual annotation is intended to supply a computer-usable description of the main information elements of a document or part of a document. CONCERTO intends then to set up a full KESE (Knowledge Engineering Software Environment) for i) performing the computer-aided construction of the conceptual annotations ; ii) using the annotations to perform high-level information retrieval operations.

CONCERTO is worked on by 8 partners from France, Greece, Italy and the UK, a mix of industrialists, universities and research centres.

2   The general CONCERTO framework (metadata)

Given their form and function, CONCERTO's conceptual annotations can be identified with 'metadata'. The term metadata — i.e., data about data — denotes, in general, any piece of knowledge that can be used in order to get information about the structure and the contents of a (usually huge) collection of documents. A traditional library catalogue is, therefore, metadata. Recently, metadata has become synonymous with machine understandable knowledge describing Web resources ; querying or retrieving digital media can be executed directly at the metadata level.

Even if several types of metadata exist, only the 'content-specific metadata' allow achieving a sufficient degree of generality. Independent of media type and media processing, they "reflect the semantics of the media object in a given context" [1 : 13]. They are then related to the 'meaning' that a given document or document component can assume for its potential users, and can then support in the best possible way their indexing and retrieval functions. In the world of digital media, expressions like 'semantic approach', 'semantic indexing', 'extraction of semantic features' etc. are, in fact, especially popular.

This sweeping use of the label 'semantic' seems, however, to be at least partly unjustified. Most of the 'semantic' features now used as metadata seem to concern only, in reality, the 'external identification framework' (the 'physical structure') of the digital documents considered, more then a description of their true 'meaning'. This is particularly well-evident for non-textual documents like images and videos, where the use of some external, physical characteristics of the media, such as colour, shape, texture, motion patterns, scene breaks, pauses in the audio, camera pans and zooms, etc. is often traded for the use of true semantic techniques. But even if we stick to textual data, the use of an approach to metadata that is still fundamentally structure-based is also well evident. Let us consider, e.g., the Dublin Core initiative [2]. In this, 15 metadata elements have been defined. They are classified in three group according to the class or scope of the information stored in the original documents : elements related to the (so-called) 'content' of the document (title, subject, description, source, language, relation and coverage) ; elements related to the intellectual property (creator, publisher, contributor, and rights) ; elements related to the instantiation of the document (date, type, format and identifier). To be totally fair, we must say that Dublin Core comes, at least initially, from the librarian community, and its format reflects then the format and contents of the usual library catalogues.

A traditional — and semantically very poor — way of supplying metadata consists in the use of keywords. We can note that keywords can be assimilated, to a certain extent, to low-level 'concepts' considered in isolation. Accordingly, several researchers have recently proposed to make use of concepts structured into an 'ontology' to describe in some depth ('annotate') the information content of the WWW objects to retrieve, see projects like Web-At-a-Glance [3] or Ontobroker [4]. Making use of ontologies constitutes, undoubtedly, an important step towards true semantic-based utilisation ; ontologies may not be sufficient, however, to fully render the semantic content of digital documents. For example, the textual documents that are of any industrial and economic interest (news stories, telex reports, corporate documents, normative and legal texts, intelligence messages, etc.) consist often of 'narratives' about 'actions', 'facts', 'events', 'states' etc. that relate the real or intended behaviour of some 'actors' (characters, personages, etc.). In this case, the simple description of concepts is not enough, and must be integrated by the description of the mutual relationships between concepts — or, in other terms, the description of the 'role' the different concepts and their instances have in the framework of the global actions, facts, events etc. Ontologies normally supply, on the contrary, a static, rigid vision of the world, i.e., a taxonomy of pinned up, 'dead' concepts. Using only them to describe the inner semantic content of a 'narrative' is not so different from the choice of describing the world using linguistic utterances that only include 'nouns', with the deliberate exclusion of any 'verb'.

From the point of view of the *specific semantic categories* proposed until now as examples of possible metadata (i.e., the 'vocabulary' of metadata, see the 15 categories of Dublin Core), the situation seems then far from being satisfactory. With respect on the contrary to the *general interoperability mechanisms* for building up metadata systems, the situation is rapidly evolving.

RDF (Resource Description Format) is a proposal for defining and processing World Wide Web metadata that is developed by a specific W3C Working Group, see "http://www.w3.org/RDF/". The model, implemented in XML (eXtensible Markup Language), makes use of Directed Labelled Graphs (DLGs) where the nodes, that represent any possible Web resource (documents, parts of documents, collections of documents etc.) are described basically by using attributes that give the named properties of the resources. No predefined 'vocabulary' (ontologies, keywords, proposals in the Dublin Core style etc.) is in itself a part of the proposal. The values of the attributes may be text strings, numbers, or other resources. Initially, the model bore a striking resemblance to some early work on semantic networks, and the examples given of RDF annotations were, as usual, in the style of "The individual whose name is X, email Y, is the creator of the resource Z". In the latest versions of the RDF Model and Syntax Specifications, new, very interesting constructs have been added. Among these, of particular interest are the 'containers' and the 'high-order statements'. Containers describe 'collections' of resources ; the higher order statements can be used to make statements about other RDF statements. RDF has then been chosen in CONCERTO as the vehicle to be used to 'move around' the system the different elements of the conceptual annotations

3   The architecture of CONCERTO

Figure 1 gives a sketchy overview of the architecture of the CONCERTO KESE. For simplicity's and readability's sake we have left out, e.g., the XML Document Translator module that provides the conversion of the original documents into XML, to be used as unique internal format within the overall KESE, and the specialised interfaces allowing a direct interaction with the repositories.

Two different types of textual documents, corresponding to the two prototype applications envisaged in the project, are entered into the CONCERTO KESE. The first are natural language (NL) abstracts, chosen among those stored in the full-text databases of Pira International (UK), one of the two CONCERTO pilot users (and the co-ordinating partner of the project). Pira wants, in general, to make use of the conceptual annotations associated with these abstracts to index them finely and, e.g., to display them to an user in a variety of ways depending on the information content ; their requirements are mainly of the type 'digital libraries and electronic publishing'.

Another category of CONCERTO documents is represented by Internet NL documents, used by our second pilot user, ASSETT (GR), to compile and commercialise written reports about emerging sectors of biotechnology (e.g., Carbohydrate Therapeutics), aimed at practitioners and decision-makers in the field.

The ultimate goal of the second pilot application of CONCERTO concerns then the identification of all the major companies in the biotechnology field and the assessment of their specific areas of involvement. After having been annotated, an initial core of Internet documents will be used as 'leads', in order to discover further information relating to the sector analysed according to an iterative and recursive process. With respect to the Pira application, ASSETT's requirements are more in the style of 'intelligent data mining on the textual component of the Web'.

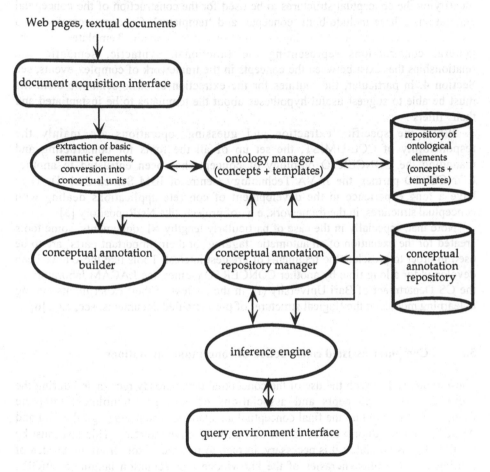

Figure 1 – Schematic architecture of the CONCERTO KESE.

We will now supply some information about the blocks of Figure 1.

3.1 Extraction of the basic semantic elements

These routines concern, firstly, the Natural Language Processing (NLP) operations intended to identify, within the NL documents, some 'basic semantic elements' like, for Pira, 'company names', 'person names and roles', 'geographic locations' etc.,

ASSETT adding to this list more specific items like, e.g., 'indication of patents'. For executing the extraction operations, we make use of the tools built up in the FACILE European project (LE 2440) ; two of the CONCERTO partners, CCL-UMIST (UK) and Quinary (IT), were in fact involved in the FACILE project.

These elements will be immediately used, by Pira, for indexing purposes in an electronic publishing context ; by ASSETT, to choose from the identified company names those that are active in the selected sector and to detect pertinent information related to these. Moreover, the basic semantic elements represent the key material for identifying the conceptual structures to be used for the construction of the conceptual annotations ; these include both 'concepts' and 'templates'. Concepts correspond to the formal representation of the important notions of the domain. Templates are more general constructions representing the functional, syntactic, semantic etc. relationships that exist between the concepts in the framework of complex events, see Section 4. In particular, the routines for the extraction of basic semantic elements must be able to suggest useful hypotheses about the templates to be instantiated and their 'fillers'.

While the specific 'extraction and guessing' operations are mainly the responsibility of CCL-UMIST, the set up of all the tools for constructing and managing the CONCERTO ontology of concepts has been entrusted to another CONCERTO partner, the JAVA Technology Centre of IBM Semea Sud (I). They have a long experience in the development of concrete applications dealing with conceptual structures, in the framework, e.g., of projects like NetRepository [5].

Note that, especially in the case of particularly lengthy NL documents, some tools created for the execution of an automatic 'tagging' of their 'important parts' are to be used in order to preselect the fragments of greatest interest. Tools like these have been developed for a long time by another CONCERTO partner, the LACAM laboratory of the CS Department of Bari University (I), in the context of their experiments aiming at learning models of the 'logical structure' of pre-classified documents, see, e.g., [6].

3.2 Computer-assisted construction of conceptual annotations

These routines deal with the use of the conceptual units already recognised during the previous phases (concepts and associations of concepts, templates, template fragments...) to build up the final conceptual annotations. The users (e.g., the Pira and ASSETT human editors) utilise to this aim an interactive interface. This last must be as 'friendly' as possible : it is necessary, in fact, to free the editors from the burden of dealing with the idiosyncrasies of the knowledge representation language, NKRL, used to represent the final conceptual annotations, see next Section. The editors introduce then the missing elements, and associate them with the already existing ones, using an input 'external' format very close to NL. The main partner responsible for the set up of the conceptual annotation builder is Quinary SpA (I).

3.3 Conceptual annotation repository

According to the metadata philosophy, all the querying and retrieving operations concerning the original documents will be executed directly at the conceptual annotations (metadata) level ; this means that the annotation repository of Figure 1 must be conceived as a standard knowledge base.

As already stated, the original texts are translated into XML by the XML Document Translator ; moreover, the internal knowledge representation language used for conceptual annotations, NKRL, is RDF-compliant, i.e., XML-compliant. To implement the repository, we must then choose a tool able to store in secondary storage XML data structures, and manage them guaranteeing good performance, high efficiency and reliability ; i.e., we must choose a Database Management System (DBMS) able to deal with XML documents. Moreover, given that NKRL is strongly object-oriented, see again next Section, our management system must also be compatible with an object-oriented or object-relational style of implementation.

All the most important DBMS producers are now proposing tools that can fulfil the above requirements. We are currently testing the XML-fitting tools proposed by the following two companies:

- Oracle Corporation: The Oracle 8i version features a set of Core XML
- Object Design: Object Design proposes eXcelon as a middle-tier data server for storing and managing XML documents.

The portability of Oracle 8i is higher than that of eXcelon – e.g., this last product is, at the moment, only supported by the NT platforms. On the other hand, given that XML is inserted in eXcelon at the physical level (the insertion is at the logical level in Oracle 8i), it becomes easier for eXcelon, e.g., to handle arbitrary XML data fully preserving the XML intrinsic hierarchical structure.

All the memorisation and access tasks related to the management of conceptual annotations are realised under the responsibility of Department of Information Sciences of Milan University (I).

3.4   Unification modules, inference engines etc

The basic building block for constructing any sort of search module and inference engine charged to perform the querying and retrieving operations on the repository is a Filtering and Unification Module (FUM). The primary data structures handled by FUM are the 'search patterns'. Search patterns are high level conceptual structures, including variables and constraints on the variables, that represent (in NKRL terms) the general properties of an information to be searched for, by filtering or unification, within the knowledge repository, see an example in the next Section.

All the work concerning the construction of the search patterns, the implementation of FUM etc. will be accomplished under the responsibility of the CS Department of Bari University (I).

4   An example of conceptual annotation

NKRL (Narrative Knowledge Representation Language) see, e.g., [7, 8], is a high-level knowledge representation language endowed with particular features which make it well suited for representing descriptive meanings like those proper to conceptual annotations. We can mention here the presence, besides the traditional 'ontology of concepts', of an 'ontology of events' (a hierarchical organisation of templates representing the formal description of general classes of real-world events, like 'move a generic object', 'formulate a need', 'be present somewhere', 'receive an information', etc.), or the possibility, see [8], of describing the temporal characteristics of the specific events (these last are represented as instances, 'occurrences', of the templates). Moreover, NKRL allows for the representation of implicit and explicit enunciative situations, of wishes, desires, and intentions, of plural situations, of causality, etc. The French National Centre for Scientific Research (CNRS, F) is the 'owner' of the NKRL methodology

Note that the NKRL ontology of events (hierarchy of templates) is described in a 'catalogue' that gives a complete account of the formal characteristics and the modalities of use of all the well-formed, 'basic templates' (like 'move a generic object' mentioned above) associated presently with the language (about 120). By means of proper specialisation operations, it is then possible to obtain directly from the catalogue all the (specific) 'derived' templates that could be concretely needed in the context of a particular, practical application. For example, from 'move a generic object' we can derive a template like 'move an industrial process', and then the corresponding occurrences — like, e.g., 'move, in a well-defined spatial-temporal framework, this particular industrial production'. This approach is particularly important for practical applications, and it implies, in particular, that : i) a system-builder does not have to create himself the syntactic structures needed to describe the events proper to a (sufficiently) large class of NL documents ; ii) it becomes easier to secure the reproduction or the sharing of previous results.

Let us now suppose we want to represent in the usual NKRL format, see Figure 2 — for clarity's sake, we do not consider here the intricacies of the RDF/XML version of NKRL — the following information that represents the essential semantic core of a Pira abstract : "On June 9, 1998, America Online announced it has finalised the acquisition of Mirabilis, an Israeli software house, for $287M cash. Mirabilis makes ICQ, an Internet tool enabling users to communicate with one another in real time".

The representation of Figure 2 is composed of a 'binding occurrence', $c1$, and three 'predicative occurrences', i.e., instances of basic templates included in the catalogue. The second-order, binding structure $c1$ makes it clear that the annotation consists of two main parts : an occurrence $c2$ relating the 'message', $c4$, transmitted by America Online (completive construction) ; an occurrence, $c3$, describing ICQ.

Occurrences $c3$ and $c4$ are both instances of basic NKRL templates pertaining to the PRODUCE branch of the hierarchy of events. In particular, $c4$ is an instance of one of the templates that translate a generic 'action' according to the syntax : PRODUCE + SUBJ *human_being_or_social_body* + OBJ <action name corresponding to the verb> (purchase_1 in this case). The presence of a 'temporal modulator', obs(erve), leads to an interpretation of $c3$ as the description of a situation that, at this particular date, is observed to exist. A 'location attribute' (a list that contains here only one element) is associated with the SUBJ(ect) arguments in $c2$, $c3$ and $c4$. The arguments introduced by the OBJ(ect) and MODAL(ity) roles include some SPECIF(ication) lists : these lists, with syntax (SPECIF e_1 p_1 ... p_n), are used to represent some of the properties which can be asserted about the first element e_1, concept or individual, of the list. In $c4$, we use one of the special SPECIF sub-lists

233

labelled in a normalised way with concepts (here, *amount_*) pertaining to the
*property_* and *attribute_value* subtrees of the hierarchy of concepts, see [7].

```
c1) (COORD  c2  c3)

c2) MOVE     SUBJ    america_online: (usa_)
             OBJ     #c4
             date-1: before-9-june-98
             date-2:

c4) PRODUCE  SUBJ    america_online: (usa_)
             OBJ     (SPECIF purchase_1 final_(SPECIF mirabilis_
                      (SPECIF software_house israeli_)))
             MODAL   (SPECIF cash_transaction_1 usa_dollar
                      (SPECIF amount_ (SPECIF million_ 287)))
             date-1: before-9-june-98
             date-2:

c3) PRODUCE  SUBJ    mirabilis_: (israeli_)
             OBJ     (SPECIF icq_ (SPECIF internet_tool (SPECIF
                      communication_tool on_line)))
             [ obs ]
             date-1: 9-june-98
             date-2:
```

Figure 2 - An example of NKRL conceptual annotation.

At least some of the concepts, e.g., *software_house*, *usa_dollar*, *internet_tool*, *communication_tool*, and of the individuals (instances of NKRL concepts), e.g., usa_, israeli_, icq_, purchase_1, of Figure 2, have been detected by the procedures for extracting the basic semantic elements and transforming them into conceptual units, see the previous Section.

To clarify now the notion of 'search pattern' introduced, before, in subsection 3.4, we reproduce in Figure 3 a simple NKRL search pattern corresponding to the question: "Who has recently acquired an Israeli software house, and according to which modalities?" that, obviously, unifies with occurrence c4 in Figure 2.

```
((?w  IS-OCCURRENCE
      :pred. PRODUCE
      :SUBJ ?x
      :OBJ  (SPECIF purchase_ (SPECIF ?y (SPECIF
             software_house israeli_)))
      :MODAL ?z)
      (1_may_98, 31_july_98)
      ((?x  IS-A  (:OR human_being social_body))
       (?y  IS-A  company_)
       (?z  IS-A  general_sale_purchase_procedures)))
```

Figure 3 - A simple search pattern.

In Figure 3, the two dates constitute the 'search interval' associated with the search pattern : this interval is used to limit the search for unification to the slice of time that it is considered appropriate to explore, see [8]. Note that the concept `purchase_` behaves here as an 'implicit variable'.

5   Conclusion

In this paper, we have provided a general overview of the European Esprit project CONCERTO (CONCEptual indexing, querying and ReTrieval Of digital documents). We have first introduced informally the notion of 'conceptual annotation' (a computer-usable description of the main information elements of a digital document, or of a part of it)). We have then explained how these annotations can represent, at least to some extent, the 'meaning' (the semantic content) of these documents. The general architecture of the CONCERTO Knowledge Engineering Software Environment (KESE) has been then introduced. We have finally supplied an example of conceptual annotation formulated according to the NKRL ('Narrative Knowledge Representation Language') format ; NKRL is a language expressly designed for representing, in a standardised way ('metadata'), the semantic characteristics of multimedia documents.

References

1. Boll, S., Klas, W., Sheth, A.: Overview on Using Metadata to Manage Multimedia Data. In: Multimedia Data Management - Using Metadata to Integrate and Apply Digital Media. McGraw Hill, New York (1998).
2. Weibel, S, Hakala, J.: DC-5 : The Helsinki Metadata Workshop - A Report on the Workshop and Subsequent Developments. D-Lib Magazine - The Magazine of Digital Library Research (February 1998).
3. Catarci, T., Iocchi, L., Nardi, D., Santucci, G.: Conceptual Views over the Web. In: Intelligent Access to Heterogeneous Information - Proc. of the 4th Knowledge Representation Meets Databases (KRDB) Workshop (1997).
4. Fensel, D., Decker, S., Erdmann, M., Studer, R.: Ontobrocker : Or How to Enable Intelligent Access to the WWW. In: Proc. of the 11th Banff Knowledge Acquisition for Knowledge-Based Systems Workshop, KAW'98. Department of Computer Science of the University, Calgary (1998).
5. Convertino, G., Di Pace, L., Leo, P., Maffione, A.: Ontological Organisation for Complex and Efficient Storage and Retrieval in the Network. In: Proc. of the Second International KRUSE'97 Symposium (1997).
6. Esposito, F., Malerba, D., Semeraro, G., Fanizzi, N., Ferilli, S.: Adding Machine Learning and Knowledge Intensive Techniques to a Digital Library Service. Int. J. Digit. Libr. 2 (1998) 1-17.
7. Zarri, G.P.: NKRL, a Knowledge Representation Tool for Encoding the 'Meaning' of Complex Narrative Texts. Natural Language Engineering 3 (1997) 231-253.
8. Zarri, G.P.: Representation of Temporal Knowledge in Events : The Formalism, and Its Potential for Legal Narratives. Information & Communications Technology Law 7 (1998) 213-241.

Text Classification Using Lattice Machine *

Hui Wang[1] and Nguyen Hung Son[2]

[1] School of Information and Software Engineering
University of Ulster
Newtownabbey, BT 37 0QB, N.Ireland
H.Wang@ulst.ac.uk
[2] Institute of Mathematics
Warsaw University
02-095, Banacha 2 Str., Warsaw Poland
son@mimuw.edu.pl

Abstract. A novel approach to supervised learning, called *Lattice Machine*, was proposed in [5]. In the Lattice Machine, it was assumed that data are structured as relations. In this paper we investigate the application of the Lattice Machine in the area of text classification, where textual data are unstructured. We represent a set of textual documents as a collection of Boolean feature vectors, where each vector corresponds to one document and each entry in a tuple indicates whether a particular term appears in the document. This is a common representation of textual documents. We show that using this representation, the Lattice Machine's operations are simply set theoretic operations. In particular, the lattice sum operation is simply set intersection and the ordering relationship is simply set inclusion. Experiments show that the Lattice Machine, under this configuration, is quite competitive with state-of-the-art learning algorithms for text classification.

1 Introduction

Lattice machine, proposed in [5], is a general framework for supervised learning. Two of its components can be specified to suit different situations. In [5] the Lattice Machine was presented to work on *structured data*, which is in the form of database relations. In this paper we re-configure the Lattice Machine so that it works on unstructured textual data. We will show that adopting the common *Boolean feature vector* representation of textual documents, two of the Lattice Machine's components – ordering relation and sum operation – are simply set inclusion and set intersection respectively. This approach will be validated by

* The authors gratefully acknowledge support by the KBN/British Council Grant No WAR/992/151

experimentation using benchmark (textual) datasets, and it will also be compared with similar approaches.

In the rest of the paper, we first of all present a brief review of the Lattice Machine. Then we specify the Lattice Machine for use with unstructured textual data. We present a detailed example to illustrate the configured Lattice Machine, along with experimental results. Finally we summarise and conclude the paper.

2 A brief review of the Lattice Machine

Given a dataset represented as a database relation, a *tuple* is a vector of attribute values, a *hyper tuple* is a vector of sets of attribute values, and a *hyper relation* is a set of hyper tuples. The notion of hyper tuple is a generalisation of database tuple. Examples of a simple relation and a hyper relation are shown in Tables 1 and 2 respectively.

It has been shown [5] that an elegant structure is implied among hyper tuples – the collection of all hyper tuples in a given domain is a semilattice under the following ordering relation $\leq$:

$$hyper\_tuple_1 \leq hyper\_tuple_2 \overset{\text{def}}{\Longleftrightarrow} hyper\_tuple_1(A) \subseteq hyper\_tuple_2(A),$$

for all $A \in U$ and U is the set of attributes. We call this *domain lattice*.

In a domain lattice, a labelled dataset (training data) corresponds to a labelling of the lattice. For example, the following labelled dataset corresponds to the labelled lattice in Figure 1.

E: $\langle Large, Red, Triangle, + \rangle$
G: $\langle Large, Blue, Circle, + \rangle$
J: $\langle Small, Blue, Triangle, - \rangle$
L: $\langle Small, Green, Rectangular, - \rangle$

Given a labelled lattice, a straightforward representation of the labelling is by sets – each set consisting of all data units with the same label, and a simple classification is by enumeration – if a new data unit is the same as one element in the set representation, then it is classified by the label of this element; otherwise, it is marked as unknown. This is in fact the idea of rote learning. Clearly there is no generalisation in this kind of learning. The nearest neighbour method goes one step further. In its basic form, the representation is also by sets, but the classification is based on some distance measure. There is generalisation in this kind of learning, but distance measures can be troublesome in cases where discrete attributes are involved.

The Lattice Machine takes a different approach to this problem. It represents the labelling by a subset of the elements in the lattice – usually much less than the number of labelled elements. These elements have the property that all elements below them have the same label or are unlabelled, and we called them *equilabelled*. The classification is governed by the following simple rule:

given an equilabeled element, any elements below it will have the same label as the equilabeled element (if any).

The hyper relation in Table 2 is in fact the set of equilabelled elements found by the Lattice Machine from the relation in Table 1.

The core of the Lattice Machine is the following algorithm [5]. Let D be a labelled dataset. The labelling implies a natural partition of the dataset with classes $\{M_0, M_1, \cdots, M_n\}$. Given M_i of labelled elements for class i, the algorithm finds a set H_i of equilabelled maximal elements (in the sense that the sum of any pair of them is not equilabelled any more). This algorithm is based on the lattice operation *sum* $(+)$ for finding the unique least upper bound of a set of elements.

Let $\mathcal{E}$ be the set of all (possible) equilabelled elements in a labelled lattice.

1. $C_1 \stackrel{\text{def}}{=} M_i$.
2. $C_{k+1} \stackrel{\text{def}}{=}$ The set of maximal elements of $[\downarrow (C_k + M_i)] \cap \mathcal{E}$.

Note that, for a lattice L and $e \in L$, $\downarrow e = \{y \in L : y \leq e\}$. It has been shown [5] that there is some n such that $C_n = C_{n+1}$, and therefore $C_n = C_r$ for all $r \geq n$. It has also been proved that $C_n = H_i$. This H_i is called *interior* of class M_i.

ID	Attribute		Class
	A_1	A_2	
t_0	a	1	0
t_1	a	2	1
t_2	a	3	1
t_3	b	1	0
t_4	b	2	1
t_5	b	3	1
t_6	c	2	0
t_7	c	3	0

Table 1. *A simple (database) relation.*

ID	Attribute		Class
	A_1	A_2	
t'_0	$\{a,b\}$	$\{1\}$	0
t'_1	$\{a,b\}$	$\{2,3\}$	1
t'_2	$\{c\}$	$\{2,3\}$	0

Table 2. *A hyper relation obtained from the relation in Table 1 by the Lattice Machine.*

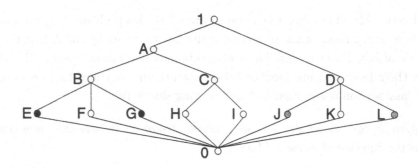

Fig. 1. *A labelled lattice.*

3   Lattice Machine for text classification

Lattice Machine is a general framework for supervised learning. The basic elements can be re-configured to suit different learning problem. In this section we are going to show how to re-configure the Lattice Machine for the task of text classification.

3.1   Representation

Lattice Machine was originally proposed to work on structured data. Text documents, however, are unstructured data. A common representation of text document is by boolean feature vector. For example, one could construct a feature for each word appearing in the corpus – a set of documents. A corpus with m documents and n words would thus be represented as a $m \times n$ matrix. This representation in fact turns unstructured datasets into structured. However, this representation is inefficient in its usage of space, since even a moderate sized corpus usually contains many different words. Lattice Machine has a natural solution to this problem.

Given two documents of a same class in Table 3, we first of all represent them by boolean feature vectors as in Table 4. Merging the two vectors by the lattice sum operation (either using set union or intersection, depending on the ordering relation), we get new vectors as in Table 5. Translating the new vectors back into word lists, we get Table 6. It is clear that the lattice sum operation is equivalent to taking the documents as sets of words and exercising the set operations (either set union or intersection).

Therefore, for the task of text classification, we represent text documents as sets (lists) of words.

England, Ireland, Poland, Scotland, Wales	Europe
Czech, Ireland, Poland, Slovia	Europe

Table 3. *Two documents of the same class.*

Czech	England	Ireland	Poland	Scotland	Slovia	Wales	Class
0	1	1	1	1	0	1	Europe
1	0	1	1	0	1	0	Europe

Table 4. *A Boolean feature vector representation of the documents in Table 3.*

Czech	England	Ireland	Poland	Scotland	Slovia	Wales	Class
1	1	1	1	1	1	1	Europe
0	0	1	1	0	0	0	Europe

Table 5. *The sum of the two tuples in Table 4. The first tuple is by set union, and the second is by set intersection. Whether these sums can be accepted depends on data in other classes.*

Czech, England, Ireland, Poland, Scotland, Slovia, Wales	Europe
Ireland, Poland	Europe

Table 6. *Set representation of results merged by the lattice sum operation.*

3.2 The ordering relation

In the original Lattice Machine the ordering relation is as follows:

$$hyper\_tuple_1 \leq hyper\_tuple_2 \overset{\text{def}}{\Longleftrightarrow} hyper\_tuple_1(A) \subseteq hyper\_tuple_2(A),$$

for all attributes A. In fact the set inclusion can be changed from $\subseteq$ to $\supseteq$, but the sum operation has also to be changed accordingly.

In the context of text classification, if the documents are relatively large hence different documents have large number of common elements, it would be more efficient to use $\supseteq$ rather than $\subseteq$ to define the ordering relation. This amounts to classifying a document using a subset of the words in the document either in a fixed order or in any order. If the documents are relatively small, however, it would be more effective to use $\subseteq$ instead. This amounts to classifying a document according to whether it is a subset of an already classified document. In what follows, our presentation is mainly for $\supseteq$. Where a result doesn't apply to $\subseteq$, we will clearly spell it out, and an alternative solution will be provided accordingly.

Since we choose to represent a document by a set of words, the ordering relation can therefore be specified as follows:

$$doc_1 \leq doc_2 \overset{\text{def}}{\Longleftrightarrow} set\_of\_words(doc_1) \supseteq set\_of\_words(doc_2),$$

where $set\_of\_words(doc_i)$ is the set of words in doc_i.

3.3 The sum operation

Now that documents are represented by sets (word list) and the ordering relation is (inverse) set inclusion, the sum operation (denoted by +) is simply set intersection. For example, the sum of the two documents in Table 3 is the intersection of the them as sets, and this results in a new document (i.e., set) $\{Ireland, Poland\}$.

4 An example

Now we use a sample of the MEMO data shown in Table 7 to illustrate our solution to the text classification problem. This dataset was used in [2]. It was 11 classes, but we use only samples from two classes. Each line corresponds to one document, and it is a list of words in the document (stemmed with the Porter Stemmer algorithm [3, 6]). Since the documents have been processed, they may not be readable to humans any more. So are the interiors to be found later.

For the "commun" class, we sum all pairs of documents using $\supseteq$ and we get the hyper tuples in Table 8. The set of maximal equilabelled hyper tuples is shown in Table 9. The same operation is applied to this table, and it is clear that the result is the same as this table. Therefore this is the interior for the "commun" class. The same is done for the "comput" class, and the interior for this class is shown in Table 9.

[1]	97 doc code r area 02 18 n america by state lewen	commun
[2]	97 j code text area 02 18 n america 2 memo by state megibow	commun
[3]	97 doc at t answer machin code 10 15 command for 1343 dave diehl	commun
[4]	97 doc at t answer machin control code 10 15 1545 r frisbi	commun
[5]	97 doc 11 at t answer machin 1339 control code text michael choi	commun
[6]	97 at code text r 02 18 2 hard drive rev sutherland	comput
[7]	97 code text r 02 18 2 xt hard drive rev sutherland	comput
[8]	97 code text 02 18 ibm irq and pc diagnost w taucher	comput
[9]	97 doc j at command 04 09 modem karam	comput
[10]	97 doc j code 02 18 7 error system mac 20k simpson	comput

Table 7. *A sample of the MEMO data.*

4.1 Discussion

Applying the classification rule on page 2, it can be easily verified that the interiors can correctly classify all the documents in Table 7. However, the generalisation

241

[1+1]	97 doc code r area 02 18 n america by state lewen	commun
[1+2]	97 code area 02 18 n america by state	commun
[1+3]	97 doc code	commun
[1+4]	97 doc code r	commun
[1+5]	97 doc code	commun
[2+2]	97 j code text area 02 18 n america 2 memo by state megibow	commun
[2+3]	97 code	commun
[2+4]	97 code	commun
[2+5]	97 code text	commun
[3+3]	97 doc at t answer machin code 10 15 command for 1343 dave diehl	commun
[3+4]	97 doc at t answer machin code 10 15	commun
[3+5]	97 doc at t answer machin code	commun
[4+4]	97 doc at t answer machin control code 10 15 1545 r frisbi	commun
[4+5]	97 doc at t answer machin control code	commun
[5+5]	97 doc 11 at t answer machin 1339 control code text michael choi	commun
[6+6]	97 at code text r 02 18 2 hard drive rev sutherland	comput
[6+7]	97 code text r 02 18 2 hard drive rev sutherland	comput
[6+8]	97 code text 02 18	comput
[6+9]	97 at	comput
[6+10]	97 code 02 18	comput
[7+7]	97 code text r 02 18 2 xt hard drive rev sutherland	comput
[7+8]	97 code text 02 18	comput
[7+9]	97	comput
[7+10]	97 code 02 18	comput
[8+8]	97 code text 02 18 ibm irq and pc diagnost w taucher	comput
[8+9]	97	comput
[8+10]	97 code 02 18	comput
[9+9]	97 doc j at command 04 09 modem karam	comput
[9+10]	97 doc j	comput
[10+10]	97 doc j code 02 18 7 error system mac 20k simpson	comput

Table 8. *The sum of all pairs of tuples in Table 7.*

[1+2]	97 code area 02 18 n america by state	commun
[1+4]	97 doc code r	commun
[3+5]	97 doc at t answer machin code	commun
[6+7]	97 code text r 02 18 2 hard drive rev sutherland	comput
[8+8]	97 code text 02 18 ibm irq and pc diagnost w taucher	comput
[9+10]	97 doc j	comput

Table 9. *Maximal equilabelled hyper tuples (interiors) obtained from Table 8.*

ability may not be very high as the dataset is very small compared with the original dataset. The generalisation ability can be seen from the experimental results to be presented in the next section.

Further processing can done to simplify the interiors obtained by the Lattice Machine. For example, since "97" appears in all interiors for both classes, it can be safely removed without affecting the classification performance. Taking this one step further, we can remove those words that appear in almost all interiors.

5 Experimental results

To evaluate the Lattice Machine as a tool for text classification, we applied it to nine benchmark problems which were used in [2]. Table 10 lists the problems and gives a summary description of each domain, the number of classes and number of terms found in each problem, and the number of training and testing examples used in the experiment. On smaller problems 10-fold cross-validation was used, and on larger problems a single holdout set of the specified size was used. The experimental results are listed in Table 11. As a comparison we cite from [2] experimental results on the same set of problems using two state-of-the-art learning algorithms – C4.5 [4], RIPPER [1].

Datasets	#Train	#Test	#Classes	#Terms	Text-valued field	Label
memos	334	10cv	11	1014	document title	category
cdroms	798	10cv	6	1133	CD-Rom game name	category
birdcom	914	10cv	22	674	common name of bird	phylogenic order
birdsci	914	10cv	22	1738	common + scientific name of bird	phylogenic order
hcoarse	1875	600	126	2098	company name	industry (coarse grain)
hfine	1875	600	228	2098	company name	industry (fine grain)
books	3501	1800	63	7019	book title	subject heading
species	3119	1600	6	7231	animal name	phylum
netvet	3596	2000	14	5460	URL title	category

Table 10. Description of benchmark problems.

6 Conclusion

The Lattice Machine is a general framework for supervised learning. Its basic components can be re-configured to suit different learning requirements. Previously the

243

Dataset	default	RIPPER	C4.5	LM/Text
memos	19.8	50.9	57.5	59.8
cdroms	26.4	38.3	39.2	40.0
birdcom	42.8	88.8	79.6	90.4
birdsci	42.8	91.0	83.3	92.3
hcoarse	11.3	28.0	30.2	20.2
hfine	4.4	16.5	17.2	13.8
books	5.7	42.3	52.2	45.3
species	51.8	90.6	89.4	89.4
netvet	22.4	67.1	68.8	67.8
Average		57.1	57.5	57.7

Table 11. Experimental results of the Lattice Machine, along with those of C4.5 and RIPPER cited from [2].

Lattice Machine works on structured data (i.e., feature vector based). In this paper the Lattice Machine is re-configured so that it can used for unstructured textual data. Under this re-configuration, the sum operation is simply set intersection, and the ordering relation is simply set inclusion. The experiments show that the Lattice Machine under this configuration is quite competitive with state-of-the-art methods for classification.

Acknowledgements We thank Prof. Ivo Düntsch, Prof. Andrzej Skowron and Prof. Ewa Orlowska for useful discussions.

References

1. William W. Cohen. Fast effective rule induction. In *Machine Learning: Procedings of the Twelfth International Conference*. Morgan Kaufmann, 1995. http://www.research.att.com/~wcohen/.
2. William W. Cohen and Haym Hirsh. Joins that generalize: Text classification using whirl. In *Proc. KDD-98, New York*, 1998. http://www.research.att.com/~wcohen/.
3. M. Porter. An algorithm for suffix stripping. *Program*, 14(3):130–137, 1980.
4. Ross Quinlan. *C4.5: Programs for Machine Learning*. Morgan Kaufmann, San Mateo, 1993.
5. Hui Wang, Ivo Düntsch, and David Bell. Data reduction based on hyper relations. In *Proceedings of KDD98, New York*, pages 349–353, 1998.
6. Jinxi Xu and W.B. Croft. Corpus-based stemming using co-occurrence of word variants. *ACM TOIS*, 16(1):61–81, Jan. 1998.

Discovering Semantic Proximity for Web Pages

Matthew Merzbacher

Mills College, Oakland CA 94613, USA
matthew@mills.edu

Abstract. *Dynamic Nearness* is a data mining algorithm that detects semantic relationships between objects in a database, based on access patterns. This approach can be applied to web pages to allow automatic dynamic reconfiguration of a web site. Worst–case storage requirements for the algorithm are quadratic (in the number of web pages), but practical reductions, such as ignoring a few long transactions that provide little information, drop storage requirements to linear. Thus, dynamic nearness scales to large systems. The methodology is validated via experiments run on a moderately–sized existing web site.

Keywords: learning and knowledge discovery, intelligent information systems, semantic distance metrics, data mining, world wide web

1 Introduction

In the World Wide Web, users navigate from page to page, following explicit links between the pages. As the number of pages on a web site grows, users must often follow a multi-hop path to get from one page to another related page. In such cases, the web server can detect the path (especially if it is well-trodden by many users) and install a direct link from the first page to the last page. Future visitors would have the opportunity to jump directly from the first to the last page, eliminating the middle steps. This paper presents the *Dynamic Nearness* (DN) algorithm and shows how it can be used to discover these implicit relationships between web pages. Based on this discovered information, previously unlinked related pages can be directly connected.

Cooperative query answering systems [4, 5, 10], help users find approximate answers, particularly when their original query cannot be precisely satisfied. One approach to finding approximate answers is *browsing*, where the user navigates the database by starting with a query. If the query answer set, A, is inadequate, then a second approximate set of answers is derived from A. The user consults with the system, identifying relevant objects in the new set, and the process can be repeated as long as necessary. At each step, the user provides feedback and discrimination.

The World Wide Web may be viewed as a very large browsing database system. In the web, users start with a *page* (corresponding to the original answer set A) and consider other pages that are *linked* to that page. The approximation of A, is the set of pages that are directly reachable from A.

In browsing systems, such as library applications [12], new material is automatically integrated into the system in a seamless manner. In the web, as new pages are added, human intervention is required to link the new information from existing pages. As a result, existing pages are seldom linked to all suitable pages and can be connected to pages that have since become immaterial. Automated techniques for discovering new links between pages in a web site are, therefore, desirable.

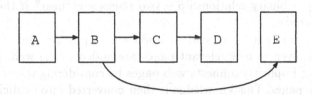

Fig. 1. Small web example

Consider a very small web (Fig. 2) with five pages, A through E. Page A is linked to B, which is linked to C, which is linked to D. Page B is also linked to page E and no other links exist. Now, suppose that a user starts at page A, moves to B, then to C. From C, the user jumps directly to E (perhaps using the link previously encountered in B). When several users follow the same path, a "smart" system should recognize patterns in user behavior and formulate new links to the pages based on the patterns. Certainly, a link from C to E would be useful, as might links from A to C and even A to E. Future users would then be able to jump straight from A to E without having to go through the inappropriate (for them) intermediary pages (Fig. 3).

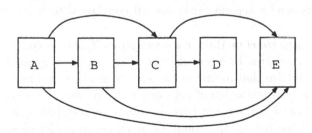

Fig. 2. Web example after knowledge discovery

Dynamic Nearness [9] is a data mining algorithm that measures the nearness between objects. This paper shows how DN can be used automatically to discover relevant links between web pages by building a sparse matrix of related web pages. From this matrix, the most valued links are selected for automatic inclusion into each web page. The algorithm discovers the most up-to-date and relevant links for each page.

Traditional browsing systems [11] rely on semantic *nearness metrics* to find the approximate answer set. Starting with a given set of objects, they use the nearness metric to find the nearest neighbors of that set based on object–object difference. The nearness metric is a function that returns a "nearness" between any pair of objects. For large domains, such as the World Wide Web, constructing such a metric is an astronomical task. However, semantic nearness between web pages is really a binary relationship – two pages are "near" if they are linked and "far" otherwise.

Since most web pages are seldom updated, in practice links are static for existing pages, even as new relevant pages are added to the web. DN discovers knowledge that implicitly connects web pages by considering the access patterns between those pages. This knowledge is then converted into explicit links.

Dynamic Nearness captures the closeness between two objects. The key features of DN are that it is:

(a) Based on transaction history;
(b) Dynamically evolving, able to reflect changes in perceptions of nearness;
(c) Efficiently computable;
(d) Suitable for use with browsing systems *and* the World Wide Web;
(e) Applicable for automatic update of existing web pages, adding new links as new relevant pages become available.

DN uses transaction history to construct a *count base* that connects semantically close objects. These objects can be tuples in a relational database system, pages in the web, or objects in an object-oriented database system. Instead of storing a value for all possible pairs, the algorithm reduces storage requirements by maintaining values for a limited number of nearest neighbors to each object; objects beyond a certain range are all considered to be remote (infinitely distant).

DN is an *a posteriori* method, constantly modifying the count base to reflect developing relationships between objects. The algorithm generates a nearness metric and maintains that metric as the system grows and changes. DN can run off-line using a transaction log of previous web accesses. Since only the nearest objects are retained in the count base, it can be represented by an efficient data structure. As time passes, the count between semantically close pages grows. Each page will have a list of high–count pages that should be linked from it. Some of these high–count pages will already be linked, but connections to new pages will be discovered automatically.

The rest of this paper is organized as follows. Section 2 discusses previous work. Section 3 introduces and explains the algorithm. Section 4 contains experimental results run on data gathered from the web server at Mills College. Section 5 contains discussion of the behavior and characteristics of Dynamic Nearness.

2 Previous Work

Most cooperative systems rely on predefined metrics for each object to determine semantic distances. Metrics are functions that return a single semantic distance between two objects and are usually either tabular or computational.

Tabular metrics use a static table to determine the distance between objects. For large domains, the number of possible pairs makes this table exceedingly large. *Computational* metrics, as the name suggests, determine semantic distance using computation instead of table lookup. Alas, for most attribute domains, reasonable computational metrics are hard to derive. For web pages and other large non-numeric domains, tabular metrics are too big and computational metrics are too complex. Worse, except in well-structured cases [7] both must be updated by an expert every time a new page is added to the web, an unacceptable burden. The metric should be able to incorporate new information automatically, dynamically and efficiently.

Considerable past effort has also gone into the related field of automatic classification, mostly concentrating on single-domain classifications, such as the symptoms in a medical expert system or the keywords in a book. Such techniques are usually a variant of the nearest-neighbor methods [3] used in vision and pattern matching, which classify objects into sets based on how well the properties of the objects match the properties of the sets.

Automatic generation of nearness functions has been used in library applications to aid catalog searching. To improve search success ratios, semantically "close" objects (in this case, books) are stored together for common reference. *Coherence*, based on shared keywords and title words, is a typical measure of the relationship between two articles [8]. This approach has been extended to web pages [6] with some success.

All of these automatic algorithms are based on the contents of the database or web pages. The DN approach is different, because it uses access patterns instead of content. While other methods are subject to difficulties when two strongly related pages use different terminology and vocabulary, the DN algorithm takes advantage of historical patterns to evaluate which objects are semantically close. Thus, objects which are frequently accessed together (because users identified them as "interesting" during the same session) are assigned strong semantic proximity, regardless of content.

Some work has been done on identifying association rules for web pages [2]. This work, which also uses transaction logs, has a heavier computational requirement than DN and does not dynamically adjust the web based on its results.

3 Dynamic Nearness for Web Pages

A web *transaction* [1] is a sequence of web pages that were accessed by the same user over a short span of time. The **Dynamic Nearness** of two web pages is the probable frequency that the pages are visited together in any single transaction. If DN is high, then the pages should be linked.

The DN algorithm is:

```
addcounts(T) :--
  initialize all counts to 0

  for each transaction T
    for each distinct pair of pages U, V in T
      increment the count between U and V
```

To save time, and because the counts need not be precise, `addcounts` can be run off–line using a transaction log. Further, it only need be run infrequently, perhaps once per month.

To illustrate DN, consider a four page web. Table 1 shows the counts after these transactions have executed:

    T1 visits pages A and C
    T2 visits pages A and D
    T3 visits all four pages
    T4 visits pages A, B and D

```
        A
      B 2 B
      C 2 1 C
      D 3 2 1
```

Table 1. Example count base

The table highlights a potential problem with the DN approach. With only four transactions, all possible pairs of pages in our mini–web have non-zero counts. In larger examples, there is a danger of proliferating links, especially if there are transactions that visit a great number of pages (e.g., T3 in the above example). Automated "web crawling" programs that catalog every page on a site leave just such a transaction footprint. However, in experiments (Sect. 4), we show that ignoring large unfocused transactions reduces the counts base to a tiny fraction of its maximum size.

Since most web pages are unrelated to one another, counts between most pairs of pages will be near zero. Frequently, unrelated pages are visited in succession by coincidence, creating a large number of pairs of pages with very low counts. To reduce the space (and time) requirements for the DN algorithm, page pairs with a count below a given threshold are ignored, allowing a sparse matrix representation. Thus, only the true nearest neighbors are stored for each page. All other pages (having count below the threshold) are considered infinitely distant. This reflects the binary relationship of web links. Experiments detailed in the next section show that pruning the sparse matrix reduces the number of links to linear in the number of pages.

3.1 Converting Counts to Links

Once the counts base is completed, it can be used to update web pages, adding additional relevant links to each page. The easiest way to do this is to identify a list of related pages for each page by selecting the pages with the best N counts for this page. Some pages have fewer than N truly close neighbors. In such cases, a second threshold value, V should be used in conjunction with N to yield reasonable results. The threshold V can be determined using the maximum count for a page or maximum overall count.

Web users accept that there can be relevant unlinked pages but do not like inappropriately linked pages. In information systems, this is known as a high–precision and low–recall environment. Raising the threshold value V reduces the likelihood of incorrect links at the risk of losing good links.

4 Experimental Results

The following experiment demonstrates the viability of DN in its space and time requirements. The experiment, using an implementation of DN written in Java, ran on monthly transaction logs for the Mills College web site. A typical monthly log contains almost a half-million accesses to over ten thousand web pages (or partial pages). Only HTML accesses were considered for this study, because other formats, such as CGI and JPEG use additional information that was not available in the log. Further, none of the non-HTML formats are suitable for having links added automatically.

The results (Fig. 4) demonstrate the sparseness of the counts base. Most pairs of pages are either unlinked or very lightly linked. Of the 60 million possible pairs of pages, only 70397 links exist and, for the pages that are linked, the average count is 1.67. This indicates that a vast majority of pages are unlinked or only linked once. Figure 4 also shows an inverse relationship between a threshold count and the number of pages having DN above that threshold. Two outlier points with extremely high counts (3863 and 6903) represent site–wide entry pages that show up in many transactions. This happens because many users start at the head of the Mills web hierarchy and many Mills web pages are linked back to the main entry pages. The other high–volume hits represent extremely popular pages[1] in the Mills hierarchy. These are pages that are often bookmarked by outside visitors and revisited directly.

DN relies on the assumption that every page should be heavily linked to a small set of nearby neighbors. In this case, transactions will return a small number of tuples. As transactions become longer, performance will degrade, since each page will be linked to too many neighbors. Fortunately, Fig. 5 shows that transaction lengths tend to be short; less than one percent of the transactions are longer than six pages. This is a promising result, since it means that "broad" information-free transactions are uncommon and will not weaken our counts base.

---

[1] One is a popular page containing pornographic short stories by one of our graduate students in creative writing.

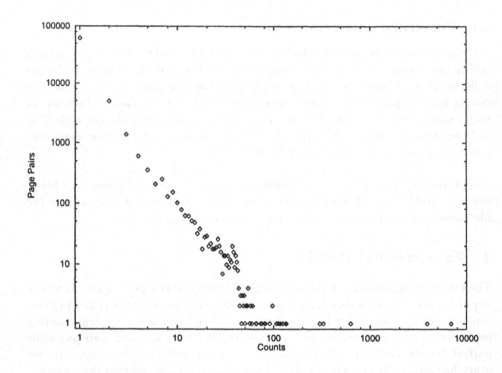

Fig. 3. Number of page pairs with count above a given threshold

5 Discussion

DN is appropriate for application domains that share a single context. When transactions span multiple contexts, results become inconsistent as truly unrelated objects are linked. However, except for the general site home page, most web transactions stay within a single context, since the user is focussed on retrieving a particular piece of information. Further, even in a multi-context domain, if multi-context transactions are rare, then they will only appear as noise without generating new links.

Although the maximum possible number of links grows quadratically with the number of pages, in practice the number of links per page remains relatively constant as long as the number of pages in each transaction remains constant. Thus, when the size of transactions is independent of the size of the web (and it usually is), DN will scale to very large systems. Even if transaction size does not remain constant, a policy of ignoring very large transactions can be applied to ensure that the size of the count base grows linearly with the number of pages. As a result, DN scales to large web sites.

When users navigate through a web, they often follow several wrong leads in the search for a particular page. This creates a transaction that is both long and filled with irrelevant intermediate sites. The appropriate action in such situations

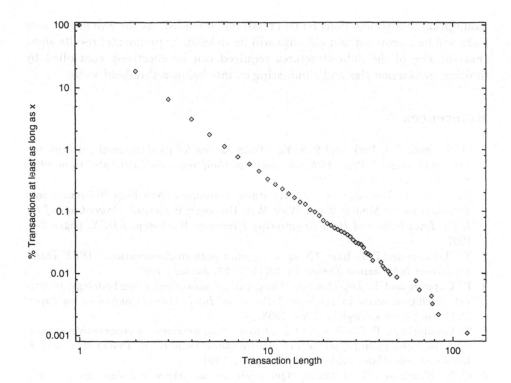

Fig. 4. Percentage of transaction lengths above a given threshold

is to connect only the start and end pages of the transaction. Then, future users will be able to jump straight to the conclusion instead of being offered pointless intermediate pages. DN can incorporate this policy, although a more sensible approach might be to connect the second page in the transaction with the last page, because the first page is often the general top-level site home page.

Existing links in DN are constantly reinforced by the counting algorithm. A user may go from page A to page B just because it is the first available link, even though it leads to a "dead end." Under the basic DN approach, such links would be counted again and again. To reduce this undesirable second-order effect, counts for existing links can be ignored or discounted by the algorithm. This shifts the focus of the algorithm entirely towards discovering new connections instead of reaffirming old ones.

As a web evolves, old links may become irrelevant. The original DN algorithm allowed deletion of old and stale links. This approach can be adapted for web pages as well.

6   Conclusion

This paper presents a method for automatically generating links in web pages based on transaction history. The method scales to large systems under the assumption that transactions remain relatively bounded. As the web grows, new links will be discovered and old links will be deleted. Experimental results show that the size of the data structures required can be effectively controlled by limiting transaction size and eliminating counts below a threshold value.

References

1. M. S. Chen, J. S. Park, and P. S. Yu, "Data mining for path traversal patterns in a web environment," *Proc. 16th International Conference on Distributed Computing Systems,* pages 385–392, 1996.
2. R. Cooley, B. Mobasher, and J. Srivastava, "Grouping Web Page References into Transactions for Mining World Wide Web Browsing Patterns," *Proceedings of the IEEE Knowledge and Data Engineering Exchange Workshop, KDEX,* pages 2–9, 1997.
3. T. M. Cover and P. E. Hart, "Nearest neighbor pattern classification," *IEEE Transactions on Information Theory.* IT-13(1):21–27, January 1967.
4. F. Cuppers and R. Demolombe, "Cooperative answering: a methodology to provide intelligent access to databases," *Proc. 2nd International Conference on Expert Database Systems,* Virginia, USA, 1988.
5. T. Gaasterland, P. Godfrey, and J. Minker, "An overview of cooperative answering," In *Nonstandard Queries and Nonstandard Answers.* R. Demolombe and T. Imielinski, eds. Oxford Science Publications, 1994.
6. C. M. Hymes and G. M. Olson, "Quick but not so dirty web design: applying empirical conceptual clustering techniques to organize hypertext content" *Proceedings of the Conference on Designing Interactive Systems: Processes, Practices, Methods, and Techniques.* pages 159–162, 1997.
7. J. A. Johnson "Semantic Relatedness," *Computer and Mathematics with Applications,* pages 51-63, 29(5), 1995.
8. L. Leydesdorff and R. Zaal, "Co-words and citations relations between document sets and environments," *Infometrics 87/88,* pages 105-119, 1988.
9. M. A. Merzbacher and W. W. Chu, "Query–Based Semantic Nearness for Cooperative Query Answering," *Proc. 1st ISMM Conference on Information and Knowledge Management: CIKM,* 1993.
10. A. Motro, "Cooperative database systems," *International Journal of Intelligent Systems.* pages 717–731, v11 n10, 1996.
11. G. Salton, *Automatic text processing: the transformation, analysis, and retrieval of information by computer,* Addison–Wesley, Reading Massachusetts, 1989.
12. D. G. Zhao, "ELINOR electronic library system," *Electronic Library,* pages 289–294, Oct 1994.

A Declarative Language Bias for Levelwise Search of First-Order Regularities

Irene Weber

Institut für Informatik, Universität Stuttgart, Breitwiesenstr. 20–22, 70565 Stuttgart, Germany. Irene.Weber@informatik.uni-stuttgart.de

Abstract. The discovery of interesting patterns in relational databases is an important data mining task. In the framework of descriptive Inductive Logic Progamming (ILP), we present a refinement operator and hypothesis language declaration formalism that successfully combine a function-free first-order hypothesis language with the levelwise search principle. In particular, the hypothesis space is structured by the subset relation between hypotheses, and the refinement operator is based on the candidate generation procedure of the Apriori algorithm which is extended to allow for user-defined constraints on the combinations of literals. Experimental results show the usefulness of the approach.

1 Introduction

An important data mining task is finding interesting patterns in databases as, for instance, association rules [1] or interesting subgroups in multi-relational databases [12]. This data mining task can become very complex when the interesting patterns are represented in dialects of first-order logic and when the mining takes place in deductive or (multi)relational databases. Due to their expressivity, first-order pattern languages usually lead to huge search spaces, while the evaluation of potentially interesting patterns can be very costly if it requires theorem proving or expensive join operations. Therefore, efficient search and pruning strategies are especially important in such task settings.

Discovery of first-order regularities can be viewed as a topic of descriptive Inductive Logic Progamming (ILP). In ILP, top-down traversal of the hypothesis space is often organized as the application of a refinement operator by repeatedly generating minimal (i.e., one-step) specializations of the currently evaluated hypothesis (i.e., a potentially interesting pattern). In general, one hypothesis can result from different sequences of refinement steps. Refinement operators that avoid producing the same hypothesis repeatedly on different refinement paths are termed *optimal* [3,12]. Practically, optimality of a refinement operator is achieved by pre-specifying the order in which the different refinements have to be applied in order to generate a particular hypothesis. Each hypothesis is marked with a label indicating the refinement steps involved in generating it, e.g., the paths of DLab [3] and the code numbers in Midos [12]. The label then determines which further refinement steps are admissible for the hypothesis. The drawback of this approach is that pruning affects only those hypotheses that are to be generated on a refinement path involving the pruned hypothesis. Specializations of the pruned hypothesis may still be reached on other refinement paths, and, consequently, have to be evaluated by possibly extensive database queries. This approach contrasts to the principle of levelwise search [7] that aims at exploiting all previously gathered informations for pruning. However, in ILP, hypothesis spaces are commonly ordered wrt. θ-subsumption which is expensive to compute [4]. Therefore, in general, direct application of levelwise search to hypothesis spaces ordered wrt. θ-subsumption is not sensible, because computation of the θ-subsumption relations costs more than it gains unless the hypothesis language is strongly restricted (as, e.g., in RDT [5]). In this paper, we present a refinement operator and a corresponding hypothesis language declaration formalism that successfully combine a function-free first-order hypothesis language with the levelwise search principle, and, in particular, with the structuring of the hypothesis space according to the subset relation. Thus, it is possible to adapt the candidate generation procedure of the well-known Apriori algorithm [1] to a first-order language, leading to significant savings of hypothesis evaluations compared to the so-called optimal refinement operators that are commonly used in descriptive ILP.

The paper is organized as follows. In the next section, the refinement operator and the language declaration formalism are introduced. In section 3, two task settings are defined that can be tackled by the developed approach, namely, finding characterising regularities and discovery of interesting subgroups. Section 4 reports results of experiments. In section 5, we discuss the approach.

2 A first-order hypothesis generator based on levelwise search

2.1 A levelwise search algorithm

A very successful algorithm employing levelwise search is the Apriori algorithm [1]. The advantages of the Apriori candidate generation are that, first, it generates each element of the hypothesis space at most once, that is, it incorporates an optimal refinement operator, and, second, that it realizes the pruning step of levelwise search by simple set operations (as opposed, for instance, to expensive computation of θ-subsumption). Table 1 shows our search algorithm with candidate generation adapted from the Apriori algorithm. The input is a database D and a set of literals L; in the first-order setting the literals are first-order function-free atoms. The hypothesis space consists of the power set of L, each subset of the literal set is interpreted as a conjunction of literals and represents a hypothesis. Accordingly, the refinement operator specializes a hypothesis by adding a literal, and a hypothesis c is a specialization of all those hypotheses that are subsets of the literals of c. The algorithm conducts a complete search of the hypothesis space, proceeding levelwise from general to specific. On each search level, the algorithm initially computes the complete set of candidate hypotheses that will be evaluated by consulting the database on that level. In the

Table 1. The search algorithm.

(1) $\underline{\text{search}(L,D) : H}$	(15) $\underline{\text{cand\_test}(C,H,D) : C'};$
(2) $H = \emptyset; \; C = \{\emptyset\};$	(16) $C' = \emptyset;$
(3) while $C \neq \emptyset$ do	(17) foreach $c \in C$:
(4) $C' = \text{cand\_det}(C,L);$	(18) if not $\text{prune}(c,D,H)$
(5) $C = \text{cand\_test}(C',H,D);$	(19) then $C' = C' \cup \{c\};$
(6) return $H;$	(20) $H = \text{accept}(c,D,H);$
	(21) return $C';$

(7) $\underline{\text{cand\_det}(C,L) : C'};$
(8) $C' = \emptyset;$
(9) foreach $c \in C$
(10) foreach $l \in L$
(11) if $\text{max\_lit}(l,c)$ then $C' = C' \cup \{c \cup \{l\}\};$
(12) foreach $c \in C'$
(13) if not $\text{subset\_prune}(c,C)$ then $C' = C' \setminus \{c\};$
(14) return $C';$

second phase of the level, the database is accessed and the candidate hypotheses are evaluated. The input to the candidate generation procedure cand_det is the literal set L and the set of hypotheses C that were generated and evaluated, but not pruned, in the previous search level. Lines (9) - (11) implement an optimal refinement operator (in the following refered to as opt_ref) that specializes a hypothesis c by appending a literal l taken from L. For the literals in L, an ordering $>_l$ is defined. A literal l is added only to such hypotheses that consist of literals smaller than l. This condition is checked by the predicate max_lit in step (11). Formally, max_lit(l,c) is true iff $l >_l l' \; \forall l' \in c$. This guarantees that each hypothesis is generated only once, so that the refinement operator is optimal. Lines (12) and (13) implement the pruning step of candidate determination (refered to as subset_prune) by verifying for each hypothesis c generated by opt_ref whether it is not a specialization of a pruned hypothesis. Specifically, subset_check(c, C) is true iff $\forall l \in c \;\; c \setminus \{l\} \in C$. The output of cand_det is the set of hypotheses C' which is the input to the procedure *cand_test* that evaluates the hypotheses and determines if a hypothesis is to be pruned or to be accepted (i.e., to be added to the set of discoveries H). The functions prune and accept depend on the task to be solved. Instantiations of these functions for two task settings are shown in section 3.

2.2 Abstracting specialization from the database representation

Applying the Apriori candidate generation procedure to first-order hypothesis languages is an attractive idea and has been followed in [2] and [10]. However, the straightforward approach as implemented in [10] implies that many redundant hypotheses, e.g., unlinked hypotheses or hypotheses with redundant literals, are generated which have to be handled by the algorithm, making candidate generation very expensive and slow. The approach of [2] avoids the problems by significant restrictions on the hypothesis language. The approach presented here aims at possibly generating only 'sensible' hypotheses while imposing less severe restrictions. The basic idea is to abstract the specialization operations from the representation of the data in the database. To this aim, we distinguish two types of literals, called linking literals and specializing literals. Linking literals are variabilisations of predicates that correspond to the database relations of D. Some of their variables occur in several linking literals and thus define the links among these literals, in database terminology, they define how to join the relations. Other variables of the linking literals occur in the specialization literals. There are two types of specialization literals, (1) literals that instantiate a variable with constant values from the corresponding relation attribute, (written $V = *$), (2) literals that represent Boolean tests (e.g., $V > 15, V1 > V2$). Specialization of a hypothesis is realised by adding specialization literals to its body. Linking literals are considered as implicitly contained in all hypotheses. Therefore, the subset-checking procedure only tests occurance of specialization literals. From the logic programming viewpoint, the unbound variables of linking literals represent existence queries; these existence queries are not put into effect when evaluating a hypothesis unless they are represented explicitly with appropriate specialization literals.

Example 1. A relational database stores phonetic data in three relations *Syllable(syl_id, word_id, next_syl, len, accent)* , *Phoneme(phon_id, syl_id, next_phon, type)*, *Word(word_id, next_word, tag)*. The hypothesis language is defined to consist of the hypotheses containing all link literals in L_l and any subset of specialization literals in L_s where

$L_l = \{$ *syllable(S_Id, W_Id, Next_S, Len, Accent)*, *word(W_Id, Next_W, Tag)*,
$\qquad$ *phoneme(P_Id1, S_Id, Type1)*, *phoneme(P_Id2, S_Id, Type2)* $\}$
$L_s = \{$ *Tag = noun, Type1 = *, Type2 = *, Len > 1, Len < 1* $\}$

2.3 Enhancing the hypothesis generator

The hypothesis language defined so far is overly general, as is illustrated by the hypothesis language defined in example 1. Since a syllable can consist of several phonemes, it is interesting to consider the types of two (or more) of its phonemes, and therefore, the two literals *Type1 = * and *Type2 = * are defined in L_s. Then, the hypothesis language L_h contains (among others) not only the intended hypothesis $\langle L_l \rangle$, *Type1 = *, Type2 = *, but also the equivalent hypotheses $\langle L_l \rangle$, *Type1 = * and $\langle L_l \rangle$, *Type2 = *. ($\langle L_l \rangle$ is an abbreviation for all linkinking literals in L_l). Furthermore, the hypothesis language L_h includes hypotheses which contain both the literals *Len > 1* and *Len < 1*. In order to alleviate these problems, additional control mechanisms are introduced which allow manual declaration of interconnections between literals. First, for each specialization literal l_s, a list of *required* literals $req(l_s)$ can be provided. The refinement operator adds the literal l_s only to such hypotheses which contain all required literals $req(l_s)$. In the example, the second phoneme type $Type2 = *$ will be allowed only in hypotheses where a first phoneme type $Type1 = *$ occurs. Second, as a means to avoid certain combinations of literals in hypotheses, *excluding* literals $excl(l_s)$ can be specified for a specialization literal $l(s)$. The refinement operator adds a literal l_s only to such hypotheses that do not contain any of its excluding literals $excl(l_s)$. As shown below, these extensions can be integrated into the procedure cand_det in table 1 such that it remains complete, i.e., it generates all potential solutions. Formally, given a set of linking literals L_l and a set of specialization literals L_s, the hypothesis language L_h is

$$L_h(L_l, L_s) = \{ L_l \cup S \mid S \subseteq L_s \text{ and if } l_s \in S \text{ then } req(l_s) \subseteq S$$
$$\text{and if } l_s \in S \text{ then } excl(l_s) \cap S = \emptyset \}$$

Completeness of excl. In step (11) in procedure cand_det, a hypothesis $h \cup \{l_s\}$ is generated only if $excl(l_s) \cap h = \emptyset$, otherwise the hypothesis is discarded. This is equivalent to pruning the hypothesis $h \cup \{l_s\}$ without a database test. As the search proceeds, the hypothesis is treated as other pruned hypotheses. As all specializations of the pruned hypothesis $h \cup \{l_s\}$ violate an exclusion restriction, they are pruned correctly. ◇

Completeness of req. The subset_check of procedure cand_det is modified as follows: subset_check(c, C) is true iff for all $l_s \in c$ it holds that if req_check$(c \setminus \{l_s\})$ then $c \setminus \{l_s\} \subseteq C$. req_check$(c)$ is true iff $\forall l_s \in c$ req$(l_s) \subseteq c$. That is, subset_check(c, C) only searches such subsets of c in C that meet the *requires* restrictions. The refinement operator in step (11) adds a literal l_s to hypothesis c if l_s is greater than all literals in c (with respect to the literal ordering $<_l$). Therefore, it is necessary to define the literal ordering such that a literal l_s *requires* only smaller literals, formally, if $l' \in req(l_s)$ then $l' <_l l$. An ordering $<_l$ with this property exists if the *requires*-relations among literals are cycle-free. ◇

3 Task settings

The approach is evaluated in two task settings, finding regularities that characterise the elements of a target group, and finding interesting subgroups (similar to Midos [12]) in a relational database. Both tasks assume that a fixed set of objects, termed the *population*, and a certain subset of the population, called the *target group* T, are prespecified. For simplicity, the objects are assumed to be represented in a relational table P; each individual object is identified by a key attribute Id of the table P. Target objects are distinguished from non-target objects by a binary class attribute *class* of the relation P taking the value 1 for target objects and the value 0 for non-target objects. Thus, the population table P takes the form $P(id, class, a_1, \ldots, a_n)$, and all hypotheses contain a linking literal $p(Id, Class, A_1, \ldots, A_n)$. In both tasks, the evaluation of hypotheses is based on their relative coverage of target and non-target objects.

Definition 1. *The coverage cov(h) of a hypothesis h containing the literal* p*(*Id, Class, $A_1, \ldots, A_n$*) is the number of individuals id $\in P$ for which the hypothesis is true in D, formally, $cov(h) = |\{id \in P | D \models h[Id/id]\}|$. $[Id/id]$ denotes the substitution of the variable Id by the constant id. The number of target objects covered by the hypothesis h is denoted tcov(h), formally, $tcov(h) = |\{id \in P | D \models h[Id/id, Class/1]\}|$.*

3.1 Finding characterising regularities

The aim of the `charac` task setting is to find all regularities that hold with a specified minimum *support* (i.e., coverage) and *confidence* (i.e., accuracy) as specified by user-defined thresholds, denoted σ_c and γ, respectively. The support of a hypothesis h is defined as its coverage of target objects relative to the *a priori* size of the target group, formally, $support(h) = \frac{tcov(h)}{|T|}$. The confidence of a hypothesis h is defined as its coverage of target objects relative to its total coverage, formally, $confidence(h) = \frac{tcov(h)}{cov(h)}$.

In the `charac` setting, the function $accept(c, D, H)$ adds a hypothesis h to the solution set H iff $support(h) \geq \sigma_c$ and $confidence(h) \geq \gamma$. Pruning is based on the minimum support requirement. If the search encounters a hypothesis with less than minimum support σ_c, all its specializations can be pruned since the more special hypotheses cannot cover more target objects than the more general hypothesis.

3.2 Finding the most interesting regularities

In the `midos` task setting, hypotheses represent descriptions of subgroups of the population. A subgroup description is considered interesting if its coverage exceeds a user-specified limit σ_m, and if its distribution of target objects differs from the *a priori* distribution of target objects in the population relation P. The interestingness function d is adapted from [12].

$$d(h) = \frac{cov(h)}{|P|} \cdot \left(\frac{tcov(h)}{cov(h)} - \frac{|T|}{|P|} \right) \text{ if } \frac{cov(h)}{|P|} \geq \sigma_m \text{ and } d(h) = -1 \text{ otherwise.}$$

Interesting subgroup discovery searches for the k most interesting hypotheses where k is a user-defined parameter. Accordingly, the search algorithm accepts a hypothesis if it belongs to the k most interesting hypotheses encountered so far. In the `midos` setting, the solution set H always contains the current (up to) k best hypotheses. If a newly evaluated hypothesis c is better than the currently weakest description $h \in H$, c replaces h.

In addition to minimum support-based pruning as above, optimistic estimate pruning is applicable in this setting [12]. For a given hypothesis, this pruning technique computes the maximum interestingness value that any specialization of the curently evaluated hypothesis is able to achieve in the best case. If the resulting optimistic estimate lies below the interestingness of the k best hypotheses found so far, the specializations of the current hypothesis are pruned. In our experiments, we use two optimistic estimate functions, $d_{oe1}(h) = \frac{cov(h)}{|P|} \cdot \left(1 - \frac{|T|}{|P|}\right)$

[12], and $d_{oe2}(h) = \frac{tcov(h)}{|P|} - \sigma_m \cdot \frac{|T|}{|P|}$. For a proof sketch of the correctness of d_{oe2} as an optimistic estimate, and an experimental comparison of d_{oe1}, d_{oe2} and minimum support pruning, see the extended version of this paper [11].

4 Experimental evaluation

The approach is incorporated in the system Laurel. Laurel is applied to SQL databases and evaluates hypotheses by SQL queries. It is implemented in C and Prolog and connects to a DB2 database via TCP/IP. The testbed is the KRK chess dataset (http://www.cs.york.ac.uk/~stephen/chess.html) that represents chess board positions in the KRK endgame with three pieces left on the board: White King, White Rook and Black King. For our experiments, the data was represented in a table with 8 attributes, *krk*(*id, class, WKcol, WKrow, WRcol, WRrow, BKcol, BKrow*). The key attribute *id* is an identifier for board positions, *class* takes the value 1 for illegal board positions and 0 for legal board positions. The remaining attributes hold the column and row of the pieces, represented as integers ranging from 0 to 7. The table contains 20,000 tuples. The background knowledge commonly used with the KRK problem are definitions of the predicates *less/2* and *adjacent/2* which define the ordering of rows and columns on the chessboard. For our experiments, this background knowledge was defined via appropriate specialization literals, namely, specialization literals encorporating conditions like *krk.WKcol < krk.WRcol* for *less* or *krk.WKcol−krk.WRcol* in $(-1, 0, 1)$ for *adjacent*. For each pair of pieces WK, WR, and BK, specialization literals for the tests =, <>, <, >, and *adjacent* where provided, both for comparing the columns and the rows. This results in a total of 30 specialization literals. The search space was restricted by *excl* conditions such that at most one of the five specialization literals concerning the columns or rows of each pair of pieces was allowed in a hypothesis. Thus, the search space consisted of $6^6 = 46\,656$ hypotheses. (Without *excludes* restrictions, the hypothesis space contains 2^{30} hypotheses.)

The test suite determines the number of candidate hypotheses (the hypotheses to be evaluated by a database test) that are generated by the optimal refinement operator and by the hypothesis generator using subset pruning, both in the charac and in the midos setting. Figure 1 depicts the results that are obtained with increasing support thresholds σ_c resp. σ_m summed up over the complete search process. The runtimes of system in the test runs are listed in table 2. On average, one database query took 3 sec. The table clearly demonstrates that the time consumed by the subset pruning step is neglectable, and that the subset pruning step leads to significant gains both in the charac and in the midos task setting.

5 Discussion and conclusion

We have proposed a hypothesis language and refinement operator that is based on the Apriori candidate determination algorithm. It is useful for various task

Table 2. The time required for hypothesis generation by the optimal refinement operator, the time consumed by subset pruning, and the total runtime for varying σ in charac and midos mode ($k = 10$). Times are in seconds (actual runtime), with Laurel running on a Sun 20/712 and the database running on a Sun Ultra I.

	charac				midos			
minimum support	0.1	0.2	0.3	0.4	0.0001	0.1	0.2	0.3
opt_ref	1	1	0	0	0	0	0	0
subset_prune	12	0	0	0	1	1	0	0
total runtime	9925	2591	1645	739	3235	1599	1102	906

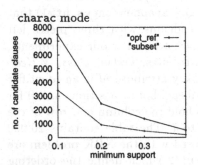
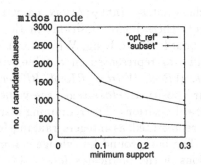

Fig. 1. Comparison of the total numbers of hypotheses generated by the optimal refinement operator opt_ref and the hypothesis generator subset in charac and midos mode ($k = 10$) for varying σ.

settings that require a complete search of the hypothesis space in a (restricted) framework of descriptive ILP. The experimental evaluation shows that levelwise search is successfully applicable in a multi-relational or ILP framework and offers significant improvements if combined with a suitable hypothesis language. The presented declarative language bias belongs to the set-oriented formalisms. The hypothesis language is defined by specifying a literal set; it allows less fine-grained specification of the hypothesis space than formalisms based on hypothesis sets as, e.g., DLab [3]. On the other hand, we expect the declarations to be more compact and, therefore, easier to define. The presented declarative language bias has some similarity to approaches based on mode declarations as the definite mode language of Progol [8]. These approaches may be regarded as a short-hand notation for an explicit listing of the literals, with the substantial difference that, in their case, the number of required variables or literals need not be fixed in advance. The important point is that Laurel's hypothesis language can be combined with a refinement operator similar to the Apriori candidate determination which is very advantageous, as the experiments reported above show. The restrictions of the hypothesis language that are made possible by the *requires* and *excludes* constructs are crucial in a first-order framework since they are neccessary for excluding many redundant hypotheses. The *requires* and *excludes* restrictions are similar to the item constraints of Srikant et al. [9]. Their item constraints take the form of a Boolean disjunctive normal form in the context of mining transaction databases, and, therefore, allow to define more general restrictions than the restrictions introduced here. On the other hand, the *requires* and *excludes* mechanisms are easily integrated with the Apriori candidate determination. Furthermore, we consider the presented hypothesis language as useful in its own right, as it provides a solution to the problem of mapping database relations to logical predicates that are suitable for ILP algorithms because it allows to express specialization steps abstractedly from the database schema. Due to the database design and normalization process, one database relation in a RDBMS typically stores information corresponding to several logical predicates, and it is desirable that, rather than mapping database relations directly to logical predicates, a logical language for discovery should allow to treat this information separately. This problem came up in [6], to my knowledge the first approach of coupling an ILP system with an RDBMS. In practical applications, this point is relevant since RDBMS relations often have a high arity, and the complexity of many common ILP hypothesis languages and corresponding refinement operators is exponential in the arity of predicates (e.g., refinement operators based on definite mode languages [8]). Therefore, this work contributes to the practical applicability of descriptive ILP.

References

1. R. Agrawal et al. Fast discovery of association rules. In U. Fayyad et al. (eds), *Advances in Knowledge Discovery and Data Mining*, 1996.
2. L. Dehaspe and L. De Raedt. Mining association rules in multiple relations. In *Proc. Seventh Int. Workshop on Inductive Logic Programming (ILP'97)*, 1997.
3. L. De Raedt and L. Dehaspe. Clausal discovery. *Machine Learning* 26, 1997.
4. J-U. Kietz and M. Lübbe. An efficient subsumption algorithm for inductive logic programming. In *Proc. 4th Int. Workshop on Inductive Logic Programming*, volume 237 of *GMD-Studien*, 1994.
5. J-U. Kietz and S. Wrobel. Controlling the complexity of learning in logic through syntactic and task-oriented models. In S. Muggleton, (ed.), *Proc. 1st Int. Workshop on Inductive Logic Programming*, 1991.
6. G. Lindner and K. Morik. Coupling a relational learning algorithm with a database system. In Y. Kodratoff et al., (eds), *Workshop Notes of the ECML-95 Workshop Statistics, Machine Learning and Knowledge Discovery in Databases*, 1995.
7. H. Mannila and H. Toivonen. Levelwise search and borders of theories in knowledge discovery. *Data Mining and Knowledge Discovery* 1(3), 1997.
8. S. Muggleton. Inverse entailment and Progol. *New Generation Computing* 13(3-4), 1995.
9. R. Srikant, Q. Vu, and R. Agrawal. Mining association rules with item constraints. In *Proc. KDD-97*, 1997.
10. I. Weber. Discovery of first-order regularities in a relational database using offline candidate determination. In *Proc. 7th Int. Workshop on ILP*, 1997.
11. I. Weber. A declarative language bias for levelwise search of first-order regularities. In F. Wysotzki et al. (eds), *Proc. FGML-98*, Technical Report 98/11 des Fachbereiches Informatik, TU Berlin, 1998.
12. Stefan Wrobel. An algorithm for multi-relational discovery of subgroups. In *Proc. 1st Europ. Symp. on Principles of Knowledge Discovery and Data Mining*, 1997.

The More We Learn the Less We Know?
On Inductive Learning from Examples

Piotr Ejdys and Grzegorz Góra

Institute of Mathematics
Warsaw University
ul. Banacha 2
02-097 Warsaw, Poland
pe146810@zodiac2.mimuw.edu.pl, gg153390@zodiac2.mimuw.edu.pl

Abstract. We consider the average error rate of classification as a function of the number of training examples. We investigate the upper and lower bounds of this error in the class of commonly used algorithms based on inductive learning from examples. As a result we arrive at the astonishing conclusion, that, contrary to what one could expect, the error rate of some algorithms does not decrease monotonically with number of training examples; it rather, initially increases up to a certain point and then it starts to decrease. Furthermore, the classification quality of some algorithms is as poor as that of a *naive* algorithm. We show that for simple monomials, even if we take an exponentially large training data set, the classification quality of some methods will not be better than if we took just one or several training examples.

1 Introduction

Classification can be understood as the assignment of an object to one of predetermined classes on the basis of observations. There have been developed a number of systems that learn from experience to classify objects automatically.

Many machine learning systems use symbolic methods for inductive learning from examples. The examples are in the form of vectors of attribute-value pairs associated with a given decision class. A set of examples, called training data, may be presented in the form of a table, in which columns are labelled by attributes, while rows represent examples. One of the attributes is decision. The most important goal of machine learning is to induce a description of concepts (called also decision classes or target functions) in order to use it for classification afterward. A concept is a subset of the set of all possible examples that have the same value of the decision. In this paper we assume that the set of attributes used for description of concepts is fixed.

In the area of machine learning rule induction systems play an important role. They take input training data and induce decision rules from it. Those rules can be presented in the following form:

$$\text{if} \quad (a_1 = v_1)\&(a_2 = v_2)\&...\&(a_k = v_k) \quad \text{then} \quad (d = v)$$

where a_i is an attribute, v_i is its value, $i = 1, 2..., k$; d is the decision, and v is its value. The pair $(d = v)$ denotes a decision class that is assigned to an entity if that entity fulfils the premis of a rule. A concept can have a disjunctive description if several conjunctive rules are associated with the same concept. In that way every concept can be described in a DNF form (see [16]).

From the knowledge discovery perspective, an important problem is to find all minimal rules. The reason is that minimal rules minimise the number of rule conditions and represent, in a sense, strong data patterns [19]. Thus, first step of many machine learning systems is similar. It results in the fact that the systems have some common features. We use this observation and try to characterise the possible classification results of such systems.

In our paper we consider error rates coming from classification using measures formulated in [14]. We investigate these errors as a function of the number of training examples. In the following section we give some definitions. In Section 3 we present exact computations and analysis for some target functions in case when probability distribution is uniform over the set of examples. In Section 4 we present the experimentally observed facts showing the behaviour of some commonly used algorithms and relate it to the results from Section 3.

2 Definitions

For the sake of our paper we assume that a training data set is consistent, that is, identically described training examples belong to the same decision class.

We consider a special case of decision tables using two value attributes. In this case every concept corresponds to a boolean function $f : \{0, 1\}^n \to \{0, 1\}$ for certain $n \in N$ and table represents partial specification of such a boolean function.

2.1 Minimal description algorithms

In this paper we consider commonly used algorithms, which generate rules in similar ways and then classify objects basing on these rules. The algorithms considered in our paper, called *minimal description algorithms*, work as follows. First, a set of consistent, minimal and complete decision rules is computed (see [14], [16], [10]), that is:

- every generated rule is consistent with respect to the training data, i.e. all the examples from training data matching the rule are correctly classified by it,
- every rule is minimal, i.e. if we remove any elementary condition from the rule then we will obtain inconsistent rule with regard to the training data,
- the rule set consists of all rules, which satisfy two previous conditions and are matched by at least one training example.

Rules induced from training examples are then used to classify objects. If there appears a new object to be classified, the subset of these rules which the object matches to is selected. Then, one of the following cases happens:

1. all the selected rules correspond to one concept (in case of boolean functions positive "1" or negative "0" decision class),
2. selected rules correspond to different concepts (in case of boolean functions there are rules pointing at decision class "1" and there are rules pointing at decision class "0").

In general it can happen one more case, namely, no one single rule matches the example (the set of rules which the object matches to is empty). However, it is easy to show that in the case of considered boolean functions it can not happen (see [4]).

In the second case we have situation of conflict. In order to enable classification in such situations it is necessary to decide how to resolve conflicts between sets of rules classifying tested objects to different decision classes. Different *minimal description algorithms* (see [5], [6], [7], [10], [11], [12], [17], [20]) do it in different ways. Usually, they use some measures for conflict resolving and decision class with the highest value is chosen. Here are two examples of such measures:

$$SimpleStrength(c) = \left| \bigcup_{\text{matching rules } R \text{ describing } c} support\_set(R) \right|$$

$$GlobalStrength(c) = \frac{SimpleStrength(c)}{|\text{set of training examples for } c|}$$

where c denotes concept and $support\_set(R)$ is a set of training examples matching the rule. For more details and more possibilities see e.g. [2], [6], [7], [10], [17], [20].

2.2 Errors of algorithms

We want to characterise the possible error rates of *minimal description algorithms* as a function of the number of training examples given to the algorithms. First, we present common measures for classification error of an algorithm which results with hypothesis function approximating decision function (see [14]).

The *true error* (see [1]) of hypothesis h with respect to target function f and distribution μ is the probability that h will misclassify an instance drawn at random according to μ:

$$error_\mu(h, f) = \mu\{x \in X | h(x) \neq f(x)\}$$

Average error rate of algorithm L with respect to target function f and distribution μ is the expected value of true error of algorithm L, when trained using randomly selected training sets s, with a fixed number of training examples M, drawn according to distribution μ:

$$err_\mu^M(L, f) = E_{\mu^M} error(L(s), f) = \sum_{s \in S^M(f)} \mu^M(s) \cdot error_\mu(L(s), f)$$

where $L(s)$ is the hypothesis output by learner L using training set s, $S^M(f)$ denotes the space of samples of length M consistent with the concept f, μ^M is a product of M measures μ.

Let us note that there are two cases when a *minimal description algorithm* L misclassifies an instance:

- all the selected rules correspond to one concept, which is the wrong concept,
- there occurs a conflict, which is not resolved properly, i.e. the wrong decision is chosen by the algorithm L.

Please note that the only difference in behaviour of *minimal description algorithms* is due to conflict resolving method. In other words, the only possibility to decrease the average error rate of such an algorithm is to avoid errors in the latter case. Thus it is important to know in how many points the conflict occurs, i.e. how large is the fraction of points, for which we can improve classification using certain methods for conflict resolving.

One can compare two algorithms by examining their average error rates $err_\mu^M(L, f)$. We want to investigate how the average error rate can vary for different algorithms in class of *minimal description algorithms*. For this purpose we define the upper and lower bound of the average error rate in this class:

$$errMax_\mu^M(f) = \sup_{L \in CMCAlg} err_\mu^M(L, f)$$

$$errMin_\mu^M(f) = \inf_{L \in CMCAlg} err_\mu^M(L, f)$$

where $CMCAlg$ denotes the class of *minimal description algorithms*.

Measure $errMax_\mu^M(f)$ is concerned with *naive* algorithm which, whenever conflict occurs, gives incorrect decision (see [5]). Straightforwardly from the definition we obtain, that $errMin_\mu^M(f) \le err_\mu^M(L, f) \le errMax_\mu^M(f)$. If for algorithm L first inequality becomes equality, then we can say that this algorithm always resolves conflicts correctly for a given function f. Analogously, if the second inequality becomes equality, we can say that algorithm L always fails in resolving conflicts for a given function f (it behaves as *naive* algorithm).

We define the *conflict area* as the average fraction of examples for which a conflict occurs. We can say that it expresses potential gain of using algorithms which resolve conflicts properly. As for boolean functions, every example matches at least one computed rule (see [4]), it is easy to see that by using defined measures $errMax$ and $errMin$ we can present conflict area as:

$$conflictArea_\mu^M(f) = errMax_\mu^M(f) - errMin_\mu^M(f)$$

3 Analysis of error rates for monomials

Let us define the sequence of monomials

$$f_n(x_1, x_2, ..., x_n) = x_1 \wedge x_2 \wedge ... \wedge x_n$$

where n is any natural number.

Let U denote uniform probability distribution over the set of all examples. In this case one can compute lower and upper bounds of errors in the class of *minimal description algorithms* as defined above.

Theorem 1. *For any $n \in N$ we have that*

$$errMax_U^M(f_n) = \frac{\sum_{k=0}^{n} \binom{n}{k} \left((1 + \frac{1}{2^n} - \frac{1}{2^k})^M - (1 - \frac{1}{2^k})^M \right) + a(n, M)}{2^n} \quad (1)$$

$$errMin_U^M(f_n) = \frac{\sum_{k=0}^{n} \binom{n}{k} \left((\frac{1}{2^k})^M - (\frac{1}{2^k} - \frac{1}{2^n})^M \right) + a(n, M)}{2^n} \quad (2)$$

where $a(n, M) = 2 \left(1 - \frac{1}{2^n}\right)^M - 1$

Proof. Due to the limited space, only the sketch of the proof of the equation (1) will be outlined. A complete proof of this theorem and of the foregoing corollaries may be found in [4].

We define random variable $B(s)$ over $S^M(f_n)$ being equal to the number of misclassifications that the *naive* algorithm commits for given sample s of length M consistent with f_n. Thus:

$$errMax_U^M(f_n) = \frac{1}{2^n} \cdot E_{U^M} B \quad (3)$$

Then, we define characteristic function $B_x(s)$ equal to 1 iff the *naive* algorithm misclassifies point x using a training sample s or equal to 0, otherwise. As one can see, $B(s)$ is the sum of $B_x(s)$ over all possible points x. Let us define $d(x)$ as the number of attributes of x with value 1. Then we can show that B_x depends only on $d(x)$ and thus:

$$E_{U^M} B = \sum_{k=0}^{n} |\{x : d(x) = k\}| \cdot P(B_{e^k} = 1)$$

where $e^k = (1,...,1,0,...,0)$ (k times 1 and $n - k$ times 0). Finally, defining $W^m(s)$ as the event that there are exactly m negative examples and $M - m$ positive examples in s and using Bayes formula for events W^m we obtain:

$$E_{U^M} B = \sum_{k=0}^{n} \binom{n}{k} \sum_{m=0}^{M} P(B_{e^k} = 1|W^m) \cdot P(W^m) \quad (4)$$

By combining (4) with (3), after some combinatorial calculations, we obtain (1).

It can be shown that in case of exchanging some of the variables in function f_n by their negations, Theorem 1 remains true as well. Thus, the following conclusions correspond also to monomials modified in this way.

In Figure 1 the highest and lowest graphs represent the functions $errMax_U^M(f_6)$ and $errMin_U^M(f_6)$ where M is a variable (in all figures included in the paper the X axis denotes the number of examples in training data set). As it could be expected, $errMin_U^M$ is a decreasing function, but surprisingly $errMax_U^M$ increases at the beginning. What is interesting to note here, is that $errMax_U^M$ corresponds to the average error rate of *naive* algorithm (see Section 2.2). In other words using *naive* algorithm, the bigger training data set we take to learn, the more classifying errors we initially make.

Of course, commonly used algorithms do not always fail in resolving conflicts (as *naive* algorithm does). Let us then consider, more realistically, the algorithms that fail in resolving conflicts only in p percent of cases. Error of such algorithms is equal to $\frac{p}{100} \cdot errMax_U^M + (1 - \frac{p}{100}) \cdot errMin_U^M$. In Figure 1 dotted graphs present it for p=80, 60, 30 and 10 respectively. It is easy to see, that for $p > 10$, they behave similarly to $errMax_U^M$ i.e. at the beginning the error increases with the growth of the number of training examples. And this effect is easier observable for the bigger p.

Let us now look at Figure 2 which presents the correspondence between the conflict area and the size of training set. Again, at the beginning, the more examples we have the bigger conflict area is. Note that the error rate of algorithm depends on its performance during conflict resolving. Therefore, it is clear that proper conflict resolving for f_6 is especially important when getting around 20 examples.

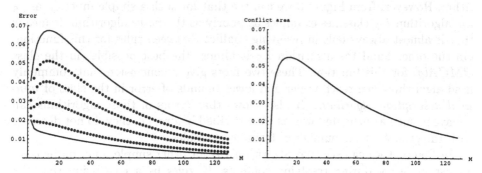

Fig. 1: Errors for algorithms that fail in conflict resolving in 100% ($errMax$), 80, 60, 30, 10 and 0% ($errMin$) for function f_6

Fig. 2: Conflict area for function f_6

The following corollaries generalise what we have seen so far.

Corollary 1. *For any $n \in N$ $errMin_U^M(f_n)$ is decreasing as a function of variable M.*

This is not true for $errMax_U^M$ function what, in special case, we have already seen in Figure 1. But we could be interested in the number of training examples for which this function is still increasing. Can this number be disregarded? The following corollary gives us the answer. And now we are about to tackle the crucial point of our paper.

Corollary 2. *For $n \geq 5$*

$$errMax_U^1(f_n) \leq errMax_U^{\sqrt{2}^{(n-4)}}(f_n)$$

Please note that having n attributes one could expect to learn the function taking not so large number of examples (for example polynomial of n). But the above corollary states that even if we took exponentially large set of training examples (that is $\sqrt{2}^{(n-4)}$) we would not achieve average error smaller than in case of taking single example as a training data. In other words in this case it would be better eiher to stop learning after presenting just one example or give to the algorithm a large number (more than $\sqrt{2}^{(n-4)}$) of training examples. It seems quite intriguing or even astonishing.

4 Error rate approximations of some algorithms

First, we want to relate the results from the previous section to some commonly used algorithms. To do it, we compute approximations of the value $err_\mu^M(L, f)$ (over a number of randomly chosen training samples) for commonly used algorithms L and few functions f. We analyse two algorithms, which use the measures *GlobalStrength* and *SimpleStrength* for conflict resolving (see Section 2.1, [2], [11]), denoted by L_G and L_S, respectively.

One can say that usually algorithms perform much better than *naive* algorithm. However, from Figure 3 we can see that for such a simple function as f_6 the algorithm L_G classifies examples as poorly as the *naive* algorithm. It means that it almost always fails in resolving conflicts between rules for this function. On the other hand the algorithm L_S is almost the best possible (in the class $CMCAlg$) for this function. These two facts give a conclusion that commonly used algorithms can reach upper and lower bounds of error in the class of *minimal description algorithms*. It also shows that errors of those algorithms can behave in such a surprising way as we described before, i.e. they do not decrease with the growth of the number of training examples.

In Figure 4 we can see that algorithm L_G for other simple function behaves almost perfectly during resolving conflicts. It gives us a conclusion that the behaviour of the same algorithm can be completely different for two different functions.

One of the most interesting challenges is to describe the class of functions for which results presented for simple monomials keep holding. Figure 5 shows the error rate of L_G for function $h(x_1, x_2, ..., x_9) = (x_1 \wedge x_2 \wedge ... \wedge x_6) \vee (x_4 \wedge x_5 \wedge ... \wedge x_9) \vee (x_7 \wedge x_8 \wedge x_9 \wedge x_1 \wedge x_2 \wedge x_3)$. Although the target function in this case is more complex than monomial, the error rate behaves similarly to the monomial case, i.e. it is increasing up to a certain point and then starts to decrease. One can see that even for samples consisting of about 100 examples the average error rate is comparable to the case when just one example is given.

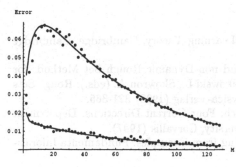

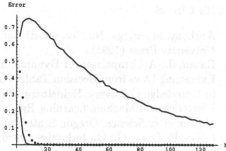

Fig. 3: Error for function f_6 for L_G and L_S algorithms (dotted), compared with $errMax$ and $errMin$ respectively

Fig. 4: Error for function $g(x_1, ..., x_6) = x_1$ for L_G algorithm (dotted), compared with approximation of $errMax$ and $errMin$

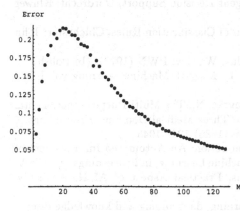

Fig. 5: Error for function $h(x_1, x_2, ..., x_9) = (x_1 \wedge x_2 \wedge ... \wedge x_6) \vee (x_4 \wedge x_5 \wedge ... \wedge x_9) \vee (x_7 \wedge x_8 \wedge x_9 \wedge x_1 \wedge x_2 \wedge x_3)$ for algorithm L_G

5 Conclusions

In this paper we discussed a behaviour of *minimal description algorithms*. We proved that the upper bound of error for simple monomials is not monotonically decreasing function. Furthermore, experiments with other functions showed that this is not an exception. In addition, errors of some commonly used algorithms reach the upper error bound and in many investigated cases the shape of error function is preserved although the error is smaller. We can conclude, that sometimes - as in real life - the more we learn the less we know.

Acknowledgments

This work was supported by the Polish State Committee for Scientific Research grant #8T11C01011 and Research Program of the European Union - ESPRIT-CRIT2 No. 20288

References

1. Anthony, M., Biggs, N.: Computational Learning Theory, Cambridge: Cambridge University Press (1992).
2. Bazan, J.: A Comparison of Dynamic and non-Dynamic Rough Set Methods for Extracting Laws from Decision Table, Polkowski L., Skowron A. (eds.): Rough Sets in Knowledge Discovery. Heidelberg: Physica-Verlag (1998) 321-365.
3. Dietterich, T.: Machine Learning Research: Four Current Directions. Department of Computer Science, Oregon State University, Corvallis (1997).
4. Ejdys, P., Góra, G.: On Inductive Learning from Examples. Fundamenta Inforaticae (submited).
5. Grzymała-Busse, J. W.: Classification of Unseen Examples under Uncertainty. Fundamenta Informaticae, 30 (1997) 255-267. Press.
6. Grzymała-Busse, J. W.: A new version of the rule induction system LERS. Fundamenta Informaticae, 31 (1997) 27-39.
7. Grzymała-Busse, J., W.: LERS - a system for learning from examples based on rough sets. In: R. Słowiński, (ed.) Intelligent Decision Support, Dordrecht: Kluwer (1992) 3-18.
8. Hand, D., J.: Construction and Assesment of Classification Rules. Chichester: John Wiley and Sons (1998).
9. Leja, F.: Differential and integeral calculus, Warsaw: PWN (1978). (In Polish)
10. Michalski, R., Carbonell, J., G. Mitchel, T., M. (ed): Machine Learning vol. I. Los Altos: Tioga/Morgan Kaufmann (1983).
11. Michalski, R.,S., Mozetic, I., Hong, J., Lavrac, N.: The Multi-Purpose Incremental Learning System AQ15 and its Testing to Three Medical Domains, Proceedings of AAAI-86. San Mateo: Morgan Kaufmann (1986) 1041-1045.
12. Michalski, R., Wnęk, J.: Constructive Induction: An Automated Improvement of Knowledge Representation Spaces for Machine Learning, in Proceedings of a Workshop on Intelligent Information Systems, Practical Aspect of AI II, Augustów (1993) 188-236.
13. Michalski, R.: A Tutorial on Machine learning, data mining and knowledge discovery Principles and Applications, Zakopane (1997).
14. Mitchell T. M.: Machine Learning, Portland: McGraw-Hill (1997).
15. Pawlak, Z.: Rough sets: Theoretical aspects of reasoning about data, Dordrecht: Kluwer (1991).
16. Skowron, A., Rauszer, C.: The Discernibility Matrices and Functions in Information Systems. R. Słowiński (ed.), Intelligent Decision Support. Handbook of Applications and Advances of the Rough Set Theory. Dordrecht: Kluwer (1992) 331-362.
17. Tsumoto, S., Tanaka H.: Incremental learning of probabilistic rules from clinical databases. Proceedings Information Processing and Management of Uncertainty on Knowledge Based Systems (IPMU-96), July 1-5, Granada, Spain, Universidad de Granada, vol. II, (1996) 1457-1462
18. Wegener, I.: The Complexity of Boolean Functions. Stuttgart: John Wiley and Sons (1987).
19. Ziarko, W., Shan, N.: Database Mining Using Rough Sets, Intelligent Information Systems IV Proceedings of the Workshop held in Augustów. Warsaw: IPIPAN (1995) 74-68.
20. Ziarko, W., Shan, N.: An incremental learning algorithm for constructing decision rules, Proceedings of the International Workshop on Rough Sets and Knowledge Discovery. Banff (1993) 335-346.

Computing MPMA Updates Using Dijkstra's Semantics

Patrick Doherty *

Department of Computer and Information Science,
Linköping University, Linköping, Sweden
email: patdo@ida.liu.se

Witold Łukaszewicz, Ewa Madalińska-Bugaj[†]

Institute of Informatics, Warsaw University
02-079 Warsaw, ul. Banacha 2, Poland
emails: witlu(ewama)@mimuw.edu.pl

Abstract

We describe a generalization of the PMA, called the modified PMA (MPMA), which permits an intuitive representation of disjunctive update and update with integrity constraints. An equivalent formulation of the MPMA in terms of Dijkstra's semantics, based on the use of the weakest precondition and the strongest postcondition formula transformers, is then provided. The Dijkstra formulation is then used as a basis for a syntactic characterization of the MPMA, which is constructed by mapping an MPMA update of a knowledge base into a command in a simple Dijkstra style programming language. This characterization provides a decision procedure for computing entailments of the MPMA and serves as a basis for relating the belief update approach with temporal logic based and more procedurally based approaches for reasoning about action and change.

1 Introduction

The classical PMA ([11, 12, 13]) is based on the assumption of minimal change when updating a knowledge base. A number of researchers ([2], [7]) have observed that this assumption may lead to unintuitive results when disjunctive update is involved. The standard example is the following. Suppose that all we know about the world is p and the effect of the performed action is $p \vee q$. Clearly, the description of the new state should be $p \vee q$ rather than p. However, according to the classical PMA, the latter of these formulas is the result of the

---

*The author was partially supported by grants from the Wallenberg Foundation and the Swedish Research Council for Engineering Sciences (TFR)

[†]The authors were partially supported by the Wallenberg Foundation and by KBN grant 8 T 11C 035 11

considered update. The reason is that defining the new world as p requires no change at all.

We provided a generalization of the PMA, called the modified PMA (MPMA), which permits the representation of disjunctive updates and the use of integrity constraints. The MPMA weakens the minimal change policy of the classical PMA by isolating a subset of atoms that are allowed to vary their truth-values during the minimization process. The technique is similar to the use of variable predicates in circumscription and the use of an *occlusion, release* or *noninert* predicate in the temporal logic paradigm.

In [6], we presented a syntactic characterization of the MPMA, constructed by mapping an MPMA update of a knowledge base into a temporal narrative in a simple temporal logic (STL). In addition, we introduced the possibility of using integrity constraints interpreted as causal constraints. The resulting representation theorem provided a basis for computing entailments of the MPMA and relating a number of temporal logic-based approaches for reasoning about action and change to the belief update paradigm.

In this paper, we provide an alternative syntactic characterization of the MPMA in terms of Dijkstra's semantics which uses the weakest precondition and the strongest postcondition formula transformers. This characterization is constructed by mapping an MPMA update of a knowledge base into a command in a simple Dijkstra style programming language.

The paper is organized as follows. In section 3 we provide the detailed decision procedure for MPMA and prove it to be correct. In section 4 the reformulation of the MPMA is extended by allowing integrity constraints IC and the detailed algorithm is provided. We illustrate our approach by number of examples. We end with conclusions in section 5.

2 The MPMA

We start with a language $\mathcal{L}_{mpma}$ of classical propositional logic based on a finite fixed set $ATM = \{p, q, r, \ldots\}$ of atoms. Formulas are built in the usual way using the connectives $\wedge, \vee, \neg, \Rightarrow, \Leftrightarrow, \top$ (truth) and $\perp$ (falsity). If α and β are formulas and p is an atom, then we write $\alpha[p \leftarrow \beta]$ to denote the formula obtained from α by replacing all occurrences of p by β. A *literal* is an atom or its negation.

Interpretations are identified with maximal consistent sets of literals. For any formula α, we write $|\alpha|$ to denote the set of all *models* of α, i.e. interpretations satisfying α. A formula α is said to *correspond* to an interpretation u iff $|\alpha| = u$. To construct such a formula, it suffices to take the conjunction of all literals occurring in u. Similarly, a formula α is said to correspond to a finite set of interpretations $\{u_1, \ldots, u_n\}$ iff $|\alpha| = \{u_1, \ldots, u_n\}$. To obtain such a formula, it suffices to take the disjunction $\beta_1 \vee \cdots \vee \beta_n$, where, for each $1 \leq i \leq n$, β_i is the formula corresponding to u_i. For instance, the formula corresponding to the set $\{\{p, \neg q\}, \{p, q\}\}$ is $(p \wedge \neg q) \vee (p \wedge q)$ which is equivalent to p.

Definition 1 Let w, v be two interpretations. The *distance* between w and v, written $DIST(w, v)$, is a set of atoms that have different values in w and u. ∎

For instance, the distance between $\{p, q, r, \neg s\}$ and $\{q, s, \neg p, \neg r\}$ is $\{p, s, r\}$.

Definition 2 Let w and v be two interpretations and suppose that P is a set of atoms. The *distance* between w and v wrt P is $DIST(w, v) - P$. ∎

For instance, the distance between $\{p, q, r, \neg s\}$ and $\{q, s, \neg p, \neg r\}$ wrt p is $\{r, s\}$.

Definition 3 The *update of an interpretation w by a set of interpretations U wrt a set of atoms P*, written $w \star^P U$, is the set of those elements of U whose distance to w wrt P is $\emptyset$. ∎

Definition 4 The *update of a set of interpretations U by a set of interpretations V wrt a set of atoms P*, written $U \star^P V$, is given by

$$U \star^P V = \bigcup_{w \in U} w \star^P V. \quad ∎$$

In the MPMA, the update $KB \star^P \alpha$ of a knowledge base KB by a formula α wrt a set of atoms P is identified with the formula corresponding to the set of interpretations $|KB| \star^P |\alpha|$.

Example 1 Let $KB = p$ and $\alpha = p \vee q$. To properly deal with this example, the atoms p and q should be allowed to vary. $|KB| \star^{\{p,q\}} |\alpha| = \{p, \neg q\} \star^{\{p,q\}}$ $\{\{p, \neg q\}, \{q, \neg p\}, \{p, q\}\} \cup \{p, q\} \star^{\{p,q\}} \{\{p, \neg q\}, \{q, \neg p\}, \{p, q\}\} = \{\{p, \neg q\},$ $\{q, \neg p\}, \{p, q\}\} \cup \{\{p, \neg q\}, \{q, \neg p\}, \{p, q\}\} = \{\{p, \neg q\}, \{q, \neg p\}, \{p, q\}\}$.
Thus $KB \star^{\{p,q\}} \alpha$ is the formula $(p \wedge \neg q) \vee (q \wedge \neg p) \vee (p \wedge q) \equiv p \vee q$. ∎

It should be noted that generally the MPMA need not preserve consistency. For instance, if $ATM = \{q\}$, $KB = \neg q$, $\alpha = q$ and $P = \emptyset$, then $KB \star^P \alpha \equiv \bot$. However, as we shall see in the next section, consistency preservation is guaranteed if variable atoms are properly chosen.

2.1 Determining variable atoms

To properly apply the MPMA, we have to provide a mechanism to determine variable atoms. It is this fundamental problem that we shall now explore.

Let KB and α be a knowledge base and the update formula, respectively. Since α represents effects of a performed action, all atoms from α are potential candidates for variable atoms. However, α may include redundant atoms and these should not be varied. The following example illustrates the point.

Example 2 Suppose that $ATM = \{p, q\}$, $KB = \neg p \wedge q$ and $\alpha = p$. Taking p as the only variable atom, we get $KB \star^{\{p\}} \alpha \equiv p \wedge q$.
Replace now α by its equivalent $\alpha' = (p \wedge q) \vee (p \wedge \neg q)$ with a redundant atom q. Taking p and q as variables, we obtain $KB \star^{\{p,q\}} \alpha' \equiv p$. This result is clearly undesirable. ∎

Definition 5 Let α be a formula. An atom p occurring in α is said to be *redundant* for α iff $\alpha[p \leftarrow \top] \equiv \alpha[p \leftarrow \bot]$. ∎

As follows from the above definition, an atom is redundant for a formula iff the logical value of the formula does not depend on the logical value of the atom.

Our choice of variable atoms is to identify them with the set of non-redundant atoms for the update formula[1]. Accordingly, in the sequel, **we always assume that all redundant atoms of the update formula have been already eliminated.**

As we noted in the previous section, the MPMA need not preserve consistency. However, if all non-redundant atoms of the update formula are considered as variable atoms, consistency preservation is assured. In the sequel, we write $atm(\alpha)$ to denote the set of all (non-redundant) atoms occurring in a formula α. The following result has been proved in [6].

Theorem 1 Let $KB \not\equiv \bot$ be a knowledge base and $\alpha \not\equiv \bot$ be the update formula such that $atm(\alpha) = P$. Then $KB *^P \alpha \not\equiv \bot$. ∎

2.2 Syntactic characterization of the MPMA

In this section, we present a syntactic characterization of the MPMA. We start with some terminology.

Let p be an atom and α be a formula. We write $\exists p.\alpha$ to denote the formula $\alpha[p \leftarrow \top] \vee \alpha[p \leftarrow \bot]$. If $P = \{p_1, \ldots, p_n\}$ is a set of atoms and α is a formula, then $\exists P.\alpha$ stands for $\exists p_1 \cdots \exists p_n.\alpha$.

A formula of the form $\exists P.\alpha$, where $P = \{p_1, \ldots, p_n\}$, is called an *eliminant of* $\{p_1, \ldots, p_n\}$ *in* α. Intuitively, such an eliminant can be viewed as a formula representing the same knowledge as α about all atoms from $ATM - P$ and providing no information about the atoms in P. The reader interested in a detailed theory of eliminants should consult [3].

We are now ready to provide a syntactic characterization of the MPMA. The following result can be found in [6].

Theorem 2 Let KB, α and $P = atm(\alpha)$ be a knowledge base, an update formula and a set of atoms, respectively. Then $KB *^P \alpha \equiv \alpha \wedge \exists P.KB$. ∎

Theorem 2 clearly shows how the MPMA works. First, we select the atoms that may vary their values when the action corresponding to the update formula α is performed. Next, we weaken the knowledge base KB by eliminating all those variable atoms. Finally, we strengthen the knowledge base $\exists P.KB$ by combining it with the update formula.

2.3 Computing the MPMA

In view of Theorem 2, all we need to compute the MPMA is the ability to compute eliminants. The following method is from [3].

---

[1] It is well-known that any propositional formula α can be constructively transformed into its equivalent, called the *Blake cannonical form of* α, which contains no redundant atoms (see [6, 3] for details).

Let α be a formula and $P = \{p_1, \ldots, p_k\}$ be a set of atoms. The eliminant $\exists P.\alpha$ is the formula obtained by the following construction.

(1) Replace α by its disjunctive normal form $t_1 \vee \cdots \vee t_n$, where $t1, \ldots, t_n$ are terms.[2] Denote the resulting formula by β.

(2) From each t_i ($1 \le i \le n$), remove all occurrences of $p_1, \ldots, p_k$. If all literals have been removed from some term t_i, stop and return $\top$ as $\exists P.\alpha$. Otherwise, return the resulting formula as $\exists P.\alpha$.

Example 3 This is the classical example from[11]. We have two atoms, b and m, standing for "a book is on the floor" and "a magazine is on the floor", respectively. $KB = (b \wedge \neg m) \vee (\neg b \wedge m)$. The update formula α is m. Since α contains no redundant atoms, the only variable atom is m. We first compute $\exists m.KB$ and we get $b \vee \neg b \equiv \top$. Hence, $KB *^m \alpha$ is $m \wedge \top \equiv m$. ∎

3 Reformulating the MPMA in Dijkstra's semantics

In this section, we provide an equivalent formulation of MPMA in terms of Dijkstra's semantics, originally developed to reason about programs [4, 5].

In [5] we are provided with a very simple programming language whose semantics is specified in terms of formula transformers, called the *weakest precondition* and the *strongest postcondition*, denoted by wp and sp, respectively. Before providing the meaning of these transformers, two remarks are in order.

Firstly, we assume here that the programming language under consideration contains one type of variables only, namely Boolean variables. No other variables will be needed for our purpose. In accord with our earlier terminology, Boolean variables will be referred to as *atoms*. Secondly, in programming language terminology, interpretations are usually referred to as *states*. We shall use this latter term here because it seems to be more appropriate in dynamic settings.

The formula transformers mentioned above are to be understood as follows. For each command S and each formula α:

- $wp(S, \alpha)$ is the formula whose models are precisely all states such that execution of S begun in any one of them is guaranteed to terminate in a state satisfying α.

- $sp(S, \alpha)$ is the formula whose models are precisely all states such that each of them can be reached by starting execution of S in some state satisfying α.

---

[2]By a term we understand a conjunction of literals.

3.1 SDPL: A Simple Dijkstra Programming Language

The programming language we shall employ consists of a *skip*, *abort* and *assignment* command, *sequential composition* of commands and a specific form of *alternative* command. Semantics of these commands is specified in terms of formula transformers as follows.

1. **The *skip* command.** This is the "empty" command in that its execution does not change the computation state.

$$wp(skip, \alpha) = sp(skip, \alpha) = \alpha.$$

2. **The *abort* command.** This command aborts the computation.

$$wp(abort, \alpha) = \left\{ \begin{array}{ll} \bot & \text{if } \alpha \not\equiv \bot \\ \top & \text{otherwise} \end{array} \right. ; \quad sp(abort, \alpha) = \bot$$

3. **The *assignment* command.** This command is of the form $x := e$, where x is a (Boolean) variable and e is a (Boolean) expression. The effect of the command is to replace the value of x by the value of e.

$$wp(x := e, \ \alpha) = \alpha[x \leftarrow e].$$

In general, the strongest postcondition is given by (here y is a fresh variable)

$$sp(x := e, \alpha) = \exists y.((x \equiv e[x \leftarrow y]) \wedge \alpha[x \leftarrow y]). \tag{1}$$

If the variable x does not occur in the expression e, the equation (1) can be simplified. In this case

$$sp(x := e, \alpha) = (x \equiv e) \wedge (\alpha[x \leftarrow T] \vee \alpha[x \leftarrow F]). \tag{2}$$

4. **The *sequential composition* command.** This command is of the form $S_1; S_2$, where S_1 and S_2 are any commands. It is executed by first executing S_1 and then executing S_2.

$$wp(S_1; S_2, \alpha) = wp(S_1, wp(S_2, \alpha)); \quad sp(S_1; S_2, \alpha) = sp(S_2, sp(S_1, \alpha)).$$

5. **The *alternative* command.** This command (denoted by IF) is of the form

$$\textbf{if} \quad B_1 \rightarrow S_1 \quad \| \quad B_2 \rightarrow S_2 \quad \| \quad \cdots \quad \| \quad B_n \rightarrow S_n \quad \textbf{fi} \tag{3}$$

where $B_1, \ldots, B_n$ are Boolean expressions called *guards* and $S_1, \ldots, S_n$ are any commands. Expressions of the form $B_i \rightarrow S_i$ are called *guarded commands*. The command is executed as follows. If none of the guards is true, the execution aborts. Otherwise, one guarded command $B_i \rightarrow S_i$ with true B_i is *randomly* selected and S_i is executed

$$wp(\text{IF}, \alpha) = \bigwedge_{i=1}^{n} (B_i \Rightarrow wp(S_i, \alpha)) \wedge \bigvee_{i=1}^{n} B_i;$$

$$sp(\text{IF}, \alpha) = \bigvee_{i=1}^{n} (sp(S_i, B_i \wedge \alpha)).$$

3.2 A Decision Procedure for MPMA

We now proceed to the reformulation of the MPMA in the context of Dijkstra's formalism.

Suppose we are given a knowledge base KB and an update formula α. Without loss of generality we may assume that α is in the disjunctive normal form (DNF). Let P be the set of all atoms occurring in α. The idea is to construct a command S such that $sp(S, KB) = KB \star^P \alpha$. In other words, we want to replace the update formula by a command which it is the effect of.

Let t be a term. We write $C(t)$ to denote the command *corresponding to t*. This is defined as follows. If t is $\top$, then $C(t)$ is *skip*. If t is $\bot$, then $C(t)$ is *abort*. Finally, if t is of the form $l_1 \wedge \cdots \wedge l_k$, then $C(t)$ is $l_1 := V_1; \ldots; l_k := V_k$, where, for each $1 \leq i \leq k$, V_i is $\top$ if l_i is positive and $\bot$ otherwise.

Let p be an atom. We write $release(p)$ as an abbreviation for the command
if $\top \to p := \top \parallel \top \to p := \bot$ **fi**.

Let $\alpha = t_1 \vee \cdots \vee t_k$ be a formula in DNF and suppose that $atm(\alpha) = \{p_1, \ldots, p_n\}$. The command corresponding to α wrt MPMA, written $C^{MPMA}(\alpha)$ is the sequential composition

$$release(p_1); \ldots; release(p_n); \textbf{if } \top \to C(t_1) \parallel \cdots \parallel \top \to C(t_k) \textbf{ fi}. \tag{4}$$

Theorem 3 Let KB be a knowledge base, $\alpha = t_1 \vee \cdots \vee t_k$ be an update formula in DNF and $P = \{p_1, \ldots, p_n\}$ is the set of all atoms occurring in α. Then

$$KB \star^P \alpha \equiv sp(C^{MPMA}, KB). \blacksquare$$

Corollary 1 Let KB be a knowledge base, $\alpha = t_1 \vee \cdots \vee t_k$ be an update formula in DNF and $P = \{p_1, \ldots, p_n\}$ be the set of all atoms occurring in α. Then for each formula β, $KB \star^P \alpha \models \beta$ iff $KB \Rightarrow wp(C^{MPMA}(\alpha), \beta)$ is a tautology. $\blacksquare$

Example 3 (continued) We now use Corollary 1 to determine whether p follows from KB updated by α in the MPMA. Since α is already in DNF, $C^{MPMA}(\alpha)$ is

$$release(p); release(q); \textbf{if } \top \to p := \top \parallel \top \to q := \top \textbf{ fi}.$$

It is easily checked that $wp(C^{MPMA}(\alpha), p) \equiv \bot$. Thus $KB \star \alpha \not\models p$. $\blacksquare$

4 MPMA and Integrity Constraints

In this section we provide the reformulation of the MPMA under integrity constraints IC. Let KB be a knowledge base satifying integrity constraints formula IC, α be an update formula and $P = atm(\alpha)$. The task is to construct an additional modification of $KB' = KB \star^P \alpha$ such that the resulting KB'' satisfies IC. The idea used below is based on [10]. We start by introducing some terminology.

By *clause* we mean a formula of the form $l_1 \vee \ldots \vee l_n$, $n \geq 1$, where l_i is a literal.

We say that a clause α *absorbs* a clause β if α is a subformula of β. For instance, the clause a absorbs the clause $a \vee l$. Let α be a formula in conjunctive normal form *CNF*. We write $ABS(\alpha)$ to denote the formula obtained from α by deleting all absorbed clauses. Clearly, α and $ABS(\alpha)$ are equivalent.

Two clauses are said to have an *opposition* if one of them contains a literal l and the other the literal $\neg l$.

Suppose that two clauses, α and β, have exactly one opposition. Then the *resolvent* of α and β, written $res(\alpha, \beta)$, is the clause obtained from the disjunction $\alpha \vee \beta$ by deleting the opposed literals as well as any repeated literals. For example, $res(\neg a \vee l, a \vee d)$ is $l \vee d$. Let α be a formula. The *canonical form of α*, written $CF(\alpha)$, is the formula obtained from α by the following construction.

1. Let β be the conjunctive normal form of α.

2. Repeat as long as possible:
   if β contains a pair δ and γ of clauses whose resolvent exists and no clause of β is a subformula of $res(\delta, \gamma)$, then $\beta := \beta \wedge res(\delta, \gamma)$.

3. Take $ABS(\beta)$. This is $CF(\alpha)$.

Theorem 4 Let α be a formula. $CF(\alpha)$ is a conjunction of all minimal clauses implied by α[3]. ∎

Assume next that we are provided with additional information on atoms, represented by an *influence relation*. It is a transitive relation $\mathcal{I} = \{(f_i, g_i)|f_i, g_i \in ATM$ for $i = 1, \ldots, n\}$. Its meaning is that any change of the atom g_i (called a *successor*) may influence the atom f_i (called a *predecessor*).

Let $\mathcal{I}$ be an influence relation, α be an update formula and β be a formula. The *canonical form of β wrt α and $\mathcal{I}$*, written $CFI(\beta, \alpha, \mathcal{I})$ is the formula obtained from β by the following construction.

1. Let γ be $CF(\beta)$ where $\gamma \equiv \gamma_1 \wedge \ldots \wedge \gamma_n$.

2. For all i, $1 \leq i \leq n$, transform γ_i into its equivalent implication $\beta_i \Rightarrow \alpha_i$, where α_i contains all atoms from γ_i which are predecessors wrt $atm(\alpha)$ in relation $\mathcal{I}$, and β_i the remaining atoms[4].

3. $CFI(\beta, \alpha, \mathcal{I}) = (\beta_1 \Rightarrow \alpha_1) \wedge \ldots \wedge (\beta_n \Rightarrow \alpha_n)$[5].

4.1 Solving Integrity Constraints in SDPL

Now we proceed to construct Dijkstra's command realizing integrity constraints.

Let KB be a knowledge base, α an update formula and $CFI(IC, \alpha, \mathcal{I}) = C_1 \wedge \ldots \wedge C_m$. Note that if a conjunct C_i contains no atoms from $atm(\alpha)$, it holds after

---

[3] A clause C is a minimal clause implied by α iff no proper subclause of C is implied by α.

[4] If a conjunct does not contain predecessors we put $\beta_i \Rightarrow F$ and if a conjunct contains only predecessors we put $T \Rightarrow \alpha_i$.

[5] Note that β_i is a clause and α_i is a term.

updating KB by α. And if $C_i = (\beta_i \Rightarrow F)$, then it cannot be realized, because there are no atoms, whose values may be modified[6]. Taking into account the above observations we should consider only those conjuncts of $CFI(IC, \alpha, \mathcal{I})$, which contain atoms from $atm(\alpha)$ and can be realized. We define

$$IC(\alpha) = \{C_i \mid C_i = \beta_i \Rightarrow \alpha_i \text{ and } atm(\alpha) \cap atm(\beta_i) \neq \emptyset\}.$$
$$IC_Q(\alpha) = \{C_i \mid C_i = \beta_i \Rightarrow F\}.$$
$$IC_{ram}(\alpha) = IC(\alpha) - IC_Q(\alpha).$$

Thus we should consider the modification of $KB' = KB *^P \alpha$ wrt $IC_{ram}(\alpha)$. Assume that $IC_{ram}(\alpha) = \{\beta_i \Rightarrow \alpha_i, 1 \leq i \leq n\}$. The semantics of this modification is as follows. If $KB' \Rightarrow \neg\beta_i \vee \alpha_i$ holds, no modification is done, otherwise all possible models of α_i are generated. This transformation may be syntacticaly characterized as

$$(KB *^P \alpha) *^{P_{ram}} IC, \text{ where } P_{ram} = \bigcup_{KB*^P\alpha \not\models \neg\beta_i \vee \alpha_i} atm(\alpha_i)$$

or equivalently

$$IC \wedge \exists P_{ram}(\alpha \wedge \exists P(KB \wedge IC)).$$

Now we formulate Dijkstra's command $C_{IC}^{MPMA}(\alpha)$ realizing update α of KB wrt IC. This is the composition of $C^{MPMA}(\alpha); C_{ram}(\alpha)$, where $C^{MPMA}(\alpha)$ is a command realizing update and C_{ram} is a command realizing integrity constraints given below (we use auxilliary variables $AUX = \{x_1, x_2, \ldots\}$ to denote conjuncts of $IC_{ram}(\alpha)$ which do not hold after the update of KB).

$$x_1 := \perp; \ldots; x_n := \perp;$$

if $\beta_1 \wedge \neg\alpha_1 \to x_1 := \top [\![\neg\beta_1 \vee \alpha_1 \to skip$ **fi**; $\quad \{x_i = \top \text{ denotes that}\}$

$\vdots$ $\qquad\qquad\qquad\qquad\qquad\qquad\qquad\qquad\quad$ {i-th element of IC_{ram}}

if $\beta_n \wedge \neg\alpha_n \to x_n := \top [\![\neg\beta_n \vee \alpha_n \to skip$ **fi**; { should be realized}

if $x_1 \to release(atm(\alpha_1)) [\![\neg x_1 \to skip$ **fi** ;

$\vdots$

if $x_n \to release(atm(\alpha_n)) [\![\neg x_n \to skip$ **fi**

$$KB' = \exists AUX.(sp(C^{MPMA}(\alpha); C_{ram}(\alpha), KB \wedge IC) \wedge IC).$$

4.2 Examples

Example 4 Let $KB = \neg a \wedge \neg b \wedge c$, an update formula $\alpha = a$, $IC = (a \Rightarrow b) \wedge (b \Rightarrow c)$ and $\mathcal{I} = \{(c, b), (b, a), (c, a)\}$.

Hence, $CFI(IC, \alpha, \mathcal{I}) = (a \Rightarrow b) \wedge (a \Rightarrow c) \wedge (\top \Rightarrow (\neg b \vee c))$, $IC(\alpha) = \{(a \Rightarrow b), (a \Rightarrow c)\}$, $IC_Q(\alpha) = \emptyset$ and $IC_{ram}(\alpha) = IC(\alpha)$.

---

[6]In reasoning about action paradigm this case is usually referred to as qualification (see [10] for details).

$IC_{ram}(\alpha)$ has two elements, thus we need x_1, x_2. $C_{IC}^{MPMA}(\alpha)$ is

$$\{C^{MPMA}(\alpha)\} \quad a := \top;$$
$$\{C_{ram}(\alpha)\} \qquad x_1 := \bot;\ x_2 := \bot;$$

if $a \wedge \neg b \to x_1 := \top [\![\neg a \vee b \to skip$ fi; if $a \wedge \neg c \to x_2 := \top [\![\neg a \vee c \to skip$ fi;
if $x_1 \to release(b) [\![\neg x_1 \to skip$ fi; if $x_2 \to release(c) [\![\neg x_2 \to skip$ fi

$KB' = \exists x_1 \exists x_2.(sp(a := \top; C_{ram}(\alpha), KB \wedge IC) \wedge IC) \equiv a \wedge b \wedge c.$ ∎

Example 5 We have three atoms: $sw1$, $sw2$, $light$, standing for positions of switch1, switch2 and the state of the light bulb, respectively. The update formula $\alpha = \neg sw1$, and $KB \equiv light \wedge sw1 \wedge sw2$. $IC = (light \Leftrightarrow (sw1 \Leftrightarrow sw2))$. $\mathcal{I} = \{(light, sw1), (light, sw2)\}$.

$$CF(IC) \equiv (\neg sw1 \vee sw2 \vee \neg light) \wedge (\neg sw2 \vee sw1 \vee \neg light)$$
$$\wedge (sw1 \vee sw2 \vee light) \wedge (\neg sw1 \vee \neg sw2 \vee light)$$

$$CFI(IC, \alpha, \mathcal{I}) \equiv (sw1 \wedge \neg sw2 \Rightarrow \neg light) \wedge (sw2 \wedge \neg sw1 \Rightarrow \neg light)$$
$$\wedge (\neg sw1 \wedge \neg sw2 \Rightarrow light) \wedge (sw1 \wedge sw2 \Rightarrow light)$$

We need here only one auxilliary variable x_1, because the right hand side of implication of all conjuncts consists of the same atom $light$. $C_{IC}^{MPMA}(\alpha)$ is

$$\{C^{MPMA}(\alpha)\} \quad sw1 := \bot;$$
$$\{C_{ram}(\alpha)\} \qquad x_1 := \bot;$$

if $sw1 \wedge \neg sw2 \wedge light \to x_1 := \top [\![\neg sw1 \vee sw2 \vee \neg light \to skip$ fi;
if $sw2 \wedge \neg sw1 \wedge light \to x_1 := \top [\![\neg sw2 \vee sw1 \vee \neg light \to skip$ fi;
if $sw1 \wedge \neg sw2 \wedge \neg light \to x_1 := \top [\![\neg sw1 \vee sw2 \vee light \to skip$ fi;
if $sw2 \wedge \neg sw1 \wedge \neg light \to x_1 := \top [\![\neg sw1 \vee sw1 \vee light \to skip$ fi;
if $x_1 \to release(light) [\![\neg x_1 \to skip$ fi

$KB' = \exists x_1.(sp(C_{IC}^{MPMA}(\alpha), KB \wedge IC) \wedge IC) \equiv \neg sw1 \wedge sw2 \wedge \neg light.$ ∎

5 Conclusions

We have provided an alternative syntactic characterization of the MPMA in terms of Dijkstra's semantics which uses the weakest precondition and the strongest postcondition formula transformers. This characterization of the MPMA, constructed by mapping an MPMA update of a knowledge base (possibly under integrity constraints) into a command in a simple Dijkstra style programming language, serves a number of useful purposes.

Besides the intrinsic interest in understanding the relation between viewing the use of update operators as executing commands in a programming language, the formal coupling between the MPMA and the Dijkstra characterization, together with the previous results describing the formal coupling between the MPMA and a number of well known nonmonotonic temporal logics for reasoning about action and change [6], serve as a basis for providing representation theorems between narrative based temporal logics and other well known approaches using formula transformers such as [8, 9, 1]. In addition, insights from both the temporal logic and formula transformer based approaches may serve to generalize the use of update operators in the belief update paradigm.

References

[1] M. Bjäreland, L. Karlsson. Reasoning by Regression: Pre- and Postcondition Operators for Logics of Action and Change. *Proc. IJCAI'97*, 1997.

[2] G. Brewka, J. Hertzberg. How to Do Things with Worlds: on Formalizing Actions and Plans. *Journal of Logic and Computation*. Vol. 3, No. 5, 517-532, 1993.

[3] F. M. Brown. *Boolean Reasoning*. Kluwer Academic Publishers, 1990.

[4] E. W. Dijkstra. *A Discipline of Programming*. Prentice Hall, 1976.

[5] E. W. Dijkstra, C. S. Scholten. *Predicate Calculus and Program Semantics*. Springer-Verlag, 1990.

[6] P. Doherty, W.Lukaszewicz, E. Madalińska-Bugaj. The PMA and Relativizing Minimal Change for Action Update. *Proceedings of KR-98*, 258-169, 1998.

[7] A. Hertzig. The PMA Revisited. *Proceedings of KR'96*, Morgan Kaufmann Publishers, Inc. San Francisco, California, 40-50, 1996.

[8] F. Lin. Embracing Causality in Specifying the Indirect Effects of Actions. *Proceedings of IJCAI'95*, 1985-1991, 1995.

[9] F. Lin. Embracing Causality in Specifying the Indeterminate Effects of Actions. *Proc. AAAI'96*, 1996.

[10] E. Madalińska-Bugaj. How to Solve Qualification and Ramification Using Dijkstra's Semantics for Programming Languages, *AI*IA-97: Advances in Artificial Intelligence*, Springer-Verlag, Lecture Notes in Artificial Intelligence, **1321**, 381-392, 1997.

[11] M. Winslett. Reasoning about Action Using a Possible Model Approach. In: *Proceedings AAAI-88*, St. Paul, MN, 89-93, 1988.

[12] M. Winslett. *Updating Logical Databases*. Cambridge Tracks in Theoretical Computer Science. Cambridge University Press, 1990.

[13] M. Winslett. Updating Logical Databases. In: D. Gabbay, A. Galton, J. A. Robinson (eds.). *Handbook of Logic in Artificial Intelligence and Logic Programming*. Vol. 4 (Epistemic and Temporal Reasoning), Oxford University Press, 133-174, 1995.

Several Extensions of Truth Values in Fuzzy Logic

Masao Mukaidono

Department of Computer Science, Meiji University
1-1-1 Higashi-mita, Tama-ku, Kawasaki-shi 214-8571 Japan
masao@cs.meiji.ac.jp

Abstract. Truth values in fuzzy logic are extended into interval truth values $\{[a,b] : 0 \le a \le b \le 1\}$ from the numerical truth values of $[0,1]$. Next we extend this interval truth values into two directions; one is to n-dimensional case such as $[a_1, \cdots, a_n]$ where $a_1 \le \cdots \le a_n$, and the other is to dropping the condition $a \le b$ in $[a,b]$. We examine the algebraic structures of these truth values on which three kinds of logic operations $AND(\cdot), OR(\vee), NOT(\sim)$ are defined, where we interpret $(x \cdot y), (x \vee y)$, and $(\sim x)$ as $min(x,y), max(x,y)$, and $(1-x)$, respectively. It is shown that we can find out structures of Kleene algebra and De Morgan algebra in these truth values.

1 Introduction

In fuzzy set theory, a membership function, which represents a degree of element belonging to a fuzzy set, takes a value in the closed interval of [0,1] apart from $\{0,1\}$ in case of classical set theory. Corre-sponding to the above situation, any statement in fuzzy logic takes a value in the closed interval of [0,1] as a truth value, where this truth value is called a numerical truth value in this paper. On the other hand, in fuzzy logic, although we can define infinite kinds of logic operations , three fundamental logic operations AND, OR, NOT have been used from the original paper of Zadeh [1].

In this paper, after surveying the relationship between set operations and logic operations in fuzzy logic, we extend the truth values of fuzzy logic from the numerical truth values of [0,1] into interval truth values $[a,b]$ where $a \le b$. Next we extend this interval truth values into two directions, one is to n-dimensional case such as $[a_1, \cdots, a_n]$ where $a_1 \le \cdots \le a_n$, and the other is to dropping the condition $a \le b$ in $[a,b]$. We examine the algebraic structures of these truth values on which three kinds of logic operations $AND(\cdot), OR(\vee), NOT(\sim)$ are defined, where we interpret $(x \cdot y), (x \vee y)$, and $(\sim x)$ such as $min(x,y), max(x,y)$, and $(1-x)$, respectively when x and y are elements of [0,1]. It is shown that we can find out structures of Kleene algebra and De Morgan algebra in these truth values.

2 Fuzzy sets and fuzzy logic

Let U be an ordinary set. Then a fuzzy set A on U is defined a mapping from U to the closed interval [0,1], which is denoted by a symbol μ_A, that is, $\mu_A : U \to [0,1]$. Here, it is said that A is a label and μ_A is a membership function of the fuzzy set. For an element e of U, $\mu_A(e)$ represents a degree of which e belongs to the fuzzy set A , where $\mu_A(e) = 1$ means the element e belongs to A completely and $\mu_A(e) = 0$ means doesn't belong completely. In fuzzy set theory, originally [1] three fundamental set operations Union($\cup$), Intersection($\cap$) and Compliment(c) were applied and defined as $\mu_{A\cup B}(e) = \mu_A(e) \vee \mu_B(e)$, $\mu_{A\cap B}(e) = \mu_A(e) \cdot \mu_B(e)$, $\mu_{A^c} =\sim \mu_A(e)$, where $\vee, \cdot$ and $\sim$ are logic operations OR, AND and NOT, and defined as follows, respectively,

Definition 1 $a \vee b = max(a, b)$, $a \cdot b = min(a, b)$, $\sim a = 1 - a$, $a, b \in [0, 1]$.

In two valued logic, the three kinds of logic operations $\vee, \cdot$ and $\sim$ are enough in the sense of that any two-valued function is representable by using these operations, that is, $\vee, \cdot$ and $\sim$ are functional complete in two-valued logic functions. But in fuzzy logic, it is not true. In fact, in fuzzy logic we can define infinite number of fuzzy functions and there is no set of finite logic operations which is functional complete for all fuzzy functions. Nevertheless, in this paper, because of the importance and fundamentality of these three logic operations we will examine the algebraic properties of a set of truth values on which only AND, OR and NOT are defined. Here, we will explain briefly the relationship between the truth value of a sentence in fuzzy logic and the degrees of a membership function in fuzzy set. [A truth value of a fuzzy statement "e is an element of a fuzzy set A" is given by the degree of the membership function $\mu_A(e)$]. This is a postulate connecting between the truth values in fuzzy logic and the degrees of a membership function in fuzzy set. Accepting this postulate in the following sections we will concentrate our researches on the logic operations and the truth values in fuzzy logic, but the results obtained here are applicable to the fuzzy sets according to the above relation.

3 Numerical truth values and logic operations[2],[3]

Let us call a value of [0,1] a numerical truth value as follows.

Definition 2 An element of [0,1] is called a numerical truth value. The set of all numerical truth values is denoted by V, that is, $V = [0, 1]$.

Property 1 For any $x, y, z \in V$, the following equalities (1) $\sim$ (9) hold concerning logic operations $\vee, \cdot$, and $\sim$.

- (1) Idempotent laws $x \vee x = x$, $x \cdot x = x$
- (2) Commutative laws $x \vee y = y \vee x$, $x \cdot y = y \cdot x$
- (3) Associative laws $(x \vee y) \vee z = x \vee (y \vee z)$, $(x \cdot y) \wedge z = x \cdot (y \cdot z)$
- (4) Absorption laws $x \cdot (x \vee y) = x$, $x \vee (x \cdot y) = x$
- (5) Distributive laws $x \cdot (y \vee z) = (x \cdot y) \vee (x \cdot z)$,
  $$x \vee (y \cdot z) = (x \vee y) \cdot (x \vee z)$$
- (6) Double negation laws $\sim\sim x = x$
- (7) De Morgan laws $\sim (x \vee y) =\sim x \cdot \sim y$, $\sim (x \cdot y) =\sim x \vee \sim y$
- (8) Maximum element $x \vee 1 = 1$, $x \cdot 1 = x$
- (9) Minimum element $x \vee 0 = x$, $x \cdot 0 = 0$

(Proof is omitted.)

Property 2 For any $x, y \in V$, the following equalities (10), called Kleene's laws,
hold   (10) Kleene's laws $(x\vee \sim x) \vee (y \cdot \sim y) = x \vee \sim x$
$$(x\vee \sim x) \cdot (y \cdot \sim y) = y \cdot \sim y.$$

Proof It is evident from $(y \cdot \sim y) \leq 1/2 \leq (x\vee \sim x)$ for any x and y when $x, y \in [0, 1]$. **Q.E.D**.

284

Definition 3 De Morgan algebra is an algebraic system in which logic operations $\cdot, \vee, \sim$ and constants 0,1 are defined and satisfy the axioms (1) $\sim$(9).

Definition 4 Kleene algebra is an algebraic system in which logic operations
$\cdot, \vee, \sim$ and constants 0,1 are defined and satisfy the axioms (1) $\sim$ (10).

Boolean algebra corresponding to two-valued logic satisfies the following
equalities (10*), called the complementary laws, adding to the axioms of De
Morgan algebra (1) $\sim$ (9).

$$(10^*) \text{ the complementary laws} \qquad x\vee \sim x = 1, \quad x\cdot \sim x = 0$$

The law of excluded middle and the law of contradiction are corresponding to
the above complementary laws. If the complementary laws hold, then Kleene's
laws holds. Therefore, Kleene algebra is weaker algebra than Boolean algebra,
where De Morgan algebra is weaker algebra than Kleene algebra. It is easily
shown that numerical truth values do not satisfy the the complementary laws
in general. For example $x\vee \sim x \neq 1$ if $x \in (0,1)$. From the above facts we can
conclude that the set of numerical truth values V and logic operations $\cdot, \vee, \sim$ on
V is not Boolean algebra, but Kleene algebra.

Proposition 1 The set of numerical truth values V with logic operations $\cdot, \vee, \sim$
satisfies Kleene algebra. (Proof is omitted.)

4   Interval truth values[4]

A numerical truth value is extended into more complicated truth values called
interval truth values for treating ambiguity more flexibly.

Definition 5 An interval truth value is a pair of two numerical truth values a, b
such as $a \leq b$, which is written as $[a, b]$. The set of all interval truth values
is written by I, that is, $I = \{[a, b] : a \leq b, \ a, b \in [0, 1]\}$.

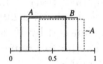

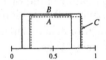

Fig. 1. An example of interval truth value

Fig. 2. $A \vee B = B, A \leq B$

Fig. 3. $A \vee B = C, A \leq\leq B$

Definition 6 Logic operations on interval truth values are defined as follows:

$AND:$ $[a, b] \cdot [c, d] = [min(a, c), min(b, d)] = [a \cdot c, b \cdot d]$,

$OR:$ $[a, b] \vee [c, d] = [max(a, c), max(b, d)] = [a \vee c, b \vee d]$,

$NOT:$ $\sim [a, b] = [1 - b, 1 - a] = [\sim b, \sim a]$, where $[a, b], [c, d] \in I$.

Example 1 Examples of logic operation OR $(A \vee B)$ for two interval truth
values A and B are show in Fig.2 and in Fig.3, and NOT operation $(\sim A)$
for A is in Fig.2.

Definition 7 Let $A = [a_1, a_2]$ and $B = [b_1, b_2]$ be two interval truth values.
Then, $A \leq B$ if and only if $a_1 \leq b_1$ and $a_2 \leq b_2$.

Definition 8 Let $A = [a_1, a_2]$ and $B = [b_1, b_2]$ be two interval truth values.
Then, $A \leq\leq B$ if and only if $b_1 \leq a_1$ and $a_2 \leq b_2$.

Example 2 $A \leq B$ is shown in Fig.2 and $A \leq\leq B$ is in Fig.3. In Fig.2 A and B
are not comparable with each other concerning to $\leq\leq$, and in Fig.3 A and
B are not comparable with each other concerning to $\leq$.

The partially ordered relation $\leq$ means "truth", that is $A \leq B$ means B is equal to or more true than A. Logic operations AND, OR and NOT defined in Definition 5 are concerning to this partially ordered relation. On the other hand, the partially relation $\leq\leq$ means "non-specificity", that is $A \leq\leq B$ means B is equal to or more non-specific than A.

4.1 Representation of interval truth values

An interval truth value is represented by a point of half set of two dimensional space $[0,1] \times [0,1]$ restricted as $a \leq b$. Therefore, instead of Fig.1, if we represent an interval truth values as a point in the triangle illustrated in Fig.4, then it will be easily understandable for us and useful for considering the relationship among interval truth values, where this triangle is described by the representative three points, $F = [0,0]$ corresponding to false, $T = [1,1]$ corresponding to true and $U = [0,1]$ corresponding to unknown. In Fig.4, for example, an interval truth value $A = [a,b]$ is represented as a point in the triangle and it means the closed interval $[a,b]$, where the lower value a (the upper value b) is mapped on the line between $F = [0,0]$ and $T = [1,1]$ which corresponds to the set of numerical truth values by projecting the point $A = [a,b]$ parallel to the line of $U = [0,1]$ and $F = [0,0]$ (the line of $U = [0,1]$ and $T = [1,1]$). Similarly, interval truth values $C = [c_1,c_2]$ and $B = [b_1,b_2]$ are represented as points in the triangle as shown in Fig.4. An interval truth value has one to one correspondence to a point of the triangle. Furthermore, this triangle is very useful for representing logic operations between interval truth values. For example, consider two interval truth values A and B illustrated in Fig.5. In this case, $A \vee B$, $A \cdot B$ and $\sim A$ can be represented by the cross points in the triangle as shown in Fig.5, where $OR(\vee)$ is right side (true side) and $AND(\cdot)$ is left side (false side) and $NOT(\sim)$ is an opposite point to the center line of $U = [0,1]$ and $[1/2,1/2]$, respectively. Hereafter, we mainly use this triangle for representing interval truth values and their logic operations. In Fig.6, the right side of an interval truth value A in the triangle is more true than A, that is $A \leq x$, and the left side of A is more false than A, that is $y \leq A$. Similarly, the upper side of A is more non-specific than A and the lower side of A is more specific than A. Any interval truth value is comparable with A concerning only one of $\leq$ or $\leq\leq$ except interval truth values on the line of A in figure (any element on the line is comparable with A concerning both $\leq$ and $\leq\leq$). The logic operations defined in Definition 5 are operations on truth side and all interval truth values are closed under these logic operations. Similarly, we can define operations AND, OR and NOT on non-specific side but unfortunately these operations are not closed for interval truth valued defined in Definition 5. For introducing three kind of operations AND, OR and NOT concerning truth and non-specificity on interval truth values simultaneously, we have to extend the definition of interval truth values. Indeed, the interval truth values will be extended into such direction in the Section 6.

4.2 Properties and algebras of interval truth values

Property 3 There is an interval truth value which does not satisfy Kleene's laws.

Proof We can find easily an example which does not satisfy Kleene's laws. For example, if $x = [0.4, 0.6]$ and $y = [0.3, 0.7]$, then $(x \vee \sim x) \cdot (y \cdot \sim y) = [0.3, 0.6] \neq y \cdot \sim y$. This is a counter example of Kleene's laws. **Q.E.D**.

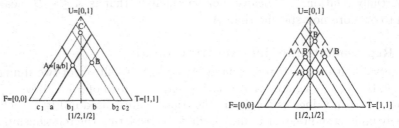

Fig. 4. Representing interval truth values in the triangle

Fig. 5. Logic operations in the triangle

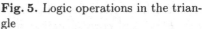
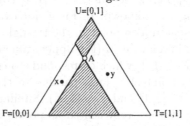

Fig. 6. Partial ordered relations on interval truth values

Proposition 2 The set of all interval truth values I with logic operations $\cdot, \vee, \sim$ satisfies De Morgan algebra. (Proof is omitted.)

Proposition 3 For any interval truth value A, $A \leq \sim A$ or $\sim A \leq A$.

Proof Let $A = [a, b]$, where $a \leq b$. Then $\sim A = [\sim b, \sim a]$. Here, $a \leq \sim b$ or $\sim b \leq a$ because $a, \sim b$, are numerical values of $[0,1]$. If $a \leq \sim b$, then $b \leq \sim a$ holds by negating both sides, that is $A = [a, b] \leq \sim A = [\sim b, \sim a]$. If $\sim b \leq a$, then $\sim a \leq b$ holds, that is $\sim A = [\sim b, \sim a] \leq A = [a, b]$. **Q.E.D.**

In Kleene algebra, treating formulas will be more easy than De Morgan algebra because Kleene algebra is near to Boolean algebra and the properties of them is well know already [2]. Please see the next Example. So it is worth to investigate the subset of interval truth values which satisfies the axiom of Kleene algebra.

Example 3 Let us consider a logic formula $F = x_1 \cdot (\sim x_3 \vee \sim x_1 \cdot \sim x_2) \vee x_1 \cdot (x_3 \vee \sim x_1 \cdot x_2)$. This formula can be expanded into the following disjunctive form in De Morgan algebra: $F = x_1 \cdot \sim x_3 \vee x_1 \cdot x_3 \vee x_1 \cdot \sim x_1 \cdot \sim x_2 \vee x_1 \cdot \sim x_1 \cdot x_2$, because the distributive laws and the commutative laws hold. But we can not simplify it more. But in Kleene algebra the above formula can be simplified into the following simpler form; $F = x_1 \cdot \sim x_3 \vee x_1 \cdot x_3$. The reason is the following: $x_1 \cdot \sim x_1 \cdot \sim x_2 \vee x_1 \cdot \sim x_1 \cdot x_2 = x_1 \cdot \sim x_1 \cdot (\sim x_2 \vee x_2) = x_1 \cdot \sim x_1$ and $x_1 \cdot \sim x_1 = x_1 \cdot \sim x_1 \cdot (\sim x_3 \vee x_3) = x_1 \cdot \sim x_1 \cdot \sim x_3 \vee x_1 \cdot \sim x_1 \cdot x_3$ holds in Kleene algebra, respectively, because the Kleene's laws and the distributive laws. Furthermore, we can omit these two terms $x_1 \cdot \sim x_1 \cdot \sim x_3$ and $x_1 \cdot \sim x_1 \cdot x_3$ because they are absorbed by $x_1 \cdot \sim x_3$ and $x_1 \cdot x_3$, respectively (In Boolean algebra, furthermore, the above formula can be simplified into

$F = x_1$, because $x_1 \cdot \sim x_3 \vee x_1 \cdot x_3 = x_1 \cdot (x_3 \vee \sim x_3) = x_1 \cdot 1 = x_1$ holds based on the complementary laws).

Property 4 In De Morgan algebra X, if x is comparable with y or $\sim y$ concerning $\leq$ for any x, y in X, then X is Kleene algebra.

Proof If x is comparable with y or $\sim y$ concerning $\leq$ in De Morgan algebra, then $x \leq y$ or $y \leq x$ or $\sim y \leq x$ or $x \leq \sim y$. Suppose $x \leq y$. Here consider $(x \vee \sim x) \cdot y \cdot \sim y$. It is evident that $(x \vee \sim x) \cdot y \cdot \sim y \leq y \cdot \sim y$. The left side of the inequality equal to $x \cdot y \cdot \sim y \vee \sim x \cdot y \cdot \sim y$. By the assumption $x \leq y$ (therefore $\sim y \leq \sim x$), $x \cdot y \cdot \sim y = x \cdot \sim y$ and $\sim x \cdot y \cdot \sim y = y \cdot \sim y$ hold. That is, the left side of the inequality becomes to $x \cdot \sim y \vee y \cdot \sim y$. Here $y \cdot \sim y \leq x \cdot \sim y \vee y \cdot \sim y$. Therefore we can get $(x \vee \sim x) \cdot y \cdot \sim y = y \cdot \sim y$, that is, Kleene's law holds. We can show it similarly in other cases of $y \leq x$ or $\sim y \leq x$ or $x \leq \sim y$. **Q.E.D.**

The converse of Property 4 is not true in general De Morgan algebra. In Fig.7, you can see a counter example of Kleene algebra in which a is non-comparable with c and $\sim c$ concerning $\leq$. But the converse of Property 4 is true in the set of interval truth values as follows.

Proposition 4 Let X be a subset of I which is closed under the logic operations $\cdot, \vee$, and $\sim$. Then, X is Kleene algebra if and only if for any x, y in X, x is comparable with y or $\sim y$ concerning $\leq$.

Proof If X be a subset of I which is closed under the logic operations $\cdot, \vee$, and $\sim$, then X is De Morgan algebra (Proposition 2). Therefore, from Property 4 for any x, y in X, x is comparable with y or $\sim y$ concerning $\leq$. Conversely, let suppose the condition "for any x, y in X, x is comparable with y or $\sim y$ concerning $\leq$" does not satisfied. It means that x are comparable strictly with y and $\sim y$ concerning $\leq$. We can suppose $x \leq y$, $\sim x \leq y$, and $\sim x \leq x$ and $\sim y \leq y$ without generality. And we can suppose $\sim x \leq x$ for all x of X without generality. Then the above fact leads that $\sim b_2 \leq b_1 \leq \sim a_2 \leq a_1$ and $\sim a_1 \leq a_2 \leq \sim b_1 \leq b_2$, where $x = [a_1, a_2]$ and $y = [b_1, b_2]$ (see Fig.8). Here consider the following two elements $c_1 = x \cdot \sim x \vee (x \vee \sim x) \cdot (y \vee \sim y)$ and $c_2 = y \cdot \sim y \vee (x \vee \sim x) \cdot (y \vee \sim y)$. In this case it becomes $c_1 = \sim x \vee x \cdot y = [\sim a_2 \vee a_1 \cdot b_1, \sim a_1 \vee a_2 \cdot b_2] = [\sim a_2, a_2]$ and $c_2 = \sim y \vee x \cdot y = [\sim b_2 \vee a_1 \cdot b_1, \sim b_1 \vee a_2 \cdot b_2] = [b_1, \sim b_1]$. Here, $c_1 \cdot \sim c_1 \vee (c_2 \vee \sim c_2) = c_1 \vee c_2 = [\sim a_2, \sim b_1] \neq [b_1, \sim b_1] = c_2 = (c_2 \vee \sim c_2)$. That is, Kleene's law does not hold. This fact means it is not Kleene algebra. **Q.E.D.**

5 Triangular truth values, trapezoid truth values and so on

An interval truth value $A = [a, b]$ is a point of two dimensional space $[0, 1] \times [0, 1]$ restricted as $a \leq b$. We can extend interval truth values into restricted three dimensional, four dimensional, $\cdots$, and n-dimensional elements.

Definition 9 A triangular truth value is a set of three numerical truth values a, b, c such as $a \leq b \leq c$, which is written as $[a, b, c]$. The set of all triangular truth values is written by T, that is, $T = \{[a, b, c] : a \leq b \leq c, a, b, c \in [0, 1]\}$ (See A in Fig.9).

Definition 10 Logic operations on triangular truth values are defined as follows: $AND: [a,b,c] \cdot [d,e,f] = [min(a,d), min(b,e), min(c,f)]$
$$= [a \cdot d, b \cdot e, c \cdot f],$$
$$OR: [a,b,c] \vee [d,e,f] = [max(a,d), max(b,e), max(c,f)]$$
$$= [a \vee d, b \vee e, c \vee f],$$
$$NOT: \quad \sim [a,b,c] \quad = [1-c, 1-b, 1-a]$$
$$= [\sim c, \sim b, \sim a], \quad \text{where } [a,b,c], [d,e,f] \in T.$$

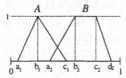

Fig. 7. An example of Kleene algebra

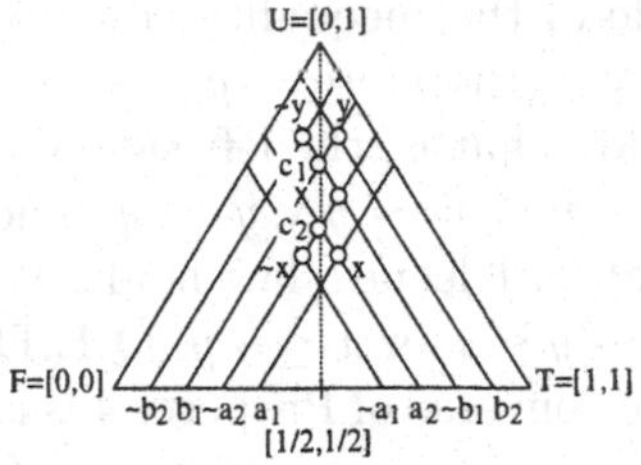

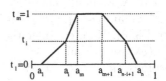

Fig. 8. x is not comparable with y and $\sim y$ concerning $\leq$

Proposition 5 The set of all triangular truth values T with logic operations $\cdot, \vee, \sim$ satisfies De Morgan algebra. (Proof is omitted)

Proposition 6 Let X be a subset of T which is closed under the logic operations $\cdot, \vee$, and $\sim$. Then, X is Kleene algebra if and only if for any $x = [a,b,c], y = [d,e,f]$ in X, $[a,c]$ is comparable with $[d,f]$ or $\sim [d,f]$ concerning $\leq$. (Proof is omitted)

Definition 11 A trapezoid truth value is a set of four numerical truth values a,b,c,d such as $a \leq b \leq c \leq d$, which is written as $[a,b,c,d]$. The set of all trapezoid truth values is written by T_P, that is, $T_P = \{[a,b,c,d] : a \leq b \leq c \leq d$, where $a,b,c,d \in [0,1]\}$.(See B in Fig.9)

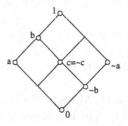

Fig. 9. Examples of triangular and trapezoid truth values

Fig. 10. $2m$ numerical truth value

Definition 12 Logic operations on trapezoid truth values are defined as follows:
$$AND: [a,b,c,d] \cdot [e,f,g,h] = [min(a,e), min(b,f), min(c,g), min(d,h)]$$
$$= [a \cdot e, b \cdot f, c \cdot g, d \cdot h],$$
$$OR: \quad [a,b,c,d] \vee [e,f,g,h] = [max(a,e), max(b,f), max(c,g), max(d,h)]$$
$$= [a \vee e, b \vee f, c \vee g, d \vee h],$$
$$NOT: \quad \sim [a,b,c,d] \quad = [1-d, 1-c, 1-b, 1-a] = [\sim d, \sim c, \sim b, \sim a],$$
where $[a,b,c,d], [e,f,g,h] \in T_P$.

Proposition 7 The set of all trapezoid truth values T_P with logic operations $\cdot, \vee, \sim$ satisfies De Morgan algebra. (Proof is omitted)

Proposition 8 Let X be a subset of T_P which is closed under the logic operations $\cdot, \vee$, and $\sim$. Then, X is Kleene algebra if and only if for any

$x = [a, b, c, d], y = [e, f, g, h]$ in X, $[a, d]$ is comparable with $[e, h]$ or $\sim [e, h]$, and $[b, c]$ is comparable with $[f, g]$ or $\sim [f, g]$ concerning $\leq$. (Proof is omitted)

Evidently, an interval truth value is a special case of a trapezoid truth value in which the first and second values are coincident and the third and fourth values are coincident. Also a triangular truth value is a special case of a trapezoid truth value in which the second value is coincident to the third truth value. We can generalize the trapezoid truth values into $2m$ dimensional case as follows.

Definition 13 Let $t_1, t_2, \cdots, t_m$ be values of $[0,1]$ such as $t_1 = 0 < t_2 < \cdots < t_m = 1$, and $a_1, a_2, \cdots, a_n$ be values of $[0,1]$ such as $a_1 \leq a_2 \leq \cdots \leq a_{n-1} \leq a_n$, where $n = 2m$. Then $A = [a_1, a_2, \cdots, a_{n-1}, a_n]$ is a $2m$ numerical truth value in which the value of the membership function is t_i at two points a_i and a_{n-i+1} ($i = 1, \cdots, n/2$) (see Fig.10). When $t_1 = 0 < t_2 < \cdots < t_m = 1$ are fixed, then the set of all $2m$ numerical truth values is written by T_{2m}, that is, $T_{2m} = \{[a_1, a_2, \cdots, a_{n-1}, a_n] : a_1 \leq a_2 \leq \cdots \leq a_{n-1} \leq a_n$, where $a_1, a_2, \cdots, a_{n-1}, a_n \in [0,1]\}$.

In a $2m$ numerical truth value the membership value ti corresponds to an interval $[a_i, a_{n-i+1}]$ for $i = 1, \cdots, n/2$. Hereafter we write a $2m$-interval truth value $[a_1, a_2, \cdots, a_{n-1}, a_n]$ as $[a_i : i = 1, \cdots, n]$ in some case.

Definition 14 Logic operations on $2m$ numerical truth values are defined as follows:

$$AND : \quad [a_i : i = 1, \cdots, n] \cdot [b_i : i = 1, \cdots, n] = [min(a_i, b_i) : i = 1, \cdots, n]$$
$$= [a_i \cdot b_i : i = 1, \cdots, n],$$
$$OR : \quad [a_i : i = 1, \cdots, n] \vee [b_i : i = 1, \cdots, n] = [max(a_i, b_i) : i = 1, \cdots, n]$$
$$= [a_i \vee b_i : i = 1, \cdots, n],$$
$$NOT : \quad \sim [a_1, a_2, \cdots, a_{n-1}, a_n] = [1 - a_n, \cdots, 1 - a_1]$$
$$= [\sim a_{n-i+1} : i = 1, \cdots, n],$$

where $[a_i : i = 1, \cdots, n]$, $[b_i : i = 1, \cdots, n] \in T_{2m}$.

Proposition 7 The set of all $2m$ numerical truth values T_{2m} with logic operations $\cdot, \vee, \sim$ satisfies De Morgan algebra. (Proof is omitted)

Proposition 8 Let X be a subset of T_{2m} which is closed under the logic operations $\cdot, \vee,$ and $\sim$. Then, X is Kleene algebra if and only if for any $A = [a_i : i = 1, \cdots, n]$, $B = [b_i : i = 1, \cdots, n]$ in X, $[a_i, a_{n-i+1}]$ is comparable with $[b_i, b_{n-i+1}]$ or $\sim [b_i, b_{n-i+1}]$ concerning $\leq$ for all $i = 1, \cdots, n/2$. (Proof is omitted)

In Definition 14 of $2m$ numerical truth values it is possible that $a_m = a_{m+1}$, that is, the middle interval $[a_m, a_{m+1}]$ reduces to a numerical value. A trapezoid truth value is a special case of a $2m$ numerical truth value putting $m = 2$, where $t_1 = 0$ and $t_2 = 1$, where if $a_2 = a_3$ then it is a triangular truth value.

If we extend the truth values in this direction in fuzzy logic, finally the truth values become fuzzy truth values, where a fuzzy truth value is a fuzzy set on the closed interval $V = [0,1]$. Linguistic truth values such as "true", "false", "very true", "more or less true" etc., which were defined firstly by L. A. Zadeh[5], are typical examples of fuzzy truth values. For fuzzy truth values, three logic operations OR($\vee$), AND($\cdot$) and NOT($\sim$) are defined by using the extension principle. But unfortunately, in general, the set of all fuzzy truth values does not satisfy the absorption laws and the distributive laws. The conditions for fuzzy truth values to satisfy the axioms of Kleene algebra and De Morgan algebra were explained in [7] ∼ [8].

6 Extended interval truth value

Here, we can extend an interval truth value to the direction of removing the condition $a \leq b$ from Definition 5, that is, an extended interval truth value is $[a, b]$, where a and b are any elements of $[0,1]$. In this section we briefly introduce the concepts of the extended interval truth values. An extended interval truth value $A = [a, b]$ is a point of two-dimensional space $[0, 1] \times [0, 1]$ and represented in a point of a lozenge as shown in Fig.12. Let E_I is a set of all extended interval truth values, that is, $E_I = \{[a, b] : a, b \in [0, 1]\}$. We can find many interpretations on a truth value $[a, b]$ of this extended interval logic. For example, we can interpret that a is a degree of affirmative assertion for a given statement and $c = (1 - b)$ is a degree of negative assertion for the same statement. That is, the degree of truth a and the degree of false c for a statement are given independently. In this extended interval logic, we can treat degrees of ambiguity $(b - a)$ and contradiction $(a - b)$ as well as degrees of truth a and false $c = (1 - b)$. Hereafter in this section an interval truth value means an extended interval truth value. We can define another operations AND ∩, OR ∪ and NOT ¬ concerning $\leq\leq$. Let us consider two interval truth values $A = [a, b]$ and $B = [a', b']$ in Fig.12. Then, $A \cap B = [a \vee a', b \cdot b']$, $A \cup B = [a \cdot a', b \vee b']$ and $\neg A = [b, a]$ in Fig.12. If a degree of negative assertion is determined uniquely from the degree of affirmative assertion through NOT operation (1-), then $b = a$ holds and this interval truth value becomes a numerical truth value. Extreme four truth values $0 = [0, 0]$, $1 = [1, 1]$, $U = [0, 1]$ and $C = [1, 0]$ of the interval logic can be considered to be false, true, unknown and contradiction, respectively. It is easily shown that the algebraic systems $\langle E_I, \cap, \cup, \neg \rangle$ and $\langle E_I, \cdot, \vee, \sim \rangle$ are models of De Morgan algebra, respectively. In E_I, we can define following three kind of negations (see Fig.13). For example letting $A = [a, b]$, $\sim A = [\sim b, \sim a]$, $\neg A = [b, a]$, $*A = [\sim a, \sim b]$, where $* = \sim \neg = \neg \sim$.

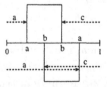

Fig. 11. An extended interval truth value $[a, b]$

Here the algebraic system $\langle E_I, \cap, \cup, * \rangle$, which is isomorphic to $\langle E_I, \cdot, \vee, * \rangle$, is isomorphic to the direct product $V \times V$ of two Kleene algebras of numerical truth values $V = \langle [0, 1], \cdot, \vee, \sim \rangle$. Therefore, algebraic systems $\langle E_I, \cap, \cup, * \rangle$ and $\langle E_I, \cdot, \vee, * \rangle$ are models of Kleene algebra, respectively. If we consider a new algebraic systems $\langle E_I, \cdot, \vee, \sim, \cap, \cup, \neg \rangle$, then we can find out interesting properties in this systems, which is a typical example of bi-lattice[9]. For the properties of this new algebra, you can see in [6].

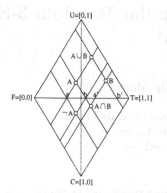

Fig. 12. Operations concerning $\leq\leq$ **Fig. 13.** 3 kinds of negations

7 Conclusion

In this paper introduced are two kinds of truth values extended from numerical truth values of $[0,1]$ in fuzzy logic. One is restricted $2m$-dimensional truth values $\{[a_1,\cdots,a_n] : 0 \leq a_1 \leq \cdots \leq a_n \leq 1\}$, where triangle and trapezoid truth values are examples of this truth values. The other is two-dimensional truth values $\{[a,b] : a,b \in [0,1]\}$, in which we can treat the degrees of truth, false, contradiction and ambiguity. Linguistic truth values such as "true", "false", very true", "more or less true", etc. firstly introduced by Zadeh are very interesting idea. These linguistic truth values are fuzzy set on $[0,1]$. We can consider any fuzzy set on $[0,1]$ as a truth value, which are called a fuzzy truth value. The truth values described in this paper are truth values between numerical truth values and fuzzy truth values. Further work will be done to clarify the properties of fuzzy truth values.

References

1. Zadeh, L. A.: Fuzzy Sets, Inf. and Control, 8, pp.304-311, 1965
2. Mukaidono, M.: On some properties of fuzzy logic, Systems Computers Controls, Vol.6, No.2, pp.36–43, 1975
3. Mukaidono, M.: A set of independent and complete axioms for a fuzzy algebra (Kleene algebra), Proceedings of the 11th International Symposium on Multiple-Valued Logic, IEEE, pp.27–34, 1981
4. Mukaidono, M.: Algebraic structures of fuzzy interval truth values, Proceedings of FUZZ-IEEE'97, Vol.II, pp.699–705, 1997
5. Zadeh, L.A.: The concept of a linguistic variable and its application to approximate reasoning (I),(II),(III), Inf. and Science, 8, pp.199-249; 8,pp.301-359;9,pp.43-80(1975)
6. Mukaidono, M. and H.Kikuchi: A Proposal on Fuzzy Interval Logic, Journal of Japan Society for Fuzzy Theory and Systems, vol.2, No.2, 1990, pp.97-11
7. Mukaidono, M.: Algebraic Structures of Truth Values in Fuzzy Logic, Fuzzy Logic and Fuzzy Control, Lecture Notes in Artificial Intelligence 833, Springer-Verlog, pp.15–21, 1994
8. Mukaidono, M.: Kleene algebras in fuzzy truth values, Proceedings of International Workshop on Rough Sets, Fuzzy Sets, and Machine Discovery, pp.37-43,1996
9. Ginsberg, M. L.: Multi-valued logics: a uniform approach to reasoning in artificial intelligence, Computational Intelligence, Vol.4, pp.265-319, 1988

Phase Transitions in the Regular Random 3-SAT Problem*

Ramón Béjar and Felip Manyà

Departament d'Informàtica, Universitat de Lleida
Jaume II 69, E-25001 Lleida, Spain
{ramon,felip}@eup.udl.es

Abstract In this paper we investigate phase transitions in the random 3-SAT problem but we move from the usual setting of classical logic to the more general setting of multiple-valued logics. We deal with regular CNF formulas and use a generalized Davis-Putnam (DP) procedure for testing their satisfiability. We establish the location of the threshold for different cardinalities of the truth value set and show experimentally that the location of the threshold increases logarithmically in the cardinality of the truth value set. We also provide a theoretical explanation of this fact. The DP procedure and the classical random 3-SAT problem appear to be a particular case of our approach.

Keywords: Multiple-valued logics, regular CNF formulas, satisfiability, phase transitions, threshold, benchmarks.

1 Introduction

Phase transitions occur in the classical propositional satisfiability problem (or SAT), as well as in other NP-hard problems [1]. Mitchell et al. [9] reported results from experiments on testing the satisfiability of classical random 3-SAT instances with the Davis-Putnam (DP) procedure [2]. They observed that (i) there is a sharp phase transition from satisfiable to unsatisfiable instances for a value of the ratio of the number of clauses to the number of variables. At lower ratios, most of the instances are under-constrained and are thus satisfiable. At higher ratios, most of the instances are over-constrained and are thus unsatisfiable. The value of that ratio where 50% of the instances are satisfiable is referred to as the threshold; and (ii) there is an easy-hard-easy pattern in the computational difficulty of solving problem instances as that ratio is varied; the hard instances occur in the area near the threshold. Nowadays, there is strong experimental evidence that the value of the threshold is around 4.25, but there are no analytical results. Only lower and upper bounds on the location of the threshold are known [7].

---

* Research partially supported by the project CICYT TIC96-1038-C04-03 and "La Paeria". The first author was supported by a doctoral fellowship of the CUR (Comissionat per a Universitat i Recerca) (1998FI00326). This work was done while the second author was at the Institute for Logic, Complexity and Deduction Systems of the University of Karlsruhe with a CUR postdoctoral fellowship (1997BEAI400138).

In this paper we investigate phase transitions in random 3-SAT but we move from the usual setting of classical logic to the more general setting of multiple-valued logics. We deal with regular CNF formulas and use a generalized DP procedure for testing their satisfiability. We establish the location of the threshold for different cardinalities of the truth value set and show experimentally that the location of the threshold increases logarithmically in the cardinality of the truth value set. We also provide a theoretical explanation of this fact. The DP procedure and classical random 3-SAT appear to be a particular case of our approach.

Regular CNF formulas are a relevant subclass of signed CNF formulas (cf. Section 2). It turns out that any finitely-valued formula can be transformed into a satisfiability equivalent signed CNF formula in polynomial time [4]. Interestingly, Hähnle [3] identified a broad class of finitely-valued logics, so-called regular logics, and showed in [4] that any formula of a regular logic can be transformed into a satisfiability equivalent regular CNF formula whose length is linear in both the length of the transformed formula and the cardinality of the truth value set. Recently, he has found a method for translating a signed CNF formula into a satisfiability equivalent regular CNF formula where the length of the latter is polynomial in the length of the former [6]. Thus, a SAT problem in any finitely-valued logic is polynomially reducible to a SAT problem in regular CNF formulas.

A generalized DP procedure (hereafter called Regular-DP) for testing the satisfiability of regular CNF formulas was described in [5]. In [8] we equipped Regular-DP with suitable data structures and showed experimentally that phase transitions occur when we run Regular-DP on regular random 3-SAT instances. There, we only considered truth values sets with cardinality 3, 4 and 5. The thresholds we obtained for such cardinalities were 5.92, 7.08 and 7.75, respectively. In view of these results, one could be tempted to conjecture that the location of the threshold increases linearly in the cardinality of the truth value set. However, in this paper we provide experimental evidence that such an increase is logarithmic. In addition, we give a theoretical explanation of this fact by providing upper bounds on the location of the unsatisfiability threshold.

Our original interest in this problem was motivated by the search for challenging benchmarks for the evaluation of satisfiability solvers for multiple-valued logics. The experimental results we report here suggest that it makes sense to test candidate algorithms on instances near the threshold. Moreover, the generator of random instances we have implemented is able to provide a large number of such hard instances easily. We believe that it is the first suitable test-bed to evaluate and compare satisfiability solvers that has been described for signed CNF formulas.

This paper is organized as follows. In Section 2 we define formally the logic of signed and regular CNF formulas; in Section 3 we describe Regular-DP; in Section 4 we present our experimental results; and in Section 5 we derive upper bounds on the location of the unsatisfiability threshold. We finish the paper with some concluding remarks.

2 Signed CNF formulas

Definition 1. truth value set *A truth value set N is a finite set $\{i_1, i_2, \ldots, i_n\}$, where $n \in \mathbb{N}$. The cardinality of N is denoted by $|N|$.*

Definition 2. signed CNF formula *Let S be a subset of N ($S \subseteq N$) and let p be a propositional variable. An expression of the form $S : p$ is a signed literal and S is its sign. A signed literal $S : p$ subsumes a signed literal $S' : p'$, denoted by $S : p \subseteq S' : p'$, iff $p = p'$ and $S \subseteq S'$. The signed literal $\overline{L} = (N \setminus S) : p$ denotes the complement of the signed literal $S : p$. A signed clause is a finite set of signed literals. A signed CNF formula is a finite set of signed clauses.*

Definition 3. length *The length of a signed clause C, denoted by $|C|$, is the total number of occurrences of signed literals in C. The length of a signed CNF formula Γ, denoted by $|\Gamma|$, is the sum of the lengths of its signed clauses.*

Definition 4. satisfiability *An interpretation is a mapping that assigns to every propositional variable an element of the truth value set. An interpretation I satisfies a signed literal $S : p$ iff $I(p) \in S$. An interpretation satisfies a signed clause iff it satisfies at least one of its signed literals. A signed CNF formula Γ is satisfiable iff there exists at least one interpretation that satisfies all the signed clauses in Γ. A signed CNF formula that is not satisfiable is unsatisfiable. The signed empty clause is always unsatisfiable and the signed empty CNF formula is always satisfiable.*

Definition 5. regular sign *Let $\boxed{\geq i}$ denote the set $\{j \in N \mid j \geq i\}$ and let $\boxed{\leq i}$ denote the set $\{j \in N \mid j \leq i\}$, where $\leq$ is a total order on the truth value set N and $i \in N$. If a sign S is equal to either $\boxed{\geq i}$ or $\boxed{\leq i}$, for some i, then it is a regular sign and i is its value.*

Definition 6. regular CNF formula *Let S be a regular sign and let p be a propositional variable. An expression of the form $S : p$ is a regular literal. If S is of the form $\boxed{\geq i}$ ($\boxed{\leq i}$), then we say that $S : p$ has positive (negative) polarity. A regular clause is a finite set of regular literals. A regular clause containing exactly one literal is a regular unit clause. A regular CNF formula is a finite set of regular clauses.*

3 The Regular-DP procedure

Regular-DP relies on the following regular versions of the branching rule and the one-literal rule:

Regular branching rule: Reduce the problem of determining whether a regular CNF formula Γ is satisfiable to the problem of determining whether $\Gamma \cup \{S : p\}$ is satisfiable or $\Gamma \cup \{(N \setminus S) : p\}$ is satisfiable, where $S : p$ is a regular literal occurring in Γ.

Regular one-literal rule: Given a regular CNF formula Γ that contains a regular unit clause $\{S\!:\!p\}$,

1. remove all clauses containing a literal $S'\!:\!p$ such that $S \subseteq S'$;
2. delete all occurrences of literals $S''\!:\!p$ such that $S \cap S'' = \emptyset$.

The pseudo-code of Regular-DP is shown in Figure 1. Regular-DP returns true if the input regular CNF formula Γ is satisfiable and returns false if Γ is unsatisfiable. Function regular-unit-resolve applies repeatedly the regular one-literal rule. Function pick-literal selects the next literal to which the regular branching rule is applied. In our implementation of Regular-DP, the heuristic used by pick-literal is a regular version of the two-sided Jeroslow-Wang rule defined in [5].

```
function Regular-DP (Γ: set of clause): boolean
var L: literal
begin
    Γ := regular-unit-resolve(Γ);
    if Γ = ∅ then return(true);
    if □ ∈ Γ then return(false);
    L := pick-literal(Γ);
    if Regular-DP (Γ ∪ {L}) then
        return(true)
    else
        return(Regular-DP (Γ ∪ {L̄}))
    endif
end


function regular-unit-resolve (Γ: set of clause): set of clause
var L: literal
var C: clause
begin
    while ∃{L} ∈ Γ and □ ∉ Γ do
        Γ := {C| ∄L' ∈ C ∈ Γ such that L ⊆ L'};
        Γ := {C − {L'|L' ∈ C and L' ⊆ L̄}|C ∈ Γ}
    endwhile;
    return(Γ)
end
```

Figure1. Pseudo-code of Regular-DP

Example 1. Let $N = \{0, \frac{1}{3}, \frac{2}{3}, 1\}$ and let Γ be the following regular CNF formula:

$$\{\{\boxed{\leq 0}:p_1, \boxed{\geq 1}:p_3, \boxed{\geq 1}:p_4\}, \{\boxed{\geq 1}:p_3, \boxed{\leq \frac{1}{3}}:p_4\}, \{\boxed{\leq 0}:p_1, \boxed{\leq \frac{1}{3}}:p_3, \boxed{\leq \frac{1}{3}}:p_4\},$$

$$\{\boxed{\geq 1}:p_1, \boxed{\leq 0}:p_5\}, \{\boxed{\geq \frac{2}{3}}:p_1, \boxed{\geq \frac{1}{3}}:p_5\}, \{\boxed{\leq \frac{1}{3}}:p_1, \boxed{\leq \frac{1}{3}}:p_3, \boxed{\geq 1}:p_4\}\}$$

Figure 2 shows the proof tree created by Regular-DP when the input formula is Γ. The root node contains Γ and the remaining nodes contain the formula obtained after applying regular-unit-resolve to the formula selected for doing branching. A node can represent several applications of the regular one-literal rule because new unit clauses can be derived during the application of this rule.

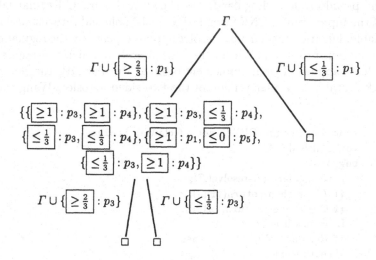

Figure2. A Regular-DP proof tree

4 Experimental results

The aim of this section is to describe, on an experimental basis, how increases the location of the threshold in regular random 3-SAT as the cardinality of the truth value set increases. To this end, we designed a series of experiments and observed that the increase is logarithmic in the cardinality of the truth value set. After describing the generator of regular random 3-SAT instances used, we report the experimental results obtained. Regular-DP was implemented in C++ and the experiments were performed on Sun Ultra-1 workstations.

4.1 Generator of regular random 3-SAT instances

The generator of regular random instances we implemented has as parameters the number of clauses (C), the number of propositional variables (V), and the cardinality of the truth value set ($|N|$). Given C and V, an instance of regular random 3-SAT is produced by generating C regular clauses of length three which are not tautologies. Each regular clause is produced by uniformly choosing three literals with different propositional variable from the set of regular literals of the form $\boxed{\leq i} : p$ or $\boxed{\geq j} : p$, where p is a propositional variable, $i \in N \setminus \{\top\}$, $j \in N \setminus \{\bot\}$, and $\top$ and $\bot$ denote the top and bottom elements of N. Observe that regular literals of the form $\boxed{\leq \top} : p$ or $\boxed{\geq \bot} : p$ are tautological.

4.2   Experiments

We applied Regular-DP to 60-variable $|N|$-valued random 3-SAT instances for $|N| = 2$–$20, 25, 30, 35, 40, 45, 50, 60, 70$. For each $|N|$, we varied the ratio of the number of clauses to the number of variables from 1 to 12 for $|N| < 7$ and from 5 to 16 for $|N| \geq 7$, incrementing the number of clauses by 5. At each setting we ran the algorithm on 300 randomly generated instances. Therefore, the number of instances executed for each $|N|$ was $39,900$ and the total number of instances executed was $1,077,300$. The thresholds obtained are shown in Table 1.

$|N|$	2	3	4	5	6	7	8	9	10	11	12	13	14	15
Threshold	4.25	6.08	7.08	7.75	8.16	8.41	8.75	8.83	9.08	9.16	9.33	9.33	9.41	9.50

$|N|$	16	17	18	19	20	25	30	35	40	45	50	60	70
Threshold	9.58	9.66	9.75	9.75	9.75	10.0	10.16	10.25	10.33	10.41	10.41	10.50	10.50

Table1. Location of the threshold for different cardinalities of N

The data indicates that the location of the threshold increases logarithmically in the cardinality of the truth value set $|N|$ as the following equation states:

$$L(|N|) = 6.30544 \ln^{0.391434}(|N|)$$

This equation was derived from the experimental thresholds by using the Levenberg-Marquardt method for obtaining a non-linear regression model implemented in the symbolic calculator Mathematica. In the remaining of this section we provide more details about our experimental results by means of figures:

Figure 3 visualizes the phase transition phenomenon in regular random 3-SAT. It shows the average number of nodes in the proof tree created by Regular-DP when $|N| = 7$. Along the horizontal axis is the ratio of the number of clauses to the number of variables in the regular 3-SAT instances tested. One can observe clearly the easy-hard-easy pattern in the computational difficulty of solving instances as that ratio is varied. The dashed line indicates the percentage of instances that were found to be satisfiable scaled in such a way that 100% corresponds to the maximum average number of nodes.

Figure 4 visualizes how increases the location of the threshold as the cardinality of the truth value set increases. It shows the average number of nodes in the proof tree created by Regular-DP when $|N| = 3$, $|N| = 4$ and $|N| = 5$. Along the horizontal axis is the ratio of the number of clauses to the number of variables in the regular random 3-SAT instances tested. Figure 5 is like Figure 4 but for $|N| = 9$, $|N| = 11$, $|N| = 13$ and $|N| = 15$. One can observe in both figures that the average number of nodes in the proof tree increases in the area near the threshold as the cardinality of the truth value set increases.

Figure 6 displays the percentage of satisfiable instances as a function of the ratio of the number clauses to the number of variables for some of the cardinalities considered in our experiments. Figure 7 shows the location of the threshold

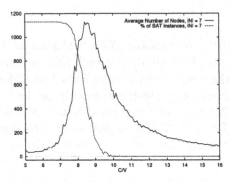

Figure3. Regular random 3-SAT, $|N| = 7$, $V = 60$

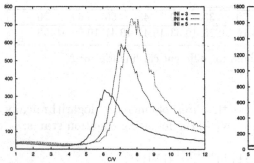

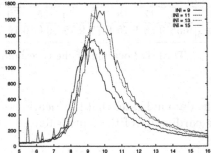

Figure4. Regular random 3-SAT, $|N| = 3, 4, 5$, $V = 60$

Figure5. Regular random 3-SAT, $|N| = 9, 11, 13, 15$, $V = 60$

as a function of $|N|$. The experimental thresholds obtained and the equation derived with Mathematica are both plotted in the graph. One can observe in both figures that the increase of the location of the threshold is not linear.

Remark: Since we had to run Regular-DP on a very large sample of regular random 3-SAT instances, we considered instances with 60 variables in order to get experimental results in a reasonable amount of time. More propositional variables occur in an instance in the area near the threshold, more time is needed to determine whether it is satisfiable.

5 Upper bounds on the unsatisfiability threshold

Let Γ be a regular random 3-SAT instance, let V be the number of propositional variables in Γ, let C be the number of regular clauses in Γ, and let $r = C/V$ be the ratio of the number of clauses to the number of variables in Γ. The problem we consider is to compute the least real number k such that if r strictly exceeds k, then the probability that Γ is satisfiable converges to 0 as V approaches infinity. We say in this case that Γ is asymptotically almost certainly unsatisfiable. A proposition stating that if r exceeds a certain constant, then Γ is asymptotically almost certainly unsatisfiable has as an immediate corollary that this constant

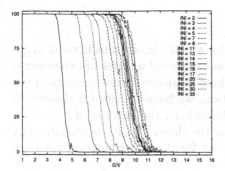
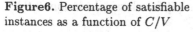
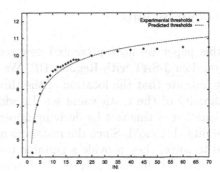

Figure6. Percentage of satisfiable instances as a function of C/V

Figure7. Location of the threshold as a function of $|N|$

is an upper bound for k. In this section we obtain upper bounds on the unsatisfiability threshold as a function of the cardinality of the truth value set. This give us a theoretical justification of our experimental results.

We consider the following model of regular random 3-SAT instances: from the sample space of non-tautological regular clauses of length three over V propositional variables and $|N|$ truth values, uniformly, independently, and with replacement select C clauses to form a regular CNF formula Γ. Given an interpretation I, the probability that I satisfies a regular random literal L is $\frac{1}{2}$; observe that the number of regular literals with positive polarity satisfied by an interpretation coincides with the number of regular literals with negative polarity that are not satisfied and vice versa. The probability that I satisfies a regular random clause (with three literals) is $1 - \left(\frac{1}{2}\right)^3 = \frac{7}{8}$. The probability that I satisfies a regular random 3-SAT instance Γ with C clauses is $\left(\frac{7}{8}\right)^C$. Since there are $|N|^V$ possible interpretations for Γ, the expected number of interpretations that satisfy Γ is

$$E[|\{I \mid I \text{ satisfies } \Gamma\}|] = |N|^V \left(\frac{7}{8}\right)^C$$

Since the expected number of interpretations that satisfy Γ is an upper bound on the probability that Γ is satisfiable, it holds that

$$Pr[\Gamma \text{ is satisfiable}] \leq E[|\{I \mid I \text{ satisfies } \Gamma\}|] = |N|^V \left(\frac{7}{8}\right)^C;$$

letting $C = rV$, an upper bound for k is found by choosing r so that the expected number of interpretations that satisfy Γ converges to 0 as V approaches infinity. Thus, if $r > \log_{\frac{8}{7}} |N|$, then Γ is almost certainly unsatisfiable.

Therefore, if an upper bound on the unsatisfiability threshold increases logarithmically in the cardinality of the truth value set, the location of the threshold cannot increase quicker than the upper bound does. For that reason, we should get experimental thresholds increasing logarithmically or less than logarithmically in the cardinality of the truth value set.

6 Conclusions

In this paper we have presented new results about phase transitions in regular random 3-SAT with Regular-DP. We have reported a series of experiments that indicate that the location of the threshold increases logarithmically in the cardinality of the truth value set. In addition, we have provided a theoretical explanation of this fact by deriving upper bounds on the location of the unsatisfiability threshold. Since the instances near the threshold are computationally hard to solve, thcy provide a suilable test-bed for the experimental evaluation of regular satisfiability solvers. As future work we plan to improve the upper bounds derived by applying the method used in [7] for classical random 3-SAT.

References

1. P. Cheeseman, B. Kanefsky, and W. M. Taylor. Where the really hard problems are. In *Proceedings of the International Joint Conference on Artificial Intelligence, IJCAI'91*, pages 331–337, 1991.
2. M. Davis, G. Logemann, and D. Loveland. A machine program for theorem-proving. *Communications of the ACM*, 5:394–397, 1962.
3. R. Hähnle. Uniform notation of tableaux rules for multiple-valued logics. In *Proc. International Symposium on Multiple-Valued Logic, Victoria*, pages 238–245. IEEE Press, 1991.
4. R. Hähnle. Short conjunctive normal forms in finitely-valued logics. *Journal of Logic and Computation*, 4(6):905–927, 1994.
5. R. Hähnle. Exploiting data dependencies in many-valued logics. *Journal of Applied Non-Classical Logics*, 6:49–69, 1996.
6. R. Hähnle. Personal communication, 1998.
7. L. M. Kirousis, E. Kranakis, and D. Krizanc. Aproximating the unsatisfiability threshold of random formulas. In *Proc. 4th Annual European Symposium on Algorithms, ESA'96*, pages 27–38, 1996.
8. F. Manyà, R. Béjar, and G. Escalada-Imaz. The satisfiability problem in regular CNF-formulas. *Soft Computing: A Fusion of Foundations, Methodologies and Applications*, 2(3):116–123, 1998.
9. D. Mitchell, B. Selman, and H. Levesque. Hard and easy distributions of SAT problems. In *Proceedings of the 10th National Conference on Artificial Intelligence AAAI'92, San Jose, CA, USA*, pages 459–465, 1992.

Improving Backtrack Search for SAT
by Means of Redundancy

Laure Brisoux, Éric Grégoire, and Lakhdar Saïs

CRIL – Université d'Artois
rue de l'Université SP16
F-62037 Lens Cedex,
France.
{brisoux, gregoire, sais}@cril.univ-artois.fr

Abstract. In this paper, a new heuristic that can be grafted to many of
the most efficient branching strategies for Davis and Putnam procedures
for SAT is described. This heuristic gives a higher weight to clauses that
have been shown unsatisfiable at some previous steps of the search process. It is shown efficient for many classes of SAT instances, in particular
structured ones.

1 Introduction

For many years, the problem of propositional satisfiability (SAT) has received
little attention in spite of the fact that it is recognized as a central issue in many
areas of artificial intelligence and other computer science domains. Recently,
there has been a surge in interest in designing new computational techniques
to address it. On the one hand, very simple stochastic search techniques have
proved efficient in solving large and hard consistent SAT problems (see e.g. [26,
25] [1] [21]). On the other hand, several people have tried to improve the best
logically complete techniques for SAT. Currently, the most efficient logically
complete techniques are still based on the classical Davis and Putnam procedure
[10]. In this paper we refer to the Davis-Logemman-Loveland procedure [9] (in
short DPLL). Some new efficient versions of DPLL have been proposed recently,
extending its practical scope to a really significant extent. Among them, let us
simply mention some of the most efficient ones, namely C-SAT [3] [12], Tableau
[8], POSIT [15], Satz [19], Relsat [2], GRASP [20] and DP+TSAT [22, 23]. Their
efficiency is based on several principal ingredients. First, a smart use of data
structures and programming skills can pay a lot with respect to this particular
problem. Some adequate local treatment before and during the search can allow
for better results for many classes of problems, in particular in detecting local
inconsistencies. Last but not least, the quality of the branching strategy appears
to be the key factor for good performance results. In this paper, it is shown that
this strategy can advantageously include a new heuristic, that gives a higher
weight to clauses that appeared unsatisfiable at some previous steps of the search
process.

Such an heuristic avoids the extra-space and computation required by techniques that use additional ingredients to avoid repetitive search (e.g. adding clauses when unsatisfiability is reached at some level of the search tree [20, 2, 16]).

The paper is organized as follows. First, the addressed formal framework is briefly recalled and DPLL with its main computational features are reviewed. Then this new heuristic is motivated and presented. Experimental results on various standard benchmarks are given to illustrate its efficiency[1]. Finally, the limits and the possible extensions of the approach, together with promising further possible paths of research are discussed.

2 Backtrack Search SAT Algorithms

Let us first recall the formal framework under consideration. SAT consists in checking the satisfiability of a boolean formula in conjunctive normal form (CNF). A CNF formula is a set (interpreted as a conjunction) of clauses, where a clause is a disjunction of literals. A literal is a positive or negated propositional variable.

An interpretation of a boolean formula is an assignment of truth values to its variables. A model is an interpretation that satisfies the formula. Accordingly, SAT consists in finding a model of a CNF formula when such a model does exist or in proving that such a model does not exist. SAT is an NP-complete problem meaning that all algorithms to solve it should be exponential in the worst cases, unless $P = NP$ [6].

However, not all SAT instances do exhibit the same difficulty, with respect to usual algorithms to solve it. Theoretical and experimental results even show good average-case performance for several classes of SAT instances (see e.g. [14]). In the following, we shall refer to a variety of benchmarks for SAT [11][2] and hard random 3-SAT instances, i.e. instances from a random generation model where the number of literals per clause is 3, the sign of each literal is randomly generated (with a probability 0.5) and the ratio of variables to clauses is 4.25 ([27], [8], [4] and [13]). Those last problems prove exponential for resolution [5].

Recently, very simple stochastic search techniques have proved efficient in solving large and hard consistent SAT problems, in particular the above mentioned hard random 3-SAT consistent instances (see e.g. [26, 25] [1] [21] [18]). However, such techniques are logically incomplete since they do not cover the whole search space. Accordingly, they cannot be used as such to prove the inconsistency of SAT instances (see however [22]). Actually, the most efficient logically complete techniques are still based on the classical DPLL procedure (see Fig. 1) [9, 10].

Some new efficient versions of DPLL have been proposed recently, extending its practical scope to a really significant extent. Among them, let us simply

---

[1] Our system is available from http://www.lifl.fr/~brisoux
[2] These benchmarks are available from http://dimacs.rutgers.edu/Challenges/index.html.

```
Procedure DPLL(S)
   Input:  a set S of clauses
   Output: a satisfying truth assignment of S if found,
           or a definitive statement that S is inconsistent.
   begin
      Propagation of unit and monotone literals;
      if the empty clause is generated then return (false)
      else if all variables are assigned then return (true)
           else begin
                p := some unassigned literal selected by a branching rule;
                return ( DPLL(S ∧ p) ∨ DPLL(S ∧ ¬p) );
                end;
end.
```

Fig. 1. DPLL procedure

mention the most efficient ones, namely C-SAT [3] [12], Tableau [8], POSIT [15], Satz [19], Relsat [2], GRASP [20] and DP+TSAT [22, 23]. One of the key features for efficiency in the DPLL procedure lies in its branching rule strategy. Accordingly, many branching rules have been proposed in the literature. Let us review the most efficient of them.

It is widely accepted that literals occurring in the shortest clauses should be preferred to some extent. Actually, for each unassigned literal l, a score $f(l)$ is defined as follows. First, a weight is assigned to each clause translating the above idea. Several measures for this weight have been proposed. Mainly, [17] proposed 2^{-r}, where r is the length of the clause. On the other hand, empirical results led Dubois and Boufkhad to adopt $-\ln(1 - \frac{1}{(2^r - 1)^2})$ as the recommended weight, increasing the weight difference between clauses of various lengths. Let S be the set of clauses.

$$f(l) = \sum_{\forall c \in S \ s.t. \ l \in c} weight(c)$$

Then the final score of a variable x is given by

$$A(x) = f(x) + f(\neg x) + \alpha \times \min(f(x), f(\neg x)) \tag{1}$$

(where α is empirically set to 1.5 [3]).

Following close motivations, Freeman [15] proposed

$$A'(x) = f(x) + f(\neg x) + \alpha' \times f(x) \times f(\neg x) \tag{2}$$

(where α' is empirically set to 1024).

Let us note that the role of the $\alpha \times \min(f(x), f(\neg x))$ and $\alpha' \times f(x) \times f(\neg x)$ terms is to balance the search tree.

These $A(x)$ and $A'(x)$ functions that are be maximized, play the role of branching rules and prove very efficient. This family of branching rules includes many variants. Let us mention Rauzy's FFIS [24] (First Failed In Shortened clauses) and also variants that attempt to explore at a minimal cost the effect of further additional resolution steps [3] or to even more exploit the power of unit propagation [19].

3 A New Heuristic

DPLL is mainly devised in such way that it attempts to cover the whole search space, exhibiting a model or showing that any branch leads to unsatisfiability.

Accordingly, the intuition behind the heuristic that we shall propose is not covered by the above branching strategy. Intuitively, it is as follows.

Whenever some clauses have been shown unsatisfiable at some steps of the search process, this information should not be neglected in the remaining search process. On the contrary, in the development of the other branches of the search tree it could be efficient to try to encounter these situations of unsatisfiability again, everywhere and as soon as possible, modulo the other factors allowing an efficient branching rule to be obtained. This can be done by selecting with a higher priority the literals occurring in these clauses.

Interestingly enough, such an heuristic can be grafted to the above efficient branching strategies. Formally, it is translated through a numerical factor β_c that is introduced in the function f in the following way.

A new generic selection function f is thus given by

$$f(l) = \sum_{\forall c \in s \ s.t. \ l \in c} \beta_c \ weight(c)$$

where β_c is set to 1, initially.

Each time DPLL selects a propositional variable that would immediately lead to inconsistency, each initial clause c of the SAT instance that would be shown unsatisfiable at this step of the search tree has its factor β_c increased by a given value γ, and its importance is thus increased in the further search .

Let us stress that such a transformed evaluation function requires an extra computing cost that is negligible and does not require additional clauses to be recorded. The β_c weight expresses the degree of redundancy of a clause c. Intuitively, increasing the weight of clauses that have been previously shown unsatisfiable directs the search towards the probable inconsistent kernels.

In the following section, we give γ the best experimental value with respect to several classes of SAT instances.

4 Experimental Results

The efficiency of most DPLL procedures does not depend on the branching strategy only but also depends on the following other principal ingredients. First, a smart use of data structures and programming skills can pay a lot with respect to this particular problem. Efficient implementations often rely on a code that is

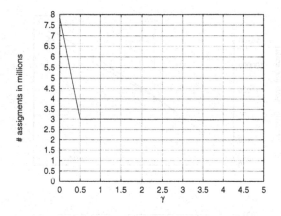

Fig. 2. Average number of assignments w.r.t. γ

often really intricate. Also, some adequate local treatment before and during the search can allow for better results for many classes of problems. In particular, it can allow us to detect inconsistencies that are local in the sense that they can be related to a small subset of clauses in the SAT instance. For instance, a call to a local search procedure can be inserted as a first step of DPLL (see [21], [7]). This step can provide us with a model or even allow for the further detection of inconsistencies that are local in the above sense. Also, a limited number of resolution steps at the root node can allow some of these inconsistencies to be detected. Accordingly, all these facets play a role in the efficiency of the satisfiability checking program.

As the heuristic described in this paper can be grafted to most branching strategies, we have experimented it with the basic one presented above, inside a straightforward implementation, allowing us to make abstraction of coding tricks. Accordingly, it should be clear that the experimental results in this paper are not expected to defeat the performance of the best SAT systems, but simply to illustrate the gain that most systems (including the best ones) could obtain, using this additional heuristic. Let us also stress that this heuristic does not intervene with local treatment at the root.

First, the heuristic has been experimented in the framework of hard random 3-SAT instances. In Figure 2, the average number of assignments obtained for various values of γ is given for 200 3-SAT instances at the threshold with 250 variables, using the standard Jeroslow and Wang 2^{-r} rule weight inside the score function $A(x) = f(x) + f(\neg x) + 1.5 \times \min(f(x), f(\neg x))$. A similar behaviour has been obtained for other 3-SAT hard instances using Boufkhad's weight rule and Freeman's score rule. A significant performance improvement is obtained when this new additional heuristic is used. Quite surprisingly, the gain does not increase in a significant way whenever γ is more than 0.5. We are currently investigating the theoretical explanation of this feature. Accordingly, we settled γ to 0.5. In Figure 3, average results for 3-SAT instances[3] (200 in-

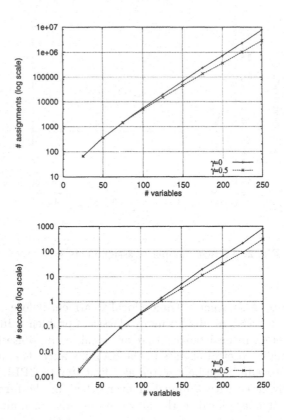

Fig. 3. Results for 3-SAT instances using the $A(x)$ branching rule (1)

stances with a variables/clauses ratio being 4.25) are illustrated; the effect of using the additional heuristic with γ set to 0.5 on the score function $A(x)$ integrating Jeroslow and Wang's weight rules and the instances as above is given. Similar figures are obtained for Freeman's score rule (2) using the same weight rule. In any case, a significant performance improvement is obtained using the heuristic. Then, this heuristic has been experimented in an extensive manner with respect to structured problems[4] , using the standard DIMACS benchmarks [11] and the Kautz and Selman's planning instances[5]. Some results are given in Table 1 and discussed below. We kept 0.5 as value for γ. Extensive results on DIMACS benchmarks are available from the authors[6].

Clearly enough, the empirical results confirm the intuition. Performance improvement is obtained with respect to most (consistent and inconsistent) problems classes. Such a result is even more important for many classes of structured

---

[3] These experimentations have been conducted on 133 Pentium PC's.
[4] These experimentations have been conducted on 166 Pentium PC's.
[5] available from `ftp://ftp.research.att.com/dist/ai`
[6] `http://www.lifl.fr/~brisoux`

Table 1. Some results for DIMACS instances: weight vs. no-weight results

Dimacs		Size		$A(x)$ branching rule (1)			
				$\gamma = 0$		$\gamma = 0.5$	
Instances	Sat.	# Var.	#Cla.	# assignments	seconds	# assignments	seconds
par16-1	Y.	1015	3310	3327186	73.85	898435	28.33
par16-4-c	Y.	324	1292	587249	23.76	282760	12.91
aim-100-2_0-no.1	N.	100	200	27056964	944.58	589	0.06
aim-200-1_6-no-2	N.	200	320	***	> 7200	1459555	211.91
hanoi4	Y.	718	4934	***	> 7200	35899827	3114.00
ssa2670-130	N.	1359	3321	***	> 7200	9023846	483.18
ssa2670-141	N.	986	2315	***	> 7200	16808521	594.90
bf1355-075	N.	2180	6778	***	> 7200	30124	5.36
bf1355-638	N.	2177	4768	***	> 7200	16737	3.48
f7hh.15	Y.	5315	140258	***	> 14400	442332	1073.40
f8h_10	N.	2459	25290	3562510	2159.16	172344	116.75
ii16e1	Y.	1245	14766	***	> 7200	77465	118.98
ii32d2	Y.	404	3153	20630465	5462.36	39993	12.16
2bitadd_12	Y.	708	1702	15508567	1363.66	1413216	109.71
e0ddr2_10by5	Y.	19500	103887	25681427	5498.15	905054	278.16
bw_large.d	Y.	6325	131973	***	> 172800	158265845	73829.20
logistics.d	Y.	2160	27242	***	> 172800	***	> 172800

Dimacs		Size		$A'(x)$ branching rule (2)			
				$\gamma = 0$		$\gamma = 0.5$	
Instances	Sat.	# Var.	# Cla.	# assignments	seconds	# assignments	seconds
par16-1	Y.	1015	33.6	3327186	74.81	757032	24.98
par16-4-c	Y.	324	1292	587249	23.30	250183	11.81
aim-100-2_0-no-1	N.	100	200	27703970	932.16	586	0.06
aim-200-1_6-no-2	N.	200	320	***	> 7200	1459555	112.98
hanoi4	Y.	718	4934	***	> 7200	43012777	3892.86
ssa2670-130	N.	1359	3321	***	> 7200	9023846	385.38
ssa2670-141	N.	986	2315	***	> 7200	16808521	628.26
bf1355-075	N.	2180	6778	***	> 7200	29129	5.00
bf1355-638	N.	2177	4768	***	> 7200	16706	3.55
f7hh.15	Y.	5315	140258	***	> 14400	***	> 14400
f8h_10	N.	2459	25290	3562510	2159.16	66625	41.60
ii16e1	Y.	1245	14766	1023	7.05	1023	7.05
ii32d2	Y.	404	3153	87651	23.18	5925	1.76
2bitadd_12	Y.	708	1702	***	> 7200	***	> 7200
e0ddr2_10by5	Y.	19500	103887	19987285	4311.01	1012918	318.45
bw_large.d	Y.	6325	131973	****	> 172800	118425586	59229.61
logistics.d	Y.	2160	27242	****	> 172800	11617271	18196.40

problems. Although our implementation of DPLL on a 166 Pentium is a straightforward one that does not use efficient coding tricks and extra features leading to greater efficiency, it is worth noting that is efficient with respect to many DIMACS instances [11].

In conclusion, it proves thus efficient to attempt to direct DPLL towards already discovered inconsistencies in the search process in most cases.

5 Conclusions

Clearly, the DPLL procedure is oriented towards the proof of inconsistency. Branching rules attempt to shorten the search tree as much as possible. Inconsistencies detected in such trees do not necessary rely on the whole path of instantiated variables leading to them. On the contrary, a same cause of inconsistency can appear several time in the search tree. Accordingly, we propose to favor the selection of literals occurring in clauses that have been shown unsatisfiable at some previous steps of the search process without the need of recording additional clauses. Interestingly enough, this can be grafted at almost no computing cost to most existing branching rules, allowing us to balance the importance of this feature with other criteria that are necessary for computational efficiency.

6 Acknowledgments

This work has been supported in part by a *Contrat d'objectif de la Région Nord/Pas-de-Calais*. Many thanks to our colleagues at CRIL, in particular O. Bailleux, Y. Boufkhad, P. Marquis and B. Mazure for fruitful discussions about this paper.

References

1. *Artificial Intelligence*, volume 81, March 1996. Special volume on frontiers in problem solving: phase transition and complexity.
2. R. J. Bayardo Jr. and R. C. Schrag. Using CSP Look-Back Techniques to Solve Real-World SAT Instances. In *Proc. of the Fourteenth National Conference on Artificial Intelligence (AAAI'97)*, pages 203–208, Providence, Rhode Island, 27-31 July 1997.
3. Y. Boufkhad. *Aspects probabilistes et algorithmiques du problème de satisfiabilité*. PhD thesis, Université de Paris VI, 1996.
4. P. Cheeseman, B. Kanefsky, and W. M. Taylor. Where the Really Hard Problems Are. In *Proc. of the Twelfth International Joint Conference on Artificial Intelligence (IJCAI'91)*, pages 163–169, 1991.
5. V. Chvátal and E. Szemerédi. Many Hard Examples for Resolution. *Journal of the Association for Computing Machinery*, 35(4):759–768, 1988.
6. S. Cook. The complexity of theorem proving procedures. In *Proc. of Third Annual ACM Symp. on Th. of Computing*, pages 151–158, 1971.
7. J. M. Crawford. Solving Satisfiability Problems Using a Combination of Systematic an Local Search, 1993. Working notes of the DIMACS challenge on SAT organized by the Center for Discrete Mathematics and Computer Science of Rutgers University.
8. J. M. Crawford and L. D. Auton. Experimental Results on the Crossover Point in Random 3-SAT. *Artificial Intelligence [1]*, 81:31–57, 1996.
9. M. Davis, G. Logemann, and D. Loveland. A Machine Program for Theorem Proving. *CACM*, 5:394–397, 1962.
10. M. Davis and H. Putnam. A Computing Procedure for Quantification Theory. *Journal of the Association for Computing Machinery*, 7:201–215, 1960.
11. Second SAT challenge organized by the Center for Discrete Mathematics and Computer Science of Rutgers University, 1993. The benchmarks used in our tests can be obtained by anonymous ftp from Rutgers University Dimacs Center: `ftp dimacs.rutgers.edu cd pub/challenge/sat/benchmarks/cnf`.

12. O. Dubois, P. Andre, Y. Boufkhad, and J. Carlier. SAT versus UNSAT. In D. S. Johnson and M. A. Trick, editors, *Cliques, Coloring, and Satisfiability: Second DIMACS Implementation Challenge*, volume 26 of *DIMACS Series in Discrete Mathematics and Theoretical Computer Science*, pages 415–436, 1996.

13. O. Dubois and J. Carlier. Probabilistic Approach to the Satisfiability Problem. *Theoretical Computer Science*, 81:65–75, 1991.

14. J. Franco and M. Paull. Probabilistic Analysis of the Davis and Putnam procedure for Solving the Satisfiability Problem. *Discrete Applied Math.*, 5:77–87, 1983.

15. J. W. Freeman. *Improvement to propositional satisfiability search*. PhD thesis, Univ. of Philadelphia, 1995.

16. J.-K. Hao and L. Tétart. CH-SAT: A Complete Heuristic Procedure for Satisfiability Problems. In *in Proc. of the ECAI'96 Workshop on Advances in Propositional Deduction*, pages 27–38, Budapest, Hungary, 13 August 1996.

17. R. G. Jeroslow and J. Wang. Solving propositional satisfiability problems. In *Annals of Mathematics and Artificial Intelligence*, pages 167–187, 1990.

18. D. S. Johnson and M. A. Trick, editors. *Cliques, Coloring, and Satisfiability: Second Dimacs Implementation Challenge*, volume 26 of *DIMACS Series in Discrete Mathematics and Theoretical Computer Science*. American Mathematical Society, 1996.

19. C. Li and Anbulagan. Heuristic Based on Unit Propagation for Satisfiability Problems. In *Proc. of the Fifteenth International Joint Conference on Artificial Intelligence (IJCAI'97)*, pages 366–371, Nagoya, Japan, 1997.

20. J. P. Marques Silva. An Overview of Backtrack Search Satisfiability Algorithms. In *Proc. of the Fifth International Symposium on Artificial Intelligence and Mathematics*, Fort Lauderdale, Florida, January 1998. available at http://rutcor.rutgers.edu/~amai/Proceedings.html.

21. B. Mazure, L. Saïs, and É. Grégoire. Tabu Search for SAT. In *Proc. of the Fourteenth National Conference on Artificial Intelligence (AAAI'97)*, pages 281–285, Rhodes Island, 27-31 July 1997.

22. B. Mazure, L. Saïs, and É. Grégoire. Boosting Complete Techniques thanks to local search methods. *Annals of Mathematics and Artificial Intelligence*, 22:319–331, 1998.

23. B. Mazure, L. Saïs, and É. Grégoire. CRIL Platform for SAT. In *Proc. of the Fifteenth International Conference on Automated Deduction(CADE-15)*, volume 1421 of LNAI, Springer, pages 124–128, 1998.

24. A. Rauzy. On the complexity of the David and Putnam's Procedure on Some Polynomial Sub-Classes of SAT. Technical Report LaBRI 806–94, Université de Bordeaux 1, 1994.

25. B. Selman, H. A. Kautz, and B. Cohen. Local Search Strategies for Satifiability Testing. In *Proc. 1993 DIMACS Workshop on Maximum Clique, Graph Coloring, and Satisfiability*, pages 521–531, 1993.

26. B. Selman, D. Mitchell, and H. Levesque. A New Method for Solving Hard Satisfiability Problems. In *Proc. of the Tenth National Conference on Artificial Intelligence (AAAI'92)*, pages 440–446, San Jose, California, 12-16 July 1992.

27. B. Selman, D. Mitchell, and H. Levesque. Hard and easy distributions of SAT problems. In *Proc. of the Tenth National Conference on Artificial Intelligence (AAAI'92)*, pages 459–465, San Jose, California, 12-16 July 1992.

Decomposition of Task Specification Problems

Hung Son Nguyen & Sinh Hoa Nguyen & Andrzej Skowron

Institute of Mathematics,
Warsaw University,
Banacha str. 2, 02-095, Warsaw, Poland

Abstract. We consider a synthesis of complex objects by multi-agent system based on rough mereological approach. Any agent can produce complex objects from parts obtained from his sub-agents using some composition rules. Agents are equipped with decision tables describing (partial) specifications of their synthesis tasks. We investigate some problems of searching for optimal task specifications for sub-agents having task specification for a super-agent. We propose a decomposition scheme consistent with given composition rules. The computational complexity of decomposition problems is discussed by showing that these problems are equivalent to some well known graph problems. We also propose some heuristics for considered problems. An illustrative example of decomposition and synthesis scheme for object assembling by multi–agent system is included. We show an upper bound of an error rate in synthesis process of our system. A preliminary results related to the presented approach have been reported in [6, 11].

Keywords: multiagent system, decomposition, rough mereology

1 Introduction

Multiagent systems (MAS) considered in the paper are simple tree structures with nodes labeled by agents and task specifications for agents. The aim of the decomposition it to find for a given specification $\mathbf{A}$ at ag such specification $\mathbf{A_i}$ for any of its child ag_i that their composition is close enough to $\mathbf{A}$.

In the rough mereological framework (see e.g. [8, 10]) any agent ag of the system S can perform tasks $st_i(ag)$, for $i = 1, ..., n(ag)$ represented in the *standard table of ag*. It is assumed that for any non-leaf agent ag there is a set of composition rules $\{R_j : st_j(ag) \leftarrow (st_j(ag_1), ..., st_j(ag_k))\}$ producing $st_j(ag)$ from standards $st_j(ag_1), ..., st_j(ag_k)$ of immediate children $ag_1, ..., ag_k$ of ag in the agent system. In addition, every composition rule R_j is given together with a tolerance composition condition $\varepsilon = \varphi_j(\varepsilon_1, \varepsilon_2, ..., \varepsilon_k)$, which means that if child-agents $ag_1, ..., ag_k$ realize their tasks satisfying specifications $st_j(ag_1), ..., st_j(ag_k)$ with closeness greater than $1 - \varepsilon_1, 1 - \varepsilon_2, ..., 1 - \varepsilon_k$, respectively, then the parent-agent ag is able to perform the task formulated by $st_j(ag)$ with closeness greater than $1 - \varepsilon$. Using such assumptions, an approximate reasoning scheme of synthesis can be developed (see e.g. [8, 10]).

We analyze the complexity of some decomposition problems and we propose for them some heuristics solutions.

2 Basic Notions

Information system [7] is a pair $\mathbf{A} = (U, A)$ where U is a non-empty, finite set called the universe and A is a non-empty, finite set of *attributes*, i.e. $a : U \to V_a$ for $a \in A$, where V_a is called the *value set* of attribute a. Elements of U are called *objects*. Every information system $\mathbf{A} = (U, A)$ and a non-empty set $B \subseteq A$ define a *B-information function* by $Inf_B^A(x) = \{(a, a(x)) : a \in B\}$ for $x \in U$. The set $\{Inf_B^A(x) : x \in U\}$ is called the *A-information set* and it is denoted by $INF^A(B)$. We also consider a special case of information systems called decision tables. A *decision table* is any information system of the form $\mathbf{A} = (U, A \cup \{d\})$, where $d \notin A$ is a distinguished attribute called *decision*. We assume that the set V_d of values of the decision d is equal to $\{1, \ldots, r(d)\}$ for some positive integer called *the range of d*. The decision d determines the partition $\{C_1, ..., C_{r(d)}\}$ of the universe U, where $C_k = \{u \in U : d(u) = k\}$ for $1 \le k \le r(d)$. The set C_k is called the *k-th decision class* of $\mathbf{A}$. We will use some relations and operations over information systems defined as follows:

1. *Restriction:* $\mathbf{A}|_B = (U, B)$ is called *the B-restriction* of $\mathbf{A}$ for $B \subseteq A$.
2. *Composition:* For given information systems $\mathbf{A_1} = (U_1, A_1)$ and $\mathbf{A_2} = (U_2, A_2)$, we define a new information system $\mathbf{A} = \mathbf{A_1} \otimes \mathbf{A_2} = (U, A)$, called *composition of $\mathbf{A_1}$ and $\mathbf{A_2}$*, by

$$U = \{(u_1, u_2) \in U_1 \times U_2 : Inf_{A_1 \cap A_2}^{\mathbf{A_1}}(u_1) = Inf_{A_1 \cap A_2}^{\mathbf{A_2}}(u_2)\}$$

$$A = A_1 \cup A_2; a(u) = \begin{cases} a(u_1) & \text{if } a \in A_1 \\ a(u_2) & \text{if } a \in A_2 \end{cases}$$

for any $u = (u_1, u_2) \in U$ and $a \in A$. By $\otimes$ we also denote the defined analogously composition of information sets.
3. *Set theoretical operations and relations*: Given two information systems $\mathbf{A_1} = (U_1, A)$ and $\mathbf{A_2} = (U_2, A)$, one can define set theoretical operations and relations like union ($\mathbf{A_1} \cup \mathbf{A_2}$), intersection ($\mathbf{A_1} \cap \mathbf{A_2}$), subtraction ($\mathbf{A_1} - \mathbf{A_2}$), inclusion ($\mathbf{A_1} \subseteq \mathbf{A_2}$) and equality ($\mathbf{A_1} = \mathbf{A_2}$) in terms of information sets $INF^{\mathbf{A_1}}(A)$ and $INF^{\mathbf{A_2}}(A)$. For example

$$\mathbf{A_1} \subseteq \mathbf{A_2} \Leftrightarrow INF^{\mathbf{A_1}}(A) \subseteq INF^{\mathbf{A_2}}(A)$$

We denote by **UNIVERSE**(A) the maximal (with respect to inclusion) among information systems having A as the attribute set.

3 Decomposition of Complete Task Specification

Let us consider an agent ag and two of his sub-agents ag_1 and ag_2. We assume agents ag, ag_1 and ag_2 can synthesize products (objects) described by attribute sets A, A_1 and A_2, respectively, where $A = A_1 \cup A_2$ and $A_1 \cap A_2 = \emptyset$. Any information system $\mathbf{A} = (U, A)$ (resp. $\mathbf{A_1} = (U_1, A_1)$ and $\mathbf{A_2} = (U_2, A_2)$) is called the *standard table* of ag (for ag_1 and ag_2, resp.).

We assume that the agent ag is obtaining a task specification in the form of an information system $\mathbf{A} = (U, A)$ (table of standards or standard table). Two standard tables $\mathbf{A_1} = (U_1, A_1)$ and $\mathbf{A_2} = (U_2, A_2)$ (of sub-agents ag_1 and ag_2, resp.) are said to be *consistent with* $\mathbf{A}$ if $\mathbf{A_1} \otimes \mathbf{A_2} \subseteq \mathbf{A}$. The set of pairs of standard tables $\mathbf{P} = \{(\mathbf{A_1^i}, \mathbf{A_2^i}) : i = 1, 2, ...\}$ is called a *consistent covering of* $\mathbf{A}$ if $\bigcup_i (\mathbf{A_1^i} \otimes \mathbf{A_2^i}) = \mathbf{A}$. A consistent covering is *optimal* if it contains a minimal number of standard pairs.

We assume there is a predefined partition of the attribute set A into disjoint non-empty subsets A_1 and A_2, which can be explored by the agent-children ag_1 or ag_2. Let $\mathbf{A}|_{A_1} = (U, A_1)$, $\mathbf{A}|_{A_2} = (U, A_2)$. In this case for any consistent covering $\mathbf{P} = \{(\mathbf{A_1^i}, \mathbf{A_2^i}) : i = 1, 2, ...\}$ of $\mathbf{A}$ we have $\bigcup \mathbf{A_1^i} = \mathbf{A}|_{A_1}$ and $\bigcup \mathbf{A_2^i} = \mathbf{A}|_{A_2}$. Hence, the problem of searching for consistent covering of specification $\mathbf{A}$ can be called the *"task decomposition problem"*. In this paper we consider some optimization problems related to the task decomposition problems which occur in multi agent systems.

1. Searching problem for a consistent (with $\mathbf{A}$) pair of standard tables $\mathbf{A_1} = (U_1, A_1)$ and $\mathbf{A_2} = (U_2, A_2)$ with maximal $card(\mathbf{A_1} \otimes \mathbf{A_2})$ (i.e. $card(U_1 \times U_2)$).
2. Searching problem for consistent covering of $\mathbf{A}$ by the minimal number of standard table pairs.

One can transform the covering problem by pairs of standard tables to the covering problem of a bipartite graph by complete subgraphs and the searching problem for a maximal consistent pair of standard tables to the searching problem for a maximal complete subgraph of a given bipartite graph. For given information systems $\mathbf{A_1}$, $\mathbf{A_2}$ we construct a bipartite graph $G = (U_1 \cup U_2, E)$, where U_1 (U_2, resp.) is the set of objects of an information system $\mathbf{A_1}$ ($\mathbf{A_2}$, resp.). A pair of vertices (v_1, v_2) belongs to E iff $Inf_{A_1}^A(v_1) \cup Inf_{A_2}^A(v_2) \in INF^A(A)$. Hence every pair of consistent with $\mathbf{A}$ standard tables $\mathbf{A_1} = (U_1, A_1)$ and $\mathbf{A_2} = (U_2, A_2)$ (i.e. satisfying $(\mathbf{A_1} \otimes \mathbf{A_2}) \subseteq \mathbf{A}$) corresponds exactly to one complete bipartite subgraph $G' = (U_1 \cup U_2, E')$ and consistent (with $\mathbf{A}$) covering $\mathbf{P}$ can be represented by a set of complete bipartite subgraphs, that covers a graph G. One can show more, namely that the considered decomposition problems are polynomially equivalent to the bipartite graph problems. Therefore computational complexity of the decomposition problems follows from complexity of corresponding graph problems (to be known as NP-hard problems).

HEURISTIC: (corresponding to the minimal covering by standard pairs)
Input: Bipartite graph $G = (V_1 \cup V_2, E)$.
Output: A set S of complete subgraphs covering the graph G.

```
1 S = ∅.
2 Search for a semi-maximal complete subgraph G_0.
3 S = S ∪ G_0; G = G - G_0.
4 If G = ∅ stop, else go to Step 2.
```

Let $N(v)$ denote the sets of objects adjacent to v. We have the following:

HEURISTIC: (corresponding to searching for maximal pair of standards)
Input: Bipartite graph $G = (V_1 \cup V_2, E)$.
Output: A complete subgraph $G' = (U_1 \cup U_2, E')$ of G with semi-maximal
   cardinality $card(U_1) \cdot card(U_2)$.

1 We construct a sequence of complete bipartite subgraphs $G^i =$
  $(V_1^i \cup V_2^i, E_i)$ of G as follows:
    $i := 0;$ $V_1^0 := \emptyset;$ $V_2^0 = V_2;$
    while $\left(N(V_2^i) \cap (V_1 - V_1^i) \neq \emptyset\right)$
       Find a vertex $v \in N(V_2^i) \cap (V_1 - V_1^i)$ with the
       maximal $card(N(v) \cap V_2^i);$
       $V_1^{i+1} := V_1^i \cup \{v\};$ $V_2^{i+1} := V_2^i \cap N(v);$ $i := i + 1;$
    endwhile
2 Return G' being the largest subgraph among complete
  subgraphs G^i (i.e. with the maximal number of edges).

---

4 Decomposition of Incomplete Task Specification

Usually in applications, we have to deal with partial specifications of tasks. The situation when we have some partial information about specification will be considered in this section.

Let $\mathbf{A} = (U, A \cup \{d\})$ be a given decision table describing a partial task specification for the agent ag, where $d : U \to \{+, -\}$. Any $u \in U$ is called an *example*. We say that u is a *positive example* (satisfies the specification) if $d(u) = $ '+', and u is a *negative example* (does not satisfy the specification) if $d(u) = $ '-'. Thus, the decision attribute d defines a partition of $\mathbf{A}$ into two information systems $\mathbf{A}^+ = (U^+, A)$ and $\mathbf{A}^- = (U^-, A)$, where

$$U^+ = \{u \in U : d(u) = \text{'+'}\} \text{ and } U^- = \{u \in U : d(u) = \text{'-'}\}$$

The tables $\underline{\mathbf{A}} = \mathbf{A}^+$ and $\overline{\overline{\mathbf{A}}} = \mathbf{UNIVERSE}(A) - \mathbf{A}^-$ are called the *lower approximation and the upper approximation*, respectively, of the specification $\mathbf{A}$.

Two standard tables $\mathbf{A_1} = (U_1, A_1)$ and $\mathbf{A_2} = (U_2, A_2)$ are said to be *satisfying the partial specification* $\mathbf{A}$ if $\mathbf{A_1} \otimes \mathbf{A_2} \subseteq \mathbf{A}^+$ and they are *consistent with the partial specification* $\mathbf{A}$ if $\mathbf{A_1} \otimes \mathbf{A_2} \cap \mathbf{A}^- = \emptyset$.

A *satisfiability degree* of any consistent pair of standard tables $(\mathbf{A_1}, \mathbf{A_2})$ with a given partial specification $\mathbf{A}$ is defined by

$$\mathbf{Sat}(\mathbf{A_1} \otimes \mathbf{A_2} | \mathbf{A}) = \frac{card(\mathbf{A_1} \otimes \mathbf{A_2} \cap \mathbf{A}^+)}{card(\mathbf{A_1} \otimes \mathbf{A_2})}.$$

According to this notation, the pair of standard tables $(\mathbf{A_1}, \mathbf{A_2})$ is satisfying $\mathbf{A}$ if and only if $\mathbf{Sat}(\mathbf{A_1} \otimes \mathbf{A_2} | \mathbf{A}) = 1$. The (consistent with $\mathbf{A}$) pair of standard tables $(\mathbf{A_1}, \mathbf{A_2})$ is *satisfying* $\mathbf{A}$ to a degree $1 - \varepsilon$ of a given partial specification $\mathbf{A}$ (is ε-consistent with $\mathbf{A}$) if $\mathbf{Sat}(\mathbf{A_1} \otimes \mathbf{A_2} | \mathbf{A}) > 1 - \varepsilon$. We have

Theorem 1. *If* $\mathbf{Sat}(\mathbf{A_1} | \mathbf{A}) > 1 - \varepsilon_1$ *and* $\mathbf{Sat}(\mathbf{A_2} | \mathbf{A}) > 1 - \varepsilon_2$ *then*
  $\mathbf{Sat}(\mathbf{A_1} \otimes \mathbf{A_2} | \mathbf{A}) > 1 - (\varepsilon_1 + \varepsilon_2).$

Let $\mathbf{A_1} = (U_1, A_1)$ and $\mathbf{A_2} = (U_2, A_2)$ be an ε-consistent (with $\mathbf{A}$) pair of standard tables. One can construct two partial specifications of tasks $\mathbf{A_1'} = (\mathbf{U_1}, A_1 \cup \{d_1\})$ and $\mathbf{A_2'} = (\mathbf{U_2}, A_2 \cup \{d_2\})$ for sub-agents ag_1 and ag_2 assuming

$$\mathbf{U_1}^+ = U_1; \quad \mathbf{U_1}^- = \{u \in \mathbf{UNIVERSE}(A_1) : (\{u\}, A_1) \otimes \mathbf{A_2} \cap \mathbf{A}^- \neq \emptyset\};$$
$$\mathbf{U_2}^+ = U_2; \quad \mathbf{U_2}^- = \{u \in \mathbf{UNIVERSE}(A_2) : \mathbf{A_1} \otimes (\{u\}, A_2) \cap \mathbf{A}^- \neq \emptyset\};$$

The defined above pair of partial specifications $\mathbf{A_1'}$ and $\mathbf{A_2'}$ is also said to be ε-consistent with $\mathbf{A}$.

Any set of ε-consistent (with a given $\mathbf{A}$) pairs of standard tables $\mathbf{P} = \{(\mathbf{A_1^i}, \mathbf{A_2^i}) : i = 1, 2, ...\}$ is called *the consistent covering of specification* $\mathbf{A}$ if $\underline{\mathbf{A}} \subset \bigcup_i (\mathbf{A_1^i} \otimes \mathbf{A_2^i}) \subset \overline{\overline{\mathbf{A}}}$ i.e. $\bigcup_i (\mathbf{A_1^i} \otimes \mathbf{A_2^i}) \cap \mathbf{A}^- = \emptyset$ and $\mathbf{A}^+ \subset \bigcup_i (\mathbf{A_1^i} \otimes \mathbf{A_2^i})$.

The *task decomposition problems* for MAS and a given parameter ε for agent ag can be now defined as follows:

1. Searching problem for an ε-consistent pair of standard tables $\mathbf{A_1} = (U_1, A_1)$ and $\mathbf{A_2} = (U_2, A_2)$ with maximal $card(\mathbf{A_1} \otimes \mathbf{A_2})$.
2. Searching problem for a consistent covering of $\mathbf{A}$ by the minimal number of ε-consistent pairs of standard tables.

4.1 Decomposition Method Based on Decision Table

In this subsection we discuss a method for ε-consistent standard tables from a partial specification according to the definition proposed in the previous section. One can see that the solutions of new decomposition problems can be found by solving some equivalent graph problems. Let the decision table $\mathbf{A} = (U, A \cup \{d\})$ define a partial specification for the agent ag, and let $A = A_1 \cup A_2$ be the predefined partition of the attribute set A into disjoint subsets. The bipartite graph $G = (V_1 \cup V_1, E)$ for a specification $\mathbf{A}$ is constructed analogously to a graph presented in Section 3 with the following modifications:

1. The pair (v_1, v_2) belongs to E iff $([Inf^{A_1}(v_1) \otimes Inf^{A_2}(v_2)]) \in INF^{\overline{\overline{A}}}(A)$.
2. The edges of a graph are labeled by 0 or 1 as follows:

$$label(v_1, v_2) = \begin{cases} 1 & \text{if } d([Inf^{A_1}(v_1) \cup Inf^{A_2}(v_2)]) = '+' \\ 0 & \text{if } [Inf^{A_1}(v_1) \cup Inf^{A_2}(v_2)] \notin INF^{\mathbf{A}}(A) \end{cases}$$

The extracting problem of an ε-consistent with $\mathbf{A}$ pair of standard tables $(\mathbf{A_1}, \mathbf{A_2})$ with the maximal value of $card(\mathbf{A_1} \otimes \mathbf{A_2})$ and $\mathbf{Sat}(\mathbf{A_1} \otimes \mathbf{A_2}|\mathbf{A}) > 1 - \varepsilon$ can be transformed to the searching problem for a complete sub-graph of $G' = (U_1 \cup U_1, E)$ with a maximal $card(U_1) \cdot card(U_2)$ and the number of edges labeled by 0 not exceeding $\varepsilon \cdot card(U_1) \cdot card(U_2)$. The considered graph problem is a modified version of the graph problem proposed in Section 4. Let $N_0(v), N_1(v)$ be the sets of objects connected with v by edges labeled by 0 and 1, respectively, and let $N(v) = N_0(v) \cup N_1(v)$. Let $Adj(v), Adj_0(v), Adj_1(v)$ denote the cardinality of $N(v), N_0(v), N_1(v)$, respectively. Starting from the empty subgraph G^0, we append to G^0 the vertices v with a maximal degree taking into consideration a proportion $\frac{Adj_1(v)}{Adj(v)}$. The algorithm can be described as follows:

HEURISTIC: (corresponding to decomposition of partial specification)

Input: Bipartite graph $G = (V_1 \cup V_2, E)$ with edges labeled by 1 or 0, $\varepsilon > 0$

Output: A semi-maximal complete bipartite subgraph $G' = (U_1 \cup U_2, E')$ of G satisfying the condition $\frac{Adj_1(U_1)}{Adj(U_1)} \geq 1 - \varepsilon$

```
1 We construct a sequence of complete bipartite subgraphs
  Gⁱ = (V₁ⁱ ∪ V₂ⁱ, Eᵢ) of G as follows:
    i := 0;      V₁⁰ := ∅;      V₂⁰ = V₂;
    while (N(V₂ⁱ) ∩ (V₁ − V₁ⁱ) ≠ ∅)
       Find a vertex v ∈ N(V₂ⁱ) ∩ (V₁ − V₁ⁱ) with the
       maximal card(N(v) ∩ V₂ⁱ);
       Let kₑ := ⌊ε · card(N₁(v) ∩ V₂ⁱ)⌋;
       Sort the set of vertices N₀(v) ∩ V₂ⁱ in the descending
       order with respect to Adj₁(.) and set
          Adjₑ(v) := the set of first kₑ vertices in N₀(v) ∩ V₂ⁱ;
       V₁ⁱ⁺¹ := V₁ⁱ ∪ {v}; V₂ⁱ⁺¹ := V₂ⁱ ∩ (Adj₁(v) ∪ Adjₑ(v)); i := i + 1;
    endwhile
2 Return the largest graph G* among complete subgraphs Gⁱ
  (i.e. with the maximal number card(V₁ⁱ) · card(V₂ⁱ) of edges)
```

4.2 Example

Now we present an illustrative example. A car (complex object) assembly room consists of five factories (agents). They are denoted by ag (the main factory), ag_1 (the factory of engines), ag_2 (the factory of bodies), ag_3 (body shop), ag_4 (paint shop) (see Figure 1). Products of agents are described by attributes from

$$A = \{\text{Engine capacity, Body type, Body color}\}.$$

Let us assume that the agent ag has obtained from the customer the examples of his favorite cars (positive examples) and the cars that he don't wont to buy (negative examples). This partial specification of the assembly task is presented in the the form of the decision table presented in the Figure 2. The decomposition problem related to the agent ag can be treated as the problem of searching for the *ENGINE* specification A_1 for the agent ag_1 and the *BODY* specification A_2 for the agent ag_2 such that if ag_1 and ag_2 independently produce their parts satisfying the specifications A_1 and A_2, then the agent ag can use these parts to compose the car satisfying (consistent) with the customer's specification.

The graph interpretation of the specification (Figure 2) is represented in Figure 3. By applying the algorithm described in the Section 4.1 for the root agent ag, we obtain the maximal pair of standard tables A_1 and A_2 presented in Figure 4. Consequently, the table A_2 can be decomposed into a pair of standard tables A_3 and A_4 (see Figure 4).

Fig. 1. The system with five agents. Attributes are denoted by: a ="Engine capacity", b ="Body type", c ="Body color"

Fig. 2. The specification of task for the root agent ag in form of the decision table

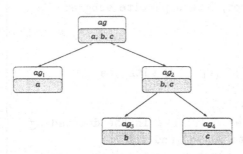

A	Engine capacity	Body type	Body color	Decision
u_1	1300	coupe	white	+
u_2	1300	coupe	gray	+
u_3	1300	coupe	green	+
u_4	1300	saloon	white	+
u_5	1300	saloon	red	−
u_6	1300	saloon	gray	+
u_7	1500	coupe	white	+
u_8	1500	coupe	gray	+
u_9	1500	coupe	green	+
u_{10}	1500	saloon	white	+
u_{11}	1500	saloon	gray	+
u_{12}	1500	saloon	black	+
u_{13}	1600	coupe	white	+
u_{14}	1600	coupe	green	+
u_{15}	1600	coupe	gray	+
u_{16}	1600	coupe	red	−
u_{17}	1600	saloon	white	+
u_{18}	1600	saloon	gray	+
u_{19}	1600	saloon	black	+
u_{20}	1600	estate	black	+
u_{21}	1600	estate	white	−
u_{22}	1800	saloon	black	+
u_{23}	1800	saloon	gray	+
u_{24}	1800	saloon	white	−
u_{25}	1800	estate	black	+
u_{26}	1800	estate	white	+
u_{27}	1800	limousine	black	+
u_{28}	1800	limousine	white	−
u_{29}	2000	limousine	black	+
u_{30}	2000	limousine	white	−

Fig. 3. The graph representation of the specification: solid lines – positive examples, dotted lines – negative examples

Fig. 4. The maximal pair of standard tables (A_1, A_2), (A_3, A_4) found for the root agent and for the agent ag_2, respectively

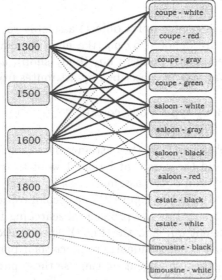

5 Decomposition of Approximate Specification

The notion of *approximate specification* has been considered in [8, 10] as an important aspect of reasoning for agents under uncertainty. Assuming that every agent ag is equipped with a function Sim_{ag} that for any object x and any specification Φ, the value $Sim_{ag}(x, \Phi) \in [0, 1]$ has an intended meaning *the satisfiability degree of Φ by x*. Then, the approximate specification of the agent ag is defined by any pair (Φ, ε), and we denote by

$$\Theta_{ag}(\Phi, \varepsilon) = \{x : Sim_{ag}(x, \Phi) > 1 - \varepsilon\}$$

the ε-neighborhood of specification Φ. The inference rules of agent ag whose children are $ag_1, ..., ag_k$ are in the form

if $(x_1 \in \Theta_{ag_1}(\Phi_1, \varepsilon_1)) \wedge ... \wedge (x_k \in \Theta_{ag_k}(\Phi_k, \varepsilon_k))$**then** $(x \in \Theta_{ag}(\Phi, \varepsilon))$

where $x_1, ..., x_k$ are objects submitted by $ag_1, ..., ag_k$, respectively, and x is the object composed by ag from $x_1, ..., x_k$.

We analyze the relationship between ε and $\varepsilon_1, ..., \varepsilon_k$ for some well known functions Sim_{Ag} in case of composition rule $\otimes$. We consider still a "binary" agent system, in which every agent has two children ag_1 and ag_2. Let the task specification be defined by an information system $\mathbf{A} = (U, A)$ stored at the root-agent. In our application every specification Φ associated with the agent ag is defined by an information system $\mathbf{A}$ equipped with this agent. Below we present some important functions defining satisfiability degrees of any object x with respect to the specification $\mathbf{A}$. We start with some basic *distance* functions $d : \mathbf{UNIVERSE}(A) \times \mathbf{UNIVERSE}(A) \to \mathbb{R}^+$ defined by

$$d_1(x, y) = card\{a(x) \neq a(y) : a \in A\} \quad (\text{the Hamming distance })$$
$$d_2(x, y) = \max_{a \in A}\{|a(x) - a(y)|\} \quad (\text{the } \infty\text{-Norm})$$
$$d_3(x, y) = \sum_{a \in A}(a(x) - a(y))^2 \quad (\text{the Euclidean distance})$$

We can see that distance functions are defined for a space $\mathbf{UNIVERSE}(A)$, where every object is characterized by all attributes in A. For any subset $B \subseteq A$ the distance functions can be modified by restriction the attribute set to B. We denote the distance function d restricted to B by $d|_B$. Having the distance function d the distance of object x to the set S is defined by $d(x, S) = min_{y \in S}d(x, y)$. Let $\mathbf{A} = (U, A)$ be a specification equipped with an agent ag. Hence the approximate specification for $\mathbf{A}$ can be defined by $\Theta(\mathbf{A}, \varepsilon) = \{x : d|_A(x, U) < \varepsilon\}$. Let $\mathbf{A}_1 = (U_1, A_1)$ and $\mathbf{A}_2 = (U_2, A_2)$ be specifications at ag_1 and ag_2, respectively. Let $\Theta(\mathbf{A}_1, \varepsilon_1)$ and $\Theta(\mathbf{A}_2, \varepsilon_2)$ be the approximate specification of $\mathbf{A}_1$ and $\mathbf{A}_2$, respectively. The following observations show the relationship between $\Theta(\mathbf{A}_1, \varepsilon_1)$, $\Theta(\mathbf{A}_2, \varepsilon_2)$ and the composed approximate specification $\Theta(\mathbf{A}, \varepsilon)$. For a given distance function d, we have the following

318

Theorem 2. *If $\Theta(A_1\varepsilon_1)$ and $\Theta(A_2,\varepsilon_2)$ are approximate specifications of subagents ag_1 and ag_2, respectively then we have*

$$\Theta(A_1,\varepsilon_1) \otimes \Theta(A_2,\varepsilon_2) \subseteq \Theta(A_1 \otimes A_2, \varepsilon)$$

where $\varepsilon = max(\varepsilon_1,\varepsilon_2)$ if d is Hamming's distance or the ∞-Norm and $\varepsilon = \varepsilon_1+\varepsilon_2$ if d is Euclidean distance.

6 Conclusions

We have investigated some decomposition problems of complex tasks in a multi-agent system assuming its specification is given. The two decomposition problems are discussed. The fist problem concerns the decomposing such tasks under a complete specification. The second problem is related to tasks with a partial specification. Both problems can be solved by transforming them to corresponding graph problems. For some predefined composition rules the proposed decomposition methods guarantee a low error rate of synthesis process.

Acknowledgments: This work was partially supported by the grant of National Committee for Scientific Research No $8T11C01011$ and by the *ESPRIT* project 20288 CRIT-2.

References

1. S.Amarel, PANEL on AI and Design, in: J.Mylopoulos and R.Reiter, eds., *Proceedings Twelfth International Conference on Artificial Intelligence* (Sydney, Australia, 1991), pp. 563–565.
2. K. Decker and V. Lesser, Quantitative modelling of complex computational task environments, in: *Proceedings AAAI-93* (Washington, DC, 1993), pp. 217–224.
3. E.H. Durfee, *Coordination of Distributed Problem Solvers* (Kluwer, Boston, 1988).
4. Garey M.R., Johnson D.S., *Computers and Interactability. A Guide to the Theory of NP-Completeness* (W.H. Freeman and Company New York, 1979).
5. M.N. Huhns, M.P. Singh, L. Gasser (eds.), *Readings in agents*, (Morgan Kaufmann, San Mateo, 1998).
6. H.S. Nguyen, S.H. Nguyen, The decomposition problem in multi-agent system. *Proceedings of the W8 Workshop at ECAI'98 on Synthesis of Intelligent Agents from Experimental Data*. Brighton August 24, 1998 (internal report).
7. Z. Pawlak, *Rough sets: Theoretical Aspects of Reasoning about Data* (Kluwer, Dordrecht, 1991).
8. L. Polkowski, A. Skowron: Rough mereology: A new paradigm for approximate reasoning. International Journal of Approximate Reasoning 15/4 (1996), pp. 333–365.
9. L. Polkowski and A. Skowron, Rough sets: A perspective, in: L. Polkowski and A. Skowron, eds., *Rough Sets in Knowledge Discovery 1: Methodology and Applications* (Physica-Verlag, Heidelberg, 1998), pp. 31–56.
10. A. Skowron and L. Polkowski. Rough mereological foundations for design, analysis, synthesis, and control in distributed systems, *Information Sciences An International Journal* 104(1-2) (1998), pp. 129-156.
11. A. Skowron, H.S. Nguyen. The Task Decomposition Problems in Multi-Agent Systems. In Proc. of CSP98, Humboldt University, Berlin, 1998 (internal report).
12. R.B. Rao and S.C.-Y. Lu, Building models to support synthesis in early stage product design, in: *Proceedings of AAAI-93; Eleventh National Conference on Artificial Intelligence* (AAAI Press/MIT Press, Menlo Park, 1993), pp. 277–282.

ORTES: The Design of a Real-Time Control Expert System

Aijun An[1], Nick Cercone[1] and Christine Chan[2]

[1] Department of Computer Science, University of Waterloo
Waterloo, Ontario N2L 3G1 Canada
[2] Department of Computer Science, University of Regina
Regina, Saskatchewan S4S 0A1 Canada

Abstract. We present ORTES, a methodology for conceptual modeling of real-time expert systems. ORTES combines advantages of current analysis methods, including structured analysis, object-oriented analysis and knowledge modeling, and circumvents their weaknesses. ORTES supports two stages, knowledge analysis and knowledge representation, in the process of knowledge acquisition. For knowledge analysis, ORTES applies both object and functional decomposition techniques. To overcome the limitations of functional decomposition, a generic task structure for real-time monitoring and control systems is proposed. For knowledge representation, ORTES makes use of object-oriented techniques which assign functions to objects and represent the system in terms of objects and their relationships. We present steps and strategies of ORTES in modeling a real-time control expert system.

1 Introduction

Software analysis methods can be generally classified into three categories: structured analysis (SA), object-oriented analysis (OOA), and knowledge modeling (KM). The major difference between OOA and SA is that the central activity in OOA is to identify objects and decompose the system in terms of objects, while SA decomposes a system based on its functionality. According to [6, 7, 9], functionally decomposed systems suffer badly when system requirements change because requirements are usually stated in terms of functionality. Functional decomposition is also somewhat arbitrary, while object decomposition tends to discover similar objects, which produces reusable components. Instead of using functional decomposition, most OOA methods use other formalisms, such as *use cases* [9], *task scripts* [7], and *event response lists* [6], to capture the system functionality. However, use cases or similar constructs are also subject to change when the requirement changes. In addition, it has been observed that use cases were very good at describing the user interface and the more superficial aspects of a system but less good for getting to the internal complexity [7]. Adams and Corriveau [1] have observed that replacing use cases with stereotypical descriptions is beneficial. Another category of software analysis methods is knowledge modeling (KM) methods for building knowledge-based systems. Most of these methods, such as IMT [4], KADS [11] and *generic tasks* [5], center around classification of knowledge items, which usually separate data and problem-solving methods and emphasize decomposing high-level problem-solving tasks into subsequent subtasks. Some KM methods, such as *generic tasks* [5], provide generic tasks to guide the decomposition process. However, the usual separation of data and problem-solving methods in knowledge representation makes it necessary to connect the different components of a conceptual model at a later stage of system development in order to make use of prevailing object-oriented tools. In addition, even if some KM methods provide generic tasks to guide modeling problem-solving knowledge, they are generally designed for diagnosis and classification tasks, which cannot be applied to real-time control systems.

We present an Object-oriented approach to analysing and modeling Real-Time process control Expert Systems (ORTES), which combines advantages of SA, OOA and KM and circumvents their weaknesses. As an expert system development tool, ORTES involves the last two of the three activities within knowledge acquisition: *knowledge elicitation, knowledge analysis* and *knowledge representation*. For knowledge analysis, ORTES applies both object and functional decomposition techniques. Object decomposition is used to structure and classify the entities that interact with the real-time system or to organise the data that are handled by the system. Functional decomposition is applied to build a task structure that captures the functional requirements of the system. For tasks that cannot be further decomposed, event response lists are used to describe the behavioral requirements for the task. To overcome the limitations of functional decomposition, a generic task structure for real-time monitoring and control systems is proposed. By suggesting generic task structures, ORTES provides guidelines for decomposing real-time control systems and therefore avoids arbitrary decomposition that may be subject to requirement changes. In terms of knowledge representation, ORTES assigns functions to objects and represents the system in terms of objects and their relationships. The final conceptual model is a set of interacting objects, each of which encapsulates a set of local data and a set of operations derived from the task structure. To build a conceptual model, ORTES conducts requirements analysis, task analysis and object-oriented conceptualization, in which four models: *environmental model, task model, object model and relationship model*, are built. In the following sections, we describe the steps and strategies for developing the four models.

2 Requirements Analysis

Requirements analysis determines the environment within which the system must operate, defines what the system should do within this environment, and describes the interactions between the system and its environment. An *environmental model* is built by identifying external objects, determining the role of each object and specifying the interaction between the system and the external objects. External objects are identified from different sources, such as the environment, the users, the external subsystems that communicate with the system,

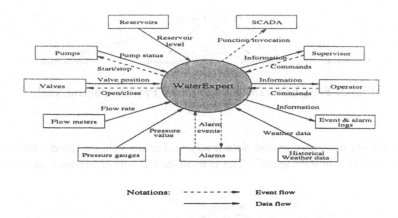

Fig. 1. Environmental Model for a Water Supply Control Expert System

and the external data elements. If an external object is a complex system and different components of this system interact with the system to be built through different signals, *object decomposition* should be used to handle the complexity. Figure 1 depicts the environmental model of an expert system that controls a water supply system. Rectangular boxes represent external objects, and the expert system is represented as a "black box", *i.e.*, we are not concerned with the internal activities of the system but rather its interactions with its environment.

3 Task Analysis

Task Analysis determines tasks the system should perform. This is where ORTES differs from other OOA methods. Rather than using *use cases* to describe the system's behavior, ORTES provides a generic task structure to help the knowledge engineer organise problem-solving knowledge in a systematic way.

3.1 Generic Task Structure

A *task* is a problem solving action. Depending on problem complexity, a task can be composite or primitive. A composite task implies a need for decomposition into sub-tasks. A primitive task can be performed directly without decomposition. The application of the task to a particular (sub-)problem results in the achievement of a goal. The goal of a process control system is to monitor and control processes. Therefore, two sub-tasks can be recognised under the task of process control: *monitoring* and *control*. Since a process control system is usually built for use by humans, *user service* is also included. In some real-time systems, handling and diagnosing malfunctions of processes is one of the objectives. In this case, real-time diagnosis is another sub-task. Therefore, the task of process control can be decomposed into four sub-tasks, as shown in Figure 2.

The *monitoring* task is responsible for continuously checking the status of various parameters of the controlled processes. It can further be decomposed into:

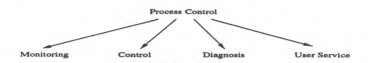

Fig. 2. First Level Decomposition of Process Control Task

data collection, *data service* and *data analysis*. Figure 3 shows the decomposition structure of the *monitoring* task. The *control* task is concerned with the system's

Fig. 3. Decomposition Structure of the *Monitoring* Task

intended behavior when reacting to events from its environment to achieve certain goals. There are two kinds of control problems. One is relatively simple and well-specified, such as cruise control or elevator control problems. This kind has deterministic, algorithmic solutions. The other kind is complex and open-ended control problems. Solutions to these problems are usually non-deterministic or heuristic. Conventional control software engineering deals with the former problems. The latter problems are addressed by knowledge engineering, which leads to knowledge-based AI approaches to control. We consider both kinds of control problems. To model problems with deterministic solutions, *domain-level control* is used. To model problems with heuristic solutions, both *domain-level control* and *meta-level control* are used. Figure 4 depicts the *control* task.

Domain level control deals with control of the external environment of the real-time system. A system may contain a number of domain-level control tasks, each of which controls a given aspect of the environment. A domain-level control task receives inputs from the environment via *monitoring* tasks and generates outputs to the environment to achieve a certain goal. Alternatively, this task may provide some data for use by other tasks. Specification of a domain-level control task consists of three parts: (1) a goal, (2) the condition under which

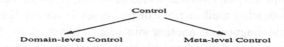

Fig. 4. Decomposition Structure of the *Control* Task

Fig. 5. Domain-level Control Task without Planning

Fig. 6. Domain-level Control Task with Planning

the goal can be achieved by the task, and (3) the task body that achieves the goal under the condition. For expert systems, expertise is usually needed to realise a certain domain-level control task. For example, in a water supply control system, maintaining a distribution pressure at a pumping station and maintaining the water level in a reservoir are domain-level control tasks, each of which concerns a given aspect of the water supply system. The knowledge about how to efficiently perform these tasks come from many years of experience. Depending on the characteristics of the knowledge, i.e., the problem-solving pattern used by the expert, a control task may consist of only *situation assessment* and *control action execution* (see Figure 5), or it may also involve a *planning* component. For the latter case, *prediction* and *plan assumption analysis* are also needed (see Figure 6). *Situation assessment* determines whether the values of some parameters formulate a situation in which a control command needs to be issued. *Control action execution* basically issues a control command when needed. *Prediction* looks ahead and estimates parameter values in the future. *Planning* analyses the current situation and the prediction results and creates a *plan*, i.e., a sequence of actions to be performed over time. *Plan assumption analyser* determines whether continuing a plan is appropriate or re-planning is necessary by checking whether assumptions under which the plan was made are still valid. Since predictions may not be accurate, a plan assumption analyser should keep checking whether the predicted parameter values are close enough to the actual values (which become available over time). If the predicted values are not accurate enough, the plan may become invalid and re-planning should be invoked.[3] Different representations can be used to describe a domain-level control task. *Event response lists, decision tables* or *decision trees* are suitable to describe situation-assessment-based control. Prediction and planning algorithms can be described using pseudo-code with iteration and selection operators.

Meta-level control is the level of control on top of the domain level, containing knowledge about determining what goals are relevant to solve a particular problem. How each goal is achieved is determined by the domain-level control

---

[3] Some end-level tasks in our generic task tree, such as *prediction* and *planning*, can be further decomposed. How they decompose depends on the methods or algorithms that implement the tasks.

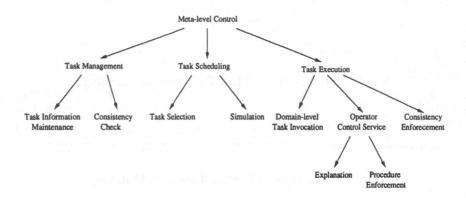

Fig. 7. Structure of the *Meta-level Control* Task

task knowledge. Meta-level control dynamically manages domain-level task execution. Given a particular problem, meta-level control determines goals to be achieved, evaluates the current situation, selects a domain-level control plan that can achieve the goal under the current situation, and executes the selected control plans. In addition, meta-level control is responsible for coordinating selected domain-level tasks, including checking the consistency among multiple control tasks and taking corrective actions when two selected domain-level tasks produce contradicting actions in some situations. Moreover, an expert system is usually required to explain its decisions. Explanation knowledge belongs to meta-level knowledge. In addition, although a process-control system is usually capable of autonomous operation, it may also be capable of being overridden by a human operator. This kind of control system is referred to as a "mixed initiative controller" [8]. For such systems, cooperation between operator and machine should be enabled, which may result in a need to restrict an operator's actions through *procedure enforcement*. In some cases, selection of domain level control tasks may require look ahead at what will happen if certain control tasks are chosen for execution. This case requires a *simulation* function be performed during selection. Thus, meta-level control consists of three sub-tasks: *task management*, *task scheduling* and *task execution*. Task management is not a real-time activity. It maintains information about domain-level control tasks, including the goal a task achieves, the condition under which it can achieve the goal, the underlying rationale, and also the timing constraints on the task. Task management also performs the consistency check among the domain-level tasks. Task scheduling is a dynamic activity, selecting domain-level control tasks according to the current goals and the status of the system, possibly making use of simulation results. Task execution gives control to the selected domain-level tasks, provides explanation for the actions taken by the tasks, and coordinates the controls between the operator and the machine. In the situation where inconsistency could appear, the execution module should also provide protective actions to resolve the conflicts. Figure 7 depicts meta-level control.

Diagnosis localises the parts of the system responsible for the abnormal behavior. Diagnosis is initiated by exceptions received from monitoring tasks. It determines problem types, finds causes of these problems, and either reports to the user or invokes a *repair* component to suggest repair solutions. *User service* provides the user interface and a set of services required by users. There may be more than one user service, one for each category of users. For example, in an automatic factory control system, there may be user services for operators, managers and engineers respectively. The services provided to the operator include displaying the status of the controlled system, printing reports or diagrams, and providing a control panel, etc. For other users, some high level interface components may be needed, such as specification of the controller (such as in state transition diagrams), visualization of the specification, and simulation of the specification. See [2] for the diagrams of the *diagnosis* and *user services* tasks.

3.2 Use of the Task Structure

The generic task structure represents types of problem-solving knowledge in a real-time control system. The tasks in the structure are not "requirements" in the sense that they are not essential for all process control applications. Nevertheless, a general-purpose tool suited to modeling process control applications should support them. This structure is designed for knowledge engineers to classify and refine knowledge for a particular application and to guide their interviews with experts. The steps for using this task structure for task analysis are as follows:

1. Determine what tasks in the task structure are needed according to the initial functional requirements obtained from the requirements analysis.
2. Classify the problem-solving knowledge obtained from knowledge sources into the tasks in the structure. If some knowledge does not suitably belong to any category of the tasks, create a new sub-task at a suitable place.
3. If a task is identified as a necessary task for the system but the knowledge about how to perform this task is not available, go to the expert or other knowledge source to elicit the knowledge.
4. For each task, specify the goal it achieves, the condition under which it can achieve the goal, the events that activate the task, other timing constraints such as the required response time to an event, and task internal structure.

This process may iterate. The refined task structure and specified tasks constitutes the *task model*, describing detailed functional requirements of the system.

4 Object-Oriented Conceptualization

After requirement and task analyses, ORTES represents the system in the form of objects. ORTES considers modeling three aspects, the *data aspect*, the *functional aspect* and the *dynamic aspect*, of a system using an object-oriented notation. Each object consists of a set of data and operations. The data aspect of a system is modeled using the data components of objects; the functional aspect of a system is modeled by functions inside objects; and the dynamic aspect of a system is described by illustrating the computational structure and timing characteristics of each function and by showing interactions between objects. To represent a system in this way, ORTES builds two models, the *object model* and the *relationship model*. The object model structures the system into objects and describe statics and dynamics of each object. The relationship model depicts the structural and interactive relationships among objects.

4.1 Building Object Model

ORTES uses two kinds of objects to model the problem domain. An *entity object* corresponds to a concrete or abstract domain object and consists of information and behavior naturally coupled to the object. A *control object* models an object in the problem-solving space that corresponds to some functionality that is not naturally tied to any entity object. A control object typically acts as a *controller* that ties and governs several other objects to perform some task. Building an object model involves identifying these two kinds of objects, assigning functions to each object, and specifying components and dynamics of each object.

Identifying Entity Objects We describe criteria for determining entity objects for the domain of real-time systems. We divide the entity objects into four categories: *device objects, external subsystem objects, user role objects* and *abstract data objects*. *Device objects* represent I/O devices in the environment that provide inputs to or receive outputs from the system. The environmental model is used to identify device objects. For every external object representing an I/O device in the environmental model diagram, there is a corresponding device object in the software system. For example, *pumps, valves*, and *reservoirs* are device objects for the expert system shown in Figure 1. *External subsystem objects* are also identified from the environmental model, representing a subsystem of the controlled system or a subsystem the communicates with the real-time system. An example of subsystem objects is the SCADA object in Figure 1. A *user role object* models a role played by a user. For each external object in the environmental model that represents a type of user, a user role object is created in the software system to model the role that this type of users plays. For example, in a factory automation system, there are operators, engineers and supervisors. For each type of user, a user role object is created. A user role object interacts with the real-world user to perform some services requested by the user. The functions of user role objects are determined by the user service task specified in the task model. *Abstract data objects* model entities in the problem domain that needs to be remembered. These objects are identified from the task specifications in the task model and also from external data elements in the environmental model. Any data element in task specifications or in the environmental model that does not belong to device objects, external subsystem objects or user role objects but needs to be remembered should be created as an abstract data object. For example, historical sensor data, alarm and event logs and statistic analysis results are possible abstract data objects for a factory automation system.

Assigning Functionality to the Entity Objects After determining entity objects, the next step is to determine the functions that these objects should offer within the system's functional requirements. ORTES provides guidance on how to assign the tasks in the task structure to the identified entity objects. For example, data collection tasks should be assigned to device objects because these tasks deal with the transition of sensor data from a device to the system to be built. [2] gives details about how to assign other tasks to entity objects.

Determining Control Objects A control object is an abstract object that belongs to the problem-solving space and controls the behavior of other objects in the system. A control object models (part of) the control structure of a system. In ORTES, a control object is identified from the control task and the diagnosis task in the task structure. Any control task in either domain level or meta level, if it is not suitable to be put in an entity object, can be modeled as a control object. A real-time system may contain several domain-level control tasks, each of which controls a certain aspect of the controlled system. For each domain-level task, a control object can be identified to encapsulate the control strategy used in the task. For example, a water supply control system involves domain-level control tasks of *maintaining the water level in a reservoir* and *maintaining the discharge pressure of a pumping station*. Each of these control tasks not only requires the information about the controlled object, i.e., the reservoir or the pumping station, but also requires information about other parts of the system, such as the status of other reservoirs or the status of other pumping stations. Thus, they are not suitable to be allocated to any single entity object. For this reason, two control objects, *reservoir controller* and *pumping station controller*, are created to model the two tasks respectively. Control objects are also created to model meta-level control tasks. For example, we can use two control objects, *task scheduler* and *task executer* to model *task scheduling* and *task execution*. These objects encapsulate the algorithms used for performing the respective task. The algorithms are represented as functions inside control objects.

Specifying Objects Once an entity or a control object is determined, the object should be explicitly specified to show its components and behavior. An object consists of data and functional components. The data component is a set of data the object encapsulates and the functional component is a set of functions the object supports. In addition, data and operations have relations among them. The relations are constraints that are imposed on data and operations in order for the object to behave properly. Declarative specification of these relations can make the requirements for the object explicit. Thus, three aspects of an object are specified: the data component, the functional component and the relations among the data and operations. See [2] for details about how to specify an object.

4.2 Specifying Relationships among Objects

After specifying the internal structure and behavior of individual objects, the global structure and behavior of the system are described by specifying the relationships among the objects. ORTES identifies 5 relationships: classification, aggregation, association, usage and constraints. The first three relationships describe the static structure of the system, while the latter two help describe the dynamic aspects. The specifications of these relationships constitute a *relationship* model. For details about how to build a relationship model, see [2].

5 Relationships between the Four Models

We have described how ORTES builds four models for modeling a process control system: the *environmental model*, the *task model*, the *object model* and the *relationship model*. These models are generated through activities of *requirement analysis, task analysis, identifying objects, assigning tasks to objects, specifying objects, and specifying relationships among objects*. The relationship among the four models and the activities is depicted in Figure 8.

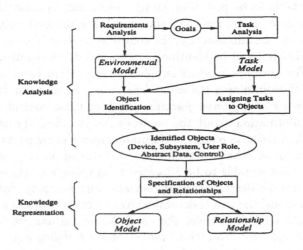

Fig. 8. Relationships of the Four Models and the Activities

6 Conclusions

We have presented ORTES as a new method for conceptual modeling of real-time expert systems. As an object-oriented analysis method, ORTES differs from other object-oriented methods since it considers object structures and task structures to be equally important and decomposes the system along both data and functional dimensions. To avoid arbitrary functional decomposition, which may cause difficulties in system maintenance, ORTES provides a generic task structure for real-time systems. With the task structure, the system functionality is better described than using low-level descriptions such as *use cases* or *event-response lists*. ORTES also provides comprehensive guidelines for identifying objects and assigning functions to objects. Compared to other KM methods, ORTES has the advantage of providing an object-oriented representation and supporting analysis of real-time systems. The object-oriented representation represents a system in terms of real-world objects and their relationships, which closely models a person's perceptions of reality and thus easy to understand. To model real-time systems, ORTES provides classification schemes for both objects and tasks that may exist in a real-time system, which help the knowledge engineer classify and organise knowledge items. Finally, as an expert system analysis method, ORTES's generic task structure helps the knowledge engineer to structure interviews with experts and to organise the obtained problem solving expertise. In particular, meta-control knowledge is addressed in the task structure, which is often needed in knowledge-based control systems. We have applied ORTES to modeling an expert system for monitoring and controlling a municipal water supply system [2]. Our experience with this application is that modeling the expert system with ORTES helps us better organise the knowledge we obtained from experts than using other conceptual modeling methods. Well-organised knowledge also leads to easy tracing of the knowledge items in the object-oriented conceptual model.

Acknowledgements

The authors are members of the Institute for Robotics and Intelligent Systems (IRIS) and wish to acknowledge the support of the Networks of Centres of Excellence Program of the Government of Canada, the Natural Sciences and Engineering Research Council, and the participation of PRECARN Associates Inc.

References

1. Adams, G. and Corriveau, J.P. 1994. "Capturing object interactions". In Magnusson, B., Meyer, B., Nerson,J.M. and Perrot, J.F.(ed.): *Tools 13*. Hemel Hempstead: Prentice-Hall.
2. An, A. 1997. "Part I: Modeling Real-time Expert Systems". *Analysis Methodologies for Integrated Enhanced Problem Solving*. Ph.D. Dissertation, Department of Computer Science, University of Regina, Canada.
3. Booch, G. 1994. *Object-Oriented Analysis and Design*, Redwood City, California: The Benjamin/Cummings.
4. Chan, C.W. 1992. *Inferential Modeling Technique for Analysis and Interpretation of Expertise*. Ph.D. Dissertation, Dept. of Computing Science, Simon Fraser University.
5. Chandrasekaran, B. 1986. " Generic Tasks in Knowledge-Based Reasoning: High-Level Building Blocks for Expert System Design". *IEEE Expert*, Fall, pp.23-30.
6. Ellis, J.R. 1994. *Objectifying Real-Time Systems*. SIGS Publications, Inc. New York.
7. Graham, I. 1992. "A Method for Integrating Object Technology with Rules", *Advanced information systems: the new technologies in today's business environment: incorporating the Sixth Int. Expert Systems Conference proceedings*, London.
8. Hayes-Roth, B., Pfleger, K., Lalanda, P., Morignot, P. and Balabanovic, M. 1995. "A Domain-Specific Software Architecture for Adaptive Intelligent Systems". *IEEE Transactions on Software Engineering*, April.
9. Jacobson, I., Christerson, M., Jonsson, P., and Overgaard, G., 1992, *Object-oriented Software Engineering*, Workingham, England: Addison-Wesley Publishing Company.
10. Rumbaugh, J., Blaha, M., Premerlani, W., Eddy, F., and Lorensen, W. 1991. *Object-oriented Modeling and Design*, Englewood Cliffs, New Jersey: Prentice-Hall.
11. Wielinga, B.J., Schreiber, A. TH. and Breuker, J.A. 1992. "KADS: A Modeling Approach to Knowledge Engineering". Knowledge Acquisition, 4(1), pp92-116.

A Statistical Approach to Rule Selection in Semantic Query Optimisation

Barry G. T. Lowden and Jerome Robinson

Department of Computer Science, The University of Essex,
Wivenhoe Park, Colchester, CO4 3SQ, Essex,
United Kingdom

Abstract. Semantic Query Optimisation makes use of the semantic knowledge of a database (rules) to perform query transformation. Rules are normally learned from former queries fired by the user. Over time, however, this can result in the rule set becoming very large thereby degrading the efficiency of the system as a whole. Such a problem is known as the *utility problem*. This paper seeks to provide a solution to the utility problem through the use of statistical techniques in selecting and maintaining an optimal rule set. Statistical methods have, in fact, been used widely in the field of Knowledge Discovery to identify and measure relationships between attributes. Here we extend the approach to Semantic Query Optimisation using the Chi-square statistical method which is integrated into a prototype query optimiser developed by the authors. We also present a new technique for calculating Chi-square, which is faster and more efficient than the traditional method in this situation.

1 Introduction

Semantic query optimization is the process of transforming a query into an alternative query that is semantically equivalent but executes in a shorter time. A semantically equivalent query returns the same result set as the original query and is generated from it by the application of rules.

Rules can consist of 'integrity constraints' that hold for all states of the database or 'dynamic rules' that hold only for a given state. Generally, rules can be supplied by the database engineer or derived automatically. Automatic rule generation methods include heuristic based systems [13], logic based systems [1], graph based systems [12] and data driven systems [7, 11].

With the development of automatic rule derivation, it becomes increasingly important to filter out ineffective rules which can lead to a deterioration in optimisation performance. The overall size of the rule set (n) is also of crucial importance since some optimisation algorithms run in $O(n^2)$ time.

The problem of a large rule set degrading the efficiency of the reformulation process is referred to as the *utility problem* [4, 8, 10, 14]. Earlier work by the authors [6] partially addressed the utility problem by time stamping rules when created, modified or used by the reformulation process. When the number of rules exceeds a specified limit, those which are recorded as unused for more than a given period of time or have a low usage count are removed from the rule set.

To further explore this problem we have examined a range of statistical tests as applied in knowledge discovery research [5, 8, 2]. In this paper we propose the use of Chi-square for the analysis and selection of effective rules for query optimisation.

In section 2 we briefly describe a prototype optimiser, developed by the authors, on which we base our experiments. We then discuss a method of calculating Chi-square which is particularly appropriate to the present application and in section 4 we present our computational results.

2 The *ARDOR* prototype

In most rule derivation systems, the characteristics of worthwhile rules are first identified and then a query issued to the database in an attempt to derive such rules. The *ARDOR* system [7] takes a different approach whereby actual queries to the system are used to learn new rules. For each query (q) an optimum alternative (q') is constructed, using a simple inductive process. The equality q ⟺ q' is then used to deduce the minimum set of rules needed to perform the transformation algorithmically and these rules added to the rule base.

The system is illustrated in Figure 1 and consists of (1) query reformulation, and (2) the rule derivation and learning modules. The query reformulation process takes the original query submitted by the user and attempts to reformulate it into a more cost effective query by matching the conditions of the query to the rule set using a 'best first' search strategy. For issues relating to bounded optimality of search strategies see [9].

By this means, the original query is transformed into a semantically equivalent query known as a reformulated query using the standard transformation rules of constraint introduction and removal [3]. This query will give the same result as the original query but with normally a shorter execution time.

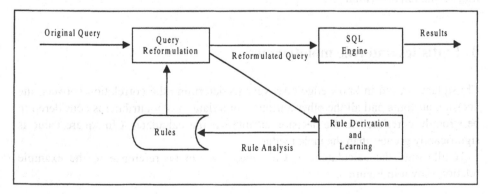

Fig. 1. Overview of Query Optimiser

It is also possible for the reformulation process to return a query result without the need to access the database at all leading to very substantial time savings. Such a situation occurs when the result of the query can be deduced from the rules alone as illustrated in Figure 2 by two simple examples.

All rules in the *ARDOR* system consist of a single antecedent and consequent. Rules sharing both common antecedent and consequent attributes are said to belong to the same *rule class*. Each time a user query is entered to the system, the learning process will attempt to generate new rules by constructing matching conditions on all attributes other than those present in the original query. Matching conditions are those which evaluate true with respect to the answer set.

Original Query(1)	: select advisor from student where uccacode = 'B70002'
Rule	: uccacode = 'B70002' $\longrightarrow$ advisor = 210
Result	: advisor = 210
Original Query(2)	: select advisor from student where uccacode = 'B70002' and advisor = 300
Rule	: uccacode = 'B70002' $\longrightarrow$ advisor = 210
Result	: null result returned

Fig. 2. Results returned without need for database lookup

Each new rule generated is added to the current rule set which, over time, may become excessively large. Also many of the rules could eventually become obsolete with respect to the present database state and should be discarded.

Having a rule set that contains entries that are not useful to the query optimizer is wasteful in storage space, and more importantly degrades the performance of the transformation algorithm.

3 Statistics and rule maintenance

Chi-square is used in knowledge discovery to determine the correlation between the decision attribute and all the other attributes in a dataset. An attribute is considered to be strongly correlated to the decision attribute if the calculated Chi-square value is significantly greater than the tabled value.

To illustrate the calculation of Chi-square, we make reference to the example relation shown in Figure 3.

dcode	dname	project	manager
ACCT	Accounting	1	ACCT01
ACCT	Accounting	1	ACCT02
ACCT	Accounting	5	ACCT01
MKTG	Marketing	2	MKTG01
MKTG	Marketing	2	MKTG04
MKTG	Marketing	2	MKTG05
MKTG	Marketing	3	MKTG02
MKTG	Marketing	4	MKTG03
MKTG	Marketing	5	MKTG01
MKTG	Marketing	5	MKTG04
MKTG	Marketing	5	MKTG05
MKTG	Marketing	6	MKTG02
MKTG	Marketing	6	MKTG03
PRSN	Personnel	7	PRSN01
PRSN	Personnel	8	PRSN02

Fig. 3. An example relation

The first step in calculating the Chi-square correlation is to arrange the data in a frequency or contingency table. Each column represents a group and each row represents a category of the sample relation. Figure 4 depicts such a table.

	Group			
Category	**1**	**2**	**3**	**Total**
1	n_{11}	n_{12}	n_{13}	R_1
2	n_{21}	n_{22}	n_{23}	R_2
3	n_{31}	n_{32}	n_{33}	R_3
Total	C_1	C_2	C_3	N

Fig. 4. A (3x3) frequency or contingency table

The Chi-square significance can be calculated by the following formula:

$$X^2 = \sum_{i=1}^{r} \sum_{j=1}^{c} \frac{\left(n_{ij} - E_{ij}\right)^2}{E_{ij}}$$

or

$$X^2 = \sum_{i=1}^{r} \sum_{j=1}^{c} \frac{n_{ij}^2}{E_{ij}} - N$$

where n_{ij} = observed number of cases of in ith row and jth column

E_{ij} = number of cases expected in the ith row and jth column.

Under the assumption of independence, the expected frequency of the observation in each cell should be proportional to the distribution of row and column totals. This expected frequency is the product of the row and column total divided by the total number of observations.

Thus E_{ij} may be calculated from the following formula:

$$E_{ij} = \frac{R_i \times C_j}{N}$$

The total frequency R_i in the ith row is

$$R_i = \sum_{j=1}^{c} n_{ij}$$

Similarly, the total frequency in the jth column is

$$C_j = \sum_{i=1}^{r} n_{ij}$$

The statistical degree of freedom (df) for the Chi-square is calculated as:

$$df = (r-1)(c-1)$$

Given, for example, the rule:

dname = 'Accounting' $\Rightarrow$ dcode = 'ACCT'

we may construct the contingency table for the associated rule class, Figure 5.

Category	Group (dcode)			
(dname)	ACCT	MKTG	PRSN	Total
Accounting	3	0	0	3
Marketing	0	10	0	10
Personnel	0	0	2	2
Total	3	10	2	15

Fig. 5. Frequency table for dname and dcode

Using the earlier expression, the Chi-square value calculated is 29.80 with degree of freedom (df) = 4. Choosing a confidence interval equal to 97.5%, the tabled Chi-square value is 11.14. Since the calculated value is greater than the value tabled, the rule is considered to be relevant and retained in the rule set.

In certain circumstances it may be appropriate to construct a contingency table limited to a restricted subset of categories where knowledge of the data indicates that this subset shows a markedly different correlation between antecedent and consequent attributes compared with other subsets in the same rule class. For example in the case of shoe size and age, it would be known that the correlation would be much greater for small shoe sizes since, in general, these would relate to children and consequently be associated with a restricted age spectrum.

3.1 Algorithm design and memory limitation

The implementation of the Chi-square statistical test normally requires the construction of a contingency table to hold the sampled frequencies of each row and column, the size of the table being dependent on the number of categories. If the size of the table becomes excessive this may well degrade the performance and efficiency of the statistical algorithm. The extreme case is where the table grows to a size beyond the memory limits of the system i.e. page swapping would then occur. These problems would imply that, in some cases, it may not be feasible to employ this technique for rule analysis and an alternative method of calculation is now presented. Consider the contingency table shown in Figure 6:

Antecedent	Consequent			Total
value(1)	n_{11}	n_{12}	n_{13}	T_{R1}
value(2)	n_{21}	n_{22}	n_{23}	T_{R2}
value(3)	n_{31}	n_{32}	n_{33}	T_{R3}
Total	T_{C1}	T_{C2}	T_{C3}	N

Fig. 6. A (3 × 3) contingency table

As before the Chi-square is given as follows:

$$X^2 = \sum_{i=1}^{r}\sum_{j=1}^{c} \frac{\left(n_{ij} - E_{ij}\right)^2}{E_{ij}}$$

applying this formula to the above table, i.e. R=3 and c=3, we have:

$$X^2 = \frac{\left(n_{11} - E_{11}\right)^2}{E_{11}} + \frac{\left(n_{21} - E_{21}\right)^2}{E_{21}} + \frac{\left(n_{31} - E_{31}\right)^2}{E_{31}} + \frac{\left(n_{12} - E_{12}\right)^2}{E_{12}} +$$

$$= \frac{\left(n_{22} - E_{22}\right)^2}{E_{22}} + \frac{\left(n_{32} - E_{32}\right)^2}{E_{32}} + \frac{\left(n_{13} - E_{13}\right)^2}{E_{13}} + \frac{\left(n_{23} - E_{23}\right)^2}{E_{23}} +$$

$$= \frac{\left(n_{33} - E_{33}\right)^2}{E_{33}}$$

where $E_{ij} = \dfrac{T_{Ri} \times T_{Cj}}{N}$.

If, for some cell $n_{ij} = 0$, then the contribution to X^2 from that cell is just $E_{ij}^2/E_{ij} = E_{ij}$. So the contribution from all the cells having zero observed frequency is simply the sum of the corresponding E_{ij}.

Furthermore, there is no need to calculate their individual values. We know that the sum of the complete set of expected frequencies is N. If we sum the expected frequency, E_{ij}, of all the non-zero cells and subtract this value from N we have the total χ^2 contribution from the cells with zero observed frequencies. Therefore the only computation needed would be for cells with non-zero frequency count.

We illustrate the method by means of the following example. Let us assume that n_{11}, n_{22} and n_{33} have values 3, 4 and 2 respectively and all other cells contain a zero. The traditional way of calculating Chi-square would be:

$$X^2 = \frac{\left(3-\frac{9}{9}\right)^2}{\frac{9}{9}} + \frac{\left(0-\frac{12}{9}\right)^2}{\frac{12}{9}} + \frac{\left(0-\frac{6}{9}\right)^2}{\frac{6}{9}} + \frac{\left(0-\frac{12}{9}\right)^2}{\frac{12}{9}} + \frac{\left(4-\frac{16}{9}\right)^2}{\frac{16}{9}}$$

$$+ \frac{\left(0-\frac{8}{9}\right)^2}{\frac{8}{9}} + \frac{\left(0-\frac{6}{9}\right)^2}{\frac{6}{9}} + \frac{\left(0-\frac{8}{9}\right)^2}{\frac{8}{9}} + \frac{\left(2-\frac{4}{9}\right)^2}{\frac{4}{9}} = 18$$

Our proposed alternative is to compute those cells that have non-zero cells separately from those that have zero frequency counts as follows.

$$\textit{Non-zero Chi-square} = \frac{\left(3-\frac{9}{9}\right)^2}{\frac{9}{9}} + \frac{\left(4-\frac{16}{9}\right)^2}{\frac{16}{9}} + \frac{\left(2-\frac{4}{9}\right)^2}{\frac{4}{9}}$$

$$= 12\frac{2}{9}$$

$$\textit{Zero Chi-square} = 9 - (1 + \frac{16}{9} + \frac{4}{9}) = 5\frac{7}{9}$$

The sum of these two values gives the same result as before without the need to construct a contingency table. This method is not restricted to diagonal tables alone and so may be used to represent rule classes of the form A $\Rightarrow$ B OR C.

4   Experimental Results

A series of experiments were carried out in order to measure any increase in optimiser performance achieved through the statistical analysis and subsequent elimination of ineffective rules.

In each case a specified query collection was executed against the database in order to generate a 'full' associated rule set using the ARDOR rule derivation and learning modules. The rule set was then subjected to the Chi-square analysis, as described in the above section, to filter out those rules considered to be weak thus creating a 'restricted rule' set. The initial query execution was then repeated first using the full rule set and then the restricted set to perform query transformation and optimisation.

In one representative experiment the following results were obtained by running a collection of ten queries, shown below, against a 7184 instance database containing real data pertaining to student records at the University of Essex.

Query Collection:

Q1) select * from student2 where status = 'A' and school = 'CSG';

Q2) select * from student2 where advisor = 479 and uccacode = 'B70002';

Q3) select * from student2 where entry < 91 and entry > 83 and examno = 0 and
 school = 'SEG';

Q4) select * from student2 where advisor = 259 and entry = 90 and status = 'A';

Q5) select scheme from student2 where entry = 90 and study = 'PHD CHEM';

Q6) select name, regno, advisor from student2 where entry = 85 and year = 'G';

Q7) select * from student2 where uccacode = 'Q10081' and entry = 90;

Q8) select advisor from student2 where uccacode = 'B70002';

Q9) select name, regno, advisor from student2 where entry = 85
 and regno <= 8556636 and regno >= 8548056;

Q10) select examno from student2 where school = 'SEG';

The queries include range, numeric and set membership conditions and make reference to both indexed attributes (name and regno) and also non-indexed attributes. The relational schema is shown in Fig. 7.

STUDENT 2	(**name**	char(30),	**regno**	integer,
	logname	char(8),	advisor	integer,
	entry	integer,	year	char(2),
	scheme	char(6),	uccacode	char(6),
	status	char(1),	examno	integer,
	study	char(8),	school	char(4))

Fig. 7. Relational Scheme of STUDENT database

Query execution resulted in the generation of 51 rules. The rule derivation module runs as a background task and so does not adversely affect the execution process.

338

Application of the Chi-square test to this rule set identified 16 rules which could be considered as weak, and therefore discarded, leaving 35 strong rules considered to be particularly effective for query optimisation.

Finally the query optimiser was run using both the full and restricted rule sets and the results shown in Figure 8. These results were averaged over 50 runs and include query transformation costs. Queries Q2, Q8 and Q10 show the greatest overall savings since they can be answered from the rule set alone without the need to access the database itself. Queries Q1, Q3 and Q4 are examples of where the transformation process cannot improve on the original query. In this case query costing routines incorporated within the optimiser would return the original query as optimal for execution.

Full rule set = 51, restricted set = 35. Timings (secs)			
QUERY	Unoptimised	Full set	Restr. set	Tot. Saving
Q1)	1.98	2.71	1.79	0.19
Q2)	1.84	0.13	0.07	1.77
Q3)	2.11	2.81	1.92	0.19
Q4)	2.21	2.22	1.82	0.39
Q5)	1.79	1.55	1.48	0.31
Q6)	1.92	1.67	1.59	0.33
Q7)	2.04	1.75	1.72	0.32
Q8)	2.31	0.15	0.17	2.14
Q9)	1.89	2.13	1.73	0.16
Q10)	2.17	0.13	0.11	2.06

Fig. 8. Experimental Results

Overall an average time saving of 30.5% was achieved across all the queries executed using the full rule set with a further improvement to 38.8% using the restricted rule set. It should be emphasised, however that the performance increase shown is as a result of applying the Chi-square rule filter to a recently derived and therefore generally relevant rule set.

Even greater savings, with respect to the use of the full rule set, may be achieved by the Chi-square analysis of rule sets which have become out of date with respect to the current database state. The use of Chi-square, therefore, ensures not only the quality of rules when they are first derived but also subsequently their relevance and effectiveness to the ongoing optimisation process.

5 Conclusions

The efficiency of a semantic optimiser is largely dependent on the number and quality of the rules used in the query transformation process. In this paper we have described how the Chi-square statistical test may be used to identify and eliminate rules which are considered to be weak and ineffective. Experimental results show significantly improved performance is achieved using this approach which can be run in conjunction with other rule selection techniques. A revised Chi-square calculation procedure has also been presented which does not require the construction of a contingency table.

References

1. U. S. CHAKRAVARTHY, J. GRANT and J. MINKER. Logic-based approach to semantic query optimisation. ACM Transactions on Database Systems, Vol. 15, No. 2, June 1990, 162-207.
2. K. C. CHAN and A. K. C. WONG. A statistical test for extracting classificatory knowledge form databases. Knowledge Discovery in Databases, Ed., The AAAI Press, 1991, 107-123.
3. G. GRAEFE and D. DEWITT. The EXODUS optimiser generator. Proceedings of the ACM-SIGMOD Conference on Management of Data, San Francisco, May 1987, 160-171.
4. J. HAN, Y. CAI and N. CERCONE. Data-driven discovery of quantitative rules in relational databases. IEEE Transactions on Knowledge and Data Engineering, Vol. 5, no. 1, February 1993, 29-40.
5. I. F. IMAM, R. S. MICHALSKI and L. KERSCHBERG. Discovering attribute dependence in database by integrating symbolic learning and statistical analysis tests. Knowledge Discovery in Databases Workshop, 1993, 264-275.
6. B. G. T. LOWDEN and K. Y. LIM. A data driven semantic optimiser, CSM 211, Internal Publication, University of Essex.
7. B. G. T. LOWDEN, J. ROBINSON and K. Y. LIM, A semantic optimiser using automatic rule derivation. Proceedings of Workshop on Information Technologies and Systems, 1995, 68-76.
8. G. PIATETSKY-SHAPIRO, and C. MATHEUS. Measuring data dependencies in large databases. Knowledge Discovery in Databases Workshop ,1993, 162-173.
9. S. RUSSELL. Rationality and Intelligence. Artificial Intelligence 94, 1997, 57-77.
10. I. SAVNIK and P. A.. FLACH. Bottom-up induction of functional dependencies from relations. Knowledge Discovery in Databases Workshop, 1993, 174-185.
11. S. SHEKHAR, B. HAMIDZADEH and A. KOHLI. Learning transformation rules for semantic query optimisation: a data-driven approach. IEEE , 1993, 949-964.
12. S. T. SHENOY and Z. M. OZSOYOGLU. Design and implementation of semantic query optimiser. IEEE Transactions on Knowledge and Data Engineering, Vol. 1, No. 3, Sept. 1989, 344-361.
13. M. D. SIEGEL, E. SCIORE and S. SALVETER. A method for automatic rule derivation to support semantic query optimisation. ACM Transactions on Database Systems, Vol. 17, No. 4, Dec. 1992, 563-600.
14. W. ZIARKO. The discovery, analysis, and representation of data dependencies in databases. In Knowledge Discovery in Databases, The AAAI Press, 1991, 195-209.

Representing and Reasoning on Conceptual Queries Over Image Databases

Mohand-Saïd Hacid[1]* and Christophe Rigotti[2]

[1] LuFg Theoretical Computer Science
RWTH Aachen, Ahornstraße 55, 52074 Aachen, Germany
hacid@@cantor.informatik.rwth-aachen.de
[2] LISI-INSA Lyon, Bâtiment 501,
F-69621 Villeurbanne Cedex
crig@@lisi.insa-lyon.fr

Abstract. The problem of content management of multimedia data types (e.g., image, video, graphics) is becoming increasingly important with the development of advanced multimedia applications. In this paper we develop a knowledge-based framework for modeling and retrieving image data. To represent the various aspects of an image object's characteristics, we propose a model which consists of three layers: (1) Feature and Content Layer, intended to contain image visual features such as contours, shapes, etc.; (2) Object Layer, which provides the (conceptual) content dimension of images; and (3) Schema Layer, which contains the structured abstractions of images. We propose two abstract languages on the basis of description logics: one for describing knowledge of the object and schema layers, and the other, more expressive, for making queries. Queries can refer to the form dimension (i.e., information of the Feature and Content Layer) or to the content dimension (i.e., information of the Object Layer). As the amount of information contained in the previous layers may be huge and operations performed at the Feature and Content Layer are time-consuming, resorting to the use of materialized views to process and optimize queries may be extremely useful. For that, we propose a formal framework for testing containment of a query in a view expressed in our query language.

1 Introduction

With recent progress in compression technology, it is possible for a computer to store huge amount of images, audio and even video. If such media are widely used in today's communication (e.g. in the form of home movies, education and training, scholarly research, and corporate enterprise solutions), efficient computer exploitation is still lacking. Many databases should be created to face the increasing development of advanced applications, such as digital libraries, archival and processing of images captured by remote-sensing satellites and air

* Work supported in part by the Deutscher Akademischer Austausch Dienst (DAAD) grant A/98/05793.

photos, training and education, entertainment, medical databases, virtual reality, Internet video, interactive TV, group-ware applications, etc. Though only a partial list, these advanced applications indicate that the problem of efficiently and user-friendly accessing to image/video data is widely encountered in real-life applications and solutions to it is significant. An important feature to be considered is content-based retrieval of the multimedia data types. For example, there are two essential questions associated with content-based query systems for imaging data [8]: (1) How to specify queries, and (2) How to access the intended data efficiently for given queries. These queries may be formulated in terms of a number of different image features, and can be grossly classified into three categories [14]: (1) *form queries*, addressing images on the basis of color, texture, sketch, or shape specifications; (2) *content queries*, focusing on domain concepts, spatial constraints, or various types of attributes; (3) *mixed queries*, which combine the two previous categories.

Despite some proposals on finding appropriate representations of image data and systems architectures able to support such representations, there is little research work on finding semantic foundations for query optimization in image databases. This paper is a contribution in this direction. We take a new look at the problem of modeling and querying image data and find that knowledge representation and reasoning techniques for concept languages developed in Artificial Intelligence provide an interesting angle to attack such problems. We exploit the possibility of using two languages: one for defining the schema (i.e. the structure) of an image database and populating it, and the other, more expressive, for querying the database through the schema.

We build on work by Chu et al. [7] to propose three layers for representing image content:

(1) *Feature and Content Layer:* It contains image features such as contours, spatial relationships, etc. This layer is characterized by a set of techniques allowing to retrieve images based on the similarity of physical features such as region, color, and shape.

(2) *Object Layer:* This layer contains objects of interest, their descriptions, and relationships among objects based on the extracted features[1]. This layer constitutes what we call the extensional part of an image database. Objects in an image are represented in the object layer as visual entities. Instances of visual objects consist of conventional attributes (e.g. name, patientID, date, etc.) as well as visual attributes (e.g. shape, size, etc.) of objects contained in the feature and content layer.

The interface between the *Feature and Content Layer* and the *Object Layer* is determined by the *Feature and Content Layer* itself and a set of predicates (e.g., similar-to predicates) over this Feature and Content Layer. Objects of the *Object Layer* are related to objects of the Feature and Content Layer via attributes.

(3) *Schema Layer:* This layer is intended to capture the structured abstractions and knowledge that are needed for image retrieval. It contains a general

---

[1] Features can be extracted *manually*, *semi-automatically* or *automatically*.

schema about the classes of objects stored in the object layer, their general properties and mutual relationships. In this layer, visual entities can be classified into a hierarchical structure known as a concept hierarchy on the basis of both conventional and visual attributes. This layer is well suited for integrating domain knowledge.

The part of a query that pertains to the Feature and Content Layer is processed by specialized signal processing procedures, and hence are time consuming. In addition, the amount of information contained in the object layer is huge. To enable quick response to the queries, the strategy based on the use of materialized[2] views to compute answers to queries can turn out to be useful. Supporting materialized views to process and optimize queries is the topic of much recent work on data-intensive applications (e.g., see [13]). Reasoning on queries in the case of image databases is not only relevant to determine views that can be used for answering queries, but it can be applied to organize large sets of queries into taxonomies which can be important to support navigation. For that, we develop an algorithm for checking the *containment*[3] between a query and a view (which is seen as a query as well) expressed in our query language.

   Although, in the basic form that we give here, the languages do not account for all aspects of image data, they constitute kernels to be extended. Showing how we can model and reason about the structure of image databases and queries is useful and significant.

Paper outline: In Section 2, we develop our languages, give their Tarski-style extensional semantics, and a calculus for query containment. Section 3 discusses related work. We conclude in Section 4 by anticipating on the necessary extensions.

2 The Languages

Before we give the syntax and semantics of our *abstract languages*, we define *concrete domains*, which are used to incorporate application-specific domains (i.e., strings, reals, integers, etc.) into the abstract domain of individuals.

Definition 1. (Concrete Domains) A concrete domain $\mathcal{D} = (\text{dom}(\mathcal{D}), \text{pred}(\mathcal{D}))$ consists of:

- the domain $\text{dom}(\mathcal{D})$,
- a set of predicate symbols $\text{pred}(\mathcal{D})$, where each predicate symbol $P \in \text{pred}(\mathcal{D})$ is associated with an arity n and an n-ary relation $P^{\mathcal{D}} \subseteq \text{dom}(\mathcal{D})^n$,

In many applications (in particular when querying databases), one would like to be able to refer to concrete domains and predicates on these domains when defining queries. An example of a concrete domain could be the set of (nonnegative) integers with comparisons $(=, <, \leq, \geq, >)$.

---

[2] A materialized view is a query whose a physical copy of each instance, answer to the query, is stored and maintained.

[3] Containment of queries is the problem of checking whether the result of one query is contained in what another query produces [1].

2.1 Schema Language ($\mathcal{SL}$)

We now introduce a simple description logic that will be used for describing the structure of an image data. Starting from atomic concepts and roles, complex concepts are built by using the universal quantification ($\forall$) and predicate restrictions. The syntax and the semantics of this description logic are given below.

Definition 2. (Syntax) Let N_C, N_R, N_f be three pairwise disjoint sets of concept names, role names, and feature (i.e., functional role) names respectively, $\mathcal{D}_1, \ldots, \mathcal{D}_k$ be concrete domains. Let P be a role name, $f, f_1, \ldots, f_n$ be feature names, A be a concept name, A' be a concept name or a concrete domain name, and P_r be an n-ary predicate name. Concept terms C, D are defined by the following rules:

$$
\begin{aligned}
C, D \longrightarrow A \mid & \qquad \text{(primitive concept)} \\
\forall P.A \mid & \qquad \text{(typing of role)} \\
\forall f.A' \mid & \qquad \text{(typing of feature)} \\
P_r(f_1, \ldots, f_n) & \quad \text{(predicate restriction)}
\end{aligned}
$$

Let A, A_1, A_2 be concept names, A_3 be a concept name or a concrete domain name, D be a concept term, P be a role name, and f be a feature name. Then $A \mathrel{\dot{\preceq}} D$ (we say A is a subconcept of D), $P \mathrel{\dot{\preceq}} A_1 \times A_2$, $f \mathrel{\dot{\preceq}} A_1 \times A_3$ are called *axioms*. A $\mathcal{SL}$ schema S consists of a finite set of axioms. In the following, we consider only *acyclic* schemas. A schema S is acyclic if no concept name occurs–neither directly nor indirectly–within its own specification.

Definition 3. (Semantics) The semantics is given by an interpretation $\mathcal{I} = (\Delta^{\mathcal{I}}, \cdot^{\mathcal{I}})$, which consists of an (abstract) interpretation domain $\Delta^{\mathcal{I}}$, and an interpretation function $\cdot^{\mathcal{I}}$. The abstract domain has to be disjoint from any given concrete domain, i.e., $\Delta^{\mathcal{I}} \cap \mathrm{dom}(\mathcal{D}_i) = \emptyset$ for all concrete domain $\mathcal{D}_i$ ($i \in [1, k]$), the concrete domains are pairwise disjoint, and $\mathrm{pred}(\mathcal{D}_i) \cap \mathrm{pred}(\mathcal{D}_j) = \emptyset$ for $i \neq j$. The interpretation function $\cdot^{\mathcal{I}}$ associates each concept C with a subset $C^{\mathcal{I}}$ of $\Delta^{\mathcal{I}}$, each role P with a binary relation $P^{\mathcal{I}}$ on $\Delta^{\mathcal{I}}$, and each feature name f with a partial function $f^{\mathcal{I}} : \Delta^{\mathcal{I}} \to (\Delta^{\mathcal{I}} \cup (\bigcup_{i=1}^{k} \mathrm{dom}(\mathcal{D}_i)))$. Additionally, $\mathcal{I}$ has to satisfy the following equations:

$$
\begin{aligned}
(\forall P.A)^{\mathcal{I}} &= \{d \in \Delta^{\mathcal{I}} \mid \forall d' \in \Delta^{\mathcal{I}} : \\
& \qquad\qquad (d^{\mathcal{I}}, d'^{\mathcal{I}}) \in P^{\mathcal{I}} \to d'^{\mathcal{I}} \in A^{\mathcal{I}}\} \\
(\forall f.A')^{\mathcal{I}} &= \{d \in \Delta^{\mathcal{I}} \mid \text{ if } f^{\mathcal{I}}(d^{\mathcal{I}}) \text{ is defined then} \\
& \qquad\qquad f^{\mathcal{I}}(d^{\mathcal{I}}) \in A'^{\mathcal{I}}\} \\
(P_r(f_1, \ldots, f_n))^{\mathcal{I}} &= \{d \in \Delta^{\mathcal{I}} \mid (f_1^{\mathcal{I}}(d^{\mathcal{I}}), \ldots, f_n^{\mathcal{I}}(d^{\mathcal{I}})) \in P_r^{\mathcal{D}}\}
\end{aligned}
$$

An interpretation $\mathcal{I}$ satisfies the axiom $A \mathrel{\dot{\preceq}} D$ iff $A^{\mathcal{I}} \subseteq D^{\mathcal{I}}$, the axiom $P \mathrel{\dot{\preceq}} A_1 \times A_2$ iff $P^{\mathcal{I}} \subseteq A_1^{\mathcal{I}} \times A_2^{\mathcal{I}}$, and the axiom $f \mathrel{\dot{\preceq}} A_1 \times A_3$ iff $f^{\mathcal{I}} \subseteq A_1^{\mathcal{I}} \times A_3^{\mathcal{I}}$. If A_3 is a concrete domain name then $A_3^{\mathcal{I}}$ stands for the domain of A_3 (i.e., $\mathrm{dom}(A_3)$) for all $\mathcal{I}$. An interpretation $\mathcal{I} = (\Delta^{\mathcal{I}}, \cdot^{\mathcal{I}})$ is a model, also called a valid interpretation, of a schema S iff it satisfies every axiom in S.

344

An interpretation $\mathcal{I}$ that satisfies all axioms in S is called an S-interpretation.

The language introduced previously allows to describe knowledge about classes of individuals and relationships between these classes. We can now turn our attention to the extensional level, which we call the *ABox*. The *ABox* essentially allows one to specify instance-of relations between individuals and classes (concepts), and between pairs of individuals and roles or features.

Definition 4. Let N_I and N_D be two disjoint alphabets of symbols, called abstract individual names and concrete individual names respectively. Instance-of relationships are expressed in terms of *membership assertions* of the form: $a : C$, $(a, b) : P$, $(a, b) : f$, $(a, z) : f$, and $(z_1, \ldots, z_n) : P_r$, where a and b are abstract individual names, $z, z_1, \ldots, z_n$ are concrete individual names, C is a concept name or an arbitrary concept, P is a role name, and P_r is an n-ary predicate name of a concrete domain. Intuitively, the first form states that a is an instance of C, and the second form states that a is related to b by means of the role P (we also say b is a P-successor of a).

An interpretation $\mathcal{I}$ is easily extended to individuals and membership assertions.

An *ABox* $\mathcal{A}$ is a finite set of membership assertions. An interpretation $\mathcal{I}$ is a model for an *ABox* $\mathcal{A}$ iff $\mathcal{I}$ satisfies all the assertions in $\mathcal{A}$.

2.2 Query Language ($\mathcal{QL}$)

Querying a database means retrieving stored objects that satisfy certain *conditions* or *qualifications* and hence are interesting for a user. In the case of relational databases, queries are constructed by means of algebra expressions defined on relations from the database. As a property, answers are also relations (i.e., sets of tuples). This correspondence between database entities and answer formats presents advantages that lead to the design and development of query optimization techniques. In object-oriented databases, classes are used to represent sets of objects. By analogy with the relational approach, classes can be used for *describing query results*. If such a possibility exists, then we can consider some kind of *reasoning* on the structure[4] of classes that will lead to reveal, for example, *subsumption* relationships between queries.

In this paper, we follow this approach. Queries are represented as concepts in our abstract language.

Definition 5. (Syntax) Let A be a concept name, P be an atomic role, d be an abstract individual name, $f_1, f_2, \ldots, g_1, g_2, \ldots$ be feature names, $P_r \in \mathrm{pred}(\mathcal{D}_i)$ for some $i \in [1, k]$ be an n-ary predicate name, and $P_{r_j} \in \mathrm{pred}(\mathcal{D}_i)$ for some $i \in [1, k]$ ($j \in [1, m]$) be a binary predicate name. Concepts C, D and roles R, R' can be formed by means of the following syntax:

$$C, D \longrightarrow \top \mid A \mid C \sqcap D \mid \{d\} \mid \exists R.C \mid P_r(f_1, \ldots, f_n) \mid$$
$$\Theta(C, D, \{\langle f_1, P_{r_1}, g_1\rangle, \ldots, \langle f_m, P_{r_m}, g_m\rangle\})$$
$$R, R' \longrightarrow P \mid P^- \mid R \circ R'$$

[4] And hence the semantics of class hierarchies.

Definition 6. (Semantics) $\mathcal{I}$ is defined as in definition 3. Additionally, $\mathcal{I}$ has to satisfy the following equations:

$$\top^{\mathcal{I}} = \Delta^{\mathcal{I}}$$

$$(\exists R.C)^{\mathcal{I}} = \{d \in \Delta^{\mathcal{I}} \mid \exists d' : (d^{\mathcal{I}}, d'^{\mathcal{I}}) \in R^{\mathcal{I}} \wedge d'^{\mathcal{I}} \in C^{\mathcal{I}}\}$$

$$P_r(f_1, \ldots, f_n)^{\mathcal{I}} = \{d \in \Delta^{\mathcal{I}} \mid (f_1^{\mathcal{I}}(d^{\mathcal{I}}), \ldots, f_n^{\mathcal{I}}(d^{\mathcal{I}})) \in P^{\mathcal{D}}\}$$

$$\{d\}^{\mathcal{I}} = \{d^{\mathcal{I}}\}$$

$$(R \circ R')^{\mathcal{I}} = \{(d, d') \in \Delta^{\mathcal{I}} \times \Delta^{\mathcal{I}} \mid \exists c \in \Delta^{\mathcal{I}} \text{ such that}$$
$$(d^{\mathcal{I}}, c^{\mathcal{I}}) \in R^{\mathcal{I}} \wedge (c^{\mathcal{I}}, d'^{\mathcal{I}}) \in R'^{\mathcal{I}}\}$$

$$(\Theta(C, D, \{\langle f_1, P_{r_1}, g_1\rangle, \ldots, \langle f_m, P_{r_m}, g_m\rangle\}))^{\mathcal{I}} =$$
$$\{d \in \Delta^{\mathcal{I}} \mid d \in C^{\mathcal{I}} \text{ and } \exists d' \, d' \in D^{\mathcal{I}} \text{ such that}$$
$$(f_1^{\mathcal{I}}(d^{\mathcal{I}}), g_1^{\mathcal{I}}(d'^{\mathcal{I}})) \in P_{r_1}^{\mathcal{D}_{P_{r_1}}} \wedge \ldots \wedge (f_m^{\mathcal{I}}(d^{\mathcal{I}}), g_m^{\mathcal{I}}(d'^{\mathcal{I}})) \in P_{r_m}^{\mathcal{D}_{P_{r_m}}}\}$$

2.3 Query Containment

Definition 7. (Containment) Given a $\mathcal{SL}$ schema $\mathcal{S}$, a query Q and a view V in $\mathcal{QL}$ language, are the answers to Q also answers to V for any database state obeying the schema $\mathcal{S}$.

A query Q is $\mathcal{S}$-satisfiable if there is an $\mathcal{S}$-interpretation $\mathcal{I}$ such that $Q^{\mathcal{I}} \neq \emptyset$. We say that Q is $\mathcal{S}$-contained in V (written $Q \preceq_S V$) if $Q^{\mathcal{I}} \subseteq V^{\mathcal{I}}$ for every $\mathcal{S}$-interpretation $\mathcal{I}$.

We have devised an algorithm (see [10]) for deciding containment of a query in a view. The basic idea for deciding the *containment* of a query Q in a view V is drawn from [4]. We take an object o and transform Q into a prototypical database state where o is an answer to Q. We do so by generating individuals, entering them into concepts in the schema, and relating them through roles and features. If o belongs to the answer of V, then Q is contained in V. If not, we have a state where an individual is in the answer to Q but not in the answer to V and therefore V does not contain Q. The details of the algorithm and the proof of the following theorem can be found in [10].

Theorem 8. *Containment of a query in a view in our query language can be decided in time polynomial to the size of Q, V and S.*

3 Related Work

Our work relates to several fields of research in databases and Artificial Intelligence. We shortly discuss the relationship to modeling and retrieving image data by content, multimedia databases and query optimization.

Modeling and Retrieving Image Data by Content. Modeling and retrieving image data by content has been considered from both database and artificial intelligence points of views. Meghini *et al.* [15] have investigated the use of a description logic as a conceptual tool for modeling and querying image data. The problem with this language is that subsumption between concepts is $PSPACE$-complete. In addition, They do not consider predicate restrictions over concrete domains. Hsu *et al.* [11] proposed a knowledge-based approach for retrieving images by content. The knowledge-based query processing is based on a query relaxation technique which exploits a Type Abstraction Hierarchy of image features. The query language is an extension of OQL[5] to include specific predicates (e.g., *similar-to* predicates).

Multimedia. Goble *et al.* [9] proposed a description logic, called, GRAIL, for describing the image and video semantic content. A set of dedicated constructors are used to capture the structural part of these media objects. The aim is to support the coherent and incremental development of a coarse index on the semantic annotations of media documents. Lambrix and Padgham [12] described an extended description logic for representing and retrieving documents. The description logic includes part-of relations and allows for ordering information between the parts.

In these two proposals, the underlying query languages support only queries based on the structure of the documents (i.e., conceptual queries). None of them supports visual queries. Together with [15] they do not take into account predicate restrictions over concrete domains, which are extremely useful when querying multimedia repositories. In addition, they did not address the questions of decidability and complexity of reasoning services in their languages.

Query Optimization in Multimedia databases. The problem of optimizing queries over multimedia repositories has been addressed in recent works (see, among others, [6]). In summary, these works consider the indexes used to search the repository and user-defined filter conditions to define an execution space that is search-minimal. Semantic query optimization considers semantic knowledge for constructing query evaluation plans, and the framework for testing query containment presented in this paper is relevant due to the incorporation of schema knowledge in our algorithm. In multimedia applications where metadata play an important role [17], these two kinds of query optimization have to cohabit.

4 Conclusion

There is now intense interest in multimedia systems. These interests span across vast areas in computer science, such as computer networks, databases, distributed computing, data compression, document processing, user interfaces, artificial intelligence, etc. In the long run, we expect that intelligent-solving systems will access information stored in a variety of formats, on a wide variety of media.

Multimedia information is inherently complex. Traditional database techniques do not apply since, for example, they do not deal with content-based retrieval. We believe that the combination of database techniques and intelligent information retrieval will contribute to the realization of intelligent multimedia systems. Artificial intelligence, and more specifically knowledge representation, will play an important role in this task.

347

Our work focuses on a fundamental problem, namely, a content-based retrieval of image data. We have merely laid a formal and flexible framework which is appropriate for modeling and reasoning about meta-data and queries in image databases. Expressiveness and services of the meta data schema are crucial for image database quality[5]. The framework is general in that little needs to be changed when making extensions or taking other constructors for the abstract languages. In addition, this framework is appropriate for supporting semantic indexing [16], conceptual queries [18] and intensional queries [3]. Indeed, as the information structure that is contained in image databases is usually complicated and amount of information is huge, users may prefer to express queries with more general and abstract information instead of primitive terms directly based on the data stored in a database.

There are many interesting directions to pursue. (1) An important direction of active research is to significantly extend this framework to support part-whole relations. The result reported in [2] constitutes a nice basis; (2) Due to the visual nature of the data, a user may be interested in results that are similar to the query, thus, the query system should be able to perform exact as well as partial or fuzzy matching.

We are investigating these important research directions.

References

1. Serge Abiteboul, Richard Hull, and Victor Vianu. *Foundations of Databases*. Addison-Wesley, 1995.
2. Alessandro Artale, Enrico Franconi, Nicola Guarino, and Luca Pazzi. Part-Whole Relations in Object-Centered Systems: An Overview. *Data & Knowledge Engineering*, 20(3):347–383, December 1996.
3. Sonia Bergamaschi, Claudio Sartori, and Maurizio Vincini. Description Logic Techniques for Intensional Query Answering in OODBs. In Franz Baader, Martin Buchheit, Manfred Jeusfeld, and Werner Nutt, editors, *Proceedings of the 2nd Workshop on Knowledge Representation meets DataBases (KRDB'95), Bielefeld, Germany*, September 1995.
4. Martin Buchheit, Manfred A. Jeusfeld, Werner Nutt, and Martin Staudt. Subsumption Between Queries to Object-Oriented Databases. In *Proceedings of the 4th International Conference on Extending Database Technology (EDBT'94), Cambridge, UK*, March 1994. (Also in Information Systems 19(1), pp. 33-54, 1994).
5. Rick Cattel. *The Object Database Standard: ODMG-93*. Morgan Kaufmann, San Mateo, CA, 1994.
6. Surajit Chaudhuri and Luis Gravano. Optimizing Queries over Multimedia Repositories. In H.V. Jagadish and Inderpal Singh Mumick, editors, *Proceedings of the 1996 ACM SIGMOD International Conference on Management of Data (SIGMOD'96), Montréal, Québec, Canada,*, pages 91–102, June 1996.

[5] Quality implies accessibility, optimization, validation, etc.

7. Wesley W. Chu, Alfonso F. Cárdinas, and Ricky K. Taira. Knowledge-Based Image Retrieval with Spatial and Temporal Constructs. In Zbigniew W. Raś and Andrzej Skowron, editors, *Proceedings of the 10th International Symposium on Methodologies for Intelligent Systems (ISMIS'97), Charlotte, North Carolina, USA*, LNAI - 1325, pages 17–34. Springer, October 1997.

8. Tzi cker Chiueh. Content-Based Image Indexing. In Jorge Bocca, Matthias Jarke, and Carlo Zaniolo, editors, *Proceedings of the 20th International Conference on Very Large Data Bases (VLDB'94), Santiago, Chile*, pages 582–593, September 1994.

9. C. A. Goble, C. Haul, and S. Bechhofer. Describing and Classifying Multimedia Using the Description Logic GRAIL. In Ishwar K. Sethi and Ramesh C. Jain, editors, *Storage and retrieval for image and video database IV (SPIE'96), San Jose, California*, pages 132–143, February 1996.

10. Mohand-Said Hacid and Christophe Rigotti. Representing and Reasoning on Conceptual Queries Over Image Databases. Research Report TCS-99-02, LuFG Theoretical Computer Science, RWTH-Aachen, Germany, 1999.

11. Chih-Cheng Hsu, Wesley W. Chu, and Ricky K. Taira. A Knowledge-Based Approach for Retrieving Images by Content. *IEEE Transactions on Knowledge and Data Engineering*, August 1996.

12. Patrick Lambrix and Lin Padgham. A Description Logic Model for Querying Knowledge Bases for Structured Documents. In Zbigniew W. Raś and Andrzej Skowron, editors, *Proceedings of the 10th International Symposium on methodologies for Intelligent Systems (ISMIS'97), Charlotte, North Carolina, USA*, LNAI 1325, pages 72–83. Springer, October 1997.

13. Alon Y. Levy, Alberto O. Mendelzon, Yehoshua Sagiv, and Divesh Srivastava. Answering Queries Using Views. In *Proceedings of the 1995 Symposium on Principles of Database Systems (PODS'95), San Jose, CA, USA*, pages 95–104, May 1995.

14. Carlo Meghini. Towards a Logical Reconstruction of Image Retrieval. In Ishwar K. Sethi and Ramesh C. Jain, editors, *Storage and retrieval for image and video database IV (SPIE'96), San Jose, California*, pages 108–119, February 1996.

15. Carlo Meghini, Fabrizio Sebastiani, and Umberto Straccia. The Terminological Image Retrieval Model. In Alberto Del Bimbo, editor, *Proceedings of ICIAP'97, 9th International Conference On Image Analysis And Processing*, volume II, pages 156–163, Florence, I, September 1997.

16. Albrecht Schmiedel. Semantic Indexing Based on Description Logics. In Franz Baader, Martin Buchheit, Manfred Jeusfeld, and Werner Nutt, editors, *Proceedings of the 1st Worshop on Knowledge Representation meets DataBases (KRDB'94), Saarbrücken, Germany*, September 1994.

17. Amit Sheth and Wolfgang Klas. *Multimedia Data Management: Using Metadata to Integrate and Apply Digital Media*. Mc Graw Hill, 1998.

18. S.C. Yoon. Towards Conceptual Query Answering. In Zbigniew W. Raś and Andrzej Skowron, editors, *Proceedings of the 10th International Symposium on methodologies for Intelligent Systems (ISMIS'97), Charlotte, North Carolina, USA*, LNAI 1325, pages 187–196. Springer, October 1997.

Knowledge Discovery in Clinical Databases: An Experiment with Rule Induction and Statistics

Shusaku Tsumoto

Department of Information Medicine, Medical Research Institute,
Tokyo Medical and Dental University
1-5-45 Yushima, Bunkyo-ku Tokyo 113 Japan
E-mail: tsumoto@computer.org

Abstract. *The main difference between empirical learning methods and KDD methods is that the latter approaches support discovery of knowledge in databases whereas the former ones focus on extraction of accurate knowledge from databases. Therefore, for application of KDD methods, domain experts' interpretation of induced results is crucial. However, conventional approaches do not focus on this issue clearly. In this paper, several KDD methods are compared by using a common database and the induced results are interpreted by a medical expert, which enables us to characterize KDD methods more concretely and to show the importance of interaction between KDD researchers and domain experts.*

1 Introduction

Empirical learning method[8] have been developed in order to acquire knowledge which is similar to that of domain experts. On the other hand, knowledge discovery in databases(KDD)[5, 7] has a different goal, to extract knowledge which is not always expected by domain experts, which will lead to a new discovery in applied domain. For this purpose, the evaluation of predictive accuracy[8] is not enough and domain experts'interpretation of induced results is crucial for discovery. However, conventional approaches do not focus on this issue clearly. In this paper, rule induction, decision tree induction and statistical methods were compared by using a common medical database on meningoencepahlitis. The induced results were interpreted by a medical expert, which showed us that rule induction methods generated unexpected results, whereas decision tree methods and statistical methods acquired knowledge corresponding to medical experts. These results enable us to characterize KDD methods more concretely and to show the importance of interaction between KDD researchers and domain experts.

2 Database on Meningoencephalitis

2.1 Characteristic of Datasets

The common datasets collect the data of patients who suffered from meningitis and were admitted to the department of emergency and neurology in several hospitals. The author worked as a domain expert for these hospitals and collecting those data from the past patient records (1979 to 1989) and the cases in which the author made a diagnosis (1990 to 1993).

The database consists of 121 cases and all the data are described by 34 attributes, including present and past history, laboratory examinations, final diagnosis, therapy, clinical courses and final status after the therapy (Table 1).[1]

Table 1. Attributes in Dataset

Category		Number of Attributes
Present History	Numerical and Categorical	7
Physical Examination	Numerical and Categorical	8
Laboratory Examination	Numerical	11
Diagnosis	Categorical	1
Therapy	Categorical	1
Clinical Course	Categorical	4
Final Status	Categorical	1
Risk Factor	Categorical	1

2.2 Statistical Analysis and Experts' Prejudice

The author analyzed the subset of this database(99 cases), which was collected until 1989 by using the t-test and χ^2-test and reported to the conference on acute medicine in Japan[9]. Before domain experts usually apply statistical methods to a database, they remove some attributes from a dataset according to their knowledge from a textbook[1] or the literature. In the case of the analysis above, age and sex are removed from a dataset since information about these attributes is not in such a textbook.

Concerning numerical data, body temperature, Kernig sign, CRP, ESR, and CSF cell count had a statistical significance between bacteria and virus meningitis. As to categorical data, loss of consciousness and the finding in CT had a statistical significance between two groups. Also, the analysis suggested that the finding in CT should be an important factor for the final status of meningitis.

However, all these results were expected by medical experts, which means that the author did not discover new knowledge.

3 Statistical Analysis

Inspired by induced results with KDD-R[10], the author applied t-test and χ^2-test again to a dataset, including age and sex.

---

[1] Except for one attribute, all the attributes do not have any missing values.

3.1 χ^2-test

The categorical attributes which have a significance between two groups are shown in Table 2. These results gives the following suggestions:

Table 2. χ^2-test

Attribute	p-value
SEX	0.00226
KERNIG (Kernig sign)	0.0144
LOC_DAT(Loss of Consciousness)	0.00760
CT_FIND(CT findings)	0.00002
CULT_FIND(Detection of Virus or Bacteria)	0.02
Risk_Factor(Risk Factor)	<0.00001

1. Male have a tendency to suffer from bacterial meningitis.
2. Kernig sign, loss of consciousness, and CT findings may be important factors for diagnosis of bacterial meningitis.
3. In the case of bacterial meningitis, the search for the bacteria is much easier than that of viral one.
4. Bacterial meningitis have several risk factors, such as DM.

3.2 Student's t-test

The numerical attributes which have a significance between two groups are shown in Table 3.

Table 3. T-test

Attribute	Bacteria	Virus	p-value
AGE	43.9	35.0	0.00247
BT (Body Temperature)	38.0	37.4	0.011
CRP	4.33	0.415	< 0.00001
ESR	8.8	3.35	0.010
CSF_CELL	4357	441	0.0005
(CSF Cell Count)			

These results show that patients suffering from bacterial meningitis have higher value of age, body temperature, CRP, ESR and CSF cell count.

These results are the same as those in [9], except for age, sex and risk factors. They are also corresponding to the results discovered by Tsumoto and Ziarko[10], although the former do not include any information about the relations between attributes.

4 Decision Tree

CART, developed by Breiman[4], was applied to a database on meningoencephalitis, the results of which are shown in Figure 1 and 2, where (a, b) denotes the number of examples of bacterial and virus meningitis, respectively. For splitting, Gini index was adopted and one-SE-rule was used for pruning.

As shown in Figure 1, the tree induced without pruning is a little complicated, where the same attributes are observed in several nodes.[2]

On the other hand, the tree induced with pruning is too simple for diagnosis of viral meningitis.

5 Rule Induction

5.1 Representation of Rule

The basic measures for rule are two conditional probabilities, accuracy, $\alpha_R(D)(= p(D|R))$ and coverage, $\kappa_R(D)(= p(R|D))$. The former shows how many examples which satisfy R belong to D and the latter does how many examples belonging to D satisfy R. They are defined as follows by using the framework of Rough Sets[6]

$$\alpha_R(D) = \frac{card\ ([x]_R \cap D)}{card\ [x]_R}, \kappa_R(D) = \frac{card\ ([x]_R \cap D)}{card\ D},$$

where R, $[x]_R$ and D denote a conjunctive formula, a set whose members satisfy R and a set belonging to D.

By the use of these two measures, a probabilistic rule is defined as: [3]

$$R \xrightarrow{\alpha, \kappa} d\ s.t.\ \alpha_R(D) > \delta_\alpha, \ and\ \kappa_R(D) > \delta_\kappa,$$

where δ_α, δ_κ are thresholds for accuracy and coverage, respectively.

From this definition, a rule induction algorithm is described as Figure 3.

5.2 Discovered Knowledge

For analysis, the thresholds for accuracy and coverage were set to 0.7 and 0.5. Rule induction method generated 67 for viral meningitis and 95 for bacterial meningitis, which included the following rules unexpected by domain experts as shown belows. Especially, rules from 5 to 7 are new induced results, compared with those discovered by Tsumoto and Ziarko[10].

---

[2] However, it is also notable that only eight attributes are used to construct the tree, which suggests that only 8 in 33 attributes be important for differential diagnosis.

[3] This rule is equivalent to association rule[2].

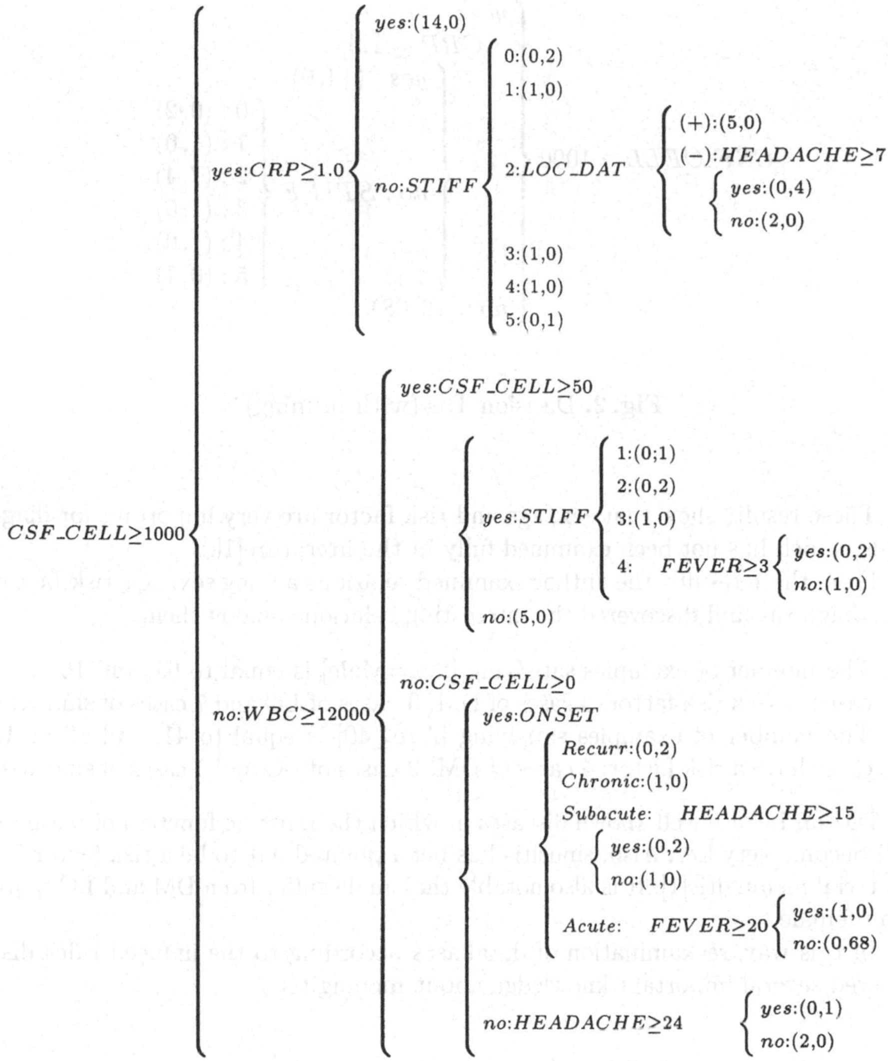

$yes:CRP \geq 1.0$
- $yes:(14,0)$
- $no:STIFF$
  - $0:(0,2)$
  - $1:(1,0)$
  - $2:LOC\_DAT$
    - $(+):(5,0)$
    - $(-):HEADACHE \geq 7$
      - $yes:(0,4)$
      - $no:(2,0)$
  - $3:(1,0)$
  - $4:(1,0)$
  - $5:(0,1)$

$CSF\_CELL \geq 1000$
- $yes:CSF\_CELL \geq 50$
  - $yes:STIFF$
    - $1:(0;1)$
    - $2:(0,2)$
    - $3:(1,0)$
    - $4: \quad FEVER \geq 3$
      - $yes:(0,2)$
      - $no:(1,0)$
  - $no:(5,0)$
- $no:WBC \geq 12000$
  - $no:CSF\_CELL \geq 0$
  - $yes:ONSET$
    - $Recurr:(0,2)$
    - $Chronic:(1,0)$
    - $Subacute: \quad HEADACHE \geq 15$
      - $yes:(0,2)$
      - $no:(1,0)$
    - $Acute: \quad FEVER \geq 20$
      - $yes:(1,0)$
      - $no:(0,68)$
  - $no:HEADACHE \geq 24$
    - $yes:(0,1)$
    - $no:(2,0)$

Fig. 1. Decision Tree(without Pruning)

```
1. [WBC < 12000]^[Sex=Female]^[CSF_CELL < 1000] -> Viral
                                 (Accuracy:0.97, Coverage:0.55)
2. [Age > 40]^[WBC > 8000] -> Bacterial   (Accuracy:0.80, Coverage:0.58)
3. [WBC > 8000]^[Sex=Male] -> Bacterial   (Accuracy:0.78, Coverage:0.58)
4. [Sex=Male]^[CSF_CELL>1000]-> Bacterial (Accuracy:0.77, Coverage:0.73)
5. [Risk_Factor=n]->Viral                 (Accuracy:0.78, Coverage:0.96)
6. [Risk_Factor=n]^[Age <40] -> Viral     (Accuracy:0.84, Coverage:0.65)
7. [Risk_Factor=n]^[Sex=Female] -> Viral  (Accuracy:0.94, Coverage:0.60)
```

354

$$CSF\_CELL \geq 1000 \begin{cases} yes: \\ \quad CRP \geq 1.0 \begin{cases} yes: (14,0) \\ \\ no: STIFF \begin{cases} 0:(0,2) \\ 1:(1,0) \\ 2:(7,4) \\ 3:(1,0) \\ 4:(1,0) \\ 5:(0,1) \end{cases} \end{cases} \\ no: (12,68) \end{cases}$$

Fig. 2. Decision Tree(with pruning)

These results show that sex, age and risk factor are very important for diagnosis, which has not been examined fully in the literature[1].

From these results, the author examined relations among sex, age, risk_factor and diagnosis and discovered the interesting relations among them:

1. The number of examples satisfying [Sex=Male] is equal to 63, and 16 of 63 cases have a risk factor: 3 cases of DM, 3 cases of LC and 7 cases of sinusitis.
2. The number of examples satisfying [Age$\geq$40] is equal to 41, and 12 of 41 cases have a risk factor: 4 cases of DM, 2 cases of LC and 4 cases of sinusitis.

DM an LC are well known diseases in which the immune function of patients will become very low. Also, sinusitis has been pointed out to be a risk factor for bacterial meningitis[1]. It is also notable that male suffer from DM and LC more than female.

In this way, reexamination of databases according to the induced rules discovered several important knowledge about meningitis.

6 Statistical Multivariate Analysis

While rule induction methods and decision tree methods can be viewed as non-parametric multivariate analysis, statistical multivariate analysis, such as logit analysis, can be viewed as parametric multivariate analysis[3].

6.1 Discriminant Analysis

Step-wise feature selection method for discriminant analysis was applied to the dataset, where the threshold for F-value is set to 3.0. The selected attributes are shown in Table 4.[4] These results show that the risk factor is the most important

---

[4] Categorical attributes were transformed into Integers.

```
procedure Induction of Classification Rules;
  var
    i : integer;   M, Lᵢ : List;
  begin
    L₁ := Lₑᵣ; /* Lₑᵣ: List of Elementary Relations */
    i := 1;   M := {};
    for i := 1 to n do      /* n: Total number of attributes */
      begin
        while ( Lᵢ ≠ {} ) do
          begin
            Sort Lᵢ with respect to the value of coverage;
            Select one pair R = ∧[aᵢ = vⱼ] from Lᵢ,
            which have the largest value on coverage;
            Lᵢ := Lᵢ − {R};
            if (κ_R(D) ≥ δ_κ)
              then do
                if (α_R(D) ≥ δ_α)
                then  do Sᵢᵣ := Sᵢᵣ + {R}; /* Include R as Classification Rule */
                else M := M + {R};
          end
        Lᵢ₊₁ := (A list of the whole combination of the conjunction formulae in M);
      end
  end {Induction of Classification Rules };
```

Fig. 3. An Algorithm for Classification Rules

factor for discriminiation and the discriminant equation obtained is represented as:

$$y = 8.40 * Risk\_Factor + 0.420 * CRP + \cdots + 2.732 * CT\_FIND - 17.32,$$

where if this function for a case is larger than 0, the case will be classified into bacterial meningitis.

6.2 Logit Analysis

Step-wise feature selection method for multiple logistic regression was also applied to the dataset, where the threshold for F-value is set to 3.0. The selected attributes are shown in Table 6.[5]

The regression equation obtained is:

$$y = 1/(1 + exp(-(5.3355 * Risk\_Factor + \cdots - 1.380 * SEX + 28.2241)),$$

where if the value of function for a case is equal to 1.0, then the case will be classified to bacterial and if the value is to 2.0, then it will be classified into viral.

---

[5] Categorical attributes were transformed into Integers.

Table 4. Selected Attributes(Discriminant Analysis)

Attributes	Coefficient	F-value	p-value
Risk_Factor	8.400	46.699	5.43E-10
CRP	0.420	21.844	8.73E-06
CSF_CELL	2.49E-04	16.748	8.35E-05
ONSET	-8.004	24.439	2.89E-06
COLD	-0.224	8.679	0.00395
HEADACHE	-0.155	7.625	0.00678
CULT_FIND	2.464	7.000	0.0110
FOCAL	2.701	6.576	0.0117
BT	0.672	5.062	0.0265
CT_FIND	2.372	4.726	0.0319
Constant	-17.342		

Table 5. Attributes Selected by Logit Analysis

Attribute	Coefficient	F-value	p-value
Risk_Factor	-5.3355	15.310	0.00016
ONSET	6.2535	11.349	0.00104
HEADACHE	0.1651	8.953	0.00342
CRP	-0.6464	7.488	0.00724
BT	-0.7696	6.462	0.01242
AGE	-0.0500	5.291	0.02333
EEG_WAVE	-3.3206	5.080	0.02618
WBC	-7.175E-05	3.563	0.06171
SEX	-1.380	3.081	0.08202
Constant	28.2241		

6.3 Summary

The results from two methods suggest that Risk_Factor, ONSET,CRP, and CSF_CELL are important for differential diagnosis,whereas SEX and AGE are not so important. If the threshold for F is set to higher values to obtain a simpler equation, then SEX and AGE will not be selected. It is because these statistical methods are based on optimization methods and the selection of attributes is influenced by the attributes selected before, which will be also observed in the case of decision tree induction[4].

7 Conclusion

In this paper, rule induction, decision tree induction and statistical methods were compared by using a common medical database on meningoencepahlitis.

The induced results were interpreted by a medical expert, which showed us that rule induction methods generated unexpected results, whereas decision tree methods and statistical methods induces only part of knowlege obtained by rule induction. This comparison shows that although decision tree and statistical methods are very fast to obtain the results from a database, some important information, which is unexpected by domain experts, cannot be discovered from the data. Thus, combination of these methods may be important to support a new discovery from a dataset, in which the interpretation of domain experts will play a crucial role.

References

1. Adams, R.D. and Victor, M. *Principles of Neurology*, 5th edition, McGraw-Hill, 1993.
2. Agrawal, R., Imielinski, T., and Swami, A.: Mining association rules between sets of items in large databases, *Proceedings of the 1993 International Conference on Management of Data (SIGMOD 93)*, pp. 207-216 (1993).
3. Anderson, T.W.: *An Introduction to Multivariate Statistical Analysis*, John Wiley & Sons (1984).
4. Breiman, L., Freidman, J., Olshen, R., and Stone, C.: *Classification And Regression Trees.*, Wadsworth International Group (1984).
5. Fayyad, U.M., et al.(eds.): *Advances in Knowledge Discovery and Data Mining*, AAAI Press (1996).
6. Pawlak, Z. *Rough Sets*, Kluwer Academic Publishers, Dordrecht (1991).
7. Piatetsky-Shapiro, G. and Frawley, W.: *Knowledge Discovery in Databases*, AAAI Press (1991).
8. *Readings in Machine Learning*, (Shavlik, J. W. and Dietterich, T.G., eds.) Morgan Kaufmann, Palo Alto (1990).
9. Tsumoto, S., et al. Examination of factors important to predict the prognosis of virus meningoencephalitis. *Japanese Kanto Journal of Acute Medicine*, **12**,710-711 (1991).
10. Tsumoto, S., Ziarko, W., Shan, N., Tanaka, H.: Knowledge Discovery in Clinical Databases based on Variable Precision Rough Set Model Proceedings of the Eighteenth Annual Symposium on Computer Applications in Medical Care, Journal of the AMIA **2**, supplement, pp.270-274 (1995).
11. Ziarko, W. Variable Precision Rough Set Model, Journal of Computer and System Sciences, **46**: 39- 59 (1993).

Reasoning and Acquisition of Knowledge in a System for Hand Wound Diagnosis and Prognosis

M.Michalewicz, M.A.Klopotek, S.T.Wierzchoń

Institute of Computer Science, Polish Academy of Sciences
Ordona 21, 01-237 Warsaw, Poland
Fax: (48 22) 37 65 64, Phone: (48 22) 36 28 85, 36 28 41 or 36 28 62 ext.45
e-mail: michalew, klopotek, stw@ipipan.waw.pl

Abstract. The paper describes a diagnostic system for hand wounds. The system shall not only propose diagnostic decisions (because this would not be sufficient for starting a complex therapeutic treatment), but shall also provide with a number of subdiagnoses describing results of subtests and makes available tools for knowledge acquisition from data. The system, implemented as a CGI service, possesses an interface based on an HTML-browser in an Internet-like network.
It consists of a bilingual database, a dictionary subsystem, a deterministic expert system, a Bayesian network base expert system, an automatic Bayesian network acquisition module and a visual Bayesian network editor.

Key words: Intelligent Information Systems, Knowledge Representation and Integration, Learning and Knowledge Discovery, reasoning, diagnostic systems, Bayesian networks, internet.

1 Introduction

This paper describes the implementation of knowledge acquisition and corresponding reasoning tools in an educational expert system in the domain of hand wound diagnosis with an interface based on an HTML-browser in an Internet-like network.

A number of medical expert systems has been described already in the literature, to mention keywords like MYCIN [3] or INTERRNIST [9]. One of important drawbacks of those systems was their inability to acquire (at least partial) knowledge from available data.

The diagnostic system for hand wounds elaborated in our research group shall not only propose diagnostic decisions (because this would not be sufficient for starting a complex therapeutic treatment), but shall also provide with a number of subdiagnoses describing results of subtests and makes available tools for knowledge acquisition from data. It should be stressed that medical knowledge required for full diagnosis of hand wounds is so vast that its normalization for purposes of an expert system had to be restricted within this project to the stage of introductory diagnosis.

Within this system, there is a distinctive difference between prognostic and diagnostic activities. The final diagnosis, given all necessary results of medical tests are collected, requires application of a few deterministic rules because of the advances of experts in the field. Data collection, however, is in itself a complex process and requires partial (deterministic) reasoning in order to determine the sequence of diagnostic tests. The prognosis of the chances of successful treatment on the other hand cannot be obtained fully deterministically. In fact it is still subject of research, so a full laboratory for probabilistic knowledge acquisition and reasoning seemed to be potentially beneficial.

Partial reasoning during the data collection stage means that if e.g. the tests done so far indicate missing activity of a particular motion nerve, then later tests of active motion for related muscles may be either pointless or should be carried out using a different technique. Other tests may indicate necessity of additional tests beyond standard set of diagnostic tests. A further constraint is the necessity to restrict patient's pain resulting from the investigation. The capability of the patient to cooperate should also be taken into account (differentiated tests for adults and children).

Another problem is the general support for the person collecting the data. Each step in data collection, each diagnostic step, each applied induction rule has to be well illustrated, so that the respective medical test would be carried out properly and the result entered correctly into the system. Also later usage of previously collected data for better understanding of future cases seems to be important, especially concerning possible outcomes of particular types of treatment. As this area of hand wound diagnosis is not well-understood, automatic knowledge generation from data may provide important insights into relationship between elements of initial diagnosis, laboratory parameters and treatment applied.

2 User's View of the System

From user's point of view, the system permits to diagnose a hand wound and to make a prognosis on the perspectives of healing.

The diagnostic steps are essentially the following: After collecting typical personal data on patient identity and history the type of the wound is asked for (e.g. a cut wound, electric shock, amputation, breakage etc.). For each type of wound its area has to be entered on a graphical screen. Depending on the type of the wound additional questions are posed (e.g. degree in case of burning wounds, chemical substance type in case of chemically caused wounds).

Subsequently the system guides the (future) physician through all necessary tests: radiological test, treatment of external blooding or tests of internal blooding, tests of feeling and motion nerves, of muscles, of passive and active motion. Finally a summary of the tests carried out is presented to the user in terms of most important data either entered by the user or deduced by the system.

The results of the consultation may be saved in a database.

After a diagnostic consultation the user may ask for a prognostic consultation provided by a (non-deterministic) Bayesian expert system.

At each stage of the work with the system the natural language used for communication can be switched (between Polish and German).

3 Technical Structure of the System

The scheme of the system has been presented in [18].

All modules have been implemented as specialized servers (CGI programs) cooperating with a HTTPd-Server under MS Windows NT.

The user communicates with the system via a frame-enabled HTML-Browser under any operational system/hardware that permits usage of Java applets.

3.1 Deterministic Educational Expert Subsystem

The system maintains so-called fact-base, which contains data stemming from fill-in forms filled in by the user, the areas indicated by the user in clickable images and results of partial reasoning run by the system. In response to data provided by the user, the system generates each time a context-(fact base-)dependent reply document guiding further data acquisition, or providing answers to user's questions or presenting final results. In the process, a hypertext knowledge base is used.

Because of the particular nature of application domain, the data collection is strongly interleaved with a graphically illustrated help system and offers the technique "clickable image" for collection of some data. The graphical images (photos, drawings) in many cases can explain the user the medical procedure better (and quicker) than dozens of lines of written text. On the other hand clicking a mouse on the image of a hand at the place of a distortion may enter data quicker and more reliably than selection of an item from a list with up to 70 entries (as in case of regions of burning wounds).

The knowledge base is split in so-called reply forms. Each reply form is encoded in a special language consisting of the standard HTML language constructions enriched by CodeBase-like expressions that may:

- evaluate to a HTML-string, or
- evaluate to an image in the .gif format, or
- update the fact base by results of some reasoning, or
- retrieve expressions from the (bilingual) dictionary

in response to recently entered user data. The result of each of these operations is of course dependent on the current content of the fact base. The system evaluates the reply form generating a reply document encoded in the pure HTML-language (and possibly several additional reply images in .gif - format) and sends this document back to the user.

The document contains usually several fill-in fields, some links to help documents, illustrative images, clickable images and some "hints" for later processing of user responses like which form to use next on the given path, which fields are to be updated automatically, whether the fact base or the data base is to be used etc. In response to the reply document the user fills in the fields and presses the submit-button or clicks on the clickable image or presses buttons leading him to auxiliary (help) information, gets again a reply document and so on. The format of a reply form is described in detail in [18].

3.2 Dictionary Subsystem

In general, there exist several possibilities for implementing multilingual interfaces. Within this system, static texts (HTML files and partially form files) are written as two copies: one in Polish and one in German. However, part of the information has to be provided dynamically: in response to specific user queries and special conditions.

The dynamic part of the bilingual interface is implemented using special functions of the educational expert system.

Nearly all the information collected from the user is encoded. Each attribute has an up to 10 characters long code name (eg. the attribute sex has a code name GESCHLECHT-). Each value of each discrete attribute has a two-digit code (for example GESCHLECHT01 encodes woman and GESCHLECHT02 encodes man). A dictionary has been created assigning each attribute and each attribute value a proper name both in Polish and in German. Beside this, the dictionary contains some phrases not necessarily associated with any of the attributes like some common warnings, e.g. one encoded PHRASE0001++. If a reply document should contain Polish or German text dependent on the data collected, the Polish-German dictionary of code names is searched and the proper decoding of the code value is presented to the user.

The system offers also the possibility to search its own dictionary to provide the user with translations of Polish and German medical terms that the human translator has provided as important in the application area.

3.3 Bayesian Expert System

By Bayesian expert system we understand a system performing inferences over a graphical knowledge base, where the knowledge base is specified by two components: the qualitative structure and the set of parameters. The qualitative structure is a directed acyclic graph $G = (V, E)$ where V is a set of nodes representing the variables involved in the problem under considerations and E is a set of directed edges of the form $X \rightarrow Y$; we say that X is the parent of Y and that Y is the son of X. Usually a parent of a node Y is interpreted as the cause of Y, hence the network G is said to be a causal network. Now for each variable X in

V we specify the conditional probability $Pr(X|\pi(X))$ where $\pi(X)$ stands for the set of parents (called a set of immediate causes) of X in the network G; if $\pi(X)$ is the empty set then $Pr(X|\emptyset) = Pr(X)$ is the a priori probability of X. We assume that all the variables have discrete domains, hence each conditional probability is stored as a table of appropriate size. The set of parameters determines the joint probability function $P(X_1, ..., X_n) = Pr(X_1|\pi(X_1))...Pr(X_n|\pi(X_n))$ specific to a given problem. For further reference we abbreviate $P(X_1 = x_1, ..., X_n = x_n)$ to $P(x_1, ..., x_n)$. Thus if $x = (x_1, ..., x_n)$ then the above formula can be rewritten in the form $P(x_1, ..., x_n) = \prod_{i=1}^{n} Pr(x_i|x_{pa_i})$ where x_{pa_i} stands for the projection of x onto the set of variables $\pi(Xi)$.

It is important to note that the separation of the qualitative and the quantitative structure makes relatively easy the process of construction of such a knowledge base. In general the knowledge base is a summarization of expert's knowledge and in our case this summarization may be acquired from a domain expert or it may be identified from a database (see Section 3.5).

Having constructed a Bayesian network, i.e. a directed acyclic graph G together with the parameters $Pr(X_i|\pi(X_i))$, $i = 1...n$, we define the two fundamental queries:

- Belief updating, or probabilistic reasoning: given an evidence o find a conditional probability $Pr(x_i|o)$. Here x_i denotes a value of i-th variable, and o is a tuple consisting of the values of the observed (clamped) variables from the set O.
- Finding the most probable explanation: given an evidence o defined for the set of variables O, let y be a set of values from the set V
  O and $x = (y, o)$ be the concatenation of y and o. The aim is to find a tuple x^* such that $P(x^*) = max_x P(x)$. Denote x^* the 1-MPE (first most probable explanation). Deleting x^* from the set of admissible configurations we can serch for another value maximizing the joint probability function; this is so-called 2-MPE. In a similiar way we can define k-MPE.

It is possible to define more complicated queries, e.g. to find the most probable explanation for a subset of variables only - this is a mixture of two previously defined tasks. However all these task are NP-complete and to solve them effectively we translate the original Bayesian network into a secondary structure, a join tree called also a Markov tree (consult [5] or [15, 16]). Within such a structure all the queries can be solved by using the idea of dynamic programming [2]. There are three main architectures implementing such a recipe: the Lauritzen- Spiegelhalter architecture [7], the Shenoy-Shafer architecture [10] and the HUGIN architecture [5]. In all these architectures the nodes of a Markov tree act as independent processors communicating with their neighbours. The communication is controlled by so-called propagation algorithm which schedules the flow of messages sent by a node to its neighbors. Intuitively the propagation is realized over the edges of the tree and the fusion of messages is performed in each node. Two operators are employed in the process: a projection operator which produces the message and a combination operator for fuzing partial information. Interestingly, dependly on how the operators are defined, the different queries may be solved [11]. Particularly, replacing the tables with the conditional probabilities by the tables representing logical truth tables we can model logical ("hard") inference.

In our system a modified Shenoy-Shafer architecture was implemented [6]. Particularly it allows for a flexible entering incremental evidence; at each step the immediate results are stored and after introducing a new piece of evidence the propagation is realized over only a fragment of the original Markov tree. Further the system allows for flexible definition of the propagation and combination operators and we can solve different types of the queries. Lastly, to find k-MPE a genetic algorithm was adopted [17].

3.4 Knowledge Acquisition Subsystem

Automatic Knowledge Acquisition Knowledge acquisition subsystem takes data from the database and generates a Bayesian knowledge base (a Bayesian network [8]), used later by the Bayesian expert system. Additionally hypertext information files are generated presenting the contents of the knowledge base in a form more acceptable by the user (so-called "production rules view of the knowledge base" - see Fig. 1). These files are attached to the server's HTML space and are available for presentation from the systems' menu.

Fig. 1. The Bayesian network can be presented also as a set of rules (here - in German)

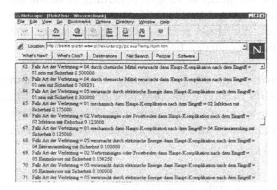

Before selecting an algorithm for generation of knowledge base from database we have carried out a feasibility study. After fixing the set of potentially useful attributes (below 30) and the potential number of cases that can be collected under real conditions (some 200 cases a year in the facility we collaborated with) we investigated algorithms of Chow/Liu [4], Pearl [8] and SGS [12]. Our choice was influenced by previous studies on stability of the Chow/Liu algorithm, on approximation of joint distributions by polytrees and by the capability of SGS to recover structure of general type Bayesian networks.

We have used the method of comparing distributions as indicated in [1]. The results, from a small (10 node) network have been summarized in Fig.2.

Fig. 2. Comparison of accuracy of Chow/Liu algorithms, Pearl's algorithm and SGS algorithm for bayesian network recovery from data for various sample sizes (horizontal axes). For comparison, the original network (from which the sample has been generated) is included.

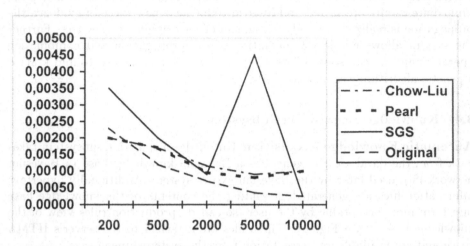

We can see that SGS has the best properties at sample size of 10,000, but with smaller samples it fails to recover some important links and gets unstable. Chow/Liu and Pearl's algorithms seem to behave well even at sample sizes as small as 200. Taking into account the realistic sample sizes it seems reasonable to consider the two latter ones. From the point of view of reasoning (translation into the Marklov tree) the networks proposed by Chow/Liu are better than the ones produced by Pearl's algorithm. For these reasons we decided to use the Chow/Liu algorithm for generation of knowledge bases.

The Chow/Liu algorithm [4] generates maximum spanning tree-like Bayesian network. The optimality and stability of this algorithm is widely known [13]. The algorithm consists essentially in forming a maximum weight spanning tree connecting all the variables, the weight of a connection being measured according to the formula:

$$WEIGHT(X,Y) = \sum_{x,y} \log \frac{Pr(x,y)}{Pr(x) \cdot Pr(y)}$$

where Pr means the "probability" (relative frequency) derived from the data. The next step is to orient randomly the undirected tree to get a directed tree. For this directed tree one needs to calculate $Pr(x|y)$ for each variable X with direct predecessor Y and this is the Bayesian network of interest. The sets of probabilities $Pr(x|y)$ are later used as potentials during Bayesian reasoning.

In case of larger databases, there exists a possibility to generate the knowledge base only from a subset of the database, according to a user-defined selection criteria.

More advanced techniques of automatic knowledge acquisition from data are currently subject of implementation.

Bayesian Network Editor/Visualizer Knowledge represenation in terms of a Bayesian network is not as intuitive as in terms of a set of rules. A totally different philosophy - in terms of causality among variables observed - has to be adopted. As the best representation of causality is in terms of a directed acyclic graph (dag), a special tool for visualization and editing of dags has been developed (see Fig. 3).

Fig. 3. Main screen of the Bayesian network editor.

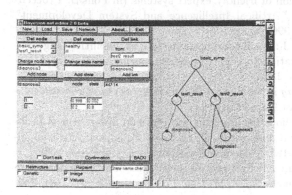

Dags can be retrieved from the server (or read locally), their structure and valuations (conditional probabilities) viewed and edited (new nodes and links inserted, removed, valuations changed), checked (for acyclicity, correctness of valuations), and subsequently stored either locally or at the server site.

A meaningful node or link removal or insertion operation is not a trivial operation. If we consider it in the widest possible generality, then this operation would require some amount of reasoning. To manage it without too large overheads, some simplifying assumptions are made (valuations are calculated and averaged in the direct vicinity only).

In future this tool should become a stand-alone module as its interface is being changed from an internal data format to an open Bayesian network interchange format.

Acknowledgement

We would like to thank Prof. J.Strużyna from Central Clinical Military Hospital of Military Medical Academy, Warsaw, who consulted us on medical aspects of the application.

References

1. Acid S., de Campos L.M.: Approximations of Causal Networks by Polytrees: an Empirical Study. IMPU'94, Information Processing and Management of Uncertainty in Knowledge-Based Systems, pp. 972-977, Paris, 1994
2. Bertele, U., and Brioschi, F. Nonserial Dynamic Programming, Academic Press, 1972,
3. Buchman B., Shortliffe E.: Rule-based Expert Systems, Addison-Wesley, 1984.
4. Chow C.K., Liu C.N.: Approximating discrete probability distributions with dependence trees, *IEEE Transactions on Information Theory*, Vol. IT-14, No.3, (1968), 462-467
5. Jensen V.F.: An introduction to Bayesian networks, University College Press, London, 1996.
6. Kłopotek M.A., Wierzchoń S.T., Michalewicz M.: Internet WWW as a new challange and chance for construction of friendly expert systems (in Polish). Proceedings of All-Polish Symposium "Artifical Intelligence and System Development" (CIR'96) Siedlce, 19-20 Sept. 1996, pp. 285-294
7. Lauritzen S.L., Spiegelhalter D.J.: Local computations with probabilities on graphical structures and their application to expert systems. Journal of the Royal Statistical Society B 50 (1988) 157-224.
8. Pearl J.: *Probabilistic Reasoning in Intelligent Systems: Networks of Plausible Inference*, Morgan Kaufmann, San Mateo CA, 1988
9. Pople, Jr., H. E.: Heuristic methods for imposing structure on ill-structured problems: The structuring of medical diagnostics. In Szolovits P., editor, Artificial Intelligence in Medicine, pp. 119-189. Westview Press, Boulder, Colorado, 1982.
10. Shafer G., Shenoy P.P., Mellouli K.: Propagating belief functions in quantitative Markov trees, *International Journal of Approximate Reasoning.* 1987:1, (4), 349-400.
11. Shenoy, P.P.: Valuation-based systems: A framework for managing uncertainty in expert systems, in: L.A. Zadeh and J. Kacprzyk (eds.), Fuzzy Logic for the Management of Uncertainty, J. Wiley & Sons, New York, 1992, pp. 83-104.
12. Spirtes P., Glymour C., Scheines R.: Causation, Prediction and Search, Lecture Notes in Statistics 81, Springer-Verlag, 1993.
13. Valiveti R.S., Oommen B.J.: On using the chi-squared statistics for determining statistic dependence, *Pattern Recognition* Vol. 25 No. 11 (1992), 1389-1400.
14. Wierzchoń S.T., Kłopotek M.A., Michalewicz M.Strużyna J.: Implementation of a bilingual educational expert system in a medical domain (in Polish), Proceedings of All-Polish AI Symposium (CIR'96) Siedlce, 19-20 Sept. 1996, pp. 235-244
15. Wierzchoń, S.T.: Constraint propagation over restricted space of configurations, in: R.R. Yager, J. Kacprzyk, and M. Fedrizzi (eds.) Advances in Dempster-Shafer Theory of Evidence, J. Wiley & Sons, New York 1994, pp. 375-394.
16. Wierzchoń S.T.: Methods for Representing and Processing Uncertain Information in the Dempster-Shafer Framework (in Polish), ICS PAS Press, Warszawa, 1996.
17. Wierzchoń S.T., Kłopotek M.A., Michalewicz M.: A genetic-based algorithm for facts explanation in graphoidal expert systems, in: Proc. of 3-rd Biennial Joint Conference on Engineering Systems Design and Analysis, Montpelier, France 1996.
18. Wierzchoń S.T., Kłopotek M.A.: A Bilingual Educational Expert System For Hand Wounds Initial Diagnosis. *Journal of Knowledge-based Intelligent Engineering Systems.* Vol. 2 No. 4 (1998), pp. 211-222.

Rough Sets as a Tool for Audio Signal Classification

Alicja Wieczorkowska

Technical University of Gdansk
ul. Narutowicza 11/12, 80-952 Gdansk, Poland and
UNC-Charlotte, Computer Science, Charlotte, NC 28223, USA
alicja@sound.eti.pg.gda.pl or awieczor@uncc.edu

Abstract: An application of RS knowledge discovery methods for automatic classification of musical instrument sounds is presented. Also, we provide basic information on acoustics of musical instruments. Since the digital record of sound contains a huge amount of data, the redundancy in the data is fixed via parameterization. The parameters extracted from sounds of musical instrument are discussed. We use quantization as a preprocessing for knowledge discovery to limit the number of parameter values. Next we show exemplary methods of quantization of parameter values. Finally, experiments concerning audio signal classification using rough set approach are presented and the results are discussed.

1 Introduction

Genesis of this work comes from sound recording and mixing. When searching through the recorded material, passages of particular instruments have to be found manually. Similar problem comes out during database searching: there is no possibility to find fragments performed by selected instruments inside files unless such information is attached to the file. Problems mentioned above are not solved so far and they gave motivation to this work.

The first problem to solve when working with digital recordings was to reduce a huge amount of data in sound files. For example, one second of 16-bit stereo recording on CD, recorded with sampling frequency 44.1kHz, contains 176.4kB of data. It is far too much so as to use such data directly for further tests. Moreover, one has to deal with the inconsistency of musical instrument sounds data, since musical instrument sound data are unrepeatable and inconsistent. The sound depends on the musical articulation, the instrument itself, arrangement of microphones, reverberation, etc. [8] Besides, sounds of different instruments can be similar, whereas sounds of one instrument may change significantly within the scale of the instrument. So as to deal with all this difficulties, sounds should be parameterized [5, 6]. This means that feature vectors that describe digital recordings will be used to compare sounds and to feed classifying algorithms. The research main goal is to check whether it is possible to recognize sounds on the basis of a limited number of parameters and to reveal which parameters are important for the classification and recognition process. Systems based on rough set theory [2, 9, 11] are good tools to test parameterization performed and to produce rules of classification, although real-value parameters should be quantized before using rough set systems [3].

2 Characteristics of musical instruments

The basic classification of musical instruments divides them into 3 main groups [4]:
• string instruments,
• wind instruments,
• percussion instruments.
In this work, the firs two groups of instruments were taken into account. From the first group, bowed string instruments have been chosen: violin, viola, cello and double bass. These instruments are commonly used in contemporary orchestras. The second group was broadly represented in experiments undertaken by lip-driven brass instruments, woodwind reed instruments and a flute.

Sounds of bowed string instruments can be performed in various ways, called articulation. The sounds used in experiments were played using bowed vibrato technique, with a mute, and pizzicato (in this case strings are plucked with fingers). Characteristics of the string sound strongly depend on the articulation technique. Sounds played pizzicato are very short and they consist of transients only. When vibrato technique is used, contents of spectrum change during the sound. The timbre of sound depends also on the material of which the string was made and on the way of leading the bow. Besides, spectra of most string sounds reveal body resonance. Another features of string instrument sounds are inharmonic partials – frequencies of partials are greater than corresponding multiples of the fundamental.

Wind instruments sounds are performed with such articulation techniques as vibrato and with a mute or muted with a player's hand. The pitch of the sound is changed through changes of the length of the horn resonator and overblowing. As far as woodwind instruments are concerned, the main way of pitch changing is reduction of the length of the horn resonator using holes between the mouthpiece and the end of the instrument body. The sound can be excited in a few ways. In flute, the sound is obtained by blowing a stream of air across a hole in the instrument body. The sounds of reed instruments are excited by vibrating reeds:
• a single reed: clarinets, saxophones;
• a double reed: oboe, English horn, bassoon, contrabassoon.

In lip-driven brass instruments, player's lips serve as a double reed. Mouthpieces only help with tone production. Mechanical valves allow changes of the length of the horn resonator. Long narrow body and extended flaring end make upper modes available, so overblowing is the main playing technique. In experiments performed, the following brass instruments have been used: trumpet, trombone, French horn, and tuba.

Spectra of trombones and trumpets sound reveal a great amount of strong partials – up to 20 partials as strong as the fundamental. French horn and tuba produce sounds with about 15 partials. The sound envelope changes with the intensity of the sound. During the starting transient of a brass sound, amplitudes of low frequency partial grow together and quite quickly, whereas amplitudes of high frequency partials grow separately – the higher partial, the slower it grows. Additionally, mutes used for trumpets and trombones also change the shape of the spectrum because of their resonant properties.

369

3 Parameters of musical sounds

Digital representation of sound is inconvenient to deal with, since it contains a huge amount of data and it is not useful to compare sounds sample by sample. After parameterization of sounds, feature vectors obtained can be used to feed intelligent classification algorithms. The database created on the basis of such parameters is useful for musical instrument pattern recognition and also in other applications.

The source of sounds used in experiments is a collection of CDs McGill University Master Samples (MUMS), prepared in McGill University [10]. These CDs include consequent sounds in the musical scale from the standard playing range of modern musical instruments. The digital representation of these sounds was prepared as 16-bit stereo sound files, recorded with sampling frequency 44.1 kHz. In experiments performed the following instruments have been used:

- bowed strings: violin, viola, cello and double bass, played vibrato and pizzicato;
- woodwinds: flute, oboe and b-flat clarinet,
- brass: c trumpet, tenor trombone and French horn, played with and without muting; also tuba without muting.

The obtained data have been gathered into 18 classes; sounds of one instrument played with one technique represent one class. The feature vector corresponds to a singular sound of one instrument. Parameters contained in the feature vector have been extracted both from time and frequency domain. When exploring time envelope of the sound, ADSR (Attack-Decay-Sustain-Release) model has been used (Fig. 1). Nevertheless, many sounds may not contain some of these stages.

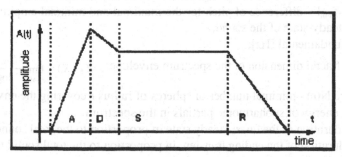

Fig. 1. ADSR model of the sound envelope

Parameterization of sounds for the automatic classification of musical instruments is difficult for many reasons. First of all, musical sounds have very complicated spectra. The main stage of the sound is the steady state. Nevertheless, spectrum changes with time evolution, even during the steady state. Another problems are caused by similarities of spectra for different instrument sounds and dissimilarities of spectra for different sounds of the same instrument. That is why the parameterization has to be done very carefully.

Spectral analyses of sounds have been performed using Fourier analysis with a frame of a few (at least 2) periods of the analyzed sound, using a rectangular window function. There are many ways of sound parameterization [1, 6, 7, 12, 15]. During the experiments performed, the following parameters have been calculated:

- at the beginning, in the middle, at the end of the starting transient (AD phases), for the maximum and the minimum amplitude during the quasi-steady state of the sound, the following feature vector describing the spectrum has been extracted:
  - h_{fd_max} – number $i \in \{1,...,5\}$ of a partial with the greatest frequency deviation,
  - fd_m – mean frequency deviation for low partials:

$$\overline{fd}_m = \sum_{k=1}^{5} A_k (\Delta f_k /(k f_1)) / \sum_{k=1}^{5} A_k \quad \text{where } A_i - \text{amplitude of } i^{th} \text{ partial,}$$

  - Tr_1 – 1st modified tristimulus parameter (energy of fundamental in proportion to the whole spectrum): $Tr_1 = A_1^2 / \sum_{n=1}^{N} A_n^2$, N – number of available partials
  - A_{1-2} – amplitude difference [dB] between 1st and 2nd partial,
  - $h_{3,4}$, $h_{5,6,7}$, $h_{8,9,10}$ – energy of the selected partials in the spectrum,
  - h_{rest} – energy of the rest partials in the spectrum,
  - Od, Ev – contents of odd/even partials in the spectrum (without the

fundamental): $Od = \sqrt{\sum_{k=2}^{L} A_{2k-1}^2} / \sqrt{\sum_{n=1}^{N} A_n^2}$, $Ev = \sqrt{\sum_{k=1}^{M} A_{2k}^2} / \sqrt{\sum_{n=1}^{N} A_n^2}$

where $M=Floor(N/2)$, $L=Floor(N/2+1)$.

  - Br – brightness of the sound: $B = \sum_{n=1}^{N} n \cdot A_n / \sum_{n=1}^{N} A_n$

- for the whole sound, the following feature vector has been calculated:
  - $|f_{max}-f_{min}|$ – difference of pitch for the maximal and minimal amplitude during the steady-state of the sound,
  - f_1 – fundamental [Hz],
  - d_{fr} – fractal dimension of the spectrum envelope: $d_{fr}(X) = \lim_{r \to 0} \dfrac{-\log N(r)}{\log r}$

where N(r) - minimal number of spheres of radius r covering the envelope,
  - $f_{1/2}$ – energy of subharmonic partials in the spectrum
  - qs – duration of the quasi-steady state in proportion to the total sound time
  - t_e – duration of the ending transient in proportion to the total sound time
  - rl – release velocity [dB/s]

Parameters described above give 62-element feature vector that is redundant for 18 classes. Rough set based knowledge discovery tools have been applied to find out how many and which parameters are sufficient to correctly classify sounds of the instruments investigated; classification rules have been extracted as well.

4 Separability of the parameters

Important reason to use soft computing techniques is that values of sound parameters are hard to separate using linear methods. Separability of the obtained parameter values can be tested using various methods. For example, separability of selected pairs of classes can be tested using Behrens-Fisher statistic [13]. Nevertheless, it is more convenient to use criteria evaluating the whole set of data.

Separability of the calculated parameters of musical instrument sounds has been tested using criterion $Q = \min\limits_{i,j} D_{i,j} \big/ \max\limits_{i} d_i$, where:

$D_{i,j}$ – measure of distances between classes i, j,

d_i – measure of dispersion in class i.

A set of parameters is satisfying if $Q>1$, since then values representing singular classes are gathered together and classes are distant one from another. Such a set of parameters is quite easy to separate and to learn classification rules.

The value of the criterion Q depends on the metrics used for calculating distances and on the definitions of distances. In the performed tests the following definitions of distances have been used:

- D_1 -   Hausdorff   metrics:
  $h(A, B) = \max\{\sup\limits_{x \in A} \inf\limits_{y \in B} d(x, y), \sup\limits_{x \in B} \inf\limits_{y \in A} d(x, y)\} \; for \; A, B \subset K$

- $D_2 / D_3 / D_4$ - max/min/mean distance between objects from different classes,
- d_1 / d_2: mean/max distance between class objects,
- d_3 / d_4: mean/max distance from the gravity center of the class.

Values of Q for the described musical instrument data are showed in Fig. 2 for the following metrics:

- Euclidean: $d(x,y) = \sqrt{\sum\limits_{i=1}^{n} (x_i - y_i)^2}$

- "city": $d(x,y) = \sum\limits_{i=1}^{n} |x_i - y_i|$

- central: $d(x,y) = \begin{cases} |x - y| \; for \; \vec{x} \parallel \vec{y} \\ |\vec{x}| + |\vec{y}| \quad else \end{cases}$

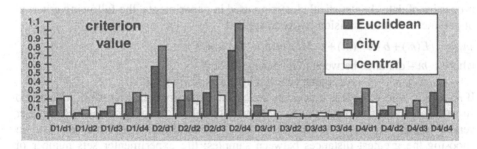

Fig. 2. Values of criterion Q for exemplary metrics, calculated for the data representing musical instrument sounds (18 classes, 62-lement feature vector)

The greatest values of Q have been obtained for D_2/d_4, so this combination of distances has been chosen for further investigations. As far as the metrics is concerned, the best choice is more difficult, since for different configurations of distance definitions, various metrics performed differently. The most popular is the Euclidean metrics, so it is usually used in most applications. For this metrics $Q<1$, so the data are too difficult to use linear methods. Therefore, soft computing techniques are more useful for classification of musical instrument sounds.

5 Quantization as a preprocessing for rough set tools

Rough set based discovery systems require small number of attribute (parameter) values, so real values of parameters should be converted first into discrete ones [2, 3, 5]. Rules obtained for real-value feature vectors can be very specific and they may not be useful for classification of unseen cases. That is why the user of rough set based tools has to perform the process of quantization or discretization that converts data sets with continuous parameters into discrete ones. This process can be omitted if neural networks are used. The neural network is able to tolerate variations in the input values, thus there is no real need for the parameter clustering in that case. On the other hand, the performance of the neural network is determined by the proper choice of its structure and the neuron transfer function. Since the training phase is time-consuming, rough set based tools are more useful.

In knowledge discovery, discretization is one of the most challenging issues. Exemplary methods of real-value parameter quantization are presented in this section. Basically, quantization methods can be divided into 2 groups:
- local methods, restricted to simple attributes,
- global methods, that simultaneously convert all continuous attributes.

The results of classification depend on the type of quantization. Therefore, it is necessary to test a variety of quantization methods and number of parameter values after quantization so as to find the most useful discrete representation of the data.

The simplest methods are local ones. For example, Equal Interval Width Method (EIWM) divides the domain of a parameter into intervals of the same length; number of intervals has to be set by an experimenter. Another methods may divide parameter domain on the basis of entropy – for instance, in Equal Frequency per Interval Method (EFIM) intervals are created in this way so that number of samples in each interval is approximately the same. Quantization can be also based on statistical properties of data. In statistical clustering used in experiments, the following criterion of parameter domain division has been applied:

$$m_l = a \cdot E(m) + b \cdot D^2(m) + c \cdot Min(m) + d \cdot Max(m) + e \cdot 1$$

where: m – distance between neighboring values,

a, b, c, d, e – parameters chosen by the experimenter.

If $m_l < const$, where $const$ is a constant set by the experimenter, points are joined into an interval. In this method the number of intervals is hard to foresee. A simpler version of this method called Maximum Distance Method (MDM) consists in choosing the greatest distances between samples; the experimenter sets number of distances. Division points are chosen from intervals represented by these distances.

All mentioned methods require experiments to choose the appropriate number of intervals or to adjust parameters of the method. Separability of musical sound data quantized using EIWM with various numbers of intervals is depicted in Fig. 3.

Exemplary global methods are described in [3] and [16]. The former method consists in cluster analysis, and the latter one is based on Boolean approach. Whereas local methods usually do not discern between points representing different classes, global methods usually take this information into account. Separability of data quantized globally is usually good, but global methods are usually time-consuming, therefore simple local methods are broadly applied anyway.

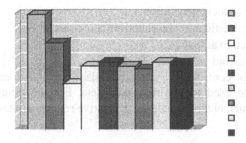

Fig. 3. Values of separability criterion Q for musical instrument sound parameters

For musical instrument sound data, separability criterion Q depends on exemplary quantization methods as follows:

- before quantization $Q=0.764308$,
- after quantization using MDM (5 intervals) $Q=1.67414$,
- for EIWM (5 intervals) $Q=1.80349$,
- for cluster analysis $Q=1.90028$.

Since cluster analysis divides parameter domains into numerous intervals, quantization obtained for EIWM was used in rough set experiments.

6 Rough set based automatic classification

Rough Set (RS) based classification systems are constructed on the following foundations [2, 11]:

Let $I=(U, A)$ - an *information system*, where $U \neq \emptyset$ - a *universe* - finite set of objects, $A \neq \emptyset$ - a finite set of *attributes* $a : U \to V_a$, $a \in A$, V_a – parameter domain. A special case of the information system is a *decision table* $T = (U, A \cup \{d\})$, where $d \notin A$ - the *decision* attribute, A - the set of *conditions*. $B \subseteq A$ implies indiscernibility relation $IND(B)$. Function $\partial_B : U \to 2^{\{1,\dots r(d)\}}$ such that $\partial_B(x) = \{i : \exists_{x' \in U} [(x'IND(B)x \wedge (d(x') = i)]\}$ is called the *generalized decision in T*. Equivalence classes of $IND(d)$ are called *concepts* and a minimal subset B such that $IND(A)=IND(B)$ is called a *reduct*. B is a *relative reduct* iff B is a minimal subset of A such that $\partial_B = \partial_A$. Reducts and relative reducts obtained for the tested sets of examples allow us to evaluate the role of particular parameters.

Although there exist several rough set based classification systems – LERS, ROSETTA, DATALOGIC etc. [2, 9, 14], we decided to create a special library of programs to facilitate and simplify research. This library, written in *Mathematica*, includes the following modules:

- parameterization of sound data, recorded in .snd format,
- separability test – criterion Q with the use of Euclidean, city and central metrics,
- data quantization with methods both local and global methods:
  - Boolean based, CAM,
  - EIWM, statistical clustering, MGM (also with threshold for minimal number of values in intervals),

- reducts and relative reducts generation,
- generation of deterministic and non-deterministic rules,
- recognition of unseen examples,
- quality test using ten-fold technique [3].

Priority of attributes is controlled. Also, redundant attributes can be removed. Discovered rules can be used to test new data sets. For the investigated base of musical instrument sounds, obtained reducts or relative reducts contain 16 parameters (Tab. 1).

Tab. 1. Parameters present in an exemplary reduct (shaded) in the investigated base of musical instrument sound data, quantized using EIWM into 5 intervals

Starting transient			Quasi-steady state		others
beginning	middle	end	max	min	
1. h_{fd_max}	12. h_{fd_max}	23. h_{fd_max}	34. h_{fd_max}	45. h_{fd_max}	56. $|f_{max}-f_{min}|$
2. fd_m	13. fd_m	24. fd_m	35. fd_m	46. fd_m	57. f_1
3. Tr_1	14. Tr_1	25. Tr_1	36. Tr_1	47. Tr_1	58. d_{fr}
4. A_{1-2}	15. A_{1-2}	26. A_{1-2}	37. A_{1-2}	48. A_{1-2}	59. $f_{1/2}$
5. $h_{3,4}$	16. $h_{3,4}$	27. $h_{3,4}$	38. $h_{3,4}$	49. $h_{3,4}$	60. qs
6. $h_{5,6,7}$	17. $h_{5,6,7}$	28. $h_{5,6,7}$	39. $h_{5,6,7}$	50. $h_{5,6,7}$	61. t_e
7. $h_{8,9,10}$	18. $h_{8,9,10}$	29. $h_{8,9,10}$	40. $h_{8,9,10}$	51. $h_{8,9,10}$	62. rl
8. h_{rest}	19. h_{rest}	30. h_{rest}	41. h_{rest}	52. h_{rest}	
9. Od	20. Od	31. Od	42. Od	53. Od	
10. Ev	21. Ev	32. Ev	43. Ev	54. Ev	
11. Br	22. Br	33. Br	44. Br	55. Br	

Most of the discovered rules contained only several attributes, for example:

$$P12 = 3 \wedge P15 = 4 \Rightarrow class\,1.$$

The accuracy of the set of discovered rules has reached 90% (we applied here DataLogic validation strategy with 10% testing data). Musical phrases consist of at least a few notes so the performing instruments can be accurately recognized. Recognition of a singular instrument in a record with the whole orchestra playing requires additional techniques, namely separating signals of the solo instrument and the orchestra, and also pitch extraction to separate consequent sounds of the solo instrument. Nevertheless, RS based classification tools can be applied to recognize/identify instruments in audio data.

7 Conclusions

The aim of the work was to investigate the possibility of the automatic classification of musical instrument sounds on the basis of a limited number of parameters. Experiments performed to classify such data consisted of a few stages. The first stage included sound processing with spectral and time-domain analysis. Huge amounts of data contained in digital sound representation required parameterization as preprocessing. Calculation of parameters allowed construction of a database that was used in further investigations. Because of the variety of musical instruments and differences in their sounds, a great number of parameters have been drawn. Inconsistency of the data implies soft computing techniques for automatic classification. As preprocessing for RS algorithms, quantization of the data was necessary. An appropriate choice of the quantization method was very important and it required many experiments. Training of RS based systems, performed as the next stage of experiments, allowed evaluation of the significance of particular parameters. The use of learning algorithm also allowed finding rules for managing classification. Non-redundant set of attributes could be found from reducts and relative reducts. Composition of parameters in RS reducts confirms that the whole evolution of the sound must be taken into account during parameterization. The performed investigation confirmed that automatic classification of musical instrument sounds on the basis of a limited number of parameters using rough set tools is possible.

References

1. Ando S., Yamaguchi K., Statistical Study of Spectral Parameters in Musical Instrument Tones, *J. Acoust. Soc. of America*, 94, 1, July 1993, 37-45.
2. Chmielewski M. R., Grzymala-Busse J. W., Peterson N. W., Than S., The Rule Induction System LERS - a Version for Personal Computers, *Foundations of Computing and Decision Sciences*, Vol. 18, No. 3-4, 1993, Institute of Computing Science, Technical University of Poznan, Poland, 181-212.
3. Chmielewski M. R., Grzymala-Busse J. W., Global Discretization of Continuous Attributes as Preprocessing for Machine Learning, *3rd International Workshop on Rough Sets and Soft Computing*, Conference Proceedings, San Jose, CA, 1994, 294-301.
4. Fletcher N. H., Rossing T. D., The Physics of Musical Instruments, Springer-Verlag, 1991.
5. Kostek B., Wieczorkowska A., A System for Musical Sound Parameter Database Creation and Analysis, *102nd AES Convention*, preprint 4498, Munich 1997.
6. Kostek B., Wieczorkowska A., Parametric Representation of Musical Sounds, *Archives of Acoustics*, 22, 1, 1997, 3-26.
7. Kronland-Martinet R., Grossmann A., Application of Time-Frequency and Time-Scale Methods (Wavelet Transforms) to the Analysis, Synthesis, and Transformation of Natural Sounds, in: De Poli G., Piccialli A., Roads C. (ed.), *Representations of Musical Signals*, MIT Press, Cambridge, Massachusetts, 1991, 45-85.
8. Meyer J., The Sound of the Orchestra, *J. Audio Eng. Soc.*, Vol. 41, No. 4, 1993, 203-213.
9. Øhrn A., Komorowski J., ROSETTA – A Rough Set Toolkit for Analysis of Data, *Proc. 3rd Int. Joint Conf. on Information Sciences*, Durham NC, 1997, Vol. 3, 403–407.
10. Opolko F., Wapnick J., MUMS – McGill University Master Samples, compact discs, McGill University, Montreal, Canada, 1987.
11. Pawlak Z., Hard and Soft Sets, *ICS Research Report* 10/94, Warsaw University of Technology, February 1994.
12. Pollard H. F., Jansson E. V., A Tristimulus Method for the Specification of Musical Timbre, *Acustica*, Vol. 51, 1982, 162-171.
13. Press W. H., Flannery B. P., Teukolsky S. A., Vetterling W. T., Numerical Recipes: The Art of Scientific Computing, Cambridge University Press, 1987.
14. Reduct Systems, DATALOGIC/R, 1990-95 Reduct Systems Inc., Regina, Saskatchewan, Canada.
15. Risset J.-C., Timbre Analysis by Synthesis: Representations, Imitations, and Variants for Musical Composition, in: De Poli G., Piccialli A., Roads C. (ed.), *Representations of Musical Signals*, MIT Press, Cambridge, Massachusetts, 1991, 7-43.
16. Skowron A., Nguyen S. H., Quantization of Real Value Attributes: Rough Set and Boolean Approach, *ICS Research Report* 11/95, Warsaw University of Technology.

Experiments with Rough Sets Approach to Speech Recognition

David Brindle and Wojciech Ziarko

Computer Science Department
University of Regina
Regina, Saskatchewan, S4S 0A2, Canada

Abstract. The paper reports work in progress on the methodology and experiments with speaker-independent speech recognition. The approach reported in the paper is based on the variable precision model of rough sets. The rough sets approach is adapted in the process of acquisition of recognition rules from training speech data whereas standard signal processing techniques are used on the level of feature extraction.

1 Introduction

The paper reports work in progress on the methodology and experiments with speaker-independent speech recognition within the frameweork of rough sets methodology. The reported experiments have been performed with the KDD-R system [1], which makes use of the Variable Precision Rough Sets model [2]. The purpose of the experiments is to investigate the feasibility of applying rough-sets methods to the problem of speech recognition. The work on the topic is still in progress and the experiments are more indicative of the problems ahead of us rather than confirming success of the approach. The results indicate the existence of the "recognition boundary" area where high precision recognition is not possible with given attributes and imposed rule size limits.

The related work on the use of rough sets methods for speech recognition have been published in [6-10]. Among other techniques that have been applied to the problem, the one which is at the forefront now is the Hidden Markov Model (HMM) [5] [3]. Neural networks [5] also have a role to play in hybrid systems, where they are used in conjunction with HMM methods.

The paper is organized as follows. In the next section we comment about data collection used in our experiments. The feature extraction methods used in the experiments are described in section three. In section four, we discuss the signal analysis and processing programs developed during the course of this project. They consist of signal visualisation, feature extraction and recognition programs. The basic processes of the KDD-R system used for computation of rules are also described although the link between the inner workings of KDD-R and underlying rough sets is not elaborated due to space limitations and the focus of this paper on the application aspect of rough sets. In section five the experiments are summarized and the results are evaluated.

2 Speech Data

For the experiments, the collection of speech recordings on the NIST Speech Disc CD1-1.1 of the TIMIT corpus [4] was used. The corpus, a data base of samples of continuous speech, was produced by a joint project-team of Texas Instruments Incorporated (TI), SRI International (SRI) and the Massachusetts Institute of Technology (MIT) under the sponsorship of DARPA, the Defense Advanced Research Projects Agency of the US government. The corpus was published in the US by NIST, the National Institute of Standards and Technology.

The material on the CD-ROM was recorded digitally using a sampling frequency of 16 kHz. The samples are 16-bit integers.

The data was collected by having the speakers read from a prompt. The data base includes machine-readable transcriptions, which mark the word- and phoneme- boundaries in the speech signals. The positioning of these boundaries is subjective and was done by trained phoneticians with the aid of computer programs which made an initial boundary determination. The transcriptions use a set of phonemes which distinguishes among 20 different vowel sounds and 32 different non-vowels.

One important function of the transcriptions is that they document what the phoneticians heard, rather than what was in the prompt. For example, for the word "Mary" in the prompt, "merry" may be what is heard for some of the speakers.

In the data base there are two sentences, each of which is spoken by each of 462 speakers. This is the part of the data base that was used in the experiments.

3 Feature Extraction

Signal processing involves transforming the signal into a form in which it is more useful for speech recognition purposes. The objective is to extract from the abundance of largely redundant information some features which are useful for classifying speech utterances. Essentially, this processing consists of mappings, $\theta : T \rightarrow D$, where θ maps from the time domain, T, where the samples are, to domain D, which may be the time domain or another domain. In current speech recognition technology, the signal processing uses sampling rates between 6.6 kHz and 20 kHz. The samples are mapped into sets called *vectors*, using any of a number of different transformations which researchers have developed. The vectors are computed every 10 or 20 msec [3] and provide the raw material for other stages of the whole recognition process. If time segments much longer than 20 msec were used, essential detail could be lost. There is extensive literature on the transformations that are used for computing vectors; descriptions and references can be found in [11] [5] [3].

Many of the transformations are based on the standard*Fourier transform* mapping from time domain to frequency domain, which is defined as follows:

$$x(n) = 1/N \sum_{r=1}^{N-1} X(r)e^{2\pi i r n/N} \tag{1}$$

$$X(r) = \sum_{n=1}^{N-1} x(n)e^{-2\pi irn/N}$$

where $x(n)$ is the value of the sample at time $t(n)$, for $0 \leq n \leq (N-1)$, and $X(r)$ is the intensity of the frequency $f(r)$, for $0 \leq r \leq (N-1)$. In these equations, i is $\sqrt{-1}$, and so $x(n)$ and $X(r)$ are series of complex terms involving $\sin(2\pi rn/N)$ and $\cos(2\pi rn/N)$. In the simplest case, for a sound consisting of a single frequency, $f(n)$, the equations reduce to $x(n) = (1/N)\sin(2\pi nf/N)$ and $X(r) = 0$ for $r \neq n$, and $X(n) = 1$.

The Fourier transform yields a power spectrum which shows how the intensity of the signal is distributed throughout the range of audible sound frequencies. Under the Fourier transform, information about time is traded for information about the power spectrum. The time information is also important, though, for speech recognition and so the two kinds of information are used in conjunction.

When building the feature vector, all non-vowel phonemes were ignored. For each vowel, a Fourier transform — as in equations 1 — was computed. The ends of the time-domain window were chosen to coincide with the boundaries of the particular vowel sound in the signal information. A feature vector with 59 elements, or attributes, was derived from the power spectrum as follows.

The power spectrum was divided into 30 overlapping bands, evenly spaced on a logarithmic scale, with the lower and upper ends of the nth band defined by

$$F_l(n) = mF_l(n-1), \quad F_u(n) = 2.0F_l$$

where $m = (F_1/F_0)^{1/30}$, $F_0 = F_l(1) = 125.0$ Hz, and $F_1 = F_u(30) = 8000.0$ Hz.

The distribution of energy among the 30 bands was computed by deriving an array of values

$$Z(n) = \sum_{r=r_l(n)}^{r_u(n)} a(r), \text{ for } 1 \leq n \leq 30$$

where $a(r) = |X(r)|$ and $r_l(n) \leq r \leq r_u(n)$ for all $F_l(n) \leq f(r) \leq F_u(n)$.

The $Z(n)$ were used to compute the values of attributes according to the formula

$$A(n) = \log(cZ(n)/w(n)Z)$$

where $Z = \sum Z(n)$ for $1 \leq n \leq 30$ normalizes among different speakers, the weight $w(n) = r_u(n) - r_l(n)$ compensates for the differences in width among the bands, and c is a constant chosen so as to make the values of the $Z(n)$ fall within a convenient range.

The other 29 attributes reflected the differences between adjacent frequency bands, that is $D(n) = A(n+1) - A(n)$, for $1 \leq n < 30$

4 The Methodology

The methodology can be divided into two major stages. In the initial stage preliminary analysis of the signal data and feature extraction was performed. In the second stage, the classification rules with probabilities were computed.

4.1 Preliminary Data Analysis

A number of signal-processing programs were written. There were two main purposes. First, there was the need to view the material in the TIMIT collection, in an understandable way, on a computer monitor. And then there was the need to process this material to produce data, or feature vectors, suitable for input to the KDD-R software used for the computation of rules. These programs were written in C, to run on a PC where the TIMIT CD-ROM could be read. Data prepared on the PC was uploaded to a Solaris mainframe computer where the KDD-R programs were run. The main two programs were the viewing program and the feature vector program.

The viewing program was written in such a way that modules for displaying pictures other than those mentioned can easily be added. When experimenting with a new function for creating feature vectors, it is useful to see pictures showing the output of the function in a visual form.

The feature-vector program navigates the DOS directory structure of the TIMIT data base to read all the required files. Each recording of one spoken instance of one sentence is a separate file. The program also reads the transcript files corresponding to each speech file to determine the start- and end-points of each required speech segment — phoneme or word. Feature vectors are extracted by an easily replaceable module of the program.

4.2 Computation of Rules

For these experiments, a feature vector was built for each vowel in each of two sentences for each of the 462 different speakers. In all, there was a total number of 57,463 vowel instances extracted from the data. (If what was transcribed corresponded exactly with what was in the prompts, the number of instances would have been a multiple of 462). In the data, there are 6,953 iy and 50,510 NOT iy instances. The array of 59-element feature vectors was input to KDD-R in the form of an ASCII text file with 57,463 records. The processing which then took place consisted of the following major steps:

- For each attribute a_i of the feature vector, the limits l_i and h_i, defined by the lowest and the highest value found for a_i in the whole set of vectors, were determined. A set of "cut points" c_{ij}, $j \leq 9$, dividing the range beween l_i and h_i into 10 equal intervals, was computed. This division initially is arbitrary and both the number and the spacing of the cut points could be varied.
- The cut points were used to construct a binary-valued vector with attributes b_{ij} which take a 0 or a 1 value depending on whether $a_i \leq c_{ij}$ or $a_i > c_{ij}$. An array of b_{ij} values corresponding to all the a_i values in the array of feature vectors was built.
- A subset B of the attributes b_{ij} was selected automatically as being the best ones to use. The selection of the best binary attributes was based on a heuristic criterion assigning to each attribute a measure characterizing

the degree of separation between positive and negative cases. The number of attributes, N_B, in the subset B should be chosen so as to be as large as possible. The limit on N_B is set by by the amount of computer time required in the subsequent processing. In these experiments $N_B \approx 30$ was usually found to be practical.

- The space consisting of all at most n'-membered subsets of B, $n' \leq N_B$, was searched to find rules for predicting the decision-attribute value iy given the values of the attributes b_{ij} in the binary-valued vector. Because the processing is based on a search, the choice of n' is severely constrained by computing-time considerations. The only values that could be used were $n' = 3$ and $n' = 4$.

There are two other parameters, apart from N_B and n' that have been used to control KDD-R's processing. These are p_{min} and C_{min}, which constrain the generation of rules with respect to to the minimum predictive probability and minimum rule strength. For any prospective rule that may be generated, there will be $(n_0 + n_1)$ instances of the feature vector satisfying the rule, where n_0 and n_1 are respectively the number of instances of the decision-attribute value 0 or 1, or NOT iy and iy in this particular case. So, a probability estimate $p = p_1/(p_0 + p_1)$ can be assigned to the rule. Only rules for which $p \geq p_{min}$ are generated. The minimum coverage parameter, C_{min}, prevents the generation of rules for which $(n_0 + n_1) < C_{min}$.

5 Experiments

The experiments were directed at the recognition of vowels. Compared to other phonemes, vowels have a long duration, a slowly changing waveform picture, and sharp spectral lines which change only slowly with time. Because of these characteristics of vowels, feature vectors were generated at intervals considerably longer than the 10 or 20 msec mentioned earlier as the norm for speech recognition.

The objective in the experiments described was to discover rules to classify all the vowel instances in the data into two classes: iy or NOT iy. The class NOT iy consists of the other 19 vowels. The experiments described are typical of many that were performed, using various feature vectors.

For the experiments shown in Table 1, numbers 1 and 2 use the feature vectors $A(n)$ and 3 and 4 use $D(n)$. And for all four:

- $p_{min} = 0.60$
- n_R is the number of rules generated
- N_0 and N_1 are, for decision-attribute values 0 and 1 respectively, the total number of instances of the feature vector for which at least one of the n_R rules is satisfied. For example, in experiment 1, there are $(50,510 - 6,858) = 43,652$ instances of decision value 0 for which none of the 895 rules is satisfied and for decision value 1 there are $(6,953 - 4,989)$, or $1,964$ instances for which no rule is satisfied.

- A_0 and A_1 are, for decision-attribute values 0 and 1 respectively, the average number of rules satisfied, for all instances which satisfy at least one rule.

In Tables 2, 3 and 4, some of the underlying detail for Table 1 can be seen. Table 2 shows for the first 407 instances of the feature vector, all instances of iy, or decision value 1. For each of the 4 experiments, the number of rules satisfied by each iy instance is shown. Table 3 shows, for the first 130 instances of the feature vector, the number of rules satisfied in each of the 4 experiments by all NOT iy instances for which at least one rule is satisfied in any of the experiments. In Table 4, a sample selection of the 895 rules generated in Experiment 1 is shown. In the table, the attributes of the subset B of the binary-valued vector are arbitrarily numbered $B_1, B_2, ... B_{30}$, and n_0, n_1, p have the meanings defined earlier.

Given a feature-vector instance selected at random, its probability of being an iy instance is $6953/57463 = 0.121$. Table 4 shows that individual rules can give a probability which is higher by a factor of at least 6 times than that achieved by random selection. However, Table 1 shows that the disjunction $R = r_1 \cup r_2 \cup ... r_n$ of all rules gives probabilities of only $4989/(4989 + 6858) = 0.421$, $5462/(5462 + 8129) = 0.402$, $4858/(4858 + 6747) = 0.419$ and $5137/(5137 + 8296) = 0.382$ for Experiments 1, 2, 3 and 4 respectively.

Rules could also be combined conjunctively — for example $R = r_a \cap r_b \cap r_c$. For the rules of Table 4, $R_1 = r_a \cap r_b$ would have the set of conditions $B_8 = 0, B_{11} = 0, B_{13} = 1, B_{16} = 1, B_{22} = 0, B_{26} = 0$ and $R_2 = r_c \cap r_f$ would have the set of conditions $B_9 = 0, B_{13} = 1, B_{15} = 0, B_{23} = 1, B_{26} = 0$. One could combine rules in this way to build more restrictive rules that are satisfied by fewer instances and could select the ones that have the highest p-values. However, in order to generate new rules systematically one would require a search process which would be impeded by the same limitations that restricted the selection of n' in the first place.

Table 1 shows the most serious difficulty of this method: that in each of the 4 experiments there is a significant proportion of iy instances that do not satisfy any rules and that there is a significant proportion of NOT iy instances that do satisfy rules. Tables 2 and 3 show that for some of the iy instances and for some of the NOT iy instances there is a consistency of the wrong decision value across the different rule-sets of the 4 experiments. It was even found in other experiments, using different feature vectors, that there was a significant number of both iy and NOT iy instances that were not correctly classified by any rule-set generated with any feature vector or for any selection of parameters that was tried.

6 Conclusions

In these experiments the feature vector was generated by an algorithm which was data-independent. In other words, the processing performed by the algorithm does not proceed along different paths according to special conditions found in

382

Experiment Number	n'	C_{min}	N_1	N_0	n_R	A_1	A_0
1	3	100	4989	6858	895	375.2	148.7
2	4	1000	5462	8129	11669	4357.7	1538.4
3	3	100	4858	6747	456	76.1	30.1
4	4	1000	5137	8296	3465	791.6	282.7

Table 1.

Instance	Expt 1	Expt 2	Expt 3	Expt 4
25	705	9143	99	1750
35	880	11667	173	1532
60	880	11667	179	1552
70	191	2828	166	1990
75	269	3190	67	504
87	603	7526	29	499
88	446	5225	32	356
98	69	1312	34	688
106	129	1544	2	40
113	191	2828	92	578
114	491	6122	61	909
119	115	1203	0	0
120	55	627	0	0
132	0	0	0	0
135	0	0	0	0
148	0	0	0	4
162	91	934	0	0
163	499	5602	10	183
175	151	2068	10	183
177	56	1037	69	657
203	130	1783	10	136
208	211	2984	39	306
209	11	238	38	546
212	400	4700	14	268
226	3	55	0	4
238	131	1938	69	657
243	705	9143	120	1319
248	421	5492	8	134
249	44	750	95	583
258	0	0	42	416
261	16	230	9	172
264	0	0	0	0
269	229	3121	22	159
272	32	558	32	384
290	43	733	23	375
293	48	791	39	297
319	56	1043	16	288
340	880	11667	100	842
341	67	1085	59	616
345	705	9143	113	1025
354	289	3244	59	673
361	60	538	0	0
374	0	0	0	0
377	0	0	0	0
382	0	0	0	0
407	25	397	15	131

Table 2.

383

Instance	Vowel	Expt 1	Expt 2	Expt 3	Expt 4
1	ix	667	8237	95	1325
2	eh			2	34
3	ih	53	960	16	169
5	ux	31	345		
6	ix	150	2222	2	36
7	ix				10
12	ih	35	620	39	557
17	ix			36	369
26	ih	13	263	2	34
27	eh				4
28	ix			9	213
29	ix	69	1312	88	922
30	uh	11	222	3	38
43	ih	27	522		9
46	eh				8
54	ey				1
58	ih		4	5	44
62	ih			7	68
63	ih			5	81
85	ix		211	5	122
86	ix			4	74
92	er	3	47		
97	ix			10	237
102	ix				88
104	ih	56	1043	2	34
105	ey	37	640	44	472
108	ix		1	62	653
110	ix	313	4315	14	95
115	ae	18	159		
116	uh		1	15	238
118	ux	3	50		
125	ix	56	1037	143	1234
130	ix	14	305		

Table 3.

Rule	Conditions	$(n_0 + n_1)$	p
r_a	$B_8 = 0, B_{16} = 1, B_{22} = 0$	2325	0.74
r_b	$B_{11} = 0, B_{13} = 1, B_{26} = 0$	2372	0.73
r_c	$B_9 = 0, B_{13} = 1, B_{26} = 0$	2318	0.74
r_d	$B_8 = 0, B_{16} = 1, B_{18} = 0$	2349	0.73
r_e	$B_3 = 0, B_{11} = 0, B_{16} = 1$	2454	0.70
r_f	$B_9 = 0, B_{15} = 0, B_{23} = 1$	2365	0.73
r_g	$B_8 = 0, B_{15} = 0, B_{21} = 1$	2437	0.70
r_h	$B_8 = 0, B_{11} = 0, B_{17} = 1$	2442	0.70

Table 4.

particular instances of the data. The experiments show that features can be found in a feature vector generated in this way that correlate well with the known decision values for the different instances of the speech data.

However, the method of using the feature vector to generate classification rules, because of the computational complexity of search algorithms, produced rules that are not restrictive enough because each rule is limited to using only 3 or 4 conditions. This conclusion appears to be confirmed by the results of further experiments, being performed now. In these latest experiments, instead of using a search process to discover rules, a decision table based on up to 16 attributes is created. The experiments show that when the number of conditions is increased the feature vector is capable of providing accurate classification. This indicates that perhaps a hierarchical rule system should be used to increase the recognition accuracy in the "recognition boundary" area.

References

1. Ziarko, W.(1998). KDD-R: rough sets-based data mining system. In: Polkowski, L., Skowron, A. (eds.). *Rough Sets in Knowledge Discovery*. Physica Verlag, vol. 2, 598-601.
2. Ziarko W. (1993). Variable precision rough sets model. *Journal of Computer and Systems Sciences*, vol. 46, no. 1, 39-59.
3. Survey of State of the Art in Human Language Technology. http://www.cse.ogi.edu/CSLU/HLTsurvey/HLTsurvey.html
4. John S. Garofolo et al. (1993). DARPA TIMIT Acoustic-Phonetic Continuous Speech Corpus, NISTIR 4930, U.S. Department of Commerce.
5. Rabiner L. and Juang B-H. (1993). *Fundamentals of Speech Recognition*. Prentice Hall.
6. Czyzewski A. and Kaczmarek. (1994). Speech Recognition System Based on Rough Sets and Neural Networks. *Proceedings of the Third International Workshop on Rough Sets and Soft Computing*, RSSC'94, San Jose 1994, pp. 97-100.
7. Czyzewski A. and Kaczmarek (1997). Speaker-Independent Recognition of Isolated Words Using Rough Sets. *Journal of Information Sciences*, vol. 104, pp. 3-14.
8. Czyzewski A. (1996). Speaker-Independent Recognition of Digits — Experiments with Neural Networks, Fuzzy Logic and Rough Sets. *Intelligent Automation and Soft Computing — an International Journal*, vol. 2, No. 2, pp. 133-146.
9. Zhao Z. (1992). A Rough Sets Approach to Speech Recognition. Master Thesis in the Dept. of Computer Science, University of Regina, Canada.
10. Brindle D. (1994). Speaker-Independent Speech Recognition by Rough Sets Analysis. *Proceedings of the Third International Workshop on Rough Sets and Soft Computing*, RSSC'94, San Jose 1994, pp. 101-106.
11. Ainsworth W. (1988). *Speech Recognition by Machine*, Peter Peregrinus Ltd.
12. Ladefoged P. (1985). The Phonetic Basis for Computer Speech Processing. In: Frank Fallside (ed.) *Computer Speech Processing*. Prentice-Hall International (UK) Ltd. pp. 3-27.

A System for Understanding A Mechanical Assembly Instruction Manual Using Virtual Space

Norihiro Abe[1], Kazuaki Tanaka[1], and Hirokazu Taki[2]

[1] Department of Mechanical Syatem Engineering, Faculty of Computer Science and
Systems Engineering, Kyushu Institute of Technology
[2] Faculty of System Engineering, Wakayama Yniversity

Abstract. The paper reports a system which builds assemblies by simulating in virtual space assembly operations specified in an assembly manual. A manual consists of both illustration and explanation.

Illustration consists of not only figures but also phrases and symbols which relate the phrases to the figures. This research uses the three dimensional models of mechanical parts generated with a modeling tool. A noun phrase in illustration specifies the name of a mechanical part and determines the model used. A verb phrase imposes an initial condition to be held before the execution of an assembly operation.

Auxiliary lines in an illustration are virtual lines, which are used to mate the parts at both ends of them. Both the assembly way and the terminal condition of the operation are elucidated in explanation.

The state of a subassembly obtained is hard to infer because an operation often occurs a side effect, which is affected with the geometries of the parts involved in the operation. Configuration obtained with simulation is propagated to inference mechanism and this allows the system recognize the state of the machine assembled.

1 Introduction

We have explored the methods for automatically assembling/disassembling mechanical objects. The methods are basically divided into two classes.

The first class is to find all possible assembling procedures by disassembling a given assembly [1],[8]. Algorithms proposed so far add only one part to a subassembly each step. As a result, it is difficult to divide one object into several groups which we refer to as subassemblies.

The second class has no problem to use the concept of subassembly but it takes too much time to find all assembly procedures with computer algorithm, that is, it is computationaly impossible. Consequently, the assembling procedures have to be given by experts or designers. The first one is considered more appropriate than the second one under the automatic assembling process because robots only need attach a part to a subassembly on a moving belt conveyer. However, when considering the case where an assembly must be disassembled for finding and repairing parts broken down, we find the second one preferable to the first one.

In fact, an instruction manual is an example of the second method. Realizing a system which understands an instruction manual and constructs the assembly is interesting to both robotics and artificial Intelligence. In this research, we intend to come up with a system which takes the similar manner that we take when reading an instruction manual.

Instruction manuals consist of illustration and explanation for people to read/see on demand. An expert can assemble a target machine even without reading explanation. But the purpose of this research is to make a model of novices who have no expertise of mechanics. Nevertheless, there are dissimilar points between human and computers. We can know no more than what we have acquired by watching how novices read/see an instruction manual.

Since no standard way of writing an instruction manual is yet admitted, we use the manual written by Health INC. [14]. Two typical examples are shown in Figures 1 and 2. The illustration contains not only figures but also description like noun and verb phrases. An auxiliary line is depicted between a part and an object to which the part is attached in order to make it easy to recognize the relation to be set between them. Consequently, illustration prescribes the initial configuration of each part or subassembly which should be held before an assembly operation is performed.

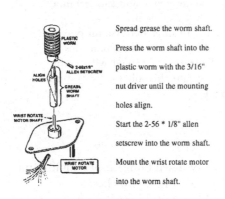

Spread grease the worm shaft.

Press the worm shaft into the

plastic worm with the 3/16"

nut driver until the mounting

holes align.

Start the 2-56 * 1/8" allen

setscrew into the worm shaft.

Mount the wrist rotate motor

into the worm shaft.

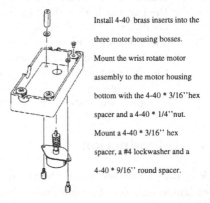

Install 4-40 brass inserts into the

three motor housing bosses.

Mount the wrist rotate motor

assembly to the motor housing

bottom with the 4-40 * 3/16"hex

spacer and a 4-40 * 1/4"nut.

Mount a 4-40 * 3/16" hex

spacer, a #4 lockwasher and a

4-40 * 9/16" round spacer.

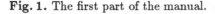

Fig. 1. The first part of the manual.   **Fig. 2.** The next part of the manual.

On the other hand, explanation specifies condition which each operation must satisfy according the assembly procedure. Each sentence prescribes which objects participate in the assembly operation and which terminal condition must hold. These facts allow the system to perform an operation at first by reading a sentence and then by determining the position and orientation of each object after recognizing it and the corresponding auxiliary line from the illustration.

It is needless to say that the system must interpret sentences in explanation and recognize the each object in illustration [5], [12]. The papers reported so far by us concerns the bottom-up method for understanding an assembly instruction manual. This research is based on them but the behavior of an assembled object is difficult to know from them because the parts depicted in the illustration are too incorrect for the system to simulate the operation specified in explanation. The system reported in this paper makes it possible to have true understanding of the instruction manual. Researches using vision and language cooperation system are proposed in [12], and this research is naturally included in them but treats not only static information but also dynamic behavior and side effects caused with assembly operations or alteration of behavior. The dynamic behavior of machinery is studied in [9], [10], but they assumed that machinery has been constructed and the representation is given in advance which is suitable for inferring behavior. On the other hand, our system constructs representation of machinery by interpreting both illustration and explanation and finds behavior of the assembly exploiting not only assembly relation built so far but also the state description discovered in the simulation of mechanism done using virtual space.

2   Presupposition of the system

At the beginning of an instruction manual there is a nominal list of mechanical parts used in an assembly, their names (hereafter, we call it p-name) are registered into the system dictionary. The set of three dimensional models of the parts used are given to the system. The models are defined using a modeling system, both of a surface model and a wire frame model are available to the system. These models are given their p-names but every component of each model is not always given a p-name in advance. Components corresponding to mounting holes, bosses and so on are not given their name in advance, though they are referred from explanation or illustration. When the system encounters such names, it must resolve what they are by comparing illustration to their parent models. The names of tools and adhesive agents and so on are given to the system but all operations concerning them are supposed to always succeed. Under these preparation, interpretation of both explanation and illustration is performed by simulating the corresponding operation using three dimensional models of parts. The resultant state of relation between parts or their surfaces is recorded in the representation referred from an inference engine.

3   Separating character strings from image

Each page is treated as image and is separated roughly into two regions, explanation and illustration. Illustration is then examined to extract character strings and figure symbols like an arrow, using the method in [3], [5]. Fig. 3 shows the result obtained from Fig. 1. The characters are recognized using OCR and sentences are analyzed with a syntactic parser using pattern matching method. In this process, all of characters are not successfully recognized, but we want to proceed to the detailed explanation of the system.

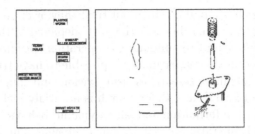

Fig. 3. (1)Phrases (2)Symboles (3)Parts.

4 Interpretation of phrases and sentences

Concerning the detail of the syntactic parser used, please see [2], [7]. Concerning interpretation of illustration, at first, phrases extracted from it are examined because the noun phrases are much the same as p-names and the verb phrases specify the initial condition to be held between subparts/components of two parts. Here, the word 'subpart' means the substructure of a parent part whose name properly includes the name of the subpart. For an example, a wrist rotate motor shaft is a subpart of a wrist rotate motor.

On the other hand, the world 'component' means the substructure of a parent part whose name does not include the name of the component. Examples are mounting holes, motor housing bosses. Although the initial state of objects to be assembled is not prescribed in explanation, it is indispensable to determine their attitudes for beginning the assembly operation.

The p-name plays an important role because it allows the system to determine the model of the part depicted in the illustration. Names except for p-names are divided into the following two classes: The first one is a set of abbreviated forms of p-names or noun phrases corresponding to their subparts. Their examples are motor, wrist rotate motor shaft and so on. The second one is a set of names corresponding to the component of a part/subassembly.

When finding a noun phrase corresponding to a subpart, the parser instructs the image analyzer to match the three dimensional model of the parent of the subpart against a figure after finding the figure relevant to the phrase from the illustration. In this case, figure symbols are used to show which figure region is related to the phrase. If the figure region has been matched to some three dimensional model, the phrase is determined to be a name of the substructure of the model. For an example, a verb phrase "align holes" in Fig. 1 means that there is a hole at the end of each arrow, and that the two holes must be aligned. Consequently, before mating the plastic worm and the worm shaft, their holes must be arranged.

In this manner, a rough initial arrangement is found by analyzing phrases given in illustration. But the precise arrangement can be unknown until the configuration of parts in illustration have been determined by matching them to their three dimensional models.

5 Determining attitude and location of parts

When a p-name appears in a sentence, its three dimensional model must be found from illustration. In the case, one of auxiliary lines attached to the model is superimposed onto one of those detected from the figure.

For an example, consider the case that auxiliary line 1 of a plastic worm in Fig. 4 (a) is selected. The figure in Fig. 4 (b) is generated by transforming the coordinate system of the original figure so as to have the auxiliary line to agree with y axis and then constructing a circumscribed rectangle which is symmetric with respect to the auxiliary line. Next one of auxiliary lines attached to the model is selected as y axis and a projected figure of the model is generated by viewing it from the same line of sight as that used when the illustration has been drawn. Then a circumscribed rectangle is generated for a figure obtained by rotating the figure around the axis. An appropriate rotation will allow the figure shown in Fig. 4 (c) to be identical to the one in Fig. 4 (b). This means that an attitude of the plastic worm has been found.

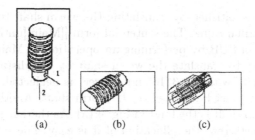

(a)   (b)   (c)

Fig. 4. (a)Plastic worm, (2)A circumscribed rectangle, (c)That for the model (a) in Fig. 5.

Here we need a method to decide if two figures are one and the same one because their scales are not the same. The scale factor is defined to be the ratio of the longitude to the width of the circumscribed rectangle. If two figures are equal then their scale factors must be also equal, and their shapes enclosed by contours must be nearly equal after the original rectangle is magnified/reduced so that it is equal to that constructed from the model. The value of magnification/reduction must be constant value k for all parts depicted in an illustration.

There may be several models passing this inspection if the external appearance is equal to the part except for the number of holes or textures. The wrong model will be surely rejected by examining assemblability along the auxiliary line between itself and the partner to be mated. If the selected model should be wrong, the system would have to backtrack. When the first object appearing in the first sentence has been correctly processed, the subsequent analysis can exploit the resultant value k and attitude of the object recognized so far.

In our example, a worm shaft is to be mated to the plastic worm through the auxiliary line2 shown in Fig. 4 (a). This means that a model of the worm shaft should be arranged so that the one of the auxiliary lines is collinear to that of the plastic worm. An attitude of the worm shaft is to be restricted using the similar way as mentioned above. But it is symmetric with respect to the auxiliary line, no rotation is needed.

At this point, it seems that an initial arrangement of the operation is completed, but the constraint from the verb phrase in the illustration must be examined. It requires two holes to be aligned, then the corresponding holes (it is hard to find them from the illustration) are found from their models and one of them is rotated around the auxiliary line until the holes align.

Here the initial arrangement has been completed. The sentence requires two operations: press the worm shaft into the plastic worm, and align the mounting holes. A virtual assembly operation required to perform the operation specified in a sentence needs only translation except for particular cases including engagement of worms or gears and so on.

6 Implementing Assembly process

The first operation is satisfied by translating the worm shaft toward the plastic worm along the auxiliary line. The sentential form [[Main][until][Sub]] instructs to attain the state of SUB by performing an operation of Main. Consequently, the system has only to translate the worm shaft by the distance between the holes. Note here that "with the 3/16" nut driver" is neglected.

Next, a setscrew must be started to the worm shaft. Another auxiliary line concerning the worm shaft is the line1 in Fig. 4 (a). As there is just one auxiliary line attached to a setscrew, the allocation of it is easy. The setscrew is located at the entrance of the hole of the plastic worm then the setscrew is inserted into the mounting hole of the worm shaft. As the result of this operation these three parts are connected and the effect is represented by merging their scene graphs into a new one of INVENTOR. This means that they are transferred together by the rule of INVENTOR if one of them is transferred.

A new object 'worm assembly' appears in the next sentence, which corresponds clearly to the assembled object. The assembly is mounted by inserting the motor shaft into the hole at the bottom of the worm shaft. Five auxiliary lines are given to the model of the motor as shown in Fig. 5, they are examined which of them corresponds to the auxiliary line in the illustration. In the similar way stated above, a circumscribed rectangle of a projected figure of the motor is generated by selecting one of them as an axis. It is then rotated around the axis to examine if the revised rectangle generated from the illustration is nearly equal to that. This revision is based on the scale factor computed so far.

The subordinate clause constraints the quantity of insertion and it is determined by detecting collision between the assembly and the motor. In this case, the condition specified in the subordinate clause is easily confirmed by examining the scene graph and the subassembly obtained so far: surely, the assembly was moved with the setscrew. Note here that the motor is not yet merged into the scene graph of the assembly. By tightening the setscrew, they are merged

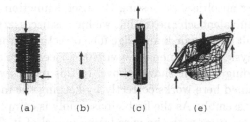

Fig. 5. The models used in Fig. 1.

into a new scene graph in Fig. 6 (a). Here mb, sf, and msa mean motor body motor shaft and motor subassembly.

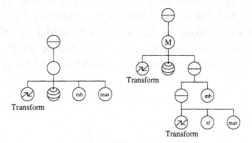

Fig. 6. A wrong scene graph (a) and a correct scene praph of the assembly constructed from Fig. 1.

7 Behavior of subassembly

Though the explanation tells nothing about the function of this subassembly, let consider what kind of function has been attained. The four parts discovered from their p-names constitute this subassembly but strictly speaking, not the motor itself but its shaft participates in the subassembly whose members are mutually locked, and there is one freedom between the motor and its shaft. Consequently the plastic worm is to rotate together with the motor shaft.

At the same time, the motor shaft is transferred if the motor is transferred. For representing these relations, the definition of a motor must be defined as shown in Fig. 6 (b). This implies that some of subparts also need their definitions in the same way as their parents are defined. Under this establishment, the result we expect is realized by the system.

Another point noted here is that the operation specified in the last sentence is wrong because the motor dose not work if the worm assembly is moved until it collides with the motor. We have common sense knowledge that a motor shaft should rotate and been taught to examine if a correct function is not violated when we encounter an object possessing the useful function. To find erroneous instruction, the equivalent scheme to that we have is necessary for the system. It is, however, difficult to prepair knowledge for correcting erroneous instruction.

To simulate physical phenomena in a virtual space, there are many problems to be solved including the one shown above. In this paper, we will assume that the assembly obtained here works correctly by keeping the motor from colliding against the worm assembly. As the first subassembly is completed, it is added to the set of models together with the wire frame model of it. The model inherits auxiliary lines from constituents constructing the assembly except for them used.

8 Treatment of missing operations

There are eleven auxiliary lines in the next illustration. Models corresponding to them are shown in Fig. 7. Note here the model (d) in Fig. 7. This corresponds to the subassembly just built but there is no auxiliary line around the worm assembly. It is not impossible for the system to add it to the model because the worm assembly inherits the function of the motor shaft, but there remain several questions which constituents of the model should be given auxiliary lines to which direction.

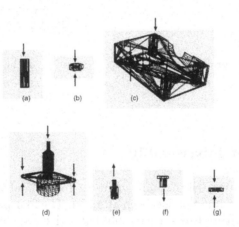

Fig. 7. The models used in Fig. 2.

The first operation has relation to the boss and motor housing bottom. It is not easy to determine the angle of incidence from the model of a boss, as the size is small, which corresponds to (f) in Fig. 7. On the other hand, as the bottom has a hole inside it, the incident angle is computable. The auxiliary line between the brass inserts and bottom in the illustration is to be selected to generate a circumscribed rectangle for comparing the figure of the bottom to the model, but the hole is also available to determine the attitude of the bottom. Fig. 8 shows the rectangle generated for the model(c) in Fig. 7 with respect to the line

L. In the same way as the previous one, the model of the bottom is rotated along the axis corresponding to L.

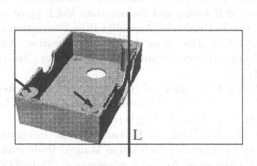

Fig. 8. Discovery of remaining bosses.

The insert operation succeeds but the instruction requires of three motor housing bosses to be inserted with brass inserts. By matching the figure and model of both the motor housing bottom and the brass insert, the location of a boss is discovered. Three bosses and inserts should be depicted in the illustration, but simplification like this is well applied to make it easy to recognize illustration. Note here that models of primitive parts must have been given all of auxiliary lines at their substructures which may be connected with something.

As a heuristic knowledge for treating this type of simplification, we know that substructures with the same function which are arranged systematically on a plane or cylinder of a parent part will be repeatedly applied with the same operation. This rule allows the system find remaining two bosses from the model. Consequently, the operations are successfully realized.

9   Conclusion

We have reported the system which integrates vision, language, and simulation in virtual environment for inferring both assembly relation between mechanical parts and behavior of an assembly constructed. There are problems to be solved for realizing the final assembly specified in the instruction manual used in this research.

References

1. S. Yamada, N. Abe, and S. Tsuji: Construction of Consulting System from Structural Description of a Mechanical Object. Proc. of IEEE on Robotics & Automation, pp.1412-1418, (4 1987).
2. N. Abe and S. Tsuji: Robot task specification in Natural Language. Proc. of Conf. & Ex. on AI, pp.586-595, (10 1987).

394

3. S. He, N. Abe, and T. Kitahashi: Understanding Assembly Illustrations in an Assembly Manual without Any Model of Mechanical Parts. Proc. of Int. Conf. on Computer Vision, pp.573-576, (12 1990).
4. N. Abe, K. Ohno, S. He, and T. Kitahashi: Task Specification Using Technical Illustration. Proc. of Robotics and Automation, Vol.2, pp.58-64, (5 1993).
5. S. He, N. Abe, and T. Kitahashi: Assembly Plan Generation by Integrating Pictorial and Textual Information in an Assembly Illustration. AAAI-94 Workshop on Integration of Natural Language and Vision Processing, Seattle Washington USA, pp.66-73, (1994).
6. N. Abe, J. Y. Zheng, K. Tanaka and H. Taki: A Training System using Virtual Machines for Teaching Assembling/Disassembling Operations to Novices. International Conference on Systems, Man, and Cybernetics(1996).
7. N. Abe, K. Tanaka, J.Y.Zheng ,S. He and H. Taki: Integration of Language and Image Processing for Assembly Instruction Manual Understanding. Proceedings of International Symposium on Artificial Intelligence. 135-140(1996).
8. L.S.Homem de Mello and A,C,Sanderson: AND/OR graph representation of assembly plan. IEEE Trans. Robotics Automat., vol.7,no.2, pp.188-199(1991)
9. L.Joskowies, E.P.Sacks: Computational Kinematics. Artif. Intell.51,1991,pp381-416.
10. A.Gelsey: Automated reasoning about machines. Artif. Intell. 74,1995,pp1-53.
11. J. Wernecke: The Inventor Mentor. Addison Weseley Publishing Company,1994.
12. P. McKevitt: Integration of Natural Language and Vision Processing. AAAI-94 workshop program.
13. K.D.Forbus and J.D.Kleer: Building Problem Solvers. MIT press, 1993.
14. HERO ROBOT arm accessary manual. HEALTH COMPANY, MICHIGAN, 1982.

Perceptual Convergence of Discrete Clamped Fractal Operator

Władysław Skarbek

Department of Electronics and Information Technology
Warsaw University of Technology
Skarbek@ire.pw.edu.pl

Abstract: While clamping the fractal operator to the grayscale range of values of the images preserves its contractivity, performing the rounding process to discrete levels spoils this property and the given iterative sequence is generally not convergent. In practice this lack of convergence is not observed by HVS (Human Visual System) on decoder's output. We explain this phenomenon by presenting a strict notion of the perceptual convergence at the given threshold. It is used to prove that any iterative sequence for a fractal operator which is contractive in l_∞ norm with contractivity $c^* < 1$, after clamping and rounding to integer levels, is perceptually convergent at the threshold $\tau \geq 1/(1 - c^*)$.

1 Introduction

Let $\mathcal{I}$ be the class of all d dimensional images, i.e. the real valued functions of the form $f : D \rightarrow [v_{min}, v_{max}]$, which are defined on a visual surface $D \subset R^d$ having values bounded to a grayscale interval $[v_{min}, v_{max}] \subset R$. Typically $d = 2$ and D is a finite discrete grid of points, so called pixels and integer values from $[v_{min}, v_{max}]$ are used as pixel grayscale values.

The idea of fractal compression of such images is based on representing the given image f by a fractal operator $F : \mathcal{I} \rightarrow \mathcal{I}$ which is defined by local operators mapping image fragments g_S defined on source domains $S \subset D, S \in \Gamma$ onto image fragments g'_T defined on target domains $T \subset D, T \in \Pi$ (cf. [2, 5]). Actually for each T there exists exactly one $S(T)$ and g'_T is obtained from $g_{S(T)}$ by reducing operation R_T, contrasting the result by c_T and offsetting o_T. Since target domains are disjoint and they cover the domain D we have:

$$F(g) \doteq \sum_{T \in \Pi} [c_T R_T(g) + o_T 1_T] \tag{1}$$

where 1_T is the characteristic function of the domain T.

The decoder receives for each T : c_T, o_T, the displacement T from $S(T)$ and optionally the permutation index p_T. It starts with arbitrary initial image $g_0 \in \mathcal{I}$ and iterates in sequence for $i > 0$:

$$F^{\circ i}(g_0) \doteq g_i = F(g_{i-1}) \tag{2}$$

In practice the process is terminated after about $i = 15$ iterations as usually no further improvement of image quality PSNR is observed.

The sufficient condition for the convergence g_i is for instance contractivity of F (cf. [2, 4]) as the Banach fixed point thorem can be applied. In the infinity norm l_∞ the contractivity in l_∞ norm is equivalent to the condition:

$$c^* \doteq \max_T |c_T| < 1 \tag{3}$$

where c^* appears to be the Lipshitz coefficient for F.

The limit image $\tilde{f} \doteq \lim_{i \to \infty} F^{oi}(g_0)$ is the fixed point of F. By the collage theorem ([1]) $\tilde{f}$ is close to the original image f as the coder builds F to minimize the distance between f and $F(f)$.

Even when g has only integer values $v = g(p), p \in D$, the image $g' = F(g)$ has already real values $v' = g'(p)$. Moreover, the result of contrasting and ofsetting can give results outside the interval $[v_{min}, v_{max}]$. In order to save image storage, the clamping operation C and the rounding operation Q is usually applied to g' before storing pixel values. If $h' = C(h)$ and for the pixel $p \in D$, $v = h(p)$ then $v' = h'(p)$ is defined by:

$$v' \doteq \begin{cases} v_{min} & \text{if } v < v_{min}, \\ v_{max} & \text{if } v > v_{max}, \\ v & \text{otherwise.} \end{cases} \tag{4}$$

Now, if $h' = Q(h)$ and for the pixel $p \in D$, $v = h(p)$ then $v' = h'(p)$ is defined by:

$$v' \doteq \begin{cases} \lfloor v \rfloor & \text{if } v < \lfloor v \rfloor + 0.5, \\ \lceil v \rceil & \text{otherwise.} \end{cases} \tag{5}$$

The composition of C and Q operations can be viewed as postprocessing step for each local operator:

$$F_{QC}(g) \doteq \sum_{T \in \Pi} QC [c_T \cdot \mathbf{R}_T(g) + o_T \cdot 1_T] \tag{6}$$

While clamping the fractal operator to the grayscale range of values of the images preserves its contractivity, performing the rounding process to discrete levels spoils this property and the given iterative sequence is generally not convergent. In practice this lack of convergence is not observed by HVS (Human Visual System) on decoder's output. We explain this phenomenon by presenting a strict notion of the perceptual convergence at the given threshold.

The sequence of images $g_i \in \mathcal{I}$ is *perceptually convergent* at threshold τ if and only if there exists i_0 such that for all $j, i > i_0$: $\|g_j - g_i\|_\infty \leq \tau$.

On the gray scale with 256 levels, the threshold $\tau = 4$ makes individual pixel values indistinguishable.

The notion of perceptual convergence was introduced by the author in [6] and applied in case of rounding process only. Here stronger notion of perceptual convergence is considered (but more suitable from the application point of view), the results are extended to the case of composition of clamping and rounding operations. Moreover, new results analyzing the discrete trajectory relatively to true trajectory, are presented.

2 Convergence analysis of discrete sequence

The clamping operation C acts independently for every pixel. If two images have for the given pixel values v_1 and v_2 respectively, then after clamping their values v_1' and v_2' are not going apart. Namely:

$$|v_1' - v_2'| \leq |v_1 - v_2| \, .$$

In terms of the infinity norm, this local property can be written in a global way:

$$\|C(g) - C(h)\| \leq \|g - h\| \tag{7}$$

Therefore if F is contractive with contractivity coefficient α then the operator $F_C \doteq C \circ F$ is contractive too:

$$\|F_C(g) - F_C(h)\| = \|C(F(g)) - C(F(h))\| \leq \|F(g) - F(h)\| \leq \alpha\|g - h\| \tag{8}$$

The rounding operation Q acts independently for every pixel too. If two images have for the given pixel close values $v_1 = \lfloor v_1 \rfloor + 0.5(1 - \epsilon)$ and $v_2 = \lfloor v_1 \rfloor + 0.5(1 + \epsilon)$ respectively, then after rounding their values v_1' and v_2' are going apart. Namely:

$$|v_1' - v_2'| = 1 > \epsilon \, .$$

In terms of the infinity norm, there exist two close images g, h such that:

$$\|g - h\| = \epsilon \text{ and } \|Q(g) - Q(h)\| > \|g - h\| \tag{9}$$

Therefore the rounding operation Q can "spoil" the contractivity of the operator F_C. Namely, if F is the contractive operator then after the clamping and rounding F_{QC} usually is not contractive. However, a modified Lipshitz condition is still true for F_{QC}:

Lemma 1.

Let c^* be the Lipshitz factor in the infinity norm of the affine fractal operator F. Then, for any $g, h \in \mathcal{I}$:

1.

$$\|F_{QC}(g) - F_{QC}(h)\|_\infty \leq c^*\|g - h\|_\infty + 1 \tag{10}$$

2.

$$\|F_{QC}^{\circ i}(g) - F_{QC}^{\circ i}(h)\|_\infty \leq c^{*i}\|g - h\|_\infty + c^{*(i-1)} + \cdots + c^* + 1 \tag{11}$$

Proof: Let $\epsilon_T(g) = QC[c_T R_T(g) + o_T 1_T] - C[c_T R_T(g) + o_T 1_T]$ and analogously $\epsilon_T(h)$ be the rounding error on subimages. The rounding error on the given pixel is not greater than 0.5. Hence the infinity norm of error subimages is not greater than 0.5. We estimate the norm of operator values:

$$\|F_{QC}(g) - F_{QC}(h)\| \; =$$

$$= \; \max_{T \in \Pi} \|QC[c_T R_T(g) + o_T 1_T] - QC[c_T R_T(h) + o_T 1_T]\|$$

$$= \; \max_{T \in \Pi} \|C[c_T R_T(g) + o_T 1_T] + \epsilon_T(g) - C[c_T R_T(h) + o_t 1_T] - \epsilon_T(h)\|$$

$$\leq \; \max_{T \in \Pi} \|C[c_T R_T(g) + o_T 1_T] - C[c_T R_T(h) + o_T 1_T]\| +$$

$$\max_{T \in \Pi} \|\epsilon_T(g) - \epsilon_T(h)\|$$

$$\leq \; \max_{T \in \Pi} \|c_T R_T(g - h)\| + \max_{T \in \Pi} \|\epsilon_T(g) - \epsilon_T(h)\|$$

$$\leq \; c^* \|g - h\|_\infty + 1$$

The second point of the lemma we get by the applications of the inequality from the point one.
□

For the contractive operator F, the Lipshitz-like condition for F_{QC} keeps the distance between images within a fixed bound. Namely, from the last lemma we get easily the following corollary:

Corollary 1.

If the affine fractal operator F has $c^* < 1$ then

$$\|g - h\|_\infty \leq \frac{1}{1 - c^*} \implies \|F_{QC}(g) - F_{QC}(h)\|_\infty \leq \frac{1}{1 - c^*} \tag{12}$$

So far, we have analyzed the mutual distance of two trajectories for the discrete clamped operator F_{QC}. It is interesting to find how the trajectory of the original operator F is related to the trajectory of the operator F_{QC}. The following lemma helps us to understand this relation in case when F is contractive fractal operator:

Lemma 2.

Let $c^* < 1$ be the contractivity coefficient in the infinity norm of the affine fractal operator F and $v_{min} = -v_{max}$. Then, for any $g, h \in \mathcal{I}$:

1.

$$\|F_{QC}(g) - F(h)\|_\infty \leq c^* \|g - h\|_\infty + 0.5 \tag{13}$$

2.

$$\|F_{QC}^{oi}(g) - F^{oi}(h)\|_\infty \leq c^{*i} \|g - h\|_\infty + 0.5[c^{*(i-1)} + \cdots + c^* + 1] \tag{14}$$

Proof: Firstly, let us observe that in case of contractivity of F we have $F_C = F$. Namely from the linearity of F and its contractivity we have in l_∞ norm we have:

$$\|F(g)\| \le c^*\|g\| < \|g\| \ .$$

Therefore if $\|g\| \le B$ then $\|F(g)\| < B$. Hence if the image g has all pixel values in $[-v_{max}, v_{max}]$ then $F(g)$ has all pixel values in the same range and the clamping operation is not needed what gives $F_C = F$.

Let $\epsilon_T(g) \doteq Q[c_T R_T(g) + o_T 1_T] - [c_T R_T(g) + o_T 1_T]$ be the rounding error on subimages. The rounding error on the given pixel is not greater than 0.5. Hence also the infinity norm of error subimages is not greater than 0.5. Similarly as before we estimate the norm of operator values:

$$\|F_{QC}(g) - F(h)\| \ = \|F_Q(g) - F(h)\| \ =$$

$$= \ \max_{T \in \Pi} \|Q[c_T R_T(g) + o_T 1_T] - [c_T R_T(h) + o_T 1_T]\|$$

$$= \ \max_{T \in \Pi} \|c_T R_T(g) + o_T 1_T + \epsilon_T(g) - c_T R_T(h) - o_t 1_T\|$$

$$\le \ \max_{T \in \Pi} \|c_T(R_T(g) - R_T(h))\| + \max_{T \in \Pi} \|\epsilon_T(g)\|$$

$$\le \ \max_{T \in \Pi} \|c_T R_T(g - h)\| + \max_{T \in \Pi} \|\epsilon_T(g)\|$$

$$\le \ c^*\|g - h\|_\infty + 0.5$$

The second point of the lemma we get directly applying the inequality from the point one.
□

For the contractive operator F, the distance between the trajectory for F_{QC} and the trajectory for F is kept within a fixed bound. Namely, from the lemma 2 we get easily the following corollary:

Corollary 2.

If the affine fractal operator F has $c^* < 1$ and $v_{min} = -v_{max}$ then

$$\|g - h\|_\infty \le \frac{0.5}{1 - c^*} \quad \Longrightarrow \quad \|F_{QC}(g) - F(h)\|_\infty \le \frac{0.5}{1 - c^*} \qquad (15)$$

From the above corollaries we conclude that trajectories starting within certain bound they are kept within the same bound. Hence, starting from the same image the discrete and the "true" trajectory are always in the distance $0.5/(1 - c^*)$. However, we are not sure whether the perceptual convergence occurs.

Due to finiteness of the space of possible discrete images with fixed domain D, any iterative sequence enters a cycle. In a rare case this cycle could consist of a single element only. It appears that the infinity distance for any two images from any cycle is bounded by the threshold $\tau = 1/(1 - c^*)$ and their distance from the fixed point $\tilde{f}$ is bounded by $\tau/2$:

Theorem 1.

Let g_0 be any initial image and g, h belong to a cycle entered by the iterative sequence $\{F^{oi}_{QC}(g_0)\}$. If $c^* < 1$ then

$$\|g - h\|_\infty \leq \frac{1}{1 - c^*} \tag{16}$$

Moreover if the pixel range is symmetric, i.e. $v_{min} = -v_{max}$ then for any g on any cycle:

$$\|g - \tilde{f}\|_\infty \leq \frac{0.5}{1 - c^*} \tag{17}$$

Hence images from all cycles are distant from each other not more than $1/(1-c^*)$.

Proof: Let elements g, h be from the cycle of length K, have the form $g = F^{oq}_{QC}(g_0)$ and $h = F^{o(q+d)}_{QC}(g_0)$ for certain iterations $q, q + d$. Using Point 2 of Lemma 1 and the periodicity of the iterative sequence, we get for any $t \geq 0$:

$$\|g - h\| = \|F^{oq}_{QC}(g_0) - F^{o(q+d)}_{QC}(g_0)\| = \|F^{o(q+tK)}_{QC}(g_0) - F^{o(q+d+tK)}_{QC}(g_0)\|$$

$$\leq (c^*)^{q+tK}\|g_0 - F^{od}_{QC}(g_0)\| + (1 - (c^*)^{q+tK})/(1 - c^*) \overset{t \to \infty}{\Longrightarrow} 1/(1 - c^*)$$

Assumming the symmetry of pixel range we can use Lemma 2:

$$\|g - F^{o(q+tK)}(g_0)\| = \|F^{oq}_{QC}(g_0) - F^{o(q+tK)}(g_0)\|$$

$$\leq \|F^{o(q+tK)}_{QC}(g_0) - F^{o(q+tK)}(g_0)\|$$

$$\leq (c^*)^{q+tK}\|g_0 - g_0\| + 0.5(1 - (c^*)^{q+tK})/(1 - c^*) \overset{t \to \infty}{\Longrightarrow} 0.5/(1 - c^*)$$

The last conclusion follows directly from the triangle inequality. $\square$

Combining Corollary 1 and Theorem 1, we have immediately:

Corollary 3.

Let $\tau \geq 1/(1 - c^*)$ be a threshold. If $c^* < 1$ then for any initial image g_0, the iterative sequence $\{F^{oi}_{QC}(g_0)\}$ is perceptually convergent at the threshold τ. In practical circumstances we get perceptual convergence for clamped discrete operator if $c^* \leq 0.75$ and $\tau = 4$.

3 Conclusions

While clamping the fractal operator to the grayscale range of values of the images preserves its contractivity, performing the rounding process to discrete levels spoils this property and the given iterative sequence is generally not convergent. In practice this lack of convergence is not observed by HVS (Human Visual System) on decoder's output. We explain this phenomenon by presenting a strict notion of the perceptual convergence at the given threshold. It is used to prove that any iterative sequence for a fractal operator which is contractive in the infinity norm with contractivity $c^* < 1$, after clamping and rounding to integer levels is perceptually convergent with threshold $\tau \geq 1/(1 - c^*)$.

In symmetric case Theorem 1 says that elements from all cycles of the operator F_{QC} can be localized in one "layer" of images and the width of this layer is not more than $1/(1 - c^*)$. The center of this layer is created by the fixed point $\tilde{f}$ of the original fractal operator F.

Acknowledgments: This work was supported by European ESPRIT INCO CRIT2 project.

References

1. Barnsley, M.F.: Fractals everywhere. Addison Wesley, Reading, MA (1988)
2. Barnsley, M.F., Hurd, L.P.: Fractal image compression. AK Peters. Ltd, Wellesley, MA (1993)
3. Dugundi, J., Granas, A.: Fixed point theory. Polish Scientific Publishers, Warszawa (1982)
4. Fisher, Y. ed.: Fractal image compression, Theory and Applications. Springer Verlag, New York (1995)
5. Jacquin, A.E.: Image coding based on a fractal theory of iterated contractive image transformations. IEEE Trans. on Image Processing **1** (1992) 18–30
6. Skarbek, W.: On convergence of affine fractal operators. Image Processing and Communications **1** (1995) 33–41

Modified Oja-RLS Algorithm – Stochastic Convergence Analysis and Application for Image Compression

Władysław Skarbek, Adam Pietrowcew, Radosław Sikora

Department of Electronics and Information Technology
Warsaw University of Technology
Skarbek@ire.pw.edu.pl

Abstract: An analysis for stochastic convergence of the modified Oja-RLS learning rule is presented. The rule is used to find Karhunen Loeve Transform. Based on this algorithm, an image compression scheme is developed by combining approximated 2D KLT transform and JPEG standard quantization and entropy coding stages.

1 Introduction

Oja-RLS algorithm as described by Kung ([2]) and Cichocki et al. ([1]) is a neural type iterative scheme

$$
\begin{aligned}
y_n &= x_n^T w_n \\
\beta_n^{-1} &= \beta_{n-1}^{-1} + y_n^2 \\
w_{n+1} &= w_n + \beta_n y_n (x_n - y_n w_n)
\end{aligned}
\tag{1}
$$

used for stochastic approximation of the principal vector $w \in R^N$ for the given random variable $X : \Omega \to R^N$ with the zero mean value (E[X]=0). The vectors are written in the column form and ^{T} denotes the matrix transposition. Components of the vector w are also called weights because they can be interpreted as weights of one linear neuron with the output $y = x^T w$. This neuron is taught to maximize the average energy of the random output signal $Y = X^T w$.

The sample $x_n \in R^N$ is a value of X chosen at the n-th moment of discrete time ($n = 1, \ldots$), randomly and independently of other samples. The real positive number β_n is called the gain or the learning rate coefficient at time n. The initial value of weight vector w_0 was not specified explicitly but heuristically a vector of length one is chosen. The value of β_0^{-1} is also suggested by the *rule of thumb* to be the variance of X.

In this work we modify Oja-RLS neural scheme by making the modification of the gain after the modification of the weight vector:

$$
\begin{aligned}
y_n &= x_n^T w_n \\
w_{n+1} &= w_n + \beta_n y_n (x_n - y_n w_n) \\
\beta_{n+1}^{-1} &= \beta_n^{-1} + y_n^2
\end{aligned}
\tag{2}
$$

In our scheme the learning sequence x_n is indexed from zero: $n = 0, 1 \ldots$. Moreover, our mathematical analysis presented leads to the following intial values for the recurrent scheme (2):

$$\beta_0^{-1} = 2B, \quad w_0 = x_0/\|x_0\| \tag{3}$$

where B is an upper bound for the learning sequence, for instance:

$$B \doteq \max_n \|x_n\|^2 \tag{4}$$

Comparing with the classical Oja rule for PCA ([5]), Oja-RLS algorithm and its modified version tend to the principal vector about one order of magnitude faster than Oja algorithm. The convergence proof for the classical Oja algorithm convergence was attempted to be shown by reducing the stochastic difference equation to the corresponding deterministic ordinary differential equation. Two basic assumptions of this theory are related to the speed of convergence to zero for β_n.

$$\sum_{n=0}^{\infty} \beta_n = \infty \text{ with probability one} \tag{5}$$

$$\sum_{n=0}^{\infty} \beta_n^2 < \infty \text{ with probability one} \tag{6}$$

Many authors (e.g.:[2]) "prove" the stochastic convergence with probability one to the principal vector of X under the conditions (5,6) for gains. Additionally it is required that the correlation matrix $C = E[XX^T]$ for X has the principal vector e_1 with the eigenvalue λ_1 of multiplicity one (i.e. $\lambda_1 > \lambda_2$) and it is not orthogonal to the initial weight vector w_0 (i.e. $w_0^T e_1 \neq 0$). These assumptions are sufficient to show the convergence of solutions for the corresponding ordinary differential equation (ODE) to the eigenvector $\pm e_1$.

However, in proofs we encountered, authors using the stochastic approximation ignored the basic condition of this theory: the existence of the compact set Z which on one hand is the basin of attraction for e_1 in the continuous dynamical system, but on the other hand Z must contain infinite number of elements of the stochastic sequence w_n defined in the corresponding discrete time dynamical system (1). Therefore their proofs were incomplete.

Recently there were some efforts to find a proof independent of the Kushner and Clark stochastic approximation theory using only general facts from martingale theory. The book of Duflo [3] includes the proof of the following theorem (Proposition 9.4.15):

Theorem 1. *Duflo's theorem*
Let $U = \{u_1, \ldots, u_L\} \subset R^N$ be a finite learning set. Suppose that (x_n) is a sequence of i.i.d. (independent and identically distributed) random variables with values in U such that the correlation matrix has the principal eigenvalue of the

multiplicity one. In Oja's algorithm, we choose w_0 with $\|w_0\|^2 \le 5$ and (β_n) to be deterministic and decreasing and such that $\beta_0 \le 1/(2B)$, $\sum \beta_n = \infty$, $\sum \beta_n^2 < \infty$. Then a.s. (almost surely) (w_n) converges either to e_1 or to $-e_1$.

The above theorem appears to be incomplete. Namely, the following example shows that at certain learning sets the algorithm fails to converge a.s. to the principal vector:

$$e_1 = [1\ 0]^T,\ e_2 = [0\ 1]^T,\ U = \{2e_1, e_2\}\ .$$

Namely the covariance matrix is now

$$C = \begin{bmatrix} 2 & 0 \\ 0 & 0.5 \end{bmatrix}$$

and its eigenvectors are e_1 and e_2 for eigenvalues 2 and 0.5, respectively. If we take as a starting point $w_0 = e_2$ then for any $n \ge 1$ w_n is parallel to e_2. Hence the sequence cannot converge to the principal vector e_1. However, the following property imposed on the learning set makes the proof complete:

Definition 1. *Let $U = \{u_1, \dots, u_L\} \subset R^N$ be a finite learning set. We say that it is admissible if and only if for each i, j:*

$$u_i^T e_j \ne 0\ ,$$

where e_j are the eigenvectors of the correlation matrix $C = 1/L \sum_i u_i u_i^T$, corresponding to positive eigenvalues.

Duflo [3] has also proved the stability of the algorithm by showing that any trajectory of Oja's dynamical system beginning from the ball $\overline{K}(0, \sqrt{5})$ (with center in zero and radius $\sqrt{5}$) will stay in this ball provided the sequence β_n is bounded by $(2B)^{-1}$.

Recently, we have shown in [6] that Oja algorithm is stable in the ball $\overline{K}(0, 9/8)$. It is more tight bound than $\overline{K}(0, \sqrt{5})$ reported by Duflo. In this paper, in case of the modified Oja-RLS algorithm, we show the stability in the ring $\overline{K}(0, 9/8) - K(0, 8/9)$. The same region of stability is valid for Oja algorithm, too.

However, the main result of this work is an analysis of convergence with the probability one for the modified Oja-RLS scheme. To this goal we have to prove that the conditions (5,6) are satisfied almost surely. Then we can use a generalized form of Duflo's theorem 1:

Theorem 2. *Generalized Duflo's theorem*
Let $U = \{u_1, \dots, u_L\} \subset R^N$ be an admissible learning set. Suppose that (x_n) is a sequence of i.i.d. random variables with values in U such that the correlation matrix has the principal eigenvalue of the multiplicity one. In Oja's algorithm, we choose w_0 with $\|w_0\|^2 \le 5$ and (β_n) to be stochastic, dependent only on w_0, $x_0, \dots x_{n-1}$, decreasing and such that

1. $\beta_0 \le 1/(2B)$,

2. $\sum \beta_n = \infty$ a.s.,

3. $\sum \beta_n^2 < \infty$ a.s.

Then a.s. (w_n) converges either to e_1 or to $-e_1$.

Proof of the above fact and all other ones given in this paper can be found in our forthcoming paper [8].

Stability of the modified Oja-RLS algorithm depends on the initial condition for w_0. The following theorem describes a set of stability for this algorithm:

Theorem 3.

1. *If $8/9 \leq \|w_n\| \leq 9/8$ then $8/9 \leq \|w_{n+1}\| \leq 9/8$;*

2. *If $S = span(U)$ is a set spanned by the learning set $U \subset R^N$ then $Z \doteq S \cap (\overline{K}(0, 9/8) - K(0, 8/9))$ is a stable set of the modified Oja-RLS dynamical system.*

2 Analysis of convergence for the modified Oja-RLS algorithm

We proceed now to analysis of convergence for the modified Oja-RLS leraning rule. Namely we want to show that the random sequence of vectors in the modified Oja-RLS dynamical system converges almost surely to the principal eigenvector e_1 of the correlation matrix for the learning set U. As we have mentioned in the introduction, to this goal it is enough to prove that the conditions (5,6) are satisfied almost surely.

To emphasize important context at which we get convergence for series of β_n^2 and lack of convergence for series of β_n, we put them together in one lemma:

Lemma 1.
Suppose that we are given:

1. *The admissible learning set $U = \{u_1, \ldots, u_L\}$ spanning the subspace $S \doteq span(U) \neq \{0\}$ and $B \doteq \max_{u \in U} \|u\|^2$;*

2. *The infinite sequence of i.i.d random variables x_n with values in U ($n = 0, 1, \ldots$) such that all elements of U is equally probable, i.e. $P(x_n = u_i) = 1/L$ and such that $\|x_n\|^2 \leq B$;*

3. *The compact set $Z \subset S - \{0\}$;*

4. *The random sequence $w_n \in R^N$, defined recursively*

$$w_{n+1} = w_n + \beta_n f(x_n, w_n)$$

where $w_0 \in Z$, $\dfrac{1}{\beta_0} = 2B$, $\dfrac{1}{\beta_{n+1}} = \dfrac{1}{\beta_n} + y_n^2$, $y_n \doteq x_n^T w_n$;

5. *The proved property: $w_n \in Z$ for each $n > 0$.*

   Then the gains β_n have the following convergence properties:

1. *Always the series $\sum_{n=0}^{\infty} \beta_n = \infty$;*

2. *Almost surely the series $\sum_{n=0}^{\infty} \beta_n^2 < \infty$.*

3. *There exist positive constants c_1 and c_2 such that:*

$$P\left(\bigcup_{m \geq 0} \bigcap_{n > m} \left\{ \frac{c_1}{n} \leq \beta_n \leq \frac{c_2}{n} \right\}\right) = 1 \qquad (7)$$

Having Theorems 2, 3, and Lemma 1, we easily get the following theorem:

Theorem 4.
Assume that the unit length principal eigenvector e_1 of the correlation matrix $C = E(XX^T))$ which corresponds to its maximum eigenvalue has multiplicity one, i.e. $\lambda_1 > \lambda_2 \geq \ldots \lambda_N \geq 0$. Suppose that we are given:

1. *The admissible learning set $U = \{u_1, \ldots, u_L\}$ spanning the subspace $S \doteq span(U) \neq \{0\}$ and $B \doteq \max_{u \in U} \|u\|^2$;*

2. *The infinite sequence of i.i.d. random variables x_n with values in U ($n = 0, 1, \ldots$) such that all elements of U is equally probable, i.e. $P(x_n = u_i) = 1/L$ and such that $\|x_n\|^2 \leq B$;*

3. *The set $Z \doteq S \cap (\overline{K}(0, 9/8) - K(0, 8/9))$;*

4. *The initial weight vector $w_0 \in Z$;*

5. *The random sequence $w_n \in R^N$, defined recursively for $n \geq 0$:*

$$w_{n+1} = w_n + \beta_n f(x_n, w_n) \text{ where } \frac{1}{\beta_0} = 2B, \quad \frac{1}{\beta_{n+1}} = \frac{1}{\beta_n} + y_n^2, \quad y_n \doteq x_n^T w_n.$$

Then the random sequence of weights w_n converges almost surely to one of the eigenvectors $\pm e_1$.

3 Image compression using the modified Oja-RLS algorithm

In order to illustrate efficiency of the modified Oja-RLS algorithm as regards the signal energy compaction, we have replaced in JPEG standard, the DCT transform C by approximated KLT transform A. At the modelling stage for each $k \times k$ image block X, we calculate the coefficient block $Y = A^T X A$. At the quantization stage in case $k = 8$, Y is quantized using the same quantization matrix as JPEG uses (cf. [4]). For $k > 8$ the quantization matrix is obtained using bilinear interpolation of the matrix in case $k = 8$. The symbols for entropy coding are created using zig-zag scan, run length and value level encoding scheme, just in the same way as JPEG does.

The KLT transform approximation for image blocks of size $k \times k$ is obtained using the algorithm (2) on the learning set which is obtained by subdivision of the given image domain into row vectors of size $1 \times k$. The extracted vectors are mean shifted by subtraction of the average vector of the learning set. Therefore for the image with N pixels we have about N/k learning vectors.

Fig. 1. The original image Barbara (left) with 8[bpp] and its reconstructions after JPEG (center) with 0.80[bpp] and after KLT (right) with 0.49[bpp].

Table 1. Results of compression for the image Barbara.

Quant. scale	Bitrate (bpp) JPEG	PSNR JPEG	Block size KLT (quant. scale 1)	Bitrate (bpp) KLT	PSNR KLT
0.50	1.16	32.20	8	0.93	32.49
0.90	0.82	29.66	12	0.63	29.75
1.00	0.77	29.18	16	0.49	29.22
1.35	0.64	27.96	32	0.32	27.94

The idea of using KLT for compression is not a new one. Actually DCT transform was invented to approximate KLT optimal energy compaction feature. It was an obvious need in seventies when computer resources such as time and memory were very limited. The technological progress gives now a chance to improve compression efficiency using optimal KLT transform giving better quality of the reconstructed image and less bitrate. Moreover, the adaptive and incremental structure of the modified Oja-RLS algorithm gives a chance to design effective compression schemes for 3D signals (i.e. time or space slices).

The possibility to apply Oja-RLS algorithm for image compression was checked by Cichocki, Kasprzak, and Skarbek in [1]. However, the authors considered there only 1D KLT transform for $k = 8 \cdot 8 = 64$ vectors and no attempts were made to join quantization and binary coding stages. Here, we make fair comparison with existing standard, by replacing only JPEG's modelling stage while preserving other coding details.

The results show a significant increase of image quality for $k = 8$. The slight decrease of bitrate in this case follows from the fact that the matrix A must be sent by the encoder to the output stream.

For $k > 8$ we have significant decrease of the bitrate in cost of decrease of PSNR. However up to $k = 16$ results are visually acceptable.

Tables 2 and 3 present comparative results of the quality of compression for the image Barbara and show great improvement after reconstruction phase made by applying KLT transform in place of DCT. The difference is apparently visible for block size $k = 16$ for KLT transform.

Table 4 compares compression bitrates between JPEG and KLT. The last row here shows also great improvements in *bpp* made by applying the KLT transform and choosing proper quantization coefficient.

Table 2. Comparison of image quality after reconstruction between JPEG and KLT for the image Barbara. Block size $k = 8$.

Quant. scale JPEG	Bitrate (bpp) JPEG	PSNR JPEG	Quant. scale KLT	Bitrate (bpp) KLT	PSNR KLT
0.80	0.88	30.13	1.05	0.87	31.89
0.90	0.82	29.66	1.20	0.82	31.40
1.00	0.77	29.18	1.30	0.77	31.07
1.20	0.69	28.41	1.60	0.69	30.24
1.35	0.64	27.96	1.80	0.65	29.75

Comparing to the JPEG standard, the developed algorithm exploiting a neural approximation of 2D KLT transform in place of the DCT, allows to obtain much better compression ratios at comparable quality.

4 Conclusions

It was shown that the discrete time dynamical system associated with the modified Oja-RLS algorithm is stable in the ring $\overline{K}(0, 9/8) - K(0, 8/9)$ if only the initial gain β_0 is bounded by $(2B)^{-1}$, where $B = b^2$ and b is the bound for the learning set.

Moreover, starting the iteration from this ring leads almost surely to the principal vector e_1 of the correlation matrix of the learning set, provided we start within the subspace spanned by the admissible learning set U.

Table 3. Comparison of image quality after reconstruction between JPEG and KLT for the image Barbara. Block size $k = 8$ for JPEG and different block sizes for KLT.

Quant. scale JPEG	Bitrate (bpp) JPEG	PSNR JPEG	Block size KLT	Quant. scale KLT	Bitrate (bpp) KLT	PSNR KLT
1.20	0.69	28.41	12	0.80	0.70	30.43
1.50	0.59	27.47	12	1.05	0.59	29.46
1.85	0.52	26.69	12	1.30	0.52	28.54
1.60	0.57	27.23	16	0.80	0.57	30.14
1.75	0.53	26.89	16	0.90	0.54	29.68
1.95	0.50	26.52	16	0.95	0.50	29.35

Assumming that the zero vectors are skipped in the training random sequence, the above results imply the following heuristic rule for the initial choice of the weight in the modified Oja-RLS algorithm:

$$w_0 \doteq \frac{x_0}{\|x_0\|}.$$

In order to get the principal vector of the covariance matrix $E[(X-E[X])(X-E[X])^T]$, the learning set U must be normalized by subtracting the mean value $\overline{U}$ from every learning vector $u \in U$.

Table 4. Comparison of compression bitrates between JPEG and KLT for the image Barbara. Block size $k = 8$ for JPEG and different block sizes for KLT.

Quant. scale JPEG	Bitrate (bpp) JPEG	PSNR JPEG	Block size KLT	Quant. scale KLT	Bitrate (bpp) KLT	PSNR KLT
0.80	0.88	30.13	8	1.65	0.68	30.08
0.95	0.80	29.41	8	1.85	0.63	29.40
1.00	0.77	29.18	12	1.25	0.54	29.12
1.30	0.65	28.11	12	1.40	0.49	28.12
1.10	0.73	28.77	16	1.10	0.46	28.78
1.50	0.59	27.47	16	1.50	0.36	27.45

This paper completes the theoretical framework of the modified Oja-RLS neural algorithm which is of great importance in KLT based adaptive applications such as: compression of multimedia information, feature extraction for pattern recognition (e.g. the face recognition), and the design of classifiers (e.g. the local subspace method).

The sound analysis of the modified Oja-RLS and the existence of convergence proof not only add more confidence to the results of our recent research but they also create a strong basis for future applications of this approach.

In order to illustrate one of such applications, the modified Oja-RLS algorithm is used to develop an image compression scheme by combining approximated 2D KLT transform and JPEG standard quantization and entropy coding stages. Though 2D KLT transform is of higher complexity than 2D DCT, the resulting PSNR quality of reconstructed images is better even by 2[dB]. Moreover at the similar level of PSNR the achieved bitrates are much lower than for JPEG.

Acknowledgments: This research has been supported in part within *Virtual Laboratory* project granted by the Dean of Electronics and Information Technology Faculty, Warsaw University of Technology (for the first two authors) and in part by European ESPRIT INCO CRIT2 project (for the third author).

References

1. Cichocki A., Kasprzak W., Skarbek W.: Adaptive learning algorithm for Principal Component Analysis with partial data. Proceedings of 13-th European Meeting on Cybernetics and Systems Research. Austrian Society for Cybernetic Studies, Vienna, Austria (1996) 1014–1019
2. Diamantaras K.I., Kung S.Y.: Principal component neural networks – theory and applications. John Wiley & Sons, Inc. (1995)
3. Duflo M.: Random iterative models. Springer (1997)
4. Pennebaker, W.B. and Mitchell, J.L.: JPEG Still Image Data Compression Standard. Prentice-Hall (1995)
5. Oja, E.: A simplified neuron model as a principal component analyzer. Journal of Mathematical Biology. **15** (1982) 267–273
6. Sikora, R. and Skarbek, W.: On stability of Oja algorithm. In: Polkowski, L., Skowron, A. (eds.): Rough Sets and Current Trends in Computing. Lecture Notes in Artificial Intelligence, Vol. 1424. Springer (1998) 354–360
7. Sikora, R., Skarbek, W.: Stability Analysis of Oja-RLS Learning Rule. Fundamenta Informaticae. **34** (1998) 441–453
8. Skarbek, W., Pietrowcew, A. and Sikora, R.: The Modified Oja-RLS Algorithm, Stochastic Convergence Analysis and Application for Image Compression. Fundamenta Informaticae. **36** (1999) xxx–yyy
9. Skarbek, W.: Local Principal Components Analysis for Transform Coding. In: Nagashino H.(ed.): Proceedings of 1996 International Symposium on Nonlinear Theory and its Applications. IEICE, Kochi, Japan, (1996) 381–384
10. Skarbek, W., Ghuwar, M., Ignasiak, K.: Local subspace method for pattern recognition. Sommer, G., Daniilidis, K., Pauli, J. (eds.): Computer Analysis of Images and Patterns. Lecture Notes in Computer Science, Vol. 1296. Springer (1997) 527–534
11. Skarbek, W., Ignasiak, K.: Handwritten digit recognition by local principal components analysis. In: Ras, Z.W., Skowron, A. (eds.): Foundations of Intelligent Systems. Lecture Notes in Artificial Intelligence, Vol. 1325. Springer (1997) 217–226

Learning from Inconsistent and Noisy Data: The AQ18 Approach*

Kenneth A. Kaufman and Ryszard S. Michalski*

Machine Learning and Inference Laboratory
George Mason University, Fairfax, VA, USA
{kaufman, michalski}@gmu.edu

* Also with Institute of Computer Science,
Polish Academy of Sciences, Warsaw, Poland

Abstract. In concept learning or data mining tasks, the learner is typically faced with a choice of many possible hypotheses characterizing the data. If one can assume that the training data are noise-free, then the generated hypothesis should be complete and consistent with regard to the data. In real-world problems, however, data are often noisy, and an insistence on full completeness and consistency is no longer valid. The problem then is to determine a hypothesis that represents the "best" trade-off between completeness and consistency. This paper presents an approach to this problem in which a learner seeks rules optimizing a *description quality criterion* that combines completeness and *consistency gain*, a measure based on consistency that reflects the rule's benefit. The method has been implemented in the AQ18 learning and data mining system and compared to several other methods. Experiments have indicated the flexibility and power of the proposed method.

1 Introduction

In concept learning and data mining tasks, a typical objective is to determine a general hypothesis characterizing training instances that will classify future instances as correctly as possible. For any non-trivial generalization problem, one can usually generate many plausible hypotheses that are complete and consistent with regard to the input data. If one can assume that the training data contain no noise, hypothesis consistency and completeness are justifiable preconditions for admissibility, but in real-world applications, data are often noisy and/or inconsistent; the completeness and consistency criteria are therefore no longer essential. One may then seek a hypothesis that is maximally consistent at the expense of completeness, maximally complete at the expense of inconsistency, or representing some combination of the two criteria.

The problem then arises as to what kind of trade-off should be chosen between completeness and consistency, or, more generally, what criteria should be used to

---

* This research was supported in part by the National Science Foundation under grants No. NSF 9904078 and IRI-9510644.

guide the learner in problems with noisy and/or inconsistent data? To illustrate this problem, suppose that a training set contains 1000 positive and 1000 negative examples of a concept to be learned. Suppose further that a learning system generated two hypotheses, one covering 600 positive examples and 2 negative examples, and the other covering 950 positive examples and 20 negative examples. Which is better?

Clearly, the choice of which hypothesis to select is not domain-independent. In some domains, the first hypothesis may be preferred because it represents a more consistent pattern. In other domains, the second hypothesis may be viewed as better, because it represents a more dominant pattern.

This paper explores issues related to the trade-off between hypothesis completeness and consistency in the case of noisy and/or inconsistent training data, and proposes a single *description quality measure*, which reflects this trade-off. This measure can be combined with a *description simplicity measure* (a reciprocal of description complexity) into a *general description quality measure* using the *lexicographical evaluation functional* (Section 2). A learning or pattern discovery process is presented as a search for a hypothesis that maximizes a given description quality measure. These measures have been implemented in the AQ18 rule learning system [9].

2 Multicriterion Ranking of Hypotheses

We explore the issue of choosing the best hypothesis or pattern in the context of a progressive covering (a.k.a. separate-and-conquer) approach to concept learning. In this approach, a complete concept description (a ruleset) is created by sequentially determining decision rules. If the training data contain errors or inconsistency, some degree of inconsistency and incompleteness of the rules may not only be acceptable, but also desirable (e.g., [2]).

Among the most important characteristics of a single rule are the *completeness* (the percentage of positive examples covered by it), and the *consistency* (the percentage of examples covered by it in the positive class). Therefore, a simple criterion for evaluating rule quality can be some function of the completeness and the consistency. Different forms of such a criterion have been presented in the literature, and appear to be adequate for problems on which they have been tested. It is, however, unrealistic to expect that any single form will fit all practical problems. For different problems, a different criterion of rule optimality may lead to better performance.

This paper views a learning process as a problem of constructing a description that optimizes a description quality criterion. This view has been implemented in the AQ18 rule learning system. To tailor the description quality measure to the problem at hand, AQ18 offers a user a range of *elementary criteria*, each representing one aspect of the hypothesis being learned. A subset of these criteria is selected from a menu of available criteria, and assembled into a *lexicographic evaluation functional* (LEF) [8], defined by a sequence:

$$<(c_1, \tau_1), (c_2, \tau_2), \ldots, (c_n, \tau_n)> .\qquad(1)$$

where c_i represents the ith elementary criterion, and τ_i is the *tolerance* associated with c_i. The latter defines the range (either absolute or relative) within which a candidate rule's c_i evaluation value can deviate from the best evaluation value of this criterion in the current set of rules. Criteria in LEF are applied sequentially to the set of hypotheses. A hypothesis passes a given criterion if its evaluation on this criterion is not outside the range as defined by the tolerance from the maximum value among the hypotheses in consideration. To illustrate LEF, let us assume that S is a set of hypotheses, and LEF consists just two elementary criteria, first to maximize the completeness, and second to maximize consistency. Let us assume further that hypotheses with completeness less than 10% below the maximum completeness achieved by any single rule in S is still acceptable, and that if two or more hypotheses satisfy this criterion, the one with the highest consistency is to be selected. Such a rule selection process can be specified by the following LEF:

$$\text{LEF} = <(\text{completeness}, 10\%), (\text{consistency}, 0\%)> . \tag{2}$$

It is possible that after applying both criteria, more than one hypothesis remains in the set of candidates. In this case the one that maximizes the first criterion is selected. The advantages of the LEF approach are that it is both very simple and very efficient; thus it is applicable where there is a very large number of candidate hypotheses. In this paper, we combine completeness and consistency gain (a measure of a rule's improvement in accuracy over a random guess) into one numerical measure, which serves as an elementary description quality criterion. Through LEFs, this criterion can be combined with a measure of description simplicity into one general description quality measure.

3 Completeness, Consistency, and Consistency Gain

An important role of a description is to classify future, unknown cases. Therefore, a useful measure of description quality is its *testing accuracy*, that is, its accuracy of classifying testing examples, as opposed to training examples. During a learning process, testing examples, by definition, are not being used; one therefore needs a criterion that is a good approximator of the testing accuracy, but uses only training examples. In order to propose such a measure, some notation needs to be introduced.

Let P and N denote the total number of positive and negative examples, respectively, of some decision class in a training set. Let R be a rule or a set of rules serving as a description of the examples of that class, and p and n be the number of positive and negative examples covered by R, (called *coverage* and *error count*, respectively). The ratio p / P, denoted compl(R), is called the *completeness* or *relative coverage* of R. The ratio $p / (p + n)$, denoted cons(R), is called the *consistency* or *training accuracy* of R. The ratio $n / (p + n)$, denoted cons(R), is called the *inconsistency* or *training error rate* of R. If the relative coverage of a ruleset (a set of rules for a single class) is 100%, then the ruleset is a *complete cover*. If the ruleset's inconsistency is 0%, then it is a *consistent cover*.

Let us return to the question posed in the Introduction as to which is preferable: a rule with 60% completeness and 99.8% consistency, or a rule with 95% completeness and 98% consistency. As indicated earlier, the answer depends on the problem at hand. In some application domains (e.g., science), a rule (law) must be consistent with all the data, unless some of the data are found erroneous. In other applications (e.g., data mining), one may seek strong patterns that hold frequently, but not always. Thus, there is no single measure of rule quality that will be good for all problems. We instead seek a flexible measure that can be easily changed to fit a given problem.

How can one define such a measure of rule quality? Let us first look at a measure based on the *information gain* criterion, which is used widely as a method for selecting attributes in decision tree learning (e.g. [11]). This criterion can also be used for selecting rules, because a rule can be viewed as a binary attribute that partitions examples into those that satisfy the rule, and those that do not satisfy it. The information gained by using rule R to partition the example space E is:

$$\text{Gain}(R) = \text{Info}(E) - \text{Info}_R(E) . \tag{3}$$

where Info(E) is the expected information from defining the class of an example in E and $\text{Info}_R(E)$ is the expected information after partitioning the space using rule R.

Information gain has one major disadvantage as a rule evaluator, namely, it relies not only on a rule's informativeness, but also on the informativeness of the complement of the rule. This is undesirable, especially in situations with more than two decision classes. Clearly, a rule may be highly valuable for classifying examples of one specific class, even if it does little to reduce the entropy of the training examples in other classes. Another disadvantage is that it does not allow one to vary the importance of consistency in relation to completeness.

Let us also observe that relative frequency of positive and negative examples in the training set of a given class should also be a factor in evaluating a rule. Clearly, a rule with 15% completeness and 75% consistency could be quite attractive if the total number of positive examples was very small, and the total number of negative examples was very large. On the other hand, the same rule would be uninformative if P was very large and N was very small.

The distribution of positive and negative examples in the training set can be measured by the ratio $P / (P + N)$. The distribution of positive and negative examples in the set covered by the rule can be measured by the consistency $p / (p + n)$. The difference between these values, $(p /(p + n)) - (P /(P + N))$ (the gain of consistency over the dataset's distribution as a whole), can be normalized by dividing it by $N /(P + N)$, so that in the case of identical distribution of positive and negative events in the set covered by the rule and in the training set, it returns 0, and in the case of perfect consistency, it will return 1. This normalized consistency thus provides an indication of the benefit of the rule over a randomly guessed assignment to the positive class/ It also allows for the possibility of negative values, in accordance with our assertion that a rule less accurate than the random guess has a negative benefit. Reorganizing the normalization term, we define the *consistency gain* of a rule R, consig(R), as:

$$\text{consig}(R) = ((p / (p + n)) - (P /(P + N))) * (P +N) /N . \tag{4}$$

4   A Formula for Description Quality

In developing a description quality measure, one may assume the desirability of maximizing both the completeness, compl(R), and the consistency gain, consig(R). Clearly, a rule with a higher compl(R) and a higher consig(R) is more desirable than a rule with lower measures. A rule with either compl(R) or consig(R) equal to 0 is worthless. It makes sense, therefore, to define a rule quality measure that evaluates to 1 when both of these components have value 1, and 0 when either is equal to 0.

A simple way to achieve such a behavior is to define rule quality as a product of compl(R) and consig(R). Such a formula, however, does not allow one to weigh these factors differently in different applications.   To achieve this flexibility, we introduce a weight, w, defined as the percentage of the description quality measure to be borne by the completeness condition.   The *description quality*, Q(R, w) with weight w, or just Q(w) if the rule R is implied, can thus be written:

$$Q(R, w) = compl(R)^w * consig(R)^{(1-w)}.$$ (5)

By changing parameter w, one can change the relative importance of the completeness and the consistency gain to fit a given problem.   The Q(w) definition satisfies all of the criteria regarding desirable features of a rule evaluation function given in [10]:

(1)   Rule quality should be 0 if the example distribution in the space covered by the rule is the same as in the entire data set.   Note that Q(R, w) = 0 when $p/(p +n)$ = $P/(P+N)$, assuming $w < 1$.

(2)   All else being equal, an increase in the rule's completeness should increase the quality of the rule.   Note that Q(R, w) increases monotonically with p.

(3)   All else being equal, rule quality should decrease when the ratio of covered positive examples in the data to either covered negative examples or total positive examples decreases.   Note that Q(R, w) decreases monotonically as either n or $(P - p)$ increases, when $P + N$ and p remain constant.

The next section compares the proposed Q(w) rule evaluation method with other methods, and Section 6 discusses its implementation in AQ18.

5   Empirical Comparison of Rule Evaluation Methods

In order to develop a sense of how the Q(w) rule rankings compare to those done by other machine learning systems, we performed a series of experiments on different datasets. In the experiments we used the Q(w) method with different weights w, the information gain criterion (Section 3), the PROMISE method [1][6], and the methods employed in CN2 [3], IREP [5], and RIPPER [4] rule learning programs.

As was mentioned above, the information gain criterion is based on the entropy of the examples in the area covered by a rule, the area not covered by the rule, and the event space as a whole.   Like the information gain criterion, the PROMISE method [1][6] was developed to evaluate the quality of attributes. It can be used, however, for rule evaluation by considering a rule to be a binary attribute that splits the space into the part covered by the rule and the part not covered by it. In this context, the value is determined based on the following expressions (which assume that $p > n$):

(1) Compute $M = \max(P - p, N - n)$

(2) Assign to T the value P if $P - p > N - n$, and value N if $P - p \leq N - n$

PROMISE returns a value of $(p / P) + (M / T) - 1$. When M is based on the positive class (when $P - p > N - n$), PROMISE returns a value of zero. Hence, PROMISE is not useful for measuring rule quality in domains in which the total number of positive examples significantly outnumbers the total number of negative ones. Note also that when p exceeds n and $P = N$, the PROMISE value reduces to:

$$(p - n) / P . \tag{6}$$

To see this, note that when $P = N$, $(p / P) + ((N - n) / N) - 1$ can be transformed into $(p / P) + ((P - n) / P) - 1$, which is equivalent to (6).

CN2 [3] builds rules using a beam search, as does the AQ-type learner, on which it was partially based. In the case of two decision classes, it minimizes the expression:

$$-((p /(p +n)) \log_2(p /(p + n)) + (n /(p + n)) \log_2(n /(p + n))) . \tag{7}$$

This expression involves only the consistency, $p / (p + n)$; it does not involve any completeness component. Thus, a rule that covers 50 positive and 5 negative examples is indistinguishable from another rule that covers 50,000 positive and 5000 negative examples. Although (7) has a somewhat different form than (4), CN2's rule evaluation can be expected to be similar to $Q(0)$ (consistency gain only). Indeed, in the examples shown below, the two methods provide identical rule rankings.

IREP's formula for rule evaluation [5] is:

$$(p + N - n) / (P + N) . \tag{8}$$

RIPPER [4] uses a slight modification of the above formula:

$$(p - n) / (P + N) . \tag{9}$$

Since P and N are constant for a given problem, a rule deemed preferable by IREP will also be preferred by RIPPER. We therefore only show RIPPER's rankings below. Comparing (9) to (6), one can notice that RIPPER evaluation function returns a value equal to half of the PROMISE value when $P = N$ and p exceeds n. Thus, in such cases, the RIPPER ranking is the same as the PROMISE ranking.

We compared the above methods on three datasets, each consisting of 1000 training examples. Dataset A has 20% positive and 80% negative examples, Dataset B has 50% positive and negative examples, and Dataset C has 80% positive examples and 20% of negative examples. In each dataset, rules with different completeness and consistency levels were ranked using the following criteria: Information Gain, PROMISE, RIPPER, CN2, $Q(0)$, $Q(.25)$, $Q(.5)$, $Q(.75)$, and $Q(1)$.

Results are shown in Table 1. The leftmost column identifies the dataset, the next two give the numbers of positive and negative examples of each class covered by a hypothetical rule, and the remaining columns list the ranks on the dataset of the rules by the various methods, where 1 indicates the best ranked rules and 7 indicates the worst. There is, of course, no one answer regarding which ranking is superior. It should be noted, however, that by modifying the Q weight, one can obtain different rule rankings, among them those identical to rankings by some other methods.

Table 1. Rule Rankings by Different Methods

Data Set	Pos	Neg	R		A		N	K	S		
			I. G.	PROM	CN2	RIPP	Q(0)	Q(.25)	Q(.5)	Q(.75)	Q(1)
A	50	5	7	7	4	7	4	7	7	7	6
	50	0	6	6	1	6	1	6	6	6	6
200	200	5	1	1	2	1	2	1	1	1	1
pos	150	10	2	2	3	2	3	2	2	2	2
	150	30	3	3	6	3	6	3	3	3	2
800	100	15	5	5	5	5	5	4	4	5	5
neg	120	25	4	4	7	4	7	5	5	4	4
B	50	5	7	7	3	7	3	7	7	7	7
	250	25	6	5	3	5	3	5	5	5	5
500	500	50	1	1	3	1	3	1	1	1	1
pos	500	150	2	3	7	3	7	6	4	2	1
	200	5	5	6	1	6	1	4	6	6	6
500	400	35	3	2	2	2	2	2	2	3	3
neg	400	55	4	4	6	4	6	3	3	4	3
C	50	5	7	–	3	7	3	6	6	6	7
	250	25	5	–	3	5	3	2	5	4	5
800	500	50	1	–	3	1	3	3	1	1	1
pos	500	150	6	–	7	3	7	7	7	7	1
	200	5	3	–	1	6	1	1	3	5	6
200	400	35	2	–	2	2	2	2	2	2	3
neg	400	55	4	–	6	4	6	5	4	3	3

6 Implementation of the Q(w) Method in AQ18

The AQ18 learning system [9] operates in two modes: the "noisy" mode (default), which relaxes the rule consistency requirement, and the "pure" mode, which accepts only fully consistent rules, and creates a complete cover. The "noisy" mode was implemented by employing the Q(w) evaluation method in two places: one—during a multi-step rule growing process (*star generation*), which repeatedly selects the best set of candidate rules for the next step of rule specialization, and second—during the completion of the process (*star termination*), which determines the best rule for output. The default value of w in Q(w) is 0.5.

During star generation, AQ18 uses a beam search strategy to find the "best" generalizations of a "seed" example by a repeated application of the "extension-against" generalization rule [8]. In the "noisy" mode, the system determines the Q value of the generated rules after each extension-against operation; the rules with $Q(w)$ lower than that of the parent rule (the rule from which they were generated through specialization), are discarded. If the $Q(w)$ value of all rules stemming from a given parent rule is lower, the parent rule is retained instead; this operation is functionally equivalent to discarding the negative example extended against as noise.

In the star termination step (i.e., after the last extension-against operation), the candidate rules are generalized additionally to determine if a resulting rule has a higher $Q(w)$ value. This chosen generalization operator may vary from among the *condition dropping, generalization tree climbing, interval extending* and the *interval closing* generalization operators depending on the type of the attributes in the rules, as described in [8]. As a result of this hill-climbing optimization step, the best rule in the resulting star is selected for output through the LEF process. Examples of the application of these generalization rules may be found in [7].

Experiments with AQ18 in the "noisy" mode revealed a difference in performance when applying different coverage criteria available in AQ18 [7]. The available criteria for defining LEF include maximizing two measures of coverage, one being the total number of positive examples covered by a rule, and the other being the coverage of positive events that have not been covered by any previously generated and retained rule for that class. The rulesets generated using the latter criterion were found to be superior, hence this criterion was adapted as a default. This idea was subsequently applied to the $Q(w)$ measure, with a hope that it may lead to a reduction of the likelihood that a rule may be supplanted by an inferior generalization. Thus we have replaced the original completeness measure, compl(R), by ncompl(R), defined as:

$$\text{ncompl(R)} = p_{new} / P . \tag{10}$$

where p_{new} is the number of positive examples newly covered by the candidate rule.

When AQ18 was applied to a medical dataset consisting of 32 attributes (all but 5 of which were of Boolean type) describing individuals' lifestyles and whether or not they had been diagnosed with various diseases, experiments were run with three different $Q(w)$ weights: 0.25, 0.5, and 0.75. For the decision class *arthritis*, the training set (7411 examples) had a highly unbalanced distribution of positive examples ($P = 1171$ or 16%) and negative examples ($N = 6240$ or 84%). The highest coverage rules learned by AQ18 for each w value in $Q(w)$ were:

For $w = 0.25$: [d =*arthritis*] <= [education ≤ vocational] &
[years in neighborhood > 26] & [rotundity ≥ low] &
[tuberculosis = no]: $p = 271, n = 903, Q = 0.111011$

For $w = 0.5$: [d =*arthritis*] <= [high blood pressure = yes] &
[education ≤ college grad] $p = 355, n = 1332, Q = 0.136516$

For $w = 0.75$: [d =*arthritis*] <= [education ≤ college grad] $p = 940, n = 4529,$
$Q = 0.303989$

Because increasing weight w in the $Q(w)$ measure gives higher importance to completeness in comparison to consistency, we see increasing p values (completeness) and decreasing values of consistency ($p /(p + n)$) in the rules above.

7 Summary

This paper introduced consistency gain as a measure of a rule's level of improvement in accuracy over a random guess, and presented a method for integrating it with the completeness criterion into one general and flexible numerical measure for guiding the process of generating inductive descriptions. This measure, $Q(w)$, allows one to change the relative importance of description coverage (completeness) in relation to consistency by varying the w parameter. The method has been implemented in AQ18 learning system and tested on a range of problems. A topic for future research and experimentation involves the quantification and integration of description simplicity into the description quality formula.

We have also introduced a mechanism especially useful for data mining applications, in which AQ18 determines negative examples to be ignored as noise. Such determinations have resulted in rules with substantially higher coverage, at a small cost to consistency, while reducing the search time.

References

1. Baim, P.W.: The PROMISE Method for Selecting Most Relevant Attributes for Inductive Learning Systems. Report No. UIUCDCS-F-82-898. Department of Computer Science, University of Illinois, Urbana (1982)
2. Bergadano, F., Matwin, S., Michalski R.S., Zhang, J.: Learning Two-tiered Descriptions of Flexible Concepts: The POSEIDON System. Machine Learning 8 (1992) 5-43
3. Clark, P., Niblett, T.: The CN2 Induction Algorithm. Machine Learning 3 (1989) 261-283
4. Cohen, W.: Fast Effective Rule Induction. Proc. 12th Intl. Conf. on Machine Learning (1995)
5. Fürnkranz, J., Widmer, G.: Incremental Reduced Error Pruning. Proc. 11th Intl. Conf. on Machine Learning (1994)
6. Kaufman, K.A.: INLEN: A Methodology and Integrated System for Knowledge Discovery in Databases. Ph.D. diss. George Mason University, Fairfax, VA (1997)
7. Kaufman, K.A., Michalski, R.S.: Learning in an Inconsistent World: Rule Selection in AQ18. Reports of the Machine Learning and Inference Laboratory. MLI 99-1. George Mason University, Fairfax, VA (1999)
8. Michalski, R.S.: A Theory and Methodology of Inductive Learning. In: Michalski, R.S. Carbonell, J.G., Mitchell, T.M. (eds.), Machine Learning: An Artificial Intelligence Approach. Tioga Publishing, Palo Alto, CA (1983) 83-129
9. Michalski, R.S.: NATURAL INDUCTION: A Theory and Methodology of the STAR Approach to Symbolic Learning and Its Application to Machine Learning and Data Mining. *Reports of the Machine Learning and Inference Laboratory*. George Mason University (1999)
10. Piatetsky-Shapiro, G.: Discovery, Analysis, and Presentation of Strong Rules. In: Piatetsky-Shapiro, G., Frawley, W. (eds.): Knowledge Discovery in Databases. AAAI Press, Menlo Park, CA (1991) 229-248
11. Quinlan, J.R.: Induction of Decision Trees. Machine Learning 1 (1986) 81-106

Learning English Grapheme Segmentation
Using the Iterated Version Space Algorithm

Jianna Jian Zhang
Department of Computer Science
University of Waterloo
Waterloo, Ontario
Canada, N2L 3G1
e-mail: j3zhang@math.uwatcrloo.ca

Howard J. Hamilton
Department of Computer Science
University of Regina
Regina, Saksatchewn
Canada, S4S 0A2
e-mail: hamilton@cs.uregina.ca

Nick J. Cercone
Department of Computer Science
University of Waterloo
Waterloo, Ontario
Canada, N2L 3G1
e-mail: ncercone@uwaterloo.ca

Abstract. Our unique approach for learning English grapheme segmentation (LE-GS) rules using the Iterated Version Space Algorithm (IVSA) is presented. After defining the problem and our representation for the instances and hypotheses, we illustrate the LE-GS approach by tracing a specific example. Experimental results, based on a ten-fold testing methodology, are given to show the performance of the LE-GS learning system.

1 Introduction

We present a learning system called LE-GS (Learning English Grapheme Segmentation), which learns how to divide the sequence of letters of an English word into a sequence of graphemes using the IVSA algorithm, which was developed and explained in our previous research [7, 1, 8]. A *grapheme* is a letter or combination of letters that represents one phoneme [5], diphthong (complex vowel sound, e.g. /ei/), or cluster (complex consonant sound, e.g. /ks/). Input words are taken from an on-line pronouncing dictionary, NTC.2, which is based on the NETalk Corpus [6] with corrections of some inconsistencies [9]. A list of target graphemes is obtained from NTC.2 and ordered by decreasing length. The learning result is a set of grapheme segmentation rules which can be used by a text-to-speech system to identify graphemes of English words to establish a serial correspondence [7, 9] between the spelling and the pronunciation.

The LE-GS technique for learning grapheme segmentation is distinct from the techniques described in [2] and [3]. First, LE-GS learns to identify existing graphemes in an on-line corpus rather than defining new graphemes according to their corresponding phonemes. Second, LE-GS does not learn to recognize single-letter graphemes because once the multi-letter graphemes are recognized, the remaining graphemes are naturally identified as single-letter graphemes. Third, LE-GS recognizes multi-letter graphemes with a small surrounding "window" of four items (either letters or previously learned graphemes) scanning from left to right for each input word. After a segmentation rule has been learned to identify a particular grapheme, this grapheme will replace its sequence of letters that may occur in the sliding window for learning a different grapheme.

LE-GS contains an example generator (EG), a grapheme learner (GL), and a grapheme translator (GT). Figure 1 illustrates the overall structure of LE-GS. The on-line pronouncing dictionary NTC.2 is a version of NETtalk Corpus (NTC) that has been transformed to achieve a serial correspondence between the graphemes and the phonemes (sound symbols) of a word [7, 9]. From the NTC.2 on-line pronouncing dictionary, EG copies the set of information needed for learning grapheme segmentation, and transforms it into training instances, as requested by LE-GS. The training instances are input to GL, which is an application of the IVSA algorithm.

Based on the training instances, GL produces candidate hypotheses for recognizing multi-syllable graphemes. Only those candidate hypotheses that effectively represent the features of grapheme segmentation are selected and placed in the temporary knowledge base. The grapheme translator GT uses the rules stored in the temporary knowledge base to classify the entire training set and determines the classification accuracy. The set of incorrectly classified instances I is used by GT as training instances for further learning until either I becomes empty or the classification accuracy stops changing. At this time, rules stored in the temporary knowledge base become the output grapheme segmentation rules, as shown at the bottom right corner of Figure 1. LE-GS accumulates an ordered list of rules for each grapheme. The rules are applied by a two-pass left-to-right translator that emits a sequence of graphemes for a given English word.

2 Problem Definition and Representation

After fifteen hundred years of development, modern English orthography has not evolved as rapidly as spoken English, in particular, its pronunciation. Modern English does not have a one-to-one correspondence between letters and sounds [4]. The relationship between the current English orthography and its pronunciation can be described as a serial correspondence between sequences of graphemes and sounds if some absent graphemes and silent morphophonemes are used [7, 9]. For example, *tough* has five letters which correspond to three phonemes. These three phonemes

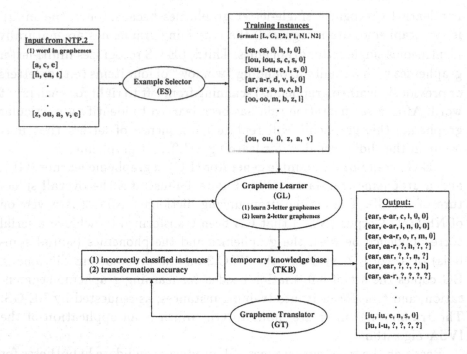

Fig. 1. An Overview of the LE-GS Learning Element

divide the word into three graphemes: <t>, <ou>, and <gh>, where each grapheme corresponds to one sound. Since grapheme <gh> in *through* is not pronounced, we call it a *silent grapheme* [7].

To establish a one-to-one serial correspondence between the graphemes of a word and its sounds, the graphemes must first be identified. An English grapheme can be one of three kinds according to the number of letters from which it is composed. Given a sequence of letters, after the three- and two-letter graphemes are identified, the remaining letters are single-letter graphemes. Based on the idea of identifying multi-letter graphemes prior to single-letter graphemes, we naturally eliminated learning single-letter graphemes. The overall task is reduced to learning rules for identifying three-letter graphemes first and then learning rules for identifying two-letter graphemes second.

2.1 Input from NTC.2

Input from the NTC.2 are words in graphemes:

Example: philosophy [ph, i, l, o, s, o, ph, y]

2.2 Creating Training and Testing Instances

The instances both for learning and testing graphemes have six attributes $A = \{A_1, A_2, A_3, A_4, A_5, A_6\}$ with different names, $A = \{L, G, P2, P1, N1, N2\}$, where P2, P1, N1, and N2 are the next preceding grapheme

Table 1. Attribute Names, Value, and Representation

Attribute Name	Information Represented
L (A_1)	sequence of letters which may form a grapheme $V_L = \{a, b, c, d, e, ..., z\}^+$
G (A_2)	sequence of grapheme composed by L $V_G = \{a, aa, ai, ..., zz\}\ [\text{-}\{a, aa, ai, ..., zz\}]^*$
P2 (A_3)	the next preceding grapheme or letter $V_{P2} = \{0, aa, ai, ar, b, ..., zz\}$
P1 (A_4)	the immediate preceding grapheme or letter $V_{P1} = \{0, a, aa, ai, ar, b, ..., zz\}$
N1 (A_5)	the immediate following grapheme or letter $V_{N1} = \{0, a, aa, ai, ar, b, ..., zz\}$
N2 (A_6)	the next following grapheme or letter $V_{N2} = \{0, a, aa, ai, ar, b, ..., zz\}$

or letter, the immediate preceding grapheme or letter, the immediate following grapheme or letter, and the next following grapheme or letter. The names of the attributes, their purposes, and their sets of possible values are given in Table 1. Previously learned graphemes may appear as values in P2, P1, N1, and N2 instead of letters because graphemes carry more information than individual letters. An attribute A_i can take any one value V_{Aij} from the set V_{A_i} where i is the index number for attributes and j is the index number for values of the attribute i. The symbol '-' in A_2 indicates a grapheme boundary, i.e., where the graphemes are divided. The '0' symbol in sets V_{P2}, V_{P1}, V_{N1}, and V_{N2} indicates no graphemes or letters are found at the specified position. The ',' symbol in the following examples is used to separate attributes. An instance derived from the word "shear" is: ⟨ear, ea-r, s, h, 0, 0⟩

2.3 The Format of Candidate Hypotheses

Because candidate hypotheses are generated from training instances, they have the same format as the training instances except that they can have 'no restriction' as a value for attributes A_3, A_4, A_5, and A_6. Each 'no restriction' value is indicated by a '?' symbol. The hypothesis ⟨e a r, ea-r, ?, ?, ?, ?⟩ indicates that the letter sequence 'e a r' should be classified as a sequence of two graphemes <ea> and <r> under all conditions.

2.4 Output

The format of the output rules is identical with that of the candidate hypotheses except that the rules are ordered according to their priority.

Examples:

⟨ear, ear, 0, 1, n, ?⟩ (learn)

⟨ear, e-a-r, o, r, m, 0⟩ (forearm)
⟨ear, ea-r, ?, h, ?, ?⟩ (hear)
⟨ear, ear, ?, ?, ?, ?⟩ (earth, pearl, search)

3 The Algorithm

Before the learning process starts, 90% of the words from NTC.2 have
been divided into 1200-word files, $F_1 \cdots F_n$ where n is the number of files,
e.g., 15 in this case. This step is necessary for speed efficiency because
IVSA uses the rules learned from F_{i-1}, where $1 < i \leq n$, to classify the
instances of the current F_i. Only those instances not correctly classified
are used for the next learning cycle. The number of incorrectly covered
instances from F_i is always less than or equal to the number of instances
in F_i if the target grapheme has already been learned during the previous
learning cycles. This is an advantage for IVSA when learning from many
instances. For example, after learning from the first 1200 words (F_1),
LE-GS has 2 rules for grapheme <ea>. Before starting to learn from the
second 1200 words (F_2), LE-GS uses the learned rules to classify the input
instances. If the classification result is 100% correct, there is no need to
learn rules from F_2 for grapheme <ea>. Therefore LE-GS starts to learn
the next grapheme.

Any sequence of letters that matches a grapheme is used by the example generator EG to form a training instance. Since <ph> is a grapheme,
training instances are created from 'alpha' and 'uphill'. The first instance
may suggest a rule for a two-letter grapheme, <ph>, while the second
may suggest a rule for two single-letter graphemes, <p> and <h>. EG is
a crucial part of the LE-GS system because the learning results depend
on how well the training instances represent English graphemes. Figure 2
shows the algorithm for creating instances for learning grapheme segmentation rules. The procedure first creates training instances for three-letter
graphemes, and then those for two-letter graphemes. Any information
learned from identifying three-letter graphemes is used when identifying
two-letter graphemes.

4 A Descriptive Example

Identifying all possible target graphemes in the input file and all the possible segmentation classes to which each target grapheme belongs precedes
LE-GS learning of segmentation rules. Consider the task of learning rules
for identifying graphemes <irr> and <rr>. First the example generator
creates instances that contain the sequences of letters {i, r, r} and {r, r},
i.e., Targets = {<irr>, <rr>}. Because grapheme <rr> can be nested
in grapheme <irr>, instances with the i-r-r letter sequence are created

Input: *File*, a sub-dictionary of NTC.2
    Targets, a set of all target graphemes
Output: I_3, a set of instances for learning 3-letter graphemes
    I_2, a set of instances for learning 2-letter graphemes

Functions:
    Sequence := Split (*Word*)
        – *Word*, current input word divided into graphemes
        – *Sequence*, the sequence of letters that composes *Word*
    G := GetSegmentation (*Word, Letters, i*)
        – *Letters*, a sequence of letters that may form some grapheme(s)
        – *i*, the position of the first letter in *Letters*
        – *G*, the actual grapheme(s) that *Letters* should be composed into
    (*Instance, Tmp*) := Parse3 (*Sequence, Letters, G, i, Tmp*)
        – *Instance*, one instance for learning 3-letter graphemes
        – *Tmp*, updated with previously processed graphemes
    (*Instance, Tmp*) := Parse2 (*Sequence, Letters, G, i, Tmp*)
        – *Instance*, one instance for learning 2-letter graphemes

$I_3 := \emptyset, I_2 := \emptyset$

for each *Word* $\in$ *File*
    Tmp := $\emptyset$, *i* := 1
    Sequence := Split (*Word*)
    for every sequence of three letters ($L_i\ L_{i+1}\ L_{i+2}$) $\in$ *Sequence*
        if ($L_i\ L_{i+1}\ L_{i+2}$) $\in$ *Targets*
            Letters := ($L_i\ L_{i+1}\ L_{i+2}$)
            G := GetSegmentation (*Word, Letters, i*)
            (*Instance, Tmp*) := Parse3 (*Letters, G, i, Tmp*)
            $I_3 := I_3 \cup$ *Instance*
        else *Tmp* = *Tmp* $\cup\ L_i$
        end if
    end for
    Sequence := *Tmp*, *Tmp* := $\emptyset$, *i* := 1
    for every sequence of two graphemes or letters ($L_i\ L_{i+1}$) $\in$ *Sequence*
        if ($L_i\ L_{i+1}$) $\in$ *Targets*
            Letters := ($L_i\ L_{i+1}$)
            G := GetSegmentation (*Word, Letters, i*)
            (*Instance, Tmp*) := Parse2 (*Letters, G, i, Tmp*)
            $I_2 := I_2 \cup$ *Instance*
        else *Tmp* = *Tmp* $\cup\ L_i$
        end if
    end for
end for each
output I_3, I_2

Fig. 2. Algorithm of the Example Generator of LE-GS

before instances with the r-r letter sequence. Rules for longer graphemes
are determined before those for shorter ones because the rules will be
used in a parser that searches for longer graphemes before shorter ones.
When LE-GS learns to identify the grapheme <rr>, instances used for
learning <irr> are not included. In our example, ES has found 41 i-r-r
and 64 additional r-r letter sequences from a set of training data (90% of
NTC.2). Independent of whether the i-r-r sequence is actually one grapheme <irr> or two graphemes <i> and <rr>, all the occurrences of i-r-r
are used to form training instances. The following illustrate 7 of the 41 instances created from i-r-r sequences (the words from which the instances
are derived are given in parentheses):

1. ⟨irr, i-rr, 0, c, u, s⟩ (cirrus)
2. ⟨irr, irr, s, t, u, p⟩ (stirrup)
3. ⟨irr, i-rr, 0, m, o, r⟩ (mirror)
4. ⟨irr, irr, s, h, 0, 0⟩ (shirr)
5. ⟨irr, irr, q, u, e, l⟩ (squirrel)
6. ⟨irr, i-rr, 0, 0, i, 0⟩ (irrigate)
7. ⟨irr, irr, w, h, 0, 0⟩ (whirr)

Because, in 37 out of 41 instances, the i-r-r letter sequence is divided
into two parts, 'i' and 'rr', and only in 4 instances is it kept as one grapheme, the first rule selected from the set of candidate hypotheses and placed
in the accepted list by the grapheme learner is

⟨irr, i-rr, ?, ?, ?, ?⟩

which means that regardless of which graphemes or letters are before or
after the sequence i-r-r, it always forms two graphemes <i> and <rr>.
This single rule yields 90.24% correct classifications for recognizing graphemes from the sequence of letters i-r-r. The next rule added is

⟨irr, irr, s, ?, ?, ?⟩

which includes 2 (out of the 4) instances that do not divide i-r-r into
two graphemes. This rule is added at the first position of the accepted
hypothesis list because this particular position causes the greatest increase in accuracy. After this rule is added, the accuracy increases to
95.12%. The grapheme learner continues creating candidate hypotheses
and placing them in appropriate places. Finally, four rules are learned
with classification accuracy of 100% on the training instances.

1. ⟨irr, irr, w, h, 0, 0⟩
2. ⟨irr, i-rr, q, u, e, l⟩
3. ⟨irr, irr, s, ?, ?, ?⟩
4. ⟨irr, i-rr, ?, ?, ?, ?⟩

After rules for the first target grapheme <irr> have been learned, the grapheme learner starts to learn rules for <rr>. Excluding any letter sequences that have been included in the previous learning, the example generator provides 64 instances. The following are 7 of these 64 instances:

1. ⟨rr, rr, 0, a, a, n⟩ (arrange)
2. ⟨rr, r-r, b, a, o, o⟩ (barroom)
3. ⟨rr, rr, b, a, o, w⟩ (barrow)
4. ⟨rr, rr, b, a, a, g⟩ (barrage)
5. ⟨rr, r-r, 0, ea, i, n⟩ (earring)
6. ⟨rr, rr, qu, a, y, 0⟩ (quarry)
7. ⟨rr, rr, w, a, a, n⟩ (warrant)

Because 62 out of the 64 instances belong to the class which combines the two letters into one grapheme <rr>, the following rule is selected first and it gives 96.88% classification accuracy:

1. ⟨rr, rr, ?, ?, ?, ?⟩

Then two more specific rules are placed before the first selected rule, and the training accuracy now is 100%.

1. ⟨rr, r-r, ?, ea, ?, ?⟩
2. ⟨rr, r-r, b, a, o, o⟩
3. ⟨rr, rr, ?, ?, ?, ?⟩

Thus far, LE-GS has learned segmentation rules for the the letter sequences i-r-r and r-r. It produced four rules for i-r-r and three for r-r with an overall classification accuracy of 100%. When these rules are applied, the translator GT scans through the input word (a sequence of letters) twice. During the first scan, GT looks for any possible three-letter graphemes by sliding the window from left to right and letter by letter, while during the second scan, it looks for any possible two-letter graphemes in a similar manner. After the second scan, all graphemes in the input word are identified. A more comprehensive example of applying grapheme segmentation rules is given in [8].

5 Experimental Results

5.1 Ten-fold Test Results

By the definition of the ten-fold test defined in [8] the NTC.2 dictionary is divided into 90% for training and 10% for testing. With the 90% and 10% words, the example generator has created an average of 29,442 training instances and 2,435 testing instances for ten runs. Only the instances relevent to learning two- and three-letter graphemes are selected. From these two- and three-letter instances, LE-GS learned an average of 1,004 rules, which is quite small (about 1 rule per 100 instances for NTC.2) compared with the resulting tree size (2,000) in [3] (about 1 rule per 18 instances for a 3,000 word-dictionary). The rules learned by LE-GS give an average accuracy of 99.60% when applied to the training instances and 95.78% when applied to the 10% previously unseen instances relevant to learning multi-letter graphemes. The average CPU time for learning 29,442 training instances is 2 hours 34 minutes and 4 seconds on a MIPS R4400 175 MHz processor. Ten-fold testing results are shown in Table 2.

Table 2. Summary of Ten-fold Testing Results

Run	# of Instances		Accuracy (90% vs 10%)		# of	CPU Time
#	Training	Test	Training	Testing	Rules	(h/m/s)
1	29,342	2,460	99.61%	95.93%	1,030	02/38/25
2	29,384	2,458	99.62%	95.57%	991	02/19/06
3	29,393	2,438	99.61%	95.73%	987	02/19/43
4	29,456	2,388	99.60%	95.56%	995	02/23/52
5	29,473	2,377	99.57%	95.79%	991	03/14/41
6	29,456	2,451	99.58%	95.47%	1,025	02/35/30
7	29,492	2,379	99.63%	96.09%	1,009	02/32/57
8	29,391	2,444	99.59%	96.28%	1,002	02/34/42
9	29,660	2,498	99.63%	95.52%	996	02/30/13
10	29,370	2,458	99.59%	95.89%	1,013	02/31/28
Ave.	29,442	2,435	99.60%	95.78%	1,004	02/34/04
S.D.	86.56	38.35	0.02	0.25	14.14	895.48

Table 3 shows the classification accuracies on all letter sequences (including single letter graphemes) before and after pruning all rules based on single training instances. After pruning, the classification accuracy for testing is lower by only 54 graphemes (0.41%) and 12 words (0.60%) than before pruning. A significant reduction in the number of rules has been achieved with little reduction in predictive accuracy. This analysis also indicates that LE-GS produces good general rules.

If the number of pruned rules is larger than the number of the words that would be incorrectly classified due to the pruning, using an exception dictionary would be more efficient than keeping the pruned rules in the knowledge base.

Table 3. Accuracy before and after Pruning Exception Rules for NTC.2

Use of	# of Instances		Training Accuracy		Testing Accuracy		# of
Pruning	Training	Testing	Graphemes	Words	Graphemes	Words	Rules
No	118,236	13,050	99.58%	99.19%	97.43%	94.89%	1,030
Yes	118,236	13,050	98.00%	96.38%	97.02%	94.29%	487

429

6 Conclusions and Future Research

We presented the LE-GS learning system that learns rules for segmenting English words into graphemes. LE-GS has learned an average of 1,004 grapheme segmentation rules from 29,442 training instances. These rules were tested on 2,435 previously unseen instances and the average classification accuracy for multi-letter graphemes is 95.78% using the ten-fold test method. The average classification accuracy on the 10% previously unseen words in NTC.2 is 94.89% before pruning (1,030 rules) and 94.29% after pruning (487 rules). A small exception dictionary could be used instead of the pruned rules to reduce the size of knowledge base.

Acknowledgments

The authors are members of the Institute for Robotics and Intelligent Systems (IRIS) and wish to acknowledge the support of the Networks of Centres of Excellence program of the Government of Canada, the Natural Sciences and Engineering Research Council, and the participation of PRECARN Associates Inc.

References

1. H. J. Hamilton and J. Zhang. The iterated version space algorithm. In *Proc. of Ninth Florida Artificial Intelligence Research Symposium (FLAIRS-96)*, pages 209–213, Daytona Beach, Florida, May 1996.
2. S. Lawrence and G. Kaye. Alignment of phonemes with their corresponding orthography. *Computer Speech and Language*, 1:153–165, 1986.
3. C. Ling and B. Zhang. Grapheme generation in learning to read English words. In R.E. Mercer and E. Neufeld, editors, *Advances in AI: 12th BCCS for the Computational Studies of Intelligence Proc.*, pages 184–195, Vancouver, Canada, 1998.
4. I. R. MacKay, editor. *Phonetics: the Science of Speech Production*. Pro-Ed, Austin, Texas, 1987.
5. I. Morris, editor. *The American Heritage Dictionary*. Houghton Mifflin, Boston, MA, 1991.
6. T. Sejnowski and C. Rosenberg. NETtalk corpus, (am6.tar.z). ftp.cognet.ucla.edu in pub/alexis, 1988.
7. J. Zhang. Automatic learning of English pronunciation rules. Master's thesis, University of Regina, Regina, Canada, 1995.
8. J. Zhang. *The LEP Learning System: An IVSA Approach*. PhD thesis, University of Regina, Regina, Canada, 1998.
9. J. Zhang, H.J. Hamilton, and B. Galloway. English graphemes and their pronunciations. In *Proceedings of Pacific Association for Computational Linguistics*, pages 351–362, Ohme, Japan, September, 1997.

Fully Automatic Acquisition of Taxonomic Knowledge from Large Corpora of Texts: Limited Syntax Knowledge Representation System Based on Natural Language

Lucja Iwańska, Naveen Mata and Kellyn Kruger

Dept. of Computer Science, Wayne State University
Detroit, Michigan 48202, USA
Ph. (313) 577-1667, Fx: (313) 577-6868
{lucja, osm, kkk}@cs.wayne.edu   http://www.cs.wayne.edu/profs/iwanska.html

Abstract. The paper presents a new method for fully automatic knowledge acquisition from large corpora of unseen texts. The approach exploits simple, efficiently, fast and reliably extractable, parsable and in-depth interpretable constructs of natural language specialized to convey taxonomic knowledge. It allows one to acquire large quantities of high quality general-purpose knowledge and practically eliminates costly and error-prone human pre&post-processing. Examples of the system-acquired concepts are discussed.

1 Introduction

1.1 Automatic Acquisition of Knowledge from Large Corpora

We present a new method for fully automatic knowledge (KN) acquisition from large corpora of unseen texts. Our *learning from clear cases* approach exploits simple, efficiently, fast and reliably extractable, parsable and in-depth interpretable constructs of natural language (NL) specialized to convey taxonomic KN. It includes type relations such as type-subtype relation and concept definitions. The approach allows the system to acquire large quantities of high quality general-purpose KN, which practically eliminates costly and error-prone human pre-processing such as hand-tagging of texts prior to their utilization and post-processing such as verification of the quality of the acquired KN.

1.2 Combination of Weak and In-Depth Methods

For the **extraction part** of our acquisition scheme, the focus of this paper, we develop weak, efficient and computationally inexpensive methods. No NL understanding or parsing is attempted because such KN acquisition can be accomplished without this kind of expensive computation, many aspects of which remain open research problems. Our engineering methods take advantage of local context, including the semantics of punctuation and presence of certain keywords.

For the **representation part**, we use (very) in-depth methods– the UNO model of NL, a KR system closely simulating the unique representational and inferential characteristics of NL [Iwańska, 1992] [Iwańska, 1993] [Iwańska et al., 1995] [Iwańska, 1996b] [Iwańska, 1997] [Iwańska, 1996a] [Iwańska, 1998]. The similarity to NL is attractive because it results in the uniformity of representation and inference, and therefore a simple and powerful computer system architecture. No interfaces to translate between incompatible representations or interfaces to access the system knowledge bases (KBs) are needed. Due to simple syntax, the NL-based UNO representation of the extracted KN can be generated automatically. It is used to also automatically update and access system KBs via NL-like mechanism.

1.3 Conjecture: *Natural Language Is A Free Lunch*

The work presented here is part of our efforts to substantiate this extremely theoretically and practically puzzling conjecture. We believe that a widely held belief in the Artificial Intelligence (AI) community that processing NL necessarily requires an apriori existing KN is misguided. This belief is often quoted as one of the main obstacles in automatic KN acquisition from NL input.

1.4 Related Work

Employing weak, local-context-based methods for processing large corpora is not a new idea. The new aspect of our approach is that we use weak methods to bootstrap the in-depth methods. We are not aware of any approach that would resemble our limited-syntax, NL-based KR system idea to acquire, represent and utilize KN from texts.

Our approach attempts to uniquely combine the advantages of the human and computer information processing– we marry the UNO framework which allows computers to process KN in the form of NL very similarly to people with the non-human computer capabilities to be precise, fast, systematic and virtually memory-unlimited.

This paper is organized as follows: Section 2 discusses NL constructs specialized to convey taxonomic KN; Sections 3 and 4 present acquisition algorithms exploiting two such constructs; it discusses the system-acquired concepts from three different corpora; Section 5 contains conclusions.

2 NL Constructs Conveying Taxonomic Knowledge

Certain NL constructs convey taxonomic KN– relations among different types and concept definitions; see Table 1. We analyze such constructs for:

1. **Frequency of occurrences** in samples of our corpora; this is indicative of the quantity of useful KN possible to acquire via each construct;

CONSTRUCT	KNOWLEDGE	EXAMPLES, COMMENTS
X and not Y	Related types	From *red and not green*, system acquires the relation between *red* and *green*
X if not Y	Scalar	From *possible if not certain*, system learns that *certain* is a stronger notion than *possible*
not only X but Y	Scalar	From *not only warm but hot*, system learns that *hot* is a stronger notion than *warm*
X– indeed Y	Scalar	From *I've seldom– indeed, hardly ever– smoked cigars*, system learns that *hardly ever* is a stronger notion than *seldom*
X, which BE Y	Definition	From *Colds are caused by viruses, which are extremely small infectious substances*, system acquires *viruses are extremely small infectious substances*
X, or Y,	Definition	From *Your child probably will have more colds, or upper respiratory infections, than any other illness* system learns *colds are upper respiratory infections*
X such as Y, ..., Z	Definition	From *With a young baby, symptoms can be misleading, and colds can quickly develop into more serious ailments such as bronchiolitis, croup, or , pneumonia.* system acquires *bronchiolitis, croup, and pneumonia are serious ailments*
X rather than Y	Related types	From *He fears that a heart attack or stroke could leave him on life support rather than kill him outright*, system learns that *life support* and *killing one outright* are related choices

Table 1. Simple, efficiently, fast and reliably extractable, parsable and in-depth interpretable constructs of natural language specialized to express taxonomic knowledge.

2. **Ease of eliminating** construct uses that do not express the desired type of KN; this is indicative of the quality of KN to be acquired via each construct.

Table 2 shows the results of the frequency analysis for the NL constructs considered in a 10%-sample of our *Time Magazine* corpus; this sample contains 137 articles with an average length of 930 words each,

NL CONSTRUCT	N_{total}	$N_{desired}$	COMMENTS
X and not Y	10	3	
X if not Y	12	4	
not only X but Y	13	5	
X– indeed Y	8	1	
X such as Y, ..., Z	18	12	Most promising
X rather than Y	17	10	Promising

Table 2. Frequency analysis of the NL constructs considered for small samples of textual corpora processed; N_{total} is the total number of the construct occurrences in the sample, and $N_{desired}$ is the number of the useful occurrences conveying the desired type of KN.

3 The *Such as* NL Construct for Knowledge Acquisition

3.1 Algorithm

A typical sentence with the *such as* construct has the following structure:

| Pre-phrase | Concept | *such as* | $T_1, T_2, ..., \text{and } T_n$ | Post-phrase |

Consider the following sentences whose structures are shown in Table 3:

1. *Caffeine produces psychological and physical dependence, including withdrawal symptoms such as headaches, depression and fatigue.*
2. *Tabloid shows such as Hard Copy and Inside Edition, for all their voyeuristic overkill, have demonstrated that there is an audience for news about celebrities that isn't publicity pap.*

PRE-PHRASE | POST-PHRASE	CONCEPT	T_1, T_2, T_3
Caffeine produces psychological and physical dependence, including | ϵ	withdrawal symptoms	headaches, depression, fatigue
ϵ | ,for all their voyeuristic overkill, have demonstrated that there is an audience for news about celebrities that isn't publicity pap	tabloid shows	Hard Copy, Inside Edition

Table 3. The *such as* structure of the sample sentences; ϵ signifies empty phrase.

The first major algorithm step is extraction. The boundaries of the structural elements of the *such as* construct are identified in order to extract the concept phrase as well as the phrase(s) that define it or relate other concepts to it. The concept resides just before the *such as* construct and is usually separated from the pre-phrase by a punctuation symbol. Specific elements of different syntactic categories often mark the boundary between the concept and the pre-phrase. They are treated as keywords and include:

Verbs	*is, are, will, can, might, could, should, would, shall, have, has, was, were*
Prepositions	*in, on, out, about, for, with, of, from, at, under, including, to, by, over*
Conjunctions	*if, and, as, or, well, whether, other, even*
Determiners	*the, many, an, a, any, some, these, those*
Pronouns	*while, which, that, where, who*

The concept defining phrases are separated by commas, with the last phrase always appearing after the word *and*. Punctuation symbols usually mark the boundaries between the defining phrases and the post-phrase. They can also be marked by similar keywords. We found that the well-performing on a large scale keyword lists facilitating identifying different boundaries are different. This good performance but little explanatory power is typical for engineering methods.

Complete lists of some of these syntactic categories available in the UNO natural language processing (NLP) system neither significantly nor in some cases, at all, improve the system's performance. Those shorter, ad-hoc lists perform better.

Once all the boundaries are identified, limited post-processing is performed. If a concept phrase has more than six words, then only the first three are used. For example, if the acquired concept is *a very lively, affectionate, extremely small animal*, then the system keeps only the *extremely small animal* part as the concept phrase. If a definitional phrase is more than six words long, it is excluded from the concept definition. The numbers were established experimentally.

The second major algorithm step is automatic generation of the UNO NL-like representation of the acquired pieces of KN; details can be found in the publications cited earlier.

We have two **implementations** of the *such as* acquisition algorithm: one in Borland C^{++} and one in Common LISP, both running on the PC and UNIX platforms. The LISP implementation, a much more natural choice for such a symbol processing task, is much smaller and easier to maintain. The much larger and harder to maintain C^{++} implementation is four times faster.

The system handles quite limited aspects of local context, yet performs well. For example, it uses extremely crude heuristics to identify sentential boundaries. This tremendously speeds up processing and, surprisingly, does not affect that much the precision of extraction.

3.2 Results: Quantity, Quality of System-Acquired Knowledge

We analyzed the the quantitity and quality and of the system-acquired KN. Table 4 sumerizes the quantitative aspects.

CORPUS	SIZE in KB	N_{total}	N_d	GRADE A CONCEPTS	GRADE B CONCEPTS	GRADE C CONCEPTS
Time Magazine	10,530	234	23	67%	22%	11%
Wall Street Journal	6,863	342	51	58%	22%	20%
Microbiology	6,327	335	54	68%	27%	5%
Total	23,720	911	39	64%	24%	12%

Table 4. Summary of the quantitative and qualitative evaluation of the system-acquired knowledge from three different corpora performed by human experts; N_{total} is the total number of concepts, N_d is the number of concepts per 1MB.

For the quality evaluation, we used human specialists. For the newspaper corpora, *Time Magazine* and *Wall Street Journal* which contain a lot of commonsense or generally known KN, a friend was the quality judge; for the *Microbiology* corpus which contains mostly highly specialized scientific KN, a specialist did the quality grading. The grades were assigned as follows: **A** fully correct KN, **B** mostly correct KN, and **C** mostly incorrect or inaccurate KN. Table 5 shows the quality evaluation.

GRADE	CONCEPT	$T_1 \mid T_2 \mid T_3$
A	core academic subjects	math | reading
A	big name computers	Compaq | IBM | Apple
A	human diseases	scrub typhus | spotted fever | typhus
A	crops	rice | soybeans | cotton
A	winter wheat states	Oklahoma | Kansas
A	category	history | comedy | tragedy
A	pass sensitive information	credit-card numbers safely over the network
B	volatile compounds	Diaceytl | its derivatives
B	underlying condition	alcoholism or some condition | malignancy
B	especially around feminist issues	abortion
B	tackle controversial topics	the environment | nuclear weapons
C	pay	Libya | Iran
C	established electronic concerns	Sun
C	abortion	abortion counseling | referrals
C	offer	Sony's

Table 5. Human experts graded the system-acquired knowledge

Less than 10% of the *Time Magazine* and *Microbiology* corpora and none of the *Wall Street Journal* corpus were used as the test & development data. This might explain why the acquisition results from *Wall Street Journal* are the worst. The *Microbiology* corpus had the best results– many more concepts were acquired and many more of them are the good ones; only about 5% are the C-grade level concepts.

4 The *Like* NL Construct for Knowledge Acquisition

4.1 Algorithm

For a different sample of the *Time Magazine* corpus, the feasibility of the *like* NL construct was compared with that of *such as*. In this four-issue sample, the *like* construct occurs much more frequently; see Table 6. The occurrences were judged as useful in virtually every instance– 12 out of 14. Not useful occurrences were often of the easy to eliminate form *such as this*.

However, *like* proved to be somewhat problematic because it is syntactically ambiguous; it can be a verb as in *We like to do this*, a noun as in *and the like*, etc. Although the majority, roughly 75%, of instances texts were judged as not useful, 42 out of 178 were considered as "likely candidates", and 11 as "possible candidates"; the higher overall incidence still resulted in a considerably larger number of likely candidates than the *such as* instances, 53 vs. 12, and therefore worth pursuing in greater depth.

NL CONSTRUCT	Jan94-1	Jan94-2	Jan94-3	Jan94-4	TOTAL
X such as Y, ..., Z	4	3	5	2	14
X like Y	44	37	52	45	178

Table 6. Frequency analysis of two NL constructs for another sample of *Time Magazine*

ISSUE	TOTAL	ELIMINATED	REMAINING	% REMAINING
Jan94-1	44	27	17	38.6%
Jan94-2	37	26	9	24.3%
Jan94-3	52	35	13	25.0%
Jan94-4	45	32	12	26.7%
TOTAL	178	127	51	28.6%

Table 7. Elimination of not useful occurrences of *like* in the sample of *Time Magazine*

Below, we outline the algorithm eliminating the not useful occurrences of *like*. It significantly reduces the number of likely candidates, losing relatively few "good" instances; see Table 7. NSU stands for *next syntactic unit*, NNSU stands for *next next syntactic unit*, PW for *preceding word*, PSU for *preceding syntactic unit*, and FSU for *following syntactic unit*:

```
Find the next occurrence of "like"; Extract NSU;
  if  (NNSU in - - " . , ; ' : ") then skip occurrence;
  else extract PSU;
      if (PW ends in - - " . , ; ' : ") or (PSU is pronoun) or (PSU is "to") or
        (PSU is adverb) or (PSU in - be, look, smell, ...") or
        (PSU in - more, most, not, less, something, lot, anything, things, nothing, on, little, much ")
      then skip occurrence;
      else extract FSU;
          if (FSU is pronoun) or (FSU is "to") or (FSU is adverb), then skip occurrence.
```

For this construct, the remaining part of the extraction algorithm is surprisingly simple. In most instances, extracting the single word preceding *like* will provide the most significant, high-level relation. For example, in the phrase *very small dogs like Pekinese and Yorkies*, taking only the immediate antecedent *dogs*, one correctly learns that *Pekinese and Yorkies are dogs*. If one only extracts one preceding word, then the more specific relation present in text is lost; here that *Pekinese and Yorkies are very small dogs*. The more antecedents one considers, the more specific KN is acquired.

However, identifying concept and its definition boundaries in general is quite tricky. It was determined that the word immediately preceding *like* was useful 100% of the time, as was the word immediately following *like*. The second word out in each direction was useful 70% of the time. For antecedents, looking one word further increases desired, but not critical specificity. For the words following *like*, roughly half cases constitute is critical pieces of KN.

For extraction of critical words following *like*, a significant proportion may be effectively delineated by identifying the next punctuation symbol, 14 out of 17, or 82%, with the occurrence of that symbol no more than a relatively short distance, maximum 6-7 words from *like*. Of those remaining occurrences of *like*, appropriate delineation would be made with the single following word.

These extremely simple steps computed after the elimination procedure conclude the algorithm.

5 Conclusions

Knowledge uniquely found in textual corpora

KN acquired from texts, especially from the newspapers and magazines, cannot be found in the existing dictionaries, encyclopedias and hand-crafted taxonomies. Most concepts acquired by the system are complex, multi-word concepts, not just simple single-word concepts; see Table 8.

CONCEPT	DEFINITION, SUBTYPES
definitive taxonomic studies	nucleic acid hybridizations method, placing filter paper strips
mammals	monkeys, sheep, goats, cats, dogs, swine
mineral medium	marine agar, yeast extract agar
complex medium	cells of all species, yeast extract broth
minimal medium	bma containing 0.2% glycerol
commonly used media	nutrient agar, blood agar
special selective bile-salt media	baby 4 medium, oxalate medium, cin medium, cal medium, ss-d agar
preferentially select known pathogens	shigella, salmonella
typing techniques	susceptibility, bacteriocin production
enterobacteria	hektoen enteric agars, xylose-lysine-deoxycholate, macconkey
natural environments	water, sewage, soil
immunologically compromised patients	multiply traumatized patients, burned, premature infants
human clinical specimens	sputum, nose, throat, urine
clinical specimens	wound swabs, blood, sputum, throat, urine
liquid enrichment media	tetrathionate broth, selenite broth
relatively noninhibitory medium	eosin methylene blue agar, macconkey
laboratory animals	rabbits, mice
potential terrorist targets	schools, bus stations
very fast action	football plays
strain your hands	knitting, bowling, cooking, gardening
activities	a pencil, a tennis racket, holding a steering wheel
life	loved ones, friends, jobs
describing possible side effects	facial ticks, uncontrollable jerky movements

Table 8. Sample of system-acquired concepts from the *Microbiology* corpus, Volume 1-5, and from the *Time Magazine* corpus, October 1994 issues

438

Possible to eliminate human pre-&post-processing, approach scales up

Overall, our system is a very useful tool for automatically acquiring large quantities of high quality general-purpose taxonomic KN from multi-source, multi-domain large-scale corpora of texts. The system-acquired KBs can subsequently support NL understanding and other in-depth AI tasks. In general, the larger the corpus, the better the acquisition results. It appears that the approach scales up easily.

We believe that the small percentage of incorrect or garbled pieces of KN acquired by our system from large scale unseen NL input justifies completely eliminating the costly, time consuming and error-prone human involvement in pre-processing of textual documents and post-processing cleanup of the acquired KN. Such human involvement, particularly the KN clean-up effort, is virtually always required by other approaches.

Context-independent and context-dependent knowledge

Concepts found in the *Microbiology* corpus are largely context-independent. This is probably because this corpus contains mostly scientific KN. Concepts found in the other two corpora were much more context-dependent. This probably reflects the commonsense and temporary nature of KN contained in these sources.

References

[Iwańska, 1992] Iwańska, L. (1992). A General Semantic Model of Negation in Natural Language: Representation and Inference. In *Proceedings of the Third International Conference on Principles of Knowledge Representation and Reasoning (KR92)*, pages 357–368.

[Iwańska, 1993] Iwańska, L. (1993). Logical Reasoning in Natural Language: It Is All About Knowledge. *International Journal of Minds and Machines, Special Issue on Knowledge Representation for Natural Language*, 3(4):475–510.

[Iwańska, 1996a] Iwańska, L. (1996a). Natural Language Is A Representational Language. In *Working Notes of the AAAI Fall Symposium on* Knowledge Representation Systems Based on Natural Language.

[Iwańska, 1996b] Iwańska, L. (1996b). Natural (Language) Temporal Logic: Reasoning about Absolute and Relative Time. *International Journal of Expert Systems*, 9(1):40–85.

[Iwańska, 1997] Iwańska, L. (1997). Reasoning with Intensional Negative Adjectivals: Semantics, Pragmatics and Context. *Computational Intelligence*, 13(3):348–390.

[Iwańska, 1998] Iwańska, L. (1998). Natural Language is a Representational Language: the UNO Model. In Iwańska, L. and Shapiro, S. C., editors, *Natural Language Processing and Knowledge Representation: Language for Knowledge and Knowledge for Language*. AAAI Press/MIT Press. Forthcoming.

[Iwańska et al., 1995] Iwańska, L., Croll, M., Yoon, T., and Adams, M. (1995). Wayne state university: Description of the uno natural language processing system as used for muc-6. In *Proceedings of the Sixth Message Understanding Conference (MUC-6)*. Morgan Kaufmann Publishers.

A Fuzzy Measure of Similarity for Instance–Based Learning

Francisco Botana

Departamento de Matemática Aplicada, Universidad de Vigo,
Campus A Xunqueira, 36005 Pontevedra, Spain
fbotana@uvigo.es

Abstract. Instance–based learning techniques are based on computing distances or similarities between instances with known classification and objects to classify. The nearest instance or instances are used to predict the class of unseen objects. In this paper we present a fuzzy measure of similarity between fuzzy sets and between elements. This measure allows us to obtain a normalized value of the proximity of objects defined by fuzzy features.

In order to test the efficiency of the proposed measure, we use it in a simple instance–based learning system and make a comparison with other measures proposed in literature.

1 Introduction

Learning to classify objects is a central problem in artificial intelligence. Quinlan [13] divides the field in five formalisms (decision trees and rule production systems, instance–based classifiers, neural networks, genetic algorithms and statistics) and settles three central issues for the second one: *i)* what training cases should be remembered?, *ii)* how can the similarity of cases be measured?, and *iii)* how should the new case be related to remembered cases? This paper addresses the second question in case there are cognitive uncertainties in the known examples.

In the fuzzy framework, machine learning has been evolved mainly following the first and third formalisms. A lot of learning algorithms that use neural networks have been proposed and also there is a growing number of rule production and tree decision systems. However, small work has been done dealing with instance–based classification. Fuzzy similarity measures and similarity relations in fuzzy relational databases have been widely studied, but little emphasis has been put in its relation with classification tasks. In [22] a comparison of similarity measures among fuzzy concepts is made and [15] proposes the use of similarity relations to define fuzzy concepts through interpolation.

The usefulness of similarity measures can be argued with Tversky's statement that similarity "may better be described as a comparison of features rather than as a computation of metric distance between points" [16]. According to that, Section 2 defines a similarity measure between fuzzy sets and between elements, and reviews other fuzzy measures of similarity. Apart from mathematical considerations, la raison d'être of a new similarity measure is its good performance on a real task. Section 3 describes a simple instance–based learning system, which serves to test the measures. Finally, Section 4 reports the experimental results of the algorithm on a well-known problem of classification.

2 A Measure of Fuzzy Similarity

2.1 Notation

We write X to denote the universal finite set of examples on which fuzzy sets are defined. Fuzzy sets are denoted with capital letters. $\mathcal{F}(X)$ is the class of fuzzy sets in X and $\mathcal{P}(X)$ the classical power set of X. $| \ |$ will denote the cardinality of a fuzzy set or the absolute value of a real number, depending on context. The membership function of the fuzzy set A is $\mu_A : X \to [0,1]$.

2.2 Similarity between fuzzy sets

In [5] we have obtained a class of entropy functions deduced from fuzzy implication operators. We have shown that Gödel and Wu [19] fuzzy implication operators lead to the function

$$E(A) = 1 - \frac{1}{|X|} \sum_{\substack{x \in X \\ \mu_A(x) \neq .5}} \max(\mu_A(x), 1 - \mu_A(x)) \ , \tag{1}$$

which is an entropy in the sense of De Luca and Termini [8]. Furthermore, we have

Proposition 1. *E is an additive entropy, that is, for any $A \in \mathcal{F}(X)$,*

$$E(A) = E(A \cap D) + E(A \cap D^C) \ , \forall D \in \mathcal{P}(X) \ .$$

Proof. For any arbitrary sets $A \in \mathcal{F}(X)$ and $D \in \mathcal{P}(X)$,

$$E(A) = 1 - \frac{1}{|X|} \sum_{\substack{x \in X \\ \mu_A(x) \neq .5}} \max(\mu_A(x), 1 - \mu_A(x))$$

$$= 1 - \frac{1}{|X|} \left(\sum_{\substack{x \in D \\ \mu_A(x) \neq .5}} \max(\mu_A(x), 1 - \mu_A(x)) + \sum_{\substack{x \notin D \\ \mu_A(x) \neq .5}} \max(\mu_A(x), 1 - \mu_A(x)) \right)$$

$$= 1 - \frac{1}{|X|} \sum_{\substack{x \in X \\ \mu_{A \cap D}(x) \neq .5}} \max(\mu_{A \cap D}(x), 1 - \mu_{A \cap D}(x))$$

$$- \frac{1}{|X|} \sum_{\substack{x \in X \\ \mu_{A \cap D^C}(x) \neq .5}} \max(\mu_{A \cap D^C}(x), 1 - \mu_{A \cap D^C}(x)) + \frac{|D|}{|X|} + \frac{|D^C|}{|X|}$$

$$= E(A \cap D) + E(A \cap D^C) \ . \ \square$$

Using the main result of [20] on this entropy we get a similarity measure between fuzzy sets $A, B \in \mathcal{F}(X)$ defined as follows:

$$S(A,B) = 1 - \frac{1}{2|X|} \cdot$$ (2)

$$\left(\sum_{\substack{x \in X \\ \mu_A(x) \geq .5, \mu_B(x) \geq .5 \\ \text{or} \\ \mu_A(x) < .5, \mu_B(x) < .5}} |\mu_A(x) - \mu_B(x)| + \sum_{\substack{x \in X \\ \mu_A(x) \geq .5, \mu_B(x) < .5 \\ \text{or} \\ \mu_A(x) < .5, \mu_B(x) \geq .5}} (1 + |\mu_A(x) - \mu_B(x)|) \right) \cdot$$

A common axiom definition states that a similarity measure between fuzzy sets should satisfy the following properties:

(P1) $S(A,B) = S(B,A), \ \forall A, B \in \mathcal{F}(X)$.
(P2) $S(A, A^C) = 0$ if and only if A is a crisp set.
(P3) $S(A, A) = 1, \forall A \in \mathcal{F}(X)$.
(P4) If $A \subset B \subset C$ then $S(A,B) \geq S(A,C)$ and $S(B,C) \geq S(A,C)$.

Proposition 2. *S is a similarity measure.*

Proof. It is easy to see that S satisfies (P1), (P2) and (P3). We prove the first inequality of (P4). Since $A \subset B \subset C$ implies $\mu_A(x) \leq \mu_B(x) \leq \mu_C(x)$, then there are only three cases:

1. If $\mu_A(x) \geq .5$ (so are $\mu_B(x)$ and $\mu_C(x)$) or $\mu_C(x) \leq .5$ then $|\mu_A(x) - \mu_B(x)| \leq |\mu_A(x) - \mu_C(x)|$.
2. If $\mu_A(x) < .5$, $\mu_B(x) < .5$ and $\mu_C(x) \geq .5$ then $|\mu_A(x) - \mu_B(x)| = \mu_B(x) - \mu_A(x) \leq 1 + \mu_C(x) - \mu_A(x) = 1 + |\mu_A(x) - \mu_C(x)|$.
3. If $\mu_A(x) < .5$ and $\mu_B(x) \geq .5$ (so is $\mu_C(x)$) then $1 + |\mu_A(x) - \mu_B(x)| \leq 1 + |\mu_A(x) - \mu_C(x)|$. $\quad\square$

2.3 Similarity between elements

The similarity measure between two elements $x, y \in X$ in fuzzy sets A_k, $k = 1, \ldots, N$ is defined as follows:

$$s(x,y) = 1 - \frac{1}{2|N|} \cdot$$ (3)

$$\left(\sum_{\substack{k=1 \\ \mu_{A_k}(x) \geq .5, \mu_{A_k}(y) \geq .5 \\ \text{or} \\ \mu_{A_k}(x) < .5, \mu_{A_k}(y) < .5}}^{N} |\mu_{A_k}(x) - \mu_{A_k}(y)| + \sum_{\substack{k=1 \\ \mu_{A_k}(x) \geq .5, \mu_{A_k}(y) < .5 \\ \text{or} \\ \mu_{A_k}(x) < .5, \mu_{A_k}(y) \geq .5}}^{N} (1 + |\mu_{A_k}(x) - \mu_{A_k}(y)|) \right) \cdot$$

The following properties are satisfied:

(p1) $s(x,y) = s(y,x)$, $\forall x, y \in X$, $\forall A_k$.
(p2) $s(x,y) = 0$ if and only if A_k, $k = 1, \ldots, N$ are crisp sets and $x \neq y$.
(p3) $s(x,x) = 1, \forall x \in X$, $\forall A_k$.
(p4) If $\mu_{A_k}(x) \leq \mu_{A_k}(y) \leq \mu_{A_k}(z)$ $\forall x, y, z \in X$, where $A_k \in \mathcal{F}(X)$, $k = 1, \ldots, N$, then $s(x,y) \geq s(x,z)$ and $s(y,z) \geq s(x,z)$.

The proofs of (p1), (p2) and (p3) are obvious. (p4) can be proved in an analogous way to (P4).

2.4 Other similarity measures

Many measures of similarity between fuzzy sets have been proposed in the literature. Zwick et al. have reviewed 19 measures in [22]. They divide the studied measures into two groups: those obtained through metric considerations taking into account the well–known one–to–one correspondence between distance and similarity measures and those obtained from a set–theoretic approach.

In the geometric model a variety of distance functions lead to fuzzy similarity measures. So, the Minkowski r–metric [2, 3], a one–parameter class of distance functions defined by

$$d_r(x,y) = [\sum_{i=1}^{n} |x_i - y_i|^r] \; , \; r \geq 1 \; , \tag{4}$$

where $x = (x_1, \ldots, x_n)$ and $y = (y_1, \ldots, y_n)$ are points in a n–dimensional space, gives the following measures of similarity between two fuzzy sets A and B.

When $r = 1$ (the Manhattan or city–block metric), Chen et al. [6] and Wang [17] propose and study the properties of the measure

$$S_1(A,B) = 1 - \frac{1}{|X|} \sum_{x \in X} |\mu_A(x) - \mu_B(x)| \; . \tag{5}$$

For the Chebychev metric, $r = \infty$, the proposed measure [6, 11, 12, 17] is

$$S_2(A,B) = 1 - \max_{x \in X} |\mu_A(x) - \mu_B(x)| \; . \tag{6}$$

The Canberra distance function [7]

$$d_C(A,B) = \sum_{x \in X} |\frac{\mu_A(x) - \mu_B(x)}{\mu_A(x) + \mu_B(x)}| \tag{7}$$

inspires the measure proposed in [12]

$$S_3(A,B) = 1 - \frac{\sum_{x \in X} |\mu_A(x) - \mu_B(x)|}{\sum_{x \in X} (\mu_A(x) + \mu_B(x))} \; , \tag{8}$$

where $S_3(A,B) = 1$ if $A = B = \phi$.

Dubois and Prade [9, p. 24] list some similarity indices that are generalizations of the classical set–theoretic similarity functions. Some of them are the measure based on the union and intersection, also proposed in [12],

$$S_4(A,B) = \frac{\sum_{x \in X} \min(\mu_A(x), \mu_B(x))}{\sum_{x \in X} \max(\mu_A(x), \mu_B(x))} = \frac{|A \cap B|}{|A \cup B|} , \qquad (9)$$

(to be taken 1 if $A = B = \phi$), or a "consistency index" [10, 22] defined as

$$S_5(A,B) = \max_{x \in X} \min(\mu_A(x), \mu_B(x)) , \qquad (10)$$

which is a subnormal similarity measure ($S_5(A,A) = 1$ if and only if A is normalized). A variant of (9) is the measure

$$S_6(A,B) = \frac{1}{|X|} \sum_{x \in X} \frac{\min(\mu_A(x), \mu_B(x))}{\max(\mu_A(x), \mu_B(x))} , \qquad (11)$$

where $0/0 = 1$, proposed in [17]. The rationale behind it is to measure the average of the similarity degree of A and B on all elements in X.

Bandler and Kohout [1] define the "degree to which the fuzzy sets A and B are the same", their "degree of sameness" as

$$S_=(A,B) = \min(A \subset B, B \subset A) , \qquad (12)$$

where $\subset \colon \mathcal{F}(X) \times \mathcal{F}(X) \to \{0,1\}$ is a fuzzy binary relation that indicates "the degree to which A is a subset of B". After criticizing the traditional definition of fuzzy set containment [21], they propose to measure the degree to which A is a subset of B by the degree of membership of A in the fuzzy power set of B, $\mathcal{F}(B)$,

$$A \subset B = \mu_{\mathcal{F}(B)}(A) , \qquad (13)$$

where

$$\mu_{\mathcal{F}(B)}(A) = \min_{x \in X}(\mu_A(x) \to \mu_B(x)) , \qquad (14)$$

for a given fuzzy implication operator $\to$.

They use six implication operators ($S^\#$, standard strict, Gödel, Goguen, Łukasiewicz and Kleene-Dienes) to obtain degrees of sameness. Wang et al. [18] note that in this way it is possible to obtain a class of similarity measures for every implication operator and study some properties of such measures. For example, they prove that the measure (6) can be obtained through the Łukasiewicz implication operator.

In order to measure the similarity between two elements $x, y \in X$ in fuzzy sets $A_k, k = 1, \ldots, N$ the extension is obvious, giving six measures $s_1, \ldots, s_6$.

3 The Learning Algorithm

Traditionally, fuzzy similarity measures have been defined and their properties studied, leaving to further papers or to other authors the study of their performance. The majority of the measures of Subsection 2.4 have been introduced this way. There are just two exceptions: in [22] a comparison between distance measures in linguistic approximation is carried out. In [17] the similarity measures S_1 and S_6 are defined and compared with other measures through a small set of four elements and three fuzzy sets. Here we use a simple instance–based learning algorithm, derived from [14], to test our measure and to compare it with the others. The algorithm has been implemented in *Mathematica* on a Unix system.

The algorithm stores a series of training instances in its memory and uses a measure of element similarity to compare new cases to those stored. New cases are classified according to the most similar instance in the memory.

3.1 Initializing and training the system

An example is described by means of its attributes and classification. In this paper only crisp classification will be considered. Each attribute is a linguistic variable which takes linguistic values $A_1, \ldots, A_n$, which are fuzzy sets in X.

We seed the memory with an example chosen at random. Once in memory, the example, called now an instance, will have a record of its efficiency: a pair {# hits, # matches}. We set this record to {1,1} for the seed.

After that, the system works incrementally, processing one new example, also chosen at random, at a time. The example is matched to all the instances in memory and the classification of the closest one is compared with the known class of the example. In case they are the same, we add one both to # hits and to # matches. Otherwise only # matches is incremented and the example is stored in memory as a new instance with efficiency {1,1}. To decide which instance is the closest to the example, the following formula is used

$$\text{instance}\left(\frac{\#hits}{\#matches}\right) \cdot \text{Sim}(\text{instance}, \text{example}) \ , \tag{15}$$

where Sim is a weighted average of fuzzy measures of similarity between elements,

$$\text{Sim}(x,y) = \sum_{i=1}^{r} w_i s_i(x,y) \ ,$$

where $0 \le w_i \le 1$, $\sum w_i = 1$ and s_i is a similarity measure between elements in fuzzy sets $A_{i_1}, \ldots, A_{i_k}$. If r is the number of used attributes to describe the objects and $A_{i_1}, \ldots, A_{i_k}$ are the values of the i–th attribute, Sim allows us to weight the relative importance of the attributes.

3.2 Learning

Once the system has been trained, learning occurs in an analogous way to training. An object is matched against all the instances in memory and its predicted class will be the one of the closest instance. Here the formula used to measure closeness is

$$\text{instance}\left(\frac{\#hits}{\#matches}\right) \cdot \text{instance}\left(1 - \frac{1}{\#matches}\right) \cdot \text{Sim}(\text{instance}, \text{example}) \ . \tag{16}$$

The reason for the second factor is to favour among all instances with equal efficiency those which have been used more times, assuming they are more paradigmatic.

4 Experimental Results

The Iris database [4] is a well-known test bench in the pattern recognition and machine learning communities. The data set contains 3 crisp classes of 50 examples each, where each class refers to a type of iris plant (*Setosa, Versicolor* and *Virginica*). There are four attributes (the length and width of plant's petal and sepal in centimeters). In Figure 1 the domains for the problem are given. Each attribute has 5 linguistic values: very_low, low, medium, high and very_high.

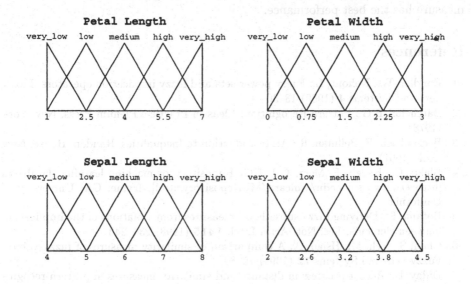

Fig. 1. Domains for iris attributes

The similarity between elements has been evaluated with equal weight for the four attributes. The methodology was the *leaving-one-out* cross–validation technique. One example is removed from data and the system is trained on the remaining examples. After a run for every example, the accuracy is measured. In addition, in each run we get the total number of instances stored in memory. The results for selected measures are shown in Table 1.

5 Conclusion

We have presented a new similarity measure between fuzzy sets and elements and tested it by means of a simple instance–based learning algorithm. The com-

Table 1. Predictive accuracy and mean number of instances

Measure	Accuracy	# instances
s	94.0	6.6
s_1	89.3	6.6
s_2	82.0	8.9
s_3	88.0	6.5
s_4	89.3	6.3
s_5	42.0	8.8
s_6	82.7	7.6

parison with other measures on a standard learning problem shows that this measure has the best performance.

References

1. Bandler, W., Kohout, L.: Fuzzy power sets and fuzzy implication operators. Fuzzy Sets and Systems **4** (1980) 13–30
2. Batchelor, B.G.: Pattern Recognition: Ideas in Practice. Plenum Press, New York (1978)
3. Beckenbach, E, Bellman, R.: An Introduction to Inequalities. Random House, New York (1961)
4. Blake, C., Keogh, E.,Merz, C.J. UCI Repository of machine learning databases [http://www.ics.uci.edu/ mlearn/MLRepository.html]. Irvine, CA: University of California.
5. Botana, F.: Deriving fuzzy subsethood measures from violations of the implication between elements. Lec. Not. Artif. Intel. **1415** (1998) 234–243
6. Chen, S., Yeh, M., Hsiao, P.: A comparison of similarity measures of fuzzy values. Fuzzy Sets and Systems **72** (1995) 79–89
7. Diday, E.: Recent progress in distance and similarity measures in pattern recognition. II Int. Joint Conf. on Pattern Recognition (1974) 534–539
8. De Luca, A., Termini, S.: A definition of a nonprobabilistic entropy in the setting of fuzzy sets theory. Inform. Control **20** (1972) 301–312
9. Dubois, D., Prade, H.: Fuzzy Sets and Systems: Theory and Applications. Academic Press, New York (1980)
10. Lee–Kwang, H., Song, Y., Lee, K.: Similarity measure between fuzzy sets and between elements. Fuzzy Sets and Systems **62** (1994) 291–293
11. Pappis, C.P.: Value approximation of fuzzy system variables. Fuzzy Sets and Systems **39** (1991) 111–115
12. Pappis, C.P., Karacapilidis, N.I.: A comparative assessment of measures of similarity of fuzzy values. Fuzzy Sets and Systems **56** (1993) 171–174
13. Quinlan, J.R.: C4.5: Programs for Machine Learning. Morgan Kaufmann, San Mateo (1993)
14. Salzberg, S.: Learning with Nested Generalized Exemplars. Kluwer Academic Publishers, Boston (1990)
15. Sudkamp, T.: Similarity, interpolation, and fuzzy rule construction. Fuzzy Sets and Systems **58** (1993) 73–86

447

16. Tversky, A.: Features of similarity. Psychological Review **84**(4) (1977) 327–353
17. Wang, W.: New similarity measures on fuzzy sets and on elements. Fuzzy Sets and Systems **85** (1997) 305–309
18. Wang, X., De Baets, B., Kerre, E.: A comparative study of similarity measures. Fuzzy Sets and Systems **73** (1995) 259–268
19. Wu, W.: Fuzzy reasoning and fuzzy relational equations. Fuzzy Sets and Systems **20** (1986) 67–78
20. Xuecheng, L.: Entropy, distance measure and similarity measure of fuzzy sets and their relations. Fuzzy Sets and Systems **52** (1992) 305–318
21. Zadeh, L.A.: Fuzzy sets. Inform. Control **8** (1965) 338–353
22. Zwick, R , Carlstein, E., Budescu, D.V.: Measures of similarity among fuzzy concepts: A comparative analysis. Int. J. Approx. Reasoning **1** (1987) 221–242

Computation of Minimal Cost Reducts

Robert Susmaga

Institute of Computing Science, Poznań University of Technology,
Piotrowo 3A, 60-965 Poznań, Poland.
Robert.Susmaga@CS.PUT.Poznan.PL

Abstract. The paper addresses the problem of computing reducts in decision tables where attributes are assigned costs. Computing reducts has been an interesting issue as the reducts may be successfully applied in further analyses of the decision table. In systems where attribute are assigned costs, the problem of reduct generation may be reformulated to that of finding reducts satisfying some additional constraints, in particular reducts of minimal attribute costs. The constraints allow to incorporate external preference into the system and, additionally, simplify the problem of interpreting the obtained results, since the number of reducts of minimal costs, as opposed to the number of all existing reducts, is usually very small. This paper introduces a new algorithm for generating all reducts of minimal costs, called minimal cost reducts or cheapest reducts. The practical behaviour of this algorithm has been tested in numerous experiments with real-life data sets, the results of which are reported here.

1 Introduction

An interesting aspect of the decision table analysis is the problem of reducing the number of attributes. The general idea of reduction, as defined e.g. in the Rough Set Theory [7], is to decrease the size of the data set while preserving some other properties of this set. Such a reduction is a useful action which may potentially reduce the expenses of collecting and storing the data, but it is not its only advantage. Reduction may also be used for identification and elimination of noise in data when constructing classifiers.

This paper addresses the problem of generating reducts which have been effectively popularized by the Rough Sets Theory [7]. The Rough Sets reducts are subsets of attributes that are minimal with regard to inclusion and which preserve the value of the quality of approximation [7]. Related papers on different aspects of decision systems analysis, e. g. [9, 10, 17] introduced further definitions of reducts [1, 11, 12, 16, 17] in different contexts.

It is important that the very mechanism used for generating reducts according to the classic definition may also be easily used for generating the other reducts as well as other exact and approximate structures that play important role in the decision table analysis, like discretizations of continuous attributes [4] and decision rules. Another application of the same mechanism could be searching for prime implicants of boolean functions [9], or, as it is demonstrated in this paper, solving 0–1 linear programming problems.

The rest of the paper is organized as follows. Section 2 presents the formal definitions of reducts, shortest reducts and cheapest reducts and an effective algorithm for generating all reducts. Sections 3 introduces the algorithm for generating cheapest reducts, while Section 4 illustrates its possible application as a tool for solving a special type of 0–1 linear programming problems. Sections 5 and 6 present the data sets and the results of the experiments. Conclusions and final remarks are included in Section 7.

2 Definitions of Reducts, Shortest Reducts and Cheapest Reducts

The main data set to be analysed has the form of a decision table. Formally, the decision table may be defined as a 4-tuple $DT = < U, Q, V, d >$, where: U is a non-empty, finite set of objects under consideration; Q is a non-empty, finite set of condition (C) and decision (D) attributes such that $C \cup D = Q$ and $C \cap D = \emptyset$; V is a non-empty, finite set of attribute values; and d is an information function, $d : U \times Q \rightarrow V$. Let $IND(P)$ denote a indiscernibility relation, defined for a set $P \subseteq Q$ as:

$$IND(P) = \{(x,y) \in U \times U : d(x,q) = d(y,q), \forall_{q \in P}\}.$$

A subset of condition attributes R $(R \subseteq C)$ is a reduct iff:

$$\forall_{p \in U \times U} \{(p \notin IND(D) \wedge p \notin IND(C)) \Rightarrow p \notin IND(R)\},$$

$$\forall_{q \in R} \exists_{p \in U \times U} \{p \notin IND(Q) \wedge p \notin IND(R) \wedge p \in IND(R - \{q\})\}.$$

The general idea of reducts is that they are subsets of attributes which allow to discern objects belonging to different classes and being discerned by all condition attributes and which are minimal with regard to inclusion. It should be noted that minimality with regard to inclusion does not imply minimality with regard to set cardinality. In fact, reducts generated for a given decision table may vary considerably as far as their cardinality is concerned. Generating all reducts that are minimal with regard to cardinality is a separate problem.

Let *Red* denote a set of all existing reducts for a given data set. A reduct R is called a k-reduct (also: a short reduct), if $|R| \leq k$. A reduct R is called the shortest reduct if it is minimal with regard to its cardinality, i.e.: $\forall_{P \in Red} |P| \geq |R|$. The shortest reduct need not be unique for a given data set.

The definitions of cheap and cheapest reducts are much like those of short and shortest reducts. The main difference is the attribute cost, introduced into the definition of the decision table. Such a system can be defined as 5-tuple $DT = < U, Q, V, d, E >$, where U, Q, V and d are defined as above and E is a non-empty, finite set of non-negative attribute costs $c(q)$. The following additive function $Cost(P)$ computes the cost of a given attribute subset P as: $Cost(P) = \sum_{q \in P} c(q)$. A reduct R is called a c-reduct (also: a cheap reduct), if $Cost(R) \leq c$. A reduct R is called the cheapest reduct (also: a minimal cost reduct) if it is minimal with regard to its cost, i.e.: $\forall_{P \in Red}\ Cost(P) \geq Cost(R)$. As it was the case with the shortest reducts, the cheapest reduct need not be unique for the given data set. It is also obvious that when all the attribute costs are equal to one another, the shortest reducts are also the cheapest ones.

The constraints to the reduct generating process are not confined to minimizing the attribute costs or reduct cardinalities. An equally interesting problem is generating reducts which are minimal with regard to the cardinality of the partition induced on the objects.

There have been many approaches to the problem of generating reducts, but there are relatively few propositions of algorithms capable of generating all reducts in an effective way [3, 5, 9, 15]. Many other approaches are heuristics designed to generate various approximate solutions, i.e. single reducts or their small but representative populations.

This paper is concerned with exact algorithms. Due to the paper size restrictions, only one of the employed algorithms may be presented in full here. It is a representative of the family of algorithms based on the notion of discernibility matrix. The reader is referenced to [9, 13, 14, 15] for detailed descriptions of these algorithms. The algorithm presented in Fig. 1 is a Fast Reduct Generating Algorithm and was introduced originally in [14]. Its function $FPI(R)$ (see [14] for details) checks if the set R is minimal with regard to inclusion.

Fig. 1. The Fast Reduct Generating Algorithm

Input: A set of objects U ($|U| = N$);
           the objects are described by values of attributes from the set Q.
Output: The set Red of all reducts for the set U.

PHASE I – Creation of the Absorbed Discernibility List (ADL)
  Step 1
  Create the ADL for $i = 1..N$, $j = 1..N$:
  $ADL := \{C_{i,j} : C_{i,j} \neq \emptyset\}$ and for no $C_{l,m} \in ADL$: $C_{l,m} \subset C_{i,j}\}$, where:
  $C_{i,j} := \{q \in Q : d(u_i, q) \neq d(u_j, q)$, for each pair i, j$\}$.
  The resulting ADL contains $(C_1, C_2, ..., C_d)$, where $d \in [1, N(N-1)/2]$.
  Usually $d \ll N(N-1)/2$.
  Step 2
  Sort the ADL in the ascending order of the cardinality of its elements.

PHASE II – Breadth-First Search for Reducts
  Step 1
  $Red_0 := \emptyset$.
  Step 2
  For every $i = 1..d$ compute:
  $S_i := \{R \in Red_{i-1} : R \cap C_i \neq \emptyset\}$.
  $Tmp_i := \{\{F\} : F = \{R \cup \{q\}\}$, where $R \in Red_{i-1}$ and $R \cap C_i = \emptyset\}$.
  $MIN_i := \{R \in F, F \in Tmp_i : FPI(R) = true\}$.
  $Red_i := S_i \cup MIN_i$.

The final result is $Red := Red_d$.

3 Generating All Cheap and Cheapest Reducts

This section presents algorithms for generating cheap reducts (c-reducts) and cheapest reducts (minimal cost reducts). The algorithm for generating c-reducts is used by the algorithm for generating cheapest reducts as one of its two main internal procedures. The other main procedure is the algorithm for generating the shortest reducts [13].

The c-Reduct Generation Algorithm may be easily created from the Fast Reduct Generation Algorithm by introducing an additional control parameter, c, which specifies the maximal allowed cost of reducts to be generated ($c \geq 0$). The idea is to employ the breadth-first type of search used in PHASE II of the FRGA. In each iteration of the loop, the cardinality of the elements of Red_i may either increase or remain constant. If so, the same must apply to the reduct's cost (assuming that the attribute costs are all non-negative). In consequence, if the cost of the elements of Red_d is to remain not greater than c, in iteration i those elements of Red_i whose cost exceeds c are discarded (they are not added to MIN_i).

The only difference between the c-RGA and the FRGA, which is presented in Fig. 1, is the definition of the set MIN_i. In case of the c-RGA the formula is:

$$MIN_i := \{R \in F, F \in Tmp_i : FPI(R) = true \wedge Cost(R) \leq c\}.$$

The simplest approach for generating cheapest reducts resolves itself into generating all the existing reducts and then selecting those of minimal costs. But this algorithm is simple only as far as its idea is concerned. In fact, the time required for generating all the reducts is big enough to render this approach useless in most practical applications.

A more effective approach generates only c-reducts, thus reducing immensely the number of reducts to be generated and subsequently considered for selecting the cheapest ones. The main problem here is choosing the cost c, which must be high enough (otherwise there will be no c-reducts) and, additionally, as small as possible (increasing c will increase the number of generated c-reducts, which may dramatically increase both the time required for generating all the c-reducts as well as that required for selecting the cheapest ones). Thus c cannot be an *ad hoc* chosen value.

In a simple approach c may be obtained as the cost of a randomly generated reduct. This solution, however, runs the risk of arriving at a value that will be far from minimal, thus increasing the computing time of the algorithm for generating all c-reducts.

A much better idea seems to be establishing c as the minimal cost of all of the shortest reducts. The shortest reducts consists of fewest attributes and, unless the data configuration is very unfortunate, they have the best chance of providing a reasonable value of c.

The general outline of the C-RGA is as follows:

- Create the *ADL*,
- Generate all shortest reducts,
- Establish c as the minimal cost of all shortest reducts,
- Generate all c-reducts,
- Select the cheapest reducts of all generated c-reducts.

It may be added that the problem of generating shortest reducts may be considered as a special case of generating cheapest reducts and may be solved after assigning the same (non-negative) costs to all the attributes in the table. The cost of a reduct will be then proportional to the cardinality of the reduct, so reducts of lowest costs will also be reducts of lowest cardinalities. This, however, is a rather complicated way of obtaining the result that may be much more effectively obtained by a specialized algorithm. In all the experiments reported below the algorithm for generating all the shortest reducts was the Shortest Reduct Generating Algorithm (S-RGA) [13].

4 Cheapest Reducts as a Solution to a 0–1 Linear Programming Problem

As it is shown in [2], some of the problems related to decision table analysis may be expressed in form of linear integer programming problems. In case of reduct generation the link between reduct generation and mathematical programming is possible thanks to the discernibility list. After creating and absorbing the discernibility list the problem of reduct generation resolves itself into finding minimal subsets of attributes that have non-empty intersections with each element of the list and may be viewed as an example of the set covering problem [6]. It is shown below how the same problem could be solved by employing 0–1 linear programming.

Let $\mathbf{x}$ be a vector of m variables x_i, such that $x_i \in \{0, 1\}$, $i \in \{1, ..., m\}$, and each x_i corresponds to the attribute $q_i \in C$ in the decision table, $|C| = m$. Let $\mathbf{A} = [a_{i,j}]$ be a $d \times m$-sized matrix, such that $a_{i,j} \in 0, 1$, $\mathbf{1}$ be a d-sized vector consisting of 1's: $\mathbf{1}^T = (1, 1, ..., 1)$, and $\mathbf{c}$ be a d-sized vector of non-negative values (attribute costs). Solving the following 0–1 linear programming problem:

$$min \sum_{i=1}^{m} c_i x_i \text{ subject to} : \mathbf{Ax} \geq \mathbf{1}$$

is equivalent to finding a reduct of minimal cost (a cheapest reduct). In case where all the costs are equal to one another, the result is a reduct of minimal cardinality (a shortest reduct).

The constraint $\mathbf{Ax} \geq \mathbf{1}$, which ensures the feasibility of the solution, is equivalent to checking for consistency in reduct generation. The matrix $\mathbf{A}$ is constructed from the discernibility list and has the of size $d \times m$, where d is the length of the list and m is the number of attributes. Each row $r = (r_1, r_2, ..., r_m)$ of the matrix corresponds to the element C of the discernibility list and its elements are defined as follows: $r_i = 1$ if $q_i \in C$ and $r_i = 0$ otherwise.

5 Presentation of the Data Sets

The data sets used in experiments are all real-life data sets of various origin. The basic characteristics of the data sets are presented in Table 1. It must be stressed that the experiments were designed and conducted with the main purpose of demonstrating the computational characteristics of different reduct generating algorithms and not the potential usefulness of the generated results.

The computing platform in all the experiments was a SUN SPARCstation 5 running at 110 MHz.

Table 1. Basic characteristics and number of reducts in the data sets used in the experiments

Data Set	#Cond. attr.	#Objects	#Classes	Length of the ADL	Avg card. of the ADL	#All Reducts	#Shortest Reducts
Elc444	30	444	2	6170	17.1	355971	20
Eswl	26	500	2	112	4.5	963	3
Iono4	33	351	2	1390	15.6	640466	1
Livdpl	22	80	2	80	5.6	1295	4
Lsd265	35	265	15	117	7.9	6509	37
Mushroom	21	8124	2	37	6.5	572	5
Urod2	33	343	2	593	7.1	38207	42
Urology1	33	500	2	299	7.7	5508	5
Urology2	33	500	3	226	6.7	3325	10
Urology3	33	500	6	524	7.3	1332	30

6 Results of Experiments

The following two subsections present an experimental evaluation of the C-RGA used for generating all cheapest reducts and for solving the presented 0–1 linear programming problems. The same collection of different data sets has been used in both experiments.

In the experiment concerned with computing all the cheapest reducts, the C-RGA has been run 5 times in 5 series for each of the considered data sets (thus there were 25 runs for each data set and 250 runs in total). Each run was characterized by a randomly generated set of costs. The costs were generated according to a uniform distribution in the range 1..Max, with the value of Max being equal to 10, 20 , 40, 80 and 160 in the five series.

The results averaged over each set of 25 runs are presented in Table 2 and include:

- Average number of cheapest reducts,
- Average computing time (with relative deviations) of the whole C-RGA algorithm [seconds of CPU] (column 3),
- Average memory requirements the algorithm [relative units] (column 4).

Table 2. Averaged results of experiments with C-RGA

Data Set	Avg no. of cheapest reducts	(Reducts)		(0–1 Problem)	
		Avg comp. time [s] [units]	Avg memory requirements	Avg comp. time [s] [units]	Avg memory requirements
Elc444	1.44	2.98E+1 ± 14%	1.55E+4	6.05E+0 ± 38%	8.73E+3
Eswl	1.28	1.06E+0 ± 03%	2.21E+3	4.86E-2 ± 43%	1.75E+2
Iono4	1.20	7.85E+1 ± 82%	3.49E+4	7.61E+1 ± 76%	3.31E+4
Livdpl	1.40	1.10E-1 ± 17%	2.88E+2	4.15E-2 ± 32%	2.19E+2
Lsd265	1.12	2.14E+0 ± 19%	3.16E+3	1.75E-3 ± 39%	2.26E+2
Mushroom	1.44	2.30E+2 ± 01%	1.47E+3	6.87E+0 ± 16%	6.95E+1
Urod2	1.20	3.57E+0 ± 05%	4.47E+3	1.48E+0 ± 09%	1.38E+3
Urology1	1.00	3.72E+0 ± 01%	5.75E+3	1.27E+0 ± 03%	3.04E+2
Urology2	1.00	2.82E+0 ± 01%	5.03E+3	7.80E-1 ± 05%	2.31E+2
Urology3	1.00	6.96E+0 ± 01%	8.21E+3	4.44E+0 ± 02%	5.29E+2

The number of cheapest reducts generated in each run was very small (predominantly 1, with some exceptions). This characteristics certainly depends on the particular set of attribute costs.

Both the computing time as well as the memory requirements are mostly determined by the number of c-reducts generated prior to selecting cheapest reducts. This, in turn, is determined by the value of c established after the algorithm for generating shortest reducts is run. The quality of results obtained by this algorithm influences also the overall computing time of C-RGA.

The somewhat exceptional computing time of the data set 'Mushroom' is mainly determined by the large number of objects which is the direct reason for the long time required to create the absorbed discernibility list.

In the second experiment the C-RGA algorithm was treated as a tool for solving 0–1 linear programming problems. The overall computing times quoted here are shorter because the time required for creating, absorbing and sorting the discernibility list (which is polynomial) is not taken into account. The discernibility list represents the set of reduced constraints and these are assumed to be given in advance. The results are presented in Table 2 and include:

- Average computing time (with relative deviations) of solving the 0–1 linear programming problem [seconds of CPU] (column 5),
- Average memory requirements the algorithm [relative units] (column 6).

455

The parameters of the integer programming problem may be read from Table 1, where the number of attributes of the data set corresponds to the number of variables while the length of the ADL corresponds to the number of absorbed (and thus reduced in number) linear constraints of this problem. The average cardinality of the ADL elements is the average 'density' of the constraints, understood as the average number of non-zero elements in the constraint. It must be stressed that the number of variables and the reduced number of constraints together with their densities are the main factors that decide about the difficulty of the problem to be solved.

7 Conclusions

The main purpose of the research reported in this paper has been the introduction and experimental evaluation of an effective algorithm for generating all reducts that are minimal with respect to their cost (cheapest reducts). The main idea of the presented algorithm is that of employing an algorithm for generating shortest reducts. This algorithm is used to generate the cost value, c, that is subsequently used for generating all reducts whose cost does not exceed c (c-reducts). Finally, the cheapest reducts are selected from among the c-reducts as those of minimal cost.

The introduction of attribute cost allows to increase the amount of control over the reduction process. This may be useful e.g. when designing classifiers like decision trees or rules, which are usually constructed using measures that optimize the discriminating abilities but do not always take into account other characteristics of attributes, like their costs or availability. Using a pre-generated c-reduct for building a decision tree guarantees that the cost of classifying a new object by the decision tree will not exceed c.

The conducted comprehensive experimental evaluation of the C-RGA allowed to conclude that practical behaviour of the presented algorithm is very promising. The obtained computing times were all confined to several minutes of CPU.

Another aspect of the C-RGA that has been presented in this paper was the ability of this algorithm to solve 0–1 linear programming problems of particular type, which produced also very interesting results.

Future research concerning the same domain may be directed towards designing further effective algorithms for the computation of reduct with other types of constraints imposed.

Acknowledgements

This paper has been supported by the KBN grant No. 8T11C–013–13. Parts of the reported computations were conducted at the Supercomputing and Networking Centre of Poznań, Poland.

456

References

1. Bazan J., Skowron A. & Synak P.: 'Dynamic Reducts as a Tool for Extracting Laws from Decision Tables', In: *Methodologies for Intelligent Systems. Proceedings of the 8th International Symposium ISMIS'94*, Charlotte, NG, LNAI Vol. 869, Springer-Verlag (1994), 346–355.
2. Boros E., Hammer P. L., Ibaraki T. & Kogan A.: 'Logical Analysis of Numerical Data', *Mathematical Programming*, Vol. 79 (1997), 163–190.
3. Kryszkiewicz M. & Rybiński H.: 'Finding Reducts in Composed Information Systems', *Fundamenta Informaticae*, Vol. 2, No 2/3, (1996), 183–196.
4. Nguyen, H. S. & Skowron A.: 'Quantization of Real Value Attributes. Rough Set and Boolean Reasoning Approaches', In: *Proceedings of the Second Annual Join Conference on Information Sciences*, September/October 1995, Wrightsville Beach, NC (1995), 34–37.
5. Orłowska M. & Orłowski M.: 'Maintenance of Knowledge in Dynamic Information Systems', In: Słowinski R., (ed.), *Intelligent Decision Support. Handbook of Applications and Advances of the Rough Set Theory*, Kluwer Academic Publishers, Dordrecht, (1992), 315–330.
6. Padberg, M. W.: 'Covering, packing and knapsack problems', *Annuals of Discrete Mathematics*, Vol. 4, (1979), 265–278.
7. Pawlak Z.: *Rough Sets. Theoretical Aspects of Reasoning About Data*, Kluwer Academic Publishers, Dordrecht, (1991).
8. Romański S.: 'Operations on Families of Sets for Exhaustive Search Given a Monotonic Function', In: Beeri, C., Smith, J.W., Dayal, U., (eds), *Proceedings of the 3rd International Conference on Data and Knowledge Bases*, Jerusalem, Israel, (1988), 28–30.
9. Skowron A. & Rauszer C.: 'The Discernibility Matrices and Functions in Information Systems', In: Słowinski R., (ed.), *Intelligent Decision Support. Handbook of Applications and Advances of the Rough Set Theory*, Kluwer Academic Publishers, Dordrecht, (1992), 331–362.
10. Skowron A. & Polkowski L.: 'Decision Algorithms: A Survey of Rough Set–Theoretic Methods', *Fundamenta Informaticae*, Vol. 30, No. 3/4, (1997), 345–358.
11. Ślęzak D.: 'Searching for Frequential Reducts in Decision Tables with Uncertain Objects', In: Polkowski L., Skowron A., (eds), *Proceedings of the First International Conference RSCTC'98*, Warsaw, June 1998, Springer-Verlag, Berlin (1998), 52–59.
12. Słowinski R. & Stefanowski J.: 'Rough-Set Reasoning about Uncertain Data', *Fundamenta Informaticae*, Vol. 27, No. 2/3, (1996), 229–244.
13. Susmaga R.: 'Computation of Shortest Reducts', *Foundations of Computing and Decision Sciences*, Poznań, Poland, Vol. 23, No. 2, (1998), 119–137.
14. Susmaga, R.: 'Effective Tests for Inclusion Minimality in Reduct Generation', *Foundations of Computing and Decision Sciences*, Poznań, Poland, (to appear).
15. Tannhäuser M.: Efficient Reduct Computation (in Polish), M. Sc. Thesis, Institute of Mathematics, Warsaw University, Warsaw, Poland, (1994).
16. Wróblewski J.: 'Covering with Reducts – A Fast Algorithm for Rule Generation', In: Polkowski L., Skowron A., (eds), *Proceedings of the First International Conference on Rough Sets and Current Trends in Computing*, Warsaw 1998, Springer-Verlag, Berlin (1998), 402–407.
17. Ziarko W.: 'Variable Precision Rough Set Model', *Journal of Computer and System Sciences*, Vol. 46, No. 1, (1993), 39–59.

Rough Set Data Mining of Diabetes Data

Jaroslaw Stepaniuk

Institute of Computer Science
Bialystok University of Technology
Wiejska 45A, 15-351 Bialystok, Poland
e-mail: jstepan@ii.pb.bialystok.pl

Abstract. The applications of the rough set theory to identify the most relevant attributes and to induce decision rules from a medical data set are discussed in this paper. The real life medical data set concerns children with diabetes mellitus. Three methods are considered for identification of the most relevant attributes. The first method is based on the notion of reduct and its stability. The second method is based on particular attribute significance measured by relative decrease of positive region after its removal. The third method is inspired by the wrapper approach, where the classification accuracy is used for ranking attributes. The rough set approach additionally offers the set of decision rules. For the rough set based reduced data application of nearest neighbor algorithms is also investigated. The presented methods are general and one can apply all of them to different kinds of data sets.

1 Introduction

Rough set theory was proposed [8] as a new approach to knowledge discovery from incomplete data. The rough set approach to processing of incomplete data is based on the lower and the upper approximation. The rough set is defined as the pair of two crisp sets corresponding to approximations. Some approaches to analysis of medical data sets based on the rough set theory are presented for example in [9], [10], [13], [7], [11], [12], [2], [14].

In this paper we discuss mining in diabetes mellitus data. We consider three sub-tasks:

- identification of the most relevant condition attributes,
- discovery of decision rules characterizing the dependency between values of condition attributes and decision attribute,
- application of nearest neighbor algorithms for rough set based reduced data.

The nearest neighbor paradigm provides an effective approach to classification. A major advantage of nearest neighbor algorithms is that they are nonparametric, with no assumptions imposed on the data other than the existence of a metric. However, nearest neighbor paradigm is especially susceptible to the presence of irrelevant attributes. We use the rough set approach for selection of the most relevant attributes within the diabetes data set. Next nearest neighbor algorithms are applied.

The presented approach has been applied to analyze data records of children with diabetes mellitus. This is a real life problem coming from the Second Department of Children's Diseases, Medical Academy of Bialystok, Poland.

The following features are evaluated by rough set methods and nearest neighbor algorithms on 107 patients aged 5-22 and suffering from insulin dependent diabetes for 2-13 years: sex, age of disease diagnosis, disease duration, appearance diabetes in the family, criteria of the metabolic balance, type of the applied insulin therapy, hypertension, body mass and presence or absence of microalbuminuria.

2 Description of the Clinical Data

There are two main forms of diabetes mellitus: type 1 (insulin-dependent), and the more prevalent type 2 (non-insulin-dependent). Type 1 usually occurs before age 30, although it may strike at any age. The person with this type is usually thin and needs insulin injections to live and dietary modifications to control his or her blood sugar level. Type 2 usually occurs in obese adults over age 40. It's most often treated with diet and exercise (possibly in combination with drugs that lower the blood sugar level), although treatment sometimes includes insulin therapy.

In this paper we consider data about children with insulin-dependent diabetes mellitus (type 1). Insulin-dependent diabetes mellitus is a chronic disease of the body's metabolism characterized by an inability to produce enough insulin to process carbohydrates, fat, and protein efficiently. Treatment requires injections of insulin.

Complications may happen when a person has diabetes. Some effects, such as hypoglycemia, can happen any time. Others develop when a person has had diabetes for a long time. These include damage to the retina of the eye (retinopathy), the blood vessels (angiopathy), the nervous system (neuropathy), and the kidneys (nephropathy). The typical form of diabetic nephropathy has large amounts of urine protein, hypertension, and is slowly progressive. It usually doesn't occur until after many years of diabetes, and can be delayed by tight control of the blood sugar. Usually the best lab test for early detection of diabetic nephropathy is measurement of microalbumin in the urine. If there is persistent microalbumin over several repeated tests at different times, the risk of diabetic nephropathy is higher. Normal albumin excretion is less than 20 microgram/min (less than 30 mg/day). Microalbuminuria is 20-200 microgram/min (30-300 mg/day).

Twelve condition attributes, which include the results of physical and laboratory examinations and one decision attribute (microalbuminuria) describe the database used in our experiments. The excerpt from the database is shown in Table 1. The data collection so far consists of 107 cases. The collection is growing continuously as more and more cases are analyzed and recorded. Out of twelve condition attributes eight attributes describe the results of physical examina-

Object	Sex	Age	...	Disease	...	...	HbA1c	...	Microalbuminuria
1	f	12		5	...		7.28	...	Yes
2	m	1		4	...		10.00	...	No
3	m	15		5	...		6.65	...	No
4	f	13		4	...		8.69	...	Yes
5	f	11		5	...		9.6	...	Yes
...	...	...		...	...		...	...	...
103	f	14		6	...		7.68	...	Yes
104	m	14		4	...		9.00	...	Yes
105	m	9		9	...		7.4	...	Yes
106	m	16		2	...		9.00	...	Yes
107	f	7		12	...		8.06	...	Yes

Table 1. An Excerpt of Patient Data

Symbol	Attribute	Attribute values
a_1	Sex	f, m
a_2	Age of disease diagnosis (years)	$< 7, [7, 13), [13, 16), \geq 16$
a_3	Disease duration (years)	$< 6, [6, 11), \geq 11$
a_4	Appearance diabetes in the family	yes, no
a_5	Insulin therapy type	KIT, KIT_IIT
a_6	Respiratory system infections	yes, no
a_7	Remission	yes, no
a_8	HbA1c	$< 8, [8, 10), \geq 10$
a_9	Hypertension	yes, no
a_{10}	Body mass	<3, 3-97, >97
a_{11}	Hypercholesterolemia	yes, no
a_{12}	Hypertriglyceridemia	yes, no
d	Microalbuminuria	yes, no

Table 2. Attributes and Their Values

tions, one attribute describes insulin therapy type and three attributes describe the results of laboratory examinations. The former eight attributes include sex, the age at which the disease was diagnosed and other diabetological findings. The latter three attributes include the criteria of the metabolic balance, hypercholesterolemia and hypertriglyceridemia. The decision attribute describes the presence or absence of microalbuminuria. All this information is collected during treatment of diabetes mellitus.

Additionally attributes with numeric values were discretized. Although several algorithms for automatic discretization exist (for overviews see [5]), in this analysis discretization was done manually according to medical norms. Final attributes and their values (after discretization) are presented in Table 2. Basic data information after discretization is presented in Table 3.

	%	Count
Total number of patients	100	107
Sex		
Male	54.21	58
Female	45.79	49
Age of disease diagnosis (years)		
< 7	22.43	24
[7, 13)	49.53	53
[13, 16)	22.43	24
≥ 16	5.61	6
Disease duration (years)		
< 6	51.40	55
[6, 11)	42.99	46
≥ 11	5.61	6
HbA1c		
< 8	42.99	46
[8, 10)	42.06	45
≥ 10	14.95	16
Microalbuminuria		
yes	52.34	56
no	47.66	51

Table 3. Characterization of Patients Group

3 Importance of Attributes

One can measure the importance of attributes with respect to different aspects. One can also consider different strategies searching for the most important subset of attributes. For example one can exhaust all possible subsets of the set of condition attributes and find the optimal ones. In general, its complexity (the number of subsets need to be generated) is $O\left(2^{card(A)}\right)$, where $card(A)$ is a number of attributes. This strategy is very time consuming. Therefore we consider less time consuming strategies.

In this section the importance of attributes is evaluated and compared using three methods.

3.1 Reducts Application

We compute the accuracy of approximation of decision classes. From Table 4 one can observe that both decision classes are definable by twelve condition attributes.

There are six reducts. Three reducts with nine attributes and three reducts with ten attributes. Reducts are presented in Table 5. Sign "+" means occurrence of the attribute in a reduct. Stability of reducts was verified on subtables. This idea was inspired by the concept of dynamic reducts [1]. Based on experimental verification, reducts for full data table are more stable than other attribute

Decision class	Yes	No
Number of patients	56	51
Cardinality of lower approximation	56	51
Cardinality of upper approximation	56	51
Accuracy of approximation (α)	1.0	1.0

Table 4. Accuracy of Approximation of Decision Classes

Attribute/Reduct	B1	B2	B3	B4	B5	B6
a_1	+	+	+	+	+	+
a_2	+	+	+	+	+	+
a_3	+	+	+	+	+	+
a_4	-	+	+	+	+	+
a_5	+	+	+	+	+	+
a_6	+	-	-	-	+	+
a_7	-	+	+	+	-	-
a_8	+	+	+	+	+	+
a_9	+	-	-	+	-	+
a_{10}	+	-	+	-	+	+
a_{11}	+	+	-	-	+	-
a_{12}	+	+	+	+	+	+
Stability of the reduct	65%	59%	58%	54%	47%	43%
Classification accuracy	63%	77%	71%	76%	68%	70%

Table 5. Reducts, Their Stability and Classification Accuracy

subsets. For example in one experiment we choose 30 subtables starting from 90% to 99% of all objects in data table, thus we consider 300 subtables. Six mentioned above reducts were also reducts at least in 69% from 300 subtables and other subsets were reducts in less than 10% of subtables.

In the Table 5 stability of the reducts based on four experiments is also presented. We consider 300 subtables in every experiment. The sampling strategy is the following: subtables are sampled on 10 equally spaced levels with 30 samples per level. In the following four experiments we consider different sampling levels:

Experiment 1: 60%, 64%, ..., 96% of the original table.

Experiment 2: 70%, 73%, ..., 97% of the original table.

Experiment 3: 80%, 82%, ..., 98% of the original table.

Experiment 4: 90%, 91%, ..., 99% of the original table.

In all experiments we consider subtables with at least 60% of the original table to preserve representability. On the other hand from evaluations presented in [1] we deduce that the number of at least 300 subtables is enough for good estimation of the stability coefficient.

For every reduct one can also compute classification accuracy based on leave-one-out method. The results are presented in the last row of the Table 5.

From the above analysis we infer that the reduct B2 is a relatively stable subset of attributes with high classification accuracy of generated rules.

Attribute	I	II	III	IV	V	VI
a_1	0.24	0.24	**0.15**	-	-	-
a_2	0.49	0.50	0.42	0.38	0.09	0
a_3	0.36	0.42	0.42	0.31	**0.09**	-
a_5	0.19	**0.19**	-	-	-	-
a_8	0.31	0.38	0.42	**0.31**	-	-
a_{12}	**0.02**	-	-	-	-	-
γ	0.76	0.74	0.55	0.40	0.09	0

Table 6. The Significance of Attributes in Succeeding Stages of the Analysis

3.2 Method Based on Significance of Attributes

For the set of all condition attributes the dependency coefficient is equal to 1.

In the first step we consider attributes that are in all six reducts. Thus we consider attributes in core. The degree of dependency is equal to 0.76. The significance of attributes is presented in Table 6. The idea is to evaluate each individual attribute with the significance measure. This evaluation results in a value attached to an attribute. Attributes are then sorted according to the values. The attribute with the least significance is removed and the process is repeated. One can stop the algorithm obtaining only one attribute.

3.3 Method Inspired by Wrapper Approach

We consider method inspired by wrapper approach [3]. The subsets of attributes are evaluated based on the cross-validation result. In the succeeding steps of the analysis attribute is removed which removal leads to the best result of the cross-validation test. The general scheme of the algorithm is as follows:

$B := A$;

Repeat $B := B - \{a\}$, where $a = \arg\max_{a \in B} \left\{ AC\left(DT_{B-\{a\}}\right) \right\}$.

Until Stop-Condition;

where $DT_{B-\{a\}} = (U, (B - \{a\}) \cup \{d\})$ and the resulting accuracy coefficient is $AC\left(DT_{B-\{a\}}\right)$.

The partial results of the analysis are presented in Table 7. The leave-one-out test was used for accuracy estimation. The best result 79.44% was obtained for six attributes. The further removal of attributes thus not led to the increase of classification accuracy.

Every method allows to analyze data from different angle. Combining the results of the three methods one can find the following three attributes as the most important: *Age of disease diagnosis*, *HbA1c* and *Disease duration*. This result is consistent with the general medical knowledge about this disease.

Attribute	I	II	III	IV	V	VI
a_1	63.55	62.62	64.49	62.62	62.62	60.75
a_2	67.29	64.49	68.22	66.36	71.96	65.42
a_3	69.16	66.36	67.29	66.36	66.36	69.16
a_4	64.49	63.55	71.03	71.03	71.96	69.16
a_5	69.16	69.16	68.22	71.96	72.90	**79.44**
a_6	70.09	**72.90**	-	-	-	-
a_7	69.16	68.22	71.03	72.90	71.03	74.77
a_8	62.62	62.62	64.49	65.42	66.36	62.62
a_9	**71.03**	-	-	-	-	-
a_{10}	68.22	70.09	**76.64**	-	-	-
a_{11}	68.22	70.09	71.03	73.83	**73.83**	-
a_{12}	68.22	70.09	73.83	**74.77**	-	-
γ	1.0	1.0	1.0	0.98	0.95	0.80

Table 7. Classification Accuracy and Quality of Approximation (γ)

4 Rough Set Methods as Preprocessing for Nearest Neighbors Algorithms

In this section we discuss the experiments with nearest neighbor algorithms. The nearest neighbor algorithm retains the entire training data set during learning. This algorithm assumes all objects correspond to points in n-dimensional space. The nearest neighbors of an object are defined in terms of the Euclidean distance. More precisely, let $DT = (U, A \cup \{d\})$ be a decision table, for every two objects $x, y \in U$ the Euclidean distance is defined by $E(x,y) = \sqrt{\sum_{a \in A} (a(x) - a(y))^2}$.

Nearest neighbor algorithms are especially susceptible to the inclusion of irrelevant attributes in the data set, and several studies has shown that the classification accuracy degrades as the number of irrelevant attributes is increased (see e.g. [4]).

For number $k \in \{1, \dots, 10\}$ of nearest neighbors and different attribute subsets (three most important attributes, all attributes and six reducts) we obtain the leave-one-out results presented in Table 8. The best results are obtained for the set $A3 = \{a_2, a_3, a_8\}$ and are also presented on Figure 1.

Conclusions

The diabetes mellitus data set has been drawn from a real life medical problem. The rough set based analysis showed that the most relevant features are the following: age of disease diagnosis, criteria of the metabolic balance and disease duration. The above aspects influence incidence of microalbuminuria in children suffering from diabetes type I. The results of our analysis and the extracted laws are also consistent with general clinical knowledge about diabetes type I. The presented methods go beyond the individual application to diabetes mellitus data analysis and can be applied to mining in different data sets.

k	A3	A	B1	B2	B3	B4	B5	B6
1	73.83	73.83	71.96	76.64	70.09	70.09	81.31	73.83
2	90.65	85.98	86.92	87.85	87.85	86.92	87.85	86.92
3	75.70	72.90	72.90	75.70	71.96	73.83	73.83	71.96
4	83.18	79.44	79.44	82.24	80.37	80.37	80.37	78.50
5	79.44	72.90	71.96	72.90	73.83	75.70	73.83	73.83
6	85.98	83.18	82.24	84.11	85.05	85.05	83.18	83.18
7	79.44	76.64	76.64	76.64	76.64	80.37	75.70	78.50
8	82.24	82.24	80.37	82.24	84.11	83.18	80.37	82.24
9	78.50	77.57	77.57	74.77	80.37	80.37	77.57	77.57
10	81.31	82.24	82.24	82.24	82.24	82.24	81.31	82.24

Table 8. Nearest Neighbors Method

Acknowledgments

The author would like to thank Andrzej Skowron, Jan Bazan and Dominik Slezak for valuable discussions and critical remarks. The author would like to express his gratitude to members of the Knowledge Systems Group at NTNU, Norway, and the Logic Group at Warsaw University, Poland taking part in creation of ROSETTA and to members of the Second Department of Children's Diseases, Medical Academy of Bialystok, Poland taking part in construction of the medical information system. This research was supported by the grants No. 8 T11C 023 15 and 8 T11C 010 11 from the State Committee for Scientific Research, the Bialystok University of Technology Rector's Grant W/II/3/98 and Research Program of the European Union - ESPRIT-CRIT 2 No. 20288.

References

1. Bazan J.G.: A comparison of dynamic and non–dynamic rough set methods for extracting laws from decision tables. [in:] L. Polkowski, A. Skowron, (eds.), Rough Sets in Knowledge Discovery 1. Methodology and Applications. Physica–Verlag, Heidelberg, 1998, pp. 321-365.
2. Carlin U.S., Komorowski J., Ohrn A.: Rough Set Analysis of Patients with Suspected Acute Appendicitis, Proceedings of IPMU'98, Paris, France, July 1998, pp. 1528-1533.
3. Kohavi R., John G.H.: Wrappers for Feature Subset Selection, Artificial Intelligence Journal, 97, 1997, pp. 273-324.
4. Langley P., Iba W.: Average-case Analysis of a Nearest Neighbor Algorithm, Proceedings of the 13th International Joint Conference on Artificial Intelligence, Morgan Kaufmann, San Mateo, CA, 1993, pp. 889-894.
5. Nguyen H.S., Nguyen S.H.: Discretization Methods in Data Mining, [in:] L. Polkowski, A. Skowron (eds.): Rough Sets in Knowledge Discovery 1. Methodology and Applications. Physica-Verlag, Heidelberg 1998, pp. 451-482.
6. Ohrn A., Komorowski J., Skowron A., Synak P.: The Design and Implementation of a Knowledge Discovery Toolkit Based on Rough Sets - The Rosetta System, [in:] L. Polkowski, A. Skowron (eds.): Rough Sets in Knowledge Discovery 1. Methodology and Applications. Physica-Verlag, Heidelberg 1998, pp. 376-399.

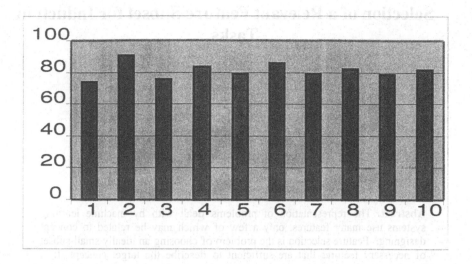

Fig. 1. Nearest Neighbors Method

7. Paszek P., Wakulicz-Deja A.: Optimization Diagnose in Progressive Encephalopathy Applying The Rough Set Theory, Proceedings of the Fourth European Congress on Intelligent Techniques and Soft Computing, Aachen, Germany, September 2-5, 1996, vol. 1, pp. 192-196.
8. Pawlak Z.: Rough Sets. Theoretical Aspects of Reasoning about Data, Kluwer Academic Publishers, Dordrecht, 1991.
9. Pawlak Z., Slowinski K., Slowinski R.: Rough classification of patients after highly selective vagotomy for duodenal ulcer. International Journal of Man-Machine Studies, 24, 1998, pp. 413-433.
10. Slowinski K.: Rough Classification of HSV Patients, (ed.) Slowinski R., Intelligent Decision Support - Handbook of Applications and Advances of the Rough Sets Theory. Kluwer Academic Publishers, Dordrecht, 1992, pp. 77-93.
11. Stefanowski J., Slowinski K.: Rough Set Theory and Rule Induction Techniques for Discovery of Attribute Dependencies in Medical Information Systems, Lecture Notes in Artificial Intelligence 1263, Springer-Verlag, 1997, pp. 36-46.
12. Stepaniuk J., Urban M., Baszun-Stepaniuk E.: The Application of Rough Set Based Data Mining Technique in the Prognostication of the Diabetic Nephropathy Prevalence, Proceedings of the Seventh International Workshop on Intelligent Information Systems, Malbork, Poland, June 15-19, 1998, pp. 388-391.
13. Tsumoto S., Ziarko W.: The Application of Rough Sets - Based Data Mining Technique to Differential Diagnosis of Meningoencephalitis, Proceedings of the 9th International Symposium, Foundations of Intelligent Systems, Zakopane, Poland, 9-13 June, 1996, Lecture Notes in Artificial Intelligence 1079, pp. 438-447.
14. Urban M., Baszun-Stepaniuk E., Stepaniuk J.: Application of the Rough Set Theory in the Prognostication of the Diabetic Nephropathy Prevalence. Preliminary Communication Endokrynologia, Diabetologia i Choroby Przemiany Materii Wieku Rozwojowego 1998, 4, 2.

Selection of a Relevant Feature Subset for Induction Tasks

Delphine Michaut[1], Pierre Baptiste[1]

[1] Laboratoire d'Automatique, Institut de Productique
CNRS - UMR 6596
25 rue Alain Savary 25000 BESANCON - FRANCE
dmichaut@ens2m.fr

Abstract. The representation of problems dealt with by machine learning systems use many features, only a few of which may be related to concept designing. Feature selection is the problem of choosing an ideally small subset of necessary features that are sufficient to describe the target concept. It is important both to speed up learning and to improve concept quality. A huge amount of work has been done to select from input data, a subset of the most relevant features. In this paper, a new algorithm of feature pre-processing for induction methods, namely induction of decision trees, and applied to symbolic objects is suggested. It selects a subset of the more relevant features, taking into account feature interaction. It is based both on the DPGoal and ODPGoal of considered variables (features). It is evaluated using three benchmark artificial domains. Then it is compared with Relief [1].

1   Introduction

The majority of real-world classification problems require supervised learning where each instance is associated with a class label. In real-world situations, relevant features are often unknown *a priori*. Therefore, many candidate features are introduced to better represent domain. Unfortunately many of these are either partially or completely irrelevant/redundant to the target concept. A relevant feature is neither irrelevant nor redundant to the target concept; an irrelevant feature does not affect the target concept in any way, and a redundant feature does not add anything new to the target concept. In many applications, the size of a data set is so large that learning might not work as well before removing these unwanted features. Reducing the number of irrelevant/redundant features drastically reduces the running time of a learning algorithm and yields a more general concept. This helps in getting a better insight into the underlying concept of a real-world classification problem.

Feature selection is the problem of choosing a small subset of features that ideally are necessary and sufficient to describe the target concept.

A huge amount of work [2], [3] has been done to select from input data, a subset of the most relevant variables and so to reduce the working space without loss of generality.

Algorithms of discrimination, namely induction of decision tree methods [4], [5], [6], [7], [8], have also treated the problem of variable selection. Concept learners, such as C4.5 [9] select relevant features by themselves, step by step. But hard concepts having feature interactions are problematic for induction algorithms [10]. Since real-world problems may involve feature interaction, it is not always enough to apply only concept learners. Data pre-processing algorithms such as Relief [11] and Focus [12] treat this problem. The first is a heuristic search algorithm; it does not always give the minimal subset. The second is exhaustive; its computational time is high.

Thus, in this paper, a new heuristic search algorithm for dealing with data sets that contain a large number of irrelevant attributes and using symbolic knowledge representation is suggested. It takes feature interaction into account and deals with redundant attributes, thus is able to determine the necessary and sufficient features. It is based both on the DPGoal (Goal Discriminant Power) and ODPGoal (Goal Original Discriminant Power) of considered features. Firstly, in section 2 the main definitions concerning symbolic objects are given. Section 3 gives the definition of the new criterion of feature selection. In section 4, a description of the proposed feature selection algorithm which is based the on the new discriminant measure is done. Then, it is applied to an example. Section 5 is an empirical evaluation of the new algorithm following by a comparison with Relief. Finally, section 6 concludes and suggests future work.

2 Symbolic Objects Representation

We chose to work with symbolic objects in order to keep things clear. A symbolic object (instance) is a description of the instance with the help of discrete values. Thus, we consider that the continuous values of some attributes have been converted into discrete values with the help of a discretization algorithm [13].

The notations used are taken from E. Diday and P. Brito [14].

Let Π a studied population,

Ω a subset of n observed objects:

$$\Omega = (\omega_1, \omega_2, \ldots, \omega_n)$$

Each element of Π is characterized by a set Y of r qualitative and significant variables $y_1, \ldots, y_k, \ldots, y_r$:

$$y_k : \Pi \to O_k$$

where O_k is a finite set of observable values for y_k, also named modalities space of y_k

$$O_k = \{v_1^k, v_2^k, \ldots, v_{m_k}^k\}$$

where v_p^k is the modality p of the variable y_k

and m_k is the y_k modality number.

Thus $O=O_1,O_2,\ldots,O_k,\ldots,O_r$ describes the working space and the application:

$$T{:}\Pi \to O$$

$$\omega \mapsto T(\omega) = \left(y_1(\omega),\dots,y_2(\omega)\right)$$

gives the description of an object ω of Ω .

3   Criteria of Feature Selection

Firstly, we define the notion of goal. To compute the *Goal Discriminant Power (DPGoal)* and the *Goal Original Discriminant Power (ODPGoal)*, the goal of the classification is considered. Thus, from the training set, we examine which objects belong to which clusters.

In order to formalize the membership of an object to one of the clusters, the variable y_{goal} is introduced. y_{goal} is a variable of the set Y of descriptive variables such that each value of y_{goal} represents one cluster of the partition; there are as many clusters as possible values of y_{goal} .

So, relationships between the considered descriptive variable values and the y_{goal} values are pointed out. Such a variable is considered relevant for the system if it is relevant in comparison to the pre-defined goal. R. Kohavi and G. H. John [15] claim that two degrees of relevance are required: weak and strong. To the authors, a feature is relevant if it is either weakly relevant or strongly relevant; otherwise, it is irrelevant. We use these definitions to define one criterion of weak relevance: the DPGoal, and another of strong relevance: the ODPGoal.

Considering two objects ω_i and ω_j that belong to different classes, the variable y_k is able to discriminate these objects if the values of y_k are different for the objects. Generalizing this idea to all object pairs (ω_i,ω_j), we define the Discriminant Power of the variable y_k , the goal variable being given.
Let $Y = \{y_1,\dots,y_{r-1},y_{goal}\}$

The **DPGoal** of a variable y_k is defined as follows:

DPGoal: Y→ℕ such that

$$\text{DPGoal}(y_k) = \sum_{i=1}^{n}\sum_{i>i}^{n} \min\!\left[\left(y_k(\omega_i) \neq y_k(\omega_j)\right),\left(y_{goal}(\omega_i) \neq y_{goal}(\omega_j)\right)\right] (1)$$

Thus, DPGoal is the number of pairs of objects discriminated by y_k as well as by y_{goal} . Its complexity is about n^2.

Let Y' a subset of Y, $Y' \subset Y - \{y_{goal}\}$.

The **DPGoal** of a subset Y' of variables is defined as follows:
DPGoal $:\mathcal{P}(Y) \to ℕ$ such that

$$\text{DPGoal}(Y') = \sum_{i=1}^{n} \sum_{j>i}^{n} \min\left[\max_{y_k \in Y'}\left(y_k(\omega_i) \neq y_k(\omega_j)\right), y_{\text{goal}}(\omega_i) \neq y_{\text{goal}}(\omega_j)\right] \quad (2)$$

DPGoal is the number of pairs of objects discriminated by both y_{goal} and at least one variable of Y'. Its complexity is about $n^2 \times \text{card}(Y')$.

Let consider two objects ω_i and ω_j that belong to different classes. y_k strongly discriminates these objects if the values of y_k are different for ω_i and ω_j and there is no variable or combination of variables that discriminates ω_i and ω_j. Generalizing this idea to all object pairs (ω_i, ω_j), we define the Original Discriminant Power of the variable y_k.

Let Y'' be a subset of Y; $Y'' \subset Y - \{y_k, y_{\text{goal}}\}$ and $\mathcal{P}(Y)$ the set of parts of Y.

The **ODPGoal** of a variable y_k in comparison with a subset of variables Y'' is defined as follows

ODPGoal : $Y \times \mathcal{P}(Y) \to \mathbb{N}$ such that

$$\text{ODPGoal}(y_k, Y'') = \sum_{i=1}^{n} \sum_{j>i}^{n} \min\left[\max\begin{bmatrix} \left(y_k(\omega_i) \neq y_k(\omega_j)\right) \\ - \max_{y_\ell \in Y''}\left(y_\ell(\omega_i) \neq y_\ell(\omega_j)\right), 0 \end{bmatrix}, \\ y_{\text{goal}}(\omega_i) \neq y_{\text{goal}}(\omega_j) \end{bmatrix} \quad (3)$$

ODPGoal is the number of pairs of objects discriminated by y_k as well as by y_{goal} and by none of the Y'' variables. Its complexity is about $n^2 \times \text{card}(Y'')$.

4 The Discriminant Power Algorithm

The algorithm that we suggest in this paper is based both on the DPGoal and the ODPGoal of the descriptive variables. From the point of view computing, it is quite similar to MINSET[16].

4.1 Algorithm

The algorithm description is as follows.

```
Initialization
```

$$B = \{y_1, y_2, \ldots, y_k, \ldots y_{r-1}\}$$
```
to_observe  ←  all the objects pairs
```

$A \leftarrow \emptyset$

❶ Essential feature selection

```
        for each variable yₖ of B do
```

$\quad\quad\quad \text{if } ODPGoal\left(y_k, B - \{y_k\}\right) \neq 0$

```
            then A ← A+{ yₖ }
                 B ← B-{ yₖ }
            end if
        end for
        updating of to_observe


while to_observe ≠ ∅ do
            ❷ Selection of the staying features
            ODPGoalmax=0
            for each variable yₖ of B do
                if ODPGoal(yₖ,A)>ODPGoalmax
                then   ODPGoal max ← ODPGoal (yₖ,A)
                            Higher ← yₖ
            end if
            end for
            updating of to_observe
            A ← A+{Higher}
            B ← B-{Higher}
            ❸ Redundant feature deletion
                for each variable yₖ of A on all object
                pairs do
                    if ODPGoal(yₖ,A-{yₖ})=0
                    then A ← A- yₖ
                    end if
                end for
    end while
```

4.2   Method

❶ Essential feature selection

The first step consists of selecting essential variables. Such a variable has the characteristic that it is the only variable that is capable of discriminating objects of some pairs of objects. Thus, this variable is definitively selected. The search for an optimal subset of features will start from this (or these) variable(s). The algorithm continues (step ❷) without the pairs for which the objects have been discriminated. If none of the variables is essential, go to the step ❷.

❷ Selection of the staying features

The second step adds the most relevant variable to the current subset of selected features. If the ODPGoal of each variable is equal to 0, then the DPGoal is used to find the best variable.

❸ redundant feature deletion

The ultimate step allows to remove variables from the current subset that have become redundant after the second step. This step is crucial to obtain an optimal subset.

At each step of the algorithm, the number of object pairs not yet discriminated is quantified by   DPGoal ($\{y_1, \ldots, y_{r-1}\}$) - DPGoal(A).

4.3 Complexity

Its complexity is about $\theta(r \cdot c)$ where

- r is the number of features;
- c is the number of objects pairs to discriminate.

5   Experimental Results

Three benchmark artificial domains were used for evaluating the discriminant power algorithm that is described section 4: LED [4], Bool and Parity. Then a comparison between Relief and the Disciminant Power Algorithm is presented.

These data sets have been chosen because they underline the algorithm behavior when features interact. Parity domain is especially interesting in that none of the relevant variables in isolation can be distinguished from irrelevant one.

5.1   LED Display Domain

Seven meaningful features, corresponding to the seven segments, and sixteen random features compose the considered data set. Each feature, except goal feature, has the value 0 or 1. The goal of this domain, i.e. the goal variable, is the description of digits 0 to 9. Table 1 shows which feature values are 1 for each digit. The number of training instances is 200.

Table 1. LED Display Domain: digit description

digit	y_1	y_2	y_3	y_4	y_5	y_6	y_7
0	1	1	1	0	1	1	1
1	0	0	1	0	0	1	0
2	1	0	1	1	1	0	1
3	1	0	1	1	0	1	1
4	0	1	1	1	0	1	0
5	1	1	0	1	0	1	1
6	1	1	0	1	1	1	1
7	1	0	1	0	0	1	0
8	1	1	1	1	1	1	1
9	1	1	1	1	0	1	1

The Discriminant Power Algorithm estimates that features 1 to 5 are necessary and sufficient to discriminate all the objects. Indeed, it estimates that features 6 and 7 are redundant in comparison with the features 1 to 5 while features 8 to 24 are estimated as completely irrelevant. Thus, the algorithm finds the minimal feature set.

5.2 Bool

The initial data set was used by Smyth et al. [17] and has been modified as follows. 12 binary features compose the data set and the goal feature is determined by the function:

$$y_{goal} = (y_1 \oplus y_2) \vee (y_3 \wedge y_4) \vee (y_5 \wedge y_6)$$

The features y_7 to y_{12} are randomly generated. The number of training instances is 200.

The Discriminant Power Algorithm gives the following results: the features y_1 to y_6 are relevant while the features y_7 to y_{12} are completely irrelevant.

5.3 Parity

Parity problem consists of 3 relevant features and 7 irrelevant features. The goal of the classification is given by:

$$y_{goal} = y_1 \oplus y_2 \oplus y_3$$

The features y_4 to y_{10} are randomly generated. The number of training instances is 200.

The Discriminant Power Algorithm estimates that the features y_1 to y_3 are relevant while the features y_4 to y_{10} are completely irrelevant.

5.4 Comparison

As A. L. Blum and P. Langley in their paper [18], the feature-selection methods are considered "grouped into three classes: those that embed the selection within the basic induction algorithm, those that use feature selection to filter features passed to induction, and those that treat feature selection as a wrapper around the induction process". The Discriminant Power Algorithm belongs to the second one. It allows data pre-processing in order to design decision trees.

Much work on filtering methods carried out. K. Kira and L. A. Rendell [8] describe and analyze different approaches. The authors concluded that concept learners as well as heuristic search algorithms and feature weight based approaches perform poorly with feature interaction, whereas algorithms of exhaustive search give the smallest feature relevant subset but at the expense of their complexity.

That is why they introduced a new algorithm Relief that selects relevant features using a statistical method. Relief is accurate even if features interact. The Relief algorithm assigns a relevance weight to each feature, which is meant to denote the relevance of the feature to the target concept. Relief samples instances randomly from the training set and updates the relevance values based on the difference between the selected instance and the two nearest instances of the same and opposite class (the "near-hit" and "near-miss"). It selects those features whose average weight is above a given threshold.

I. Kononenko extended Relief to deal with incomplete and multi-class problems: ReliefF [19]. Nevertheless, neither Relief nor ReliefF finds a minimal subset.

A comparison between Relief and the Discriminant Power Algorithm on the three domains is realized.

The first data set emphasizes the capacity of the two algorithms to deal with irrelevant features.

The results obtained from the parity domain are as follows. Both algorithms establish that features 1, 2 and 3 are relevant and features 4 to 10 are completely irrelevant. Thus, like Relief, the Discriminant Power Algorithm is efficiently when features interact, i.e. when none of the relevant attributes in isolation has any power to discriminate the classes.

On the LED Display Domain, the new algorithm finds a subset composed by 5 features against 7 given by Relief for the discrimination of all the digits. For the description of the digit 2, it estimates that one feature is sufficient (feature 6) against 3 for Relief. This result can be explained as follows. Relief does not help with redundant features. If most of the given features are relevant to the concept, it would select most of the given features even though only a small number of them are necessary for concept description [8]. The Discriminant Power Algorithm deals with redundant features; the selected features that become redundant are removed from the relevant feature subset (step ❸).

Thus, the use of such benchmark data sets, which contain a large number of irrelevant attributes, emphasizes that the Discriminant Power Algorithm deals with feature interaction and redundant features and finds a minimal subset of relevant features.

6 Conclusion and Further Work

The algorithm we suggested in this paper selects a subset of the more relevant features using two numerical selection criteria: the DPGoal and the ODPGoal. It allows a reduction in working space for designing decision trees and thus, optimizes the learning time of the concepts. The three crucial points of this algorithm are as follows:

First, the algorithm takes into account feature interaction. Indeed, one of the selection criteria is the ODPGoal which computes the relevance of one feature considering the others. Second, it deals with redundant features; at each selection of a new feature, it estimates all the selected features and removes from the relevant set those that have become redundant. Finally, it gives a minimal subset of relevant features.

We are studying the behavior of our algorithm with noisy data and are working to improve it. Furthermore, we are evaluating the proposed method on real learning tasks.

References

1. Kira, K., Rendell, L. A.: The Feature Selection Problem: Traditional Methods and a New Algorithm. Proc. AAAI-92, San Jose (1992)
2. Dash, M., Liu, H.: Feature Selection for Classification. Intelligent Data Analysis, Vol. 1, no. 3 (1997)
3. Bratko, I., Cestnik, B., Kononenko, I.: Attribute-based learning. AI Communications, Vol. 9 (1996), 27-32
4. Breiman, L., Friedman, J. H., Olshen, R. A., Stone, C. J.: Classification and Regression Trees. Wadsworth, (1984)
5. Buntine, W., Niblett, T.: A Further Comparison of Splitting Rules for Decision Tree Induction. Machine Learning, Vol. 8 (1992), 75-85
6. White, A. P., liu, W. Z.: Bias in Information-Based Measures in Decision Tree Induction. Machine Learning, Vol. 15 (1994), 321-329
7. Mingers, J. : An Empirical Comparison of Selection Measures for Decision Tree Induction. Machine Learning, 3 (1989), 319-342
8. Liu, W. Z., White, A. P.: The Importance of Attribute Selection Measures in Decision Tree Induction. Machine Learning, Vol. 15 (1994), 25-41
9. Quinlan, J. R., C4.5: programs for machine learning, Morgan Kaufmann (1993)
10. Langley, P., Sage, S.: scaling to Domains with Irrelevant features. Computational learning theory and natural learning systems, Vol. 4, MA: MIT Press, Cambridge (1997), 17-29
11. Kira, K., Rendell, L. A.: A Practical Approach to Feature Selection. Machine Learning (1992), 249-255
12. Almuallim, H., Dietterich, T. G.: Learning With Many Irrelevant Features. Ninth National Conference on Artificial Intelligence (1991), 547-552
13. Dougherty, J., Kohavi, R., Sahami, M.: Supervised and Unsupervised Discretization of Continuous Features. Proc. of the 12th ICML, San Francisco (1994), 194-202
14. Brito, P., Diday, E.: Pyramidal representation of symbolic objects. In Schalder, M. & Gaul, W. (eds.): Knowledge, Data and Computer-Assisted DecisionsSpringer-Verlag, Berlin (1990), 3-16,
15. Kohavi, R., John, G. H.: Wrappers for feature subset selection. Artificial Intelligence (1997), 273-324
16. Ziani, D., Khalil, Z., Vignes, R.: Recherche de sous-ensembles minimaux de variables à partir d'objets symboliques. Proc. 5èmes journées "Symbolique-Numérique", IPMU-94, Paris (1994), 794-799
17. Smyth, P., Goodman, R.M., Higgins, C.: A hybrid rule-based Bayesian classifier. Proc. of ECAI, Stockholm (1990), 610-615
18. Blum, A. L., Langley, P. : Selection of relevant features and examples in machine learning. Artificial Intelligence (1997), 245-271
19. Kononenko, I.: Estimating Attributes: Analysis and Extensions of RELIEF. ECML-94, Catania, Italy (1994), 171-182

A Data Structure for Subsumption-Based Tabling in Top-Down Resolution Engines for Data-Intensive Logic Applications

Jacques Calmet and Peter Kullmann

Institut für Algorithmen und Kognitive Systeme (IAKS)
Fakultät für Informatik, Universität Karlsruhe
Am Fasanengarten 5, D-76131 Karlsruhe, Germany

Abstract. Using tables in top-down resolution engines is an effective way of optimization by avoiding recomputation of formerly derived facts. This effect can be even more exploited if, instead of considering only identical subgoals, facts from subsuming sugoals are reused. This is particularly of interest if recalculation is expensive, e.g. due to data transmission cost or the mere volume of data to be processed.

We present a data structure for subsumption-based tabling in subgoal-oriented resolution. Our data structure is based on hB-Trees, a multi-attribute indexing structure which emerged from research on database management systems. Hence, our data structure inherits desirable properties such as its use as efficient indexing structure for secondary storage.

Keywords: Logic for Artificial Intelligence, Intelligent Information Retrieval, Subsumption-based Tabling, Information Integration

1 Introduction

Tabling in top-down proof procedures has originally been proposed to guarantee the termination of recursive programs and thus allow their evaluation [TS86]. The general effect of using tables is that the recalculation of answer substitutions can be avoided if a subgoal has already been calculated in the resolution process or its calculation is currently in process. The new subgoal can be fed with answers from the existing subgoal. Thus, answer tables serve as a cache. This aspect makes the use of tables also interesting for non-recursive subgoals as an optimization technique if the cost for calculating answers is high. This might be the case if remote sites have to be contacted via a network in order to retrieve facts from a specific information source or the data volume is extremely high.

In connection with our research on the integration of heterogeneous information systems we have developed the logic-based mediator system KOMET [CJKS97]. The core of KOMET is a highly flexible resolution engine which processes many-sorted annotated logic programs [KS92]. It uses SLG resolution [CW93] which has been extended for annotated logic. SLG resolution makes extensive use of answer tables for program evaluation under the well-founded semantics. In the context of a mediator system like KOMET, tables can play a central role in the query optimization strategy by using them as cache for expensive subgoal calls. Ideally the tables are kept across queries to maximally exploit their effect. For certain applications it might even be worth-while to use local secondary storage devices for maintaining answer tables. Such a mechanism can make a mediator system highly suitable as a data warehouse system where the gathering, preprocessing and locally storing of information is done implicitly by the mediator engine in contrast to one or more explicit preprocessing steps as it is done in traditional data warehouse systems.

2 Data Structures for Tabling

In our paper we adopt the notion of subgoals as answer *producers* whereas the selected literals in clauses are regarded as answer *consumers*. Upon selection of a literal in a clause body it is necessary to find a producer which generates appropriate answers to be able to resolve the clause. This producer can either already exist from previous calculations or it has to be created which usually implies that program clause resolution is initiated.

Common approaches to tabling rely on variant-based tabling. In variant-based tabling an existing subgoal is accepted as producer if it equals the selected literal up to variable renaming. Variant-based tabling has several properties which make the use and processing of answer tables straight-forward and efficient. Variant-based tabling schemes mostly adopt a structure-sharing approach to represent subgoal answer tables in the form of indexing tries [RRR96]. Since tries share representations of atoms, they are very efficient in terms of space requirements and exhibit very good performance for insert and lookup operations.

The main drawback of variant-based tabling is the fact that the potential of tables as caching facility is not fully exploited. Using variant-based tabling tends to produce a large number of subgoal answer tables while performing many redundant computations. By exploiting the subsumption of subgoal calls, performance of a subgoal-based resolution engine can be drastically improved. This has recently been shown in [RRR96] where tries have been extended for subsumption-based tabling.

We believe, a tabling data structure suitable for a data-intensive logic-based applications should have the following properties:

Support for specific needs of subsumptive tabling: Subsumptive tabling requires retrieval of subsets of the table contents according to a query literal which is more specific than the subgoal but still may contain variables. This requires all answers to be indexed on all arguments in some way, since it cannot be foreseen what binding information is supplied by consumers. As another requirement, a mechanism for registering consumers is needed, since a subgoal calculation might still be in process when a subsumed literal is selected.

Reduction of subsumed answers: On the one hand, a new answer should be ignored if it is subsumed by another answer in the data structure. On the other hand, if a new answer subsumes one or more answers in the data structure they should be removed from the table.

Support for secondary storage: Main memory should not limit the data volume which can be processed in a deductive system. However, disk accesses must be sufficiently efficient.

Support for persistence: To maximally exploit tabling it might be sensible to store answer tables over a longer period of time (not only across queries, but as well across query sessions). In a concrete system, tables could be recalculated regularly (e.g. weekly) in order to reduce resource consumption in a productive environment.

The use of tries as data structure for subsumption-based tabling has an essential drawback. As they are one-dimensional indexes, the concatenation of attributes are used as index keys. Tries inherently index on prefixes of the stored information, i.e. lookup is the more efficient the longer the prefix of the query is. Partial-match queries will degenerate to traversals of the entire data structure in the worst case, even in the presence of bound arguments. A class of access methods applicable to our scenario are hash-based methods. However they present several problems. The one is the poor space efficiency which is even worse in the case of multi-dimensional methods. Another is that they are not suitable for the efficient incorporation of secondary storage devices. Finally the dynamic growth of hash tables usually involves expensive reorganization processes.

3   Multi-attribute Indexing Structures

Multi-attribute indexing structures have been mainly the concern of work in database research. Usually, ordering access methods applicable to arbitrary sets of key values are based on tree search. The classical indexing structure for one-dimensional access is the B-tree which is an approximately balanced, page-oriented binary tree. A naive way to achieve multi-attribute indexing is to use a one-dimensional index for each dimension. The greatest disadvantages of this approach are the poor space efficiency and the high cost for insertions and deletions, since these operations have to be performed for each dimension individually. The fact that cost increases proportionally with the dimension of the search space is not generally acceptable. Grid files, K-D-B-trees and R-trees and variants are well-known data structures for multi-attribute indexing. More recently, X-trees [BKK96], hB-trees [LS90,ELS95] and UB-trees [Bay97] have been discussed, each with specific strengths and weaknesses. Our requirements for a tabling data structure are good average storage utilization, efficient dynamic reorganization, support for partial-match queries and robustness with respect to data distribution and key space dimension. Most of the above indexing structures exhibit these properties only partially. For our purposes we have found hB-trees to be a data structure which guarantees these properties all of the time in the face of arbitrary data. A more detailed analysis of multi-attribute indexing methods can be found in [Lom92].

4   hB-Trees

The hB-Tree, introduced by Lomet and Salzberg [ELS95] exhibits several properties in addition to our requirements.

- For small data sets, hB-trees can easily be modified for complete storage and management within the physical main memory.
- hB-Trees have recently been extended for concurrent access [ELS95]. This property would make them suitable for a multi-threaded resolution engine. Note, that SLG resolution is also well-suited for concurrent processing.

The hB-tree is derived from the K-D-B-tree. hB-Trees are composed of pages which contain a k-d-tree each. A k-d-tree basically consists of two types of nodes. *Data nodes* contain data objects and represent rectangular subspaces. *Index nodes* contain an index term and references to the left and right subtree and divide a subspace along one dimension. A hB-tree page is the unit for storage on disk. In contrast to K-D-B-Trees, the goal of the hB-Tree structure is to avoid downward cascading of page splits, hence avoiding both restructuring cost and adverse storage utilization. When a page becomes full, splitting is done based on the exisiting boundaries within the subspace. This results in the removal of a smaller brick-like subspace from the larger brick-like subspace of the original full page. The result is a "holey brick", which is where the name comes from.

In the remainder of the paper we will describe the modifications necessary in order to use hb-Trees as tabling structure for subsumptive tabling. We will first define an abstract tabling engine and then describe our data structure in terms of this definition. Our work is currently restricted to logical languages without free function symbols but includes non-monotonic reasoning. In addition we require the domains of all predicate arguments to be fully ordered.

5   Tabled Resolution

In this section we abstractly describe a resolution engine with tabling. This abstract view will help us to understand the central properties and difficulties of tabled resolution. Our definition is similar, but in details different to the one given in [RRR96] and emphasizes other aspects of tabled resolution. For this presentation we use a simplified version of our model which is restricted to programs without negation.

We divide a tabled resolution engine in two subsystems: the resolution engine $\mathcal{RE}$ and the tabling engine $\mathcal{TE}$. Neither of the two systems is a true subsystem of the other. Depending on the evaluation strategy they may call each other. Due do the decoupling of the two subsystems, which is achieved by using input queues, this framework may well serve as a model for a multi-threaded resolution engine.

A tabling engine $\mathcal{TE}$ is given by the set of tabled subgoals S, of which each subgoal s is given by the tuple

$$\langle l, A, C, Q \rangle$$

l denotes a subgoal literal, A represents a set of answers, C represents a set of pending clauses with selected literal and associated subgoal for the head literal, Q stands for a queue of waiting answers to be inserted into the subgoal table. A contains all facts subsumed by l found up to the current state of processing. If substitution factoring is used for tabling, A is a set of answer subtitutions over the set of variables in l. Substitution factoring can be employed transparently in this framework, we can neglect it here without loss of generality.

A resolution engine $\mathcal{RE}$ is given by the tuple

$$\langle P, Q_c, Q_s, Q_r \rangle$$

P is a logic program, Q_c, Q_s and Q_r represent queues of elements waiting for further processing. Q_c is a queue of pending pairs $\langle s, Cl \rangle$, where Cl is a clause and s an associated subgoal table for its head. Q_s is a queue of new subgoals waiting for program clause resolution. Q_r is a queue of triples $\langle s, Cl, \theta \rangle$. Such a triple is formed by a clause Cl with a selected literal, an associated subgoal table s for the clause head and a substitution θ for answer resolution.

$\mathcal{RE}$ supports following operations:

$NewClause(s, Cl)$: This operation takes a clause Cl and its associated subgoal table s. If the clause body is empty, $\mathcal{TE} :: NewAnswer$ will be called, otherwise a literal is selected and $\mathcal{TE} :: FindOrCreateSubgoal$ is called.

$NewSubgoal(s)$: This operation determines the appropriate program clauses for resolution with a subgoal literal s. For each clause it performs the appropriate substitution and calls $\mathcal{RE} :: NewClause$.

$ResolveAnswer(s, Cl, Cl_s, \theta)$: This operation performs answer resolution on the clause Cl with selected literal Cl_s using the given substitution θ. It then calls $\mathcal{RE} :: NewClause$ with s and the resolved clause.

$\mathcal{TE}$ supports following operations:

$NewAnswer(s, A)$: This operation inserts an answer A into the specified subgoal table s, if it is not subsumed. It determines all approriate consumers in C and calls $\mathcal{RE} :: ResolveAnswer$ with each consumer.

$FindOrCreateSubgoal(l, Cl)$: This operation first determines, if an appropriate subgoal call already exists in S. If it does exist, all subsumed answers are sent to the consuming clause Cl. If the subgoal evaluation is still in process, Cl is registered as consumer. If the call does not yet exist, a new subgoal table is created and $\mathcal{RE} :: NewSubgoal$ is invoked.

These operations parallel a subset of the transformations of SLG resolution as defined in [CW93]. The termination property of SLG can be directly transferred to our tabled resolution engine, if we ensure that all elements in any of the queues are processed until there are no more elements in any of the queues.

6 hBT-Tables

We depart from the hB-Tree data structure as it is given in [LS90,ELS95]. As it is documented in the algorithms for the tabled resolution engine, our data structure has to provide for following mechanisms:

- Insertion of answers with variable arguments,
- Determination of subsumed answers (partial match queries),
- Registration of consumers,
- Correct page splitting in the presence of above modifications.

Insertion Answers with no variable arguments are inserted as in the standard insert operation, that is, the appropriate leaf node is determined by descending the hB-Tree. As answers with variables in their arguments represent a region in the index space, they are inserted in all data nodes which overlap with the given region[1]. Since a search only finds data nodes as a whole, it is neccesary to regard the answers in a data node as candidate answers and to check them individually against the search literal. A special treatment is given to answers which have only variable arguments, such as $A(X,Y)$ or $A(X,X)$ for a subgoal $A(X,Y)$. Otherwise they would need to be inserted in all data nodes. To reduce redundancy and to be able to guarantee the correctness of our page split algorithm, we store these answers in a separate list at the root of the tree. The pseudocode algorithm is given in the following.

```
Insert(Answer)
  InsertAnswer(Root,Answer)
  if Answer was inserted
    SendToConsumers(Answer)
end

InsertAnswer(Node,Answer)
  if Node is an index node
    SDim is the splitting dimension of the index term
    if Answer is not ground at argument position SDim
      InsertAnswer(left child,Answer)
      InsertAnswer(right child,Answer)
    else if the argument value of Answer at position SDim is less than index term
      InsertAnswer(left child,Answer)
    else
      InsertAnswer(right child,Answer)
  else Node is data node
    forall answers B in the answer container
      Perform reduction
    end forall
    if Answer was not subsumed
      Insert Answer in answer container
    if container overruns
      split node
  end if
end
```

---

[1] This technique is used in R+-trees as well as in UB-trees.

Finding subsumed or unifiable answers The search for subsumed (unifiable) answers in general corresponds to a partial match query. Such a query defines a subspace within the search space. As result all entries that are enclosed in (overlap) the subspace are returned. The candidate data pages are determined in the same way as in the insertion algorithm. The algorithm for subsumed answers is given below. The algorithm for unifiable answers works accordingly.

```
GetSubsumed(Node,Query,Subsumed)
begin
    if Node is an index node
        SDim is the splitting dimension of the index term
        if Query is not ground at argument position SDim
            GetSubsumed(left child,Query,Subsumed)
            GetSubsumed(right child,Query,Subsumed)
        else if the argument value of Query at position SDim is less than index term
            GetSubsumed(left child,Query,Subsumed)
        else
            GetSubsumed(right child,Query,Subsumed)
    else Node is data node
        add all subsumed answers in container to Subsumed
    end if
end
```

Consumer registration We supplement our data structure with a K-D-B-tree in which consumers for answers of the particular subgoal are stored. After a new answer has been inserted into the answer tree, the consumer entries that unify with the new answer are determined. The answer is then queued in $\mathcal{RE}$ for resolution.

Page splitting The general algorithm for page splitting remains as given for the hB-tree. The general idea is that upon node overrun the content of the node is evenly split into two parts. In [LS90] it has been shown that in a node with point data[2] such a split is always possible with a ratio of $2:1$ or better. Note, that the splitting criterion may involve more than one dimension of the search space. In the presence of *spatial data*[3] we have a different situation. If an answer or a consumer is variable in the argument position of the split dimension, or, generally speaking, overlaps both subspaces, it is duplicated and inserted in both pages. This is the technique which is used in R^+-trees [SRF87]. A problem arises when all entries in a data node cover the entire subspace defined by the node. It will then not be possible to find an appropriate splitting criterion. However, by exploiting the special structure of non-ground answers in our application domain we can guarantee valid data node splits, if the capacity of data nodes is at least $\frac{(dim-2)(dim-1)}{2} + 1$. This number corresponds to the maximum possible number of non-ground entries in the presence of answer reduction due to subsumption.

---

[2] i.e. there are no entries with variable arguments

[3] here, answers with non-ground arguments such as $A(1, X, Y)$

```
SplitNode(DataNode)
begin
    Find splitting criterion which splits with 2 : 1 ratio
    NewNode is a new index node with subnodes realizing the criterion
    forall answers B in answer container
        Insert B in NewNode
    end forall
    Exchange NewNode with DataNode
end
```

7 Results

We have implemented a version of hbT-tables for complete in-memory tabling. The implementation of our system additionally supports negation and handles many-sorted annotated logic programs according to the well-founded semantics using SLG resolution. There is no other system that we are aware of which implements the calculation of the well-founded semantics for annotated logic programs. The only inference engine we know that (partially) implements SLG resolution is the PROLOG system XSB. Due to the additional features of our engine, it performs approximately an order of magnitude worse than XSB. In the table below we compare the performance of using subsumptive hbT-tables with a variant-based version of our engine.

Size of parent relation	KOMET 1.2, Variant-based	KOMET 1.2 Subsumption-based	Relative Speedup
512	4.29	0.82	5.23
1024	15.81	2.5	6.32
2048	59.19	8.92	6.63
4096	235.89	33.7	7.0
8192	963.93	128.84	7.4

Table 1. Performance comparison

As benchmark the calculation of the *ancestor* relation from a complete binary tree realized by the *parent* relation with different sizes was used[4]. The tests were run on a Intel Pentium 233 MMX with 128MB of main memory. Execution times are given in seconds. In our experiments hBT-tables exhibit substantial speed-ups in comparison to our previous variant-based tabling technique. It proves to be robust under different circumstances such as data distribution and arity of predicates.

---

[4] ancr(X,Y):[t] <- par(X,Y):[t]
ancr(X,Z):[t] <- par(X,Y):[t] & ancr(Y,Z):[t]
The query anc(X,Y):[t] computes all solutions

483

8 Conclusion

We have presented a data structure for subsumption-based tabling for subgoal-oriented resolution strategies. This data structure is based on a multi-attribute indexing data structure called hB-tree. The necessary adaptations could be achieved while preserving the general properties of hB-Trees such as node utilization and high fan-out. hBT-tables can be used for secondary-storage tabling which opens a wealth of possibilities for optimization in deductive systems in distributed, heterogeneous environments. hBT-tables will be incorporated in KOMET, a logic-based mediator system for the integration of distributed, heterogeneous information systems [CJKS97]. In this context we will further explore the optimization potential of subsumption-based tabling.

References

[Bay97] R. Bayer. The Universal B-Tree for Multidimensional Indexing. In *Proceedings of the WWAC Conference*, pages B-3-2-1-B-3-2-12, 1997.

[BKK96] S. Berchthold, D. A. Keim, and H.-P. Kriegel. The X-Tree: An Index Structure for High-dimensional Data. In *Proceedings of the International Conference on Very Large Data Bases (VLDB)*, pages 28–39, 1996.

[CJKS97] J. Calmet, S. Jekutsch, P. Kullmann, and J. Schü. KOMET – a System for the Integration of Heterogeneous Information Sources. In *10th International Symposium on Methodologies for Intelligent Systems (ISMIS)*, 1997.

[CW93] W. Chen and D. S. Warren. Query Evaluation Under the Well-founded Semantics. In *ACM Symposium on Principles of Database Systems*. ACM Press, 1993.

[ELS95] G. Evangelidis, D. Lomet, and B. Salzberg. A Multi-attribute Index Supporting Concurrency, Recovery and Node Consolidation. In *Proceedings of the International Conference on Very Large Data Bases (VLDB)*, 1995.

[KS92] M. Kifer and V. S. Subrahmanian. Theory of Generalized Annotated Logic Programming. *Journal of Logic Programming*, 12(1):335–367, 1992.

[Lom92] D. Lomet. A Review of Recent Work on Multi-attribute Access Methods. *SIGMOD Record*, 20(3), September 1992.

[LS90] D. Lomet and B. Salzberg. The hB-Tree: A Multiattribute Indexing Method with Good Guaranteed Performance. *ACM Transactions on Database Systems*, 15(4), December 1990.

[RRR96] P. Rao, C. R. Ramakrishnan, and I. V. Ramakrishnan. A Thread in Time Saves Tabling Time. In *Proceedings of the Joint International Conference and Symposium on Logic Programming*, 1996.

[SRF87] T. Sellis, N. Roussopoulus, and C. Faloutsus. The R+-Tree: A Dynamic Index for Multi-dimensional Objects. In *Proceedings of the International Conference on Very Large Data Bases (VLDB)*, 1987.

[TS86] H. Tamaki and T. Sato. OLD Resolution with Tabulation. In *International Conference on Logic Programming*, pages 84–98, 1986.

Modelling and Reasoning about Multi-dimensional Information

M. A. Orgun

Department of Computing, Macquarie University, Sydney, NSW 2109, Australia
mehmet@mpce.mq.edu.au

Abstract. This paper presents a formalism based on logic programming for modelling and reasoning about multidimensional information. It is supported by a rule-based system based on multidimensional logic. It can be used in applications such as multidimensional spreadsheets and multidimensional databases usually found in decision suport systems. In order to enhance the appreciation of representations and computations in the rule-based system, we also propose a flexible visual user interface (VUI) allowing the user to view and analyse a multidimensional object from different viewpoints.

1 Introduction

Multidimensional information is pervasive in many computer applications, for example, time series, geographical information and data warehousing. Such applications also demand sophisticated techniques for the representation and manipulation of multidimensional information, which is context-sensitive by nature. However, most of the proposed approaches to modelling multi-dimensional information have been application-dependent, severely lacking a clear and well-defined underlying formalism. Hence they do not easily generalise to other application domains [2, 6]. These shortcomings restrict their wide acceptance and use. One area of continuing research is therefore the development of an application-independent formalism capable of representing multidimensional information in a natural manner.

It has been shown that non-classical logics such as temporal and modal logic provide a natural formalism for studying the properties of dynamic information in many applications. For instance, temporal logics have been successfully used in many applications such as temporal reasoning[11] and temporal databases[7]. Multidimensional logic (logics with multiple dimensions such as time, location and so on) also provide a natural formalism for reasoning about multidimensional properties of certain applications [9, 10]. In multidimensional logic, values from different contexts are combined through the use of contextual operators, not by explicit references to context. The use of a well-defined formalism based on multidimensional logics can provide an application-independent basis for modelling multidimensional information. Therefore lessons learned from one application can be potentially used in another application through generalizations and abstractions in the formalism [9, 10].

Multi-dimensional logics can also provide a formal basis for modelling multidimensional databases [5]. A recent development in database systems is the emergence of multidimensional database systems to support decision support systems [12]. Data warehousing and on-line analytical processing (OLAP) are essential elements of decision support, which has increasingly become a focus in the database industry [4]. A multidimensional view to a data warehouse is a popular conceptual model that influences database design and query engines for OLAP. Multidimensional databases are a different conceptual way of considering a relational database; it has been shown that the relational model of data, which conventional databases are based on, is not suitable for analysing data from multiple perspectives [5, 12]. For instance, the perspectives of sale values for a retail company may include dates, stores, products and so on. In the relational model, these perspective factors are stored as attributes with individual data values and together they constitute a record of a relation. However, records and relations have no clear relationships or organization in terms of perspective factors of data values. For analysis purposes, retrieving and aggregating data values based on selected perspectives, are important.

A multidimensional database is a collection of multidimensional relations (or hypercubes) defined over a number of dimensions of interest. It is not surprising, therefore, that most of the recent approaches to multidimensional data models offer hypercube-based data models. For instance, Agarwal *et al* [1] proposed a simple hypercube data model oriented towards a direct SQL implementation into a relational database. Libkin *et al* [8] defined a query language based on multidimensional arrays, which is oriented towards physical implementation. Cabibbo and Torlone [3] proposed a multidimensional data model based on *f*-tables, a logical abstraction of multidimensional arrays. These approaches, among others, are steps in the right direction towards a systematic approach to modelling multidimensional information in the database context, however, currently available multidimensional databases are not yet as powerful and widely accepted as relational databases. This failure is partly due to their lack of an *application-independent* basis whose underlying model generalized the relational model, which treats each dimension uniformly, and enables the declarative specification and optimization of queries. Multidimensional logics, enriched with features designed to cater for the special requirements of OLAP technology, have the potential to provide such a basis for multidimensional databases.

In this paper, we propose a rule-based programming language based on multidimensional logic, which can be used as a powerful tool for representing and manipulating multidimensional objects. A program of the language is a rule-based system formalizing our knowledge of a multi-dimensional target application and it can also be considered a (deductive) multidimensional database on its own right. The language is based on an executable subset of multidimensional logic[10], just like Prolog is based on an executable subset of first-order logic. We can also reason about properties of multidimensional objects in the multidimensional logic using theorem proving techniques.

In the following, section 2 summarizes the multi-dimensional logic we use in our formalism, and gives a brief introduction to multidimensional logic programs (MLP). Section 3 outlines an application of multidimensional programming to multidimensional databases. Section 4 discusses a visual user interface (VUI) in the form of a 2D spreadsheet. The VUI allows the user to view and analyse a multidimensional object from different viewpoints. Section 5 concludes the paper with a brief summary.

2 Multi-Dimensional Programming

This section discusses multi-dimensional logic ML(n), multidimensional logic programs based on ML(n) and presents an example program in 2D, that of the Sieve of Erastosthenes for generating prime numbers.

2.1 Multi-Dimensional Logic

Multi-dimensional logic is a form of modal logic [9]. The set of possible contexts (possible worlds) is modeled by $\mathcal{Z}^\omega$, the countably infinite Cartesian product $\mathcal{Z} \times \mathcal{Z} \times \mathcal{Z} \times \cdots$. For a given $x \in \mathcal{Z}^\omega$, we write $x = \langle x_0, x_1, x_2, \ldots \rangle$ where each x_k is the coordinate (value) for the kth dimension. For each dimension $k \geq 0$, there are three contextual operators: init_k, prior_k, and next_k operating on dimension k. Informally, init_k refers to the origin, prior_k the previous point, and next_k the next point, along dimension k.

The syntax of multi-dimensional logic extends that of first-order logic with three formation rules: if A is a formula, so are $\text{init}_k A$, $\text{prior}_k A$, and $\text{next}_k A$, for all $k \geq 0$. For any given $m \geq 0$, we write $\text{prior}_k[m]$ and $\text{next}_k[m]$ for m successive applications of prior_k and next_k.

We write ML(ω) for the multi-dimensional logic with countably infinite dimensions. We are especially interested in multi-dimensional logics with a finite number of dimensions. For instance, ML(n) is a logic with n dimensions (for $n \geq 0$) for which $\mathcal{Z}^n$ is the set of possible contexts. We write A^n for n-folded Cartesian product of set A.

The meaning of a formula is naturally context-dependent. The semantics of formulas of ML(ω) are provided by multidimensional interpretations [10]. A multidimensional interpretation assigns meanings at all possible contexts to all the basic elements of the language such as function and predicate symbols, and variables. Interpretations are extended upward to all elements of the language by a satisfaction relation $\models$.

2.2 MLP(n)

The basic building blocks in multi-dimensional logic programs are *contextual units* defined inductively as follows.

Definition 1.

- *All atomic formulas are contextual units.*
- *If A is a contextual unit and ∇ is a contextual operator of ML, then ∇A is a contextual unit.*

For convenience, we use upper-case letters for variables, and lower-case letters for function and predicate symbols. Program and goal clauses are defined as follows.

Definition 2.

- *A program clause is the universal closure of a clause of the form $A <- B_1, \ldots, B_m$ ($m >= 0$) where each B_i and A are contextual units.*
- *A goal clause (query) is the universal closure of a clause of the form $<- B_1, \ldots, B_m$ ($m >= 0$) where each B_i is a contextual unit.*

A multi-dimensional logic program consists of (the conjunction of) a finite set of program and unit clauses regarded as axioms true at all contexts in Z^ω.

For practical purposes, we restrict the following discussion to MLP with a finite number of dimensions. There is a dimensionality analysis technique to determine the dimensionality of a given MLP program P. The dimensionality of P is determined by the dimensionalities of the contextual operators that appear in it. If the dimensionality of P is n, then we say it is in MLP(n). We refer the reader to [10] for details.

We also need the following definitions:

Definition 3. *Let A be a contextual unit of MLP(n). We say that A is canonical if it is of the form $\text{init}_0 \nabla_0[m_0]\text{init}_1 \nabla_1[m_1]\ldots\text{init}_{n-1}\nabla_{n-1}[m_{n-1}] B$ where B is an atomic formula and each ∇_i is either next_i or prior_i.*

Definition 4. *Let $A <- B_1, \ldots, B_m$ be a program clause of MLP(n). We say that the clause is canonical if all of A and $B_1, \ldots, B_m$ are canonical contextual units. Similarly for goal clauses (queries).*

Programs in MLP(n) are executed using a proof procedure called MSLD-resolution (for multi-dimensional SLD-resolution). MSLD-resolution is applied to a set of *canonical instances* of program clauses and queries. See [10] for more details.

2.3 An Example Program in 2D

The Sieve of Erastosthenes is a popular prime number generation technique. It operates by putting all of the natural numbers from 2 onwards into a "sieve". We then perform the following steps ad infinitum:

- Remove the smallest number from the sieve. This is our prime number; and
- Remove all the multiples of this number from the sieve.

Each step naturally corresponds to a moment in time. We can model the notion of time using, say, the positive fragment of dimension 0.

Below we present a solution to generating prime numbers using the Sieve of Erastosthenes. Note that all program clauses are interpreted as assertions true at all points in the hyperfield of contexts.

```
init₁ ints(2) <- !.
next₁ ints(X) <- ints(Y), X is Y+1.

init₀ sieve(X) <- ints(X), !.
next₀ sieve(X)<- init₁ sieve(Y),smallest(X),(X mod Y)=\= 0,!.

init₁ smallest(X) <- newsmallest(X).
smallest(X) <- next₀ prior₁ sieve(Y),newsmallest(X),X =\= Y.

newsmallest(X) <- sieve(X).
newsmallest(X) <- next₁ newsmallest(X).

prime(X) <- init₁ sieve(X).
```

As shown in Figure 1, the `sieve` predicate represents all the natural numbers left in the sieve at each moment in time, along dimension 1. The `prime` predicate just picks the smallest number from the sieve at each point along dimension 0. Figure 2 shows the `prime/1` relation in two dimensions.

Since the definition of `sieve` involves contextual operators operating on dimensions 0 and 1, the value of `sieve` varies only in those dimensions while the `prime` predicate varies along dimension 0 only. The dimensionality of the program is 2, that is, it is in MLP(2).

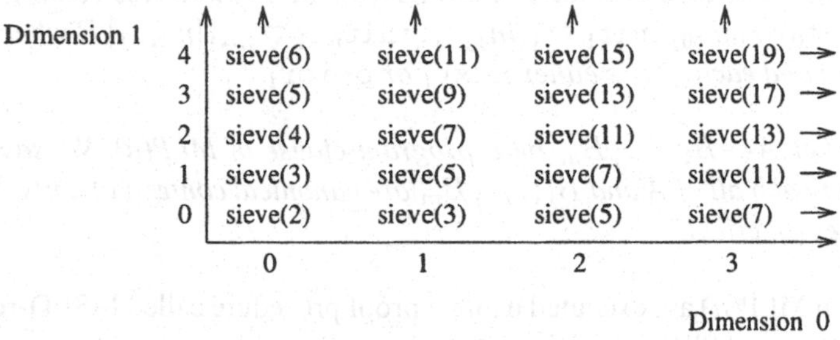

Dimension 1

4	sieve(6)	sieve(11)	sieve(15)	sieve(19)	→
3	sieve(5)	sieve(9)	sieve(13)	sieve(17)	→
2	sieve(4)	sieve(7)	sieve(11)	sieve(13)	→
1	sieve(3)	sieve(5)	sieve(7)	sieve(11)	→
0	sieve(2)	sieve(3)	sieve(5)	sieve(7)	→
	0	1	2	3	

Dimension 0

Fig. 1. The `sieve/1` relation in two dimensions

Dimension 1

4	prime(2)	prime(3)	prime(5)	prime(7)	→
3	prime(2)	prime(3)	prime(5)	prime(7)	→
2	prime(2)	prime(3)	prime(5)	prime(7)	→
1	prime(2)	prime(3)	prime(5)	prime(7)	→
0	prime(2)	prime(3)	prime(5)	prime(7)	→
	0	1	2	3	

Dimension 0

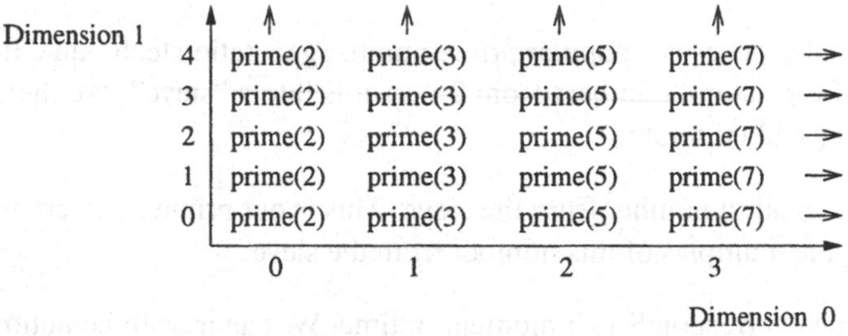

Fig. 2. The `prime/1` relation in two dimensions

Given a goal like `<- prime(X)`, the question then is how to produce the canonical instances of the goal (instances that are fixed to specific coordinates on the two dimensions) to obtain answers. Since the `prime` predicate varies only along the dimension 0, we generate the following canonical instances of the goal:

```
<- init_0 init_1 prime(X).
<- init_0 next_0[1] init_1 prime(X).
<- init_0 next_0[2] init_1 prime(X).
```

and so on. Here each X is an independent variable. However, for a given goal such as `<- sieve(X)`, there is no apriori ordering imposed on the way in which canonical instances are produced. The user should guide the implementation in generating the canonical instances of the goal.

3 Multidimensional Databases

A multidimensional database is a collection of multidimensional relations where each relation looks like a hypercube defined over a number of dimensions of interest. Each dimension may represent a perspective to data stored in say a (relational) database. For *sales* data, the dimensions of interest may be: product sold, date of sale, location of sale and so on. A sales value (eg., quantity sold) is stored in a cell in the hypercube indexed by the actual values of all the perspectives to the database. Figure 3 shows the sales hypercube in three dimensions. In the figure, not all the sales values are shown.

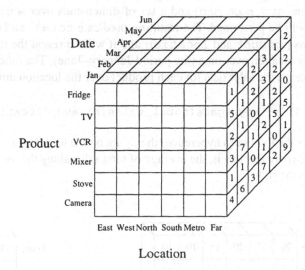

Fig. 3. Sales data over 3 dimensions

In MLP(n), each predicate naturally represents a multidimensional relation over $\mathcal{Z}^n$. Some base relations may be coming from a data warehouse (eg., a multidimensional database) and therefore do not need to be included in programs. Using MLP, we can provide a deductive capability on top of multidimensional databases.

In a multidimensional database, each dimension is defined over a finite domain of values (eg., products), which can be easily mapped to an actual dimension in MLP(n) using enumerated types as follows.

```
Dim time = {jan,feb,mar,apr,may,jun}
Dim product = {camera,stove,mixer,vcr,tv,fridge}
Dim location = {east,west,north,south,metro,far}
```

We can easily provide a mapping from the dimensions given above to dimensions in MLP(n) by providing a function, say actual, as follows:

```
actual = { time↦ 0, product↦ 1, location↦ 2}
```

Here we call date dimension as `time` dimension. In a given program, the contextual operators may be indexed by numeric dimension values or by symbolic names of the dimensions involved, eg., the operator $init_0$ is identical to $init_{product}$.

A distinctive feature of the data model for OLAP is its stress on aggregation of perspectives by one or more dimensions as a key operation [4]. Aggregation operations can be introduced into MLP(n) using meta-programming techniques. For example, consider the following clause:

```
total_sales(X) <- aggregate(sales(X), sum, {time}).
```

The `aggregate` meta-predicate takes 3 arguments, a goal argument, an aggregation function (e.g., `sum`, `avg`, `max`, `min`) and a set of dimensions over which the aggregation operation will be performed. The resulting predicate `total_sales` will only vary in dimensions `product` and `location` and it will represent the total sales for any product at any location over time (the period January–June). The following clause can be used to average the sales data for each product over the location dimension.

```
avg_sales(X) <- aggregate(total_sales(X),avg,{location}).
```

Figure 4 shows the total sales hypercube (the figure on the left). Figure 4 also shows the average sales hypercube, that is, the average of total sales along the location dimension (the figure on the right).

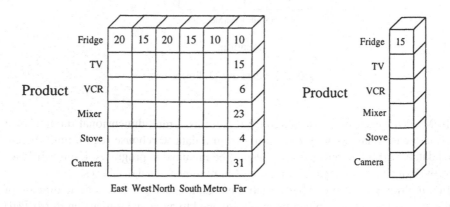

Fig. 4. Total and average sales data

Note that the above form of aggregation only works for finite dimensions (eg., time dimension over Jan–Jun). In MLP, all dimensions are infinite, therefore, we would need to provide a mapping from finite sets of index values for any given dimension to an index value over the same dimension. This approach is in line with the approach taken in OLAP technology.

4 A Visual User Interface

A spreadsheet-like 2-D visual interface is a natural choice as a visual user interface (VUI) to MLP. Each cell in the interface corresponds to a context. The interface can be used to define clauses and display results of goals. We can define a clause in a cell (context), a dimension (row or column), or the entire plane. If a context has two or more defining clauses, the finer one, say cell, will override the coarser one, say dimension.

For programs of MLP(n) where $n \geq 2$, any two dimensions can be chosen for the visual interface. This would allow the user to view a multi-dimensional object from different points of view by selecting two appropriate dimensions and their relative ordering. Any unary predicate can be designated as the *goal predicate*, that is, the predicate whose values will be displayed in the interface.

Consider the Sieve of Erastosthenes program of ML(2) given earlier. The value of sieve at each context in $\mathcal{Z} \times \mathcal{Z}$ corresponds to the value displayed in a cell in a 2D spreadsheet. We regard a 2D interface as a window through which finite portions of the infinite plane $\mathcal{Z} \times \mathcal{Z}$ can be observed. Using the interface, we can define the clause for predicate sieve(X) as follows. For all the cells on the plane, we define

```
next0 sieve(X)<- init1 sieve(Y),smallest(X),(X mod Y)=\= 0,!.
```

For all cells in column 0, we define

```
next1 ints(X) <- ints(Y), X is Y+1.
```

which override their plane definitions. Each cell definition corresponds to a canonical instance of the defined clause in that context.

Figure 5 shows how the result of the computation initiated by the open-ended goal <- sieve(X) is displayed in a 8 × 8 spreadsheet. The sieve predicate is designated as the goal predicate. Origin refers to the left-most cell in the top row, and it gives the coordinate of the possible context chosen to be displayed in that position. The cells (contexts) at which sieve(X) fails are left blank.

Consider the 3-D sales data example given earlier. If we choose product and time dimensions for the VUI, then we can view each Product's sales over time (see Figure 6). If we were interested in sales data over store locations, then we could choose the product and location dimensions for Dim.

The multidimensional interface also provides an elegant solution to the goal convention problem: canonical instances of a given open-ended goal are produced for all the cells chosen for the interface. For the above example, the following canonical instances (up to the reordering of contextual operators) would be produced:

```
Cell (d0,d1)=(0,0): <- init0 init1 sales(X)
Cell (d0,d1)=(0,1): <- init0 init1 next1 sales(X)
Cell (d0,d1)=(0,2): <- init0 init1 next1[2] sales(X)
Cell (d0,d1)=(0,3): <- init0 init1 next1[3] sales(X)
```

and so on. As mentioned before, the variable X is assumed to be different for each canonical instance.

Origin: (d0, d1) = (-1, 6)	Dim:					Goal: sieve(X)	
d1 \ d0	-1	0	1	2	3	4	5	6
6		8	15	23	29	31	37	41
5		7	13	19	23	29	31	37
4		6	11	17	19	23	29	31
3		5	9	13	17	19	23	29
2		4	7	11	13	17	19	23
1		3	5	7	11	13	17	19
0		2	3	5	7	11	13	17
-1								

Fig. 5. `sieve/1` on a 2-dimensional spreadsheet

5 Concluding Remarks

We have presented a formalism based on multidimensional logic which can be used to model and reason about multidimensional objects in a natural manner. The formalism provides an application-independent and sound basis for representing and reasoning about multidimensional properties of certain applications. Future work includes the development of the VUI which can be built on top of an implementation of MLP using a GUI. We plan to add such facilities as incremental compilation techniques to the VUI that the user will be able to see (partial) results from a rule-based system while it is still under development.

Acknowledgments

This research has been supported in part by an Australian Research Council (ARC) grant and a Macquarie University Research Grant (MURG). Thanks are also due to W. Du and R. K. Wong for many fruitful discussions.

References

1. S. Agrawal, A. Gupta, and S. Sarawagi. Modeling multidimensional databases. Technical report, IBM Almaden Research Center, San Jose, California, 1995.
2. E. A. Ashcroft, A. A. Faustini, R. Jagannathan, and W. W. Wadge. *Multidimensional Programming*. Oxford University Press, 1995.
3. L. Cabibbo and R. Torlone. Querying multidimensional databases. In *Proceedings of the Sixth Workshop on Database Programming Languages*, 1997.
4. S. Chaudhuri and U. Dayal. An overview of data warehousing and OLAP technology. *SIGMOD RECORD*, 26(1):65–74, 1997.

d1 \\ d0	0	1	2	3	4	5	6	7
5	1	1	2	3	1	2		
4	5	1	2	3	2	2		
3	2	1	0	1	2	0		
2	3	7	1	2	5	5		
1	1	1	0	1	0	1		
0	4	6	3	7	2	9		
-1								
-2								

Origin: (d0, d1) = (0,6)   Dim: (time,product)   Goal: sales(X)

Fig. 6. `sales/1` over product and time dimensions

5. G. Colliat. OLAP, Relational, and multidimensional database systems. *SIGMOD RECORD*, 25(3):64–69, September 1996.
6. W. Du. MQL - A definition and query language for multidimensional databases. In *Proceedings of the Tenth International Symposium on Lucid and Intensional Programming*, University of Victoria, Britis Columbia, Canada, 1997.
7. D. Gabbay and P. McBrien. Temporal logic & historical databases. In *Proceedings of the 17th Very Large Data Bases Conference*, pages 423–430, Barcelona, Spain, September 1991. Morgan Kauffman, Los Altos, Calif.
8. L. Libkin and L. Wong. A query language for multidimensional arrays: Design, implementation and optimization techniques. In *Proceedings of the 1996 ACM SIGMOD International Conference on Management of Data*, pages 228–239. ACM Press, 1996.
9. M. Marx and Y. Venema. *Multi-dimensional modal logic*. Kluwer Academic Publishers, 1996.
10. M. A. Orgun and W. Du. Multidimensional logic programming: Theoretical foundations. *Theoretical Computer Science*, 185(2):319–345, 1997.
11. Y. Shoham. *Reasoning About Change*. MIT Press, 1988.
12. Kenan Technologies. An introduction to multidimensional database technology. http://www.kenan.com/acumate/mddb.htm.

An Interpretation for the Conditional Belief Function in the Theory of Evidence

Mieczyslaw A. Klopotek and Sławomir T. Wierzchoń

Institute of Computer Science
Polish Academmy of Sciences,
ul. Ordona 21, PL 01-237 Warsaw, Poland
Fax: (48 22) 37 65 64, Phone: (48 22) 36 28 85, 36 28 41 or 36 28 62 ext.45
e-mail: klopotek, stw@ipipan.waw.pl
http://www.ipipan.waw.pl/klopotek, štw

Abstract. The paper provides a frequency-based interpretation for conditional belief functions that overcomes the well-formedness problem of DST belief networks by identifying a class of conditional belief functions for which well-formedness is granted.
Key words: Knowledge Representation and Integration, Soft Computing, evidence theory, graphoidal structures, conditional belief functions, well-formedness

1 Introduction

It is commonly acknowledged that we need to accept and handle uncertainty when reasoning with real world data, including vagueness and incompleteness of knowledge. The Mathematical Theory of Evidence or the Dempster-Shafer Theory (DST) [2, 14] has been intensely investigated in the past as a means of expressing incomplete knowledge. A number of implementations in various fields apparently confirm the usefulness of this model of representation and processing of uncertainty (e.g. reliability in real-time X-ray radioscopy and ultrasounds [3], multisensor image segmentation [1], safety control in large plants [4], map construction and maintenance [12], just to mention a few).

The belief functions in DST formally fit into the framework of VBS system [15, 9] which enables efficient reasoning by local computations [15, 18]. VBS implies however a concept of conditional belief functions which possess negative valued probability masses. Hence it is generally unusable for representation of belief functions in learning and sample generation as composition of conditional belief functions is not granted to yield joint multivariate belief distribution [6, 15, 17]. We call this the well-formedness problem of decomposition into conditional belief functions. The paper provides a frequency-based (probability- based) interpretation for conditional belief functions that overcomes this difficulty by identifying a class of conditional belief functions for which well-formedness is granted.

Let us recall the definition of a DST (Bayesian) belief network, based on the graphoidal properties of a DST belief function.

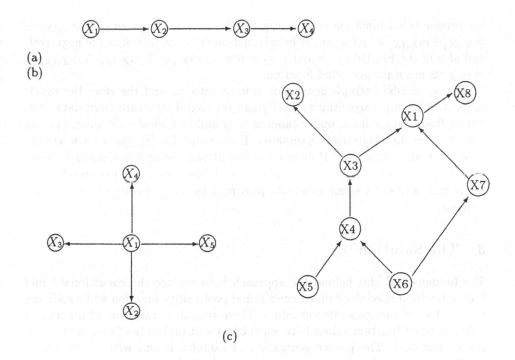

(a)

(b)

(c)

Fig. 1. a) A chain-like Bayesian network. b) A star-like Bayesian network c) A general Bayesian network, with generated data available at $http://www.ipipan.waw.pl/~klopotek/ds/szampony.zip$

Definition 1 *[10] A DST (Bayesian) belief network is a pair (D, Bel) where D is a dag (directed acyclic graph) and Bel is a belief function called the underlying distribution. Each node i in D corresponds to a variable X_i in Bel, a set of nodes I corresponds to a set of variables X_I and x_i, x_I denote values drawn from the domain of X_i and from the (cross product) domain of X_I respectively. Each node in the network is regarded as a storage cell for any distribution $Bel^{\downarrow\{X_i\}\cup X_{\pi(i)}|X_{\pi(i)}}$ where $X_{\pi(i)}$ is a set of nodes corresponding to the parent nodes $\pi(i)$ of i. The underlying distribution represented by a DST (Bayesian) belief network is computed via:*

$$Bel = \bigoplus_{i=1}^{n} (Bel^{\downarrow\{X_i\}\cup X_{\pi(i)}})^{|X_{\pi(i)}}$$

2 The problem

The well-formedness problem of belief networks for DST has been illustrated in [7]. For Bayesian networks in Fig.1a) and b), we can construct such conditional probabilities that marginals of all variables are identical, and at the same time in Fig.1a) $m_{X_1} \oplus m_{X_2|X_1} \oplus m_{X_3|X_2}$ and in Fig.1b) $m_{X_1} \oplus m_{X_2|X_1} \oplus m_{X_3|X_1} \oplus m_{X_4|X_1}$

are proper belief functions; but in Fig.1a) the function $m = m_{X_1} \oplus m_{X_2|X_1} \oplus m_{X_3|X_2} \oplus m_{X_4|X_3}$ is not a proper belief function (some values of m are negative); and also in the Fig.1b) the function $m = m_{X_1} \oplus m_{X_2|X_1} \oplus m_{X_3|X_1} \oplus m_{X_4|X_1} \oplus m_{X_5|X_1}$ is not a proper belief function.

Hence, in DST, sample generation from a network and therefore the development of learning algorithms identifying graphoidal structure from data, reasoning from sample data, understanding of causality and of mechanisms giving rise to belief distributions is hampered. E.g. except for [8], the known sample generation algorithms [5, 11] do not use conditional belief functions and therefore (1) conditional independence between variables cannot be pre-specified for the sample and (2) a single generator pass may fail to generate a single sample element.

3 The Solution

The fundamental idea behind the approach is to replace the conditional belief function with a specially defined conditional probability function while splitting some values of variables into subvalues. These subvalues take care of differences between belief function values between subsets and supersets of elementary values of variables. The proper generation of samples is run with these special conditional probability functions in a very traditional way, and after completion of sample generation the split values are again joined.

The main difficulties we encounter with handling conditional belief functions is that the conditional independence in DST is radically different from probabilistic independence and that the conditional mass functions m take negative values.

To overcome negativeness, we assume that the conditional belief functions are represented in terms of so-called K functions as introduced in [8]. Given that X is the set of all variables in the conditional belief function and q the set of conditioning variables, we have:

$$K_{|q}(A) = \sum_{B; A^{\downarrow q} \subseteq B^{\downarrow q}, A^{\downarrow X-q}=B^{\downarrow X-q},} m(B)$$

For example, given m in table 1 (a) we get K in table 1 (b): K-function is nonnegative. For any level of conditioning variables the conditioned variables form a probability distribution.

To justify our approach, we assume that a (large) sample has been generated from a Bayesian network. We have as the result a sample of independent individuals. Now these individuals start to interact (note that after that process they stop to be independent in statistical sense). We assume that objects merge if they differ only by the value of a single attribute. In Fig. 2 we indicate this with the assumption that the objects differ by the value of an attribute X1 (called "current") and share the values of the collection of attributes Xa preceding X1 in the Bayesian network and of Xp succeeding it in the Bayesian network. Out of two objects we get a single one with a set-valued attribute X1={k,l}. These

Table 1. A conditional mass function m (a) and its corresponding cumulative mass function K (b).

<table>
<tr><td colspan="3">

(a)

X1	X2	m
{a} ×	{a}	0.166667
{a} ×	{b}	-0.0833333
{a} ×	{a,b}	-0.0833333
{b} ×	{a}	-0.0833333
{b} ×	{b}	0.166667
{b} ×	{a,b}	-0.0833333
{a,b} ×	{a}	0.35
{a,b} ×	{b}	0.35
{a,b} ×	{a,b}	0.3

</td><td colspan="3">

(b)

X1	X2	K
{a} ×	{a}	0.516667
{a} ×	{b}	0.266667
{a} ×	{a,b}	0.216667
{b} ×	{a}	0.266667
{b} ×	{b}	0.516667
{b} ×	{a,b}	0.216667
{a,b} ×	{a}	0.35
{a,b} ×	{b}	0.35
{a,b} ×	{a,b}	0.3

</td></tr>
</table>

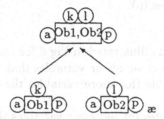

Fig. 2. Merging two objects with common predecessor attribute values (a) successor attribute values (p) and distinct current values (k and l)

complex objects may also merge yielding still larger objects, but with the side effect of splitting into smaller ones. To get an object with a set of cardinality n ($n > 2$) as the value of the attribute X1, we need n objects with value-set cardinality $n-1$. Upon merger we get one object with value-set cardinality n and n objects with value-set cardinality $n-2$. Figs 3, 4 illustrate this for $n = 3, 4$ resp. Note that if we define an "unnormalized" commonality function Q'_{X1} as $Q'_{X1}(A) =$ number of objects with the value of X1 being superset or equal to the set A, then $Q'(A)$ remains unchanged for any A with $card(A) < n$. The proportions of objects merging should depend only on the values of parents of X1.

Finally we get a reduced number of objects. The objects then split in such a way (Fig.5) that only one of them keeps the value of X1 and Xp, and the remaining ones loose these values. We get the original number of objects. In the subpopulation of "losers" the Bayesian network process is repeated starting with the variable X1, and themerging and splitting is repeated there until the "losers" subpopulation vanishes. The same happens with respect to other variables.

As only objects of identical values of previous and successive attributes may merge, the population needs to "stratify" over the distribution of successive at-

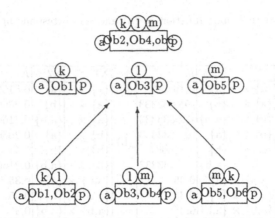

Fig. 3. Merging three "double-objects" with common predecessor attribute values (a) and successor attribute values (p).

tributes prior to merging as illustrated in Fig 6 for one direct successor variable only and Fig 7 for two direct successor variables that are conditionally independent on the current variable (for more variables the stratification proceeds by analogy).

This stratification ensures for successor variables that conditionally independent variables remain conditionally independent in the sense of DST (though they will be no more independent in the traditional statistical sense).

The requirement of split of complex objects into simple ones and re-running of the Bayesian network process ensures that conditional DST independence among predecessor variables is kept. The special merger operation retaining Q' values secures the conditional DST independence between predecessor and successor variables. Proofs of this statement will be given in a forthcoming paper.

The above argument leads to the following proposal: First we extend the set of values of every variable.

If the set Ξ_i is a set of values of an attribute X_i, then we define the set $PS(\Xi_i)$ such that it contains as elements:

1. all not empty subsets A of Ξ_i,
2. all expressions of the form $A' \copyright A''$, where A' is not empty and $A' \subset A'' \subseteq \Xi_i$ with $card(A') \geq card(A'') - 2$, and
3. all expressions of the form $A' @ A''$, where A' is not empty and $A' \subset A'' \subseteq \Xi_i$ with $card(A') = card(A'') - 1$.

Any element of the set $PS(\Xi_i)$ shall be called a V-expression. For any n let us define $PS_n(\Xi_i)$ as a union of sets:

1. $\{A\}^n$ for all not empty subsets A of Ξ_i,
2. $\{A' \copyright A''\}^n$ for all A', A'', where A' is not empty and $A' \subset A'' \subseteq \Xi_i$ with $card(A') = card(A'') - 2$, and

499

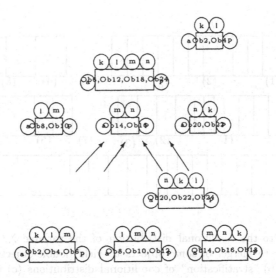

Fig. 4. Merging four "triple-objects" with common predecessor attribute values (a) and successor attribute values (p).

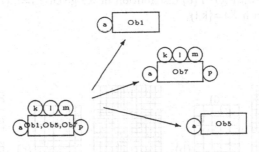

Fig. 5. Splitting a "triple-object" into three simple objects with only one retaining current and successor values.

3. $\{A'\copyright A", A'@A"\}^n - \{A'\copyright A"\}^n$ for all $A', A"$ where A' is not empty and $A' \subset A" \subseteq \Xi_i$ with $card(A') = card(A") - 1$.

So a $V(n)$-expression is a vector of n V-expressions (but not vice versa). Let $MY(A) = A$, $SU(A) = \emptyset$, $MY(A'\copyright A") = A'$, $SU(A'\copyright A") = A"$, $MY(A'@A") = A'$, $SU(A'@A") = A"$, same for $V(n)$ expressions.

We assume a positive real number α is defined.

Let X_j be a node in the belief network with n successors and let $\pi(X_j)$ be the set of its predecessors in the network. Let $K_{X_j|\pi(X_j)}$ be the K-function associated with this node. We transform it into a conditional probability function by replacing X_j with X'_j taking its values from the set of $V(n)$-expressions over the set of values of X_j, and every variable $X_i \in \pi(X_j)$ is replaced with $X_i"$ taking its values

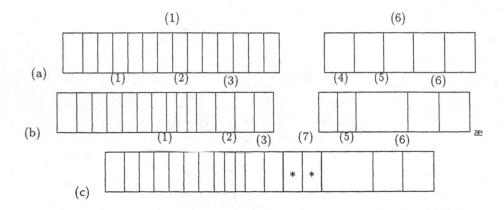

Fig. 6. Changes to the conditional distribution of the variable X2 given X1=k and given X1=l prior to merger of some objects to yield double-objects with X1={k,l}. (a) initial state (b) "stratification" of conditional distributions (c) merger. Areas (1) distribution of X2 given X1=k, (2) distribution of X2 compensating distribution of X2 given X1={k,l} to yield distribution of X2 given X1=k; with X1=k (3) distribution of X2 given X1={k,l}; with X1=k (3) distribution of X2 given X1={k,l}; with X1=l (4) distribution of X2 compensating distribution of X2 given X1={k,l} to yield distribution of X2 given X1=l; with X1=l (6) distribution of X2 given X1=l, (7) distribution of X2 given X1={k,l}; with X1={k,l},

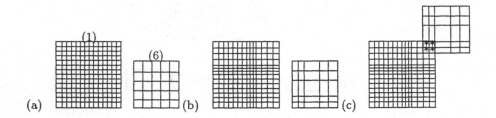

Fig. 7. Changes to the conditional distribution of the variables X2 and X3 given X1=k and given X1=l prior to merger of some objects to yield double-objects with X1={k,l}. (X2 and X3 independent given X1). (a) initial state (b) "stratification" of conditional distributions (independly for X2 and X3) (c) merger

from the set of V-expressions over the set of values of X_j. Let $x'_j, x_{i1}", \ldots, x_{ik}"$ represent any values from $PS_n(\Xi_j), PS(\Xi_{i1}), \ldots, PS(\Xi_{ik}))$. $P(x'_j | x_{i1}", \ldots, x_{ik}")$ is calculated as follows:

1. If $SU(x_{i1}") = \ldots = SU(x_{ik}") = \emptyset$ then for any subset of values s from the domain of X_j $\sum_{x'_j; MY(x'_j)=s} P(x'_j | x_{i1}", \ldots, x_{ik}") = K_{X_j | \pi(X_j)}(x'_j | x_{i1}", \ldots, x_{ik}")$.

2. $P(A' \copyright A" | x_{i1}", \ldots, x_{ik}")) = \sum_{x'_j; A" \subseteq MY(x_j)} P(x'_j | x_{i1}", \ldots, x_{ik}"))$ for all $A', A"$, where A' is not empty and $A' \subset A" \subseteq \Xi_j$ with $card(A') = card(A") - 2$,

3. $\alpha \cdot P(A'@A"|x_{i1}",\ldots,x_{ik}")) = \sum_{x'_j;A"\subseteq MY(x_j)} P(x'_j|x_{i1}",\ldots,x_{ik}"))$ for all $A', A"$, where A' is not empty and $A' \subset A" \subseteq \Xi_j$ with $card(A') = card(A") - 1$,

4. If $x_{il}" = MY(x_{il}")\copyright SU(x_{il}")$ then
   $P(x'_j|x_{i1}",\ldots,x_{il}",\ldots,x_{ik}") = P(x'_j|x_{i1}",\ldots,SU(x_{il}"),\ldots,x_{ik}")$

5. if $x_{il}" = MY(x_{il}")@SU(x_{il}")$ let x^*_{il} denote either $x_{il}"$ or $SU(x_{il}")$ and otherwise let x^*_{il} denote only $x_{il}"$. if $x_{il}" = MY(x_{il}")@SU(x_{il}")$ let x^+_{il} denote $MY(x_{il}")$ and otherwise let x^+_{il} denote $x_{il}"$. Then
   $P(x'_j|x^+_{i1},\ldots,x^+_{ik}) = average_{x^*_{i1},\ldots,x^*_{ik}}(P(x'_j|x^*_{i1},\ldots,x^*_{ik}) \cdot \alpha^{count@})$ with $count@$ being the number of @ among $x_{il}"$.

To meet the well-formedness criterion, $P(x'_j|x_{i1}",\ldots,x_{ik}") \cdot \prod_{l=1..k} \gamma_k$ where

- $\gamma_l = 1$ if the variable X_{il} does not depend on any other variable in $\pi(X_j)$ and $x_{il}" = MY(x_{il}")\copyright SU(x_{il}")$ or $x_{il}" = MY(x_{il}")$
- $\gamma_l = \alpha$ if the variable X_{il} does not depend on any other variable in $\pi(X_j)$ and $x_{il}" = MY(x_{il}")@SU(x_{il}")$
- $\gamma_l = P(x_{il}"|....)$ if the variable X_{il} depends on some other variable in $\pi(X_j)$ and $x_{il}" = MY(x_{il}")\copyright SU(x_{il}")$ or $x_{il}" = MY(x_{il}")$ (for all combinations of values of variables outside of $\pi(X_j)$)
- $\gamma_l = P(x_{il}"|....) \cdot \alpha$ if the variable X_{il} depends on some other variable in $\pi(X_j)$ and $x_{il}" = MY(x_{il}")@SU(x_{il}")$ (for all combinations of values of variables outside of $\pi(X_j)$)

has to be non-negative everywhere.

If X_j is a parent of another node in the network on the $h-th$ outgoing edge, then the respective $x_j"$ acts as the $h-th$ element of the vector x'_j.

With such a transformed probability distribution we generate the sample and then replace all the V- and V(n) expressions V with $MY(V)$.

If X_j is the conditioning variable in the nth branch then the composite (vector) values act as if they were the nth component of the vector.

After random generation the variable values collapse back to what they were before.

4 Concluding Remarks

To verify the above sample generation algorithm, and hence the well-formedness criterion, a program has been implemented allowing to generate the sample from conditional belief functions and to test DST conditional independence properties of the sample. The independence test is based on a previously elaborated layered independence test [6]. The PC algorithm of Spirtes/Glymour/Scheines [16] has been successfully tested for multivariate belief distributions for samples generated by our approach. Fig.1c) represents one of the networks recovered.

References

1. Bendjebbour A., Pieczynski W.: *Traitement du Signal*, Vol. 14, No.5, 1997, pp. 453-464.
2. Dempster A.P.: *Upper and lower probabilities induced by a multi-valued mapping*, Ann. Math. Stat. 38 (1967), 325-339
3. DromignyBadin A,Rossato S,Zhu Y.M.: Radioscopic and ultrasonic data fusion via the evidence theory, *Traitement du Signal*, Vol. 14, No.5, 1997, pp.499-510.
4. Itoh M., Inagaki T.: Evidential theoretic revision of beliefs under a mixerd strategy for safety-control of a large-complex plant. *Transactions of the Society of Instrumental and Control Engineering*, Vol. 34, no.5, 1998, pp. 415-421
5. Kaempke T.: About assessing and evaluating uncertain information within the theory of evidence. Decision Support Systems 4:433-439, 1988
6. Kłopotek M.A., Matuszewski A., Wierzchoń S.T.: Overcoming negative-valued conditional belief functions when adapting traditional knowledge acquisition tools to Dempster-Shafer Theory, Proc. CESA'96 IMACS Multiconference (Conference on Expert System Applications), Lille-France, 9-12 July 1996, Vol.2, pp.948-953.
7. Kłopotek M.A.: Non-Destructive Sample Generation From Conditional Belief Functions. [in:]: Z. Bubnicki, A. Grzech eds: Proc. 13th International Conference on Systems Science. September 15-18, 1998, Wrocław. Oficyna Wydawnicza Politechniki Wrocławskiej, Wrocław 1998, Vol. I, pp 115-120.
8. Kłopotek M.A.: *Methods of Identification and Interpretations of Belief Distributions in the Dempster-Shafer Theory* (in Polish). Publisher: Institute of Computer Science, Polish Academy of Sciences, Warsaw, Poland, 1998, ISBN 83-900820-8-x.
9. Kłopotek M.A.: On (Anti)Conditional Independence in Dempster-Shafer Theory. *Journal Mathware and Softcomputing* 5(1998)1, 69-89.
10. Kłopotek M.A.: Beliefs in Markov Trees - From Local Computations to Local Valuation. [in:]R. Trappl, Ed.: *Cybernetics and Systems Research*, Proc. 12th European Meeting on Cybernetics and System Research, Vienna 5-8 April 1994, World Scientific Publishers, Vol.1. 351-358.
11. Moral S, Wilson N. Importance sampling Monte-Carlo algorithm for the calculation of Dempster-Shafer belief, Proc. 6th Int.Conf. IPMU'96, Granada 1-5.7.1996, Vol. III, pp. 1337-1344
12. Pagac D,Nebot E.M.,Durrant-Whyte H: An evidential approach to map-building for autonomous vehicles. IEEE Transactions on Robotics & Automastion, vol.14, no. 4, 1998, pp.623-629.
13. Pearl J.: *Probabilistic Reasoning in Intelligent Systems:Networks of Plausible Inference*, Morgan Kaufmann, San Mateo CA, 1988.
14. Shafer G.: *A Mathematical Theory of Evidence*, Princeton University Press, Princeton, 1976
15. Shenoy P.P.: Conditional Independence in Valuation-based Systems. *International Journal of Approximate Reasoning*, 10, 203-234, 1994.
16. Spirtes P., Glymour C., Scheines R.: *Causation, Prediction and Search*, Lecture Notes in Statistics 81, Springer-Verlag, 1993.
17. Studeny M.: Formal properties of conditional independence in different calculi of AI, Sonderforschungsbericht 343, Diskrete Strukturen in der Mathematik, Universität Bielefeld, 1994.
18. Wierzchoń S.T., Kłopotek M.A.: Modified Component Valuations in Valuation Based Systems As A Way to Optimize Query Processing. *Journal of Intelligent Information Systems* 9(1997), 157-180.

Artificial Neural Networks Aid the Design of Non-carcinogenic Azo Dyes

Les M. Sztandera[1], Charles Bock[2], Mendel Trachtman[2], and Janardhan Velga[3]

[1] Computer Science Department, Philadelphia College of Textiles and Science,
Philadelphia, PA 19144, USA
SztanderaL@philacol.edu
[2] Chemistry Department, Philadelphia College of Textiles and Science,
Philadelphia, PA 19144, USA
BockC@philacol.edu, mendel@spartan.texsci.edu
[3] Fibrous Materials Science Program, Philadelphia College of Textiles and Science,
Philadelphia, PA 19144, USA
Velga2@philacol.edu

Abstract. This research involves the integration of fuzzy entropies (used in the context of measuring uncertainty and information) with computational neural networks. An algorithm for the creation and manipulation of fuzzy entropies, extracted by a neural network from a data set, is designed and implemented. The neural network is used to find patterns in terms of structural features and properties that correspond to a desired level of activity in various azo dyes. Each molecule is described by a set of structural features, a set of physical properties and the strength of some activity under consideration. After developing an appropriate set of input parameters, the neural network is trained with selected molecules, then a search is carried out for compounds that exhibit the desired level of activity. High level molecular orbital and density functional techniques are employed to establish databases of various molecular properties required by the neural network approach.

1 Introduction

This research focuses on the use of neural networks to aid in the development of novel, state-of-the-art dyes which are of commercial importance to the U.S. textile industry. Where appropriate, modern molecular orbital (MO) and density functional (DF) techniques are employed to establish the necessary databases of molecular properties to be used in conjunction with the neural network approach.

We concentrated on: 1) using molecular modeling to establish databases of various molecular properties required as input for our neural network approach; and 2) designing and implementing a neural network architecture suitable to process these databases.

1.1 Molecular Modeling

Properties of various molecules of interest to the textile industry are established using density functional calculations at the BP/DN** computational level. This approach uses non-local corrections for the functional according to the method of Becke and Perdew [1-3]. The DN** numerical basis set is very flexible and includes polarization functions on all the atoms [4]. Complete geometry optimization with no constraints are performed on all the molecules in this research.

We decided to concentrate initially on azo dyes which account for more than 50% of the commercial dye market. One advantage of azo dyes is that they have been studied more than any other class of dyes, and a significant amount of experimental data currently exists on them [5]. This experimental data serves as a check on the results of our calculations, and also augments our database. It should be mentioned that the toxicological results of Freeman and coworkers [6] have been very useful in this regard.

Studies on approximately 50 azo derivatives were completed. We calculated a variety of molecular properties, including dipole moments, HOMO and LUMO energies, and charge distributions.

2 Neural Network Approach

In the last several years there has been a large and energetic upswing in research efforts aimed at synthesizing fuzzy logic with computational neural networks in the emerging field of soft computing in AI. The enormous success of commercial applications (primarily by Japanese companies), which are dependent to a large extend on soft computing technologies, has led to a surge of interest in these techniques for possible applications throughout the US textile industry.

The marriage of fuzzy logic with computational neural networks has a sound technical basis, because these two approaches generally attack the design of "intelligent" systems from quite different angles. Neural networks are essentially low level, computational algorithms that offer good performance in dealing with large quantities of data often required in pattern recognition and control. Fuzzy logic, introduced in 1965 by Zadeh [7], is a means for representing, manipulating and utilizing data and information that possess non-statistical uncertainty. Thus, fuzzy methods often deal with issues such as reasoning on a higher (i.e., on a semantic or linguistic) level than do neural networks. Consequently, the two technologies often complement each other: neural networks supply the brute force necessary to accommodate and interpret large amounts of data and fuzzy logic provides a structural framework that utilizes and exploits these low level results.

This research is concerned with the integration of fuzzy logic and computational neural networks. Therefore, an algorithm for the creation and manipulation of fuzzy membership functions, which have previously been learned by a neural network from some data set under consideration, is designed and implemented. In the opposite direction we are able to use fuzzy tree architecture to construct neural networks and take advantage of the learning capability of neural networks to manipulate those membership functions for classification and recognition processes. In this research, membership functions are used to calculate fuzzy entropies for measuring uncertainty and information. That is, the amount of uncertainty regarding some situation represents the total amount of potential information in this situation. The reduction of uncertainty by a certain amount (due to new evidence) indicates the gain of an equal amount of information.

2.1 Fuzzy Entropy Measures

In general, a fuzzy entropy measure is a function $f: P(X) \rightarrow R$, where $P(X)$ denotes the set of all fuzzy subsets of X. That is, the function f assigns a value $f(A)$ to each fuzzy subset A of X that characterizes the degree of fuzziness of A. Thus, f is a set-to-point map, or in other words, a fuzzy set defined on fuzzy sets [8].

DeLuca and Termini [9] first axiomatized non-probabilistic entropy. Their axioms are intuitive and have been widely accepted in the fuzzy literature. We adopt them here. In order to qualify as a meaningful measure of fuzziness, f must satisfy the following axiomatic requirements:

Axiom 1. $f(A) = 0$ if and only if A is a crisp (non-fuzzy) set.
Axiom 2. $f(A)$ assumes the maximum if and only if A is maximally fuzzy.
Axiom 3. If A is less fuzzy than B, then $f(A) \leq f(B)$.
Axiom 4. $f(A) = f(A^C)$.

Only the first axiom is unique; axioms two and three depend on the meaning given to he concept of the degree of fuzziness. For example, assume that the "less fuzzy" relation is defined, after DeLuca and Termini [9], as follows:

$$\mu_A(x) \leq \mu_B(x) \text{ for } \mu_B(x) \leq 1/2$$

$$\mu_A(x) \geq \mu_B(x) \text{ for } \mu_B(x) \geq 1/2,$$

and the term maximally fuzzy is defined by the membership grade 0.5 for all $x \in X$. Motivated by the classical Shannon entropy function DeLuca and Termini proposed the following fuzzy entropy function [9]:

$$f(A) = -\sum (\mu_A(x)\log_2\mu_A(x) + (1 - (\mu_A(x))\log_2 (1 - \mu_A(x))).$$

Its normalized version is given by $f(A)/ |X|$, where $|X|$ denotes the cardinality of the universal set X. Similarly, taking into account the distance from set A to its complement A^C another measure of fuzziness, referred to as an index of fuzziness [10], can be introduced. If the "less fuzzy" relation of axiom 3 is defined by:

$$\mu_C(x) = 0 \text{ if } \mu_A(x) \leq 1/2$$

$$\mu_C(x) = 1 \text{ if } \mu_A(x) > 1/2,$$

where C is the crisp set nearest to the fuzzy set A, then the measure of fuzziness is expressed by the function [10]:

$$f(A) = \sum (\mu_A(x) - \mu_C(x))$$

when the Hamming distance is used, and by the function [10]:

$$f(A) = (\sum (\mu_A(x) - \mu_C(x))^2)^{1/2}$$

when the Euclidean distance is employed.

It is clear that other metric distances may be used as well [11]. For example, the Minkowski class of distances yields a class of fuzzy measures:

$$f_w(A) = (\sum (\mu_A(x) - \mu_C(x))^w)^{1/w}$$

where $w \in [1, \infty)$.

However, both DeLuca and Termini measure, and Kaufmann measure are only special cases of measures sugested by Knopfmacher [12] and Loo [13], expressed in the form [11]:

$$f(A) = h(\sum g_x(\mu_A(x))),$$

where g_x ($x \in X$) are functions

$$g_x : [0, 1] \rightarrow R^+,$$

which are all monotonically increasing in [0, 0.5], monotonically decreasing in [0.5, 1], and satisfy the requirements that $g_x(0) = g_x(1) = 0$, and that $g_x(0.5)$ is the unique maximum of g_x, and h is a monotonically increasing function.

It has been shown that the degree of fuzziness of a fuzzy set can be expressed in terms of the lack of distinction between the set and its complement [14-16]. It has been also established that a general class of measures of fuzziness based on this lack of distinction is exactly the same as the class of measures of fuzziness expressed in terms of a metric distance based on some form of aggregating the individual differences [11]:

$$f_C(A) = |X| - \sum (\mu_A(x) - c(\mu_A(x))).$$

To obtain the normalized version of a fuzzy entropy the above expression is divided by the cardinality of a fuzzy set.

The previous definitions can also be extended to infinite sets [11].

Another fuzzy entropy measure was proposed and investigated by Kosko [8, 17]. He established that

$$f(A) = (\sum\text{count } (A \cap A^C)) / (\sum\text{count } (A \cup A^C)),$$

where $\sum$count (sigma-count) is a fuzzy cardinality [18, 19].

Kosko [17] claims that his entropy measure, and corresponding fuzzy entropy theorem does not hold when we substitute Zadeh's operations [7] with any other generalized fuzzy operations. If any of the generalized Dombi's operations [20] are used, the resulting measure is an entropy measure, it is maximized, however it does not equal unity at the midpoints [21].

The generalized Dombi's operations proved to do well in different applications, and were used by Sztandera [22] for detecting coronary artery disease, and were suggested for image analysis by Sztandera [23]. However, we still have to use Zadeh's complement [7], since the Kosko's theorem does not hold for any other class of fuzzy complements.

2.2 A New Concept of Fuzzy Entropy

In our experiments we used fuzzy entropy suggested by Kosko [17] and generalized fuzzy operations introduced by Dombi [20].

Generalized Dombi's operations form one of the several classes of functions, which possess appropriate axiomatic properties of fuzzy unions and intersections. The operations are defined below. From our experience the parameter $\lambda = 4$ gives the best results [21].

Dombi's Fuzzy Union

$$\{1 + [(1/\mu_A(x) - 1)^{-\lambda} + [(1/\mu_B(x) - 1)^{-\lambda}]^{-1/\lambda}\}^{-1}$$

where λ is a parameter by which different unions are distinguished, and $\lambda \in (0, \infty)$.

Dombi's Fuzzy Intersection

$$\{1 + [(1/\mu_A(x) - 1)^{\lambda} + [(1/\mu_B(x) - 1)^{\lambda}]^{1/\lambda}\}^{-1}$$

where λ is a parameter by which different intersections are distinguished, and $\lambda \in (0, \infty)$.

It is interesting to examine the properties of these operations. By definition, generalized fuzzy union and intersection operations are commutative, associative, and monotonic. It can be shown that they neither satisfy the law of the excluded middle nor the law of contradiction. They are also not idempotent, nor distributive. However, they are continuous and satisfy the de Morgan's laws (when the standard Zadeh's complement is used)[20]. Zadeh's complement (c(a) = 1 - a) is by definition monotonic nonincreasing. It is also continuous and involutive. Other properties and the proofs can be found in Dombi's [20] and Zadeh's [7] papers.

3 Feed-Forward Neural Network Architecture

The proposed algorithm generates a feed forward network architecture for a given data set, and after having generated fuzzy entropies at each node of the network, it switches to fuzzy decision making on those entropies. The nodes and hidden layers are added until a learning task is accomplished. The algorithm operates on numerical data and equates a decision tree with a hidden layer of a neural network [21]. A learning strategy used in this approach is based on achieving the optimal goodness function. This process of optimization of the goodness function translates into adding new nodes to the network until the desired values are achieved. When this is the case then all training examples are regarded as correctly recognized. The incorporation of fuzzy entropies into the algorithm seems to result in a drastic reduction of the number of nodes in the network, and in decrease of the convergence time. Connections between the nodes have a "cost" function being equal to the weights of a neural network. The directional vector of a hyperplane, which divides decision regions, is taken as the weight vector of a node.

The outline of the algorithm follows:

Step i) For a given problem with N samples, choose a random initial weight vector .

Step ii) Make use of learning rule

$$\Delta w_{ij} = - \rho \, \partial f(F)/\partial \, w_{ij}$$

where ρ is a learning rate, $f(F)$ is a fuzzy entropy function; and search for a hyperplane that minimizes the fuzzy entropy function:

$$\min f(F) = \sum N_r/N \text{ entropy}(L, r)$$

where: L - level of a decision tree, R - total number of nodes in a layer, r - number of nodes, f (F) - fuzzy entropy.

Step iii) If the minimized fuzzy entropy is not zero, but it is smaller than the previous value compute a new node in the current layer and repeat the previous step. Otherwise go to the next step.

Step iv) If there is more than one node in a layer compute a new layer with inputs from all previous nodes including the input data, then go to step ii). Otherwise terminate.

4 Azo Dye Database

In our research we conclusively demonstrated that density functional techniques can efficiently be used to investigate the structure and properties (charge distribution, band gap, logP, etc.) of a wide range of azo dyes. (Most prior calculations on dyes have used lower level semi-empirical methods). We employed the gradient-corrected density functional (Becke-Perdew) method incorporated into the Spartan 5.0 molecular modeling package [4] using the polarized numerical DN** basis set (BP/DN**//BP/DN** level), which provides an exceptionally good description of the bonding in most organic molecules. (This computational level can also be used with dyes that contain metals such as Cr, Co, Cu, etc.). The calculated structural and physicochemical properties of these dyes, augmented with experimental results (optical properties, toxicological activity, etc.) were incorporated into a database that was used to train the neural network.

Preliminary results from several trials suggest that given a collection of dye molecules, each described by a set of structural features, a set of physical properties, and the strength of some activity under consideration, a neural network algorithm could be used to find patterns in terms of the structural features and properties that correspond to a desired level of activity.

To determine the effectiveness of the proposed algorithm, the performance was evaluated on a database of molecular properties involving nearly 50 azo dyes. As a simple example, using only the detailed BP/DN** geometry of some azo dyes, in conjunction with experimental toxicological data, the network has been able to learn and differentiate between mutagenic/carcinogenic and non-mutagenic/non-carcinogenic dyes. We expect the neural network to predict the mutagenic/carcinogenic nature of other chemical structures. The resulting neural network architecture, for the example mentioned above, is shown in Figure 1. Figure 2 depicts fuzzy entropy values at all hidden nodes for the generated neural network.

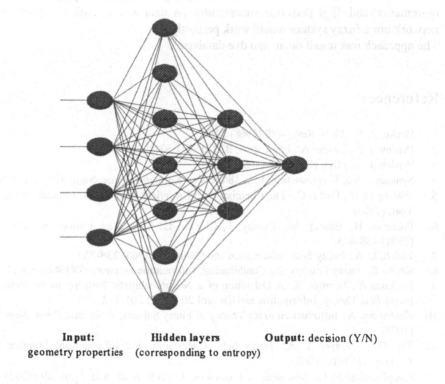

Input:　　　　**Hidden layers**　　　**Output:** decision (Y/N)
geometry properties　(corresponding to entropy)

Fig. 1. The resulting neural network architecture for indication of mutagenicity/carcinogenicity.

5 Summary

The proposed approach shows a way in which neural network technology can be used as a "tool" within the framework of a fuzzy set theory. Generating membership functions with the aid of a neural network has been shown to be an extremely powerful and promising technology. In this research, membership functions are used to calculate fuzzy entropies for measuring uncertainty and information. The proposed neural network is a building block towards combining the two soft computing paradigms. It allows for a self-generation of a neural network architecture suited for a particular problem.

The main features and advantages of the proposed approach are: 1) it is a general method of how to use numerical information, via neural networks, to provide good approximations to the membership functions; 2) it is a simple and straightforward quick-pass build-up procedure, where no time-consuming iterative training is required, resulting in much shorter design time than most of neural networks; 3) there is a lot of freedom in choosing the membership functions and corresponding fuzzy entropies; this provides flexibility for designing systems satisfying different requirements; and 4) it performs successfully on data where neither a pure neural network nor a fuzzy system would work perfectly.

The approach was tested on an azo dye database.

References

1. Becke, A. D.: Phys. Rev., A38 (1968) 3098
2. Perdew J. P., Zunger A.: Phys. Rev., B23 (1981) 5048
3. Perdew J. P.: Phys. Rev., B33 (1986) 8822
4. Spartan v. 5.0, Wavefunction, Inc., 18401 Von Karman Avenue, Suite 370, CA (1996)
5. Waring D. R., Hallas G.: The Chemistry and Application of Dyes, Plenum Press, New York (1990)
6. Freeman, H., Esancy, M., Esancy, J., Claxton L.: Color Yes, Cancer No, Chemtech (1991) 438-445
7. Zadeh, L. A.: Fuzzy Sets, Information and Control 8 (1965) 338-353
8. Kosko B.: Fuzzy Entropy and Conditioning, Information Sciences 40(1986)165-174
9. De Luca A., Termini, S.: A Definition of a Nonprobabilistic Entropy in the Setting of Fuzzy Sets Theory, Information and Control 20 (1972) 301-312
10. Kaufmann, A.: Introduction to the Theory of Fuzzy Subsets, Academic Press, New York (1975)
11. Klir G. J., Folger T. A.: Fuzzy Sets, Uncertainty and Information, Prentice Hall, Englewood Cliffs (1988)
12. Knopfmacher J.: On Measures of Fuzziness, J. Math. Anal. and Appl. 49 (1975) 529-534
13. Loo S. G.: Measures of Fuzziness, Cybernetica 20 (1977) 201-210
14. Yager R. R.: On the Measure of Fuzziness and Negation. Part I: Membership in the Unit Interval, International Journal of General Systems 5 (1979) 221-229
15. Yager R. R.: On the Measure of Fuzziness and Negation. Part II: Lattices, Information and Control 44 (1980) 236-260
16. Higashi M., Klir G. J.: On Measures of Fuzziness and Fuzzy Complements, International Journal of General Systems 8 (1982)169-180
17. Kosko B.: Neural Networks and Fuzzy Systems, Prentice Hall, Englewood Cliffs (1992)
18. Zadeh L.: A Computational Approach to Fuzzy Quantifiers in Natural Languages, Comput. Math. Appl. 9 (1983)149-184
19. Zadeh L.: The Role of Fuzzy Logic in the Management of Uncertainty in Expert Systems, Fuzzy Sets and Systems 11 (1983) 199-227

20. Dombi, J.: A General Class of Fuzzy Operators, the De Morgan Class of Fuzzy Operators and Fuzziness Measures, Fuzzy Sets and Systems 8 (1982)149-163
21. Cios K. J., Sztandera, L. M.: Continuous ID3 Algorithm with Fuzzy Entropy Measures, Proceedings of the 1st International Conference on Fuzzy Systems and Neural Networks, IEEE Press, San Diego (1992) 469- 476
22. Cios, K. J., Goodenday, L. S., Sztandera, L. M.: Hybrid Intelligence Systems for Diagnosing Coronary Stenosis, IEEE Engineering in Medicine and Biology 13 (1994) 723-729
23. Sztandera L. M.: Relative Position Among Fuzzy Subsets of an Image, M.S. Thesis, Computer Science and Engineering Department, University of Missouri-Columbia, Columbia, MO (1990)

Values of fuzzy entropy

Hidden layers of a feed-forward neural network

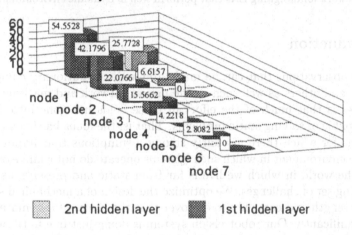

Fig. 2. Fuzzy entropy values at hidden nodes for the neural network shown in Fig. 1.

Acknowledgement

This research was supported by US Department of Commerce grant to National Textile Center. Authors acknowledge support of I98-P01 grant.

Evolving in a Changing World

Kenneth De Jong

George Mason University
Fairfax, VA 22003 USA
kdejong@gmu.edu

Abstract. There is increasing interest in using evolutionary algorithms to solve problems in which the fitness landscape is nonstationary. Not surprisingly our favorite EAs developed for static optimization problems don't fare too well in changing worlds. In this paper we explore the issues involved, identify some key elements, and provide a more structured framework for designing EAs that perform well in dynamic environments.

1 Introduction

One of the observations that can be made about the evolutionary computation community and others as well such as the neural network and machine learning communities is that much of the effort in these fields has gone into designing systems capable of solving static problems. That is, the focus has been primarily on problems for which there are fairly strong assumptions that important features of the environment in which such systems operate do not change over time. However, the world in which we live is far from static and presents us with an ever changing set of challenges. We optimize the design of a mechanical structure based on strength and cost only to discover that the prices of raw materials has changed significantly. Our robot vision system is doing just fine until new lighting is installed. An automated stock trader's performance suddenly degrades as a side effect of a foreign country's monetary crisis.

In each case human intervention is required to repose the problem and redesign the system on the basis of the changed environment. Since in many of these cases we are using evolutionary and machine learning techniques to solve the statically posed versions of these problems, a natural question is whether or not we can use these techniques to design systems capable of self-tuning over time.

In this paper we explore this possibility for the specific case of evolutionary computation. However, many of the insights obtained apply to neural networks and machine learning as well.

2 Background

It shouldn't come as much of a surprise that many of our algorithms don't perform particularly well in a changing environment. In a very real sense we have often "over fit" our algorithms to various classes of static optimization problems, with the focus on getting the representation and the operators to produce rapid convergence to (near) optimal points. However, this rapid telescoping down from a diverse initial population to a highly fit homogeneous one can be a significant detriment if the fitness landscape suddenly changes. In such cases this lack of diversity results in rather weak capabilities to respond and adapt to change.

In the evolutionary computation community there has been sporadic interest in these issues. In one of the earliest published studies Goldberg and Smith looked at biologically motivated diploid representations (two strands of genetic material) as a kind of memory function to improve the response of GAs to an environment that oscillated between two quite different landscapes (Goldberg and Smith 1987). Dasgupta and McGregor attacked this problem by modifying a GA to use a tree-structured population (sGA) in which higher level nodes control lower level ones (Dasgupta and McGregor 1992). Cobb and Grefenstette adopted a quite different strategy that introduced the notions of triggered hypermutation and random migration (Cobb and Grefenstette 1993). More recently, Angeline has looked at the ability of EP-style evolutionary algorithms to track moving optima (Angeline 1997), and Bäck has done a similar study for Evolutionary Strategies (ESs) (Bäck 1998).

Although these studies take quite different approaches to dealing with changing environments, taken collectively they present a picture with some emerging coherence. In the remainder of the paper we explore this coherence in more detail, using it to understand existing results and suggest new directions for further research.

3   Nonstationary Landscapes

One of the difficulties we encounter immediately is that the term "nonstationary landscapes" leaves us with a rather large and unstructured set of possibilities. Clearly, if landscapes are changing in arbitrarily random ways, there is likely to be a "no free lunch" result lurking in the background. Fortunately, real world problems don't appear to have such properties and exhibit patterns of change that can be discovered and exploited. There are several such representative categories that appear to be important.

The first category involves drifting landscapes whose topology doesn't change much over time. This is reflective of situations such as the control of a large chemical production process in which aging equipment, minor changes in the quality of raw materials, etc. results in gradual movement of the optimal control point over a high dimensional parameter space. The goal is to develop an algorithm capable of "tracking" this moving optimum.

A second category of interest are landscapes that are undergoing significant morphological changes over time in which interesting peaks of high fitness shrink and new regions of high fitness emerge from previously uninteresting regions. This is reflective of competitive marketplaces in which opportunities for significant profit come and go as the levels of competition change. The goal here is to develop algorithms capable of responding to such changes and maintaining high levels of fitness (profit) over time.

A third category involves landscapes that exhibit cyclic patterns in which a landscape spends most of its time repeatedly visiting a relatively small number of states. This is reflective of things involving seasonal climate changes, political election cycles, etc. The goal here is to develop algorithms capable of detecting and exploiting such cycles.

A final type of change to be considered here are those that are abrupt and discontinuous, reflective of cataclysmic events such as the effects of a power station failure on a power distribution grid or the effects of a multi-vehicle accident on traffic flow.

There are, of course, many other ways in which landscapes can be nonstationary. However, these four categories are motivated by real world problems with similar characteristics, they cover a wide range of dynamic changes, and they present distinct challenges to traditional EAs.

4   EAs for Changing Landscapes

It is helpful to illustrate these issues with very simple experimental setups. Figure 1 depicts a two state landscape in which each of the two states, A and B, are simple piecewise linear functions over the interval $[0, 4]$, and have a global maximum of 10.0 at $x = 3.5$ and $x = 0.5$ respectively.

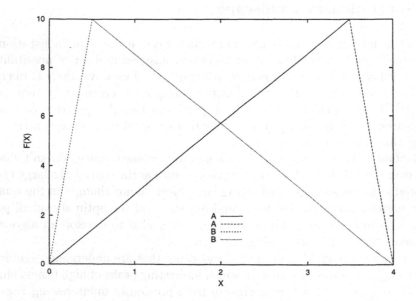

Fig. 1. A simple two state landscape.

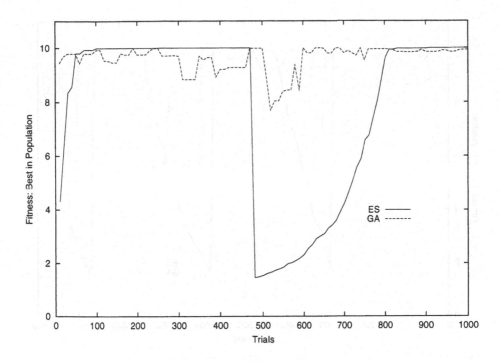

Fig. 2. EA response to a single abrupt change.

Alone, neither landscape poses a particularly difficult challenge for any EA, but abruptly switching from one to the other during evolution presents some difficulties. An interesting exercise is to try your favorite EA on something as simple as this. Figure 2 illustrates the sort of behavior you are likely to see by running two simple EAs with standard settings for 1000 trials. About half way through the landscape abruptly switches from state A to state B.

A $(1 + 10) - ES$ starts approximately in the middle of the interval $[0, 4]$ and quickly climbs to the top of A's peak located at 3.5. The disadvantage of maintaining only one parent is seen about 500 trials in when the landscape abruptly changes from A to B and the parent's fitness drops from 10 to less than 2. It does manage to recover and find the new peak at 0.5, however, more slowly than before primarily because the self-adapting mutation operator had evolved to very small step size.

By contrast, a GA (generational with a population of size 10, using fitness proportional selection) maintains a fair amount of diversity. The fact that it is non-elitist means that the fitness of the best individual in the population can actually decrease from one generation to the next yielding additional diversity. Consequently, an abrupt change has less effect on it.

Clearly there are parameter changes we could make to both algorithms that would improve their performance on such abrupt landscape changes. The point

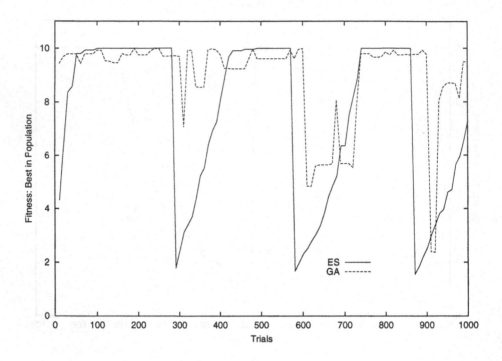

Fig. 3. EA response to oscillating change.

here is simply that tuning EAs for dynamic landscapes is likely to decrease performance on static problems and vise versa.

Additional insight can be obtained by changing the landscape dynamics slightly so that it oscillates between A and B roughly every 300 trials. Figure 3 illustrates how the same two EAs handle these dynamics. The period between landscape changes is sufficiently long that both EAs have time to recover. In the case of the ES we see a very regular oscillating pattern that corresponds to the landscape dynamics. In the case of the GA notice how each change produces a more pronounced effect and a longer recovery time. This is because after each recovery there is less diversity than before, making the population more sensitive to change.

This raises an important point. In addition to the type of nonstationarity, the rate of change of the environment relative to the evolutionary clock is also an important factor. One can imagine rates of change ranging from very rapid (within a generation) to very slow (many generations between changes). These effects are illustrated in Figure 4 in which the frequency of oscillation of our simple landscape is increased to approximately every 100 trials.

As we increase the rate of change, we see signs that both EAs are struggling to keep up. Slower and suboptimal recovery is frequently observed. As we increase the rate of change, these trends become even more evident.

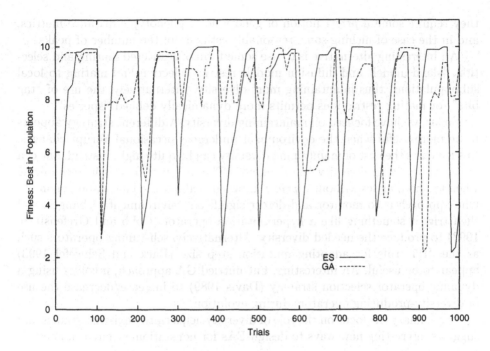

Fig. 4. EA response to more rapid oscillating change.

In a similar manner, this simple landscape can be easily modified to test the ability of an EA to track a drifting peak (e.g., between A and B), or to test its ability to handle peaks whose heights are changing (by raising/lowering A and B). In each case we see the need for modifying and tuning our EAs in quite different ways than we do for static optimization. We focus now on this issue.

4.1 The role of diversity

The dominant theme that emerges from these studies is the critical role that diversity plays in adapting to changing landscapes. However, the dynamics of the landscape determine whether an EA needs to maintain some diversity or is better off generating diversity on demand.

The need for maintaining diversity is most evident for landscapes exhibiting high rates of change. This can be accomplished in a number of ways.

The first, and most obvious, strategy is to weaken selection pressure. The difficulty with this approach is getting the right amount of selection pressure without *a priori* knowledge about the dynamics of the environment. Too much pressure (typical of many static optimizers) results in poor recovery performance. Too little pressure produces overall mediocre performance.

An alternative is to use some form of crowding or niching. Both approaches allow for strong initial selection, but restrict considerably the ability for individuals to "take over" the population. The difficulty with these approaches is that they require some *a priori* notion of genotypic or phenotypic distance metrics, and in the case of niching some reasonable estimate of the number of peaks.

An interesting alternative is to use some form of restricted mating and selection. Island models and diffusion models restrict selection and mating to local subpopulations, thus maintaining more diversity. Alternatively, the use of "tag bits" for mating restrictions permits more dynamically defined "species".

So far, we have focused on maintaining diversity. A different strategy appears to be more useful when the environment undergoes occasional abrupt changes. In such cases the cost of maintaining diversity can be quite high. Instead, one can focus on providing diversity "on demand". The difficulty here is in recognizing when the need arises without *a priori* knowledge about the landscape dynamics. One approach is to monitor and detect significant environmental changes, and then trigger something like a hypermutation operator (Cobb and Grefenstette 1993) to produce the needed diversity. Alternatively, self-tuning operators such as the "1:5" rule for adapting mutation step size (Bäck and Schwefel 1993) appear to be useful. An interesting, but untried GA approach, involves using a dynamic operator selection strategy (Davis 1989) to increase/decrease the use of diversity-producing operators during evolution.

In summary the focus on the role of diversity helps clarify existing studies and suggests interesting new ways to design EAs for nonstationary environments.

5   Conclusion

We have surveyed briefly and explored via a simple set of experiments the issues involved in applying EAs to problems involving nonstationary landscapes. We have seen that there is a fairly consistent tension between designing and tuning EAs for static optimization problems vice dynamic ones. Improving performance on one invariably decreases performance on the other.

An important insight into understanding these issues is in appreciating the key role that population diversity plays. Depending on the particular landscape dynamics, an EA may need to maintain fairly high levels of diversity or produce useful diversity when needed. This allows us to think in a more focused manner as to the kinds of mechanisms one might use to improve the performance of EA-based systems that need to operate in changing worlds.

One of the difficult open questions is how to measure performance on dynamic landscapes in more precise and meaningful ways. Most of our insights to date tend to be more visual than systematic and statistical. Having both standard measures and standard test problems is necessary for future progress.

References

[Angeline 1997] Angeline, P. (1997). Tracking extrema in dynamic environments. In *Sixth International Conference on Evolutionary Programming*, pp. 335–345. Springer Verlag.

[Bäck 1998] Bäck, T. (1998). On the behavior of evolutionary algorithms in dynamic fitness landscapes. In *IEEE International Conference on Evolutionary Computation*, pp. 446–451. IEEE Press.

[Bäck and Schwefel 1993] Bäck, T. and H.-P. Schwefel (1993). An overview of evolutionary algorithms for parameter optimization. *Evolutionary Computation 1*(1), 1–23.

[Cobb and Grefenstette 1993] Cobb, H. and J. Grefenstette (1993). Genetic algorithms for tracking changing environments. In *Fifth International Conference on Genetic Algorithms*, pp. 523–530. Morgan Kaufmann.

[Dasgupta and McGregor 1992] Dasgupta, D. and D. McGregor (1992). Nonstationary function optimization using the structured genetic algorithm. In R. Männer and B. Manderick (Eds.), *Parallel Problem Solving from Nature*, pp. 145–154. Elsevier.

[Davis 1989] Davis, L. D. (1989). Adapting operator probabilities in genetic algorithms. In *Third International Conference on Genetic Algorithms*, pp. 61–69. Morgan Kaufmann.

[Goldberg and Smith 1987] Goldberg, D. and R. Smith (1987). Nonstationary function optimization using genetic dominance and diploidy. In *Second International Conference on Genetic Algorithms*, pp. 59–68. Morgan Kaufmann.

High-Performance Data Mining on Networks of Workstations

Cosimo Anglano[1], Attilio Giordana[1], and Giuseppe Lo Bello[2]

[1] DSTA, Università del Piemonte Orientale, Alessandria, Italy
{mino,attilio}@di.unito.it
[2] Data Mining Lab, CSELT S.p.A., Torino, Italy
lobello@cselt.it

Abstract. In this paper we present G-Net, a distributed algorithm able to infer classifiers from pre-collected data, and its implementation on Networks of Workstations (NOWs). In order to effectively exploit the computing power provided by NOWs, G-Net incorporates a set of dynamic load distribution techniques that allow it to adapt its behavior to variations in the computing power due to resource contention.

1 Introduction

The induction of classification rules from a database of instances pre-classified by a teacher is a task widely investigated both in Pattern Recognition and in Artificial Intelligence. The popularity recently gained by the Knowledge Discovery and Data Mining field has brought a renovated interest on this topic, and has set up new requirements that started a new trend aimed at developing new algorithms. As a matter of fact, most Data Mining applications are characterized by huge amounts of data that exceed the capabilities of most existing algorithms. Therefore, a new generation of induction algorithms have been recently proposed in the literature. Among the emerging approaches, evolutionary algorithms are gaining more and more interest since they naturally lend themselves to exploit large computational resources such as the ones offered by networks of workstations (NOWs).

In this paper we will present G-Net [1], a distributed evolutive algorithm for learning classifiers, and we will discuss its implementation on NOWs. By using NOWs, relatively large systems can be built without massive investments in hardware resources, since NOWs are relatively inexpensive and, more importantly, already existing machines can be exploited as well. So-doing, the learning algorithm can be used to solve problems of considerable complexity without the need of massive investments in computing resources.

In order to exploit the opportunities provided by NOWs, it is necessary to develop applications able to deal with some peculiar features of these platforms. In particular, applications must be able to tolerate the effects of resource contention due to the presence of several users sharing the machines. Therefore, the main part of the work required to port G-Net on NOWs platforms was devoted to the development of techniques allowing the application to effectively deal with this issue.

The paper is organized as follows. Section 2 gives a brief presentation of the G-Net algorithm. In Section 3 we discuss the main issues that we had to face when we designed and implemented G-Net on a NOW. Section 4 presents some experimental results, and Section 5 concludes the paper.

2 The G-Net Algorithm

In this section we give a brief description of the G-Net algorithm, focusing on the logical behavior of its various computational entities (the interested reader may refer to [1] for a more detailed presentation of its features).

G-Net learns classification rules for a class h of objects starting from a dataset $D = D^+ \cup D^-$, being D^+ and D^- sets of elements belonging and not belonging to h, respectively.

G-Net has a distributed architecture that encompasses two levels. The lower level is a distributed genetic algorithm that stochastically explores the search space, while the upper level applies a coevolutive strategy [6] that directs the search process of the genetic algorithm towards globally best solutions. The above architecture (schematically depicted in Fig. 1) encompasses three kind of processes, namely Genetic Nodes (G-Nodes), Evaluator Nodes (E-Nodes), and a Supervisor Node. Each G-Node corresponds to a particular element $d \in D^+$, and

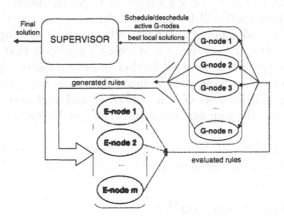

Fig. 1. Distributed architecture of G-Net

is in charge of finding rules covering d, which are stored into the G-Node's *local memory*, by executing a genetic algorithm schematically working as follows:

1. Select 2 rules from the local memory with probability proportional to their fitness;
2. Generate 2 new rules φ_1 and φ_2 by applying suitable genetic operators;
3. Send φ_1 and φ_2 to an E-Node for evaluation in order to obtain their fitness values

4. Receive from the E-Nodes a set of evaluated rules (if available) and stochastically replace some of the rules already in the local memory with them.
5. Go to step 1

As indicated in the above algorithm, E-Nodes perform *rule evaluation*: Each time a G-Node generates a new rule, sends it to an E-Node that matches it against each element of the dataset D, and assigns it a numerical quantity expressing the "goodness" of the rule (fitness). When the evaluation of a rule is completed, the E-Node broadcasts it to all the G-Nodes, so during Step 4 of the genetic algorithm a G-Node may receive also rules generated by other G-Nodes. G-Nodes and E-Nodes work asynchronously, that is a G-Node can continue generating new rules while already-generated ones are still under evaluation.

The Supervisor Node coordinates the execution of the various G-Nodes according to the coevolutive strategy. Its activity basically goes through a cycle (called *macro-cycle*), having period measured in terms of iterations performed by the G-Nodes (*micro-cycles*), in which it receives the best rules found by the G-Nodes, selects the subset of rules that together give the best classification accuracy for class h, and chooses the subset of G-Nodes that will be *active* during the next macro-cycle. As a matter of fact, although in principle all the G-Nodes might be simultaneously active if enough computational resources were available, in real situations the number of processors is limited. Since in a typical Data Mining application the number of G-Nodes ranges from hundred of thousands to several millions, it is evident that even a very large NOW cannot provide enough resources, so each machine will be shared among several G-Nodes. In order to deal with this issue, only a subset of G-Nodes (henceforth referred to as *G-Nodes working pool*) will be activated during each macro-cycle, and the composition of the working pool is dynamically varied by the Supervisor (across different macro-cycles) by means of a stochastic criterion that tends to favor those G-Nodes whose best rules need further improvement (see [1] for more details). The size of the working pool is specified by the user, and the duration of a macro-cycle is defined as $G \times \mu$, where G and μ denote the number of active G-Nodes and the number of micro-cycles per G-Node per macro-cycle, respectively.

The execution of the algorithm terminates when the quality of the found classifier does not improve for an assigned number of macro-cycles.

3 Porting G-Net on NOWs

Let us now discuss the issues involved in the design of the NOW version of G-Net. Porting G-Net on a traditional parallel computing system is relatively simple, since the distributed architecture of the algorithm can be easily translated into a set of parallel processes. Our implementation, however, was targeted to NOWs, and this required to take into considerations several aspects that can be disregarded in the case of traditional parallel computers.

In particular, since the workstations making up a NOW may deliver different performance from each other, and their performance may vary over time, it was necessary to adopt a dynamic load distribution policy able to assign to each machine an amount of work proportional to its speed, and to keep the above distribution balanced during the execution of the application.

In the following of this section we present in detail the two load balancing mechanisms we introduced in G-Net.

3.1 Software Architecture

The software architecture of our implementation of G-Net on NOWs, schematically depicted in Fig. 2, encompasses two kinds of processes, namely *Searchers* (that generate rules) and *Matchers* (that perform rule evaluation).

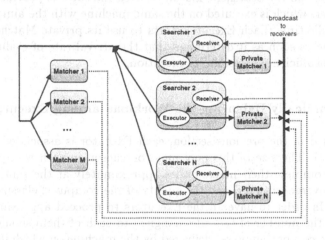

Fig. 2. Software architecture of G-Net; continuous arrows correspond to rules sent for evaluation, and dotted arrows to evaluated rules

Searcher processes are made up by two threads, called *Executor* and *Receiver*, respectively, and split among them the computation load required by the G-Nodes. In particular, each Executor receives a portion of the G-Nodes working pool (called *local working pool*), multiplexes the processor among its locally active G-Nodes, and alters across different macro-cycles the composition of the local working pool. The duration of the macro-cycle of Executor E_i is $wps(E_i) \cdot \mu$, where $wps(E_i)$ is the size of its local working pool.

The Receiver thread is in charge of receiving evaluated rules from the set of Matchers, and acts as a filter for the corresponding Executor. In particular, it does not forward to its Executor all the evaluated rules generated elsewhere (*non-local* rules) since, for the sake of convergence, it is necessary that a) the percentage of non local rules used by an Executor does not exceed a given threshold and b) the difference between the micro-cycle executed by the Executor and the micro-cycle during which the rule was generated does not exceed a predefined value (i.e., the rule is not too *old*). Finally, Matchers correspond to E-Nodes, and are in charge of evaluating on the dataset D the rules generated by the various Searchers.

The last issue that needs to be discussed is concerned with the choice of the number of Searchers and Matchers. Rather then trying to find an optimal allocation, we have followed the following approach: We require the user to specify the number of Searchers and hosts and we use a flexible allocation scheme that allows G-Net to exploit the computing power that may be left unused as a consequence of a poor distribution. In particular, given N Searchers and P hosts ($N < P$), the Searchers are scheduled on the N fastest machines, while Matchers are executed on the remaining $P - N$ machines. Since the above mapping may yield idle time on the Searchers' machines, each Executor is provided with a *private* Matcher, which is executed on the same machine with the aim of exploiting the above idle time. Each Executor starts to use its private Matcher instead of a shared one as soon as it determines that the arrival rate of evaluated rules is becoming insufficient to sustain its execution.

3.2 Dynamically Balancing the Workload among Executors

As mentioned in the previous section, each Executor is associated with a local working pool. The size of this pool must be chosen in such a way that all the Executors complete their macro-cycles approximately at the same rate, otherwise the convergence speed and the quality of the computed classifiers would be hampered. In order to have all the Executors to proceed approximately at the same pace, the number of G-Nodes assigned to each of them should be proportional to the computing power delivered by the machine on which it is allocated. Moreover, since the above power varies as the load due to other users varies, the local working pool size must vary as well. To achieve this goal, we have developed a dynamic load balancing algorithm based on the *hydrodynamic approach* proposed by Hui and Chanson [4].

The hydrodynamic approach defines a framework for the development of *nearest-neighbor* dynamic load balancing algorithms, that is algorithms that allow the workstations to migrate tasks with their immediate neighbors only. Each workstation W_i is associated with two real functions, the *load* $l_i(t)$ and the *capacity* $c_i(t)$ (reflecting its workload and its speed in processing it at time t, respectively), and is represented as a cylinder having a cross-sectional area given by $c_i(t)$ and containing a quantity of liquid given by $l_i(t)$. The *height* of the liquid in cylinder i at time t is defined as $h_i(t) = l_i(t)/c_i(t)$ (for the sake of readability, in what follows we denote capacity, load, and height of workstation W_i as c_i, l_i and h_i, respectively). The network connections among workstations correspond to infinitely thin liquid channels that allow the liquid to flow from one cylinder to another. The goal of the dynamic load balancing algorithm is to distribute the liquid among the various cylinders in such a way that their heights are equal.

The load balancing algorithm developed for G-Net is executed only by Executors. In particular, given a set of Executors $\{E_1, E_2, \ldots, E_n\}$, we associate with each E_i its capacity c_i, measured in terms of micro-cycles executed per second, and its load l_i, that corresponds to the number of micro-cycles that have to be performed to complete a macro-cycle (computed as $wps(E_i) \cdot \mu$). Consequently, the height h_i corresponds to the amount of seconds needed to E_i to complete a macro-cycle, so the goal of having the same height for all the Executors corresponds, as expected, to keep the Executors proceeding at the same speed.

Initially, $wps(E_i) = c_i \cdot (\sum_{j=1}^{n} l_j / \sum_{j=1}^{n} c_j)/\mu$, so all the Executors have the same height $h_i = \sum_{j=1}^{n} l_j / \sum_{j=1}^{n} c_j$. During the execution of each macro-cycle, E_i periodically measures the average speed s_i at which it completes the micro-cycles and broadcasts it to the other Executors. At the end of each macro-cycle, E_i builds a list in which all Executors are ranked in increasing order according to their speed, and divides it into two parts of equal size. Therefore, the upper part of the list will contain *overloaded* Executors that are slower than the *underloaded* Executors contained into the lower part. If E_i is overloaded, it decreases the size of its local working pool of a suitable amount x of active G-Nodes (see below), i.e. $wps(E_i) = wps(E_i) - x$, and chooses an underloaded Executor to assign the execution of this surplus. If, conversely, E_i is underloaded, it waits for a notification, sent by some overloaded Executor, concerning the amount x of active G-Nodes that must be added to its local working pool.

Each overloaded Executor E_i whose position in the list is $pos(E_i)$ ($pos(E_i) < n/2$) balances its workload with the underloaded Executor listed at the position $n - pos(E_i) + 1$. In this way, a given underloaded Executor may be chosen only by a single overloaded Executor.

The amount of active G-Nodes sent by the overloaded Executor E_i to an underloaded Executor E_j is computed as $\gamma(c_i * c_j/(c_i + c_j))(h_i - h_j)$, where $\gamma = 0.7$ (the minimum value recommended by [4]), $c_j = 1/s_j$, and h_i is computed by setting $l_j = wps(E_j) \cdot \mu$.

3.3 Dynamically Distributing Rule Evaluations among Matchers

As discussed in Section 3.1, it is crucial for G-Net that rule distribution is performed is such a way that all the Matchers proceed at the same evaluation rate in spite of possible differences in the speed of the corresponding machines, otherwise it may happen that the work performed by the slower Matchers is completely wasted.

In order to select a suitable rule distribution policy, we have considered three different policies. The first policy, henceforth referred to as *work stealing*, was adopted in the first implementation of G-Net [1], and is based on a client/server scheme in which an Executor sends a new rule to a Matcher only if there is a Matcher immediately available for evaluation, otherwise stores it into a local FIFO queue. When a Matcher finishes to evaluate a rule, it signals to the Executor that generated it that it is willing to accept a new rule for evaluation. Each Matcher servers the various Executor in a round robin fashion, in order to avoid that an Executor has exclusive use of the Matcher resources. The rationale behind this algorithm is that faster Matchers will reply more often than slower Matchers and, consequently, will receive more rules to evaluate.

The second policy we consider is the *Join the Shortest Queue* [7] (JSQ) policy. In this case, Executors do not store locally a new rule if no free Matchers are available, but rather they send it to a Matcher as soon as it is generated. If the chosen Matcher is busy, the rule waits into a FIFO queue and is evaluated later. Each time an Executor has to send a rule, it chooses the Matcher with the shortest queue, since a shorter queue indicates that the Matcher is able to process its rules faster than Matchers with longer queues.

Finally, the last policy we analyzed is called *Join the Fastest Queue* (JFQ) [7]. This policy is similar to the JSQ one, with the difference that now an Executor chooses the Matcher that minimizes the expected time required to evaluate a new rule.

In order to evaluate the effectiveness of these policies, we have developed a discrete event simulator, and we have evaluated their performance for various scenarios. As will be shown by our results, the JFQ policy results in the best performance for various system configurations that represent the opposite extremes of the whole spectrum, so it has been chosen for use in G-Net.

Our analysis focused on two performance indices that allow to assess the suitability of each policy to the needs of G-Net. The first one is the average *rule round trip time* (RTT), defined as the time elapsing from when a rule is generated to when the evaluated rule is received by the Executor that generated it, and indicates the speed at which evaluated rules are received by the Executors. The second index is the *evaluation time range*, and is computed as follows. Let ET_{M_i} be the average time elapsing from when a rule is generated to when its evaluation is completed by M_i, and M_{min}, M_{max} the slowest and fastest Matchers, respectively. The evaluation time range is computed as $ET_{M_{max}} - ET_{M_{min}}$, and indicates the maximal difference in the speeds of Matchers and, hence, the probability of discarding rules because of their age.

Let us describe one evaluation scenario, corresponding to the graphs shown in Figs. 3 and 4, in which we have kept fixed the number of Executors (8), and we have progressively increased the number of Matchers from 8 to 24. The rule generation speed has been kept equal to a given value S_G for all the Executors. Also, we have used 4 "slow" Matchers, having an evaluation speed 100 times smaller than S_G, while we have progressively increased the number of "fast" Matchers having a speed only 5 times smaller than S_G. As can be observed from the graph in Fig. 3, all the three policies have practically the same average rule RTT, while the results for the evaluation time range (Fig. 4) are quite different. In particular, we can observe that the JSQ policy has the largest evaluation time range, that corresponds in the highest probability that evaluated rules are discarded because of their age, while the best performance is provided by the JFQ policy.

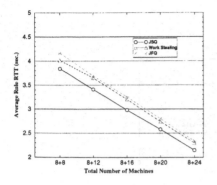

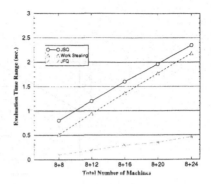

Fig. 3. Average rule RTT   **Fig. 4.** Evaluation Time Range

4 Experimental Evaluation

In this section we present some experimental results concerning the performance of G-Net on the *Mutagenesis* problem [5], for which the task consists in learning rules for discriminating substances having cancerogenetic properties on the basis of their chemical structure. This task is a specific instance of the more general problem called *Predictive Toxicology Evaluation*, recently proposed as a challenging Data Mining application [3], and is very hard since the rules are expressed using First Order Logics, and the complexity of matching formulas in First Order Logics limits the exploration capabilities of any induction system.

When assessing the performance of systems for classifiers induction, two different aspects must be considered. The first one is related to the quality of the classifiers that the system is able to find, that is expressed in terms of the number of disjuncts (rules) contained in the classifiers (the smaller the number of disjuncts, the better the classifiers) and of the relative error (misclassification of objects). In [2] we have shown that G-Net is able to find classifiers whose quality is significantly better than those generated by other systems representative of the state of the art.

The second one is instead related to the efficiency of the system, and is measured in terms of the time taken to find the above solution. The graph shown in Fig. 5 reports the speed-up obtained when running G-Net on a NOW made up by 8 PentiumII 400 Mhz PCs, connected by a switched Fast Ethernet. In the above experiments we have kept fixed the number of Searchers (2), while we have progressively increased that of Matchers (from 2 to 6). As can be seen by the graph the speed-up, although sub-optimal (because of the presence of serialization points), can be considered reasonable, meaning that G-Net's performance scaled reasonably well with the number of machines dedicated to the execution of Matchers. This is due to the fact that the evaluation task is significantly demanding in terms of computing power. Consequently, the evaluation time dominates over communication time, so an increase in the number of Matchers results in a significant reduction of the execution time.

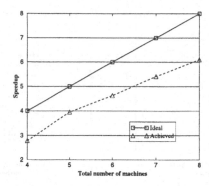

Fig. 5. Speedup achieved by G-Net on the Mutagenesis dataset

5 Conclusions

In this paper we have presented G-Net, a parallel system for learning classifiers, whose implementation has been targeted to NOWs. G-Net is able to deliver performance higher than other systems of the same type for what concerns both the quality of the found classifiers and the achieved speed-up. Thanks to the dynamic load balancing strategies it incorporates, G-Net is able to profitably exploit the computing power provided by non-dedicated NOWs, with the consequence that it can be effectively used to address real problems characterized by a very high complexity.

References

1. C. Anglano, A. Giordana, G. Lo Bello, and L. Saitta. A Network Genetic Algorithm for Concept Learning. In *Proceedings of the 7th International Conference on Genetic Algorithms*, East Lansing, MI, July 1997. Morgan Kaufman.
2. C. Anglano, A. Giordana, G. Lo Bello, and L. Saitta. An Experimental Evaluation of Coevolutive Concept Learning. In *Proceedings of the 15th International Conference on Machine Learning*, Madison, WI, July 1998. Morgan Kaufman.
3. L. Dehaspe, H. Toivonen, and R.D. King. Finding Frequent Substructures in Chemical Compounds. In *Proceedings of the 4th International Conference on Knoweldge Discovery and Data Mining*, pages 30–36, New York, NY, August 1998. AAAI Press.
4. C. Hui and S.T. Chanson. Theoretical Analysis of the Heterogeneous Dynamic Load-Balancing Problem Using a Hydrodynamic Approach. *Journal of Parallel and Distributed Computing*, 43(2), June 1997.
5. R.D. King, A. Srinivasan, and M.J.E. Stenberg. Relating chemical activity to structure: an examination of ILP successes. *New Generation Computing*, 13, 1995.
6. M.A. Potter, K.A. De Jong, and J.J. Grefenstette. A coevolutionary approach to learning sequential decision rules. In *Proceedings of the 6th International Conference on Genetic Algorithms*, pages 366–372, Pittsburgh, PA, 1995. Morgan Kaufmann.
7. R.W. Weber. On the Optimal Assignment of Customers to Parallel Servers. *Journal of Applied Probability*, 15:406–413, 1978.

Virus-Enhanced Genetic Algorithms Inspired by DNA Computing

Jan J. Mulawka, Piotr Wąsiewicz, Katarzyna Piętak

Warsaw University of Technology, Nowowiejska 15/19, Warsaw, Poland
{jml,pwas}@ipe.pw.edu.pl

Abstract. DNA computing is a new promising paradigm to develop an alternative generation of computers. Such approach is based on biochemical reactions using DNA strands which should be carefully designed. To this purpose a special DNA sequences design tool is required. The primary objective of this contribution is to present a virus-enhanced genetic algorithms for global optimization to create a set of DNA strands. The main feature of the algorithms are mechanisms included specially for searching solution space of problems with complex bounds. Formulae, describing bounds of power of sequences' sets, which satisfy criteria and estimation functions are expressed. A computer program, called Mismatch, was implemented in C++ and runs on Windows NT platform.

1 Introduction

1.1 The development of molecular computing

Traditional computer systems are implemented with electronic networks comprising transistors. This technique has been under development for recent 50 years. A couple of years ago however, a new technique of computing based on molecules (called molecular computing) has appeared [1,2,3]. In this approach different chemical compounds can be used to store and process information. The calculations are performed in vitro by adequate interpretation of chemical reactions. Investigations indicate that organic substances used in biology are well suited for this purpose, especially nucleic acids and proteins. For example DNA molecules provide high degree of selectivity of biochemical reaction and therefore can serve as an information carriers. The approach based on DNA molecules is an interesting alternative for electronic computation.

The molecular method of computing has been initiated by Adleman [1] who demonstrated how to solve NP-complete combinatorial and graph problems which are difficult for conventional computers. A number of possible applications of DNA computing has been repored so far. For example it has been demonstrated that DNA computing is suitable for programming in logic [4]. Expert systems can also be realized by this technique. In [5] implementation of the inference engine based on a backward chaining algorithm has been discussed. However, other paradigms of reasoning also may be used.

A single-strand has a phospho-sugar backbone and four bases Adenine, Thymine, Cytosine, Guanine denoted by the symbols A, T, C, and G, respectively. A double-strand may be formed of two single-strands due to hybridization or in other words annealing reaction, because A is complementary with T and C is complementary with G. Due to this reaction the oligonucleotides may connect with each other forming longer double-strand DNA chains.

1.2   Potentials of DNA computing

Molecular technology offers the following potential advantages over the classical electronic computers.

Speed of operation. In a single test tube there may exist 10^{20} DNA strands. Average reaction time of biological operation performed on a strand is 1000s. The speed of parallel operations [6] performed may amount $V=10^{14}$ MIPS. By automatization of the biological operations and by reducing the reaction time below 1000s gives a chance to speed up the performance. It should be noted that existing supercomputers comprising a couple of thousand of processors may achieve the speed up to 10^6MIPS (ASCI Red - 1,8Tflops, 9256 processors) [7].

Data capacity. Assuming that in molecular computing particular strand is coded with about 500-800 bits, data memory realized on DNA strands in a single test tube ($1dm^3$ of water solution comprises approximately 10^{20} strands) may amount to 1 bit/nm^3. It allows to achieve the memory about 10^8 times greater than current magnetic memories ($250*10^9$ bit/$inch^2$). A concept of DNA memory exceeding about 10^6 times human memory has been proposed by Baum [8]. An important feature of such approach is that the DNA memory is of an associative type.

Energy saving. In molecular technology the calculations are performed on DNA molecules. For biochemical reactions adequate temperatures are required. The energetic efficiency of these operations is high. It amounts approximately 10^{19} op/J [9] comparing to 10^9 op/J for traditional supercomputers.

2 Limitations of DNA computing

DNA computing is based on the technology of genetic engineering which suffers a number of drawbacks. DNA operations initiated by a human are using biochemical reactions prone to errors [10,11]. Unexpected results in these reactions are due to many factors such as not exact temperature, specifity of the chemical reaction performed in a solution, etc. The main factors which cause mistakes of biological operations are the following:

Extraction - 5 % errors. It may happen that during extraction unproper strand is selected. To decrease the chance for such mistake it is proposed to keep a constant amount of reacting strands in a vessel. It may be accomplished by replicating the strands during reaction. Some improvements are also achieved by making change in coding manner, by taking double quantity of the input data, etc.

Replication by PCR (Polymerase Chain Reaction) - 0,001 % errors. During biochemical reactions strands may be replicated with an error caused by different speeds in connecting complementary nucleotides.

Ligation. Sometimes it happens that ligase enzyme causes connections of unproper strands. To improve this mistake it is proposed to select the proper enzyme for a given set of DNA strands.

Annealing. In ideal case during annealing two single-strands are connected to produce double-strand of DNA. However, occasionally single strands are folding and anneal with themself, or particular pairs of strands create irregular shapes. These are so called hybridization mistakes. To eliminate annealing errors the proper coding of input data is recommended.

As follows from the above considerations in molecular computing the proper encoding and selection of DNA strands is necessary to minimize the disadvantages of biological technology.

3 Description of virus-enhanced genetic algorithm for design of DNA strands

Genetic algorithms [12] belong to techniques that can be successfully applied to NP-hard optimization problems e.g. for optimizing functions with many local and one global optima. They consist of selections and different types of genetic operations which are repeated in cycles. It is assumed that genetic algorithms search for the global optimum [13] of such functions with complex constraints. In addition our algorithm implements an idea of viruses (autonomous DNA strands) to optimization problems. We assume two different types of viruses: fitness and reproduction ones. Each of the former has a unique fixed transition position in an overwritten DNA strand and a fixed length. The latter are created during reproduction and they have no fixed position in a victim strand and random lengths. Both types have a fixed lifetime, but the latter can die if they are not effective in action this means in improving the fitness of individual by overwriting the part of its original chromosome (in order to be copied with the infected individual and infect other).

The algorithm of Fig. 1 has been applied in the task of choosing DNA sequences for molecular computing. In this problem the sequence of nucleotides is binary coded. Each of these nucleotides is described by two bits as shown in Fig. 2. They are ordered by their atomic weights.

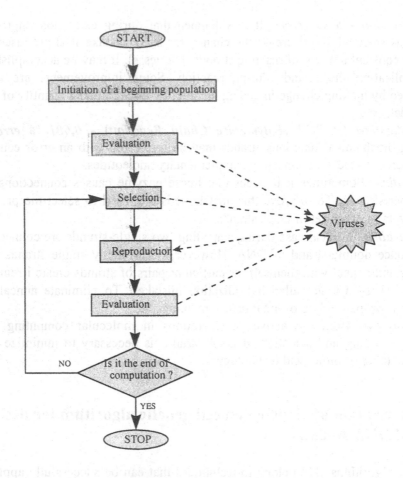

Fig. 1. The structure of a virus enhanced genetic algorithm

```
C -------> 00 -------> 288,2 [dalton]
T -------> 01 -------> 303,2 [dalton]
A -------> 10 -------> 312,2 [dalton]
G -------> 11 -------> 328,2 [dalton]
```

Fig. 2 Binary coding of nucleotides

Thus every four nucleotides are coded in one byte. In Fig. 3 a process of their coding is explained. The advantages of this approach are the following: maximum density of information makes computation more easy, one change of a bit causes a change of a non-complementary type of a nucleotide, very quick testing of complementary strings with a logic function XOR as shown below.

```
C ≡ G complementary pairs        00 XOR 11 = 11
T = A complementary pairs        01 XOR 10 = 11
```

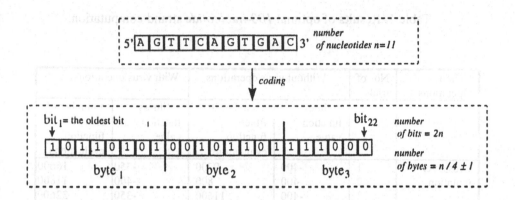

Fig. 3 The process of coding DNA strands into binary strings

Here a fitness of such strand is a number of strand mishybridizations with itself and other strands. The less mishybridizations the better value of this fitness function is obtained. It can be easy described when it is only the largest mishybridization taken into consideration and such the fitness function of a single oligonucleotide e.g. with number one is as follows

$$f_1(a_i) = -\left(100 \cdot k_{max} + 50 \cdot not\_unique - c_{min}\right)$$

where $f_1(a_i)$ - a fitness function of a DNA strand, k_{max} - length of the longest mishybridization, c_{min} - the smallest value of a fitness function in a strand population, *not_unique* - equals 1 if there are more mishybridizations with the same length, otherwise - 0. It is important to have always values above 0, therefore c_{min} is subtracted.

5 Results of Experiments

In our experiments the first task was to find one DNA strand of η nucleotides with the smallest own complementarity. The solution has to be energeticly stabilized. This means the capacity of GC pairs (%GC) has to be equal to 50% with ± *GCMaxInequality[%]*. During computation these strands are transformed into 2η binary strings and are decoded only when they are presented on a screen or written to a file. In order to have solutions within constraints connected with energy (%GC) and weight (%CT) stability before analyzing of such a string fitness this string has to be repaired.

$$\begin{cases} |gc(a_i)| \le GCMaxInequality \\ |ct(a_i)| \le CTMaxInequality \end{cases}$$

Table 1. Results of optimal *100-nucleotide* strand computation.

Genetic Operations	No of trials	Without virus operations		With virus operations	
		a fitness function value	a number of fitness function evaluations	a fitness function value	a number of fitness function evaluations
Crossover	1	-400	9700	-350	16600
mutation	2	-400	800	-400	11800
	3	-400	11600	-350	32600
	4	-400	2300	-400	7300
	5	-350	17200	-350	8400
uniform	1	-350	45700	-350	17700
crossover	2	-350	49300	-400	3800
mutation	3	-400	11500	-350	4900
	4	-400	13300	-400	400
	5	-350	23000	-350	9000
uniform	1	-350	1567	-350	2848
crossover	2	-350	3829	-350	4485
subinversion	3	-450	100	-350	3158
	4	-350	6611	-350	6120
	5	-350	2025	-350	2920

The experiments were performed with the following values of parameters of analysis

MinMatch   3   and ones of the genetic algorithm:
EnergeticRestrict   1
GCMaxInequality   10   GA_PopulationSize   100
CTMaxInequality   15   GA_NumberOfGenerations   500
    MutationProbability   0.1
    CrossoverProbability   0.4
    RVirusCreationProbability   0.5
    VirusInfectionProbability   0.2

and for $\eta=100$ and five trials, the results are depicted in Table 1.
In Fig. 5 it is shown how to process the analysis of selfcomplementarity of a strand.

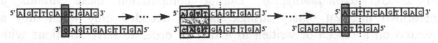

Fig. 5 Strand selfcomplementarity analysis

535

CAGACACGGCCACTCACCGGACTCTCACAGAAGCGCTCACGGAAAGATGGAA
TACTCGGGACAGAACCACAGCAAACAGGAACACACTACATACAGACGT

Fig. 6 One of the best strands selected

One of the best strings found during optimization is depicted in Fig. 6.
Value of the function fitness is equal to 350 (the longest mishybridization of
three nucleotides and there are several the same sequences).

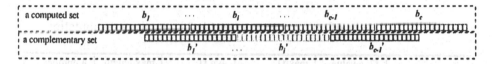

Fig. 7 The only allowed DNA set hybridization

The next task of the optimization was to find a set of $|c|$ DNA η-*nucleotide*
strands which hybridize only in one way (Fig. 7) . The process of coding into
one $2|c|\eta$ binary string is depicted in Fig. 8. Its fitness function is described by
the formula shown below.

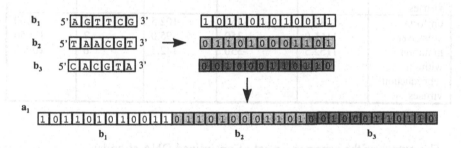

Fig. 8 Binary coding of a DNA strand set into one binary string

$$f_2(a_i) = -\left(100 \cdot k_{all\,max} + 20 \cdot others\_count\right) + f_{1\,max}(b) + \frac{\sum_{j=1}^{c} f_1(b_j)}{c}$$

where $f_2(a_i)$ - a fitness function of a DNA strand, k_{allmax} - length of the longest
mishybridization in the strand set, *others_count* - equals 1 if there are more
mishybridizations with the same length in the strand set, otherwise - 0 (for > 4
equals 4), $f_{1\,max}(b)$ - the largest value of the single strand fitness function,
$\frac{\sum_{j=1}^{c} f_1(b_j)}{c}$ - average of the single strand fitness function in the strand set.

With the same bounds and parameters for virus operations:

MaxVirusLife   10,   parameters for GA:
WeekVirus   5,
RVirusCreationProbability   0,   GoodComplementarity   2,
(these viruses cause mishybridizations)   GA_PopulationSize   20

and for $\eta = 20$ the results described in Table 2 were obtained.

Table 1. Results of optimal 20-*nucleotide* 20-strand *set* computation.

Genetic Operations	f2: a value of DNA set fitness	max f1 max. value of the single strand fitness	avg f1 avg. value of the single strand fitness	max length of mishybridization	a number of fitness function evaluations
uniform crossover mutation without reproduction viruses	-1140.0 -1175.0 -1190.0	-350 -350 -400	-110.0 -125.0 -130.0	6 7 6	6300 4400 1200
uniform crossover mutation without reproduction viruses	-1132.5 -1165.0 -1152.5	-350 -350 -350	-102.5 -95.0 -142.5	6 7 6	6000 10050 10900

The output of the program - a set of optimized DNA strands:

ACAACCTTGACGCAATTCGT   TACTAATAGAGGAAGCATCG
GTGTTGAAGGGTCTTATGTA   TAAAGCTCGGTCCCCCTGTA
GAGAAGAGGCCGTGTTCGAG   TTCGGCGAAGAATGTGCCCA
CGAAAGGCTTGGCAGGATTA   TTATCGAGTACAAGACCTAG
CATGAAGAAGTCGAACGGTA   GGTGGAGCTACGAGTCTGTT
TTGAGCTGCACTGCTTGAAC   AGTGAGAGCCGCCTATCTTA
GGCTGCTCCTGAACGTAGTT   GCAACTTACTAGCGCTATAT
TTGAGACGGCGGTACTGAGA   AGCCTACCAATGCAATCAAT
GAATCCTCCTCTAGTAGGCC   TTACGCTCTATCACACGAAC
CGCTGATGTACTGTGTTGTC   AATGATGTCTCAACGTGTCT

6 Conclusions

We have presented the method of optimizing DNA strands suitable for DNA computing by special designed genetic algorithms. In description of molecular computing, applications, profits and problems relevant to DNA-based technology were discussed and need for creation of a special DNA sequences design tool is explained. Changes in sequences of oligonucleotides can be well-controlled by viruses. They are to remember single strands with small own complementarity and within constraints connected with weight and energy stability. Viruses can have a variable length or are equal to 2η and overwrite oligonucleotides. Proper design of oligonucleotide sequences is very important for further development and applications of DNA computing.

Acknowledgments

This work was supported by the KBN Grant No 8T11F00816

References

[1] L.M. Adleman, Molecular Computation of Solutions to Combinatorial Problems, Science 266 (11/1994), 1021-1024
[2] J.J. Mulawka, Molecular Computing - promise for new generation of computers, Proc. Workshop on Circuit Theory, Signal Processing and Appl., Budapest, 94-99, Warsaw University of Technology, 1997
[3] J.J. Mulawka, P. Wąsiewicz, Obliczenia molekularne - nowy kierunek technik informacyjnych, Informatyka 7/8, 1998
[4] M. Ogihara, A. Ray, Simulating Boolean Circuits on a DNA Computer, University of Rochester, USA, 1996
[5] J.J. Mulawka, P. Borsuk , P. Węgleński: Implementation of the inference engine based on molecular computing technique, Proc. IEEE Int. Conf. Evolutionary Computation (ICEC'98), Anchorage 493-498(1998)
[6] L.M. Adleman, On Constructing a Molecular Computer, University of Southern California, Los Angeles, USA, 1995
[7] T. Glanville, The Intel ASCI Red Supercomputer, 1997
      http://www.frontiernet.net/~tglanvil/ASCI/Report.htm
[8] E. Baum, Building an Associative Memory Vastly Larger Than the Brain, Science, vol.268, 583-585, April 1996
[9] T.A. Bass, Gene Genie, 1995
      http://www.cs.princeton.edu/~dabo/biocomp/molecular.html
[10] K. Langohr, Sources of Error in DNA Computation, University of Ontario, 1997
[11] R. Lipton et al., Making DNA Computers Error Resistant, Princeton University, 1996
[12] D.E. Goldberg, Algorytmy genetyczne i ich zastosowania, WNT, 1995
[13] Z. Michalewicz, Algorytmy genetyczne + struktury danych = programy ewolucyjne, WNT, 1996

Evolutionary Approach to Non-stationary Optimisation Tasks

Krzysztof Trojanowski,[1] Zbigniew Michalewicz,[2,1]
trojanow@ipipan.waw.pl, zbyszek@uncc.edu

[1] Institute of Computer Science, Polish Academy of Sciences,
ul. Ordona 21, 01-237 Warsaw, Poland
[2] Department of Computer Science, University of North Carolina,
Charlotte, NC 28223, USA

Abstract. Most real-world applications operate in dynamic environments. In such environments often it is necessary to modify the current solution due to various changes in the environment (e.g., machine breakdowns, sickness of employees, etc). Thus it is important to investigate properties of adaptive algorithms which do not require re-start every time a change is recorded. In this paper non-stationary problems (i.e., problems, which change in time) are discussed. We describe different types of changes in the environment. A new model for non-stationary problems and a classification of these problems by the type of changes is proposed. A brief review of existing applied measures of obtained results is also presented.

1 Introduction

Most optimization algorithms assume static objective function; they search for a near-optimum solution with respect to some fixed measure (or set of measures), whether it is maximization of profits, minimization of a completion time for some tasks, minimization of production costs, etc. However, real-world applications operate in dynamic environments, where it is often necessary to modify the current solution due to various changes in the environment (e.g., machine breakdowns, sickness of employees, etc). Thus it is important to investigate properties of adaptive algorithms which do not require re-start every time a change is recorded.

We are interested in solving such non-stationary problems with evolutionary computation techniques. It would be interesting to investigate, which extensions of evolutionary algorithms are useful in these scenarios. In this paper we discuss the nature of non-stationary problems especially from the point of view of evolutionary search process.

The paper is organized as follows. In section 2 a model of a problem is proposed. The model includes stationary and non-stationary problems as well. Section 3 provides a discussion of types of changes, whereas Section 4 presents a brief review of existing approaches to non-stationary problem optimization. In Section 5 existing applied measures of obtained results are discussed. Some conclusions are drawn in section 6.

2 The Model

Most real-world optimization problems can be modelled by specifying the variables of the problem together with their domains, the objective function to be optimized, and a set of constraints the solution must satisfy. We assume that the problem has n decision variables, $\overline{x} = (x_1, \ldots, x_n)$. There is also an additional discrete variable t, which plays the role of time.[3]

Thus, a model $\mathcal{M}$ of a problem P can be expressed as:

$$\mathcal{M}(P) = (\mathcal{D}, \mathcal{F}, \mathcal{C})$$

where:

- $\mathcal{D}$ – domain of the variables of the problem. It is a $(n+1)$-dimensional search-space: $\mathcal{D} = \prod_{i=1}^{n}\langle q_i(t), r_i(t)\rangle \times \mathbb{N}$, where $x_i \in \langle q_i(t), r_i(t)\rangle$ for $1 \leq i \leq n$ ($\langle q_i(t), r_i(t)\rangle$ is a range for the i-th variable at time t).
- F – an evaluation function (implied by the problem), possibly extended by the time dimension: $F = f(\overline{x}, t) : \mathcal{D} \to R$.
- $\mathcal{C}$ – set of constraints: $\mathcal{C} = \{c_i(\overline{x}, t) \leq 0\}$, $i = 1, \ldots, v(t)$.

There are two forms of changes of the domain during the search process:

1. the intervals for domain variables can change, and
2. the number of dimensions of the search space can change in time — some variables may disappear or a new variables can be introduced.

Changes of the number of dimensions as well as changes of the of intervals for domain variables modify the nature of the problem. In that situation it is usually necessary to re-start the search procedure and to tune the optimization tool to the new problem after a change has occurred. So in further text we do not discuss this form of changes and we assume that the domains is constant in time, i.e., $q_i(t) = q_i$ and $r_i(t) = r_i$.

The model discussed above represents both stationary and non-stationary problems. The difference is in the role of time in the evaluation function and constraints. If the variable of time t is present in the formula of evaluation function, i.e., $\mathcal{F} = f(\overline{x}, t)$ or in constraint inequalities (i.e., $c_i = c_i(\overline{x}, t)$ for some i), then the model represents a non-stationary problem, otherwise we deal with a stationary one.

Note that all problems represented in the model can be divided further into six categories, since there are two categories of objective function and three categories of the set of constraints:

- the objective function may or may not depend on the time variable t, and
- the set of constraints $\mathcal{C}$ can be empty, non-empty and time independent, and non-empty and time dependent.

Table 1 provides a classification of all possible cases.

---

[3] Note, that time is continuous, however, any changes are usually recorded in discrete intervals.

Table 1. Classification of changes in a process. The symbol ∅ denotes the case where the set of constraints is empty; *const* — there are no changes in time; *var* — there are some changes in time

No.	*objective function*	*constraints*
1	*const*	∅
2	*const*	*const*
3	*const*	*var*
4	*var*	∅
5	*var*	*const*
6	*var*	*var*

The first and the second class of problems are the stationary cases, i.e., they represent situations where the problem do not have any time context. These two classes were investigated heavily in the EA community.

In 1975 De Jong studied usefulness of evolutionary techniques to five different evaluation functions which belonged to the first class of problems (i.e., the objective function is constant; the set of constraints is empty). Since that time a large group of researchers continued studying properties of evolutionary algorithms, proposed new operators of selection and variability, new population maintenance techniques, and other extensions of basic evolutionary algorithm for many different but stationary problems from the first class of problems. For the second class of problems many constraint-handling methods (e.g., methods based on preserving feasibility of solutions, penalty functions, repair algorithms, specialized operators, etc.) were proposed [15]. Clearly, the largest effort of the researchers of evolutionary computation community has been focused exclusively on these two classes of problems.

However, as discussed in Introduction, most real-world applications operate in dynamic environments, which are modeled by classes 3–6. Thus in the rest of the paper we concentrate on these.

3 Discussion of types of changes

The model of a problem discussed in the previous section introduced a time variable t. At any time there might be a change in the evaluation function or in the set of constraints. The first issue to consider is the visibility of a change. It is necessary to investigate whether the change which occurred in the environment is known to the system or if it must be detected first. In further discussion we will assume that all necessary informations about changes are given to the system and are known just after the change appeared. In the following two subsections we consider cases where a change occurs in (1) the objective function or (2) constraints of the problem.

3.1 Changes of a function landscape

Changes of a function landscape represent real-world optimization tasks where values of proposed solutions change in time and thus demand continuous optimization process. An example of a situation of this type is a (real-time) traveling salesperson problem. The level of traffic in the streets change in time respectively to the hours of a day. The salesperson plans the route taking into account the time of the journey (as a longer route can take less time than the shorter one performed on the crowded streets), and the total time depends on the time of the day. In other words, the same solution (in terms of a route) may have different merit at different times.

Changes in the function landscape can be classified in many ways. One of them is based on the regularity of changes:

1. **random changes** — where the next change of the landscape does not depend of the previous change and the time t. If changes are too large we have a situation of optimization of a completely different new problem.
2. **non-random and non-predictable changes** — where the next change do depend of the previous changes, but the dependency is so complex that we consider these changes not predictable.
3. **non-random and predictable changes** — where the change of the landscape is deterministic. This class of non-random and predictable changes can be divided into two additional subclasses: (a) cyclical changes, and (b) non-cyclical changes.

The next criterion of classification is the continuous or discrete nature of changes. We can distinguish two areas of this classification: the time of search and the search space. Changes which are continuous in time make the environment at least a little different every time we measure it. Discrete changes appear in the environment from time to time and there are periods of stagnations between them. Changes which have a continuous nature in the search space move the optimum to the other point which is close enough to be found again by the local search mechanisms without a risk of becoming trapped in a local optimum. Discrete changes in the space represent situation when optimum skips from one point to another during a single change. The distance between these two coordinates before and after skip is big enough to make the local search inefficient or too expensive.

3.2 Changes of problem constraints

Changes of a set of constraints simulate other real-world situations where some feasible solutions become unacceptable or — in the opposite case — unacceptable solutions become feasible. An example is a factory with a set of machines producing some goods. List of tasks and list of machines are the input data for a system optimizing task management in the factory. A case when some of machines break and need time to be repaired is the situation where a new constraint appears in the optimizing system. Task allocations for the broken machine are not feasible till the machine is repaired.

Changes of problem constraints can be constant or discrete in time and in the search space as well. Additionally they can be classified by the change of capacity of the feasible part of search space.

For a discrete search space $\mathcal{S}$ its capacity $V(\mathcal{S})$ is equal to the number of possible solutions in the domain; similarly, the capacity of the feasible part $V(\mathcal{F})$ is equal to the number of feasible solutions in the domain. For continuous spaces we can measure these capacities using integrals.

As the feasible part $\mathcal{F}$ of the search space is defined by a set of constraints $\mathcal{C}$ (which are time dependent), the capacity of the feasible part of the search space can change over time. For better control of constraints behavior during the search process two measures of changes can be very useful: (1) a feasible part of the search space capacity ratio, and (2) a gradient of change. Let $\rho(t)$ is a feasible search space ratio for a given time t; for dynamic constraints this ratio is a function of t:

$$\rho(t) = \frac{V(\mathcal{F}(t))}{V(\mathcal{S})}.$$

For dynamic constraints we can also measure a gradient of change $\mathcal{G}(t)$:

$$\mathcal{G}(t) = \frac{V((\mathcal{F}(t) \cup \mathcal{F}(t-1)) - (\mathcal{F}(t) \cap \mathcal{F}(t-1)))}{V(\mathcal{F}(t) \cup \mathcal{F}(t-1))}$$

It's value is in the range $\langle 0, 1 \rangle$ and equal 1 when the feasible search space changed completely and 0 when the feasible space for the time t is the same as the feasible space for the time $t-1$.

4 Existing evolutionary approaches to non-stationary problem optimization

Extensions of evolutionary algorithm to consider changes which may occur during the search process and to track the optimum efficiently in spite of this changes have been studied by several researchers over the last few years. These extensions can be grouped into three general categories:

○ Maintenance of the diversity level. The presence of many potential solutions during the evolutionary search seems to be a useful feature in optimization in changing environments. As long as some level of the population diversity is uphold we could expect the algorithm to adapt easier to changes. Hence maintaining diversity of the population could increase search performance of the algorithm.
   Among many maintaining population diversity techniques we can select:
   • sharing and crowding techniques [11, 4],
   • techniques based on the concepts of temperature and entropy [16],
   • techniques based on the concept of the age of individuals [8],
   • a random immigrants mechanism [12],

- a mechanism of variable range local search around the current locations [20].

o **Adaptation and self-adaptation mechanism.** Dynamical adjustment of the algorithm to the non-stationary environment is the next feature of the efficient optimization. So adaptive and self-adaptive techniques are the next significant extension of evolutionary algorithm [1, 3, 7]. In adaptation the parameters of the algorithm are updated using statistic or heuristic rules to determine how to update. Update of the parameters in the genetic process in parallel with searching of the optimum is called a self-adaptation. Both these techniques of parameters update were applied to non-stationary optimization tasks.

o **Redundancy of genetic material.** One of the most important abilities in adaptation to changes is reasoning from previous experiences. If we want to reason from past a place to collect experiences is needed. So the next good idea of enforcement of efficiency in dynamic optimization is adding memory structures to the algorithm.

One of the earliest forms of memory although not used for non-stationary optimization was the *tabu-search* strategy [9]. Beside TS a considerable number of other ideas using past experience and the forms of memory were proposed. We can classify them into several types [18]:

- **numerical memory** — where the modification of algorithm parameters is performed using experience of previous generations [17, 18]. This type of memory has a form of additional numerical parameters. They are updated every generation using the results of the previous search. Their influence on the search process is realized by modification of the behavior of search operators: mutation or crossover.

- **symbolic memory** — where the algorithm gradually learns from the individuals in the populations and thus constructs beliefs about the relevance of schemas (Machine Learning theory is exploited) [19]. The symbolic type of memory encodes some knowledge in its structures which have a form of rules used to guide search operators.

- **exact memory** — where existing structures are enhanced by additional genes, chromosomes (diploidy) or groups of chromosomes (polyploidy) [5, 10, 13, 16]. The memory is utilized during the search process and between the search tasks as well. Change of the current active chromosome of the individual by the data from memory is controlled by some dominance functions which behavior depends on the type of stored data (chromosomes or just single genes), the structure of memory (linear, hierarchical, etc.) and a form of access — it is common for the whole population, an individual or a single gene only.

5 Measures for comparisons of algorithms

When the problem is stationary (neither an evaluation function nor a set of constraints change in time) it is relatively easy to compare the results of various algorithms. However, when a problem is non-stationary, the situation is more complex, as it is necessary to measure not the final result (which does not exist in the continuous process of tracking the moving optimum), but rather the search process itself (e.g., its reactions to different types of changes).

In evolutionary computation community some measures of obtained results have been proposed; these measures exploited the iterational nature of the search process and the presence of continuously modified and improved population of solutions. One of the first measures were on-line and off-line performance proposed by De Jong in 1975 [6].

- **off-line performance** — is the best value in the current population averaged over the entire run. It represents the efficiency of the algorithm in the given time of run.
- **on-line performance** — is the average of all evaluation of the entire run. It shows the impact of the population on the focus of the search.

These two measures, although designed for static environments, were employed in experiments with non-stationary ones [2, 12, 20].

For results estimations of non-stationary optimization process we proposed the following two measures: *Accuracy* — *Acc* and *Adaptability* — *Ada*. They are based on a measure proposed by De Jong [6]: *off-line performance* but evaluate difference between the value of the current best individual and the optimum value instead of evaluation of the value of just the best individual.

• Accuracy — Accuracy is a measure dedicated exclusively for dynamic environments. It is a difference between the value of the current best individual in the population of the "just before the change" generation and the optimum value averaged over the entire run.

$$Acc = \frac{1}{K} \sum_{i=1}^{K} (err_{i,\tau-1})$$

• Adaptability — difference between the value of the current best individual of each generation and the optimum value averaged over the entire run.

$$Ada = \frac{1}{K} \sum_{i=1}^{K} \left[\frac{1}{\tau} \sum_{j=0}^{\tau-1} (err_{i,j}) \right]$$

where:

$err_{i,j}$ — a difference between the value of the current best individual in the population of j-th generation after the last change ($j \in [0, \tau - 1]$), and the optimum value for the fitness landscape after the i-th change ($i \in [0, K - 1]$),

τ — the number of generations between two consequtive changes,

K — the number of changes of the fitness landscape during the run.

Clearly, the smaller the measured values are (for both Accuracy and Adaptability), the better the result is. In particular, a value of 0 for Accuracy means that the algorithm found the optimum every time before the landscape was changed (i.e., τ generations were sufficient to track the optimum) On the other hand, a value of 0 for Adaptability means that the best individual in the population was at the optimum for all generations, i.,e., the optimum was never lost by the algorithm.

6 Conclusions

In this paper a model for non-stationary problems was proposed. Two components of the problem can be changed in time: evaluation function and problem constraints. We discussed and classified different types of components changes. A brief review of existing evolutionary approaches to non-stationary problem optimization was presented. They were divided into three main groups representing (1) population diversity maintenance techniques, (2) adaptation and self–adaptation techniques, and (3) redundant genetic material approaches. In the last section different measures for comparisons of obtained results were discussed. They mostly exploited the iterational nature of the search process and observed values of individuals changing in time. Some measures controlled diversity of the population of solutions which is continuously modified and improved by the algorithm. Two new measures of non-stationary optimization results were also proposed.

Acknowledgments

The research reported in this paper was supported by the ESPRIT Project 20288 Cooperation Research in Information Technology (CRIT-2): "Evolutionary Real-time Optimization System for Ecological Power Control".

References

1. Angeline, P., "Tracking Extrema in Dynamic Environments", Proceedings of the Sixth International Conference on Evolutionary Programming - EP'97, vol. 1213 in LNCS, Springer, 1997, pp 335-346.
2. Baeck, T., "On the Behavior of Evolutionary Algorithms in Dynamic Environments", Proceedings of the 5nd IEEE International Conference on Evolutionary Computation - ICEC'98, IEEE Publishing, pp 446-451.
3. Baeck, T., Schutz, M., "Intelligent Mutation Rate Control in Canonical Genetic Algorithm", Proceedings of the 9th International Symposium – ISMIS'96, vol. 1079 in LNAI, Springer, 1996, pp 158-167.
4. Cedeno, W., Vemuri, V., R., "On the Use of Niching for Dynamic Landscapes", Proceedings of the 4th IEEE International Conference on Evolutionary Computation - ICEC'97, IEEE Publishing, Inc., pp 361-366.

5. Dasgupta, D., McGregor, D. R., "Nonstationary Function Optimization using the Structured Genetic Algorithm", 2PPSN: Parallel Problem Solving from Nature, Elsevier Science Publishers B. V., 1992, pp 145-154.

6. De Jong, K., A., "An Analysis of the Behavior of a Class of Genetic Adaptive systems", (Doctoral Dissertation, University of Michigan), Dissertation Abstract International 36(10), 5140B. (University Microfilms No 76-9381).

7. Eiben, A., E., Hinterding, R., Michalewicz, Z., "Parameter Control in Evolutionary Algorithms", Technical Report TR98-07, Department of Computer Science, Leiden University, Netherlands, 1998.

8. Ghosh, A., Tsutsui, S., Tanaka, H., "Function Optimization in Nonstationary Environment using Steady-State Genetic Algorithms with Aging of Individuals", Proceedings of the 5th IEEE International Conference on Evolutionary Computation - ICEC'98, IEEE Publishing, Inc., pp 666-671.

9. Glover, F., Laguna, M., "Tabu Search" in *Modern Heuristic Techniques for Combinatorial Problems*, edited by Colin R. Reeves BSc. MPhil, Halsted Press: an Imprint of John Wiley & Sons Inc.

10. Goldberg, D., E., Smith, R., E., "Nonstationary Function Optimization Using Genetic Algorithms with Dominance and Diploidy", Proceedings of the 2nd IEEE International Conference on Genetic Algorithms - II ICGA'87, Lawrence Erlbaum Associates, pp 59-68.

11. Goldberg, D., E., Richardson, J., "Genetic Algorithms with Sharing for Multimodal Function Optimization", Proceedings of the 2nd IEEE International Conference on Genetic Algorithms - II ICGA'87, Lawrence Erlbaum Associates, pp 41-49.

12. Grefenstette, J., J., "Genetic algorithms for changing environments", Parallel Problem Solving from Nature, Elsevier Science Publishers B. V., 1992, pp 137-144.

13. Kwasnicka H., "Redundancy of Genotypes as the Way for Some Advanced Operators in Evolutionary Algorithms - Simulation Study", *VIVEK A Quarterly in Artificial Intelligence*, Vol. 10, No. 3, July 1997, National Centre for Software Technology, Mumbai, pp 2-11.

14. Michalewicz, Z., *Genetic Algorithms + Data Structures = Evolution Programs*, 3-rd edition, Springer-Verlag, New York, 1996.

15. Mori, N., Imanishi, S., Kita, H., Nishikawa, Y., "Adaptation to a Changing Environments by Means of the Memory Based Thermodynamical Genetic Algorithm", Proceedings of the 7th IEEE International Conference on Genetic Algorithms - VII ICGA'97, Morgan Kauffman, pp 299-306.

16. Reynolds R., G., Chung C., J., "Knowledge-based Self-adaptation in Evolutionary Programming using Cultural Algorithms", Proceedings of the 4th IEEE International Conference on Evolutionary Computation - ICEC'97, IEEE Publishing, Inc., pp 71-76.

17. Sebag, M., Schoenauer, M., Ravise, C., "Toward Civilized Evolution: Developing Inhibitions", Proceedings of the 7th IEEE International Conference on Genetic Algorithms - VII ICGA'97, Morgan Kauffman, pp 291-298.

18. Sebag, M., Schoenauer, M., Ravise, C., "Inductive Learning of Mutation Step-Size in Evolutionary Parameter Optimization", Proceedings of the Sixth International Conference on Evolutionary Programming - EP'97, vol. 1213 in LNCS, Springer, 1997, pp 247-261.

19. Vavak F., Fogarty T.C., Jukes K., "Learning the Local Search Range for Genetic Optimization in Nonstationary Environments" , Proceedings of the 4th IEEE International Conference on Evolutionary Computation - ICEC'97, IEEE Publishing, Inc., pp 355-360.

On Discovering Functional Relationships When Observations Are Noisy: 2D Case

J. Ćwik[1], J. Koronacki[1,2] and J.M Żytkow[1,3]

[1] Institute of Computer Science, Polish Academy of Sciences,
[2] Polish-Japanese Institute of Computer Techniques
[3] Computer Science Department, UNC Charlotte
jc, korona@ipipan.waw.pl, zytkow@uncc.edu

Abstract. A heuristic method of model selection for a nonlinear regression problem on R^2 is proposed and discussed. The method is based on combining nonparametric statistical techniques for generalized additive models with an implementation of the Equation Finder of Zembowicz and Żytkow (1992). Given the inherent instability of such approaches to model selection when data are noisy, a special procedure for stabilization of the selection is an important target of the method proposed.

1 Introduction

Discovering functional relationships from data in presence of random errors should be an inherent capability of every data mining and, more generally, knowledge discovery system. Such discoveries are particularly challenging when data carry relatively large errors. The challenge becomes aggravated when function argument is of a dimension greater than one.

In statistical terms, the problem amounts to choosing a model in a regression set-up. That is, given a random sample of pairs was: sample of random pairs $(\mathbf{x}_1, y_1), \ldots, (\mathbf{x}_n, y_n)$, where

$$y_i = f(\mathbf{x}_i) + \varepsilon_i, \tag{1}$$

$i = 1, 2, \ldots, n$, ε_i's are zero-mean random variables and f is an unknown (regression) function on R^d, $d > 1$, the task is to estimate f by a member of a given family of functions. We assume that the $\mathbf{x}_i$'s come from some probability distribution on a compact set in R^d and that they are independent of the ε's. Functions $\hat{f}$ estimating unknown f will be called predictors.

Ćwik and Koronacki (1998) have dealt with one-dimensional case, $d = 1$. In that study, the Equation Finder (EF), a discovery system of Zembowicz and Żytkow (see Zembowicz and Żytkow (1992) for a detailed description and discussion of the system and Moulet (1997) for EF's evaluation and comparisons), has been used almost directly, since EF is capable of discovering functions of one variable. The only problem was to propose and include a procedure stabilizing the choice of acceptable models for data at hand. Indeed, it was revealed by simulations that, for different samples from the same distribution, EF provides results that differ substantially from sample to sample if random errors are not small enough. This sort of instability is common to practically all the well-known methods of model selection in nonlinear regression.

To be more specific, let us recall first that EF finds "acceptable" models by means of a systematic search among polynomials of transformed data, when transformations – such as logarithm, exponent and inverse – of both the independent and response variable are conducted. The family of all models to be considered is decided upon in advance by listing possible transformations of the data and choosing the possible order of the polynomials. Initial part of simulation study by Ćwik and Koronacki (1998) consisted in generating random samples drawn from regression model (1) with fixed (and known) f's which belonged to the family of models recognizable by EF. For each fixed f, a set of samples of the same size n was generated from the same probability distribution (the distributions of ε_i's was always normal while the distribution of $\mathbf{x}_i$'s was uniform on a fixed interval). Then, for each such sample, predictors found by EF as acceptable or close to acceptable were subjected to two additional rankings, one based on the empirical mean squared error,

$$\text{EMSE} = \frac{1}{n} \sum_{i=1}^{n} (\hat{f}(x_i) - f(x_i))^2,$$

and another on the mean squared residual error,

$$\text{MSRE} = \frac{\text{SSR}}{n} = \frac{1}{n} \sum_{i=1}^{n} (y_i - \hat{f}(x_i))^2.$$

It turned out that, for each f used for data generation, each predictor's ranks based on MSRE differed substantially from sample to sample while its EMSE ranks behaved very stably. Interestingly, for most samples, the EMSE ranks were relatively low when the equation for $\hat{f}$ (with the predictor's parameters unspecified) could be made close or equal to f by properly specifying its parameters, and these ranks were relatively large when no specification of parameters of $\hat{f}$ could make the predictor close to f in the L_2 distance.

From the above observations there follows a simple idea for a more stable model selection when $d = 1$. As should have been expected, MSRE has been shown to be a poor basis for evaluating predictors' accuracy. However, for most samples, we can hope that predictors $\hat{f}$ are relatively close to f if the space searched by EF includes the right form. Thus, for most samples, such predictors can be close one to another or, to put it otherwise, to appear in clusters in a suitably defined space. Note that this last observation makes the values of the EMSE of predictors, unknown in real life situations, irrelevant. This very observation has been used to advantage by Ćwik and Koronacki (1998) who consider as acceptable those predictors which appear in clusters for most samples. Since in practice one has just one sample of data, $(\mathbf{x}_1, y_1), \ldots, (\mathbf{x}_n, y_n)$, a set of pseudosamples is first generated from the original sample by resampling combined with leave-many-out procedure, and EF is run on the speudosamples. The approach can be traced back to Breiman (1996a and 1996b).

Model selection for nonlinear regression, with suitable stabilization procedures included, is grossly aggravated when the argument's dimensionality is increased to two. In the next section, we propose to adopt the projection pursuit regression (PPR) of Friedman and Stuetzle (1981). Using PPR with one-dimensional projections turns the original regression problem into a combination of one-dimensional tasks, so that EF can then be applied. Stabilization of selection of projections is proposed and incorporated into the estimation process. At this stage of our research, the whole process of discovering functional relationship from data at hand is not yet integrated into one system. In particular, algorithms for (nonparametric) estimation of a regression function on R^2 are borrowed from the statistical system S-Plus.

Simulation results are discussed in Sect. 3. Although we confine ourselves to discussing in detail just one example, several other have been investigated, leading to essentially the same conclusions. The simulations show that the methodology proposed can be considered a useful tool for model selection in the nonlinear regression context, at least when the argument's dimensionality is one or two. In fact, the method should work well for 3D and, perhaps, 4D problems. So far, our modest experience seems to confirm this claim for the 3D case.

2 The Method – 2D Case

The true model can be written as

$$E(y|\mathbf{X} = \mathbf{x}) = f(\mathbf{x})$$

with $E(\cdot|\mathbf{X} = \mathbf{x})$ denoting conditional expectation given $\mathbf{X} = \mathbf{x}$, $\mathbf{x} \in R^2$. We will approximate the true model by a so-called generalized additive model

$$\hat{f}(\mathbf{x}) = \mu_y + \sum_{m=1}^{M_0} \beta_m \phi_m(\mathbf{a}_m^T \mathbf{x}), \tag{2}$$

where μ_y is the overall expectation of y, the β_m are constants, $\mathbf{a}_m$ are two-dimensional unit vectors (projection directions), ϕ_m are functions of one variable such that

$$E\phi_m(\mathbf{a}_m^T \mathbf{x}) = 0, \quad E\phi_m^2(\mathbf{a}_m^T \mathbf{x}) = 1 \tag{3}$$

and M_0 is a fixed number of additive terms in the model. It follows, e.g., from Diaconis and Shahshahani (1984) that each continuous function on R^2 can be written in this form. It should be emphasized that we do not require the ϕ's to be of any known general form with only some parameters unspecified (in this sense, the given estimator is "nonparametric").

The most interesting method of estimating an unknown regression function of several variables by an estimator of the form given by (2) is PPR of Friedman and Stuetzle. In that method, the a_m's are found by pursuing "most interesting" directions in some sense. In our method of model selection, we use PPR repeatedly, in a version implemented in S-Plus. If the a_m's are considered fixed in advance, other nonparametric estimators of the form given by (2) can be used. In what follows, we use the technique of alternating conditional expectations, or ACE, developed by Breiman and Friedman (1985), again in the form implemented in S-Plus.

The process of finding "the most interesting" directions requires some sort of stabilization since its result depends heavily on a sample at hand. In effect, our proposal for choosing a model in the 2D case can be summarized as follows:

1. Generate a set of pseudosamples from the original sample (x_i, y_i), $i = 1, \ldots, n$.
2. Apply the PPR algorithm to each pseudosample.
3. Determine "stable projections of high merit" by properly "averaging" projection directions obtained for different pseudosamples.
4. Substitute the projection directions thus determined into the additive model given by (2), and fit that model to the original sample using the ACE algorithm.
5. Use EF to approximate the $\phi_m(a_m^T x)$, $m = 1, \ldots, M_0$, by parametric functions. Use the form of equations, but disregard the parameter values.
6. Fit the parametric model obtained (with the a_m's kept fixed) to the original sample using the least squares (LS) method.

Let us now explain the process in detail.

As to 1: A set of pseudosamples is obtained by the folowing resampling procedure: the original data are randomly permuted and the first pseudosample is obtained by leaving-out the first 2% of the data; then the second 2% is left-out to obtain the second pseudosample, again of the size equal to 98% of the size of the original data, and so on, each time giving a pseudosample of the same size; (e.g., if the sample size is 100, each permutation enables one to obtain 50 pseudosamples of size 98). The whole process, starting with permuting the original data, is repeated as many times as needed

As to 2: The PPR algorithm is applied separately to each pseudosample. Given the results, a new and single M_0 (see (2)) is determined and PPR is rerun on those samples for which it had earlier chosen another value of M_0. (M_0 should preferably be determined by the user upon inspecting a randomly chosen part of the results for pseudosamples; it can also be the M_0 which had been chosen most often by the algorithm.)

As to 3: "Averaging" the directions a_m, $m = 1, \ldots, M_0$, over all pseudosamples should be robust against too high variability of the directions found and, hence, should be confined to a cluster (or clusters) where the bulk of directions lie. Thus, "averaging" decomposes into (i) running a clustering algorithm based on the notion of similarity and (ii) averaging within a cluster (or, separately, within clusters) obtained:

Clustering uses the following steps:

- Let the M_0 directions found for a j-th pseudosample be called the j-th set of directions and let directions in this set be denoted by $\mathbf{a}_m^{(j)}$, $m = 1, \ldots, M_0$; $j = 1, \ldots, J$ with J denoting the number of pseudosamples. In order to define similarity between any pair of two sets of directions, say, sets j and k, note first that each of the two sets determines M_0 lines coming through zero and having the given directions. Now, find the smallest possible angle between a line from set j and that from set k. Exclude the two lines involved from further considerations and find the smallest possible angle between one of the remaining lines in set j and one of the remaining lines in set k. Repeat this process until M_0 angles are found and define the sum of these angles as the similarity between set j and set k. Repeat for all pairs of the sets of directions.
- Construct a complete linkage dendrogram (see, e.g., Krzanowski (1988) for the dendrogram's description).
- Cut the dendrogram at half of its height and stop if the greatest cluster contains more than 30% but less than 70% of all sets of directions.
- If the greatest cluster contains 70% of sets or more, increase the number of clusters by one and continue until less than 70% of sets are in the greatest cluster.
- If the greatest cluster contains 30% of sets or less, decrease the number of clusters by one and continue until more than 30% of sets are in the greatest cluster.
- Accept for further consideration clusters with more than 20% of sets.

Averaging within a cluster consists in the following:

- For each cluster separately, find the set of "median" or "averaged" directions: Choose a j-th set of directions and sort its directions arbitrarily from 1 to M_0; for each other set in the cluster, sort its directions in the way consistent with how the similarity between this set and set j has been calculated; for each m-th direction, $m = 1, \ldots, M_0$, take the i-th ($i = 1, 2$) coordinate of all $\mathbf{a}_m^{(j)}$, $j = 1, \ldots, J$, sort them and find their median (for a given m, this gives the median coordinates (in R^2) for this direction).

As to 4: Most of the time, more than one set of "stable" directions is obtained at stage 3. When this happens, ACE is run on the original sample repeatedly, each time using another stable set of averaged directions. The estimate retained for further analysis is determined by inspecting the results provided by running ACE: the smoothest estimate of a regression function sought is chosen.

As to 5: The estimate obtained at stage 4 is uniquely determined but it is nonparametric. Moreover, while it is possible to give $\hat{f}(\mathbf{x})$ for each $\mathbf{x}$, the analytical form of $\hat{f}$ remains unknown. We therefore apply EF along each direction $\mathbf{a}_m$ to estimate parametrically the ϕ's. For each m, only a model which best fits corresponding funcion ϕ is chosen. Once all the additive terms in the model are thus given parametric forms, only the general formulas are preserved while the parameter values provided by EF are disregarded.

As to 6: Parameters of the additive model obtained at stage 5 are estimated by running the LS method for the original data. Earlier determined projection directions a_m, $m = 1, \ldots, M_0$, are kept fixed, but it should be emphasized that this step of our algorithm can be made more general by adding the a_m's to the set of parameters to be specified by the LS method (see discussion in Sect. 3).

Two more points need explanation. First, disregarding parameter values provided by EF and adding stage 6 usually leads to a dramatic improvement of the accuracy of the model finally chosen. And second, it is in principle possible to choose more than one model in each direction at stage 5, in particular by fitting the additive model (with directions fixed) to pseudosamples. Clearly, this would lead to a family of plausible models, much in the spirit of our analysis in the one-dimensional case. It seems likely that such an approach can help when the algorithm presented in this report fails to find a satisfactory model (a likely possibility only when f is not recognizable by EF or noise is "very large").

3 Simulation Results

In our example, the regression function was of the form

$$f(\mathbf{x}) = 2x_{(1)}x_{(2)} + x_{(1)}^3, \tag{4}$$

$x_{(p)} \in [-1, 1]$, and the ε's were normally distributed with zero mean and standard deviation equal to 0.05. Equation Finder was set at search depth equal to one, with transformations SQR, SQRT, EXP, LOG, INV, MULTIPLICATION and DIVISION, and with maximum polynomial degree equal to three. Hundred random samples $(\mathbf{x}_1, y_1), (\mathbf{x}_2, y_2), \ldots, (\mathbf{x}_{100}, y_{100})$ of size 100 were generated from model (1).

It is worth noting that f in (4) is equal to

$$(1/2)(x_{(1)} + x_{(2)})^2 - (1/2)(x_{(1)} - x_{(2)})^2 + x_{(1)}^3.$$

Thus, ideally, M_0 in (2) should be equal to 3 and the ϕ's should be of the form $a(x_{(1)} + x_{(2)})^2$, $b(x_{(1)} - x_{(2)})^2$ and $cx_{(1)}^3$, where a, b, c are normalizing constants (cf. (3)).

In the simulations, 80 pseudosamples were generated from each sample, each of size 98 (the size of pseudosamples should be specified by the user – it should be such that the variability of directions provided by PPR be clearly visible but not "too wild"). For all samples, $M_0 = 3$ was chosen upon inspection – it was always clear that the fourth direction introduces only noise into the model (i.e., ϕ_4 provided by PPR behaved very erratically and $\phi_4(\mathbf{x})$ could be considered negligible for all $\mathbf{x}$'s). Typically, 2 or 3 clusters were obtained by step 3 of the general algorithm. Only in a very few cases 4 clusters had to be taken into account. The best cluster (cf. our comment to step 4) was always easy to choose.

553

For some of the original samples, PPR failed to provide satisfactory results. For one such example sample, the situation is illustrated in figure 1. In the first line, the three ϕ's provided by PPR applied to the original sample are given. In the subsequent lines, the three ϕ's provided by step 4 of the general algorithm are depicted: since running step 3 resulted in obtaining two sets of directions, ACE was applied to the original sample twice (i.e., with each set used once in model (2)). Clearly, the second set of directions provides a satisfactory result.

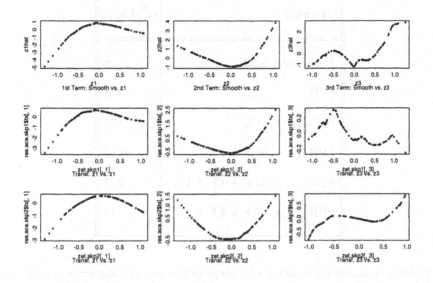

Fig. 1. The ϕ's provided by PPR and by ACE with averaged directions

Results from the third line of figure 1 are typical for most samples. The three ϕ's provided by step 4 of the general algorithm, which are depicted in the figure, approximated in turn in step 5 by EF, have been found to be, respectively, quadratic functions of $a_{1,(1)}x_{(1)} + a_{1,(2)}x_{(2)}$ and of $a_{2,(1)}x_{(1)} + a_{2,(2)}x_{(2)}$, and a polynomial of degree 3 of $a_{3,(1)}x_{(1)} + a_{3,(2)}x_{(2)}$; moreover, the projection directions determined in step 3 (and kept fixed from then on) have been found by the algorithm as one would like them to be: all the $a_{i,(j)}$, $i,j = 1,2$, are of approximately the same magnitude $(1/\sqrt{2})$ with only one of them being negative, $a_{3,(1)} \simeq 1$ and $a_{3,(2)} \simeq 0$.

The results for all samples are summarized in table 1. In its second column, the mean (over all samples) of EMSE is given. In the first line of the table, the result for fitting the true model by LS is provided. Subsequent lines give results for: PPR applied to the original sample; running steps 1–4 of the general algorithm (in the table, symbol PPR_{clust} refers to the fact that the a_m's in (2) come from the previous steps of the algorithm); running steps 1–5 with parameter values provided by EF considered as the final parameters of the model (i.e., $\hat{f}$ provided by using EF is considered to be the final estimate of f); running all 6 steps of the general algorithm (symbol LS_{dir} refers to keeping the a_m's fixed); running all 6 steps with the a_m's added in step 6 to the set of parameters to be specified by the LS method.

Table 1.

Algorithm	10^5 EMSE
True Model + LS	8
PPR	398
PPR_{clust} + ACE	175
PPR_{clust} + ACE + EF	2651
PPR_{clust} + ACE + EF + LS_{dir}	203
PPR_{clust} + ACE + EF + LS	26

Results obtained by running all 6 steps of the general algorithm (with step 6 in its original form) can be considered truly satsifactory. First, EMSE obtained for PPR_{clust} + ACE + EF + LS_{dir} is comparable with that for PPR_{clust} + ACE, what should be seen as a desirable result. While the latter estimator gives as good a fit to the data as is possible in the presence of random errors, it does not provide an analytical form of $\hat{f}$; it is the former estimator which does. And second, our general algorithm has proved capable of correctly recognizing the general form of the two terms in (4).

At the same time, one should not hope for obtaining low values of EMSE without readjusting model parameters by implementing the LS method. This point is well illustrated by the results for PPR_{clust} + ACE + EF at the one extreme and for PPR_{clust} + ACE + EF + LS at the other. It is well-known that, whenever possible, parameter readjustment after each modification of a model is a must when random errors are present.

In particular, if it is feasible, the a_m's, which appear in the additive model obtained in step 5, should be added to the set of parameters to be specified by the LS method. This could readily be done in our example since EF proved capable of discovering that the f given by (4) is in fact a polynomial of order 3 in two variables. It is another matter that the generalization mentioned can turn the least squares minimization into a highly nonlinear problem whose numerical solution can be hard to obtain.

Let us turn briefly to one more example. Let

$$f(\mathbf{x}) = 3x_{(1)}^3 + \frac{1}{x_{(2)} + 1.2}$$

and all the other conditions be as in the former example. In this case, the general algorithm described in section 2 cannot lead to EMSE as low as that obtained in the earlier example, unless the sample size is made sufficiently larger. For the sample size of 100, it is not unusual to obtain in step 6 of the algorithm parameters like 1.15 or 1.25 instead of the true value 1.2 in the second term of f; but then, for $x_{(2)} = -1$, the differences

$$\frac{1}{x_{(2)} + 1.2} - \frac{1}{x_{(2)} + 1.15} \quad \text{and} \quad \frac{1}{x_{(2)} + 1.2} - \frac{1}{x_{(2)} + 1.25}$$

become -1.66... and 1, respectively. Since the values in the denominator are not far enough from zero, the fraction's contribution to the mean squared error will be large unless an estimate of the constant 1.2 is very close to 1.2. But, for a given level of random ε's, this can only be achieved by increasing the sample size. Interestingly, however, already for sample size of 100, the shape of the two functions contributing to f is again generally well recognized by our algorithm.

References

Breiman, L.: Heuristics of instability and stabilization in model selection. Ann. Statist. **24** (1996a) 2350–2393

Breiman, L.: Bagging predictors. Machine Learning **26** (1996b) 123–140

Breiman, L. and Friedman, J.H: Estimating optimal transformations for multiple regression and correlation. J. American Statist. Assoc. **80** (1985) 580–619

Ćwik, J. and Koronacki, J.: A heuristic method of model choice for nonlinear regression. In: Rough Sets and Current Trends in Computing, L. Polkowski and A. Skowron (eds.), Springer, LNAI 1424 (1998) 68-74

Diaconis, P. and Shahshahani, M.: On nonlinear functions of linear combinations. SIAM J. on Scientific and Statistical Computing 5 (1984) 175-191

Friedman, J.H. and Stuetzle, W.: Projection pursuit regression. J. American Statist. Assoc. **76** (1981) 817-823

Krzanowski, W.J.: Principles of multivariate analysis: A user's perspective. Oxford Univ. Press, 1988.

Moulet, M.: Comparison of three inductive numerical law discovery systems. In: Machine learning and statistics, G. Nakhaeizadeh and C.C. Taylor (eds.), Wiley, 1997, 293-317

Zembowicz, R. and Żytkow, J.M.: Discovery of equations: Experimental evaluation of convergence. In: Proceedings of the 10th National Conference on Artificial Intelligence, AAAI Press, 1992, 70-75

Approximate Time Rough Software Cost Decision System: Multicriteria Decision-Making Approach*

J.F. Peters[1], L. Han[1], S. Ramanna[2]

[1] Department of Electrical and Computer Engineering,
University of Manitoba, Winnipeg, Manitoba R3T 2N2 Canada
jfpeters@ee.umanitoba.ca
[2] Department of Business Computing,
University of Winnipeg, Winnipeg, R3B 2E9, Canada
sramanna@io.uwinnipeg.ca

Abstract. This paper introduces an approximate time rough software cost control system based on a multicriteria decision-making approach using the Choquet integral as well as refinements of the Albrecht-Gaffney function points cost model. Estimated project durations are measured with approximate time windows, which compute the degree of membership of each estimate in a number of temporal information granules which contribute to our knowledge of the time required for software development. An application of the Choquet integral in a rough set approach to controlling software cost is presented in this paper. The Choquet integral provides global evaluations of coalitions of timesaving software development technologies used during a software project. Such global evaluations pave the way for the construction of decision system tables and the use of rough set theory in deriving rules to control the duration of a software process. A sample rough software cost decision system is given.

1 Introduction

The function points approach to software cost estimation was developed by Allan Albrecht at IBM and published for the first time in 1979 [1], refined by Albrecht and Gaffney in 1983 [2], and standardized by the International Function Points Group. Function Points measure software functionality from a user's point of view based on what a user requests and what a user receives in return. This paper introduces an approximate time software cost control system based on a multicriteria decision-making approach using the Choquet integral as well as refinements of the Albrecht-Gaffney function points cost model. Estimates of project durations are evaluated in the context of approximate time windows, which were introduced in [3] and have been used in the design of adaptive control of systems with time-varying behavior [4]. The multicriteria decision-making

* Research supported by NSERC Individual Research Grant Nos:OGP0170398 and 202700

approach provides an application of the Choquet integral in software cost estimation based on an extension of the Albrecht function points model. A fuzzy measure which models the importance of coalitions of software development technologies provides the basis for the use of the Choquet integral in arriving at an estimate of software cost. The Choquet integral provides a global evaluation, which takes into account numerical preferences for various coalitions of software development technologies relative to the percentage of usage of each of the technologies in a software development effort. The concept of a fuzzy measure was introduced by Sugeno [5]. Considerable work has been done on the Choquet integral and its application [6]-[7], especially in software cost estimation in [8]-[9]. The paper is organized as follows. In Section 2, a brief introduction to the Albrecht-Gaffney cost estimation model is given. An overview of a software cost control methodology is also given in Section 2. In connection with an algorithm underlying the feedback system model for software cost estimation, fuzzy measures and the Choquet integral are presented in Section 3. An application of the software cost estimation system is given in Section 4. The contribution of this paper is the introduction of a rough software cost estimation system based on the Choquet integral and approximate time windows.

2 Overview of Cost Estimation Method

An approximate reasoning approach to making software release decisions relative to the impact of measured applications of recent software development technologies and software cost estimates are investigated in this paper. For simplicity, approximate reasoning has been limited to measurements of processing complexity used in software cost estimates by Albrecht and Gaffney [2]. A prevalent problem in software system cost estimation models is the assessment of the impact of interacting system components on the total work (a Man Month (MM) measurement) required to completing a project. Usually, one MM equals 152 hours. In the case of Albrecht's Function Points (FPs) approach to estimating software cost, software development time estimates are based on assessing the impact of Technical Complexity Factors (TCFs) on the functionality of software and on a measurement of function counts (FCs). The functionality of a software system is assessed relative to what are known as Function Counts (FC). Briefly, FC is a weighted sum based on based on estimates of the number of external inputs, internal inputs, logical internal files, external interface files, and external inquiries for a given software system.

$$FC = \sum_{i=1}^{n}[(itemCount_i)(complexityLevel_i)] \tag{1}$$

Each itemCount$_i$ equals the number of occurrences of an item such as number of external inputs in the behavioral (functional) description of software. Item counts can be obtained from software descriptions (e.g., dataflow diagrams or coloured Petri nets) during the early phases of a software process, which makes it possible to use Albrecht's function points method to derive preliminary software cost estimates. A complexity level is assigned to each itemCount$_i$. The technical complexity (TCF) of software is estimated by computing an adjusted sum of estimates of the degree of influence (DI) of data communication, reusability, installation ease, and so on as in (2).

$$TCF = 0.65 + (0.01) \sum_{i=1}^{n} \qquad (2)$$

TCF represents an estimate of the cumulative effect of sources of processing complexity on a software development effort. The influence of FC is moderated by a TCF estimate in arriving at W (a MM estimate) required to complete a project using (3).

$$W = 54(FC)(TCF) - 13390 \qquad (3)$$

DI Factors affecting technical complexity estimates are assumed to be independent of each other as well as independent of system size [2]. The formulas in (2) and (3) come from [2]. Notice that the TCF estimate in Albrecht does not take into account the aggregative effect of newer software development technologies, which tend to mitigate "processing complexity" and which significantly influence software design, accelerate the coding phase thanks to code generation, and contribute to speedup due to parallel processing. FP estimates of project durations have been shown to have significant relative error, and to be sensitive to system size, particularly whenever the functionality of smaller projects is in the 50 to 100 man-month (MM) range. In addition, the TCFs used in FP analysis of a project fail to take into account the impact of coalitions of technologies such as integrated development environments, code generation, web browsers, applet viewers and concurrent engineering on MM project requirements. The key point to notice in FP analysis is that it depends on subjective multicriteria evaluation, and that it fails to take into the relation between factors underlying estimates of the functionality of a computer program as well as the importance of various coalitions of software development technologies in shortening the duration of a software process. In this paper, Albrecht's approach to assessing processing complexity has been refined. The approach taken in this paper is based on the design of a software process, which has been "sensitized" relative to a planned software cost. This is accomplished in a number of ways. A high-level view of the steps in software cost estimation is given in Fig. 1. The first step in the algorithm in Fig. 1 is to use input values to construct an information granule, which is pair (S_u, $\leq_u$) where S_u is a set of vectors of values of conditional sensors in a decision system and $\leq_u$ is a partial order defined over S_u [10]-[11]. Let X $\subseteq$ U be a subset of objects in a universe U, and let V be a set of values. A sensor is a mapping of X to V. A conditional sensor is a sensor, which computes a value used in the premise of a decision system rule. Objects in the universe are perceived through available information u provided by a value vector of conditional sensors. The information u is used to classify objects by matching the left-hand sides of decision rules. The cost estimation process in Fig 1. is initialized with

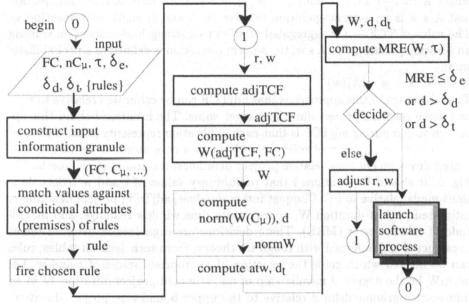

Fig. 1 Software Cost Estimation Model

FC, global evaluation C_μ of the impact of using software technologies, maximum error level δ_e, minimum degree-of-acceptability of duration estimates δ_d, minimum approximate time δ_t, a set rules of decision rules and a reference duration t, which is an upper bound on the time allowed to develop a software product. Cost estimation is governed by rules derived from decision system tables using rough set theory [12]. Hence, the method described in Fig. 1 provides the basis for a rough software cost estimation system. The Choquet integral (represented by C_μ in Fig. 1) is used in a multicriteria decision approach to assessing the impact of various percentages of usage of software development technologies on technical complexity as in [8]. The notation nC_μ represents degree of membership of C_μ in an information granule representing "normal" Choquet integral values in the global evaluation of software development technologies. It is nC_μ, which provides the basis of an estimate of the technical complexity of software (TCF). We make the simplifying assumption (4).

$$TCF = 1 - nC_\mu \qquad (4)$$

This approach to computing TCF stems from the view that a value of 1 for TCF represents maximum, "complete" technical complexity. Values of TCF less than 1 represent the beneficial influence of various combinations of software development technologies, which have the effect of decreasing technical complexity. An adjusted TCF (adjTCF) is computing using (5).

$$adjTCF = ((r \to TCF)sw) \qquad (5)$$

where $A := r \to TCF = \min(1, TCF/r)$ is a Goguen form of fuzzy implication and A s w is an s-norm operation relative to A and strength-of-connection w. The value of $TCF \to r$ is aggregated relative to a strength-of-connection w using an s-norm operation. For A s w, the s-norm operation is defined as a probabilistic sum:

$A \text{ s } w = A + w - (A)(w)$

The advantage to this approach is that adjTCF can be calibrated relative to r, w, and some software project duration target value. The intuition behind this approach to computing adjTCF is that each calibration represents either increased or decreased application of software technologies as a means of adjusting estimated development time relative project deadlines. Returning to the method in Fig. 1, it should be mentioned that preliminary values of r and w reflect decisions made relative to FC, Choquet integral values, adjTCF, project deadline τ, estimated project duration W, approximate time window readings, and magnitude of relative error (MRE). These decisions are organized in decision tables constructed and analyzed with rough set theory. From such decision tables, rules can be derived which guide the selection of appropriate values of r and w. Let normW be the degree of membership of an estimated project duration W in an information granule defined relative to the upper bound t on project duration. Further, let d, d_t be the degree of acceptability of normW, and assessment of the approximate time readings, respectively. Briefly, the particular form of approximate time window used in this paper computes the degree of membership of each estimate W in a number of temporal information granules with functions such as early(W), ontime(W), late(W), which contribute to our knowledge of the time required for software development. Approximate time windows are explained in [3]. In its simplest form, the cost estimation process consists in measurement of the magnitude of relative error (MRE) relative to a required and estimated software development times τ and W, a value of d (degree of acceptability of estimate W), and the value of d_t (assessment of approximate time window reading). MRE and d values are useful in cases where W values exceed a project duration requirement t. An unacceptable MRE or d value results in adjustments in r and w, which reflect the changing influence of percent usage of software development technologies used in arriving at an estimated man-month estimate for a project. The value of d_t (atw assessment) is useful in cases where W has a value less than (early) or (ontime) very nearly equal to upper bound τ.

3 Fuzzy Measures and the Choquet Integral

This section introduces the beginnings of an approach to assessing the aggregative effect of the usage of software development technologies based on a fuzzy measure defined relative to coalitions of software development technologies and the Choquet integral. A fuzzy measure is represented by μ. A fuzzy measure μ is a non-negative, monotone set function introduced by Sugeno in 1974 [5]. Let X, P(X), A, B be a set of elements, the power set of X, and subsets of X, respectively.

Definition [Discrete Choquet Integral]

Let the elements of a set X be denoted by $x_1, ..., x_n$ and let μ be a fuzzy measure on X. The discrete Choquet integral of $f : X \to [0, 1]$ with respect to μ is defined by

$$(C) \int f d\mu := \sum_{i=1}^{n} (f(x_{(i)}) - f(x_{i-1}))\mu(A_{(i)}) \tag{6}$$

where $._{(i)}$ specifies that indices have been permuted so that $0 \leq f(x_{(i)}) \leq ... \leq f(x_{(n)})$, $A(i) := x_{(i)}, ..., x_{(n)}$, and $f(x_{(0)}) = 0$. The definition of the discrete Choquet integral is based on a formulation in Grabisch. The notation $C\mu$ denotes a Choquet integral. In an effort to provide an uncertainty measure of processing complexity in the context of more recent developments in software engineering, a subjective multicriteria evaluation methodology is introduced using the concept of fuzzy measure and the Choquet integral. This effort is in keeping with the original application of the fuzzy integral by Sugeno [5], and the use of the fuzzy integral as an aggregation tool in multicriteria decision-making [6]. This approach offers a means of assessing the combined influence of more recent software development methodologies on software cost.

Example. Let X = {ide, team, web} be a collection containing ide (integrated development environment), team (coordinated development method), and web (world-wide web browser). In addition, let e : X $\to$ [0, 1] where e(x) equals the percent usage of the technology x in X. Let X = {ide, team, av, web, awt} be a collection of software development technologies explained in Table 1. The lattice of fuzzy measure coefficients in Fig. 2 reflect preferences (perceived strengths) for various software technology coalitions in relation to a particular software project. In this context, the value of $\mu(A)$ for $A \subseteq X$ reflects a subjective evaluation of the effectiveness of technologies in coalition A in saving time during a particular software development project.

Table 1 *Software Development Technologies*

Technology	Description
ide	integrated development environment (usually includes editor, error checker, debugger, graphical user interface, ability to link files, compiler)
team	cooperating software engineering teams, e.g., cleanroom engineering model.
web	use of web to maintain software requirement descriptions

4 Case Study

We consider sample data from a collection of 25 Java development projects with function counts (FCs) varying between 200 and 1300, and target duration τ

Table 2 Global Evaluation Table

% use strategy	ide	team	web	global evaluation
strategy 1	0.1(1)	0.3(2)	0.8(3)	0.505
strategy 2	0.4(2)	0.3(1)	0.8(3)	0.565
strategy 3	0.6(2)	0.7(3)	0.5(1)	0.600
strategy 4	0.65(2)	0.7(3)	0.6(1)	0.650

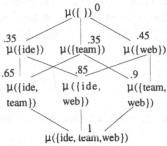

Fig. 2 Lattice of μ values

ranging between 1800 and 9700 hours. The degrees-of-membership of Choquet integral values (denoted nCμ) relative to a granule named normal ranged from 0.4 to 0.8. In setting up decision system tables used to derive rules, values of decision d ranged from 0.01 to 0.1. Sample d and r estimates relative to a representative set of software development projects are given in Table 3.

Table 3. Sample Software Cost Decision Table

FC	τ	nCμ	W	s	early (W)	ontime (W)	MRE	d	r
400	3600	.413	3552	160	.509	.912	0.014	.01	**0.6**
550	7200	.413	7113	320	.483	.929	0.112	.03	**0.9**
1200	7200	.755	7178	640	.756	.999	0.003	.10	**0.9**

Entry s in this table is the standard deviation in a Guassian distribution of Choquet integral values. MRE values in Table 3 result from a comparison of upper bound τ and estimated duration W. Table 3 instantiates a decision system table for software cost estimation relative to decision r. A similar table is constructed for decision w values. Rules derived from these decision system table provide a basis for selecting r and w. Rules are discretized relative to interval rather than individual sensor values. This is made possible by the quantization of the real values of software cost estimation sensors so that sensor values are partitioned into intervals using the method described by H.S. Nguyen. To illustrate this approach to rule formation in the context of software cost estimation, let x[*, b) for values of a sensor x so that $* \leq x < b$, where the lower bound * is indeterminate. Similarly, x[a, *) represents values of x in $a \leq x < *$ where the upper bound is left indeterminate. The notation x(a < x ≤ b) asserts that sensor x is defined relative to the set (a, b) — $a < x \leq b$. Further, let fc, tau, ncu, d represent function count, time limit, degree-of-membership of Choquet integral value in a granule named normal, and degree-of-acceptability, respectively.

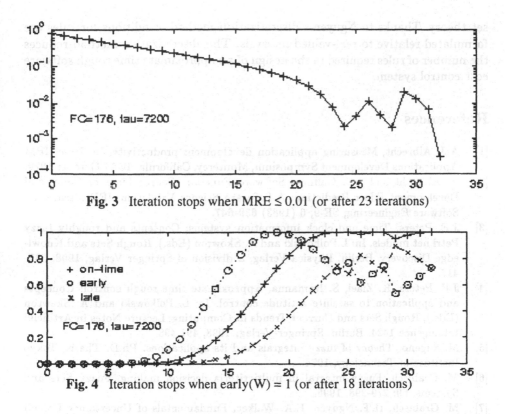

Fig. 3 Iteration stops when MRE ≤ 0.01 (or after 23 iterations)

Fig. 4 Iteration stops when early(W) = 1 (or after 18 iterations)

The notation fc([*, 400)), for example, specifies that * ≤ fc < 400. Rules for selecting w have the form given in (6). Similar rules are derived for selecting w (weight) values used to estimate adjTCF.

$$fc([*, 310.0)) AND\ tau([*, 2700)) AND\ ncu([*, 0.584)) AND\ s(s = 160)$$
$$AND\ d([0.10, *]) \rightarrow r(0.6) \quad (7)$$

The rule with conditions closest to the experimental condition values is selected for firing. The estimation of project duration W continues until either MRE is less than δ_e (see Fig. 3) or $W \leq \tau$ (when $d_t = 1$) in cases where a project can be completed sooner than expected (see Fig. 4).

5 Concluding Remarks

An approach to estimating software project durations based multicriteria decision-making using the Choquet integral and approximate time evaluation of duration estimates has been given in this paper. The Choquet integral provides a global evaluation of the grade of importance of the percentage of use of various coalitions of software development technologies. It has been found that this evaluation is helpful in arriving at software project duration estimates. The estimation process is guided by decision rules derived from decision system tables using rough set theory. Thanks to Nguyen's discretization method, conditions for rules are formulated relative to real-valued intervals. This discretization method reduces the number of rules required in the design of an approximate time rough software cost control system.

References

[1]   A.J. Albrecht, Measuring application development productivity. In: Proc. IBM Applications Development Symposium, Monterey, California, 14-17 October 1979.

[2]   A. Albrecht and J.E. Gaffney: Software Function, Source Lines of Code, and Development Effort Prediction: A Software Science Validation. IEEE Trans. on Software Engineering, SE-9, 6 (1983) 639-647.

[3]   J.F. Peters, Time and clock information systems: Concepts and roughly fuzzy Petri net models. In: L.Polkowski and A. Skowron (Eds.), Rough Sets and Knowledge Discovery. Berlin, Physica Verlag, a division of Springer Verlag, 1998, 385-417.

[4]   J.F. Peters, K. Ziaei, S. Ramanna, Approximate time rough control: Concepts and application to satellite attitude control. In: L. Polkowski and A. Skowron (Eds.), Rough Sets and Current Trends in Computing, Lecture Notes in Artificial Intelligence 1424. Berlin, Springer-Verlag, 1998, 491-498.

[5]   M. Sugeno, Theory of fuzzy integrals and its applications. Ph.D. Thesis, Tokyo Institute of Technology, 1974.

[6]   M. Grabisch, Fuzzy integral in multicriteria decision making. Fuzzy Sets and Systems, 69: 279-298, 1995.

[7]   M. Grabisch, H.T. Nguyen, E.A. Walker, Fundamentals of Uncertainty Calculi with Applications to Fuzzy Inference. Boston, Kluwer Academic Publishers, 1995.

[8]   J.F. Peters and S. Ramanna: Application of Choquet Integral in Software Cost Estimation. In: Proc. IEEE Int. Conf. on Fuzzy Systems, New Orleans, 1996, 862-866.

[9]   J.F. Peters, S. Ramanna, Application of the Choquet integral in a software deployability control system. Proc. of the 5th Int. Conf. on Soft Computing and Information/Intelligent Systems, Iizuka, Fukuoka Japan, 16-20 October 1998, vol. 1, 386-389.

[10] A. Skowron and J. Stepaniuk, Constructive information granules. In: Proc. of the 15th IMACS World Congress on Scientific Computation, Modelling and Applied Mathematics, Berlin, Germany, 24-29 August 1997. Artificial Intelligence and Computer Science 4, 1997, 625-630.

[11] A. Skowron and J. Stepaniuk, Information granules and approximation spaces. In: Proc. 7th Int. Conf. on Information Processing and Management of Uncertainty in Knowledge-based Systems (IPMU'98), Paris, La Sorbonne, 6-10 July 1998, 1354-1361.

[12] Z. Pawlak, Rough Sets: Theoretical Aspects of Reasoning About Data. Boston, MA, Kluwer Academic Publishers, 1991.

Machine Learning Method for Software Quality Model Building

Maurício Amaral de Almeida[1] and Stan Matwin

School of Information Technology and Engineering
University of Ottawa
150 Louis Pasteur, Ottawa
Ontario, K1N 6N5 Canada
{malmeida,stan}@csi.uottawa.ca

Abstract. We discuss the full cycle of an application of Machine Learning to software quality prediction and show how software quality prediction can be cast as a concept learning problem. Significant part of the project was devoted to activities outside the learning process: data acquisition, feature engineering, labeling of the examples, etc. The method proposed here is applied to a set of real-life COBOL programs and discussion of the results is presented.

1 Introduction

Lack of adequate tools to evaluate and estimate software quality is one of the main challenges in Software Engineering. Historically, there have been numerous attempts to develop robust, analytical models based on the knowledge of factors influencing software quality [11]. Many of these approaches adapt to software the general engineering reliability models (e.g. The Raleigh Model [11]). The results, however, have not produced tools whose use has proven itself in practice. A different approach posited that rather than looking for analytical models, one should treat the problem as an empirical experiment, and try to predict quality based on past experience. The existing models (e.g. [12]) typically use statistical approaches, e.g. regression techniques, on data that represents the past experience of some organization concerning selected aspects of software quality. In our experience, statistical models

---

[1] Faculdade de Tecnologia de São Paulo, São Paulo, Brazil.

have two drawbacks. Firstly, these methods behave like "black boxes". The user enters the values of the model's parameters, and obtains an answer quantifying some aspect of software quality. It is difficult for the user to see the connection between the inputs of the model and the quantitative answers it provides: interpretability of the model is questionable. Secondly, the empirical data available about both the organization, and the software, may be drastically different from the kind of organization and the kind of software whose quality is to be predicted. Consequently, these methods are often criticized for being based on assumptions that do not apply to the project at hand, and for the difficulties with the interpretation of their estimates.

We propose an approach that derives simple estimates of selected aspects of software quality. The method that we have developed builds a quality model based on the organization's own past experience with similar type of software projects. The underlying model-building technique is concept induction from examples. This allows us to draw on a rich body of techniques for learning concepts from examples. Low maintainability, for instance, becomes a concept to be learned from positive and negative examples. These are software components whose maintenance effort can be labeled as low or high.

In this paper, we discuss the full cycle of an application of Machine Learning. As it often happens in real-life applications, significant part of the project was devoted to activities outside the learning process: data acquisition, feature engineering, labeling of the examples, etc. We believe that in projects that reach out to real data (rather than rely on the prepared data sets from the existing repositories), these activities often decide about the success or a failure of the project. Consequently, it is important to present and discuss them, with the goal of producing generally recognized methodologies for data mining activities that precede and follow the learning step.

2 Prior and related work

There is a small, but growing body of work in which ML is applied in the software quality prediction task. Porter and Selby [15] have used ID3 to identify the attributes that are the best predictor of interface errors likely to be encountered during maintenance. Briand [2], [3] built cost models for isolation and correction using an approach that combines statistical and machine learning classification methods. In this work, values of metrics were used for the first time to represent the properties of the code believed relevant to the task. The metrics were extracted by the ASAP tool form a set of ADA components from the NASA SEL. Jorgensen [10] has constructed a predictive model of the cost of corrective maintenance using Briand's approach [3] for generating a logical classification model, and has compared the symbolic ML approach to neural networks and lest square regression. Basili [1] has built maintenance cost using the C4.5 and metrics extracted by the AMADEUS tool.

Cohen [5] presents a comparison between the FLIPPER and the FOIL using data from class declarations in C++.

De Almeida, Lounis and Melo [6] have continued the work by Basili [1] comparing the models built with C4.5 with models built with NewID, CN2 and FOIL. The metrics was extracted with the ASAP tool from a set of ADA components from the NASA SEL.

3 Methodology

We view software quality as a multi-dimensional concept, consisting of such properties of the software as modifiability, changeability, error proneness, etc. The approach we are proposing is to treat each quality dimension as an *unknown* function from the observable attributes of the software to a value in a selected quality dimension. This function clearly depends on the characteristics of the software organization that develops and maintains the software. We treat these characteristics, such as development tools for software and hardware, software project methodologies, software life cycle, specific characteristics of the software development team as non-observable: not only are they often unavailable or uncertain, but their precise influence on software quality is difficult to quantify. We will refer to the collection of non-observables as context. We rely on experience, which is represented as a certain number of quality values, known from past experience, and the observables that resulted in these values. We are then predicting the unknown values of the quality function, using ML techniques. In this manner, we do not need to work with the context. We assume that it implicitly influences the observables, and that this influence is captured by the induction process. Consequently, ML-generated software quality models are adaptable to a given context that influences the quality.

In the experiment described in this paper, we view the prediction of a selected measure of software quality as a classification problem. We assume that software units (modules, procedures, and files, whatever are the units in a given programming language) can be described by a number of attributes, and that the values of these attributes are available, e.g. from software metrics. Moreover, for each unit we know, from past experience, the value of the quality measure that we are seeking to model. We can therefore describe the empirical data for this problem as a set of pairs: a collection of attribute values for a given unit, and the corresponding value (class label) of the quality measure. Predicting the quality measure class can then be handled as a classification problem: given the set of known classifications, inductive learning will build a model allowing class prediction for unseen data, i.e. for data describing the software which was not used in the training (but which shares the same context with the training data). Fig. 1 presents this process.

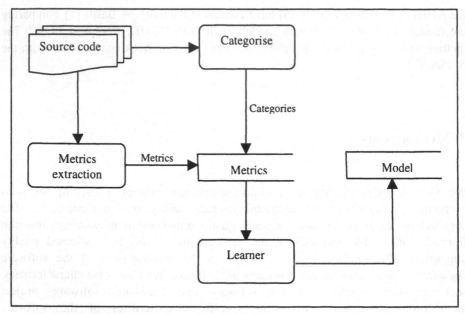

Figure 1. Quality model construction process.

3.1 Case selection

When building dedicated quality models one should pay special attention to the definition of the specific conditions under which the model is being built. Several aspects have to be considered here. The first one is the dimension of quality to be modeled. Enough reliable historical information about that attribute is necessary for model induction. Furthermore, the context should be well defined, and all cases must belong to the same context to assure the comprehensibility, reliability and applicability of the model. The context characteristics to be considered include the software and hardware used, the team, and the project. The software component aspects to be considered include the granularity, the accessibility, and the quantity of the components.

569

3.2 Metric selection and extraction

After the cases selection the metrics to be used should be chosen. In many cases the metrics have already being extracted by the software organization, and we do not have even access to the source code of the components.

The metrics to be chosen depends on the programming languages, the available extraction tools, the attribute to be modeled, and others. Usually classical metrics [4], [7] are included in the metrics set, such as size metrics (KLOC, function points), code documentation metrics (comment lines, blank lines, Halstead metrics [8], cyclomatic complexity [14], specific syntactic structures (IF-THEN-ELSE, WHILE, DO-WHILE, FOR), structural metrics (Fan-in, Fan-out), object oriented metrics (methods/class, inheritance tree depth, coupling), data structure metrics (number of operands [8], DATA [3].)

In our experiment, we have used 19 metrics, based on the metrics from the list above.

3.3 Labeling

Due to a number of factors, i.e. the granularity and imprecision of the available information, difficulty to automatically retrieve the available information, and incoherent data, in our experience the labeling is the hardest phase of the quality model building. For instance, it is quite common that the historical data are presented in a different granularity then the one used in the metrics extraction.

The source code, extraction methods, and evaluation methods for the labeling process must be clearly established. Finally the classes and a mapping scheme must be defined. Frequently the classes are defined as "high" and "low" for many of the most common dimensions of software quality modeling like maintainability, faut-proness, changeabilirty, and others.

In our experiment, there was a need to attribute the cost to units of smaller granularity than the units for which cost data was available. We have achieved this by attributing costs to sub-units proportionally to the length of the code. This was consistent with the experts' (maintainers') intuition about the influence of the size of units maintained to the cost of maintenance.

3.4 Data analysis

After the metrics extraction and the case labeling, the data set should be analyzed to assure the data quality and consequent reliability of the model. The tools to analyze the data include the outlier analysis, the Pareto chart and the distribution of the classes and attributes. A deeper discussion of the techniques for analyzing software data can be found in [4].

Since we need to discretize the quality into a small number of label values, some discretization process is necessary. In our experiments the median of the values of the attribute that is being modeled is used as the boundary between the high and low labels.

A presentation of the de distribution of each of the attributes, containing maximums, minimums, average, standard deviation, median, upper and lower quartiles and the histogram may be a valuable tool in the interpretation of the model. In section 4, we present these measures obtained in our experiment.

3.5 Using the model

Software quality models may by applied in a number of ways, for example for evaluating the software components generated inside the organization, evaluating the software components generated by a third party, or for construction of guidelines for the development process.

Firstly, the evaluation and prediction of software components generated inside de organization is the most obvious application of the software quality models.

Secondly, sometimes when dealing with sub-contracting of software, one whishes to be able to evaluate quality attributes of the software product before accepting it. In such cases during the relation with each sub-contacted it is possible to build quality models that relates the internal attributes of the sub-contracted software with its external behavior in the context of the contracting organization.

Thirdly, the analysis of the model may allow a better comprehension of the reasons that leads some quality aspect to be bellow the accepted level, allowing the organization to build or refine it's software development guidelines.

It is important to notice that although the method presented here was primarily exemplified using metrics of internal attributes of the software source code, this method can be extended to any metric of any phase of the software life-cycle.

4. A specific application

The method proposed above was applied to a set of programs from Bell Canada, the company responsible for the local and phone traffic, as well as for the majority (60%) of long-distance and overseas market in Canada.

Bell Canada has implemented a set of functional changes in the billing system. The system is composed of hundreds of COBOL programs from which 355 were altered. The metrics extracted form those programs are presented in the figure 4.

Large values in the standard deviation column, when compared with the average, of the table indicate considerable degree of variance in the data. This large variance makes us believe that the sample programs were well selected.

During the change of the billing system the cost of specification and development of the changes were registered to entire sets of programs. The attribute to be modeled was the changeability of the programs. To do so, the cost for changing was spread among the individual programs. Different forms of spreading the cost were considered. The chosen method was to divide the cost attributed to each program set in a weighed way to each program in the set, using as weight the "Total lines of Code".

$$\text{Alteration cost}_i = \frac{\text{Set cost} \cdot \text{Total lines of code}_i}{\sum_{Set} \text{Total lines of code}}$$

The dichotomization of the cost in two classes was made using the median of the costs. Alteration cost above the median was classified as "high" otherwise they were categorized as "low". In that manner 176 programs were classified as "high" and 179 as "low".

Using this data, five different models were generated using for NewID, CN2, C4.5, C4.5 rules and FOI. The models were tested using the one-out cross validation for NewID, CN2 and C4.5 and 3-fold cross validations for FOIL. The results from all the learning systems were evaluated using the standard accuracy, as well as completeness and correctness. Setting FOIL aside, the results from the other learners were very close, with correctness between 74% and 77%, completeness between 74 and 74% and 76%, and accuracy between 75% and 77%. For FOIL, correctness, completeness and accuracy were 61.4%, 60.7%, and 64.5, respectively.

The results show that even though four different inductive systems with five representations of the learned classifiers were used, are no significant differences in the model correctness were observed. The results are reported, for each of the two classes of the cost, in terms of completeness and correctness. The overall accuracy for NewID, CN2, C4.5 trees and C4.5 rules is almost identical, while the accuracy for

FOIL is lower. It has to be observed, however, that FOIL was at a disadvantage because no relational attributes were involved in the representation used, and FOIL worked essentially as an attribute-value learner.

The results show that, on unseen data, the high vs. low cost of alteration can be predicted correctly three times out of four.

5 Conclusion

The results shown in sec. 4 indicate that the correctness and completeness do not differ significantly between the different learningt systems used. The values obtained for C4.5 (trees and rules), NewID, and CN2 are virtually identical. The results for FOIL are lower, likely due to the fact that there are no truly relational attributes among the metrics that represent the programs, and therefore FOIL is used as a non-relational learning system.

A criterion under which the results between different learners differ is comprehensibility. The difference, however, is difficult to quantify, as there are no generally agreed upon measures to express comprehensibility [9]. To us, the C4.5 rules results seemed most comprehensible.

This is consistent with the overall conclusion of the recent review of Machine Learning applications [16]. In our paper, we have indicated how we dealt with some of these issues. We believe that more work in this area needs to be done, leading to a systematic approach to all the steps that precede model building by ML techniques.

Acknowledgements

The authors acknowledge the support of Bell Canada and the Natural Sciences and Engineering Research Council of Canada for this work.

References

1. Basili , V., Condon, K., El Emam, K., Hendrick, W., Melo, W., Characterizing and Modeling the Cost of Rework in a Library of reusable Software Components. In Procs. Of the IEEE 19th Int'l. Conf. On Software Engineering, Boston, 1997.
2. Briand, L.; Basili, V.; Hetmansky, C. J. A pattern recognition approach for software engineering data analysis. IEEE transactions on software engineering, n. 18, v. 1, Nov. 1992.

3. Briand, L.; Thomas, W. M.; Hetmanski, C. J. Modeling and managing risk early in software development In proceedings IEEE 15th International Conference on software engineering, Baltimore, May 1993.
4. Boehm, B. W. Software engineering economics, Prentice Hall, Englewood Cliffs, NJ 1981.
5. Cohen, W., Devanbu, P., A comparative Study of Inductive Logic Programming Methods for Software Fault Prediction, Procs. of the 14th Int'l. Conf. On Machine Learning, Nashville, 1997.
6. de Almeida, M., Lounis, H., Meolo, W., An Investigation on the Use of Machine Learned Models for Estimating Correction Costs, Procs. of the 20th Int'l. Conf. On Software Engineering, Kyoto, 1998.
7. Fenton, N. E.; Pfleeger, S. L. Software metrics: A rigorous & practical approach International Thomson computer press, London, 1996.
8. Halstead, M. H. Elements of software science Elsevier North Holland, New York, 1977.
9. IJCAI'95 workshop Machine learning and comprehensibility 14th International Joint Conference on Artificial Intelligence, Montreal, 1995.
10. Jorgensen, M. Experience with the accuracy of software maintenance task effort prediction models IEEE Transactions on software engineering, v. 21, n. 8, p. 674-81, Aug. 1995.
11. Kan, S. H. Metrics and models in software quality engineering. 1. Ed. Readings Massachusetts, Addison-Wesley Publishing Company, 1995.
12. Khoshgoftaar, T. M. at all Using process history to predict software quality IEEE Computer p. 66-72, April 1998.
13. Michalski, R. S. A theory and methodology of inductive learning endgames In Carbonel, J.G.; Michalski, R. S.; Mitchell, T. M. Machine learning. An artificial intelligence approach, v.1, Tioga, Palo Alto, California, p. 83-134, 1983.
14. McCabe, T. J. A complexity measure IEEE Transactions on software engineering, v. 2, n.4 p. 308-20, Dec 1976.
15. Porter, A.; Selby, R. Empirically guided software development using metric-based classification trees IEEE Software, v. 7, n. 2, p. 463-81, March 1991.
16.Provost, F.; Kohavi, R. On applied research in machine learning Machine learning, v. 30, n.2/3, p. 127-32, 1998.

Discovery of Generalized Patterns

Sinh Hoa Nguyen

Institute of Computer Sciences
Warsaw University
Banacha str. 2, 02-095, Warsaw, Poland

Abstract. The pattern extraction is one of the main problem in data mining. Usually, patterns are defined by a conjunction of simple descriptors of the form (*variable* = *value*). In this paper we consider a more general form of descriptors, namely (*variable* ∈ *valueset*), where *valueset* is a subset of the variable domain. We present methods for generalized pattern extraction. We also investigate the problem of data table covering by a semi-optimal set of patterns. The proposed methods return more universal features satisfied by a large number of objects in data table (or in a given subset of objects). We also present applications of extracted patterns for two important tasks of KDD: prediction of new unseen cases and description of decision classes.

1 Introduction

Patterns are often seen as statements in a logic language describing a subsets of data. In many applications, patterns are understood as the "**if ... then ...**" rules [2], [3], [10]. In this paper we consider patterns called *templates* (see e.g. [5]). Methods for template extraction from data, where templates are defined as conjunctions of clauses of the form (*attribute* = *value*) have been developed in [5], [6], [8]. In some cases there is a need to discover more general patterns. In this paper we investigate a general form of templates. Such patterns, called *generalized templates*, are defined by conjunctions of clauses (descriptors) of the form (*variable* ∈ *valueset*). We present methods searching for (semi-)optimal generalized templates with respect to measures expressing some of the following requirements:

(i) the templates are supported by "large" number of objects;
(ii) the number of descriptors in templates is "large"
(iii) the *valueset* in any descriptor (*variable* ∈ *valueset*) is "small";
(iv) the templates should be "close" to the approximated concept.

The generalized template extraction methods proposed in this paper are quite universal. It is possible to generate different kinds of templates depending on the specific application domain. We also present searching methods for data set covering using minimal number of templates. The advantage of template concept is illustrated by their applications to the two crucial problems i.e. *classification* and *description of decision classes*.

2   Basic notions

The subject of study is an *information system* $\mathbf{S} = (U, A)$, where U is a set of objects, A is a set of attributes. A value set V_a called the *domain* is associated to any attribute $a \in A$. We distinguish two attribute categories *numerical* and *symbolic*. A *decision table* is a system $\mathbf{S} = (U, A \cup \{d\})$, where $d \notin A$ is called *decision*. Assume that $d : U \to V_d = \{1, ..., m\}$. For any $i \in V_d$, the set $C_i = \{x \in U : d(u) = i\}$ is called the ith *decision class*.

Let $\mathbf{S} = (U, A)$ be an information system. Any clause of the form $D = (a \in S_a)$ is called a *descriptor* and the value set S_a ($S_a \subseteq V_a$) is called the *range* of D. If a is a numerical attribute, the range S_a is defined by a real interval, that means $S_a = [v_1, v_2] \subseteq V_a$. In case of symbolic attributes, S_a can be any finite subset $S_a \subseteq V_a$. The *volume* of a given descriptor $D = (a \in S_a)$ is defined by $Volume(D) = card(S_a \cap a(U))$. By $Prob(D)$, we denote the hitting probability of the set S_a i.e.

$$Prob(D) = \begin{cases} \frac{card(S_a)}{card(V_a)} & \text{if } a \text{ is a symbolic attribute} \\ \frac{v_2 - v_1}{max(V_a) - min(V_a)} & \text{if } a \text{ is a numerical attribute} \end{cases}$$

Any propositional formula $T = \bigwedge_{a \in A} (a \in S_a)$ (i.e. any conjunction of descriptors) will be called *the template* of $\mathbf{S}$. The template T is *simple*, if any descriptor of T has one element range, otherwise it is called *generalized*. For any $X \subseteq U$, $[T]_X$ denotes the set of objects $\{x \in X : \forall_i a_i(x) \in S_{a_i}\}$ from X satisfying T. Let $support_X(T) = card([T]_X)$. Any template $T = D_1 \wedge ... \wedge D_k$, is characterized by:

1. $length(T) = k$ – the number of descriptors occurring in T;
2. $support(T) = support_U(T)$ – the number of objects satisfying T;
3. $precision(T) = \sum_{1 \leq i \leq k} \frac{1}{Volume(D_i)}$;

   In some applications we are interested in searching for templates "well matching" some chosen decision classes. Such templates are called the *decision templates*. The template associated to a single decision class is called *decision rule*. The precision of any decision template (e.g. $T \to (d \in V)$), is estimated by its accuracy ratio. For example, the accuracy of decision rule $R \equiv T \to (d = i)$ (associated with decision class C_i) is defined by $accuracy(R) = \frac{support_{C_i}(T)}{support_U(T)}$.

3   Template extraction

In this section, we present the methods for optimal template extraction from data. First at all, we introduce the notion of template *quality*.

3.1   The quality functions

The quality of any template T can be estimated by parameters $support(T)$, $length(T)$ and $precision(T)$. One of the effective function is:

$$quality(T) = support(T) \cdot precision(T)$$

In case of decision templates, we should take into consideration their accuracy ratio. The quality of $[T \to (d = i)]$ can be measured by the following functions:

$$quality(R) = accuracy(R) \tag{1}$$

$$quality(R) = support_{C_i}(T) \cdot length(T) \tag{2}$$

$$quality(R) = support_{C_i}(T) \cdot accuracy(T) \tag{3}$$

To estimate the chance that the descriptor D can be chosen to extend the template T in searching for the template with the best quality, we use the fitness function. The descriptor $(a \in S_a)$ is a *good candidate*, if it is supported by many objects and the condition set S_a is *small*. Thus, the fitness the descriptor $(a \in S_a)$ can be estimated by $fitness_T(a \in S_a) = support_{[T]_U}(a \in S_a) \cdot Prob^{-1}(S_a)$.

3.2 The general scheme

We consider the searching scheme called the *template lengthening strategy*. Starting from the empty template T we gradually extend T by adding to it the new descriptors maximizing the quality of the resulting template. For the temporary template T, the descriptor D is chosen according to the fitness function $fitness_T(D)$ (see Section 3.1).

TEMPLATE LENGTHENING STRATEGY
1. $i := 0$; $T_i = \emptyset$; $T_{best} = \emptyset$.
2.while $(A \neq \emptyset)$
3.   choose the attribute $a \in A$ and the corresponding value set $S_a \subseteq V_a$
      such that $(a \in S_a)$ is the best descriptor according to $fitness_{T_i}(.)$;
4. $T_i := T_i \wedge (a \in S_a)$; $i := i + 1$;
5.   if $(quality(T_{best}) < quality(T_i))$ then $T_{best} := T_i$;
6.   remove the attribute a from the attribute set A;
7.endwhile.
8.return the template T_{best} with the maximal quality.

For any algorithm based on the presented scheme two parameters should be fixed, namely the *estimation of the quality of templates* and the *strategy of searching for the best descriptor* $(a \in S_a)$ of a given attribute a (Step 3).

4   Searching for optimal descriptors

Let $\mathbf{S} = (U, A \cup \{d\})$ be a given decision table and let $a \in A$ be a fixed attribute. We consider a searching problem for the range S_a of the best descriptor $(a \in S_a)$.

Let $R_a \subseteq V_a \times V_a$ be a given similarity relation (we assume the *reflexivity* of R_a only). We define the *similarity class* of v by $[v]_{R_a} = \{u \in V_a : vR_au\}$ for any value $v \in V_a$. The similarity classes establish the covering of V_a. In our consideration, the range S_a is computed by taking the similarity class $[v^*]_{R_a}$ of the chosen *generator* v^*. The searching algorithm for the optimal range S_a often needs square time with respect to the number of objects, so it is not efficient for large data tables. We propose in this section some algorithms returning the semi-optimal descriptors in time reduced to $O(n \log n)$, where n is the number of values in V_a. In the next sections we present two main types of searching strategies for optimal descriptors. They are called *global* and *local strategies*.

4.1 Global strategies

For a need of the section, we introduce some notations related to a simple descriptor $(a = v)$. Let $[a = v]_U$ and $[a = v]_{C_i}$ denote the set of objects satisfying $(a = v)$ in the whole data set and in the decision class C_i, respectively. Let $support_U(a = v) = card([a = v]_U)$ and $support_{C_i}(a = v) = card([a = v]_{C_i})$. By $P(C_i|a = v) = \frac{support_{C_i}(a=v)}{support_U(a=v)}$ we denote the conditional probability of the event that the randomly chosen object from $[a = v]_U$ belongs to C_i. It is obvious that $\mu_a(v) = \langle P(C_1|a = v), .., P(C_m|a = v) \rangle$ defines the probabilistic distribution on $[a = v]_U$. The decision class C_i is called *predominant* in the set $[a = v]_U$ if $P(C_i|a = v)$ is maximal in $\mu_a(v)$.

Let $v_{\max}^a$ be the most frequently occurring value in $a(U)$. For any similarity relation R_a, if a is symbolic attribute, then the range S_a is computed by $S_a = [v_{\max}^a]_{R_a}$, otherwise S_a is the largest real interval $[v_1, v_2]$, that $v_{\max}^a \in S_a$ and $\forall_{v \in a(U)}(v \in [v_1, v_2]) \Rightarrow (v_{\max}^a \ R_a \ v)$.

Similar Frequency (SF): The frequency strategy is used in *unsupervised learning model*. We use the value frequencies to determine the similarity of them. For given real number $\varepsilon \in \mathbb{R}$, we define similarity relation $R_a^\varepsilon \subseteq V_a \times V_a$ by

$$\forall_{u,v \in V_a} \left(uR_a^\varepsilon v \Leftrightarrow \frac{|support_U(a = u) - support_U(a = v)|}{support_U(a = u)} \leq \varepsilon \right)$$

The similar frequency can be used as a tool for extracting *regular blocks* of objects with similar values in condition attributes. The advantage of the method is a possibility to operate without any knowledge about classes.

Similar Distribution relatively to Decisions (SDD): This is one of the *supervised learning* methods. The similarity relation R_a^ε is defined by distribution $\mu_a(v)$ of decision classes i.e.

$$\forall_{u,v \in V_a}(uR_a^\varepsilon v \Leftrightarrow distance(\mu_a(u), \mu_a(v)) \leq \epsilon)$$

To measure the *distance* between distribution vectors, one can use any distance function defined in m-dimensional space $\mathbb{R}^m$ (e.g. the *Euclidean distance*). The **SDD** strategy is an important tool for extracting similar objects with respect to distribution among decision classes defined by them.

Similar Predominant Decision Class (SPDC): The Similar Predominant Decision Class techniques are used for extracting the *decision rules*. The definition of similarity relation R_a^ε is also based on the distribution vectors with the following modification:

$$\forall_{u,v \in V_a}(uR_a^\varepsilon v \Leftrightarrow distance\left(P(C_{a=u}^*|a = u), P(C_{a=v}^*|a = v)\right) \leq \epsilon)$$

where $C^*_{a=v}$ is the predominant decision class in $[a = v]_U$. The similar pre-dominant decision class strategy is a used for extracting decision rules associated with one decision class.

4.2 Local strategies

The *local strategy* searches for a template related to a single object $x \in U$. The purpose is to find a good template T_x, that covers a given object $x \in U$ and as many as possible other objects with the same decision as x. Local techniques often use the similarity of a given object to its neighbors. The range S_a of the best descriptor will be defined analogously to the definition of S_a in the previous section with the following modification: instead of $v_{\max}$, the value $a(x)$ will be chosen as the generator of the condition set S_a.

Let R_a be a predefined similarity on V_a for a given attribute $a \in A$. If a is a symbolic attribute, then $S_a = [a(x)]_{R_a}$. If a is numerical, the set S_a is a maximal real interval $[v_1, v_2]$ such that $a(x) \in S_a$ and $\forall_{v \in V_a}(v \in [v_1, v_2]) \Rightarrow (a(x) \ R_a \ v)$.

The local versions of **SDD** and **SPDC** strategies, presented in the previous section, are denoted by **L-SDD** and **L-SPDC**. The experimental results show that the local strategies help to extract decision rules of high quality.

One can see that all proposed algorithms can be implemented effectively by sorting attribute values in time $O(kn \log n)$, where n is the number of objects and k is the number of attributes in the data set.

5 Template set extraction

We focus our considerations on finding the minimal set of templates, that covers whole data table. In [6] we have discussed the covering methods by *global templates*. In this paper the covering problem by *local templates* will be considered.

Any local template is generated by an object called *generator*. The generator x is "good" if the local template T_x has high quality. The set of generators is called optimal if the template set generated from them covers whole data set and is of the minimal cardinality. The general covering scheme can be presented as a greedy process searching in every iteration step for the template with the best quality. This process is continued until all objects are covered.

MINIMAL COVERING ALGORITHM
Input: A decision table $\mathbf{S} = (U, A \cup d)$.
Output: A (semi-)minimal covering of U i.e. such a set $\mathbf{T_S}$ of templates that
  $\forall_{x \in U} \exists_{T \in \mathbf{T_S}} x \in [T]_U$.
1. $S := \emptyset$;
2. Find a local template T_x of the best quality, where $x \in U$;
3. $S := S \cup \{T\}$;
4. Remove from U all objects matching T;
5. If $U \neq \emptyset$ then **go to** Step 2, else **stop**.

The main problem is to find the optimal set of generators. High quality generators should have the following properties:

(i) Generator must be *typical*, i.e. *close* to many objects from the data set.
(ii) For decision templates, generator should be *close* to many objects from the same decision class (and *different* from objects from other decision classes).
(iii) Generator should be *representative*: that means the intersection of supporting sets of different generators must be as small as possible.

In our approach, the generators are selected according the *weight functions*. Let $dist : U \times U \to \mathbb{R}_0^+$ be a given distance function defined on object space U. (e.g. the normal Euclidean or Hamming function (see [8])). The weight function $W : U \to \mathbb{R}$ can be defined by one of the following formulas:

$$W(x) = \frac{1}{n} \sum_{y \neq x} dist(x, y) \qquad \text{(Ave. Distance Weight)}$$

$$W(x) = \sum_{d(y)=d(x)} dist(x, y) - \sum_{d(z) \neq d(x)} dist(x, z) \quad \text{(Dec. Distance Weight)}$$

$$W(x) = dist(x, G) = \min_{y \in G} \{dist(x, y)\} \qquad \text{(Dynamic Distance Weight)}$$

where $G = \{x_1, ..., x_i\}$ is the set of generators in the current step.

6 Template applications and experiment results

We present in this section the applications of the template concept to the description and classification problems.

6.1 Description of decision classes

Suppose, that a decision table **S** is given. We are interested in the description of its decision classes. The decision class can be approximated by covering it with templates. For a given decision class C_i, the problem is to search for the optimal set of generators covering C_i. One can use the *Decision Distance Weight* to measure the quality of generators in C_i. Having the best generator x, the template T_x can be extracted by **L-SPDC** strategy.

We include the experimental results of *description quality* over tables chosen from U.C. Irvine repository [4]. We adopted the approach based on five-fold cross-validation(CV-5) to generate the *training* and *testing* sets. The quality of description is estimated by *compression ratio* and *accuracy degree*. The compression ratio depends on two factors: the number of covering templates and their average length. For a given decision class C_i, let $\mathbf{T}_i$ be the set of templates covering C_i and let k be the number of condition attributes in **S**. The *object compression ratio* is defined by $\frac{card(C_i)}{card(\mathbf{T}_{C_i})}$ and the *attribute compression ratio* is defined by $\frac{k}{Ave(length(\mathbf{T}_i))}$. In Figure 1, we show both compression ratios for *predominate decision class* in the training data tables.

Fig. 1. The compression ratios of decision class description

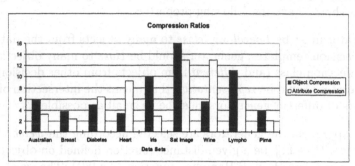

Fig. 2. The correctness of decision class description

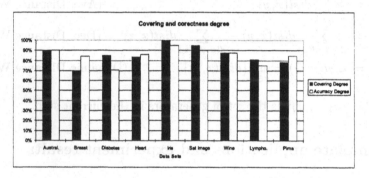

The quality of the covering set is estimated by two coefficients, namely the *covering degree* and *correctness*. The *covering degree* of the template set T_i is defined by $\dfrac{card(\bigcup_{T \in T_{C_i}} [C_i]_T)}{card C_i}$ and the *correctness* is defined by $\dfrac{card(\bigcup_{T \in T_{C_i}} [C_i]_T)}{card(\bigcup_{T \in T_{C_i}} [U]_T)}$.

In our experiments, the template set has been generated for *predominate decision class* in the training table. Figure 2 shows the covering degree and the correctness degree of the template set in the *testing table*.

6.2 New case classification

The goal is to classify unseen objects to proper decision classes. We are using templates as the main classifiers. The classification process consists of two phases.

Phase 1 Generation of a decision template set. The suggested method is **L-SDD** or **L-SPDC** and preferred weight functions for generator selection are *Dynamic Distance based* or *Decision Distance based* functions.

Phase 2 Classification of a new object x based on template set matching x. In conflicting case, the *fitness function* is used to resolve conflicts.

Table 1. Classification quality: Average accuracy

Data Sets	Majority Voting	Ave. Accuracy	Total Support
Australian	86.11%	84.25%	86.11%
Breast	73.60%	75.50%	73.60%
Diabetes	74.20%	71.40%	74.28%
Limphography	72.40%	82.75%	75.80%
Heart	87.00%	80.00%	85.00%
Iris	97.70%	97.70%	97.70%
Pima	72.00%	75.00%	72.00%
Tic-Tac-Toe	98.85%	98.20%	98.80%
Sat. Image	81.00%	86.02%	81.59%
Wine	95.60%	92.60%	95.60%
Ave. Quality	**83.74%**	**84.24%**	**83.95%**

Let $\mathbf{T}(x)$ and $\mathbf{T}_{C_i}(x)$ denote the set of templates supported by x and the set of templates associated with decision class C_i, respectively. We use the following fitness functions (see also [2]) for conflict resolving:

$$fitness(C_i, x) = card\{\mathbf{T}_{C_i}(x)\} \qquad \text{(Majority Voting)}$$
$$fitness(C_i, x) = \sum_{T \in \mathbf{T}_{C_i}(x)} support_{C_i}(T) \qquad \text{(Total Support)}$$
$$fitness(C_i, x) = \frac{\sum_{T \in \mathbf{T}_{C_i}(x)} accuracy(T \to (d=i))}{card\{\mathbf{T}_{C_i}(x)\}} \qquad \text{(Average Accuracy)}$$

where C_i is a given decision class and x is an object.

In Table 1 we present the classification results. Data tables have been partitioned into *training* and *testing* sub-tables by CV-5 strategy (except Sat. Image). Local Similar Decision Distribution **L-SDD** for template generation and the *Dynamic Distance Weight* for selecting the optimal generators has been used. In Table 1 we compare the quality of three voting strategies: Majority Voting, Maximal Average Accuracy and Maximal Total Support.

In the second column of Table 2 we show the *covering degree* in the testing set. The classification accuracy for the *recognized set* is shown in the third column. In the last column we present the *classification quality* for *individual decision classes*. Some decision classes are recognized with high accuracy.

7 Conclusion

We have presented a scheme for generalized pattern extraction. An interesting aspect of our approach is that, on the one hand, searching methods are oriented towards uncertainty reduction in constructed descriptions of decision classes, but at the same time, uncertainty in temporary synthesized descriptions of decision classes is the main "driving force" for the searching methods. The results of computer experiments are showing that the presented methods for template generation are promising for large data tables. The presented results also create a step for further experiments and research on adaptive decision system synthesis.

Table 2. Classification quality: Accuracy in decision classes

Data Sets	Covering Degree	Average Accuracy	Accuracy in Decision Classes
Australian	80.0%	91.6%	**95.1%** 86.9%
Breast	84.2%	72.9%	76.9% 55.5%
Diabetes	100.0%	65.0%	63.9% 66.7%
Heart	83.3%	92.0%	**100%** 83.3%
Iris	100.0%	96.7%	**100% 90% 100%**
Wine	72.0%	92.0%	**100% 100%** 75%
Limpho.	82.8%	91.7%	**92.3% 90% 100%**
Pima	93.5%	71.3%	70.7% 75%
Tic-Tac-Toe	98%	100.0%	**100% 100%**
Sat. Image	99.5%	86.0%	**97.4% 96.34%** 80.5% 60.13% **91.46%** 83.97%

Acknowledgments: The author would like to express the deepest gratitude to Prof. A. Skowron for valuable comments, criticisms and proofreading this paper. This work was partially supported by the grant No 8T11C01011 from Polish National Committee for Scientific Research and by the ESPRIT project 20288 CRIT-2.

References

1. Agrawal R., Mannila H., Srikant R., Toivonen H., Verkamo A.I., 1996. Fast discovery of assocation rules. In V.M. Fayad, G.Piatetsky Shapiro, P. Smyth, R. Uthurusamy (Eds.): *Advanced in Knowledge Discovery and Data Mining*, AAAI/MIT Press, pp. 307-328.
2. Bazan J. 1998. A comparision of dynamic and non-dynamic rough set methods for extracting laws from decision tables. In L. Polkowski, A. Skowron (Eds.): *Rough Sets in Knowledge Discovery* 1, Springer Physica-Verlag, Heidelberg, pp. 321-365.
3. Grzymala Busse J., 1997. A new version of the rule induction system LERS. *Fundamenta Informatice* 31/1, pp. 27-39.
4. Murthy S., Aha D., 1996. UCI repository of machine learning data tables. http://www/ics.uci.edu/~mlearn.
5. Nguyen S. H., Nguyen T.T., Skowron A., Synak P., 1996. Knowledge Discovery by Rough Set Methods, *Proc. of The International Conference On Information Systems Analysis and Synthesis*, Orlando, USA, pp. 26-33.
6. Nguyen S. H., Polkowski L., Skowron A., Synak P., Wróblewski J., 1996. Searching for Approximate Description of Decision Classes. In: *Proc.of The Fourth International Workshop on Rough Sets,Fuzzy Sets,and Machine Discovery*, Tokyo, Japan, pp.153-161.
7. Nguyen S. H., Skowron A., 1997. Searching for Relational Pattern on Data. In: J. Komorowski, J. Zytkow (eds.), Proceedings of First European Symposium on Principles of Data Mining and Knowledge Discovery - PKDD'97, Trondheim, Norway. **LNAI 1263**, Berlin, Springer Verlag, pp. 265-276.
8. Nguyen S. H., Skowron A., Synak P. 1998. Discovery of Data Patterns with Applications to Decomposition and Classification Problems. In L. Polkowski, A. Skowron (Eds.): *Rough Sets in Knowledge Discovery* 2, Springer Physica-Verlag, Heidelberg, pp. 55-97.
9. Pawlak Z., 1991. *Rough Sets. Theoretical Aspects of Reasoning about Data*, Kluwer Academic Publishers, Dordrecht.
10. Ziarko W. 1998. Rough sets as a methodology for data mining. In L. Polkowski, A. Skowron (Eds.): *Rough Sets in Knowledge Discovery* 1, Springer Physica-Verlag, Heidelberg, pp. 554-576.

Incomplete Database Issues
for Representative Association Rules

Marzena Kryszkiewicz and Henryk Rybinski

Institute of Computer Science, Warsaw University of Technology
Nowowiejska 15/19, 00-665 Warsaw, Poland
e-mails: mkr@ii.pw.edu.pl, rybinski@mimuw.edu.pl

Abstract. Discovering association rules among items in large databases is recognized as an important database mining problem. It was originally introduced for sales transaction database. Usually the data mining research refers to complete databases. However, missing data often occur in relational databases, especially in business ones. In this paper, we investigate applicability of representative association rules in the context of incomplete databases. Relationship between the classes of representative and association rules satisfying conditions for optimistic, expected and pessimistic support and confidence is shown. In addition we discuss necessary modifications of the *Apriori* algorithm that enable mining for association rules in incomplete databases.

1 Introduction

Discovering *association rules* among items in large databases is recognized as an important database mining problem. The problem was introduced in [1] for sales transaction database. The association rules identify sets of items that are purchased together with other sets of items, e.g. "80% of customers that buy fish, buy also white wine". Applications of association rules range from decision support to telecommunications alarm diagnosis and prediction.

In the context of transaction databases, *missing* (*unknown*) *values* have not been considered. However, in many other applications, when one tries to discover associations between values of different attributes, one may often face the problem of missing values. The problem is especially serious in the cases of (though not restricted to) management support systems, scientific databases, or medical data files. Missing data may result from errors, measurement failures, changes in the database schema etc.

The problem of missing values has been investigated in the area of artificial intelligence (e.g. [3, 4, 5, 7, 8, 10, 12]). The simplest approach consists in removing examples with missing values or replacing missing values with the most common values. In [11] a way of generating association rules from incomplete data was proposed. The main idea was to cut a database into several *valid databases* without missing values. The drawbacks of the approach have been shown in [9], where a framework for treating missing values in data mining has been provided. In [9] formulae for pessimistic and optimistic support and confidence of an association rule were derived. In addition, notions of expected support and confidence of a rule were proposed and justified. In this paper we refer to the notions and results from [9].

Several extensions and variations of the notion of an association rule were offered in the literature (see e.g. [6, 13]). One of such extensions is *a representative rule* (introduced in [6]). The idea of representative rules is to find a least set of rules covering all association rules. It was shown that all association rules could be generated by a cover operator without accessing a database.

In this paper, we investigate applicability of representative association rules in the context of incomplete databases. In addition we discuss necessary modifications of the *Apriori* algorithm [2] mining for association rules in large databases.

2 Association Rules

2.1 Association Rules in Transaction Databases

The definition of a class of regularities called *association rules* and the problem of their discovering were introduced in [1]. Here, we describe this problem after [1, 2]. Let $I = \{i_1, i_2, ..., i_m\}$ be a set of distinct literals, called *items*. In general, any set of items is called an *itemset*. Let D be a set of transactions, where each transaction T is a set of items such that $T \subseteq I$. An *association rule* is an expression of the form:

$$X \Rightarrow Y, \text{ where } \varnothing \neq X, Y \subset I \text{ and } X \cap Y = \varnothing.$$

X is called the *antecedent* and Y is called the *consequent* of the rule. Statistical significance of an itemset X is called *support* and is denoted by $sup(X)$. $sup(X)$ is defined as the percentage (or the number) of transactions in D that contain X. Statistical significance (*support*) of a rule $X \Rightarrow Y$ is denoted by $sup(X \Rightarrow Y)$ and is defined as follows:

$$sup(X \Rightarrow Y) = sup(X \cup Y).$$

Additionally, an association rule is characterized by *confidence*, which expresses its strength. The confidence of an association rule $X \Rightarrow Y$ is denoted by $conf(X \Rightarrow Y)$ and is defined as follows:

$$conf(X \Rightarrow Y) = sup(X \Rightarrow Y) / sup(X).$$

The problem of mining association rules is to generate all rules that have support greater than some user specified minimum support s and confidence not less than a user specified minimum confidence c. Such set of rules we denote by $AR(s,c)$, i.e.

$$AR(s,c) = \{r| sup(r) > s \text{ and } conf(r) \geq c\}).$$

Several efficient solutions applicable for large databases were proposed to solve this problem (see [2]). The problem of generating association rules is usually decomposed into two subproblems:
1. Generate all itemsets whose support exceeds the minimum support s. The itemsets of this property are called *frequent* (*large*).
2. Generate all association rules from frequent itemsets. Let X be a frequent itemset and $\varnothing \neq Y \subset X$. Then any candidate rule $X \setminus Y \Rightarrow Y$ is an association rule if $(sup(X) / sup(X \setminus Y)) \geq c$.

One may easily notice that $sup(X) \geq sup(Y)$ for $X \subset Y$. This property implies that all subsets of a frequent itemset are frequent and all supersets of an infrequent itemset are infrequent. The property is commonly used in algorithms solving the subproblems.

2.2 Association Rules in Relational Databases

Relational table is a pair $D = (O, AT)$, where O - is a non-empty finite set of *tuples* and AT is a non-empty finite set of *attributes*, such that $a: O \rightarrow V_a$ for any $a \in AT$, where V_a is called the *domain* of a. The notion of a tuple corresponds to the notion of a transaction, but the size of a tuple is fixed. A *relational item* is meant to be an *attribute-value pair* (a,v), where $a \in AT$ and $v \in V_a$. In the paper, we assume that a *relational itemset* is any set of relational items in which no attribute occurs more than once. *Relational association rules* are constructed in usual way, but only from relational itemsets. The definitions of support and confidence are the same as for a transaction database.

Example 1. Fig. 1 (a) presents some database D with all attribute values known. Fig. 1 (b) contains some association rules induced from D.

Id	X1	X2	X3	X4
1	a	a	a	c
2	a	a	b	d
3	a	b	c	c
4	a	b	d	c
5	b	b	e	d
6	b	b	f	c
7	b	c	g	c
8	b	c	h	d

$X \to Y$	$sup(X \Rightarrow Y)$	$conf(X \to Y)$
$\{(X1,a)\} \Rightarrow \{(X4,c)\}$	3/8	3/4
$\{(X4,c)\} \Rightarrow \{(X1,a)\}$	3/8	3/5
$\{(X1,a),(X2,b)\} \Rightarrow \{(X4,c)\}$	2/8	2/2
$\{(X2,b),(X4,c)\} \Rightarrow \{(X1,a)\}$	2/8	2/3

Fig. 1: (a) Exemplary database D; **(b)** association rules in D

3 Incomplete Databases

3.1 Basic Notions

Computation of support and confidence of an association rule is not obvious in the case of databases with missing attribute values. Below, we introduce some notions that will be useful in expressing properties of such rules. Missing values will be denoted by "*".

Any itemset X without missing attribute values may play a role of a *pattern*: The *maximal set of tuples that match the pattern X necessarily* is denoted by $n(X)$ and is defined as follows:

$$n(X) = \{x \in D \mid \forall (a,v) \in X: a(x)=v\}.$$

By $m(X)$ we denote the *maximal set of tuples may match the pattern X* in D, i.e.

$$m(X) = \{x \in D \mid \forall (a,v) \in X: a(x) \in \{v,*\}\}.$$

The difference $m(X) - n(X)$ is denoted by $d(X)$, that is $d(X)$ is the set of tuples in D that are likely to match pattern X but this is not certain. By $n(-X)$ we denote the *maximal set of tuples that certainly do not match the pattern X* in D, i.e.

$$n(-X) = D \setminus m(X).$$

By $m(-X)$ we denote the *maximal set of tuples that may not match X* in D:

$$m(-X) = D \setminus n(X).$$

The difference $m(-X) - n(-X)$ is denoted by $d(-X)$. Note that $-X$ may be understood as the set of all patterns having the same attributes as X that differ from X on at least one item. $-X$ is also called *anti-pattern* of X.

Example 2. Given the incomplete database D presented in Table 1, we illustrate the introduced notions of necessary and possible patterns matching in Table 2. Let us note that e.g. tuple 5 does not match the pattern $\{(X1,a),(X4,c)\}$ certainly, though the value of attribute X1 is missing. Nevertheless, the value of attribute X4 for tuple 5 is known and it is equal to d, which is different from the value c related to attribute X4 in the pattern {(X1,a),(X4,c)}. So, whatever is the real value of tuple 5 for attribute X1, the tuple will not match the pattern {(X1,a),(X4,c)}.

Id	X1	X2	X3	X4
1	*	a	a	c
2	a	a	b	*
3	a	b	c	c
4	a	b	d	c
5	*	b	e	d
6	b	b	f	*
7	b	c	g	*
8	b	c	h	*

Table 1: Exemplary database with missing values

Itemset X	n(X)	m(X)	d(X)	n(-X)	m(-X)	d(-X)
{(X1,a)}	{2,3,4}	{1,2,3,4,5}	{1,5}	{6,7,8}	{1,5,6,7,8}	{1,5}
{(X4,c)}	{1,3,4}	{1,2,3,4,6,7,8}	{2,6,7,8}	{5}	{2,5,6,7,8}	{2,6,7,8}
{(X1,a),(X4,c)}	{3,4}	{1,2,3,4}	{1,2}	{5,6,7,8}	{1,2,5,6,7,8}	{1,2}
{(X1,a),(X2,b)}	{3,4}	{3,4,5}	{5}	{1,2,6,7,8}	{1,2,5,6,7,8}	{5}
{(X2,b),(X4,c)}	{3,4}	{3,4,6}	{6}	{1,2,5,7,8}	{1,2,5,6,7,8}	{6}
{(X1,a),(X2,b),(X4,c)}	{3,4}	{3,4}	∅	{1,2,5,6,7,8}	{1,2,5,6,7,8}	∅

Table 2: Tuples matching (anti)pattern X

Below some properties of the introduced notions of pattern matching are provided.

Property 1. Let X be an itemset in D.
(a) $n(-X) = \{x \in D | \exists (a,v) \in X: a(x) \notin \{v,*\}\}$
(b) $m(-X) = \{x \in D | \exists (a,v) \in X: a(x) \neq v\}$
(c) $d(X) = \{x \in D | \forall (a,v) \in X: a(x) \in \{v,*\} \text{ and } \exists (a,w) \in X: a(x)=*\}$
(d) $m(X) \cap m(-X) = d(X) = d(-X)$
(e) $n(X) \cup d(X) \cup n(-X) = D$

Property 2. Let X, Y be itemsets in D and $X \subset Y$. Then:
(a) $n(X) \supseteq n(Y)$
(b) $m(X) \supseteq m(Y)$
(c) $n(-X) \subseteq n(-Y)$
(d) $m(-X) \subseteq m(-Y)$

Property 3. Let X, Y be itemsets in D. Then:
(a) $m(X \cup Y) = m(X) \cap m(Y)$
(b) $n(X \cup Y) = n(X) \cap n(Y)$
(c) $d(X \cup Y) = [n(X) \cap d(Y)] \cup [d(X) \cap n(Y)] \cup [d(X) \cap d(Y)]$

3.2 Estimations of Support and Confidence

In the case of an incomplete information system one may not be able to compute support of an itemset X precisely. Nevertheless, one can estimate the actual support by the pair of two numbers meaning the *lowest possible support* (*pessimistic* case) and the *greatest possible support* (*optimistic* case). We denote these two numbers by pSup(X) and oSup(X), respectively and define as follows:

$$pSup(X) = |n(X)| / |D|, \qquad oSup(X) = |m(X)| / |D|.$$

The difference oSup(X) - pSup(X) will be denoted by dSup(X).

Property 4. Let X, Y be itemsets in D and $X \subset Y$. Then:

(a) $pSup(X) \geq pSup(Y)$

(b) $oSup(X) \geq oSup(Y)$

A similar problem arises when one tries to compute the confidence of a rule in an incomplete database. Let $pConf(X \Rightarrow Y)$ and $oConf(X \Rightarrow Y)$ denote the *lowest possible confidence* and *greatest possible confidence* of $X \Rightarrow Y$, respectively. The property below shows how to compute these values.

Property 5 [9]. Let $X \Rightarrow Y$ be a rule in an incomplete database D.

(a) $pConf(X \Rightarrow Y) = |n(X) \cap n(Y)| / (|n(X) \cap n(Y)| + |m(X) \cap m(-Y)|)$

(b) $oConf(X \Rightarrow Y) = |m(X) \cap m(Y)| / (|m(X) \cap m(Y)| + |n(X) \cap n(-Y)|)$

Tables 3-4 contain estimations of itemset support and rule confidence.

3.3 Expected Values of Support and Confidence

The difference between optimistic and pessimistic estimations for rules can be high. It would be useful to be able to predict values of support and confidence close to real (though unknown) ones. Below we provide definitions of the notions and the properties of expected support and confidence of an association rule after [9].

The *expected support* for pattern X is denoted by $eSup(X)$ and is defined as follows:

$$eSup(X) = pSup(X) / (pSup(X) + pSup(-X)).$$

The definition of the expected support was based on the following assumptions:

$$eSup(X) / eSup(-X) = pSup(X) / pSup(-X) \quad \text{and} \quad eSup(X) + eSup(-X) = 1.$$

Property 6. Let X be an itemset in D.

(a) $eSup(X) = pSup(X) / (1 - dSup(X))$

(b) $pSup(X) \leq eSup(X) \leq oSup(X)$

Property 7. Let X, Y be itemsets in D and $X \subset Y$. Then:

$$eSup(X) \geq eSup(Y).$$

The *expected confidence* of a rule $X \Rightarrow Y$ will be denoted by $eConf(X \Rightarrow Y)$ and is defined in usual way:

$$eConf(X \Rightarrow Y) = eSup(X \cup Y) / eSup(X).$$

Property 8. Let $X \Rightarrow Y$ be a rule in an incomplete database D.

$$pConf(X \Rightarrow Y) \leq eConf(X \Rightarrow Y) \leq oConf(X \Rightarrow Y).$$

Example 3. Let us consider the incomplete database D from Table 1. In Table 3, we place estimated supports for exemplary itemsets. These values can be quickly computed when applying extracted information on D that is contained in Table 2.

Itemset X	$pSup(X)$	$oSup(X)$	$dSup(X)$	$pSup(-X)$	$eSup(X)$
{(X1,a)}	3/8	5/8	2/8	3/8	3/6
{(X4,c)}	3/8	7/8	4/8	1/8	3/4
{(X1,a),(X4,c)}	2/8	4/8	2/8	4/8	2/6
{(X1,a),(X2,b)}	2/8	3/8	1/8	5/8	2/7
{(X2,b),(X4,c)}	2/8	3/8	1/8	5/8	2/7
{(X1,a),(X2,b),(X4,c)}	2/8	2/8	0	6/8	2/8

Table 3: Estimated and expected values of support of exemplary itemsets

Table 4 is filled with pessimistic, optimistic and expected values of confidence of rules from Example 1. One may use information in Tables 2-3 to derive respective supports of the rules and their antecedents.

$X \Rightarrow Y$	$pConf(X \Rightarrow Y)$	$oConf(X \Rightarrow Y)$	$eConf(X \Rightarrow Y)$
$\{(X1,a)\} \Rightarrow \{(X4,c)\}$	2/4	4/4	2/3
$\{(X4,c)\} \Rightarrow \{(X1,a)\}$	2/6	4/4	4/9
$\{(X1,a),(X2,b)\} \Rightarrow \{(X4,c)\}$	2/3	2/2	7/8
$\{(X2,b),(X4,c)\} \Rightarrow \{(X1,a)\}$	2/3	2/2	7/8

Table 4: Estimated and expected values of confidence of rules

3.4 Implications of Incompleteness

Incompleteness of the data introduces a confusion how to treat requests for a given user-specified support and confidence of rules. One can imagine that a user is interested in the rules whose pessimistic support and expected confidence are above requested thresholds, or in the rules whose pessimistic support and pessimistic confidence are above the thresholds. Other variations of the requirements are also likely. To this end we propose a generic definition of classes of association rules:

$$AR_{\alpha\beta}(s,c) = \{r \mid \alpha Sup(r) > s \text{ and } \beta Conf(r) \geq c\},$$

where α / β can be substituted by either by p, or o, or e (pessimistic, optimistic, expected support / confidence), e.g.: $AR_{pe}(s,c) = \{r \mid pSup(r) > s \text{ and } eConf(r) \geq c\}$.

Obviously, the most natural combinations of requests for support and confidence of rules are: $AR_{pp}(s,c)$, $AR_{oo}(s,c)$, $AR_{ee}(s,c)$. We call them *pessimistic*, *optimistic* and *expected association rules*, respectively.

Incompleteness of data complicates the mining algorithms. The main problems refer to (i) counting optimistic support of itemsets; (ii) computing the pessimistic and optimistic confidence of rules.

In order to implement (i) efficiently, data mining algorithms apply hash tree for fast finding itemsets that match a tuple [2]. For a tuple with unknown attributes (*), a number of values is returned by the hash function, so that a number of nodes has to be visited for each unknown item in the tuple.

In the case of (ii), in order to calculate the pessimistic confidence we have to refer to the database (directly or by means of indexes) in order to calculate $|m(X) \cap m(-Y)|$ (see Property 5). A similar problem appears for the optimistic confidence, where $|n(X) \cap n(-Y)|$ requires accessing the database[1].

4 Representative Association Rules

In this section we describe a notion of representative association rules, which was introduced in [6]. Informally speaking, a set of all representative association rules is a least set of rules that covers all association rules by means of a *cover operator* as defined originally in [6].

The *cover C* of the rule $X \Rightarrow Y$, $Y \neq \varnothing$, is defined as follows:

---

[1] The other parts of the formulae expressing pessimistic and optimistic confidence are known as supports of respective frequent itemsets.

$$C(X \Rightarrow Y) = \{X \cup Z \Rightarrow V|\, Z, V \subseteq Y \text{ and } Z \cap V = \varnothing \text{ and } V \neq \varnothing\}.$$

Each rule in $C(X \Rightarrow Y)$ consists of a subset of items occurring in the rule $X \Rightarrow Y$. The antecedent of any rule r covered by $X \Rightarrow Y$ contains X and perhaps some items from Y, whereas r's consequent is a non-empty subset of the remaining items in Y. It was proved in [6] that each rule r in the cover $C(r')$, where r' is an association rule having support s and confidence c, belongs to $AR(s,c)$. Hence, if r belongs to $AR(s,c)$ then every rule r' in $C(r)$ also belongs to $AR(s,c)$. The number of different rules in the cover of the association rule $X \Rightarrow Y$ is equal to $3^m - 2^m$, where $m = |Y|$ (see [6]).

Example 4. Let us consider transaction database D containing 5 transactions: $T_1 = \{A,B,C,D,E\}$, $T_2 = \{A,B,C,D,E,F\}$, $T_3 = \{A,B,C,D,E,H,I\}$, $T_4 = \{A,B,E\}$ and $T_5 = \{B,C,D,E,H,I\}$. Let r: $(AB \Rightarrow CDE)$ (sup.=3, conf.=75%). Then, the following rules:

- $(AB \Rightarrow E)$ (support=4, confidence=100%)
- $(ABC \Rightarrow E)$ (support=3, confidence=100%)
- $(ABE \Rightarrow CD)$ (support=3, confidence=75%)

belong to $C(r)$. There are altogether 19 association rules in $C(r)$. Their support and confidence are not less than the support and confidence of r.

Below, we present a simple property, which will be used further in the paper.

Property 9. Let r: $(X \Rightarrow Y)$ and r': $(X' \Rightarrow Y')$ be association rules. Then:

$$r \in C(r') \text{ iff } X \cup Y \subseteq X' \cup Y' \text{ and } X \supseteq X'.$$

Now, we recall the notion of representative rules:
A set of *representative association rules* wrt. minimum support s and minimum confidence c is denoted by $RR(s,c)$ and is defined as follows:

$$RR(s,c) = \{r \in AR(s,c)|\, \neg \exists r' \in AR(s,c), r' \neq r \text{ and } r \in C(r')\}.$$

Each rule in RR is called a *representative association rule*. By the definition of RR no representative association rule may belong to the cover of another association rule.

Property 10.

$$AR(s,c) = \bigcup_{r \in RR(s,c)} C(r).$$

Example 5. Given minimum support $s = 2$ and minimum confidence $c = 75\%$, the following representative rules $RR(s,c)$ would be found for the database D from Example 4: $\{A \Rightarrow BCDE, C \Rightarrow ABDE, D \Rightarrow ABCE, B \Rightarrow CDE, E \Rightarrow BCD, B \Rightarrow AE, E \Rightarrow AB\}$.

There are 7 representative association rules in $RR(s,c)$, whereas the number of all association rules in $AR(s,c)$ is 165. Hence, the representative association rules constitute 4.24% of all association rules.

As verified in [14], the ratio between the number of representative RR and association rules AR (being in the cover of RR) is high in the case when frequent itemsets are long. For example, a test in [14] on synthetic data indicated that for frequent itemsets with expected number of items equal to 8 the ratio reached 100. This feature seems to be promising for the rules generated from databases with taxonomies [13], where frequent itemsets are usually long.

5 Representative Rules in Incomplete Databases

Analogically to RR for complete database, we define below the notion of representative rules for databases with missing values. We introduce the same generic notation as we did for $AR_{\alpha\beta}$ above. A set of *representative association rules* for $AR_{\alpha\beta}(s,c)$ wrt. minimum support s and minimum confidence c is denoted by $RR_{\alpha\beta}(s,c)$ and is defined as follows:

$$RR_{\alpha\beta}(s,c) = \{r \in AR_{\alpha\beta}(s,c) | \neg \exists r' \in AR_{\alpha\beta}(s,c), \ r' \neq r \text{ and } r \in C(r')\}.$$

We start this section with providing a few useful properties, which express relationship between a rule r and another rule r' from the cover of r.

Property 11. Let r, r' be rules and $r' \in C(r)$. Then:
 (a) $pSup(r') \geq pSup(r)$
 (b) $oSup(r') \geq oSup(r)$
 (c) $eSup(r') \geq eSup(r)$

Proof. Ad. (a). Let $r: X \Rightarrow Y$, $r': X' \Rightarrow Y'$ and $r' \in C(r)$. Since $(X' \Rightarrow Y') \in C(X \Rightarrow Y)$ then $X' \cup Y' \subseteq X \cup Y$. Hence, $pSup(X' \Rightarrow Y') \geq pSup(X \cup Y)$ (by Property 4(a)). So, $pConf(X' \Rightarrow Y') \geq pConf(X \Rightarrow Y)$.

Ad. (b), (c). Can be proved analogously to the proof of property (a) by applying Properties 4(b) and 7, respectively.

Property 12. Let r, r' be rules and $r' \in C(r)$. Then:
 (a) $pConf(r') \geq pConf(r)$
 (b) $oConf(r') \geq oConf(r)$
 (c) $eConf(r') \geq eConf(r)$

Proof. Further on in the proof we assume that $r: X \Rightarrow Y$, $r': X' \Rightarrow Y'$ and $r' \in C(r)$. As $(X' \Rightarrow Y') \in C(X \Rightarrow Y)$, then by Property 9 we obtain the following properties:
 • $X' \cup Y' \subseteq X \cup Y$, $X' \supseteq X$, and $Y' \subseteq Y$,
which will be used throughout the proof.

Ad. (a). By Property 5(a) and 3(b), we have: $pConf(X' \Rightarrow Y') = |n(X' \cup Y')| / [|n(X' \cup Y')| + |m(X') \cap m(-Y')|]$ and $pConf(X \Rightarrow Y) = |n(X \cup Y)| / [|n(X \cup Y)| + |m(X) \cap m(-Y)|)]$. Hence:
 • $1 / pConf(X' \Rightarrow Y') = 1 + [|m(X') \cap m(-Y')| / |n(X' \cup Y')|]$,
 • $1 / pConf(X \Rightarrow Y) = 1 + [|m(X) \cap m(-Y)| / |n(X \cup Y)|]$.
By applying Property 2 we obtain:
 • $n(X' \cup Y') \supseteq n(X \cup Y)$, $m(X') \subseteq m(X)$, $m(Y') \supseteq m(Y)$, and $m(-Y') \subseteq m(-Y)$.
This allows inferring: $|m(X') \cap m(-Y')| \leq |m(X) \cap m(-Y)|$ and $|n(X' \cup Y')| \geq |n(X \cup Y)|$. Thus, $(1 / pConf(X' \Rightarrow Y')) \leq (1 / pConf(X \Rightarrow Y))$. Finally, $pConf(X' \Rightarrow Y') \geq pConf(X \Rightarrow Y)$.

Ad. (b). Can be proved analogically to the proof of property (a).
Ad. (c). $eConf(X' \Rightarrow Y') = eSup(X' \cup Y') / eSup(X')$ and $eConf(X \Rightarrow Y) = eSup(X \cup Y) / eSup(X)$. By Property 7 we infer: $eSup(X' \cup Y') \geq eSup(X \cup Y)$ and $eSup(X') \leq eSup(X)$. This allows concluding: $eConf(X' \Rightarrow Y') \geq eConf(X \Rightarrow Y)$.

From Properties 11-12 results the following:

Property 13. Let r, r' be rules and $r' \in C(r)$.

$$\text{If } r \in AR_{\alpha\beta}(s,c) \text{ then } r' \in AR_{\alpha\beta}(s,c).$$

Directly from this property and the definition of $RR_{\alpha\beta}(s,c)$ the property below can be inferred.

Property 14.

$$AR_{\alpha\beta}(s,c) = \bigcup_{r \in RR_{\alpha\beta}(s,c)} C(r).$$

6 Conclusions

Support and confidence of association rules induced from incomplete databases may not be computable, but they can be precisely estimated. In the paper, we investigated applicability of representative association rules in the context of incomplete databases. It was shown the relationship between the classes of representative and association rules satisfying conditions for optimistic, expected and pessimistic support and confidence. We discussed necessary modifications of the *Apriori* algorithm that enable mining for association rules in large incomplete databases.

References

[1] Agraval, R., Imielinski, T., Swami, A.: Mining Associations Rules between Sets of Items in Large Databases. In: Proc. of the ACM SIGMOD Conference on Management of Data. Washington, D.C. (1993) 207-216

[2] Agraval, R., Mannila, H., Srikant, R., Toivonen, H., Verkamo A.I.: Fast Discovery of Association Rules. In: Fayyad, U.M., Piatetsky-Shapiro, G., Smyth, P., Uthurusamy, R. (eds.): Advances in Knowledge Discovery and Data Mining. AAAI, CA (1996) 307-328

[3] Chmielewski, M.R., Grzymala-Busse, J.W., Peterson, N.W., Than S.: The Rule Induction System LERS - A Version for Personal Computers. In: Foundations of Computing and Decision Sciences, Vol. 18, No. 3-4 (1993) 181-212.

[4] Deogun, J.S., Raghavan, V.V., Sarkar, A., Sever, H.: Data Mining: Trends in Research and Development. In: Lin, T.Y., Cercone, N. (eds.): Rough Sets and Data Mining. Kluwer Academic Publishers (1997) 9-45

[5] Kononenko, I. , Bratko, I. , Roskar, E.: Experiments in Automatic Learning of Medical Diagnostic Rules. Technical Report. Jozef Stefan Institute, Ljubljana, Yugoslavia (1984)

[6] Kryszkiewicz, M.: Representative Association Rules. In: Proc. of PAKDD '98. Melbourne, Australia. LNAI 1394. Research and Development in Knowledge Discovery and Data Mining. Springer-Verlag (1998) 198-209

[7] Kryszkiewicz, M.: Properties of Incomplete Information Systems in the Framework of Rough Sets: In Polkowski, L., Skowron, A. (eds.): Studies in Fuzziness and Soft Computing 18. Rough Sets in Knowledge Discovery 1. Physica-Verlag, Heidelberg (1998) 442-450

[8] Kryszkiewicz, M., Rybinski H.: Incompleteness Aspects in the Rough Set Approach. In: Proc. of JCIS '98. Raleigh, USA (1998) 371-374

[9] Kryszkiewicz, M.: Association Rules in Incomplete Databases. In: Proc. of PAKDD-99. Beijing, China (1999)

[10] Quinlan J.R.: Induction of Decision Trees. In: Shavlik J. W., Dietterich T. G. (eds.): Readings in Machine Learning. Morgan Kaufmann Publishers (1990) 57-69

[11] Ragel A., Cremilleux B.: Treatment of Missing Values for Association Rules. In: Proc. of Second Pacific Asia Conference, PAKDD '98. Melbourne, Australia. LNAI 1394. Research and Development in Knowledge Discovery and Data Mining. Springer (1998) 258-270

[12] Slowinski R., Stefanowski J., Rough-Set Reasoning about Uncertain Data. In: Fundamenta Informaticae, Vol. 27, No. 2-3 (1996) 229-244

[13] Srikant, R., Agraval, R.: Mining Generalized Association Rules. In: Proc. of the 21st VLDB Conference. Zurich, Swizerland (1995) 407-419

[14] Walczak, Z., Selected Problems and Algorithms of Data Mining. M.Sc. Thesis (1998) Warsaw University of Technology (in Polish)

A Dynamic Integration Algorithm for an Ensemble of Classifiers

Seppo Puuronen[1], Vagan Terziyan[2], Alexey Tsymbal[1]

[1] University of Jyväskylä, P.O.Box 35, FIN-40351 Jyväskylä, Finland
{sepi, alexey}@jytko.jyu.fi
[2] Kharkov State Technical University of Radioelectronics, 14 Lenin av.,
310166 Kharkov, Ukraine
vagan@kture.cit-ua.net

Abstract. Numerous data mining methods have recently been developed, and there is often a need to select the most appropriate data mining method or methods. The method selection can be done statically or dynamically. Dynamic selection takes into account characteristics of a new instance and usually results in higher classification accuracy. We discuss a dynamic integration algorithm for an ensemble of classifiers. Our algorithm is a new variation of the stacked generalization method and is based on the basic assumption that each basic classifier is best inside certain subareas of the application domain. The algorithm includes two main phases: a learning phase, which collects information about the quality of classifications made by the basic classifiers into a performance matrix, and an application phase, which predicts the goodness of classification for a new instance produced by the basic classifiers using the performance matrix. In this paper we present also experiments made on three machine learning data sets, which show promising results.

1 Introduction

Currently electronic data repositories are growing quickly and contain huge amount of data. The capabilities to collect and store all kinds of data totally exceed the abilities to analyze, summarize, and extract knowledge from this data. Data mining or knowledge discovery is the process of finding previously unknown and potentially interesting patterns and relations in large databases [6]. Numerous data mining methods have recently been developed, and there is often a need to select the most appropriate data mining method or methods. The method selection can be done statically or dynamically. Dynamic selection takes into account characteristics of a new instance and usually results in higher classification accuracy.

During the past several years, researchers have discovered that ensembles are often able to produce more accurate results than individual classifiers alone. For example, Skalak [17] has shown that the two advantages that can be reached through combining classifiers are: 1) combining a set of simple classifiers may result in better classification than any single sophisticated classifier alone, and 2) the accuracy of a sophisticated classifier may be increased by combining its classification with those made by unsophisticated classifiers.

Our basic assumption is that each data mining method is the most competent one inside subareas of the application domain, and we try to estimate these competence areas so that this information can be used in the dynamic integration of methods. This view-point has much in common with the use of multiple experts as in voting-type techniques and recursive statistical analysis [18] to handle knowledge obtained from multiple medical experts and in meta-statistical tools to manage different statistical techniques [19] in knowledge acquisition.

In this paper, we apply this kind of thinking to the dynamic integration of classifiers. Classification is a typical data mining task where the value of some attribute for a new instance is predicted based on the given collection of instances for which all the attribute values are known [2]. Chapter 2 discusses the dynamic integration of classifiers and considers basic approaches suggested. The third chapter presents our dynamic classifier integration approach and its implementation as an algorithm using classification error estimates. In chapter 4, we present some experimental results of the approach, and chapter 5 concludes with a brief summary and further research topics.

2 Dynamic Integration of Multiple Classifiers

In this chapter, integration of multiple classifiers and particularly dynamic integration of classifiers is discussed and suggested solutions are described.

The integration of multiple classifiers has been under active research in machine learning and neural networks, and different approaches have been considered for example in [2, 5, 7, 9-11, 13, 14, 16-21]. The challenge of integration is to decide which classifier to rely on or how to combine classifications produced by several classifiers.

Two main approaches have lately been used: *selection* of the best classifier and *combining* the classifications produced by the basic classifiers. One of the most popular and simplest selection approaches is CVM (Cross-Validation Majority) [10], which estimates the accuracy of each basic classifier using cross-validation and selects a classifier with the highest accuracy. More sophisticated selection approaches use estimates of the local accuracy of the basic classifiers by considering errors made in similar instances [10] or the meta-level classifiers ("referees"), which predict the correctness of the basic classifiers for a new instance [13]. We have used prediction of the local accuracy of basic classifiers by analyzing the accuracy in near-by instances [14, 18-20]. This paper considers an enhancement of our classifier selection approach.

Classifier selection methods can also be divided into two subsets: *static* and *dynamic* methods. A static method propose one "best" method for the whole data space (as for example CVM), while a dynamic method takes into account characteristics of a new instance to be classified (as for example the more sophisticated selection methods above).

The most popular and simplest method of combining classifiers is voting (also called majority voting and Select All Majority, SAM) [10]. The classifications produced by the basic classifiers are handled as equally weighted votes for those particular classifications and the classification with most votes is selected as the final classification. More sophisticated classification algorithms that use combination of classifiers include the stacking (stacked generalization) architecture [21], SCANN method that is based on the correspondence analysis and the nearest neighbor procedure [11], combining minimal nearest neighbor classifiers within the stacked generalization framework [17], different versions of resampling (boosting, bagging, and cross-validated resampling) that use one learning algorithm to train different classifiers on subsamples of the training set and then simple voting to combine those classifiers [5,16]. Two effective classifiers' combining strategies based on stacked generalization (called an arbiter and combiner) were analyzed in [2] showing experimentally that the hierarchical combination approach is able to sustain the same level of accuracy as a global classifier trained on the entire data set.

Nevertheless, there are still many open questions even with the widely used stacked generalization architecture, as which basic classifiers should be used, what attributes should be used at the meta-level training, and what combining classifier should be used. Different combining algorithms have been considered by various researchers, as classic boosting with simple voting [16], ID3 for combining nearest neighbor classifiers [17], and the nearest neighbor classification in the space of correspondence analysis results (not directly on the predictions) [11].

3 An Algorithm for Dynamic Integration of Classifiers

In this chapter, we consider a new variation of stacked generalization, which uses a metric to locally estimate the errors of component classifiers. This algorithm has been presented also in [14]. Instead of training a meta-level classifier that will derive the final classification using the classifications of the basic classifiers as in stacked generalization, we propose to train a meta-level classifier that will estimate the errors of the basic classifiers for each new instance and then use these errors to derive the final classification. Our goal is to use each basic classifier just in that subdomain for which it is the most reliable one. Our dynamic approach to the integration of multiple classifiers attempts to create a meta-model that describes subspaces correctly classified by the corresponding component classifiers. Our approach is closely related to that considered by Ortega, Koppel, and Argamon-Engelson [13]. The main difference between these two approaches is in the combining algorithm. In [13] the C4.5 decision tree induction algorithm was used to predict the errors of the basic classifiers, but we use weighted nearest neighbor classification (WNN) [1,3], which simplifies the learning phase of the composite classifier. It is enough to calculate the performance matrix for the basic classifiers during the learning phase. In the application phase, nearest neighbors of a new instance among the training instances are found out and the corresponding basic classifiers' performances are used to calculate the predicted classifiers' performance for each basic classifier. This is done by summing up the corresponding performance values of a classifier using weights that depend on the distances between a new instance and its nearest neighbors.

Thus our approach contains two phases. In the learning phase (procedure *learning_phase* in Fig. 1), the training set T is partitioned into v folds. The cross-validation technique is used to estimate the errors of the basic classifiers $E_j(x^*)$ on the training set and the meta-level training set T^* is formed. It contains the attributes of the training instances x_i and the estimates of the errors of the basic classifiers on those instances $E_j(x^*)$. The learning phase finishes with training the component classifiers C_j on the whole training set.

In the application phase, the combining classifier (either the function *DS_application_phase* or the function *DV_application_phase* in Fig. 1) is used to predict the performance of each component classifier for a new instance. The first function DS implements Dynamic Selection. In the DS application phase the classification error E_j^* is predicted for each basic classifier C_j using the WNN procedure and a classifier with the smallest error (with the least global error in the case of ties) is selected to make the final classification. The second function DV implements Dynamic Voting. In the DV application phase each component classifier C_j receives a weight W_j that depends on the local classifier's performance and the final classification is conducted by voting classifier predictions $C_j(x)$ with their weights W_j.

```
T component classifier training set
T_i i-th fold of the training set
T* meta-level training set for the combining algorithm
x attributes of an instance
c(x) classification of the instance with attributes x
C set of component classifiers
C_j j-th component classifier
C_j(x) prediction produced by C_j on instance x
E_j(x) estimation of error of C_j on instance x
E*_j(x) prediction of error of C_j on instance x
m number of component classifiers
W vector of weights for component classifiers
nn number of near-by instances for error prediction
W_NNi weight of i-th near-by instance
procedure learning_phase(T,C)
     begin {fills in the meta-level training set T*}
          partition T into v folds
          loop for T_i ⊂ T, i = 1,...,v
             loop for j from 1 to m
                 train(C_j, T-T_i)
             loop for x ∈ T_i
                loop for j from 1 to m
                    compare C_j(x) with c(x) and derive E_j(x)
                collect (x, E_1(x),...,E_m(x)) into T*
          loop for j from 1 to m
              train(C_j, T)
     end
```

```
function DS_application_phase(T',C,x) returns class of x
    begin
        loop for j from 1 to m
```

$$E_j^* \leftarrow \frac{1}{nn} \sum_{i=1}^{nn} W_{NN_i} \cdot E_j(\mathbf{x}_{NN_i}) \quad \{\text{WNN estimation}\}$$

$$l \leftarrow \text{argmin}_j E_j^* \quad \{\text{number of cl-er with min. } E_j^*\}$$

```
        {with the least global error in the case of ties}
        return C_l(x)
    end
function DV_application_phase(T',C,x) returns class of x
    begin
        loop for j from 1 to m
```

$$W_j \leftarrow 1 - \frac{1}{nn} \sum_{i=1}^{nn} W_{NN_i} \cdot E_j(\mathbf{x}_{NN_i}) \quad \{\text{WNN estimation}\}$$

```
        return Weighted_Voting(W, C_1(x), ..., C_m(x))
    end
```

Fig. 1. Our algorithm for dynamic integration of classifiers

4 Experiments

In this chapter, we present our experiments with the algorithm. We considered some preliminary experiments already in [14]. The two above variations (DS and DV) of the algorithm are evaluated and compared with each other, and with weighted voting (WV) and cross-validation majority (CVM) [10]. In this chapter, we first present the experiment setting and then describe the data sets and results of our experiments.

We made replications of 30 runs with the number of neighbors varying from 1 to 9 for each selected data set. In each run about 22% of the given instances are first randomly picked up for test purposes. The rest 78% of the instances are divided using stratified random sampling into 10 folds and then we use 10-fold cross-validation as described above (Fig.1). In these experiments, we use only the Euclidean distance metrics (the standard squared-difference metrics) because we noticed in our preliminary experiments [14] that there were no statistically significant difference in the accuracy of the DS and DV variations between the two tested distance metrics (the Euclidean metrics and probabilistic metrics of the PEBLS classification algorithm [3]) on the three data sets used there. The values of continuous attributes are discretised dividing the interval of the values of the attribute into intervals with equal length.

The comparison of the accuracy of algorithms is done using the paired differences t-test based on 30 random train/test splits. The null hypothesis, which we are testing, is that the two classification algorithms compared have the same average accuracy. Under the null hypothesis, this statistic has approximately a t distribution with 29 degrees of freedom. Because Dietterich [4] has strongly criticized the use of this test, we applied also the McNemar's test and a test for the difference of two proportions [4,pp.1901-1902] to check whether they give the same results.

We use in the experiments three basic classification algorithms: PEBLS [3], C4.5 [15], and BAYES [1]. The experiments were implemented within the MLC++ framework, the machine learning library in C++ [8]. We have conducted experiments on three data sets: (1) the Glass Identification database, (2) the BUPA Liver Disorders database, and (3) the Pima Indians Diabetes database from the UCI machine learning repository [12]. SCANN and other classifier integration algorithms have been shown to perform worst in the Glass and Liver domains out of all 18 domains in [11]. Voting performed significantly better than other integration methods (and SCANN) in these domains. Voting has been also shown to perform significantly better than other sophisticated integration methods in these domains in [10].

First we noticed that there were no statistically significant differences with respect to the different number of neighbors taken into account. There seemed to be a slight trend that the accuracy of our algorithm decreased when the number of neighbors grew, but this needs deeper analysis. Because this was not statistically significant, we present here only the results when one neighbor is used in our algorithm.

The Glass Identification database contains 214 instances with 9 numeric attributes, which describe a certain glass, and no missing values. The variable to be predicted is the type of glass. The second column of Table 1 shows the averages of the classification accuracy of our integration techniques (DS, DV), CVM, WV, and the basic classifiers for the 30 runs for the Glass domain. The second, third, and fourth columns show the t-test values for the difference of averages and their statistical significance, where *** means that the H_0 hypotheses can be rejected at a 0.001 level of significance, ** means that the H_0 hypotheses can be rejected at a 0.01 level of significance, * means that the H_0 hypotheses can be rejected at a 0.05 level of significance, and (no star) means that the H_0 hypotheses cannot be rejected at a 0.05 level of significance.

Table 1 shows that both DS and DV outperform WV and that DV outperforms WV statistically at a 0.001 level of significance. DV also outperforms CVM statistically at a 0.01 level of significance. The results of the McNemar's test were the same except that in the comparison of DS and DV the difference was found at a 0.05 level of significance.

Table 1. Classification accuracy and t-test values for the Glass domain

	Average accuracy	DV	CVM	WV
DS	0.6194	-0.89	4.39***	3.54**
DV	0.6271		4.42***	4.68***
CVM	0.5771			0.06
WV	0.5764			
PEBLS	0.5847			
C4.5	0.5938			
BAYES	0.3215			

The BUPA Liver Disorders database created by BUPA Medical Research Ltd. contains 345 instances with 6 numeric attributes and no missing values. The variable to be predicted is a selector that is used to split the database into two sets. Table 2 shows test results for the Liver database using the same notation as in Table 1.

Table 2 shows that the DS version of our dynamic integration algorithm outperforms both WV and CVM statistically at a 0.001 level of significance. DV also outperforms WV statistically at a 0.01 level of significance. There is no statistically significant difference between DV and CVM. The test results using the McNemar's test were similar except that this test found that DV outperforms CVM at a 0.001 level of significance! In this comparison we also applied a test for the difference of two proportions [4, p.1902] and it found the statistically significant difference at a 0.01 level of significance.

The Pima Indians Diabetes database includes 768 instances that classifies patients into two classes according to World Health Organization criteria with respect of

Table 2. Classification accuracy and *t*-test values for the Liver domain

	Average accuracy	DV	CVM	WV
DS	0.6225	1.32	3.99***	4.18***
DV	0.6100		1.25	3.22**
CVM	0.5939			1.32
WV	0.5814			
PEBLS	0.5468			
C4.5	0.6065			
BAYES	0.5732			

diabetes diagnoses. There are 8 continuous attributes and no missing values in this data set. Table 3 shows experimental results for the Diabetes database.

Table 3. Classification accuracy and *t*-test values for the Diabetes domain

	Average accuracy	DV	CVM	WV
DS	0.7454	5.43***	0.49	-0.42
DV	0.7216		-4.42***	-5.69***
CVM	0.7441			-0.74
WV	0.7472			
PEBLS	0.7177			
C4.5	0.7049			
BAYES	0.7429			

Table 3 shows that the DS version of our dynamic integration algorithm gives as good results as WV and CVM. It also shows that the DV version is outperformed by all the three other algorithms statistically at a 0.001 level of significance. The test results using the McNemar's test were similar.

We considered here test results on three data sets with the paired differences t-test based on 30 random train/test splits. With two of these sets, our algorithm outperformed significantly weighted voting and cross validation majority. The results were also supported by the McNemar's test and a test for the difference of two proportions. However, with the third data set results show that our algorithm does not always produce significant benefit over the two other methods. But even in that domain DS did not perform significantly worse than the other integration methods. The dependence between the accuracy of our algorithm and different characteristics of the application domain is a topic for further research. It could be discovered from the tests also that the accuracy is not changed significantly with different numbers of nearest neighbors. But further research is also needed to make deeper investigation of this dependency.

5   Conclusion

In data mining one of the key problems is the selection of the most appropriate data-mining method. Often the method selection is done statically without paying any attention to the values of attributes of a new instance. The dynamic integration that takes into account the new instance has been researched actively recently.

Our goal in this paper is to further enhance dynamic integration of multiple classifiers. We discussed basic suggested approaches of integration and represented our dynamic integration algorithm. This approach consists of two phases: a learning phase and an application phase. The basic assumption behind our algorithm is that each basic classifier is best inside certain subareas of the application domain. Our algorithm is a new variation of the stacked generalization method.

We presented experimental results on three data sets. With two of these sets, our algorithm outperforms significantly the weighted voting and cross validation majority methods. With the third data set, the results show that our algorithm does not always (not for every data set) produce significant benefit over the two other methods.

Further research is needed to make deeper comparisons of the algorithm with others on large databases to analyze the characteristics of the domains that can take benefit of our algorithm. In further research, the combination of the algorithm with other integration methods as boosting, bagging, and minimal nearest neighbor classifiers is another interesting future research topic.

Acknowledgments: This research is partly supported by the Academy of Finland. We are thankful to the COMAS Graduate School and Kharkov State Technical University of Radioelectronics and particularly to the Deputy of Vice-Rector on International Cooperation Dr. Helena Kaikova that made it possible for Alexey Tsymbal to work in Jyväskylä during the preparation of this article. We would like to thank the UCI machine learning repository of databases, domain theories and data generators for the data sets and the machine learning library in C++ for the source code used in this study. We are grateful to Mr. Artyom Katasonov for considerable help in programming the algorithm and the anonymous referees for their constructive criticism.

References

1. Aivazyan, S.A.: Applied Statistics: Classification and Dimension Reduction. Finance and Statistics, Moscow (1989).
2. Chan, P., Stolfo, S.: On the Accuracy of Meta-Learning for Scalable Data Mining. Intelligent Information Systems, Vol. 8 (1997) 5-28.
3. Cost, S., Salzberg, S.: A Weighted Nearest Neighbor Algorithm for Learning with Symbolic Features. Machine Learning, Vol. 10, No. 1 (1993) 57-78.
4. Dietterich, T.G.: Approximate Statistical Tests for Comparing Supervised Classification Learning Algorithms. Neural Computation, Vol. 10, No. 7 (1998) 1895-1923.
5. Dietterich, T.G.: Machine Learning Research: Four Current Directions. AI Magazine, Vol. 18, No. 4 (1997) 97-136.
6. Fayyad, U., Piatetsky-Shapiro, G., Smyth, P., Uthurusamy, R.: Advances in Knowledge Discovery and Data Mining. AAAI/ MIT Press (1997).
7. Kohavi, R.: A Study of Cross-Validation and Bootstrap for Accuracy Estimation and Model Selection. In: Proceedings of IJCAI'95 (1995).
8. Kohavi, R., Sommerfield, D., Dougherty, J.: Data Mining Using MLC++: A Machine Learning Library in C++. Tools with Artificial Intelligence, IEEE CS Press (1996) 234-245.
9. Koppel, M., Engelson, S.P.: Integrating Multiple Classifiers by Finding their Areas of Expertise. In: AAAI-96 Workshop On Integrating Multiple Learning Models (1996) 53-58.
10. Merz, C.: Dynamical Selection of Learning Algorithms. In: D.Fisher, H.-J.Lenz (Eds.), Learning from Data, Artificial Intelligence and Statistics, Springer Verlag, NY (1996).
11. Merz, C.J.: Combining Classifiers Using Correspondence Analysis. In: Advances in Neural Information Processing Systems 10, M.I.Jordan, M.J.Kearns, S.A.Solla, eds., MIT Press, 1998.
12. Merz, C.J., Murphy, P.M.: UCI Repository of Machine Learning Databases [http:// www.ics.uci.edu/ ~mlearn/ MLRepository.html]. Dep-t of Information and CS, Un-ty of California, Irvine, CA (1998).
13. Ortega, J., Koppel, M., Argamon-Engelson, S.: Arbitrating Among Competing Classifiers Using Learned Referees, Machine Learning (1998) to appear.
14. Puuronen, S., Terziyan, V., Katasonov, A., Tsymbal, A.: Dynamic Integration of Multiple Data Mining Techniques in a Knowledge Discovery Management System. In: SPIE Conf. on Data Mining and Knowledge Discovery, 5-9 April 1999, Orlando. Florida (to appear).
15. Quinlan, J.R.: C4.5 Programs for Machine Learning. Morgan Kaufmann, San Mateo, CA (1993).
16. Schapire, R.E.: Using Output Codes to Boost Multiclass Learning Problems. In: Machine Learning: Proceedings of the Fourteenth International Conference (1997) 313-321.
17. Skalak, D.B.: Combining Nearest Neighbor Classifiers. Ph.D. Thesis, Dept. of Computer Science, University of Massachusetts, Amherst, MA (1997).
18. Terziyan, V., Tsymbal, A., Puuronen, S.: The Decision Support System for Telemedicine Based on Multiple Expertise. Int. J. of Medical Informatics, Vol. 49, No. 2 (1998) 217-229.
19. Terziyan, V., Tsymbal, A., Tkachuk, A., Puuronen, S.: Intelligent Medical Diagnostics System Based on Integration of Statistical Methods. In: Informatica Medica Slovenica, Journal of Slovenian Society of Medical Informatics, Vol.3, Ns. 1,2,3 (1996) 109-114.
20. Tsymbal, A., Puuronen, S., Terziyan, V.: Advanced Dynamic Selection of Diagnostic Methods. In: Proceedings 11th IEEE Symp. on Computer-Based Medical Systems CBMS'98, IEEE CS Press, Lubbock, Texas, June (1998) 50-54.
21. Wolpert, D.: Stacked Generalization. Neural Networks, Vol. 5 (1992) 241-259.

UIB-IK: A Computer System for Decision Trees Induction[1]

Gabriel Fiol-Roig

University of the Balearic Islands.
Departament de Ciències Matemàtiques i Informàtica.
Crra. de Valldemosa, Km. 7.5
07071 Palma de Mallorca. Baleares. Spain
E-mail: dmigfr0@ps.uib.es
Fax: +34-71 173003

Abstract. Decision Trees constitute a common knowledge structure to express the results of an Inductive Process. A computer system called UIB-IK, to induce decision trees from an initial collection of examples is presented. General properties of this tool are compared to those from some very known systems, such as the ID3, ID5, C4.5 and AQ11 systems. Performance qualities of UIB-IK are exposed on the basis of its functional model, and a synthesized description of two complex real applications is presented. The modular design together with the programming techniques used to implement the final program, makes UIB-IK to be a consistent and parameterized software tool, capable to cope a large range of problems.

1 Introduction

Looking into new ways to obtain Intensional Descriptions of Concepts described initially in an extensional way, also called Induction from Examples or concrete portions of knowledge is, perhaps, the most explored Artificial Intelligence Area. A lot of contributions are found in literature, specially those representing intensional descriptions through a decision tree structure.

Limitations of inductive methods are well known [26]; however that may be, most of them are not optimal, in the sense that the resultant induced structure does not constitute, in general, the best description in the space of possible solutions. It is the case of systems ID3 [19] and C4.5 [18] of Quinlan, to induce decision tree structures, the method of Cestnik and Karalic, presented in [2], based on probabilistic measures to select the attributes in tree induction, and the ILS system [17] of Wong, based on the Rough Sets approach of Pawlak [27], to induce abstractions in the form of decision rules. Other methods, such as the classical AQ11 [24] system of Michalski, based on finding one of the most reduced expressions to describe a set of initial concepts and the Rough Sets Theory [27] of Pawlak, in which a technique to find expressions without superfluous information is defined, go after an specific aim when performing their inductive procedure. However, none of these methods considers the particular nature of the problem in hand, concentrating on developping specific

---

[1] This paper has been partially supported by the *Comision Interministerial de Ciencia y Tecnología* through the *TAP96-1114-C03-02 Project*.

inductive techniques. Fiol and Miró have presented some works on induction of decision trees from examples [6], [9], [13], focussed on the particular nature of the problem in hand, in the sense that the characteristics of the final results (decision tree) depend on the demands of the situation to be solved. Practical results of these works are expressed through the UIB-IK computer tool [21], whose characteristics make possible to face a large variety of problems.

The presence of large collections of examples in the initial extensional knowledge base, also called the environment, constitutes another important limitation of inductive systems, since the complexity of the system response may become exponential, particularly when trying to obtain optimal decision trees. Incremental Learning constitutes perhaps the best technique to face such a problem. Classical examples are found in [22] and [25], where an extension of methods described in [20] and [19] respectively, based on an incremental learning approach, is presented. Other systems such as the C4.5 tool of Quinlan [18] apply a windowing methodology, in order to make the inductive process efficient. The UIB-IK system allows both techniques: incremental learning (also called structural incremental learning) and windowing, to be incorporated. In particular, windowing strategies are based on a selected model of the initial extensional knowledge base, guaranteeing its essential properties to be satisfied, whereas the structural incremental learning technique considers all the initial extensional knowledge.

Other aspects are available in the present version of UIB-IK, thus its modular design and structured programming methodology used, allow to include new software modules, such as those considering new optimality criteria in order to solve a wider range of problems; a technique [13] to discretize multivalued attributes so that unnecessary information about their values may be discarded, is also provided; and a powerful mechanism to administrate the initial knowledge base has been implemented.

Future considerations are focussed essentially on including inductive methods allowing incomplete information [14] in the environment to be treated and new discretization techniques for multivalued attributes to be available.

An outstanding aspect of the UIB-IK tool is the wide range of research and development fields which it may be applied to, thus Diagnosis [3], [7], Monitorization and Decision [10], Evaluation of the Quality of Knowledge Bases [4], [5], [15], [16] constitute some important examples of such application areas.

2 Theoretical Foundations of UIB-IK

UIB-IK is a computer tool conceived to develop an Inductive Acquisition of Knowledge from Examples Process. Initial extensional information is given in the form of concrete portions of knowledge about some concepts, also called examples, which is generalized by the inductive procedure in order to obtain intensional descriptions of the given concepts expressed, as a decision tree structure.

Theoretical foundations of UIB-IK are found in [6], [9], [13]; however, a synthesis of the main aspects is presented below.

Formulation of the Problem of Induction. Let $D = \{d_1, d_2, ..., d_m\}$ be an extensionally defined set of elements or examples and $R = \{r_1, r_2, ..., r_n\}$ an extensionally defined set of attributes (binary or multivalued), such that for each

$d_j \in D$ the values of these attributes are known. Given the extensional subsets $D_i = \{d_a, d_b, ..., d_c\}$, $i = 1, 2, ..., k$, $D \supseteq D_i$ we want to find an intensional description P_i, $i = 1, 2, ..., k$, of these subsets, $D_i = \{d_j \in D / P_i\}$, $i = 1, 2, ..., k$, expressed as a decision tree structure, satisfying a given criterion; moreover, P_i will be expressed in terms of a subset R_x, $R \supseteq R_x$, of attributes.

An *Enlarged Object Attribute Table (EOAT)* constitutes an adequate knowledge representation for the just mentioned problem, such as definitions 1 and 2 indicate.

Definition 1. An *Object Attribute Table (OAT)* is defined as a four-tuple as follows:

OAT = <D, R, V, F>, where

$D = \{d_1, d_2, ..., d_m\}$ is a set of elements or concrete objects of knowledge.

$R = \{r_1, r_2, ..., r_n\}$ is a set of qualities or attributes, also called *condition attributes.*

$V = \{V_1, V_2, ..., V_n\}$ is a family of sets, such that V_i is the set of values of attribute r_i adopted by the elements of D. In database literature V_i is called the domain of r_i.

$F = \{f_1, f_2, ..., f_n\}$ is a set of functions defining extensionally the values adopted by elements $d_i \in D$ for each attribute $r_j \in R$, that is, $f_i: D \times \{r_i\} \rightarrow V_i$, $i = 1...n$.

The *Subset Definition Table (SDT)* establishes, in a format compatible with that of the OAT, the subsets (or concepts) whose intensional description is desired, by means of the characteristic function f.

Definition 2. The SDT is defined as a three-tuple as follows:

SDT = <D, C, f>, where D has the same meaning as in definition 1, $C = \{D_1, D_2, ..., D_w\}$, $D \supseteq D_i$, $i = 1...w$, is a set of w subsets of D, also called concepts, $1 \leq w \leq m$, and the function f assigns to each element of D its corresponding subsets, that is, $f: D \rightarrow P(C)$, where P(C) denotes the set of parts of C.

The discussion of the problem becomes easier by representing the OAT and the SDT graphically, such as figure 1 indicates. We will refer to the Enlarged Object Attribute Table (EOAT); where $t_i{}^k \in V_k$, $k = 1...n$, $i = 1...m$, is the value of attribute r_k associated to element d_i through function f_k, $C_i \in P(C)$, denotes the subsets of C associated with element $d_i \in D$, $i = 1...m$. Note that P(C) can be interpreted as an attribute, called consequence attribute. However, more than one consequence attribute may be present in the EOAT.

D	r_1	r_2				r_n	P(C)
d_1	$t_1{}^1$	$t_1{}^2$	.	.	.	$t_1{}^n$	C_1
d_2	$t_2{}^1$	$t_2{}^2$		.	.	$t_2{}^n$	C_2
.	.	.				.	.
d_m	$t_m{}^1$	$t_m{}^2$	.	.	.	$t_m{}^n$	C_m

Fig. 1. Enlarged OAT

The choice of the subset R_x, $R \supseteq R_x$, of attributes to be used to describe intensionally the subsets or concepts of C constitutes one of the main stages of the inductive acquisition of knowledge process. In fact, an adequate subset R_x must be found before proceeding to generate a desired intensional description, expressed in terms of the attributes of R_x.

An important notion arising from the above theoretical considerations is the concept of *attribute basis*. An attribute basis of set R in relation to set C of concepts is a subset R_y, $R \supseteq R_y$, allowing to describe the concepts in C without any kind of confussion (contradiction).

There is a close connection between the concepts of *attribute basis* and *reduct* [27] of Pawlak, in the sense that a reduct defines a particular kind of attribute bases: those bases without *superfluous attributes*. However, in some cases such as those problems demanding an optimal intensional description to be found, the concept of reduct may lose significance, since an optimal description (for example, an optimal decision tree) may contain superfluous attributes. This is the reason for which the inductive procedure of UIB-IK is based on the concept of attribute basis instead of on a reduct approach.

3 Functional Structure and Performance Qualities of UIB-IK

The most accepted definition for Learning Systems suggests that such systems must be capable of improving its behaviour over time. This means that a learning system should be able to consider experiences about new situations, such as accepting new data coming from the external environment and interpreting the results when applied to the real world.

A unified general model to describe any learning system is still far from being found, in spite of the efforts of researchers. Figure 2 [23] illustrates a general sketch showing the main functional units of a learning system, selected as the basic standard which UIB-IK is based on. Circles in the model denote declarative knowledge elements (e.g. predicate calculus rules or statements made by an expert), whereas boxes represent procedures. Arrows show the data flow in the learning system. The Environment provides extensional information to the Knowledge Acquisition Element in the form of particular examples about some given concepts. The Knowledge Acquisition Element is in charge of transforming the extensional description of the concepts coming from the Environment into an adequate intensional knowledge structure, stored in the Knowledge Base. Finally, the Performance Element sees about performing the task of the system, whose acquired experience serves as feedback to the Knowledge Acquisition Element.

Performance qualities of UIB-IK try to cover the main aspects of the new perspective in the inductive acquisition of knowledge presented in [6], [13]. A synthesized description of each individual component of the functional structure of UIB-IK is given below.

The Environment. The Environment is made up of two essential knowledge components:
- The *EOAT*, such as it has been described in section 2.
- The *Additional Information (AI)* about the examples and concepts in the EOAT.

UIB-IK has a powerful mechanism to administrate the EOAT through a menu structure, allowing the following operations:

• To create a new EOAT.

• To load an EOAT placed in a file in secondary storage.

• To modify an EOAT by adding, deleting or changing data about the examples, such as the values of some attributes, the subsets (concepts) associated to some examples and the Additional Information about the examples.

• To display and print a given EOAT.

• To save a current EOAT.

Particular characteristics of each option in the menu are exposed in [21].

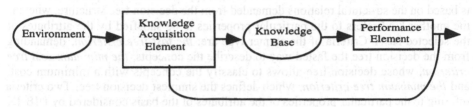

Fig. 2. A simple model for learning systems

UIB-IK allows binary and multivalued attributes to be included in the EOAT. Multivalued attributes may be qualitative or quantitative and no constraints on their domains are imposed. This fact makes the presence of continuous and discrete attributes to be possible, allowing also to include vague knowledge about their values (such as fuzzy, rough or incomplete knowledge).

When a very large amount of examples or condition attributes is to be processed, then a new arrangement of information in the EOAT may be necessary, so that learning techniques can be applied in an effient way. In particular, the methods implemented to process large EOAT's are based on two strategies:

• Windowing strategies [11], [12], which try to find an adequate model of the EOAT according to some criteria established, allowing to cover all the examples.

• Structural incremental learning strategies [11], [12], based on breaking the EOAT into portions and applying the learning process to each portion.

Additional Information (AI) includes those aspects to do with the examples and concepts in the EOAT and with the characteristics of the final decision tree to be obtained, which are considered by the Knowledge Acquisition Element in order to perform its task. The main AI considered by UIB-IK are:

i. Information about the cost of the condition attributes in the EOAT. Each attribute is supposed to have a cost associated. What this cost mean, depend on the particular case in hand.

ii. Information to do with the processing strategy of multivalued condition attributes.

iii. Information about alternative measures to describe the concepts when their initial description provided by the EOAT do not allow suitable decision trees to be induced.

iv. Information specifying the characteristics that the decision tree must satisfy. These characteristics are expressed in the form of criteria.

v. Information about the most adequate model of the EOAT to consider when windowing strategies are to be applied, or about the particular characteristics of the structural incremental learning strategy to apply, if it is the case.

The Knowledge Acquisition Element (KAE). The KAE constitutes the main procedural component of the learning system, as it is in charge of performing the inductive task according to suggestions given by the AI. Final results are expressed in the form of a decision tree structure.

General heuristics methods including efficient tree prunning techniques heve been used to implement the inductive process. These gencral algorithms will allow UIB-IK to cope with a lot of different problems. In particular, two kinds of optimality criteria have been considered by UIB-IK in several real applications developed; one of them is based on the structural relations demanded from the decision tree structure, whereas the another kind refers to the particular properties to be satisfied by the attributes of the selected basis. Criteria of the former type are: *the fast tree criterion,* demanding from the decision tree the fasted way to describe the concepts, *the minimum cost tree criterion,* whose decision tree allows to classify the concepts with a minimum cost, and *the minimum tree criterion,* which defines the simplest decision tree. Two criteria refering to the particular properties of the attributes of the basis considered by UIB-IK are: *the minimum cost basis criterion,* whose cost of the selected basis is minimum and *the minimum basis criterion,* defining an optimal basis as that containing a minimum number of attributes. However, the modular and parameterized design of UIB-IK allows new criteria to be considered in an easy way. The specific nature of the above mentioned criteria together with the characteristics of the inductive algorithms are described in detail in [13] and [21].

The KAE provides a complete menu structure allowing to perform the aspects included in Additional Information, which is described in detail in the user guide of UIB-IK [21].

The Knowledge Base (KB). The KB stores the intensional description of the concepts of the EOAT in the form of a decision tree structure, generated by the KAE.

UIB-IK also provides a powerful mechanism with a nice graphical user interface to perform the resultant decision tree in an interactive way, which has been developed for three different hardware systems: SUN Workstation, IBM PC computers and Apple computers.

4 Technical Aspects of UIB-IK

UIB-IK has been designed from the three following fundamental programming and design techniques:
- Modular Design Techniques.
- Structured Programming Techniques.
- Abstract Data Types Techniques.

At present, UIB-IK is made up of ten software modules interacting each other; however, the use of the above mentioned techniques allows an easy future extension of UIB-IK by adding new functional modules.

Moreover, the complex data structures used demand an explicit control of information, in order to avoid uncontrolled situations, leading to programming errors.

This may be avoided through the application of the concepts of visibility and encapsulation provided by the Abstract Data Types methodology.

UIB-IK is a user-friendly tool, with a powerful menu structure guiding the user and making its task easy.

The selection of the hardware resources to implement UIB-IK has been guided by the results of previous experiences, with an special attention to the processing capacity. Thus, Sparc Stations computers have been selected to cover the aims. In particular, two Sparc Station models have been used, whose main technical characteristics are illustrated in table 1.

NAME:	SUN Microsystems	Hyundai Electronics
MODEL:	SPARCstation IPC	SPARCstation IPX2
PROCESSOR:	1 x SPARC	1 x SPARC
FREQUENZY (in Mhz):	25	40
MIPS:	17'7	28'5
MFLOPS:	2'1	4'2
CACHE MEM. (in Kb):	64	64
RAM MEM. (in Mb):	24-32	32
RESOLUTION:	1152 x 900	1152 x 900
OPERATING SYSTEM:	SunOS 4.1.1	SunOS 4.1.1

Table 1. Hardware Resources

The C programming language was used to implement UIB-IK, providing important advantages such as transportability, low level instructions, recursive character and modularity.

5 Comparing Decision Trees from UIB-IK and ID3 Systems

In this section a comparison of the results obtained by the UIB-IK and ID3 systems is described, according to the minimum tree criterion (see section 3), which demands a simplest decision tree, in the sense that it contains a minimum number of nodes.

The initial sample, illustrated through figure 3, has been obtained from [17]. It contains four discrete multivalued condition attributes, r_1, r_2, r_3 and r_4, and two concepts, $\{0, 1\}$, to be described intensionally, represented by the consequence attribute C.

Figure 4 illustrates the decision tree obtained by UIB-IK. This tree contains 7 inner nodes and 8 leaf nodes. Inner nodes are represented by attributes r_1 and r_3, but note that only subsets $\{2, 3\}$ and $\{2, 3\}$ of values of the domains of these attributes respectively, appear in the decision tree. Leaf nodes identified by the G1 value denote the subset of D whose elements have associated the value 1 for the consequence attribute C, whereas G2 leaf nodes denote the subset of D represented by the value 0 of attribute C. Each branch in the tree represents one decision rule, thus the tree contains 8 rules. Notice that this is a binary tree induced after applying the discretization procedure of UIB-IK. Such as the applied criterion demands, no other decision tree with a minimum number of nodes exists.

Figure 5 represents the decision tree obtained by the ID3 system. This tree contains 9 inner nodes and 20 leaf nodes (rules), considering for inner nodes all the values of their domains. This means that superabundance of information is not

608

avoided by ID3. In fact, this tree is far of being the best one according to the established criterion. What is more, design characteristics of the ID3 system do not allow to include new attribute selection criteria in an easy way, which is not the case of UIB-IK, whose ability to adapt to circumstances has been proved.

6 Experimental Results

Successful experimental results have been obtained in developing real applications through UIB-IK. A medical application [3] to do with the diagnosis of ascites, a common disease known to lead to the formation of free fluid within the peritoneal cavity, was developed by members of the Computer Science Department of the Balearic Islands University and the 'Son Dureta Hospital', in Palma de Mallorca, Balearic Islands.

The initial sample provided by the expert Doctors of the hospital (that is, the EOAT), contains 3605 examples of particular cases of ascites and 35 condition attributes, and covers 14 possible diagnosis (causes of ascites). Due to the large amound of examples and attributes, structural incremental learning techniques were applied.

202 patients were diagnosed through the decision tree obtained by UIB-IK, in order to evaluate the accuracy of the results. 193 cases (95.5%) were diagnosed correctly, whereas 9 cases (4.5%) were missclassified. The analysis of the missclassified cases showed a lack of information in the initial sample about the corresponding patients. Moreover, UIB-IK was also submitted to another rigorous performance evaluation, one of the main stages of this evaluation procedure consisting of comparing the results obtained by UIB-IK to those obtained by four hepatology experts. The main conclusions of physicians were as follows: a) in spite of the fact that the medical application of UIB-IK was conceived initially as a prototype, its usefulness as a pedagogical tool or even more, as an aid system for clinical cases, was considered; b) time spent by the computer application in classifying the considered patients is much shorter than that spent by the doctors; c) although the medical application was not completed with regard to the medical cases covered, its capability to establish the right conclusion concerning the cause of ascites was shown.

Another significant experiment supported by a research project of the Spanish Government[1] to do with Real Time Supervision of Dynamic Control Systems [10] has also been developed through UIB-IK. The experiment is based on a lab pilot plant, made up of two liquid tanks, interconnected through a control valve, which regulates the level of liquid inside the two tanks. The aim of the control system consist of keeping the level of liquid of the two tanks in a satisfactory volume interval, according to a preestablished objective function. However, satisfying suitably this objective depend, among other reasons, on the existence of disturbances during the process, whose causes must be diagnosed according to preestablished time constraints, so that the behaviour of the dynamic system may be led to an acceptable situation.

The task of UIB-IK consisted of generating an adequate decision tree defining the possible causes of disturbances of the dynamic system in terms of the variables provided by the experts, in such a way that time constraints are satisfied for any considered cause. This experiment pointed up the powerful capacity of UIB-IK to consider real time based criteria, extending so its application range to the field of supervision of dynamic processes.

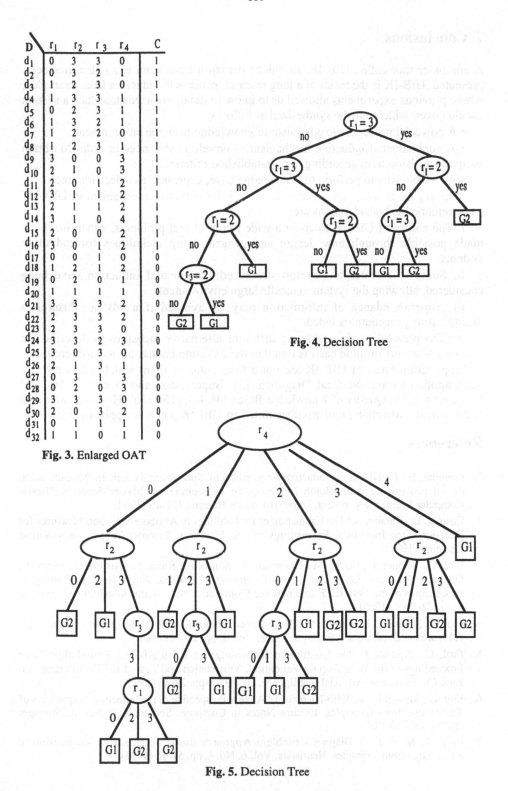

D	r_1	r_2	r_3	r_4	C
d_1	0	3	3	0	1
d_2	0	3	2	1	1
d_3	1	2	3	0	1
d_4	1	3	3	1	1
d_5	0	2	3	1	1
d_6	1	3	2	1	1
d_7	1	2	2	0	1
d_8	1	2	3	1	1
d_9	3	0	0	3	1
d_{10}	2	1	0	3	1
d_{11}	2	0	1	2	1
d_{12}	3	1	1	1	1
d_{13}	2	1	1	2	1
d_{14}	3	1	0	4	1
d_{15}	2	0	0	2	1
d_{16}	2	0	1	2	1
d_{17}	0	0	1	0	0
d_{18}	1	2	1	2	0
d_{19}	2	2	0	1	0
d_{20}	1	1	1	1	0
d_{21}	3	3	3	0	0
d_{22}	2	3	3	2	0
d_{23}	2	3	3	0	0
d_{24}	3	2	2	3	0
d_{25}	3	0	3	0	0
d_{26}	2	1	3	1	0
d_{27}	0	3	1	3	0
d_{28}	0	2	0	3	0
d_{29}	3	3	3	0	0
d_{30}	2	0	3	2	0
d_{31}	0	1	1	1	0
d_{32}	1	1	0	1	0

Fig. 3. Enlarged OAT

Fig. 4. Decision Tree

Fig. 5. Decision Tree

7 Conclusions

A computer tool called UIB-IK, to induce decision trees from examples, has been presented. UIB-IK is the result of a long research process in induction from examples, whose previous experiments allowed us to know in detail the needs that such a system should cover, which may be synthesized as follows:

• A powerful procedure to administrate knowledge from the environment.

• A sophisticated inductive mechanism to develop inferences in order to obtain adequate decision trees according to preestablished criteria.

• A flexible way to perform the knowledge base, expressed as a decision tree.

With regard to the main aspects to do with the inductive mechanism of UIB-IK, some remarkable considerations are:

i. The ability of UIB-IK to cover a wide range of real problems, which has been made possible through new design and programming techniques for inductive systems.

ii. Some techniques to develop structured incremental induction have been considered, allowing the system to handle large environments.

iii. Superabundance of information may be avoided if needs be, through a discretization procedure included.

iv. The possibility of considering different alternative measures to describe the concepts when no attribute basis is found in the environment has been considered.

Application areas of UIB-IK are not a few, some of them which it has already been applied to are: Medical Diagnosis [3], Supervision and Decision [10] and Evaluation of the Quality of Knowledge Bases [4], [5], [15], [16]. However, any area to do with classification problems constitutes an UIB-IK potential application field.

References

1. Canudas, B.: CONEIX, An Inductive Acquisition of Knowledge System, in Mecanización de un proceso de Adquisición Inductiva de Conocimiento. Master Science Thesis. Computer Science Department, University of the Balearic Islands (1992)
2. Cestnik, B., Karalic, A.: The Estimation of Probabilities in Attribute Selection Measures for Decision Tree Induction. Proceedings of the European Summer School on Machine Learning (1991)
3. Fiol, G., Vaquer, P., Ferrer, M., Llompart, A., Sansó, A., Riera, J., Garrido, C., Gayà, J., Obrador, A.: Computer-Aided Causal Diagnosis of Ascites. Analysis of a Prototype. Proceedings of the 1996 IEEE International Conference on Systems, Man and Cybernetics, pp. 1102-1107 (1996)
4. Fiol, G., Aguiló, I., Ferrer, M.: Rule-Based Diagnostic Systems Quality Assurance. Advances in Database and Expert Systems, Vol. 3, pp. 29-34 (1996)
5. Fiol, G., Aguiló, I.: On Qualitative Knowledge in a Rule-Based Knowledge Base. Proceedings of the Workshop on Validation, Verification and Test of KBS's. International Joint Conference on Artificial Intelligence, IJCAI'93. pp. 27-36 (1993)
6. Fiol, G., Miró-Julià, J., Miró-Nicolau, J.: A New Perspective in the Inductive Acquisition of Knowledge from Examples. Lecture Notes in Computer Science 687. Berlin: Springer (1993), pp. 219-228
7. Fiol, G., Miró, J.: A Diagnosis Problem Approach Based on Inductive Acquisition of Knowledge from Examples. Heuristics, Vol. 6, No. 3, pp. 54-65 (1993)

8. Fiol, G., Miró, J.: S.A.I.C., An Inductive Acquisition of Knowledge System. Revista de Ciència 7, pp. 61-78 (1988)

9. Fiol, G., Miró, J.: Theoretical Considerations about Subset Descriptions. Lecture Notes in Computer Science 763. Berlin: Springer (1993), pp. 111-117.

10. Fiol, G., Ferrer, M.: Expert System for Supervision of Real Time Dynamic Processes. Proceedings of the 1997 IEEE International Conference on Systems, Man and Cybernetics, Orlando (USA), pp. 1966-1971, (1997).

11. Fiol, G., Ferrer, M.: Learning from Examples I: Longitudinal Learning. Abstracts of the Fifth International Conference on Computer Aided Systems, EUROCAST'95 (1995)

12. Fiol, G., Ferrer, M.: Learning from Examples II: Transverse Learning. Abstracts of the Fifth International Conference on Computer Aided Systems, EUROCAST'95 (1995)

13. Fiol, G.: Contribution to the Inductive Acquisition of Knowledge. Ph.D. Thesis. Computer Science Department, University of the Balearic Islands (1991)

14. Fiol, G.: Inductive Systems with Incomplete Information. Internal Report. Computer Science Department, University of the Balearic Islands (1998)

15. Aguiló, I., Fiol, G.: Evaluation of the Quality of a Knowledge Base. Proceedings of Cybernetics and Systems'96, pp. 1217-1221 (1996)

16. Aguiló, I., Fiol, G.: Qualitative Aspects about System Diagnosis. Advances in Systems Studies, Vol. 2, pp. 64-68 (1995)

17. Wong, J. H.: An Inductive Learning System-ILS. A Thesis submitted to the Faculty of Graduate Studies and Research. Faculty of Science. University of Regina (1986)

18. Quinlan, J. R.: C4.5 Programs for Machine Learning. Morgan Kaufmann Pub. (1993)

19. Quinlan, J. R.: Induction of Decision Trees. Machine Learning, Vol. 1, No. 1, pp. 81-106 (1986)

20. Breiman, L., Friedman, J., Olsen, R., Stone, C.: Classification and Regression Trees. Wadsworth International Group (1984)

21. Ferrer, M.: UIB-IK, an Inductive Acquisition of Knowledge System, in Prototipo de un Sistema de Adquisición Inductiva de Conocimiento para la descripción de la Ascitis. Master Science Thesis. Computer Science Department, University of the Balearic Islands (1993)

22. Utgoff:, P.: ID5: An Incremental ID3. International Conference on Machine Learning, pp. 107-120 (1988)

23. Cohen, R., Feigenbaum, E. (eds.): The Handbook of Artificial Intelligence, Vol. 3. Pitman (1982)

24. Michalski, R. S., Larson, J. B.: Selection of most Representative Training Examples and Incremental Generation of VL1 Hypothesis: The Underlying Methodology and the Description of Programs ESEL and AQ11. Report No. 867, Dep. of Computer Science, University of Illinois (1987)

25. Crawford, S.: Extensions to the CART Algorithms. International Journal of Man-Machine Studies 31, pp. 197-217 (1989)

26. Weiss, S., Kulikowski, C.: Computer Systems that learn. Morgan Kaufmann Pub. (1991)

27. Pawlak, Z.: Rough Sets. International Journal of Computer and Information Sciences, Vol. 11, No. 5, pp. 341-356 (1982)

Preterm Birth Risk Assessed by a New Method of Classification Using Selective Partial Matching*

Jerzy W. Grzymala-Busse[1], Linda K. Goodwin[2], and Xiaohui Zhang[1]

[1] Department of Electrical Engineering and Computer Science,
University of Kansas, Lawrence, KS 66045
[2] Department of Information Services and the School of Nursing,
Duke University, Durham, NC 27710

ABSTRACT: In the United States, 8–12% of all newborns are delivered *preterm*, i.e., before 37 weeks of gestation. Most existing methods to assess preterm birth are based on risk scoring. These methods are only between 17% and 38% predictive in determining preterm birth. Hence there is need for data mining and knowledge discovery in database for predicting birth outcomes in pregnant women. This paper presents a new approach to classification (diagnosis) using selective partial matching. It is shown that our approach is more stable and, in general, more accurate than the method used so far. Our other result shows that classification based on more specific rules is worse.

KEYWORDS: Preterm birth, machine learning, knowledge discovery in databases, data mining, rough set theory, rule induction, classification of examples, system LERS.

1 Introduction

In the United States, 8–12% of all newborns are delivered before 37 weeks of gestation. Such babies are considered to be "preterm". Premature, or preterm, babies die at much higher rates than babies who remain in the womb for their normal 9 month gestation. They also have increased incidence of lifelong handicaps and disabilities that include blindness, respiratory problems, neurological problems, etc., see [3] If physicians and nurses who care for pregnant women could better predict who is at risk, then they could more appropriately intervene with educational programs, bed rest orders, antibiotic treatment, and early symptom management to prolong gestation and improve outcomes for infants and their families. In spite of amazing medical and technological advances that can keep premature babies alive, the rate of preterm birth is increasing in a developed country where it would seem reasonable to expect a decrease in the numbers and rates of preterm birth. Most existing methods to assess preterm birth are based on risk scoring. These methods are between 17% and 38% predictive in determining preterm birth [10]. Hence data mining and knowledge discovery in database tools are being applied for predicting birth outcomes in pregnant women [7].

---

* This work was supported in part by the National Library of Medicine, USA, Grant No. RO1 LM-O6488-02 and by the Committee for Scientific Research, Warsaw, Poland, Grant No. 8T11C00512.

The most persistent limitation for preterm birth risk classification is our
continued lack of understanding about the causes of preterm birth. The role of specific
risk factors and of the possible synergistic relationships between risk factor patterns is
an area where knowledge discovery in databases may offer improved prediction over
experts' heuristics. In our study, using experts for rule verification proved to be a
non-trivial task. Experts had great difficulty in verifying rules that appeared (to them)
to be incomplete, that is, the rules were not implausible and did not contain irrelevant
conditions, per se, but the information contained in an individual rule did not appear
to have enough information to make a judgment about preterm or full term birth.
The challenge is that perinatal experts believe prediction based on rules containing
more conditions, i.e., more specific, are better. Experts perceive that less specific
rules are "too simplistic". Rules are considered less specific if the numbers of
attribute-value pairs, or conditions, are limited to a small number within the rule.
Our results show that prediction of preterm birth based on less specific rules is not
worse. While the predictive accuracies using more specific versus less specific rules
were not large, from a decision support standpoint the shorter less specific rules are
computationally more efficient and easier for the human to comprehend and remember
[7, 8].

Usually classification (or diagnosis) of unseen cases is based on complete and
partial matching of rules against unseen cases. The main objective of the paper is
comparison of two different approaches to partial matching: *mixed matching*, used so
far, with a new approach, called *selective matching*, introduced in the paper.

2 Rule induction by LERS

Historical datasets describing the length of pregnancy, collected by commercial data
providers, present each patient as a *case* (or an *example*) characterized by a vector of
values of many variables. A simplified version of such a dataset, just to illustrate the
problem, is presented in Table 1. In practice the number of variables is bigger,
similarly, the number of cases is also much bigger. The first variable, *Identifier*, can
be considered an attribute, but it should be ignored in the process of data mining,
anyway.

Variables are either independent (*attributes*) or dependent (*decisions*). For this
application, the decision *delivery* was single and it had two values (*classes* or
concepts): *fullterm* and *preterm*.

Frequently, datasets describing pregnant women have conflicting cases (or,
briefly, datasets are *inconsistent*). Examples are conflicting if values for all attributes
are pairwise equal but decision values are different. In Table 1, the case_1 and case_6

Table 1. Dataset

	Attributes			Decision
Identifier	Age	Complications	Pregnancy	Delivery
Case_1	25–30	none	second	fullterm
Case_2	25–30	smoking	first	preterm
Case_3	<25	bleeding	first	fullterm
Case_4	>30	none	third	fullterm
Case_5	<25	none	first	fullterm
Case_6	25–30	none	second	preterm

are conflicting. In other words, the data sets are imperfect. Knowledge discovery from such data is affected by uncertainty. The best tool to deal with inconsistency is rough set theory [12, 13]. Thus a choice of the data mining tool based on rough set theory was natural and the system LERS (Learning from Examples based on Rough Set theory) was selected. The system has been developed at the University of Kansas [5]. Let us recall a few definitions from rough set theory.

Let U denote the set of all cases of the dataset and let P denote a nonempty subset of the set Q of all variables, i.e., attributes and decisions. Let P be a subset of Q. An *indiscernibility relation* ρ on U is defined for all $x, y \in U$ by $x \rho y$ if and only if for both x and y the values for all variables from P are identical. Equivalence classes of ρ are called *elementary sets* of P. An equivalence class of ρ containing x is denoted $[x]_P$. Any finite union of elementary sets of P is called a *definable set* in P. Let X be a class. In general, X is not a definable set in P. However, set X may be approximated by two definable sets in P, the first one is called a *lower approximation of* X *in* P, denoted by $\underline{P}X$ and defined as follows

$$\{x \in U \mid [x]_P \subseteq X \}.$$

The second set is called an *upper approximation of* X *in* P, denoted by $\overline{P}X$ and defined as follows

$$\{x \in U \mid [x]_P \cap X \neq \emptyset \}.$$

The lower approximation of X in P is the greatest definable set in P, contained in X. The upper approximation of X in P is the least definable set in P containing X. A *rough set* of X is the family of all subsets of U having the same lower and the same upper approximations of X.

In our example (Table 1), $U = \{\text{case\_1, case\_2,..., case\_6}\}$, say that $P = \{Age, Complications, Pregnancy\}$. An indiscernibility relation ρ may be presented by a partition on U that uniquely defines ρ:

$$\{\{\text{case\_1, case\_6}\}, \{\text{case\_2}\}, \{\text{case\_3}\}, \{\text{case\_4}\}, \{\text{case\_5}\}\}.$$

The interpretation of the above partition is: the only two distinct cases that are indiscernible are case_1 and case_6. The blocks of the partition are elementary sets of P.

For the class *preterm*, i.e., the set {case_2, case_3, case_6}, the lower approximation is the set {case_2, case_3}, and the upper approximation is the set {case_1, case_2, case_3, case_6}.

Rules induced from the lower approximation of the concept *certainly* describe the concept, so they are called *certain*. On the other hand, rules induced from the upper

Table 2. Dataset in the LERS format

< x [dentifier	a Age	a Complications	a Pregnancy	d > Delivery]
Case_1	25–30	none	second	fullterm
Case_2	25–30	smoking	first	preterm
Case_3	<25	bleeding	first	fullterm
Case_4	>30	none	third	fullterm
Case_5	<25	none	first	fullterm
Case_6	25–30	none	second	preterm

Table 3. Dataset in the LERS format

< x [Identifier	a Age	a Complications	a Pregnancy	d > Delivery]
Case_1	25–30	none	second	fullterm
Case_2	25–30	smoking	first	preterm
Case_3	<25	bleeding	first	preterm
Case_4	>30	none	third	fullterm
Case_5	<25	none	first	fullterm
Case_6	25–30	none	second	fullterm

approximation of the concept describe the concept only *possibly* (or *plausibly*), so they are called *possible* [4]. LERS checks input data for consistency. If a class is not involved in conflicts with other classes, rules are induced directly for the class. For a class involved in conflicts, lower and upper approximations are computed.

Table 2 presents the input data from Table 1 in the LERS format. The first row of the Table 2, starting from "<", declares which variables are attributes (those denoted by *a*s) and which are decisions (denoted by *d*s). This line ends with ">". The first line may contain the letter *x* (corresponding variable and variable values will be ignored in all subsequent computations). The second line, starting from "[" and ending with "]", contains names of all variables. The following lines contain vectors of variable values. Table 3 presents the input data for LERS for computing certain rules for class *preterm* from Table 1, and Table 4 presents the input data for computing possible rules for the same class.

In this project the algorithm LEM2 [2, 5] was used to induce rule sets. We cite basic definitions necessary to explain principles of LEM2 algorithm. Let *B* be a nonempty lower or upper approximation of a concept represented by a decision-value pair (*d*, *w*). Set *B depends on a set T* of attribute-value pairs *t* if and only if

$$\emptyset \neq [T] = \bigcap_{t \in T} [t] \subseteq B,$$

where [(*a*, *v*)] denoted the set of all examples such that for attribute *a* its values are *v*. Set *T* is a *minimal complex* of *B* if and only if *B* depends on *T* and no proper subset *T'* of *T* exists such that *B* depends on *T'*. Let $\mathbb{T}$ be a nonempty collection of nonempty sets of attribute-value pairs. Then $\mathbb{T}$ is a *local covering of B* if and only if the following conditions are satisfied:

(1) each member *T* of $\mathbb{T}$ is a minimal complex of *B*,

Table 4. Dataset in the LERS format

< x [Identifier	a Age	a Complications	a Pregnancy	d > Delivery]
Case_1	25–30	none	second	preterm
Case_2	25–30	smoking	first	preterm
Case_3	<25	bleeding	first	preterm
Case_4	>30	none	third	fullterm
Case_5	<25	none	first	fullterm
Case_6	25–30	none	second	preterm

(2) $\bigcup_{T \in \mathbb{T}} [T] = B$, and

(3) $\mathbb{T}$ is minimal, i.e., $\mathbb{T}$ has the smallest possible number of members.

The user may select an option of LEM2 with or without taking into account attribute priorities. The procedure LEM2 with attribute priorities is presented below. The other option differs from the one presented below in the selection of a pair $t \in T(G)$ in the inner loop WHILE. When LEM2 is not to take attribute priorities into account, the first criterion is ignored. In our experiments all attribute priorities were equal to each other.

Procedure LEM2
(**input:** a set B,
output: a single local covering $\mathbb{T}$ of set B);
begin
    G := B;
    $\mathbb{T}$:= ∅;
    while G ≠ ∅
    begin
    T := ∅;
    T(G) := {t | [t] ∩ G ≠ ∅};
    while T = ∅ **or** [T] ⊈ B
        begin
        select a pair t ∈ T(G) with the highest attribute
          priority, if a tie occurs, select a pair t ∈ T(G)
          such that $\left| [t] \cap G \right|$ is maximum; if another tie
          occurs, select a pair t ∈ T(G) with the smallest
          cardinality of [t]; if a further tie occurs, select
          first pair;
                T := T ∪ {t};
                G := [t] ∩ G;
                T(G) := {t | [t] ∩ G ≠ ∅};
                T(G) := T(G) – T;
        end {while}
        for each t in T **do**
          if [T – {t}] ⊆ B **then** T := T – {t};
        $\mathbb{T}$:= $\mathbb{T}$ ∪ {T};

        G := B $- \bigcup_{T \in \mathbb{T}} [T]$;

    end {while};
    for each T in $\mathbb{T}$ **do**

        if $\bigcup_{S \in \mathbb{T}-\{T\}} [S] = B$ **then** $\mathbb{T}$:= $\mathbb{T}$ – {T};

end {procedure}.

3. Classification system of LERS

For classification of new cases system LERS uses a modification of the "bucket brigade algorithm" [1, 6]. The decision to which concept an example belongs is made on the basis of three factors: strength, specificity, and support. They are defined as follows: *Strength* is the total number of examples correctly classified by the rule during training. *Specificity* is the total number of attribute-value pairs on the left-hand side of the rule. The matching rules with a larger number of attribute-value pairs are considered more specific. The third factor, *support*, is defined as the sum of scores of all matching rules from the concept. The concept C for which the support, i.e., the following expression

$$\sum_{\text{matching rules } R \text{ describing } C} \text{Strength}(R) * \text{Specificity}(R)$$

is the largest is a winner and the example is classified as being a member of C.

If an example is not completely matched by any rule, some classification systems use *partial matching*. System AQ15, during partial matching, uses the probabilistic sum of all measures of fit for rules [11]. Another approach to partial matching is presented in [14]. Holland *et al.* [9] do not consider partial matching as a viable alternative of complete matching and rely on a default hierarchy instead. In LERS partial matching does not rely on the input of the user. If complete matching is impossible, all partially matching rules are identified. These are rules with at least one attribute-value pair matching the corresponding attribute-value pair of an example.

For any partially matching rule R, the additional factor, called *Matching factor* (R), is computed. In partial matching, the concept C for which the following expression is the largest

$$\sum_{\text{partially matching rules } R \text{ describing } C} \text{Matching\_factor}(R) * \text{Strength } (R) * \text{Specificity}(R)$$

is the winner and the example is classified as being a member of C. All rules, induced by LERS, are preceded by three numbers: specificity, strength, and the total number of training examples matched by the rule.

The above approach to partial matching, used so far in LERS, will be called *mixed*. The name comes from its application: all rules with one missing condition (i.e., all rule conditions match the example except one), two missing conditions, etc., are used simultaneously.

In this paper we introduce a new approach to partial matching. In this approach, in partial matching, for a given example, all rules with one missing condition are identified first. If at least one rule with exactly one missing condition matches the example, classification is performed. Rules that could match the example with two or more missing conditions are ignored. On the other hand, if there is no one rule with one missing condition that matches the example, rules with two missing conditions are searched for. If the search is successful, the classification is performed on the basis of such rules and rules with three or more missing conditions are ignored. If there is no one rule with two missing conditions that match the example, rules with three missing conditions are looked for, etc. The new approach is called a *selective partial matching*.

4 Experiments

For our experiments three perinatal datasets were used. These datasets are characterized in Tables 5 and 6.

Table 5. Training data

	Dataset 1	Dataset 2	Dataset 3
Number of cases	1,654	1,218	6,608
Number of cases in the class *fullterm*	1,482	307	4,096
Number of cases in the class *preterm*	172	911	2,512
Number of conflicting cases	179	0	16
Number of attributes	13	73	67

Table 6. Unseen (testing) data

	Dataset 1	Dataset 2	Dataset 3
Number of cases	1,953	1,218	6,608
Number of cases in the class *fullterm*	1,199	330	4,268
Number of cases in the class *preterm*	394	888	2,340

Two main strategies were used for classification of unseen cases: complete matching first, then partial matching and complete matching and partial matching at the same time. Within each strategy, four approaches were tested: using specificity and not using specificity combined with selective partial matching and mixed partial matching. Results are presented in Tables 7 and 8.

Table 7. Error rate for complete matching first, then partial matching

	Using specificity		Not using specificity	
	Selective partial matching	Mixed partial matching	Selective partial matching	Mixed partial matching
Dataset 1	9.92	9.92	9.54	9.54
Dataset 2	28.0	28.0	28.0	28.0
Dataset 3	31.63	32.01	31.07	31.46

Table 8. Error rate for complete matching and partial matching at the same time

	Using specificity		Not using specificity	
	Selective partial matching	Mixed partial matching	Selective partial matching	Mixed partial matching
Dataset 1	10.04	24.73	9.67	24.73
Dataset 2	28.0	27.09	28.0	27.09
Dataset 3	31.63	35.04	31.07	35.41

5 Conclusions

Selective partial matching gives more stable results of classification than mixed partial matching. The mixed partial matching is surprisingly unstable: it may substantially increase the error rate, for example, by switching from *complete matching first, then partial matching* to *complete matching and partial matching at the same time*, not using specificity, for selective partial matching, the error rate increases from 9.54% to 9.67%, while, under the same circumstances, for mixed partial matching increases from 9.54% to 24.73%.

Roughly speaking, using the strategy *complete matching first, then partial matching* gives better results than classification with using *complete matching and partial matching at the same time*.

In general, the error rate in classification of unseen cases is larger when factor *specificity* is used. By using specificity priority is given to rules with larger number of conditions. Such rules are weaker, so it should be not surprising that resulting classification is worse.

An additional observation: in our experiments for the three perinatal data sets, in selective partial matching, only one missing condition was used all the time, i.e., partial matching was always performed with only one missing condition on the left hand side of rules. This may explain why selective partial matching gives more stable results of classification—rules with larger number of missing conditions may cause only "noise", their contribution to final classification is misleading.

A conclusion for diagnosis of preterm birth is that the more missing conditions in rules are taken into account the more erroneous final diagnosis is.

The information explosion of the past decade has created a situation where health care providers are unable to assimilate the volumes of information available to make decisions in optimal fashion. Traditional methods of science have not yielded satisfactory solutions for the problem. Ongoing knowledge discovery in database work to analyze perinatal clinical data may someday offer improved decision support for identifying women at risk for preterm birth. Progress toward this goal continues to be a nontrivial research problem that benefits from combined efforts between clinical domain experts and knowledge engineers.

Acknowledgment. Special thanks to St Luke's Regional Perinatal Center (Kansas City, MO), HealthDyne Perinatal Services, Inc. (Marietta, GA), and TOKOS Corporation (Santa Ana, CA) for providing data.

References

[1] Booker, L. B., Goldberg, D. E., and Holland, J. F.: Classifier systems and genetic algorithms. In *Machine Learning. Paradigms and Methods*. Carbonell, J. G. (ed.), The MIT Press (1990) 235–282.

[2] Chan, C. C. and Grzymala-Busse, J. W.: On the attribute redundancy and the learning programs ID3, PRISM, and LEM2. Department of Computer Science, University of Kansas, TR-91-14 (1991) 20 pp.

[3] Feldman, W. E. and Wood, B.: The economic impact of high-risk pregnancies. *Journal of Health Care Finance* 24 (1997) 64–71.

[4] Grzymala-Busse, J. W. *Managing Uncertainty in Expert Systems*. Kluwer Academic Publishers (1991).

[5] Grzymala-Busse, J. W.: LERS—A system for learning from examples based on rough sets. In *Intelligent Decision Support. Handbook of Applications and Advances of the Rough Sets Theory*. Slowinski, R. (ed.), Kluwer Academic Publishers (1992) 3–18.

[6] Grzymala-Busse, J. W.: Managing uncertainty in machine learning from examples. *Proc. of the Third Intelligent Information Systems Workshop*, Wigry, Poland, June 6–11, 1994, 70–84.

[7] Grzymala-Busse, J. W., and Goodwin, L. K.: Improving prediction of preterm birth using a new classification scheme and rule induction. Proc. of the 18-th Annual Symposium on Computer Applications in Medical Care (SCAMC), Washington, DC, November 5–9, 1994, 730–734.

[8] Grzymala-Busse, J. W., and Goodwin, L. K.: A comparison of less specific versus more specific rules for preterm birth prediction. Proc. of the First Online Workshop on Soft Computing WSC1 on the Internet, Nagoya University, Japan, Aug. 19–30, 1996, 129–133.

[9] Holland, J. H., Holyoak K. J., and Nisbett, R. E.: *Induction. Processes of Inference, Learning, and Discovery*. The MIT Press (1986).

[10] McLean, M., Walters, W. A. and Smith, R. Prediction and early diagnosis of preterm labor: a critical review. *Obstetrical & Gynecological Survey* 48 (1993) 209–225.

[11] Michalski, R. S., Mozetic, I., Hong, J. and Lavrac, N.: The AQ15 inductive learning system: An overview and experiments. Department of Computer Science, University of Illinois, Rep. UIUCDCD-R-86-1260 (1986).

[12] Pawlak, Z.: Rough sets. *International Journal Computer and Information Sciences* 11 (1982) 341–356.

[13] Pawlak, Z.: *Rough Sets. Theoretical Aspects of Reasoning about Data*. Kluwer Academic Publishers (1991).

[14] Slowinski, R. and Stefanowski, J.: Handling various types of uncertainty in the rough set approach. *Proc of the RKSD–93, International Workshop on Rough Sets and Knowledge Discovery* (1993) 395–397.

Probabilistic Rough Induction: The GDT-RS Methodology and Algorithms

Juzhen Dong[1], Ning Zhong[1], and Setsuo Ohsuga[2]

[1] Dept. of Computer Science and Sys. Eng., Yamaguchi University
[2] Dept. of Information and Computer Science, Waseda University

Abstract. In this paper, we introduce a probabilistic rough induction methodology and discuss two algorithms for its implementation. This methodology is based on the combination of *Generalization Distribution Table (GDT)* and the *Rough Set* theory (GDT-RS for short). A GDT is a table in which the probabilistic relationships between concepts and instances over discrete domains are represented. The GDT provides a probabilistic basis for evaluating the strength of a rule. The rough set theory is used to find minimal relative reducts from the set of rules with larger strength. Main features of the GDT-RS are (1) biases can be selected flexibly for search control, and background knowledge can be used as a bias to control the creation of a GDT and the rule induction process; (2) the uncertainty of a rule including the prediction of possible instances can be represented explicitly in the strength of the rule.

1 Introduction

Over the last two decades, many researchers have investigated inductive methods to learn *if-then* rules and concepts from instances. Based on the viewpoint of the value of information, these methods can be divided into two types. The first type is based on the *formal* value of information, that is, the real meaning of data is not considered in the learning process. ID3 is a typical method belonging to this type [Quinlan-86]. Although *if-then* rules can be discovered by using the methods, it is difficult to use background knowledge in the learning process. The other type of inductive methods is based on the *semantic* value of information, that is, the real meaning of data must be considered by using some background knowledge in the learning process. Dblearn is a typical method belonging to this type [Han-93]. It can discover rules by means of background knowledge represented by concept hierarchies, but if there is no background knowledge, it can do nothing.

In this paper, we introduce a new methodology called GDT-RS, in which both the formal value and the semantic value of information are considered, for learning *if-then* rules in data with uncertainty and incompleteness, as well as discuss two algorithms for its implementation. GDT-RS is based on the combination of *Generalization Distribution Table (GDT)* and the *Rough Set* theory. The main features of the GDT-RS are: biases can be selected flexibly for search control; background knowledge can be used as a bias to control the creation of a GDT and the rule induction process; unseen instances can be predicted and the uncertainty of a rule including the prediction of possible instances can be represented explicitly in the strength of the rule.

2 The GDT Methodology

The central idea of our methodology is using a variant of transition matrix, which is called *Generalization Distribution Table (GDT)*, as a hypothesis search space for generalization, in which the probabilistic relationships between concepts and instances over discrete domains are represented [Zhong-96]. This section describes the basic concepts and principles of the GDT methodology.

2.1 GDT

We define a GDT consisting of three components: *possible instances, possible generalizations* for instances, and *probabilistic relationships* between possible instances and possible generalizations.

The *possible instances*, which are denoted in the top row of a GDT, are all possible combinations of attribute values in a database.

The *possible generalizations* for instances, which are denoted in the left column of a GDT, are all possible cases of generalization for all possible instances.

The *probabilistic relationships* between the possible instances and the possible generalizations, which are denoted in the elements G_{ij} of a GDT, are the probabilistic distribution for describing the strength of the relationship between every possible instance and every possible generalization. The prior distribution is equiprobable, if we do not use any prior background knowledge.

$$G_{ij} = p(PI_j | PG_i) = \begin{cases} \dfrac{1}{N_{PG_i}} & \text{if } PG_i \supset PI_j \\ \\ 0 & \text{otherwise} \end{cases} \tag{1}$$

where PI_j is the jth possible instance, PG_i is the ith possible generalization, and N_{PG_i} is the number of the possible instances satisfying the ith possible generalization, that is, N_{PG_i} is the product of number of values of attribute that are not contained in PG_i. Let m be the number of attributes, n_k the number of different attribute values in attribute k, N_{PG_i} is given by

$$N_{PG_i} = \prod_1^m (n_k : \ PG_i[k] = *) \tag{2}$$

Here, we need to distinguish two kinds of attributes: *condition* attributes and *decision* attributes (sometimes called class attributes) in a database. Condition attributes as possible instances are used to create the GDT but the decision attribute is not. The decision attribute is usually used to distinguish which concept (class) should be described in a rule.

Table 2 is an example of the GDT, which is generated by using three condition attributes, A, B, C, in a sample database shown in Table 1, and $A \in \{a_0, a_1\}$, $B \in \{b_0, b_1, b_2\}$, $C \in \{c_0, c_1\}$. Furthermore, "$*$" in Table 2, which specifies a wild card, denotes the generalization for instances[3]. For example, the generalization $*b_0 c_1$ means the attribute A is unimportant for describing a concept.

Table 2.
A GDT generated from the sample database

	$a_0b_0c_0$	$a_0b_0c_1$	$a_0b_1c_0$	$a_0b_1c_1$	...	$a_1b_2c_1$
$*b_0c_0$	1/2				...	
$*b_0c_1$		1/2			...	
$*b_1c_0$			1/2		...	
$*b_1c_1$				1/2	...	
$*b_2c_0$					...	
$*b_2c_1$					...	1/2
a_0*c_0	1/3		1/3		...	
a_0*c_1		1/3		1/3	...	
a_1*c_0					...	
a_1*c_1					...	1/3
a_0b_0*	1/2	1/2			...	
a_0b_1*			1/2	1/2	...	
a_0b_2*					...	
a_1b_0*					...	
a_1b_1*					...	
a_1b_2*					...	1/2
$*\ *c_0$	1/6		1/6		...	
$*\ *c_1$		1/6		1/6	...	1/6
$*b_0*$	1/4	1/4			...	
$*b_1*$			1/4	1/4	...	
$*b_2*$					...	1/4
$a_0*\ *$	1/6	1/6	1/6	1/6	...	
$a_1*\ *$					...	1/6

Table 1. A sample database

No.	A	B	C	D
u1	a_0	b_0	c_1	y
u2	a_0	b_1	c_1	y
u3	a_0	b_0	c_1	y
u4	a_1	b_1	c_0	n
u5	a_0	b_0	c_1	n
u6	a_0	b_2	c_1	y

2.2 Biases

Since our approach is based on the GDT, rule discovery can be constrained by three types of biases corresponding to three components of the GDT defined in Section 2.1.

The first type of biases is related to the possible generalizations in a GDT. It is used to decide which concept description should be first considered. We divide possible generalizations (concept descriptions) into several levels of generalization according to the number of "$*$" in a generalization, and the more the number of "$*$", the higher the level. According to the preference, you can select more general concept descriptions in an upper level or more specific ones in a lower level.

The second type of biases is related to the probability values denoted in G_{ij} in a GDT. It is used to adjust the strength of the relationship between an instance and a generalization. If no prior background knowledge as a bias is available, as default, we consider that the possibility of which all possible instances appear are equiprobable to create the prior distribution of a GDT. However, a bias such as background knowledge and/or meta knowledge can be used while creating a GDT, and the probability distribution can be dynamically revised for acquiring the posterior distribution.

---

[3] For simplicity, we would like to omit the wild card in some places in this paper. That is, $*b_0 c_1 = b_0 c_1$

The third type of biases is related to the possible instances in a GDT. In our approach, the strength of the relationship between every possible instance and every possible generalization depends on a certain extent how to create and define the possible instances. In particular, this bias is useful to represent the instances with missing data in a GDT.

Furthermore, background knowledge can be used as a bias to constrain the possible instances and the prior distributions. For example, if we use a background knowledge,

"when the air temperature is very high, it is not possible there exists some frost at ground level",

to learn rules from a earthquake database in which there are attributes such as the air temperature, frost at ground level, two centimeters below ground level, the atmospheric pressure etc., then we do not consider the possible instances that are contradictory with this background knowledge in all possible combination of different attribute values in a database for creating a GDT. Thus, we can get the more refined result by using background knowledge in the learning process.

2.3 Rule Strength

In our approach, a learned rule is typically expressed in $X \rightarrow Y$ with S. Where X denotes the conjunction of the conditions that a concept must satisfy, Y denotes a concept that the rule describes, and S is a "measure of strength" of which the rule holds.

The strength S of a rule $X \rightarrow Y$ is defined as follows:

$$S(X \rightarrow Y) = s(X) \times (1 - r(X \rightarrow Y)) \qquad (3)$$

where $s(X)$ is the strength of the generalization X, (i.e., the condition of the rule), r is the rate of noises. In other words, the strength of a rule represents the incompleteness and uncertainty of the rule, which is influenced by both unseen instances and noises.

Let $X = PG_i$. The strength of the generalization PG_i, $s(PG_i)$, is given by Eq. (4),

$$s(PG_i) = \sum_j G_{ij} = \sum_j p(PI_j | PG_i) = \frac{N_{ins-rel}(PG_i)}{N_{PG_i}} \qquad (4)$$

where $N_{ins-rel}(PG_i)$ is the number of the observed instances satisfying the generalization PG_i. The initial value of $s(X)$ is 0. The value will be dynamically updated according to the real data in a database. If all of the possible instances satisfying generalization X appear, the strength will be the maximal value, 1. In other words, the strength of the generalization X represents explicitly the prediction for unseen instances.

On the other hand, the rate of noises, r, shows the quality of classification, that is, how many instances satisfying generalization X can not be classified into class Y.

$$r(X \rightarrow Y) = \frac{N_{ins-rel}(X) - N_{ins-class}(X,Y)}{N_{ins-rel}(X)}, \tag{5}$$

where $N_{ins-class}(X,Y)$ is the number of the instances belonging to the class Y within the instances satisfying the generalization X.

A user can specify an allowed noise rate as the threshold value. Thus, the rules with the larger rates than the threshold value will be deleted.

It merits our attention that Eq. (4) is not suitable for duplicate instances. Hence the duplicate instances should be handled before using this equation.

3 Combining the GDT with Rough Sets

This section describes a way of implementing the GDT methodology by combining the GDT with the *rough set* methodology (GDT-RS for short). By using GDT-RS, we can first find the rules with larger strengths from possible rules, and then find minimal relative reducts from the set of rules with larger strengths.

3.1 Simplifying a Decision Table by GDT-RS

By using the GDT, it is obvious that one instance can be expressed by several generalizations, and several instances can be generalized into one generalization. Simplifying a decision table is to find such a set of generalizations, which covers all of the instances in a decision table and the number of generalizations is minimal. The method of computing the reducts of condition attributes in GDT-RS, in principle, is equivalent to the discernibility matrix method [Skowron-92, Pawlak-91]. However, we do not find dispensable attributes. This is because

- Finding dispensable attributes benefits the *core* finding, but does not benefits the best solution acquiring. The greater the number of dispensable attributes, the more difficult it is to acquire the best solution.
- Some values of a dispensable attribute may be indispensable for some values of a decision attribute.

For the generalization generated by instances in different classes should be checked. If the noise rate $r(X \rightarrow Y)$ is smaller than a threshold value, the generalization X is regarded as a consistent generalization of class Y. Otherwise, the generalization is contradictory. Furthermore, if two generalizations in the same level have different strengths, the one with larger strength will be selected first.

Figure 1 shows the relationship between generalizations and instances. Instance $\{a_0b_1c_1\}$ can be generalized into $\{a_0\}$, $\{b_1\}$, $\{c_1\}$, $\{a_0b_1\}$, $\{a_0c_1\}$, or $\{b_1c_1\}$. $\{b_1\}$ and $\{a_0c_1\}$ are contradictory due to the generalizations with the instances belonging to different classes. Furthermore, $\{a_0\}$ and $\{c_1\}$ are also contradictory because $\{a_0c_1\}$ is contradictory. Although $\{a_0b_1\}$ and $\{b_1c_1\}$ can be used as generalizations for the instance, we select $\{b_1c_1\}$ because the strength $S(\{b_1c_1\}) = 1$ is larger than the strength $S(\{a_0b_1\}) = 0.5$.

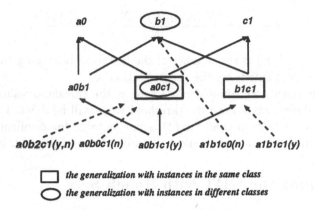

the generalization with instances in the same class

the generalization with instances in different classes

Fig. 1. Probability of a generalization rule

3.2 Rule Selection

There are several possible ways for rule selection. For example,

- Selecting the rules that contain as many instances as possible;
- Selecting the rules in the levels as high as possible ;
- Selecting the rules with larger strengths.

What kind of rules are best can be decided by user according to their preference.

3.3 Algorithms

We have developed two algorithms called *"Optimal Set of Rules"* and *"Sub Optimal Solution"* respectively for implementing the GDT-RS methodology. We briefly describe the algorithms as follows.

Algorithm 1 (Optimal Set of Rules)

Step 1. Create one or more GDTs.
 In fact, this step can be omitted because the prior distribution of a generalization can be calculated by Eq. (1) and Eq. (2).
Step 2. Handle duplicate instances as shown in following table, so that the probability of generalization can be calculated correctly.
Step 3. For each instance, find out all generalizations with other instances, and put consistent generalizations into G_+, contradictory generalizations into G_-.
Step 4. Acquire the rules that discern current instance and the instances in other classes by complement of G_-, and the result is denoted in G_T. That is, $G_T = \overline{G_-}$. For the instance $\{a_0 b_1 c_1\}$, $G_T = \overline{G_-} = \overline{\{a_0 c_1\} \cup \{b_1\}} = \{b_1\} \cap (\{a_0\} \cup \{c_1\}) = \{b_1 a_0\} \cup \{b_1 c_1\}$.
Step 5. Revise the strengths of the generalizations in G_T in Eq. (4).

Step 6. Select the generalizations by using one of the methods stated in Section 3.2 as the discovered rules covering some instances.

Step 7. Go back to *Step 3* until all of instances are handled.

The time complexity of Algorithm 1 is $O(mn^3 + mn^2 N(G_T))$, where n is the number of instances in a database, m is the number of attributes, $N(G_T)$ is the number of generalizations in G_T.

We can see that the algorithm is not suitable for the database with a lot of attributes. A possible method to solve the issue is to find a reduct (subset) of condition attributes as a preprocessing before using the algorithm [Zhong-99]. In the remainder of this section, we would like to discuss another algorithm called *Sub Optimal Solution* that is more suitable for the database with a lot of attributes.

Algorithm 2 (Sub Optimal Solution)

The Sub Optimal Solution algorithm is a greedy one. It can be described briefly as follows:

Let R be conjunction of conditions of a rule, RS a set of rules and initial RS = {}, $COVERED$ a ID list of instances covered by a rule in RS, SS a ID list of instances that satisfy the conditions of R.

Step 1. Same as *Step 1* of **Algorithm 1**.

Step 2. Same as *Step 2* of **Algorithm 1**.

Step 3. Set $R = \{\}$, $COVERED = \{\}$, and $SS = \{$all instances IDs$\}$.
For each class D_c, divide the decision table T into two part: current class T_+ and other classes T_-.

Step 4. From the attribute values v_{ij} of the instance I_k (where v_{ij} means the jth value of attribute i, $I_k \in T_+$, $I_k \in SS$), choose a value v with the maximal number of occurrence within the instances contained in T_+, and the minimal number of occurrence within the instances contained in T_-.

Step 5. Insert v into R. $R = R \cap v$.

Step 6. Delete the instance ID from SS if the instance does not contain the attribute value v.

Step 7. Go back to *Step 4* until the noise rate obtained in Eq. (5) is less than the threshold value.

Step 8. Find out a minimal sub-set R' of R according to their strengths. Insert $(R' \rightarrow D_c)$ into RS. Set $R = \{\}$, copy the instance IDs in SS to $COVERED$, and set $SS = \{$all instance IDs$\}$ - $\{COVERED\}$.

Step 9. Go back to *Step 4* until all instance of T_+ are in $COVERED$.

Step 10. Go back to *Step 3* until all classes are handled.

The time complexity of Algorithm 2 is $O(m^2 n^2)$. Here we would like to emphasize that not every greedy approach succeeds in producing the best result overall. Just as in life, a greedy strategy may produce a good result for a while, yet the overall result may be poor. However, it is a better way for solving very-large, complex problems that we just find the sub optimal solution by using some greedy approach.

4 An Application

Some of databases such as postoperative patient, earthquake, weather, cancer, meningitis, mushroom have been tested for our approach. We would like to use the mushroom database as an example.

The mushroom database includes descriptions of hypothetical samples corresponding to 23 species of gilled mushrooms in the Agaricus and Lepiota Family. Each species is identified as definitely edible, definitely poisonous, or of unknown edibility and not recommended. This latter class was combined with the poisonous one. The guide clearly states that there is no simple rule for determining the edibility of a mushroom; no rule like "leaflets three, let it be" for Poisonous Oak and Ivy.

In the mushroom database, there are 8124 instances, not any contradictory instances and duplicate instances. The threshold value for the noise rate is 0, because we don't want to acquire a rule with noise rate greater than 0 to discern edible and poisonous.

In this paper, we only list the result of poisonous in Table 3 because of limitation of space. The number in column *No.* is the number of instances covered by the rule, the *Stren* column indicates the strength of the rule.

Table 3. The conditions for poisonous

Conditions	No.	Stren
gill-spacing(c) ∧ stalk-surface-above-ring(k)	2228	8/T
odor(f)	2160	9/T
stalk-surface-below-ring(k) ∧ ring-number(o)	2160	12/T
gill-spacing(c) ∧ ring-type(e) ∧ population(v)	1760	60/T
cap-surface(s) ∧ gill-spacing(c) ∧ veil-color(w) ∧ ring-number(o) ∧ population(v)	1096	576/T
cap-surface(s) ∧ gill-spacing(c) ∧ gill-size(n)	1040	16/T
cap-surface(s) ∧ bruises(f) ∧ gill-size(n)	960	16/T
stalk-color-below-ring(w) ∧ ring-number(o) ∧ spore-print-color(w)	872	243/T
cap-color(g) ∧ bruises(f) ∧ stalk-root(b)	712	100/T
cap-color(y) ∧ bruises(f)	672	20/T
stalk-root(b) ∧ habitat(g)	612	35/T
cap-surface(y) ∧ gill-spacing(c) ∧ gill-size(n) ∧ stalk-surface-below-ring(s)	560	64/T
gill-color(g) ∧ stalk-root(b)	504	60/T
cap-color(w) ∧ gill-spacing(c) ∧ stalk-root(b)	152	100/T
spore-print-color(r)	72	9/T
bruises(f) ∧ gill-spacing(c) ∧ stalk-root(b) ∧ ring-number(o) or gill-spacing(c) ∧ stalk-shape(e) ∧ stalk-root(b) ∧ ring-number(o)	1392	60/T
bruises(f) ∧ stalk-root(b) ∧ ring-number(o) ∧ habitat(d) or stalk-shape(e) ∧ stalk-root(b) ∧ ring-number(o) ∧ habitat(d)	624	210/T

$T = \prod_{i=1}^{m} n_i$, n_i is the number of value of attribute i.

n=(2,6,4,10,2,9,2,2,2,12,2,5,4,4,9,9,1,4,3,5,9,6,7).

We prefer the rules that contain as many instances as possible. If there are two or more rules contain same instances, we prefer the rules with larger strength.

629

If the rules contain same instances and have the same strength (such as the last two group rules with *or* in Table 3), each of them are select-able.

The result of our method is not same as C4.5 [Quinlan-93]. By comparing with the result of C4.5, we can see that the rule *"odor(m) → poisonous"* is not in our result, because all of the instances containing *odor(m)* are covered by other rules with higher strength. By using our method, the rule

gill-spacing(c) ∧ stalk-surface-above-ring(k) → poisonous

that covers 2228 instances is acquired. But using C4.5, no rule can cover instances over 2160.

5 Conclusion

In this paper, we presented a probabilistic rough induction methodology called GDT-RS that is based on the combination of *Generalization Distribution Table (GDT)* and the *Rough Set* theory, as well as discussed two algorithms for its implementation. We described that our approach is *very soft*, that is, both the formal value and the semantic value of information are considered in the GDT-RS. Some of databases such as postoperative patient, earthquake, weather, mushroom, meningitis, and cancer have been tested or are being tested for our approaches. By using the GDT-RS, we can first find the rules with larger strengths from possible rules, and then find minimal relative reducts from the set of rules with larger strengths. Thus, a minimal set of rules with larger strengths can be acquired from databases with noisy, incomplete data.

References

[Han-93] J. Han, et al. Data-Driven Discovery of Quantitative Rules in Relational Databases. *IEEE Trans. Knowl. Data Eng.*, Vol.5 (No.1) (1993) 29-40.
[Mitchell-77] T.M. Mitchell. Version Spaces: A Candidate Elimination Approach to Rule Learning. *Proc. 5th Int. Joint Conf. Artificial Intelligence* (1977) 305-310.
[Skowron-92] A. Skowron and C. Rauszer. The discernibility matrics and functions in information systems, *Intelligent Decision Support* (1992) 331-362.
[Skowron-97] A.Skowron and L. Polkowski, Synthesis of Decision Systems from Data Tables, in T.Y. Lin and N.Cercone (eds.), *Rough Sets and Data Mining: Analysis of Imprecise Data*, Kluwer (1997) 259-299.
[Pawlak-91] Z. Pawlak. *ROUGH SETS, Theoretical Aspects of Reasoning about Data*, Kluwer Academic Publishers (1991).
[Quinlan-86] J.R. Quinlan, Induction of Decision Trees. *Machine Learning*, 1 (1986) 81-106.
[Quinlan-93] J.R. Quinlan, C4.5: Programs for Machine Learning (1993).
[Zhong-96] N. Zhong and S. Ohsuga, Using Generalization Distribution Tables as a Hypotheses Search Space for Generalization. *Proc. 4th International Workshop on Rough Sets, Fuzzy Sets, and Machine Discovery (RSFD-96)* (1996) 396-403.
[Zhong-99] N. Zhong, J.Z. Dong, and S. Ohsuga, "Using Rough Sets with Heuristics to Feature Selection" (to appear).

Cluster Evolution Strategies for Constrained Numerical Optimization

Cees H.M. van Kemenade[1] and Joost N. Kok[2]

[1] CWI,
P.O. Box 94079, 1090 GB Amsterdam, The Netherlands
Cees.van.Kemenade@cwi.nl
[2] Leiden Institute of Advanced Computer Science, Leiden University,
P.O. Box 9512, 2300 RA Leiden, The Netherlands
joost@cs.leidenuniv.nl

Abstract. We introduce cluster evolution strategies. Cluster evolution strategies are evolution strategies that use clustering together with standard selection methods to select individuals for the evolutionary operators and local optimization. We propose a method for handling constraints within cluster evolution strategies and the performance of cluster evolution strategies is assessed on a test-suite of numerical constrained optimization problems.

1 Introduction

We describe the cluster evolution strategy (Cl-ES). It is a variant of an evolution strategy [1, 2, 7]. The main idea is to use evolutionary operators and local optimization in an efficient way within the evolution strategy [9]. This is done by a special selection scheme that selects elements for local optimization. The selection scheme uses a fitness based scheme together with a clustering method. Only the optimized elements are allowed to reproduce.

The standard Cl-ES is suited for unconstrained optimization problems, but by using a penalty method we can also apply Cl-ES to constrained optimization problems [10]. We compare its performance to other evolutionary algorithms on a standard test-suite of eight constrained optimization problems.

The contents of rest of the paper are as follows. A description of the cluster evolution strategy is given in section 2. Then a brief introduction to numerical constrained optimization problems is given in section 3 and our penalty approach is described. The test-suite and the experiments are in section 4. A brief discussion of the results and a comparison to related work is given in section 5, and conclusions follow in section 6.

2 Cluster evolution strategies

The Cluster Evolution Strategy uses a two-stage selection process. During the first stage a subset of the complete population, containing the best individuals, is selected. This step results in a selective pressure which guides the search towards regions of high average fitness. Next, a clustering process is applied to the individuals selected during the first phase, and the best individual of each cluster is selected as a representative for that cluster. A new population is created by taking all selected elements from the first phase together with new elements that are obtained by applying the evolutionary operators to the representatives only. Using only representatives as parents helps in preventing premature convergence. If a region extracts relatively many individuals, then this unbalance is likely to be enlarged by the recombination operator [11]. This problem is resolved because each cluster of individuals is represented by only one representative, independent of the size of this cluster. Nearly identical individuals are likely to belong to the same cluster, and thus only one of these individuals needs to be present in the set of representatives. Because the presented two-stage selection schedule is not very sensitive to premature convergence, it is relatively safe to preserve the selected individuals. This results in population-elitism, which helps in preserving information and propagating obtained information to subsequent generations.

Within many randomized clustering methods local optimization is applied for two reasons [8]. First, if the search space around an individual is relatively smooth, there is no reason to use a slow global optimization method. Second, by applying local optimization in an early phase the potential of different individuals can be compared better. For these reasons we have incorporated local search in our algorithm too. Local optimization is applied to the representatives only, because these representatives are assumed to be typical for the current population. Local optimization happens before the application of the evolutionary operators. Applying local optimization to the (small) set of representatives reduces the amount of computation required and decreases the probability of locating the same local optimum multiple times. Because high-quality representatives are likely survive for several generations due to the population-elitism, the local optimization can be done in stages. During each generation only a limited number of local optimization steps are spent on each representative, so the maximal number of local optimization steps spend on an individual is proportional to the number of generations it is able to survive. This multi-stage local optimization process prevents that a lot of local optimization steps are spend on an individual that is discarded immediately afterwards.

Next, the pseudo-code of the algorithm for the main loop of the cluster evolution strategy is given.

```
ClusterEvolutionStrategy()
   P = randomPopulation(N);

   repeat
       B = selectBest(P);
       R = selectRepresentatives(B);
       L = localOptimization(R);
       C = produceChildren(L);
       P = (B\R) ∪ L ∪ C;
```

```
    until ready;
  end
```

Parameters are the maximal population size N and the maximal number of representatives N_{repres}. The ready predicate becomes true when the desired objective value is obtained, or when the total allowed number of function evaluations is reached, or when all clusters have a size below a certain minimal threshold.

The clustering method creates a projection of all individuals on each coordinate axis. The following clustering is then performed for each of the coordinates axes. The expected distance between adjacent (projected) individuals is computed, and a each two adjacent points are put in the same cluster if their (projected) distance is smaller than τ times the expected distance. So an increase of the value of τ can decrease the number of clusters. Next, the best performing individual of each cluster is added to the set of representatives. For the exact details see [11].

Our main evolutionary operator is a (disruptive) recombination operator. The whole population is divided in pairs. Then for each pair, a child is created as follows. For each dimension the value of one of the parents is choosen with equal probability, and some Gaussian noise is added to it. Given two different parents $x^{(p1)}$ and $x^{(p2)}$, an offspring is created according to

$$x_i^{(o)} = (x_i^{(p1)} \text{ or } x_i^{(p2)}) + N(0, \sigma^2)$$

where $N(0, \sigma^2)$ is a Gaussian distributed random variable with mean zero and standard deviation $\sigma = |x_i^{(p1)} - x_i^{(p2)}|/3$.

With a low probability $P_{discrete}$ also a recombination operator without noise is used:

$$x_i^{(o)} = x_i^{(p1)} \text{ or } x_i^{(p2)}.$$

If there is only a single representative left, then it is not possible to apply recombination. Only then a mutation operator is applied. The sampling density of the mutation operator is constant over the region that covers the cluster of the individual, and it decreases linearly outside this region. A constant density sampling over the cluster is chosen, such that the search does not become biased towards the centre of the cluster, and only selection can decrease the size of the cluster. Only if the best individuals are located in a part of the cluster, then the search will focus on this part due to selection. The sides, that are located outside the cluster, are added such that some of the newly generated samplepoints are located outside the cluster, and the cluster can grow. If there is not yet a sufficient number of elements in the population then the population is again randomly divided in pairs and more children are produced.

3   Numerical constrained optimization

Many numerical constraint optimization problems (NCOP) can be written in the following form:

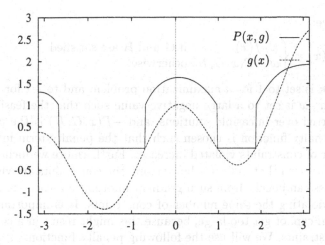

Fig. 1. The constraint $g(x) = \exp(x_i/\pi) + \cos(2 \cdot \pi \cdot x_i) - 1 \leq 0$ and an associated penalty function.

objective: MAXIMIZE $f(x)$
constraints:

$$x_{i,low} \leq x_i \leq x_{i,high} \quad \text{(box)}$$
$$G(x) \leq 0 \qquad\qquad \text{(inequality)}$$
$$H(x) = 0 \qquad\qquad \text{(equality)}$$

where $x \in \mathbb{R}^d$ is called the objective vector, $f(x)$ is the objective function, $G(x) \leq 0$ denotes the set of inequality constraints of type $g(x) \leq 0$ and $H(x) = 0$ denotes the set of equality constraints of type $h(x) = 0$. The goal is to find the objective vector x^* that maximizes the objective function and simultaneously satisfies all the constraints. Note that function optimization problems can be written as a NCOP with only box-constraints, so the class of function optimization problems is a subset of NCOP.

The complexity of the constraints can have a strong influence on the difficulty of NCOP's. Linear constraints (such as box-constraints) are relatively easy to process, because such constraints give a feasible region consisting of a single convex hull. Nonlinear constraints can result in one or more irregularly shaped feasible regions.

When applying evolutionary algorithms to a NCOP, one has to cope with the constraints. These constraints can be handled by means of penalty functions, decoders, or repair operators [5]. Penalty functions can be used to recast the original problem to a new problem having only box-constraints and using a modified objective:

$$f'(x) = \begin{cases} \kappa \cdot f(x) & \text{if G and H are satisfied} \\ \omega - P(x, G, H) & \text{otherwise.} \end{cases}$$

The parameter κ is set to 1 for a maximization problem and to -1 for a minimization problem, ω is set to a large negative value such that the feasible solutions are preferred over infeasible solutions, and $-P(x, G, H)$ is the penalty function. This penalty function is chosen such that the penalty-term increases when the number of constraints violated increases. Furthermore we included an additional gradient term that indicates how strong the constraints are violated. The search process can benefit from such gradient information when comparing two individuals violating the same number of constraints. It is important that this gradient term cannot get too large, because this might result in a competition between constraints. We will use the following penalty function:

$$P(x, G, H) = \sum_{g \in G} p(g(x)) + \sum_{h \in H} p(-|h(x)|)$$

where

$$p(y) = \begin{cases} 1 + (1 - e^{-y/\gamma}) & \text{if } y < 0 \\ 0 & \text{otherwise} \end{cases}$$

with γ a scaling factor. When using this $P(x, G, H)$ each violated constraint results in a contribution to $P(x, G, H)$ in the range [1,2]. Hence, if two different constraints are violated, then their contribution to the $P(x, G, H)$ differs by at most a factor two, and thus it is prevented that different constraints start to compete and that the evolutionary search focuses on the satisfaction of a subset of all constraints. Figure 1 shows a simple inequality constraint $g(x)$, and its corresponding penalty $P(x, g)$.

Much more information on constrained optimization problems and the way these are handled by evolutionary algorithms can be found in the book by Michalewicz [4] and in the paper by Michalewicz and Schoenauer [6].

4 Experiments

In this section results are reported of experiments that are conducted on a test-suite of numerical constrained optimization problems to assess the performance of a number of different evolutionary algorithms. The test-problems are taken from a paper by Michalewicz and Schoenauer [6]. That paper gives an overview of many different ways in which constraints can be processed. A set of different penalty based methods for handling constraints is compared by means of the Genocop system. The paper is an overview paper in the sense that it collects results from many other approaches and hence the results in that paper are a good benchmark for our cluster evolution strategies.

We put emphasis on a proper tradeoff between exploration and exploitation. Therefore a single penalty-method is used and our attention is directed towards the comparison of the different selection schemes. A comparison is made between:

1. Cl-ES with $N = 2n$ and $\tau = 1.5$ with local optimization (M1),
2. Cl-ES with $N = 2n$, $\tau = 1.5$ without local optimization (M2),
3. Cl-ES with $N = 2n$ and $\tau = 10$ with local optimization (M3),
4. (μ, λ) selection with $\mu = n$ and $\lambda = 7n$ (M4), and
5. a set of independent local optimizers of size $N = n$ (M5).

During the experiments a value $n = 100$ is used. Local optimization is performed by the $(1 + 1)$ evolution strategy using the $1/5$-succes rule [11]. The algorithm M5 uses a population of such local optimizers that are evolved in parallel. The population sizes for the different evolutionary algorithms are set such that the size of the smallest population (after a fitness-based selection) is the same for all algorithms. This means that the different algorithms are tested with different population sizes. We consider this to be a fair way of comparing the different algorithms because this minimal population size determines the bottle-neck for passing information to subsequent phases of the evolution process. For the cluster evolution strategy we set this size equal to the size of the population after fitness based selection (which is equal to the maximal number of representatives taken). For the (μ, λ) strategy we take μ (the size of the parent population). The scaling factor γ for the penalty-function is one, the probability $P_{discrete}$ that discrete recombination is applied is set to 0.1, and the maximal number of function evaluations during a single run is set to 100,000.

The test-suite is taken from Michalewicz and Schoenauer [6]. The penalty method we apply is strict in the sense that very small violations of a constraint already result in a large penalty. Equality constraints are often not satisfied exactly and therefore result in a (small) violation. Hence, the penalty approach we use here is not directly applicable to problems involving equality constraints. We decided to exclude the test-problems that involve equality constraints, and hence we use only eight out of the eleven test-problems contained in this test-suite, i.e. problems G1, G2, G4, G6, G7, G8, G9 and G10.

Problem	number dimen.	Type of $f(x)$	optimal objective	linear constraints	nonlinear constraints
G1	13	min. quadratic	-15	9	0
G2	20	max. nonlinear	**0.803603**	1	1
G4	5	min. quadratic	**-31,025.6**	0	6
G6	2	min. cubic	-6961.81381	0	2
G7	10	min. quadratic	24.3062032	0	5
G8	2	max. nonlinear	0.095825	0	2
G9	7	min polynomial	680.6300573	0	4
G10	8	min. linear	7049.3307	3	3

Table 1. Characteristics of the test-problems (the optima shown in boldface are better than the best solutions found in literature).

problem		M1	M2	M3	M4	M5
	best	-14.9997	-14.9997	-14.9999	**-15**	-9.36095
	low	0.000278185	0.00045778	0.000291878	$3 \cdot 10^{-8}$	6.41386
G1	median	0.000397222	0.000626888	0.000447622	$\mathbf{4 \cdot 10^{-8}}$	8.1346
	high	0.00061712	0.000868548	0.000631218	$7 \cdot 10^{-8}$	9.31185
	feasible	**100%**	**100%**	98.3%	**100%**	**100%**
	best	0.790802	0.80358	0.80343	**0.803603**	0.56874
	low	0.016	0.003	0.0001	-0.00004	0.26
G2	median	0.041	0.003	**0.0056**	0.01	0.35
	high	0.10	0.09	0.03	0.03	0.4
	feasible	100%	100%	100%	100%	100%
	best	-31023.9	-31018.3	**-31025.6**	-31025.5	-31012.7
	low	4.7	21.6	0.04	7.0	18.6
G4	median	38.9	79.4	**0.042**	38.8	67.0
	high	112.4	211.2	0.44	104.378	127.3
	feasible	100%	100%	100%	100%	100%
	best	**-6961.81**	-6909.36	**-6961.81**	-6954.52	**-6961.81**
	low	0.00193931	152.467	$2.5 \cdot 10^5$	123.531	0.324958
G6	median	11.7058	643.803	**0.00076073**	365.341	3.23206
	high	203.15	1572.97	0.0152746	1272.81	24.4417
	feasible	**100%**	**100%**	**100%**	**100%**	98.3%
	best	24.5112	24.324	**24.3195**	24.3634	29.3381
	low	0.249132	0.0531871	0.0210181	0.0743209	6.07777
G7	median	0.436249	0.250809	**0.125341**	0.288405	11.807
	high	0.703945	0.854894	0.377214	1.31661	45.3596
	feasible	**100%**	**100%**	**100%**	**100%**	98.3%
	best	0.09582504	0.09582504	0.09582504	0.09582504	0.09582504
	low	0.0	0.0014169	0.0	0.0	0.0
G8	median	**0.0**	0.029	**0.0**	**0.0**	**0.0**
	high	0.0	0.228	0.0	0.0	0.0
	feasible	100%	100%	100%	100%	100%
	best	680.635	**680.631**	680.632	680.634	681.903
	low	0.0148805	0.0054169	0.0024507	0.018264	2.48683
G9	median	0.0415661	0.0337994	**0.0108197**	0.0535273	5.35698
	high	0.0890875	0.232804	0.0349449	0.186989	10.4311
	feasible	100%	100%	100%	100%	100%
	best	7139.87	7066.67	**7056.52**	7094.35	7272.83
	low	162.886	82.7099	32.1858	137.109	399.114
G10	median	395.008	986.571	**201.291**	605.38	760.798
	high	765.559	4973.58	438.629	1924.59	1457.93
	feasible	**100%**	98.3%	**100%**	**100%**	**100%**

Table 2. Results obtained on the test-suite of constrained optimization problems (best reports the objective value, low, median and high report the distance to the optimum).

Table 2 shows performance measures that are based on the best solution found after the termination of the different types of evolution strategies. Each column of this table corresponds to a single type of evolution strategy and each row corresponds to one of the test-problems. For each test-problem five rows are given. The first row, which is labelled best, shows the best individual obtained over all sixty independent runs. The rows labelled low, median, and high show the statistics for the difference between the best observed fitness and the fitness of the global optimum. The row labelled median shows the median best solution at termination over all sixty runs. We use the median values instead of the average values, because the median values are less sensitive to outliers in the data-set. The lines labelled low and high give the bounds on the 90% confidence interval. This interval is obtained taking the best solution of each of the sixty independent runs, sorting these solutions on fitness and removing the 5% best solutions and the 5% worst solutions. The two end points of the remaining sequence of fitness values are reported. The last line, labelled feasible, shows the percentage of runs for which the best solution is a feasible solution. For each of the rows labelled best, median, and feasible the best result is shown in bold-face.

5 Discussion of results

The results produced by our evolution strategies are promising. On two out of eight problems we have found better solutions than the best results reported in literature (see [6]). On problem G1 our evolution strategies find the optimum easily, just like the GA's reported in the literature. On the five remaining problems our evolution strategies perform at least as good as the best other evolutionary approaches given in the overview paper [6], and often our methods even perform better in terms of the quality of the solution or the reliability of the method.

Nonlinear inequality constraints are handled: good results are produced while our approach is not tailored towards specific inequality constraints. Furthermore our method handles the constrained optimization problem as a black box problem where GA uses fitness values as the only information to guide the search. Our parameters were set by means of an educated guess, no further tuning of these parameters was performed, and all problems were handled with the same set of parameters. This suggests that our approach is quite robust, and not too sensitive to the actual settings of the different parameters.

Our penalty approach is quite powerful, using a strong penalty for violating constraints, a gradient term showing how strong these constraints are violated, and a scaled fitness-contribution for violated constraints, such that cross-competition between constraints is limited. The objective function is only computed for feasible solutions. The fact the standard algorithms perform well is due to this penalty approach.

Local search helps a lot in finding good solutions for constraint optimization problems, although one has to take care that the local search does not consume too much time.

6 Conclusions

Within the current experiments the cluster-selection performs best. It can handle more difficult problems than the other selection schedules, and it does so using less function evaluations. This scheme has a high selective pressure and the application of the clustering step and the selection of representatives prevents the over-sampling of certain parts of the search-space and hence the probability of premature convergence is reduced.

The test-results are promising. On all eight problems our set of ES M1-4 performs at least as good as the best other evolutionary approaches reported in literature. On seven of these problems all other evolutionary approaches are outperformed, and on two problems we even find optima that are better than the best results reported in [6]. Given that a standard ES-selection (M4) performs well with our penalty-function approach, it seems that our penalty-function approach is quite powerful. Furthermore, when comparing the different evolutionary algorithms, we observe that the Cluster evolution strategies outperform other algorithms, and that local optimization really is beneficial on the test-suite.

References

1. T. Bäck, F. Hoffmeister, and H.-P. Schwefel. A survey of evolution strategies. In Belew and Booker [3], pages 2–9.
2. Th. Bäck. *Evolutionary Algorithms in Theory and Practice.* Oxford University Press, 1996.
3. R.K. Belew and L.B. Booker, editors. *Proceedings of the 4th International Conference on Genetic Algorithms.* Morgan Kaufmann, 1991.
4. Z. Michalewicz. *Genetic Algorithms + Data structures = Evolution programs.* Springer, Berlin, 3rd edition, 1996.
5. Z. Michalewicz and C.Z. Janikow. Handling constraints in genetic algorithms. In Belew and Booker [3], pages 151–157.
6. Z. Michalewicz and M. Schoenauer. Evolutionary algorithms for constrained parameter optimization problems. *Journal of Evolutionary Computation*, 4(1):1–32, 1996.
7. H.-P. Schwefel. *Evolution and Optimum Seeking.* Sixth-Generation Computer Technology Series. Wiley, New York, 1995.
8. A. Törn and A. Žilinskas. *Global optimization*, volume 350 of *Lecture Notes in Computer Science.* Springer, 1989.
9. C.H.M. van Kemenade. Cluster evolution strategies, enhancing the sampling density function using representatives. In *Proceedings of the 3rd IEEE Conference on Evolutionary Computation*, pages 637–642. IEEE Press, 1996.
10. C.H.M. van Kemenade. Comparison of selection schemes for evolutionary constrained optimization. In *Proceedings of the Eighth Dutch Conference on Artificial Intelligence*, pages 245–254, 1996.
11. C.H.M. van Kemenade. *Recombinative Evolutionary Search.* Doctoral dissertation, LIACS, faculty of Mathematics and Natural Sciences, Leiden University, the Netherlands, 1999.

Evolutionary Algorithms as
Fitness Function Debuggers

F. Mansanne[1], F. Carrère[2], A . Ehinger[2], and M. Schoenauer[3]

Abstract. All Evolutionary Algorithms experienced practitioners emphasize the need for a careful design of the fitness function. It is commonly heard, for instance, that *"If there is a bug in your fitness function, the EA will find it"*. This paper presents a case study of such a situation in the domain of geophysical underground identification: some weird solutions are found by the Evolutionary Algorithm, obviously physically absurd, but fulfilling almost perfectly the geophysical criterion.

1 Introduction

Among the crucial steps of the design of an Evolutionary Algorithm, practitioners mostly focus on parameter tuning, with work ranging from good-old systematic trial-and-error [16] to meta-optimization [7] and to more recent self-adaptive strategies (initiated in [20], see [8] for a recent survey). The design of an efficient representation is also recognized as a crucial step, as witnessed by the never-ending debate binary vs real for real-parameter search spaces [6, 1, 9], or more recent attempts to actually separate representation from operators [22]. The choice of operators, somehow dual of the choice of representation [2], also raised a lot of discussions [5, 11]. And, to a less extend, some works addressed the initialization issue [23, 12]. But it is amazing to see that the design of the fitness function is generally omitted from the discussions. One exception is given by the field of constraint handling, for which a range of penalty methods (see [14] for a survey) can be seen as addressing the issue, though somehow indirectly: the fitness function is modified in order to take into account the constraints, but the main objective function is itself hardly discussed.

Of course, only real-world problems make the issue of the objective function worth investigating: when the function to optimize is a given analytic function, little room is left for improvement. But in complex domains, a blind use of "state-of-the-art" objective function within an Evolutionary Algorithm may sometimes lead to unexpected results: The optimization algorithm lacks the "common sense" that implicitly prevents the experts to even think of looking for solutions in some yet unexplored regions of the search space. On the other hand, such unexpected strange results might allow for new insights into some yet unquestioned long-used criterion, yielding to a better understanding of the problem at hand.

---

[1] Laboratoire de Mathématiques Appliquées, Université de Pau, France
[2] Geophysics and Instrumentation, IFP, Pau, France
[3] Centre de Mathématiques Apliquées, UMR CNRS 7641, Ecole Polytechnique, Palaiseau, France

This paper presents a case study of "fitness debugging" using Evolutionary Computation in the domain of geophysical inverse problem solving: The goal is to identify the velocity distribution in the underground from surface records of reflection profiles of elastic waves. The problem is presented in section 2, together with the fitness function derived from the "aligned iso-X" criterion that geophysicists have been using for a long time. The evolutionary algorithm, using the variable length representation based on Voronoï diagram introduced in [17] and used on the same geophysical problem, but with a different fitness function, in [18], is described in section 3. Results on simple synthetic 2D simulated data of section 4 illustrate the weaknesses of the iso-X criterion: the algorithms exhibits weird solutions that are better than the known synthetic solution with respect to the iso-X criterion – and that would clearly be immediately eliminated by human eyes. But is it that easy to introduce "common sense" in evolutionary algorithms? The conclusion section discusses this issue.

2 The geophysical problem

The goal of the inverse problem in geophysical prospection is to identify the velocity distribution in the underground from recorded reflection profiles of elastic waves. A seismic experiment starts with an artificial explosion (a *shot*) at some point of the surface. The acoustic waves propagate through the underground medium, eventually being reflected by multiple interfaces between different media (see Figure 1). The reflected waves are measured by some receptors on the surface, actually recording pressure variations along time, termed *seismograms*. The aim is to identify the repartition of the velocities in the underground domain from the seismograms obtained from a sequence of shots.

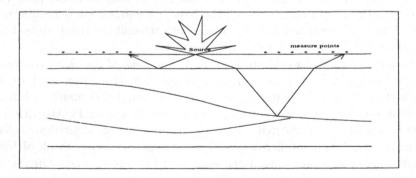

Fig. 1. *A two-dimensional view of a typical seismic-reflection experiment.*

Several methods for the determination of underground velocities have been proposed. The most successful [4] makes a clever use of migration velocity analysis, a method for determining long wavelength velocity structure, which is successfully applied to 2D data from North Sea. However, a prerequisite to the efficient description of a model in this method is the identification of regions of smooth variation.

Another way to handle the problem is to directly compute the difference between observed and simulated wave fields, as has been done in [21] (as well as in [18], using the same evolutionary approach based on Voronoï diagrams described in section 3). But such approach requires solving the wave equation in the whole domain, which is highly resource consuming when accuracy matters. Moreover, the velocity information can be derived solely from travel times. Hence, it has been decided here to work with migrated data rather than with original data: only the "useful" part of the wave field has to be computed, for each shot receptor pair.

2.1 Migrated images

The principle of a prestack shot record migration is the following (see [24] for a more detailed presentation): Two wave fields are considered: the wave propagated from the seismic source (the explosion of figure 1), and the virtual wave obtained by backward propagation from the receptors down to the diffracting obstacles of the upward traveling diffracted wave.

The key idea is that diffracting points are the only points where these two waves coincide in time. Hence, the so-called *Clearbout imaging principle* can be applied. It answers the question of, telling whether, at a certain point in space, there is time coincidence of the source wave and the backward-propagated diffracted wave.

Thus, a migrated image can be considered as a map of coefficients of reflection, the highest coefficients assessing the presence of reflectors. The imaging step finally concludes the migration process, yielding an image of the subsurface. The inverse problem of underground identification can then be addressed through as a maximization problem based on the *semblance* of the migrated images.

2.2 The objective function

Most practical underground velocity determinations are based on image gathers analysis (for example, migration velocity analysis in [4]). In an image gather each trace represents a migrated image of the subsurface at the same horizontal position. The objective function relies on the fact that reflection events in an image gather are horizontally aligned if the underground velocity model is correct (Figure 2). To measure the horizontal alignment of the reflection events in an image gather, the criterion first proposed in [24], and applied with success in [10] to 1D seismic profile from the North Sea, will be used hereafter, yielding the following expression, where ξ represents the set of receptors:

$$Fitness = \sum_{X \in \xi} \frac{|| \sum_{i=1}^{i=nshots} trace_i(X,Z)||}{\sum_{i=1}^{i=nshots} ||trace_i^2(X,Z)||} \qquad (1)$$

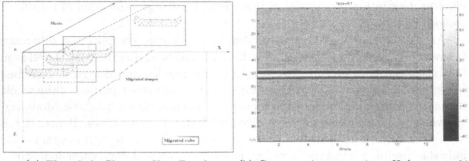

(a) The whole Shots × X × Z cube   (b) Cross-section at a given X (receptor 61)

Fig. 2. *The aligned events in the plane Shots × Z (plot b) correspond to the simple test case of section 4.*

If the underground velocity repartition is correct, traces for different positions at the surface location are aligned in the *Shot × X* cross-sections (Figure 2-b) and the fitness is hence maximal. Next section introduces the the evolutionary algorithm used to optimize the above fitness.

3 Evolutionary underground velocity identification

A number of authors recently addressed seismic processing problems with EA techniques. In [21], a genetic algorithm with multiple crossover locations is developed for the inversion of plane-wave seismograms; in this work, the underground is represented by a series of layers. In [3], the 'pseudo-subspace' method for the inversion of geophysical data is proposed: the complexity of models is progressively increased, but following a user-defined evolution. In [4], a classical GA algorithm is used with spline coefficients encoded into a binary string.

The central issue when addressing such inverse problem is the trade-off one has to make between the complexity of the representation and the accuracy of the models in the resulting search space. Whatever underground velocity model is used, it has to be later translated into a regular mesh which is the input data to the finite difference wave propagation algorithm. As an example, a grid of 400x400=160,000 points can be represented as a full 160,000-long vector in the full parametric approach (one velocity per element of the mesh), packed into 40x20=800 spline coefficients if spline approximation is preferred, or into a few dozens of Voronoï sites, each involving 3 real coefficients in the approach chosen here.

3.1 Voronoï representation

The underlying hypothesis in this work is that the underground domain can be partitioned into regions of homogeneous velocity, i.e. the velocity is supposed

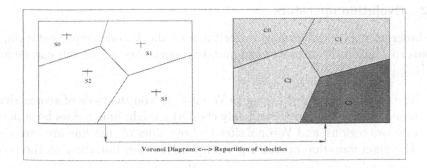

Fig. 3. *The Voronoï representation: Voronoï sites S_i define a partition of the domain into polygonal subsets in (a). Associate a velocity v_i to each cell C_i to obtain the piecewise constant function shown in (b).*

piecewise constant. The idea is to evolve both the partition and the real-valued velocities.

A possible way of representing partitions of a given domain comes from computational geometry, more precisely from the Voronoï diagram theory (see [15] for a detailed introduction to Voronoï diagrams). The representation of partitions by Voronoï diagrams has been introduced to tackle Optimum Design problems [17], identification problems in Structural Mechanics [19], and, recently, to address the geophysical inverse problem of section 2 [18].

Voronoï diagrams Consider a finite number of points $S_0, \dots, S_N$ (the *Voronoï sites*) of a given subset of $\mathbb{R}^n$ (the design domain). To each site S_i is associated the set C_i of all points of the design domain for which the closest Voronoï site is S_i, termed *Voronoï cell*. The *Voronoï diagram* is the partition of the design domain defined by the Voronoï cells. Each cell C_i is a convex polyhedral subset of the design domain, and any partition of a domain of $\mathbb{R}^n$ into convex polyhedral subsets is the Voronoï diagram of at least one set of Voronoï sites.

The genotype Consider now a (variable length) list of Voronoï sites, in which each site S_i is given a real valued coefficient v_i. The corresponding Voronoï diagram represents real-valued piecewise constant function if all points in each Voronoï cell are given the velocity value of the associated site (here the Voronoï diagram is supposed regular, i.e. to each cell corresponds exactly one site). Example of Voronoï representations can be seen in Figure 3, where the Voronoï sites are the dots in the center of the cells.

Note that the complexity of this representation does not depend in any way on the discretization that will be used to compute the response of the model to wave propagation. Moreover, as the number of Voronoï sites is adjusted by the algorithm itself, the complexity is in fact *self-adaptive*.

3.2 Evolution operators

In order to apply evolutionary algorithms to the Voronoï representation, one needs to define some crossover and mutation operators. All details can be found in [17], [19] or [18].

- The crossover operator exchange Voronoï sites on the basis of geometrically-based choice. The same (randomly chosen) straight line divides both parents into two regions, and Voronoï sites on both sides of that line are exchanged.
- The main mutation operator performs a Gaussian mutation on the coordinates and/or on the velocities of the sites. As in Evolution Strategies, the standard deviation is self-adapted, i.e. undergoes a log-normally distributed random mutation, as proposed by Schwefel [20].
- Mutation operators for variable-length representations must include random addition and destruction of some items in the list.

3.3 The algorithm

The evolution paradigm used in all experiments is similar to "traditional" Genetic Algorithm: population size of 30; binary tournament selection and generational replacement (with elitism); crossover rate of 0.7 and mutation rate of 0.6. The algorithm stops after a fixed number of evaluation without improvement of the best fitness.

The value of the mutation rate may seem high in the light of GA standards. But first this is the *individual* mutation rate, as opposed to usual probability to flip each bit; Second, it should be related to the self-adaptation of standard deviations: The underlying hypothesis of the self-adaptation mechanism is that there exists some correlation between the value of the standard deviations of an individual and the location of that individual on the fitness landscape. Such correlation is obviously lost if mutations happen too rarely. Several experiments (see [13]) witness for that – and also enforce the usefulness of crossover in that framework.

4 Results on a synthetic problem

4.1 Experimental conditions

The chosen synthetic test starts from an homogeneous repartition of velocity ($2000ms^{-1}$) in a 2D area of depth $1000m$ and width $3100m$, with one single horizontal reflector at depth $500m$ across the whole domain. For all 12 shots that are considered, the acquisition system consists in 101 receptors. Shot sources and receptors are equi-distributed on the surface with respective spacings of $50m$ and $25m$. Sampling rate is $4ms$ and the record length is $2s$. Velocities are searched between $1000ms^{-1}$ and $3000ms^{-1}$.

The direct problem is solved using the IFP dedicated solver. The cost of one fitness evaluation is $70s$ on a Dec Alpha 500 workstation, which will be reduced to

$35s$ on a Nec vector calculator (most of the computing time is obviously devoted in the evaluation of the fitnesses). Hence the maximum number of evaluations has to be severely limited to 2500 in all runs of section 4 and a single run still takes around 24h.

4.2 Validation results

In the first experiments, the number of Voronoï sites was severely limited (2 or 5 sites at most). The reflector was perfectly identified, and the homogeneous velocity approached within a few percent.

The migrated images are horizontal at the depth of $500ms^{-1}$, exactly at the position of the only reflector, and the iso-X plots are strictly horizontal (see figure 2-b). The conclusion of these early experiments was that the chosen algorithmic approach seemed to work quite right.

4.3 A bug in the fitness?

To further illustrate the actual effectiveness of the proposed approach, the constraint on the maximum number of Voronoï sites was relaxed. And strange results began to emerge, as the one plotted in Figure 4-a. Indeed this individual cannot be thought as a solution by anyone having even the smallest experience in seismic data. But it did give optimal values of the fitness function defined in section 2, as witnessed by a sample Iso-X diagram of Figure 4-b, almost "as horizontal as" the one of the perfect solution of Figure 2-b.

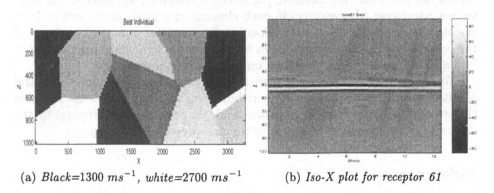

(a) $Black=1300\ ms^{-1}$, $white=2700\ ms^{-1}$ (b) Iso-X plot for receptor 61

Fig. 4. *The absurd underground velocity repartition (a) is miles away from the exact solution (homogeneous $2000ms^{-1}$ velocity), and nevertheless gives almost perfect iso-X plot – compare (b) with Figure 2-b!*

At this stage, it is not possible to say if the model itself is too simple compared to the degrees of freedom of the individuals, or if the formula of equation (1) used to test the horizontality is too raw, or, more dramatically, if the horizontality criterion itself should be questioned. But these results did raise many issues among the expert geophysicists, who are how trying to understand the case.

Conclusion

The above results clearly enlighten the need for some guidelines when transposing human-designed criterion to computer optimization: human experts in fact use a lot of implicit criteria when tackling complex problems. Those criteria usually don't need to be explicitly written down as long as other experts with the same scientific background are addressing the same kind of problem. But computer programs don't have any scientific background – unless explicitly programmed.

The question thus becomes how to incorporate "common sense" in our favorite algorithms? As for the seismic inversion problem addressed in this paper, some straightforward partial answers can be given to avoid weird underground velocities like the one of Figure 4: the idea would be to forbid velocity distribution that look too chaotic – but roughness is not easy to measure. A first could be to forbid too high discontinuities between adjacent Voronoï cells. But the implementation of such constraint is not straightforward (see [14]): should one penalize high jumps in velocities – with fixed or dynamic penalties? – or repair bad individuals by modifying their genotype, ... ? Moreover, whatever the constraints on the genotype, there is absolutely no guarantee at all that other types of weirdos will not emerge, meeting these artificial constraints, but finding other unguarded common sense holes.

On the other hand, such additional constraints, though difficult to design and to incorporate efficiently are reliably in the algorithm, might prove beneficial for the whole search process, by limiting the size of the space to be searched. As a matter of fact, even if complexity was not its main drawback, the mesh-based representation, where the unknown parameters to identify are made of one real-valued parameter (the velocity) in each element of a given mesh, suffers from the high uncorrelation of adjacent velocities. For instance, pure random choice of the one velocity per element results in highly non-physical underground models (see also [12] for a related discussion on initialization procedures).

To conclude, let us say that, even though experts are sometimes doubtful about the ability of Evolutionary Algorithms to efficiently optimize the function that took them years to begin to understand, they are indeed convinced by the discovery of unbelievable cases such as the one presented in that paper.

References

1. J. Antonisse. A new interpretation of schema notation that overturns the binary encoding constraint. In J. D. Schaffer, editor, *Proceedings of the 3rd International Conference on Genetic Algorithms*, pages 86–91. Morgan Kaufmann, June 1989.
2. D.L. Battle and M.D. Vose. Isomorphisms of genetic algorithms. In G. J. E. Rawlins, editor, *Foundations of Genetic Algorithms*, pages 242–251. Morgan Kaufmann, 1991.
3. F. Boschetti. *Application of genetic algorithms to the inversion of geophysical data*. PhD thesis, University of Western Australia, 1995.
4. P. Docherty, R. Silva, S. Singh, Z. Song, and M. Wood. Migration velocity analysis using a genetic algorithm. *Geophysical Prospecting*, 45:865–878, 1997.

5. D.B. Fogel and L.C. Stayton. On the effectiveness of crossover in simulated evolutionary optimization. *BioSystems*, 32:171–182, 1994.
6. D. E. Goldberg. A theory of virtual alphabets. In Hans-Paul Schwefel and Reinhard Männer, editors, *Proceedings of the 1st Parallel Problem Solving from Nature*, pages 13–22, 1991.
7. J. J. Grefenstette. Optimization of control parameters for genetic algorithms. *IEEE Trans. on Systems, Man and Cybernetics*, SMC-16, 1986.
8. R. Hinterding, Z. Michalewicz, and A. E. Eiben. Adaptation in evolutionary computation: A survey. In *Proceedings of the 4th IEEE International Conference on Evolutionary Computation*, pages 65–69. IEEE Press, 1997.
9. C. Z. Janikow and Z. Michalewicz. An experimental comparison of binary and floating point representations in genetic algorithms. In R. K. Belew and L. B. Booker, editors, *Proceedings of the 4th International Conference on Genetic Algorithms*, pages 31–36. Morgan Kaufmann, 1991.
10. S. Jin and P. Madariaga. Background velocity inversion with a genetic algorithm. *Geophysical research letters*, 20(2):93–96, 1993.
11. T. Jones. Crossover, macromutation and population-based search. In L. J. Eshelman, editor, *Proceedings of the 6th International Conference on Genetic Algorithms*, pages 73–80. Morgan Kaufmann, 1995.
12. L. Kallel and M. Schoenauer. Alternative random initialization in genetic algorithms. In Th. Bäck, editor, *Proceedings of the 7th International Conference on Genetic Algorithms*, pages 268–275. Morgan Kaufmann, 1997.
13. F. Mansanne. . PhD thesis, Université de Pau, In preparation.
14. Z. Michalewicz and M. Schoenauer. Evolutionary Algorithms for Constrained Parameter Optimization Problems. *Evolutionary Computation*, 4(1):1–32, 1996.
15. F. P. Preparata and M. I. Shamos. *Computational Geometry: an introduction*. Springer Verlag, 1985.
16. J. D. Schaffer, R. A. Caruana, L. Eshelman, and R. Das. A study of control parameters affecting on-line performance of genetic algorithms for function optimization. In J. D. Schaffer, editor, *Proceedings of the 3rd International Conference on Genetic Algorithms*, pages 51–60. Morgan Kaufmann, 1989.
17. M. Schoenauer. Representations for evolutionary optimization and identification in structural mechanics. In J. Périaux and G. Winter, editors, *Genetic Algorithms in Engineering and Computer Sciences*, pages 443–464. John Wiley, 1995.
18. M. Schoenauer, A. Ehinger, and B. Braunschweig. Non-parametric identification of geological models. In *Proceedings of the 5th IEEE International Conference on Evolutionary Computation*. IEEE Press, 1998.
19. M. Schoenauer, L. Kallel, and F. Jouve. Mechanical inclusions identification by evolutionary computation. *European J. of Finite Elements*, 5(5-6):619–648, 1996.
20. H.-P. Schwefel. *Numerical Optimization of Computer Models*. John Wiley & Sons, New-York, 1981. 1995 – 2nd edition.
21. P.L. Stoffa and M.K. Sen. Nonlinear multiparameter optimization using genetic algorithms : inversion of plane-wave seismograms. *Geophysics*, 56, 1991.
22. P.D. Surry and N.J. Radcliffe. Formal algorithms + formal representations = search strategies. In H.-M. Voigt et al., editors, *Proceedings of the 4th Parallel Problems Solving from Nature*, pages 366–375. Springer Verlag, 1996.
23. P.D. Surry and N.J. Radcliffe. Inoculation to initialise evolutionary search. In *AISB Evolutionary Computing*, LNCS 1141, pages 269–285. Springer Verlag, 1996.
24. M.T. Taner and F. Koehler. Velocity spectra-digital computer derivation and applications to velocity functions. *Geophysics*, 56:1794–1810, 1969.

Solving Real-Life Time-Tabling Problems

Martin Schmidt

Dept. of Computer Science, University of Aarhus, Denmark

Email: marsch@daimi.au.dk and msc@bording.dk

Abstract. We will compare the performance of a Genetic Algorithm and Simulated Annealing on instances of difficult real-life Time-Tabling Problems. We will further explain how the performance can be increased significantly by applying a general and very effective genotype-to-phenotype decoding. Furthermore, we will contrast the performance of Lamarckian Learning to the performance of Baldwin Learning. Finally, we test and comment on the benefits of adaptive operators for both Genetic Algorithms and Simulated Annealing.

1 Introduction

Time-Tabling Problems (TTP's) are scheduling problems that with an overwhelming frequency are found in business and academia (see [2], [3], [4] and [5] for good overviews). This paper shows how to solve difficult real-life TTP's with Genetic Algorithms (GA's) and Simulated Annealing (SA). We will show how to increase the performance with a general and effective genotype-to-phenotype decoder, and we will furthermore contrast the performance of Lamarckian Learning to Baldwin Learning. We will further argue for and against adaptive operators for both GA's and SA. Finally, we comment on using a GA or a SA in order to solve TTP's.

The paper contains the following sections: 1. Introduction, 2. Time-Tabling Problems, 3. Description of Algorithms, 4. Results and Analysis, and 5. Conclusions.

2 Time-Tabling Problems

TTP's are a general class of difficult real-life problems where one has to schedule a number of tasks on the basis on both soft constraints and hard constraints. The soft constraints may be broken while the hard constraints may *not* be broken since they invalidate the whole schedule. The following matrix exemplifies a TTP:

	Person			
Timeslot		Job		

Table 1: Time-Tabling Problem

Some examples of TTP's are (Timeslot / Person / Job):
- Teaching hour / Teacher / Class, i.e. University Time-Tabling Problems.
- Hour / Machine / Job, i.e. Job-Shop Scheduling Problems.
- Day / Worker / Job. This is our case.

Our goal is to schedule jobs for workers such that a particular ship can sail between Denmark and Germany [1]. Every job can be one of six jobs:

1. Morning job (6 hours).
2. Lunch job (6 hours).
3. Evening job (6 hours).
4. Morning + lunch job (11 hours and not as expected 12 hours).
5. Lunch + evening job (11 hours).
6. Day off.

There are 3 different categories of workers and they are paid differently:

- Workers of category 1 are on regular salary.
- Workers of category 2 and category 3 [2] are paid on hourly basis according to union agreements e.g. 6 hours work is paid as 8 hours while 11 hours work is paid as 11 hours.

Before a ship may sail all the hard constraints *must* be obeyed; otherwise the ship is not allowed to sail. The soft constraints *should* be obeyed as well as possible because of worker preferences. The following *hard constraints* were applied:

- No worker may work more than 161 hours a month.
- No worker may work more than 3 days consecutively.
- The desired days off (e.g. vacation) of every worker must be respected.
- The required workers with security training must be on board the ship.
- No worker is allowed to work late one day and early the following day.
- Workers of category 1 must at least have one weekend off a month.
- There is a max limit of 20 days of work a month for workers of category 1.
- Category 1 workers are credited for 5.37 hours for each day off.
- Workers of category 2 and 3 are paid 8 hours even if they work less than 8 hours (while e.g. 11 hours are paid as 11 hours).

The following *soft constraints* were applied:

- Workers prefer to work 2 days followed by 2 days off.
- Workers prefer many hours a few days a month.
- Workers of category 1 are preferred over workers of category 2, which again are preferred over workers of category 3.

3 Description of Algorithms

3.1 Encoding

The used encoding was: Concatenate all jobs in Table 1 row-wise into a list. This encoding describes the genotype and the *no. genes* is the length of the list, i.e. *no. genes* = no. columns * no. rows. Every gene holds one of 6 values. However, the phenotype is not a list but a matrix like the one shown in Table 1. To evaluate a genotype it is decoded into the phenotype and the fitness function is applied.

---

[1] The trip from Denmark to Germany and back takes only a few hours.
[2] Category 2 workers work more frequently than category 3 workers.

3.2 Simple Decoder and Locally Optimal Decoder

During the decoding, every single allele was compared to the hard constraints. If the allele did not break any hard constraint then it was used directly. Nevertheless, if it breaks a hard constraint then the worker was assigned a day off. This *simple decoder* removes many constraint violations in the start of the timetable but not in the end.

Instead of just giving the worker a day off as in the simple decoder, one can choose the following *locally optimal decoder*: If a constraint is violated, find the best possible alternative by exhaustive search [3]. If no constraint is broken then use the allele directly. This decoder focuses on the local level such that the optimisation technique can concentrate on the global improvements. Note that this general strategy is very effective and can be applied to all problems that have a *set* of possible alleles for each gene [4]. The locally optimal decoder has an interesting effect: It forms attractors towards local optima ! This happens since many genotype "errors" are "removed" during the decoding and will never appear in the phenotype. Hence, the solutions receive (most probably) an increased fitness. This is deterministic Baldwin Learning. Based on the decoder improvements one can use Lamarckian Learning, i.e. with probability $P_{Lamarckian}$ an improvement is coded back from phenotype to genotype.

3.3 Fitness and Operators

The overall goal of the optimisation system is to minimise the salary for workers of category 2 and 3, while obeying the hard and soft constraints. The *salary* of workers of category 1 can not be optimised since they are on regular salary.

Every optimisation technique *minimised* the following fitness function:
```
Fitness = 50 * (MissingWorkers + MissingCards)
          + 2 * WorkedHoursCategory3
          + WorkedHoursCategory2
          + NormalisingDistanceFactor * DistToSequence2
where
  MissingWorkers = total no. workers that are missing
  MissingCards = total no. security cards that are missing
  WorkedHoursCategory3 = total no. paid hours for category 3
  WorkedHoursCategory2 = total no. paid hours for category 2
  DistToSequence2 = distance to "2 days work then 2 days off"
  NormalisingDistanceFactor = normalise DistToSequence2 in [0:1]
```
The fitness function is achieving the following: Mainly, avoid hard constraints by penalising MissingWorkers and MissingCards [5]. Further, both category 2 and 3 workers cost money so try to avoid using them. Nevertheless, if you cannot avoid

---

[3] According to the hard constraints and the fitness function, which are only evaluated for the current gene. The exhaustive search is in our case only searching 6 different possibilities.
[4] The set should not be too large since the exhaustive search would become too ineffective.
[5] The company has an estimate of the minimal number of needed workers for every day.

using them, prefer category 2 workers to category 3 workers. Finally, try to find a solution that resembles a solution with 2 days work followed by 2 days off.

We tested several "standard" operators and some problem specific operators. Some operators were binary, i.e. they take 2 parents and create 1 child, and some operators were unary, i.e. they take 1 parent and create 1 child. The GA is the only investigated technique that can use the binary operators. We tested the following operators:

- **Binary operators:** (1) *1X*: One-point crossover, (2) *2X*: Two-point crossover, (3) *UX*: Uniform crossover, (4) *2RC*: Two-point row crossover (whole rows were exchanged), (5) *URC*: Uniform row crossover (whole rows were exchanged), (6) *2CC*: Two-point column crossover (whole columns were exchanged), (7) *UCC*: Uniform column crossover (whole columns were exchanged).
- **Unary operators:** (1) *RM*: Random mutation of genes. Expected number of mutations is 2, (2) *2To1*: Swap jobs for a day between workers of category 2 and 1, (3) *3To2*: Swap jobs for a day between workers of category 3 and 2, (4) *RSwap*: Swap jobs for a day (Row) between randomly chosen workers, (5) *CSwap*: Swap jobs for a worker (Column) between randomly chosen days.

3.4 Simulated Annealing and Genetic Algorithm

We used a relatively standard SA with the following characteristics [6]:
1. Exponential annealing schedule i.e. $T_{Time} = k * T_{Time-1}$, where $k = 0.975$.
2. Variable Markov chain length L:
   $L = k * Number of genes$, where $k = 6$ (6 different values).
3. Stop optimisation after N transitions without improvement of the best solution: $N = k * Number of genes$, where $k = 250$.
4. Automatic calculation of start temperature such that the number of accepted transitions initially is in the range 80% - 85%.
5. The unary operators (see section 3.3) define the neighbourhood.

These characteristics resulted in a very stable implementation i.e. the SA algorithm did not need to be changed although the problem size was increased significantly.

The used Steady State Genetic Algorithm (ssGA) had the following characteristics [7]:
1. Every generation only 1 new individual was generated.
2. We used a fixed population size P: $P = k * Number of genes$, where $k = 6$.
3. Stop optimisation after N generations without improvements:
   $N = k * P$, where $k = 100$.
4. Binary tournament selection and binary tournament replacement.

With these characteristics problems of varying size can be solved without re-coding.

---

[6] The SA constants where found easily during preliminary tests.
[7] The GA constants where found easily during preliminary tests.

4. Results and Analysis

This section presents the tested operators, tests using the simple decoder, tests using the locally optimal decoder, results of Baldwin Learning and Lamarckian Learning, and results on a very large real-life test case.

All the following results present the average over 10 runs. In general, the fitness corresponds approximately to the salary for the workers of category 2 and 3. The smaller the salary the better, and hence the smaller the fitness the better.

The following sections refer to two different types of TTP's:

1. *Medium Size TTP*: This is a real-life TTP were one must assign jobs for 41 workers for the next month (30 days). This gives a total of 1230 jobs in the timetable, which results in a total search space of the size $6^{1230} \approx 10^{957}$. The GA population for this TTP is $P = 6*1230 = 7380$.

2. *Large Size TTP*: This is another real-life TTP were one must assign jobs for 205 workers for the next month (30 days). This gives a total of 6150 jobs in the timetable, which results in a total search space of the size $6^{6150} \approx 10^{4786}$. The GA population for this TTP is $P = 6*6150 = 36900$.

Both test cases are based on real timetable data from a customer (a Ship Company).

4.1 Simple Decoder

We tested *every operator alone* for both the GA and the SA using the simple decoder on the medium size TTP. We found the following results as shown in Figure 1:

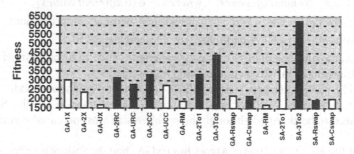

Figure 1: Fitness Using one Operator.

White columns represent methods that always gave valid results [8], while black columns represent methods that did not. The smaller the fitness the better.
Figure 1 shows that:

1. A GA using 1X, 2X and UX gave always valid results.
2. GA using special crossovers 2RC, URC, 2CC resulted in invalid results. An analysis showed that the GA converged to fast and got stuck in illegal optima.
3. Mutation alone gave very good results for the GA and the SA.

The best performances were GA-UX with fitness 1661 and SA-RM with fitness 1679.

---

[8] This means that no hard constraints were broken.

Given the many invalid results (black columns in Figure 1) due to a too fast convergence, and given the quite good performance of mutation alone, we decided to perform some more tests were we *always use mutation plus one other operator* [9]. We found the following results as shown in Figure 2:

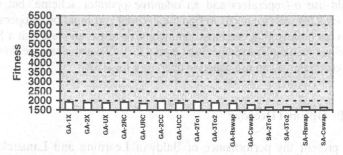

Figure 2: Fitness Using Mutation Plus one Other Operator.

Figure 2 shows that all results are valid if we use mutation as one of two operators. Further, all performances are more alike. Nevertheless, the earlier best fitness of the GA (see GA-UX in Figure 1) is worsened and is 1838 using the crossover operator UCR together with mutation (see GA-UCR). On the contrary, the best SA fitness is improved to 1640 using the operators mutation and CSwap (see SA-CSwap).

The worsened best GA performance might be a result of a decreased convergence due to mutations. To verify this we performed the same tests using a selection and replacement size of 3. This results in a polynomial selection and replacement pressure instead of a linear selection and replacement pressure. Hence, the divergence influence of mutation will be reduced and the convergence speed will be increased. Surprisingly we found *no* improvement of the GA performance.

Hence we found (see Figure 2):

- The best GA fitness is 1838 using mutation and URC (see GA-URC). The best GA performance is significantly worsened using mutation, while the average GA performance is increased.
- The best SA fitness is 1640 using mutation and CSwap (see SA-CSwap). The best SA performance is significantly increased using mutation, and the average SA performance is also increased.

The so-far best GA uses UX only, and the best SA uses mutation and CSwap.

Finally, we tried to use all possible operators and an adaptive operator scheme (see [1]) in order to see whether this gave better results. We found the following results: GA fitness of 1762 and SA fitness of 1649.

Compared to the *best* results found earlier we found that:

1. The best GA performance is worsened by 6.1% from 1661 (see Figure 1) to 1762 using all operators.
2. The best SA performance is worsened by 0.5% from 1640 (see Figure 2) to 1649 using all operators.

---

[9] We used Davis' adaptive operator scheme [1].

Based on these results one can question the optimality of the adaptive operator scheme. Nevertheless, it is easier, faster and more convenient to use an adaptive operator scheme and all operators, than to use thousands of CPU and man hours to find the optimal combination of operators. Hence, if one wants rapid development, one should use *all* operators and an *adaptive* operator scheme, but if one wants sublime performance, one needs to find the optimal combination of operators.

We do not believe that one based on the above tests can state that a SA in general is more robust using adaptive operators than a GA. Nevertheless, we do conclude that one with good results can use adaptive operators for a SA.

4.2 Locally Optimal Decoder

We now present the performance of Baldwin Learning and Lamarckian Learning using the locally optimal decoder on the medium size TTP. Baldwin Learning is achieved with $P_{Lamarckian} = 0.0$. In Figure 4, 5 and 6 the x-axis shows $P_{Lamarckian}$.

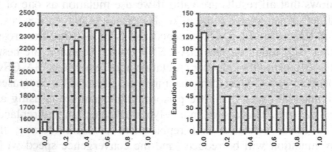

Figure 4: Genetic Algorithm Using UX as the Only Operator.

Figure 4 shows that even a weak form of Lamarckian Learning reduces the execution time, but also dramatically decreases the performance. Furthermore, we find that our locally optimal decoder finds far better solutions than those found in section 4.1, see $P_{Lamarckian} = 0.0$ with a fitness of 1578. Since Lamarckian Learning quickly destroys the diversity a mutation operator seems to be appropriate to increase the diversity (hopefully still with a reduced execution time). Hence, we also tested a GA with UX and the mutation operator, and found the following results:

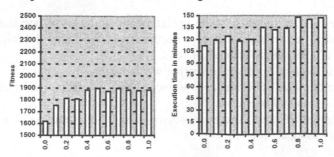

Figure 5: Genetic Algorithm Using UX and the Mutation Operator.

Our hopes were not fulfilled. In Figure 5 we see that the added mutation operator did increase the diversity and hence the mean performance is improved, but the best performance is worsened and the execution time is significantly increased. Therefor, using a GA with UX and without mutation seems to perform best (see Figure 4).

SA with Baldwin Learning and Lamarckian Learning gave the following results:

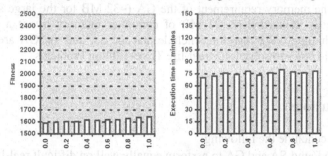

Figure 6: Simulated Annealing Using Mutation and CSwap.

Figure 6 shows a very stable performance of the SA. Pure Baldwin Learning performs best, but Lamarckian Learning does not dramatically decrease the performance. The execution time is very robust and does not change dramatically. The best performance was found with pure Baldwin Learning with a fitness of 1588. We conclude that Baldwin Learning increases the performance while Lamarckian Learning destroys the performance achievements found with the locally optimal decoder.

Compared to the best results found with the simple decoder we find that:

1. The GA is improved by 4.9% from 1661 to 1578 using Baldwin Learning.
2. The SA is improved by 3.1% from 1640 to 1588 using Baldwin Learning.

4.3 Large Size Time Tabling Problem

Finally we test our GA, SA and a simple iterated random next-ascent hillclimber (HC) on a large TTP with 6150 jobs using the locally optimal decoder. The HC is allowed to run approximately the same number of iterations as the SA and the GA.

We found the following results using the best GA and SA settings so-far (section 4.2):

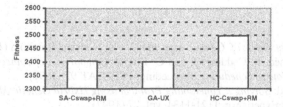

Figure 7: Results on a Large Time-Tabling Problem.

Figure 7 shows that a SA with mutation and CSwap performs as well as a GA with UX. The SA finds solutions with a fitness of 2404 and the GA finds solutions with a fitness of 2401. Surprisingly the HC (using the same operators as the SA) performs

656

quite well with a fitness of 2498 which is only ~4 % worse than the GA. This is most probably due to the effective locally optima decoder.

In order to declare the "best" method we cannot exclusively look at the performance since the SA and the GA perform equally well. Hence, we have to look at the memory requirements and the execution time. The GA is ~9 % faster than the SA, but this could be changed with a faster annealing method. What one cannot change is the memory requirement of the GA (~32 MB for the large size TTP) that the GA needs. Nevertheless, 32 MB of computer memory is not a problem with current technology. We therefor conclude that the SA and the GA are equally well applicable in order to solve large real-life Time-Tabling Problems.

5. Conclusions

We finally conclude the following:
- We found SA and GA to perform equally well on difficult real-life TTP's.
- We found high quality solutions that fully satisfied our customer.
- A general and locally optimal decoder resulted in a significant improvement of the performance. The locally optimal decoder can easily be applied to almost every TTP where it would improve the performance considerably.
- Baldwin Learning results in slower convergence than Lamarckian Learning but finds far better solutions than Lamarckian Learning. We advice using Baldwin Learning since we experienced problems with Lamarckian Learning but never with Baldwin Learning.
- Both SA and GA performed very well when extended with Baldwin Learning.
- Adaptive operators speeded up the development time significantly, since we did not have to use many weeks on fine-tuning operator probabilities.

Regards

Thanks to the software company Bording Data A/S for their support and to Zbigniew Michalewicz for comments on drafts of this paper.

References

1. L. Davis: *Handbook of Genetic Algorithms*, Van Nostrand Reinhold (1991)
2. S. Elmohamed, P. Coddington and G. Fox: *A Comparison of Annealing Techniques for Academic Course Scheduling*, Proceedings of PATAT'97 (1997)
3. L. Kragelund: *Solving a Timetabling Problem using Hybrid Genetic Algorithms*, Software-Practice and Experience, 1121-1134, vol. 27 (1997)
4. A. Schaerf: *A survey of automated timetabling*, Department of Software Technology, Report CS-R9567, CWI, Amsterdam, The Netherlands (1995)
5. D. de Werra: *An intoduction to timetabling*, European Journal of Operational Research, 19, 151-162 (1985)

On Measures of Search Features

Roger Jonsson

Department of Computer Engineering, Mälardalens University, Box 883,
721 23 Västerås, Sweden, roger.jonsson@mdh.se

Abstract. This paper describes several measures that can be useful
when analyzing features of search in genetic algorithms. Results obtained
by different researchers are often hard to compare and it is often difficult
to draw general conclusions from them. This means that non-experienced
users of genetic algorithms have little help in constructing their own effective solutions for a particular problem. The article contains a sugges-
tion about possible ways of investigating features of search in genetic
algorithms. These features are defined together with descriptions how to
measure them.

1 Introduction

Imagine the following scenario: an engineer needs to construct a static scheduler for tasks to be run on a particular computer system. The engineer has read
about genetic algorithms and thinks they would be applicable to this optimization problem. Unfortunately there is little information about how to construct
the algorithm for this specific problem, which representation, operators and parameters should be used? Also, if an algorithm would be constructed, how could
the algorithm be altered to perform better or is the current setup the best?

Today there are results from application areas using various genetic algorithms with different parameter values, operators and representations. They
often have encouraging results but there is rarely any proof or theory that a
particular parameter or operator is optimal or good for their kind of problem.
The results are often compared to other methods taking into account either
convergence rate, execution speed or both. Unfortunately, this usually provides
little help to an engineer that wants to solve a practical optimization problem
since convergence rate is tightly coupled to the problem it is solving.

This article proposes five general measures that could be used to compare
performance and features of different genetic algorithms. The features described
are not new in the genetic algorithm community but some of the measures are
not defined as far as we know.

The table of search properties (Table 1), quoted from [3], shows clear differences in how an optimization algorithm should perform depending on the
type of problem (in the table called objective function) it is solving. A natural procedure should be to explore as much as possible while also investigating
the currently most promising area of the search space. This implies a tradeoff
between exploration and exploitation.

Our study contains research regarding the dependencies between parameter values, different operators and exploration and exploitation of the population. Hopefully, results from this research may lead to a theory of how operators and parameters affect the search during the evolution. By using this theory, an engineer would be able to use parameters and/or operators to tune the search towards either more extensive exploration or exploitation.

Table 1. Unimodal and modal search properties.

unimodal objective function	multimodal objective function
convergence velocity	convergence confidence
"hard" selection scheme	"soft" selection scheme
small genotypic diversity	large genotypic diversity
path oriented	volume oriented
exploitative character	explorative character

2 The Current State of Research

An introduction to genetic algorithms and a good overview of the current state of research in the domain can be found in [2, 11, 4, 5, 14], all with extensive lists of references. They all give descriptions in how to construct a genetic algorithm, problems that occur and, for some problems, ways to avoid them.

In the above mentioned overviews the following problems are described: representation, deception, epistasis, premature convergence, slow convergence, construction of the fitness function, invalid genes and choice of operators and parameters. All these issues are important when constructing a genetic algorithm, but in what way do the design decissions affect the genetic search or, more specificly, exploration and exploitation?

In what follows a presentation of the problems and some lines of research that try to deal with them is given.

Representation: This is one of the key issues. In our opinion the representation does not directly affect the explorative or exploitative behavior but many of the following problems and design choices (regarding the construction of a genetic algorithm) have their origin and depend on the representation.

Holland formalized the "schema theorem" saying that binary coding is the most effective one due to the building block theory. Although it may be the most effective representation for problems where binary representation has a natural translation to the problem search space, many problems incorporate either deception (see below), or epistasis (see below), or both when using binary coding.

An algebra for GA is presented by Radcliffe in [15]. He shows that a single characteristic of a search space leads to a unique genetic representation.

Deception: This problem can be explained by Holland's building block theory and basically amounts to that the genetic algorithm is being fooled into a local optimum. There are two solutions to this problem: use another representation or try to spread the population. Louis and Rawlings have tried to deal with this problem by inverting the worst gene [10] and thereby spreading the population.

Epistasis: The phenomenon called epistasis occurs when there is strong interaction between loci (parts of genes). The interaction can be described as when the same change in a locus produces different fitness depending on other loci. It can be classified into three levels [5]: no interaction, mild interaction and epistasis. A high interaction between loci prohibit good building blocks to form and thus effective search.

Beasley, Bull and Martin point out that two ways of solving this problem are possible (similarly to deception): produce new theory with new algorithms or change the representation. Expansive coding [6] describes a method to transform a representation with high epistasis to a representation with a low one.

Premature convergence: This problem appears when a "super-individual" takes over the entire population. That means less differing gene material in the population and that reduces the effect of crossover. In the end the population gets stuck in a local optimum. From this point only mutation can make individuals diverse from the population. This problem can be handled by altering the selection procedure (see below), the fitness function (see below) or by mate preference [13].

Mate preference is used by Schaffer & Eshelman (described in [13]). It is called "incest avoidance" and prevents mating between individuals that are too similar, which means that one super-individual never has the possibility to occupy the whole population.

The main objective, regardless of solution, is to maintain diversity in the early generations.

Slow convergence: A somewhat opposite problem to the previous one but the key issue for most real world applications. Regardless of how a problem is solved or reduced, measuring convergence speed is usually done by calculating number of individuals processed or number of operations performed. Convergence naturally depends on how well the algorithm exploits the currently best solution.

Construction of the fitness function: Although one can build heuristics and application knowledge into the different operators, the fitness function is usually the only part that has contact with the optimization search space (in contrast to the search space that the representation works in). The type of problems that arise in the fitness function construction often have a close connection to the representation or the selection method.

Invalid genes: When the fitness function has problems in evaluating a gene (due to missing important gene material) it can be said to be invalid. Another way of describing it would be to say that there are invalid regions in the representation space. This problem can be dealt with by assigning a penalty to the gene (the hardest penalty being death), using some kind of decoder (to transform invalid parts to valid parts of the search space) or repair function (this can be computationally expensive), or using another representation with operators that keep the gene in valid parts of the search space. All four techniques are described in [12] and exemplified in three applications.

Parameters: Most parameters arc probabilities of using an operator, but there are also the size of the population and some stop criteria (often the maximum number of generations). Bäck argues that the parameters should vary during the evolution and that the most efficient parameter setting depends on at least the fitness function [1], which in turn depends on the application. This is also supported by [7] and by the fact that researchers have come up with different "optimal" parameter settings [2].

Operators: This area includes operators like selection, crossover and mutation. The problem here is to choose which operator to use, since several operators can be used with the same representation. Bäck compares selection mechanisms with the property of how preservative different selection schemes are [3] by using convergence rate and diversity. Selection methods have also been thoroughly compared using only convergence rate as a measure [8]. Unfortunately, as Hancock writes in the beginning of his article, convergence rate is not easy to define in other way than relative to a problem.

Spears [17] gives guidelines and a theory of how to construct operators (crossover and mutation) and their effect on search (Spears and de Jong have made a lot of research on this topic [16, 18, 9]).

3 Features of Search

It is important to provide a framework with theories and suggestions about how to use genetic algorithms in an effective and robust way. A framework should contain as general theories as possible of how search properties could be measured and altered. Fortunately there is plenty of research going on in this area, but it is still hard to compare results from several problem domains using different operators and parameters.

Below is a summary of measures that describe different features of search; the list is ordered by frequency of use.

Convergence rate. One definition of convergence can be found in [4] (originally from K. de Jong's PhD thesis): "A gene is said to have converged when 95% of the population share the same value. The population is said to have converged when all of the genes have converged". This definition is not practical in all applications though, for instance [19] presents a method where the goal is to produce different solutions (genes).

Also, as stated by Hancock [8], convergence rate is relative to the problem, which makes comparisons between different problems futile.
Correctness of solution. An intuitive description could be the distance to the optimal solution, or how often the algorithm finds a optimal solution. However, this causes problems when the optimal solution is not known or can not be estimated.
This measure is relative to the population size and number of generations (or number of processed individuals, see below) since the more genes that are considered the likelihood of finding a better individual increase. This measure only provides information about the final state, not about how the search is performed. The last thing is usually not important in real problems but interesting when understanding how the search in genetic algorithms work. However, it should be useful for validation.
Number of individuals processed. This says something about how effective the search is. However, some caution has to be taken when using operators that discard invalid genes and retry to produce an offspring. The number of individuals processed should be seen as a measure of the number of samples considered in search space. Then all individuals considered should be counted, regardless whether they were valid or not. This could be calculated in three ways: all individuals considered during the search, all different individuals considered during the search and all new individuals considered in one generation.
The first measure describes the amount of work the algorithm has done (if all individuals are equally hard to produce, see above on invalid genes), the second says how much of the representation space is explored and the last describes how effective the algorithm is between generations. Note that neither say anything about the amount of time the search has taken.
Exploration (diversity). A possible measure could be the variance in the population (when using real valued alleles) in each locus of a gene. A high variance indicates a population with differing individuals. The variance for locus j at time (generation) t is defined as:

$$v_j^t = \frac{1}{\lambda - 1} \sum_{i=0}^{\lambda} \left(\frac{1}{\lambda} \sum_{i=0}^{\lambda} \alpha_{i,j}^t - \alpha_{i,j}^t \right)^2 \tag{1}$$

where λ = population size, t = generations elapsed and $\alpha_{i,j}^t$ is locus j in gene i at generation t.
When using binary representation, either the variance in Hamming-distance could be applicable or Bäck's definition of diversity [3], called bias:

$$bias = \frac{1}{l\lambda} \sum_{j=1}^{l} \max \left(\sum_{i=1}^{\lambda} (1 - \alpha_{i,j}^t), \sum_{i=1}^{\lambda} \alpha_{i,j}^t \right) \tag{2}$$

where l denotes the length (number of alleles) of the gene. Bias have the bounds 0.5 – 1.0 where 1.0 indicates a population with equal individuals and 0.5 a population with maximum diversity.

These equations measure the diversity of the representation, not of the problem search space. To be able to measure the exploration in the problem search space, one must know the mapping between the representation and the problem. Unfortunately, this mapping is usually not known.

Exploitation. This measure should reflect the intensity of exploitation by calculating the percentage of genes in the neighborhood of the current best gene in representation space. To specify the neighborhood a parameter, d, is used to describe the maximum distance from the best gene. The function Γ_d below checks wether a gene (g_i^t) is in the d-neighborhood of the current best gene (b^t).

$$\Gamma_d(g_i^t) = \begin{cases} 1 \text{ if } \Delta(g_i^t, b^t) < d \\ 0 \text{ otherwise} \end{cases} \tag{3}$$

where $\Delta(g_1, g_2)$ is a distance between two genes. Now the intensity in the d-neighborhood of b^t can be calculated as:

$$I_d^t = \frac{1}{\lambda} \sum_{i=0}^{\lambda} \Gamma_d(g_i^t) \tag{4}$$

where λ is the size of the population. This measure does not take into account that several genes can be identical, thus a more interesting measure would be the relative amount of *different* genes in the d-neighborhood of the best gene.

$$J_d^t = \frac{1}{\lambda} \sum_{i=0}^{\lambda} f(g_i^t) \Gamma_d(g_i^t) \tag{5}$$

where the function $f(g_i^t)$ returns one only once per group of identical individuals:

$$f(g_i^t) = \begin{cases} 1 \text{ if } \sum_{k=i+1}^{\lambda} h(g_i^t, g_k^t) = 0 \\ 0 \text{ otherwise} \end{cases} \tag{6}$$

and where in turn $h(g_1, g_2)$ returns one if the two genes are identical:

$$h(g_1, g_2) = \begin{cases} 1 \text{ if } \Delta(g_1, g_2) = 0 \\ 0 \text{ otherwise} . \end{cases} \tag{7}$$

A natural objective when imposing fast convergence should be to exploit as many different points as possible in the neighborhood of the current best gene.

4 Conclusion

How can we compare similar genetic algorithms when they are solving different problems? Well, only the last three measures (number of different individuals, exploration and exploitation) seem to be adequate, although they only compare the search in a specific representation. But this may also be useful because the effect different operators and parameters have on the search (in the representation search space) can be calculated and compared.

In an ideal situation genetic algorithms combines exploration and exploitation in an optimal way, but that requires an infinitely large population, low interaction between loci and a fitness function that perfectly reflects the problem [4]. Since at least the first requirement can not be met in computer algorithms, measures for exploration and exploitation are necessary to be able to tune the search. Unfortunately, another parameter (a distance to the current best solution) is required when measuring exploitation.

The above described measures can contribute in at least four ways:

- When testing operators and their parameters, number of new individuals considered, exploration and exploitation should be measured for comparison with other operators.
- Solutions to problems with deception could be measured by exploration.
- If there are dependencies between certain operators and diversity, premature convergence could be reduced by using those operators.
- When fine tuning a genetic algorithm for an specific application, exploitation and convergence rate should be useful.

An interesting question is how different operators affect the diversity, especially crossover and selection. Naturally, selection can only decrease the diversity of the population but how fast? It is also relatively clear that high probability of mutation causes diversity of the population but how large compared to crossover? Are exploration and exploitation features that should be calculated during the run-time and immediately affect the parameters?

The measures described above are suggestions how we could learn more about the relationships between individual operators and search in genetic algorithms. There should also be a continued quest for more measures and more precise definitions of the terms above.

I hope the knowledge found by using these measures can be used to augment the current theory of genetic algorithms.

Acknowledgments

I would like to thank Jacek Malec and Baran Çürüklü for reviewing earlier drafts of this paper. This work was supported by Volvo Research Foundation, Volvo Educational Foundation and Dr. Pehr G. Gyllenhammar Research Foundation.

References

1. T. Bäck. The interaction of mutation rate, selection, and self-adaption within a genetic algorithm. *Parallel Problem Solving from Nature*, 2:85–94, 1992.
2. T. Bäck, U. Hammel, and H.-P. Schwefel. Evolutionary computation: Comments on the history and current state. *IEEE Transaction on Evolutionary Computation*, 1(1), 1997.
3. T. Bäck and F. Hoffmeister. Extended selection mechanisms in genetic algorithms. In *Proceedings of the Fourth International Conference on Genetic Algorithms and their Applications*, 1991.
4. D. Beasley, D. R. Bull, and R. R. Martin. An overview of genetic algorithms: Part 1, fundamentals. *University Computing*, 15(2):58–69, 1993.
5. D. Beasley, D. R. Bull, and R. R. Martin. An overview of genetic algorithms: Part 2, research topics. *University Computing*, 15(2):170–181, 1993.
6. D. Beasley, D. R. Bull, and R. R. Martin. Reducing epistatis in combinatorial problems by expansive coding. *The Proceeding of the Fifth International Conference on Genetic Algorithms*, 1993.
7. A. E. Eiben, R. Hinterding, and Z. Michalewicz. Parameter control in evolutionary algorithms. *IEEE Transactions on Evolutionary Computation*, 2(4), 1998.
8. P. J. Hancock. An empirical comparision of selection methods in evolutionary algorithms. *Evolutionary Computing: AISB Workshop*, 1994.
9. K. A. D. Jong and W. M. Spears. A formal analysis of the role of multi-point crossover in genetic algorithms. *Annals of Mathematics and Artificial Intelligence Journal*, 1992.
10. S. J. Louis and G. J. E. Rawlins. Predicting convergence time for genetic algorithms. Technical report, University of Waterloo, 1993.
11. Z. Michalewicz. *Genetic algorithms + data structures = evolution programs.* Springer, 1996.
12. Z. Michalewicz, S. Esquivel, R. Gallard, M. Michalewicz, and G. Ta. The spirit of evolutionary algorithms. *Journal of Heuristics*, 1(2):177–206, 1995.
13. G. F. Miller. Exploiting mate choice in evolutionary computation: Sexual selection as a process of search, optimization, and diversification. *Lecture Notes in Computer Science*, 865:65–79, 1994.
14. M. Mitchell. *An introduction to genetic algorithms.* MIT Press, 1998.
15. N. J. Radcliffe. The algebra of genetic algorithms. *Annals of Maths and Artificial Intelligence*, 1994.
16. W. M. Spears. Crossover or mutation? *Foundations of Genetic Algorithms*, 2, 1992.
17. W. M. Spears. Recombination parameters. *Handbook of evolutionary computation*, 1995.
18. W. M. Spears and K. A. D. Jong. An analysis of multi-point crossover. *Proceedings of the Foundations of Genetic Algorithms Workshop*, 1990.
19. S. Tsutsui and A. Ghosh. Genetic algorithms with a robust solution searching scheme. *IEEE Transaction on Evolutionary Computation*, 1(3), 1997.

Genetic Algorithms in Constructive Induction

Jacek Jelonek and Maciej Komosiński

Institute of Computing Science, Poznan University of Technology
Piotrowo 3A, 60-965 Poznan, Poland
{jacek.jelonek, macko}@cs.put.poznan.pl

Abstract. In this paper, genetic algorithms are used in machine learning classification task. They act as a constructive induction engine, which selects features and adjusts weights of attributes, in order to obtain the highest classification accuracy. We compare two classification approaches: a single 1-NN and a n^2 meta-classifier. For the n^2-classifier, the idea of an improvement of classification accuracy is based on independent modification of descriptions of examples for each pair of n classes. Finally, it gives $(n^2 - n)/2$ spaces of attributes dedicated for discrimination of pairs of classes. The computational experiment was performed on a medical data set. Its results reveal the utility of using genetic algorithms for feature selection and weight adjusting, and point out the advantage of using a multi-classification model (n^2-classifier) with constructive induction in relation to the analogous single-classifier approach.

Keywords: evolutionary computation, machine learning, knowledge representation, feature selection, multi/meta-classification systems.

1 Introduction

The main problem concerning usage of any classification system is definition of a set of features, which allows obtaining the highest possible classification accuracy. In many practical applications of machine learning, such as pictorial image classification, speech recognition, identification tasks etc., it is easy to suggest (or even automatically generate) many features. However, only a part of them is usually relevant. An influence on the accuracy of those remaining may be not significant; sometimes using them may even deteriorate the classification result.

In order to solve that problem many feature selection algorithms have been developed [2], [14], [23], [10]. In general, feature selection can be treated as a search problem. Each state in the search space represents a subset of possible features. Following the typical view of feature selection algorithms [2] one can define: *search algorithm* - which looks through the space of feature subsets; *evaluation function* - used to evaluate examined subsets of features; and *classifier* - which is constructed basing on final subset of features. These elements can be integrated in two basic ways forming *filter* or *wrapper model* [4]. In the filter model, features are selected as a pre-processing step before a classifier is used, depending on the properties of the data itself. In the wrapper model, the search algorithm conducts a search for a good subset of features using a classifier itself as the evaluation function. Evaluation is usually done by estimating classification accuracy.

Feature selection and attribute weighting can be treated as the basic methods belonging to *constructive induction* (CI) methodology - regarded as supporting automatic, problem-oriented transformation of representation space to facilitate learning [21], [18], [24]. An improvement of accuracy in CI is usually obtained by construction of new features, modification of existing ones and reduction of irrelevant ones. Most systems use specific techniques within one basic computational method: data-driven, hypothesis-driven or knowledge-driven [24].

In this paper we employ a multi-classification system, n^2-classifier (proposed by Jelonek and Stefanowski [9]), in a constructive induction framework. The n^2-classifier is composed of $(n^2 - n)/2$ binary base classifiers (n is a number of classes). Each base classifier is specialized to discriminate one pair of decision classes. A quite similar approach was independently proposed by Friedman [6], and later extended and modified [8], [19]. Our previous experiments have shown that the n^2-classifier with inherent capability of reducing irrelevant features usually yields better classification results than the analogous, single classification model [10], [12]. This observation led us to the hypothesis that creation of dedicated sets of features (e.g. by CI) for discrimination of pairs of classes by independent classifiers gives higher accuracy than using a single set of features dedicated for classification of all classes simultaneously. That was verified on a medical data set in [13], where a genetic algorithm was used for feature selection. Here we extend the capabilities of a genetic algorithm, so that it can not only select features, but also adjust their weights in a nearest-neighbor classification and the wrapper model.

To sum up, we compare here a constructive induction process for both single classifier and n^2-classifier. CI is performed by a genetic algorithm, which provides a global, evolutionary technique for finding best descriptions of examples [15]. In the n^2-classifier case, CI process is repeated $(n^2 - n)/2$ times in order to obtain best-discriminating description spaces for all pairs of classes. Finally, the best sets of weighted features found during the GA runs are used for constructing the n^2-classifier. Our computational experiment based on medical data set confirms the advantage of using a multiple CI algorithm instead of a single CI algorithm. Furthermore, the results obtained show that extending the capabilities of genetic algorithm by weight adjusting yields greater improvements in n^2-classifier, than in a single classifier.

The paper is organized as follows: in the next section we describe a constructive induction framework based on the feature selection. Going into details in subsections 2.1 and 2.2 we present two main components of the CI loop, i.e. *function optimization engine* (a genetic algorithm) and *features evaluation* obtained by using a single or a multi-classification model. The details of computational experiments are included in section 3, where we describe the medical data set, our implementation of the classifiers, the parameters of genetic algorithms and the results of a single and a multi-classifier approach. Section 4 groups final remarks and conclusions.

2 Constructive induction based on feature selection

Figure 1 shows a typical loop of a constructive induction framework. In this scheme function optimization is based on maximization of classification accuracy by modification of input data space (feature selection and their weighting is applied here). In each iteration the function optimization engine calls the features evaluation module to estimate the quality of the features. We applied genetic algorithms as a function optimization engine and a typical k-nearest neighbor classifier (1-NN) as features evaluator [1]. The 1-NN algorithm was used both in a single and in a multi-classifier (n^2-classifier) model.

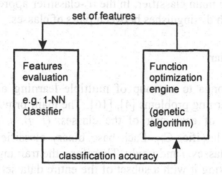

Fig. 1. Main loop of a constructive induction framework

2.1 Genetic algorithms for function optimization

Genetic algorithms (GA) have been successfully applied to many difficult optimization problems. This search method was proved efficient and robust [7]. GA simulate natural mechanisms, like selection and reproduction, while processing a *population* of *individuals* – each individual representing one solution. The algorithm is iterative – in each *generation* best individuals are promoted (*selection*), information between them is exchanged (*crossover*) and *mutation* takes place [5]. Those operations are conducted in order to improve fitness of the next population and to avoid premature convergence to local optima. The operations are usually non-deterministic – they happen with certain probabilities. Despite this non-determinism, GA manage to find the neighborhood of optimal solutions where other search algorithms cannot be applied or do not work effectively [20].

Genetic algorithm is a good tool for feature selection problems. It is not a greedy algorithm - it can search the space of solutions in a global manner, discovering important features and their weights, and passing them to future generations. In our case, each individual represents a weight vector (each weight corresponds to one attribute). In a feature selection task, weights can be equal to 0 or 1 only. Evaluation of each individual (a vector of weights of features) is done by estimating the classification accuracy it yields. Best individuals are the best weight vectors – the weights that give the highest classification accuracy in the classification problem.

2.2 Classifiers

2.2.1 Single classifier

In the wrapper model, the classifier is used to estimate sets of features. It is called every time an individual is evaluated. In GA, a population of individuals is evaluated in each generation, so the classifier should be quick. As we want the CI to be performed by the GA only, the classifier should be simple – should not adapt to the data, remove redundant features nor modify them (i.e., by weighting). If it did, the classification accuracy would not concern original features, but an altered solution.

This is why we used 1-NN classifier (nearest neighbor). In a single-classifier approach, 1-NN is the main classifier. In the n^2-classifier approach, 1-NN is used as a binary classifier which distinguishes between pairs of classes.

2.2.2 The n^2-classifier

The n^2-classifier belongs to a group of multiple learning algorithms dedicated to solving multiclass learning problems [4], [16]. The main principle of the n^2-classifier is the discrimination of each pair of the classes: (i, j), $i, j \in \langle 1..n \rangle$, $i \neq j$, by an independent binary classifier $C_{i,j}$. Each base binary classifier $C_{i,j}$ corresponds to a combination of two classes: i and j only. Therefore, the training of each base classifier $C_{i,j}$ consists in presenting it with a subset of the entire data set that contains examples from class i and j only. The classifier $C_{i,j}$ yields a binary classification indicating whether a new example, x, belongs to class i or j. Let $C_{i,j}(x)$ be the classification of example x by the base classifier $C_{i,j}$. We assume that if $C_{i,j}(x)$ equals 1, then the example x is classified by $C_{i,j}$ to class i, otherwise $(C_{i,j}(x) = 0)$ x is classified to class j.

The complementary classifiers: $C_{i,j}$ and $C_{j,i}$ (where $i, j \in \langle 1..n \rangle$, $i \neq j$) solve the same classification problem. Their predictions can be computed as the opposite predictions of their complementary equivalents:

$$C_{i,j}(x) = 1 - C_{j,i}(x) . \tag{1}$$

The final decision is obtained by aggregation of votes of binary classifiers. In order to accomplish this, the credibility of each base classifier is estimated. It can be done in several ways, however in this study we associate with each classifier $C_{i,j}$ its credibility coefficient, $P_{i,j}$, defined in the following way:

$$P_{i,j} = \frac{v_i}{e_j + v_i} , \tag{2}$$

where e_j is a number of misclassified examples from class j, and v_i is a number of correctly classified examples from class i. The computation of the credibility coefficients is performed during the learning phase of the classification task (in our case, it is done on the training data set, during the feature selection stage).

The aggregation rule should take into account the reliability of each base classifier. We decided to treat the credibility coefficients $P_{i,j}$ as weights of the sum of the responses yielded by base classifiers for each row of classifier matrix **C**. Now, the whole process of classification can be described in the following steps:

1. Apply example x to all classifiers, $C_{i,j}$ $(i < j)$, and obtain their predictions $C_{i,j}(x)$.
2. Determine classification of the remaining classifiers, $C_{i,j}$ $(i > j)$, using formula (1).
3. For each class i, $i \in \langle 1..n \rangle$, compute weighted sum:

$$S_i = \sum_{\substack{j=1; \\ j \neq i}}^{n} P_{i,j} \cdot C_{i,j}. \tag{3}$$

4. Find the greatest value of S_i and return its index, i, as a final classification (break ties arbitrarily in favor of the class that comes first in the class order).

In the context of constructive induction, presented in this paper, the n^2-classifier acts both as a framework in which feature selection is performed and as the final classifier.

3 Experiments

3.1 Data set

The data set used in our experiment is composed of 700 histological images. The images have been collected and classified by Janusz Szymaś, medical senior expert from the Department of Pathology, University School of Medicine in Poznan. The whole data set includes 50 images for each of 14 classes of brain tumors (*tumors of neurepithelial tissue*). Each class is represented by 10 images of 5 patients. To avoid undesirable appearance of the data, coming from the same patient in learning and testing data set, we were obliged to perform a 5-fold cross validation technique. Neglecting this restriction leads to overoptimistic results, as it was shown in [11].

Our previous experiments showed that the histogram of intensities of three principal color components (RGB – red, green, blue) is a simple feature which gives a relatively good classification results. Thus, we have 3 (R, G, B) × 256 attributes. After a simple quantization (replacing each of four consecutive values by their sum), we obtained 192 features. 68 of them were redundant (equal to zero for all cases). Finally, our data set contains 700 objects described by 124 attributes.

3.2 Implementation

In our genetic algorithm, each individual is represented by a genotype string of 124 digits. In the feature selection task, the genes are binary: '1' gene means that the corresponding attribute is chosen, '0' means that it is discarded. In a weight-adjusting task, each gene can be a digit '0' to '9', which is the integer weight of the corresponding attribute. In a single-classifier approach, there is only one run of GA – we look for features that discriminate all the classes best. In a n^2-classifier approach, each run is to find the optimal features subset for a binary classifier, which distinguishes between two classes only. $(n^2 - n)/2$ classifiers and as many evolutions are needed. In our case, for 14 classes, we need 91 binary classifiers.

We carried out separate experiments with a single classifier and n^2-classifier. For each of those approaches, we examined feature selection without attribute domain normalization, feature selection with normalization, and attribute weighting with normalization. The attribute normalization process (adjusting the domain of each attribute to a <0,1> interval) was very time-consuming, so we had to shorten the corresponding evolutions.

Most of the genetic algorithm's parameters were identical for all runs and based on our previous experiences. Population size was constant (80 individuals for experiments without normalization and 40 individuals for experiments with normalization, due to the time constraints). Selection was carried out according to the remainder with repetitions rule. To achieve more stable and certain evaluation of individuals, cross-validation tests were repeated 10 times and the mean value was computed. Despite this, due to the random nature of cross-validation tests, the mean could vary a few percent depending on a fold distribution during those 10 repetitions. In a n^2-classifier experiment, the mean varied more because the number of examples was much smaller (only two classes for a binary classifier).

Crossing-over probability was 100%. Two-point crossing-over was used. For feature selection task, mutation was a simple bit-flipping (0 to 1 or 1 to 0). For feature weighting, mutation turned a gene to 0 when it was greater than 0, or set it randomly to a 1-9 digit when it was 0.

In our experiments, mutation probability was variable during the evolution. It was 5% in the beginning to diversify the population and prevent premature convergence, and decreased linearly to 1/(population size) [7] to allow more precise tuning of solutions. However, we do not expect convergence to a single solution; we keep track of the best individual found so far during the evolution. This is an *off-line* process.

Standard deviation (sigma) truncation scaling was used. The scaling coefficient decreased non-linearly from 5 in the beginning to 1 at the end of the evolution. Non-linear decrease yields a shorter low-pressure period and a longer high-pressure period.

3.3 Results

3.3.1 Single classifier

The evolution in "feature selection with no attribute normalization" task was supposed to last at most 500 generations. Mutation probability reached 1/80 after 50 generations, z reached 1 after 500 generations. The evolution lasted less than 500 generations, and was finished because there was no improvement during the last 100 generations.

Full search space for feature selection consisted of 2^{124} solutions (more than 10^{37}). In 500 generations and with 80 individuals, we examine 500×80 solutions only, which is less than 10^{-33} of the full space. For a weight-adjusting problem, the full search space size is 10^{124}.

The experiments with normalization of attribute domains were more complex and time consuming, and so the populations were smaller and the evolutions shorter. The results are shown in Table 1 (best classification accuracy and standard deviations).

3.3.2 n^2-classifier

In this multi-classifier approach, we needed 91 evolutions (one for each pair of classes). Figure 2 presents best-so-far classification accuracy for some sample binary classifiers, each distinguishing between a pair of classes.

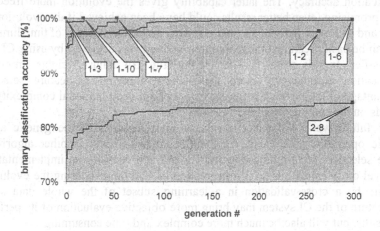

Fig. 2. Evolution of subsets of features in a n^2-classifier model (best-so-far accuracy).

There was no need to evolve discriminant subsets of features for classes 1 and 3; in the first generation, a random subset of features could separate them with 100% accuracy. Pair 1-10 could be 100%-discriminated after a few generations only. Pair 2-8 was hard to distinguish; classes 1 and 6 were easier, but not perfectly distinguishable. The evolution of subsets of features for pair 1-2 was finished due to no improvement in the last 200 generations.

The whole n^2-classifier system yielded 75% classification accuracy in feature selection task; this was still improved in the experiment with attributes' weighting. Table 1 summarizes all results.

Table 1. Classification accuracy for a single and n^2-classifiers

Data characteristics	Classification accuracy [%]		
	Single classifier	n^2-classifier	Improvement n^2 vs. single
all features no normalization	35.34 ± 0.97	35.81 ± 1.20	-
feature selection no normalization	49.89 ± 1.32	75.03 ± 0.88	25.14
feature selection normalized	52.49 ± 0.87	74.05 ± 1.38	21.56
weighting normalized	53.00 ± 0.74	81.61 ± 0.81	28.61

4 Conclusions

The experiments we have performed show the ability of using evolutionary algorithms for constructive induction tasks. The genetic algorithm described in this paper is capable of both selecting features and adjusting their weights for best classification accuracy. The latter capability gives the evolution more freedom and seems promising (even better results could have been achieved if the evolutions lasted longer and had more individuals; that was not carried out because of time limitations).

It can be easily seen that the main improvement was achieved by using CI within a n^2-classifier. In this meta-classifier, letting the GA adjust weights improved the classification accuracy by more than 6%, comparing to feature selection. A disadvantage of the meta-classifier may be its high computational complexity (which depends on the complexity of the base classifiers).

Our future work will concern various improvements of the genetic algorithm (genetic operators, parameters, etc.), and comparison with another algorithms for feature selection, weight adjusting and CI. We are working on implementation of a two-level cross-validation, so that evaluation of individuals during the evolution will be done by a cross-validation in a learning subset of the whole data set. Such architecture of the CI system may bring more objective evaluation of its performance and results, but will also be much more complex and time consuming.

It would be worthwhile to extend our approach by more "constructive", evolutionary induction (including creation of new attributes, rules etc. [15]). A tradeoff between the number of features, their easy interpretation and classification accuracy could also be introduced. This approach should also be tested on more known data sets to validate its promising utility.

Acknowledgements

The computational experiments have been carried out at the Poznan Supercomputing and Networking Centre affiliated to the Institute of Bioorganic Chemistry at the Polish Academy of Science. This work has been supported from State Committee for Scientific Research, KBN research grant no. 8T11C 013 13 and from CRIT 2 – Esprit Project no. 20288.

References

1. Aha, D.W., Kibler E., Albert M.K.: Instance-based learning algorithms. Machine Learning 6 (1991) 37-66.
2. Aha, D.W., Bankert R.L.: Feature Selection for Case-based Classification of Cloud Types: An Empirical Comparison, *Proceedings AAAI-94 Workshop Case-Based Reasoning*, (1994), 106-112.
3. Bloedorn, E., Michalski, R.S, Wnek, J.: Multistrategy Constructive Induction: AQ17-MCI. *Proceedings of the 2nd International Workshop on Multi-Strategy Learning*, Harper's Ferry, WV, (1993).

4. Chan, P.K., Stolfo, S.J.: Experiments on multistrategy learning by meta-learning. *In Proceedings of the Second International Conference on Information and Knowledge Management*, (1993), 314-323.
5. Davis, L.: *Handbook of genetic algorithms*, Van Nostrand Reinhold, New York, (1991).
6. Friedman, J.H.: Another approach to polychotomous classification, Technical Report, Stanford University, (1996).
7. Goldberg, D.E.: *Genetic Algorithms in Search, Optimization, and Machine Learning*, Addison-Wesley Publishing Co. (1989).
8. Hastie, T., Tibshirani R.: Classification by pairwise coupling, *Proc. NIPS97*.
9. Jelonek, J., Stefanowski J.: Using n^2-classifier to solve multiclass learning problems. Technical Report, Poznan University of Technology, (1997).
10. Jelonek, J., Stefanowski J.: Feature subset selection for classification of histological images, *Artificial Intelligence in Medicine* **9** (1997) 227-239.
11. Jelonek, J., Krawiec, K., Słowiński, R., Stefanowski, J., Szymaś, J.: Computer-assisted diagnosis of neurepithelial tumours based on clinical and pictorial data, *Computers in Medicine* **4** (1997) 170-175, Polish Society of Medical Informatics, Łódź.
12. Jelonek, J., Stefanowski J.: Experiments on solving multiclass learning problems by n^2-classifier, *Proceedings 10th European Conference on Machine Learning*, Chemnitz, Germany, (1998).
13. Jelonek, J., Komosiński, M.: Using n^2-classifier in constructive induction. In: Ch. Giraud-Carrier, M. Hilario (eds.), *ECML '98 Workshop on Upgrading Learning to the Meta-Level: Model Selection and Data Transformation*, Chemitzer Informatik-Berichte, Chemnitz, (1998), 21-29.
14. John, G., Kohavi R., Pfleger K.: Irrelevant features and the subset selection problem, *In Proceedings 11th International Machine Learning Conference*, (1994), 121-129.
15. Komosiński, M.: ECIS – Evolutionary Constructive Induction System, http://www-idss.cs.put.poznan.pl/ecis/
16. Littlestone, N., Warmuth, M.K.: The weighted majority algorithm. *Information and Computation*, 108 (2), (1994), 212-261.
17. Matheus, Ch.J.: The need for constructive induction, *In Proceedings 8th International Workshop on Machine Learning*.
18. Matheus, C.J. and Rendell, L.: Constructive Induction on Decision Trees, *Proceedings of IJCAI-89*, pp. 645-650, Detroit, MI, (1989).
19. Mayoraz, E., Moreira, M.: On the decomposition of polychotomies into dichotomies, *In Proceedings 14th International Conference on Machine Learning*, (1997), 219-226.
20. Michalewicz, Z.: *Genetic Algorithms + Data Structures = Evolution Programs*, Springer-Verlag, (1996).
21. Michalski, R.S.: Pattern recognition as knowledge-guided computer induction, Departament of Computer Science Reports, No. 927, University of Illinois, Urbana, June 1978.
22. Michalski, R.S., Tecuci, G.: *Machine Learning. A multistrategy approach*. Volume IV, Morgan Kaufmann (1994).
23. Pudil, P., Novovicova J., Kittler J., Floating Search methods in feature selection, *Pattern Recognition Letters* **15** (1994) 1119-1125.
24. Wnek, J. and Michalski, R.S.: Hypothesis-driven constructive induction in AQ17: a method and experiments, *Proceedings of IJCAI-91*, Workshop on Evaluating and Changing Representation in Machine Learning, Sydney, Australia, (1991).

Author Index

N. Abe	385	G. Fiol-Roig	601
T. Aida	163		
M.A. de Almeida	565	A. Giordana	76, 520
A.H. Alsaffar	114	L.K. Goodwin	612
A. An	319	G. Góra	262
C. Anglano	520	E. Grègoire	301
		J.W. Grzymala-Busse	612
A. Badia	94		
P. Baptiste	466	M.-S. Hacid	340
R. Basili	199	H.J. Hamilton	420
R. Béjar	292	L. Han	556
E. Bertino	226		
B. Black	226	L. Iwańska	430
C. Bock	503		
F. Botana	439	S. Jacobsen	123
A. Brasher	226	J. Jelonek	665
D. Brindle	376	C.A. Johnson	144
L. Brisoux	301	R. Jonsson	657
J. Calmet	475	K.A. Kaufman	411
F. Carrère	639	C.H.M. van Kemenade	630
B. Catania	226	W. Klösgen	1
N.J. Cercone	319, 420	M.A. Klopotek	358, 494
C. Chan	319	Y. Kodratoff	16
J. Chen	67	J.N. Kok	630
M.F. Costabile	208	M. Komosiński	665
J. Ćwik	547	J. Koronacki	547
		K. Kruger	430
D. Deavin	226	M. Kryszkiewicz	583
S.M. Deen	144	P. Kullmann	475
K. De Jong	512	S. Kundu	217
J.S. Deogun	114		
B.C. Desai	154	P. Lambrix	123
M. Di Nanni	199	P. Leo	226
L. Di Pace	226	F.A. Lisi	103
P. Doherty	271	G. Lo Bello	520
J. Dong	621	B.G.T. Lowden	330
		W. Łukaszewicz	271
A. Ehinger	639		
P. Ejdys	262	E. Madalińska-Bugaj	271
F. Esposito	103, 208, 226	D. Malerba	103
		F. Mansanne	639
N. Fanizzi	208	F. Manyà	292
S. Ferilli	208	N. Mata	430

S. Matwin 565
J. McNaught 226
R.A. Meersman 30
M. Merzbacher 244
M. Michalewicz 358
Z. Michalewicz 538
R.S. Michalski 411
D. Michaut 466
M. Mukaidono 282
J.J. Mulawka 529

H.S. Nguyen 310
S.H. Nguyen 235, 310, 574

S. Ohsuga 163, 621
M.A. Orgun 484

D. Pacholczyk 181
M.T. Pazienza 199
A. Persidis 226
J.F. Peters 556
K. Piętak 529
A. Pietrowcew 402
B. Prędki 172
S. Puuronen 592

V.V. Raghavan 114
S. Ramanna 556
C. Rigotti 340
F. Rinaldi 226
J. Robinson 330
H. Rybinski 583

L. Saïs 301
L. Saitta 76
M. Schmidt 648
M. Schoenauer 639
F. Sebastiani 133
G. Semeraro 208, 226
H. Sever 114
N. Shahmehri 123
N. Shayan 154
R. Shinghal 154
R. Sikora 402
W. Skarbek 395, 402
A. Skowron 310

J. Stepaniuk 457
V.S. Subrahmanian 46
R. Susmaga 448
L.M. Sztandera 503

H. Taki 385
K. Tanaka 385
V. Terziyan 592
B. Thomas 190
M. Trachtman 503
K. Trojanowski 538
S. Tsumoto 349
A. Tsymbal 592

J. Velga 503

H. Wang 235
P. Wąsiewicz 529
I. Weber 253
A. Wieczorkowska 367
G. Wiederhold 56
S.T. Wierzchoń 358, 494
S. Wilk 172
C.-M. Wu 85

G.P. Zarri 226
J.J. Zhang 420
X. Zhang 612
Y. Zhang 85
N. Zhong 621
Y. Zhou 154
W. Ziarko 376
J.M. Żytkow 547

Springer
and the
environment

At Springer we firmly believe that an
international science publisher has a
special obligation to the environment,
and our corporate policies consistently
reflect this conviction.
We also expect our business partners –
paper mills, printers, packaging
manufacturers, etc. – to commit
themselves to using materials and
production processes that do not harm
the environment. The paper in this
book is made from low- or no-chlorine
pulp and is acid free, in conformance
with international standards for paper
permanency.

 Springer

Lecture Notes in Artificial Intelligence (LNAI)

Vol. 1446: D. Page (Ed.), Inductive Logic Programming. Proceedings, 1998. VIII, 301 pages. 1998.

Vol. 1453: M.-L. Mugnier, M. Chein (Eds.), Conceptual Structures: Theory, Tools and Applications. Proceedings, 1998. XIII, 439 pages. 1998.

Vol. 1454: I. Smith (Ed.), Artificial Intelligence in Structural Engineering. XI, 497 pages. 1998.

Vol. 1455: A. Hunter, S. Parsons (Eds.), Applications of Uncertainty Formalisms. VIII, 474 pages. 1998.

Vol. 1456: A. Drogoul, M. Tambe, T. Fukuda (Eds.), Collective Robotics. Proceedings, 1998. VII, 161 pages. 1998.

Vol. 1458: V.O. Mittal, H.A. Yanco, J. Aronis, R. Simpson (Eds.), Assistive Technology in Artificial Intelligence. X, 273 pages. 1998.

Vol. 1471: J. Dix, L. Moniz Pereira, T.C. Przymusinski (Eds.), Logic Programming and Knowledge Representation. Proceedings, 1997. IX, 246 pages. 1998.

Vol. 1476: J. Calmet, J. Plaza (Eds.), Artificial Intelligence and Symbolic Computation. Proceedings, 1998. XI, 309 pages. 1998.

Vol. 1480: F. Giunchiglia (Ed.), Artificial Intelligence: Methodology, Systems, and Applications. Proceedings, 1998. IX, 502 pages. 1998.

Vol. 1484: H. Coelho (Ed.), Progress in Artificial Intelligence – IBERAMIA 98. Proceedings, 1998. XIII, 421 pages. 1998.

Vol. 1488: B. Smyth, P. Cunningham (Eds.), Advances in Case-Based Reasoning. Proceedings, 1998. XI, 482 pages. 1998.

Vol. 1489: J. Dix, L. Fariñas del Cerro, U. Furbach (Eds.), Logics in Artificial Intelligence. Proceedings, 1998. X, 391 pages. 1998.

Vol. 1495: T. Andreasen, H. Christiansen, H.L. Larsen (Eds.), Flexible Query Answering Systems. Proceedings, 1998. IX, 393 pages. 1998.

Vol. 1501: M.M. Richter, C.H. Smith, R. Wiehagen, T. Zeugmann (Eds.), Algorithmic Learning Theory. Proceedings, 1998. XI, 439 pages. 1998.

Vol. 1502: G. Antoniou, J. Slaney (Eds.), Advanced Topics in Artificial Intelligence. Proceedings, 1998. XI, 333 pages. 1998.

Vol. 1504: O. Herzog, A. Günter (Eds.), KI-98: Advances in Artificial Intelligence. Proceedings, 1998. XI, 355 pages. 1998.

Vol. 1510: J.M. Zytkow, M. Quafafou (Eds.), Principles of Data Mining and Knowledge Discovery. Proceedings, 1998. XI, 482 pages. 1998.

Vol. 1515: F. Moreira de Oliveira (Ed.), Advances in Artificial Intelligence. Proceedings, 1998. X, 259 pages. 1998.

Vol. 1527: P. Baumgartner, Theory Reasoning in Connection Calculi. IX, 283 pages. 1999.

Vol. 1529: D. Farwell, L. Gerber, E. Hovy (Eds.), Machine Translation and the Information Soup. Proceedings, 1998. XIX, 532 pages. 1998.

Vol. 1531: H.-Y. Lee, H. Motoda (Eds.), PRICAI'98: Topics in Artificial Intelligence. XIX, 646 pages. 1998.

Vol. 1532: S. Arikawa, H. Motoda (Eds.), Discovery Science. Proceedings, 1998. XI, 456 pages. 1998.

Vol. 1534: J.S. Sichman, R. Conte, N. Gilbert (Eds.), Multi-Agent Systems and Agent-Based Simulation. Proceedings, 1998. VIII, 237 pages. 1998.

Vol. 1535: S. Ossowski, Co-ordination in Artificial Agent Societies. XVI, 221 pages. 1999.

Vol. 1537: N. Magnenat-Thalmann, D. Thalmann (Eds.), Modelling and Motion Capture Techniques for Virtual Environments. Proceedings, 1998. IX, 273 pages. 1998.

Vol. 1544: C. Zhang, D. Lukose (Eds.), Multi-Agent Systems. Proceedings, 1998. VII, 195 pages. 1998.

Vol. 1545: A. Birk, J. Demiris (Eds.), Learning Robots. Proceedings, 1996. IX, 188 pages. 1998.

Vol. 1555: J.P. Müller, M.P. Singh, A.S. Rao (Eds.), Intelligent Agents V. Proceedings, 1998. XXIV, 455 pages. 1999.

Vol. 1562: C.L. Nehaniv (Ed.), Computation for Metaphors, Analogy, and Agents. X, 389 pages. 1999.

Vol. 1570: F. Puppe (Ed.), XPS-99: Knowledge-Based Systems. VIII, 227 pages. 1999.

Vol. 1571: P. Noriega, C. Sierra (Eds.), Agent Mediated Electronic Commerce. Proceedings, 1998. IX, 207 pages. 1999.

Vol. 1572: P. Fischer, H.U. Simon (Eds.), Computational Learning Theory. Proceedings, 1999. X, 301 pages. 1999.

Vol. 1574: N. Zhong, L. Zhou (Eds.), Methodologies for Knowledge Discovery and Data Mining. Proceedings, 1999. XV, 533 pages. 1999.

Vol. 1582: A. Lecomte, F. Lamarche, G. Perrier (Eds.), Logical Aspects of Computational Linguistics. Proceedings, 1997. XI, 251 pages. 1999.

Vol. 1599: T. Ishida (Ed.), Multiagent Platforms. Proceedings, 1998. VIII, 187 pages. 1999.

Vol. 1609: Z. W. Raś, A. Skowron (Eds.), Foundations of Intelligent Systems. Proceedings, 1999. XII, 676 pages. 1999.

Lecture Notes in Computer Science

Vol. 1557: P. Zinterhof, M. Vajteršic, A. Uhl (Eds.), Parallel Computation. Proceedings, 1999. XV, 604 pages. 1999.

Vol. 1558: H. J.v.d. Herik, H. Iida (Eds.), Computers and Games. Proceedings, 1998. XVIII, 337 pages. 1999.

Vol. 1559: P. Flener (Ed.), Logic-Based Program Synthesis and Transformation. Proceedings, 1998. X, 331 pages. 1999.

Vol. 1560: K. Imai, Y. Zheng (Eds.), Public Key Cryptography. Proceedings, 1999. IX, 327 pages. 1999.

Vol. 1561: I. Damgård (Ed.), Lectures on Data Security.VII, 250 pages. 1999.

Vol. 1562: C.L. Nehaniv (Ed.), Computation for Metaphors, Analogy, and Agents. X, 389 pages. 1999. (Subseries LNAI).

Vol. 1563: Ch. Meinel, S. Tison (Eds.), STACS 99. Proceedings, 1999. XIV, 582 pages. 1999.

Vol. 1565: P. P. Chen, J. Akoka, H. Kangassalo, B. Thalheim (Eds.), Conceptual Modeling. XXIV, 303 pages. 1999.

Vol. 1567: P. Antsaklis, W. Kohn, M. Lemmon, A. Nerode, S. Sastry (Eds.), Hybrid Systems V. X, 445 pages. 1999.

Vol. 1568: G. Bertrand, M. Couprie, L. Perroton (Eds.), Discrete Geometry for Computer Imagery. Proceedings, 1999. XI, 459 pages. 1999.

Vol. 1569: F.W. Vaandrager, J.H. van Schuppen (Eds.), Hybrid Systems: Computation and Control. Proceedings, 1999. X, 271 pages. 1999.

Vol. 1570: F. Puppe (Ed.), XPS-99: Knowledge-Based Systems. VIII, 227 pages. 1999. (Subseries LNAI).

Vol. 1571: P. Noriega, C. Sierra (Eds.), Agent Mediated Electronic Commerce. Proceedings, 1998. IX, 207 pages. 1999. (Subseries LNAI).

Vol. 1572: P. Fischer, H.U. Simon (Eds.), Computational Learning Theory. Proceedings, 1999. X, 301 pages. 1999. (Subseries LNAI).

Vol. 1574: N. Zhong, L. Zhou (Eds.), Methodologies for Knowledge Discovery and Data Mining. Proceedings, 1999. XV, 533 pages. 1999. (Subseries LNAI).

Vol. 1575: S. Jähnichen (Ed.), Compiler Construction. Proceedings, 1999. X, 301 pages. 1999.

Vol. 1576: S.D. Swierstra (Ed.), Programming Languages and Systems. Proceedings, 1999. X, 307 pages. 1999.

Vol. 1577: J.-P. Finance (Ed.), Fundamental Approaches to Software Engineering. Proceedings, 1999. X, 245 pages. 1999.

Vol. 1578: W. Thomas (Ed.), Foundations of Software Science and Computation Structures. Proceedings, 1999. X, 323 pages. 1999.

Vol. 1579: W.R. Cleaveland (Ed.), Tools and Algorithms for the Construction and Analysis of Systems. Proceedings, 1999. XI, 445 pages. 1999.

Vol. 1580: A. Včkovski, K.E. Brassel, H.-J. Schek (Eds.), Interoperating Geographic Information Systems. Proceedings, 1999. XI, 329 pages. 1999.

Vol. 1581: J.-Y. Girard (Ed.), Typed Lambda Calculi and Applications. Proceedings, 1999. VIII, 397 pages. 1999.

Vol. 1582: A. Lecomte, F. Lamarche, G. Perrier (Eds.), Logical Aspects of Computational Linguistics. Proceedings, 1997. XI, 251 pages. 1999. (Subseries LNAI).

Vol. 1584: G. Gottlob, E. Grandjean, K. Seyr (Eds.), Computer Science Logic. Proceedings, 1998. X, 431 pages. 1999.

Vol. 1586: J. Rolim et al. (Eds.), Parallel and Distributed Processing. Proceedings, 1999. XVII, 1443 pages. 1999.

Vol. 1587: J. Pieprzyk, R. Safavi-Naini, J. Seberry (Eds.), Information Security and Privacy. Proceedings, 1999. XI, 327 pages. 1999.

Vol. 1590: P. Atzeni, A. Mendelzon, G. Mecca (Eds.), The World Wide Web and Databases. Proceedings, 1998. VIII, 213 pages. 1999.

Vol. 1592: J. Stern (Ed.), Advances in Cryptology – EUROCRYPT '99. Proceedings, 1999. XII, 475 pages. 1999.

Vol. 1593: P. Sloot, M. Bubak, A. Hoekstra, B. Hertzberger (Eds.), High-Performance Computing and Networking. Proceedings, 1999. XXIII, 1318 pages. 1999.

Vol. 1594: P. Ciancarini, A.L. Wolf (Eds.), Coordination Languages and Models. Proceedings, 1999. IX, 420 pages. 1999.

Vol. 1596: R. Poli, H.-M. Voigt, S. Cagnoni, D. Corne, G.D. Smith, T.C. Fogarty (Eds.), Evolutionary Image Analysis, Signal Processing and Telecommunications. Proceedings, 1999. X, 225 pages. 1999.

Vol. 1597: H. Zuidweg, M. Campolargo, J. Delgado, A. Mullery (Eds.), Intelligence in Services and Networks. Proceedings, 1999. XII, 552 pages. 1999.

Vol. 1599: T. Ishida (Ed.), Multiagent Platforms. Proceedings, 1998. VIII, 187 pages. 1999. (Subseries LNAI).

Vol. 1602: A. Sivasubramaniam, M. Lauria (Eds.), Network-Based Parallel Computing. Proceedings, 1999. VIII, 225 pages. 1999.

Vol. 1605: J. Billington, M. Diaz, G. Rozenberg (Eds.), Application of Petri Nets to Communication Networks. IX, 303 pages. 1999.

Vol. 1609: Z. W. Raś, A. Skowron (Eds.), Foundations of Intelligent Systems. Proceedings, 1999. XII, 676 pages. 1999. (Subseries LNAI).